In Search of the Labyrinth

NEW DIRECTIONS IN CLASSICS

Editors

Duncan F. Kennedy (Emeritus Professor of Latin Literature and the Theory of Criticism, University of Bristol) and Charles Martindale (Emeritus Professor of Latin, University of Bristol)

Editorial board

Published in association with the Institute of Greece, Rome and the Classical Tradition, University of Bristol.

In the last generation, Classics has changed almost beyond recognition. The subject as taught thirty years ago involved enormous concentration on just two periods: fifth-century Athens and late Republican Rome. There was no reception, virtually no study of women or popular culture, and little attention given to late antiquity. Today, Classics at its best again has an unusually broad interdisciplinary scope, and reaches out to the arts and humanities generally as well as beyond. It is just such a 'New Classics' that this exciting series seeks to promote – an open-minded Classics committed to debate and dialogue, with a leading role in the humanities; a Classics neither antiquarian nor crudely presentist; a Classics of the present, but also of the future. *New Directions in Classics* aims to do something fresh, and showcase the work of writers who are setting new agendas, working at the frontiers of the subject. It aims for a wide readership among all those, both within the academy and outside, who want to engage seriously with ideas.

TITLES IN THE SERIES

Antiquity and the Meanings of Time: A Philosophy of Ancient and Modern Literature, Duncan F. Kennedy

The Modernity of Ancient Sculpture: Greek Sculpture and Modern Art from Winckelmann to Picasso, Elizabeth Prettejohn

Thucydides and the Idea of History, Neville Morley

In Search of the Labyrinth

The Cultural Legacy of Minoan Crete

Nicoletta Momigliano

BLOOMSBURY ACADEMIC
LONDON • NEW YORK • OXFORD • NEW DELHI • SYDNEY

BLOOMSBURY ACADEMIC
Bloomsbury Publishing Plc
50 Bedford Square, London, WC1B 3DP, UK
1385 Broadway, New York, NY 10018, USA
29 Earlsfort Terrace, Dublin 2, Ireland

BLOOMSBURY, BLOOMSBURY ACADEMIC and the Diana logo are trademarks of
Bloomsbury Publishing Plc

First published in Great Britain 2020
Reprinted 2020, 2021

Cover design: Terry Woodley
Cover image © Roussetos Panagiotakis

A catalogue record for this book is available from the British Library.

Library of Congress Cataloging-in-Publication Data
Names: Momigliano, Nicoletta, author.
Title: In search of the labyrinth : the cultural legacy of Minoan Crete / Nicoletta Momigliano.
Other titles: Cultural legacy of Minoan Crete
Description: London ; New York : Bloomsbury Academic, 2020. | Series: New directions in classics |
Includes bibliographical references and index. | Summary: "In Search of the Labyrinth explores the
enduring cultural legacy of Minoan Crete by offering an overview of Minoan archaeology and modern
responses to it in literature, the visual and performing arts, and other cultural practices. The focus is on
the twentieth century, and on responses that involve a clear engagement with the material culture of
Minoan Crete, not just with mythological narratives in Classical sources, as illustrated by the works of
novelists, poets, avant-garde artists, couturiers, musicians, philosophers, architects, film directors, and
even psychoanalysts – from Sigmund Freud and Marcel Proust to D.H. Lawrence, Cecil Day-Lewis,
Oswald Spengler, Nikos Kazantzakis, Robert Graves, André Gide, Mary Renault, Christa Wolf,
Don DeLillo, Rhea Galanaki, Léon Bakst, Marc Chagall, Mariano Fortuny, Robert Wise, Martin Heidegger,
Karl Lagerfeld, and Harrison Birtwistle, among many others. The volume also explores the fascination
with things Minoan in antiquity and in the present millennium: from Minoan-inspired motifs
decorating pottery of the Greek Early Iron Age, to uses of the Minoans in twenty-first-century
music, poetry, fashion, and other media" – Provided by publisher.
Identifiers: LCCN 2020019050 (print) | LCCN 2020019051 (ebook) | ISBN 9781350156708 (paperback) |
ISBN 9781784538545 (hardback) | ISBN 9781350156715 (epub) | ISBN 9781350156722 (ebook)
Subjects: LCSH: Civilization, Western–Classical influences. | Civilization, Modern–Classical influences. |
Minoans–Greece–Crete. | Crete (Greece)–Civilization. | Minoans–Greece–Crete–Antiquities.
Classification: LCC CB245 .M579 2020 (print) | LCC CB245 (ebook) | DDC 909/.09821–dc23
LC record available at https://lccn.loc.gov/2020019050
LC ebook record available at https://lccn.loc.gov/2020019051

ISBN: HB: 978-1-7845-3854-5
       PB: 978-1-3501-5670-8
       ePDF: 978-1-3501-5672-2
       eBook: 978-1-3501-5671-5

Series: New Directions in Classics

Typeset by RefineCatch Limited, Bungay, Suffolk
Printed and bound in Great Britain

To find out more about our authors and books visit www.bloomsbury.com
and sign up for our newsletters.

To all the people who have been affected by Cretomania

Contents

List of Illustrations   viii

Preface and Acknowledgements   xii

1   Introduction: Desperately Seeking Ariadne – the Cultural Legacy of Minoan Crete   1

2   Sons of Europa: From Medical Remedies for Constipation to Bestiality, Sexually Transmitted Death, and the Dawn of the 'Minoan Age' (from Antiquity to the Mid-Nineteenth Century)   17

3   Rediscovering European Origins: Ariadne as the Great Mother Goddess (Mid-Nineteenth Century–First World War)   37

4   Minoans and the World Wars (c. 1915–49): The Aryan Revenge   87

5   The Minoans in the Cold War and Swinging Sixties: From the End of the Greek Civil War to the End of the Colonels' Dictatorship (c. 1949–74)   137

6   Minoan Paradises Lost and Regained: From Cannibalism to Postmodernism (c. 1975–99)   187

7   Minoan Cultural Legacies: Every Age Has the Minoans It Deserves and Desires   227

Notes   243

Bibliography   307

Index   347

Illustrations

Table

0.1 Chronological table for relative and approximate absolute chronology used in this volume.   xiii

Figures

1.1 Knossos, 'The Snake Goddess and her votaries': Evans's conjectural arrangement of her shrine.   2

1.2 Back and front cover of Elizabeth Lawton's 1977 pamphlet.   4

1.3 Marc Chagall, *L'écuyère* (1925).   7

1.4 Knossos, the Toreador fresco.   7

1.5 Knossos, The Ivory Acrobat.   8

1.6 Black-figure Attic vase with Minotaur image.   9

1.7 Three different drawings of the same clay seal impression from Knossos, reproduced at different times, which according to Evans showed a seated young Minotaur, but in fact represents a monkey.   11

1.8a–b Gustav Klimt, *Medicine*, and detail of Hygieia, University of Vienna ceiling paintings (presented in March 1901 at the tenth Secession Exhibition).   13

1.9 Paul Klee, *The Snake Goddess and her Foe* (1940).   14

2.1 Detail from a scene depicting foreigners bringing gifts in the tomb of Rekhmire (TT 100) at Thebes, Egypt.   19

2.2 Cartoon of Santorini eruption as Mycenaean plot.   23

2.3 The Burgon ring.   32

3.1 Bust of Heinrich Schliemann in the Neues Museum, Berlin.   39

3.2 The so-called Treasure of Priam.   39

3.3 Pithos from Minos Kalokairinos's 1878 excavations at Knossos donated to the British Museum.   43

3.4   Sir Arthur Evans at Knossos.   46

3.5   Seal-stone with pictographic signs donated to the Ashmolean
      Museum in 1889.   48

3.6   Plan of the Palace at Knossos.   52

3.7   The Throne Room at Knossos.   53

3.8a–c Examples of Pictographic, Linear A, and Linear B scripts.   53

3.9   Knossos, The Cup Bearer fresco.   55

3.10 Knossos, Dancing Lady fresco.   55

3.11 Knossos, mason's marks in the shape of double-axes.   58

3.12 Knossos, the Theatral Area.   58

3.13 Knossos, The Priest King or Prince of Lilies fresco.   64

3.14 The Harvester Vase from Hagia Triada.   67

3.15 Knossos, La Parisienne fresco.   70

3.16 Mariano Fortuny's 1935 portrait of his wife, wearing dress and
      scarf with Minoan motifs, in the Fortuny Museum, Venice.   78

3.17 One of F. Kupka's Minoan-inspired illustrations for the 1908
      edition of Leconte de Lisle's tragedy *Erinnyes*.   79

3.18 L. Bakst, sketch of costume for Ida Rubinstein as Helen in
      the drama *Hélène de Sparte* (1912), showing Minoan sacral ivy
      combined with crocus motif.   80

3.19 L. Bakst, set design for Ida Rubinstein's 1923 production of
      D'Annunzio's tragedy *Phédre* (*Fedra*), Thyssen-Bornemisza Museum.   81

3.20a–c D. Chaineaux's sketches for costumes in Jules Bois's
      La Furie (1909), on display at the 2014 exhibition *La Grèce des origins:
      entre rêve et archéologie*, Musée d'Archéologie Nationale, Château
      Saint-Germain-en-Laye, Paris.   82

3.21 Illustration of some costumes used in Richard Strauss's *Elektra*,
      based on Minoan and Mycenaean artefacts.   84

3.22 John Collier (1850–1934), *Clytemnestra* 1884 and 1914.   85

4.1a–b Examples of Fritz Krischen's illustrations for Bossert (1921).   96

4.2   Ocean liner *Aramis*: grand staircase of the first-class dining room.   104

4.3a–b Two illustrations from Berry's *The Winged Girl of Knossos* (1933), one
      modelled on the well-known Knossian fresco 'Ladies in Blue' (after Evans
      1921: fig. 397), the other using Minoan elements and Berry's imagination.   108

4.4   Detail of one illustration by Edna F. Hart-Hubon in Lamprey's
      Children of Ancient Greece (1928).   109

4.5   Detail of illustration from Mitchison's *Boys and Girls and Gods* (1931).   109

4.6   One of Massimo Campigli's illustration for Gide's *Theseus* (1949),
      showing the twins Phaedra and Glaucus exchanging their clothes.   113

4.7   Massimo Campigli, test lithography for Gide's *Theseus*.   113

4.8a–b (a) Knossos, the North Entrance, with replica of charging
      bull fresco. (b) This replica reminded Mario Praz of Bovril
      posters, such as the one illustrated here.   117

4.9   Knossos, west view of the North Lustral Basin, which reminded
      Mario Praz of public lavatories.   117

4.10 Norman Lindsay, *Crete*, 1940.   125

4.11a–b Joan Junyer, two designs (screenprints) for the ballet
      Minotaur (1947); (a) Handmaidens. (b) Ariadne.   127

4.12a–b Photograph from the 1934 production of the drama *Medea*, designed
      by Otte Sköld and cartoon from *Stockholms-Tidningen* (23 February 1934)
      (reproduced by kind permission of the Archive of the Royal Dramatic
      Theatre in Stockholm).   128

4.13a–b (a) Still from the silent film *The Private life of Helen
      of Troy* (First National Pictures, 1927), directed by Alexander
      Korda, showing Maria Corda as Helen wearing a Minoan-inspired
      dress decorated with sprays of lilies (photo: © Getty images / General
      Photographic Agency / Stringer). (b) Jars decorated with lilies
      from Knossos (after Evans 1921: 603, fig. 443).   130

4.14a–b Dimitrios Kyriakos's Heroon building in Heraklion (1930), including
      detail of Minoanizing iron gate. For a picture of the Heroon in its prime,
      see cover of Momigliano and Farnoux (2017).   131

4.15 Octopus vase by Charles Catteau (1932), on display at the
      2014 exhibition *La Grèce des origins: entre rêve et archéologie*, Musée
      d'Archéologie Nationale, Château Saint-Germain-en-Laye, Paris.   132

4.16a–b (a) Samples of black and white versions of Josef Frank's
      fabric 'Anakreon' created for Svenskt Tenn in 1938. (b) Knossos,
      'Blue Bird Fresco' (after Evans 1928: 454, colour plate XI).   133

4.17 Woven gown by Florentini Kaloutsi, alluding to the Prince of
      Lilies fresco from Knossos.   134

5.1   Dust jacket of Mary Renault's 1958 edition of the *King Must Die*.   155

5.2   Knossos, Saffron Gatherer fresco, as originally restored by Evans,
      with blue boy instead of a monkey.   174

5.3   Detail of illustration accompanying the poem 'Keftiu' by Aris Diktaios
      (Diktaios 1974), showing Spring naming the youth/poet her king.   177

5.4   Dimarchio (City Hall) of Ierapetra, Crete.   179

5.5   Screenshots from *Helen of Troy* (Warner Bros., 1956), directed by
      Robert Wise.   181

5.6   Wooden replica of the throne in the Throne Room at Knossos in
      Doctor Who's TARDIS: still from first episode, 23 November 1963.   182

5.7   Trading cards with Minoan images created for the Liebig Extract
      of Meat Company in the 1950s, on display in the Virtual Museum
      Vallée, which includes the Museo della Mucca (Cow Museum).   184

6.1   The Isopata Ring.   201

6.2   Minoan Brotherhood shrine for the grove Temenos ta Theia of
      Minos Hermes, Chicago, IL, 2018.   206

6.3   Cover of English paperback edition of Wolf's *Kassandra* (1984).   208

6.4   The Hagia Triada sarcophagus, detail of side showing bull sacrifice.   215

6.5   Roussetos Panagiotakis, *The Upbringing of Zeus* (1997).   219

6.6   Roussetos Panagiotakis, *Theophania* (1996).   219

6.7   Roussetos Panagiotakis, *Throne Room* (1999).   220

6.8   Roussetos Panagiotakis, *The Great Mother* (1997).   220

6.9   Vignette from U. Cossu's *Le Ninfe* (1989) showing
      CippaCola billboard.   223

6.10a–b Coca-Cola seasonal limited edition bottle dedicated
      to Crete, inspired by Minoan decorations and Greek mythology.   223

7.1a–c (a) Céline Murphy's mural before defacement
      (April 2018); (b) after defacement (July 2018); and (c) after retouch
      by the artist (July 2018). Murphy's work indicates how this image,
      which has become like a poster-girl for Minoan Crete, has
      been heavily reconstructed.   234

7.2   Roussetos Panagiotakis, *Minotaur* (2014). The setting recalls
      the lustral basin area in the Throne Room at Knossos.   235

7.3   Snake Priestess in Harrison Birtwistle's *Minotaur* (2008).   236

7.4   Minoan Theater, Crete: performance inspired by the Minoan past.   239

7.5   Ermioni Dova impersonating the Knossos 'Snake Goddess' in the
      main square of Heraklion, summer 2019.   240

Preface and Acknowledgements

In the mid-nineteenth century, the Darwinian revolution and the discovery of the antiquity of mankind sparked a widespread interest in the remote human past and a vigorous search for origins not only of biological but also of cultural phenomena. A generation later, in the 1870s, Schliemann's excavations at Troy, Mycenae, Tiryns, and other Aegean sites opened a new chapter in our understanding of the origins of Classical Greece (itself commonly regarded as the foundation of European/Western culture), by seemingly providing Homeric heroes with flesh and blood. This was largely thanks to Schliemann's claim that he had discovered buildings, artefacts, tombs, and skeletal remains belonging to the age in which the Homeric Trojan War was thought to have occurred, even if his finds often dated from much earlier periods of Aegean antiquity. Similarly, in the early twentieth century, the excavations by Sir Arthur Evans and other archaeologists on Crete provided an even longer perspective on the roots and development of the 'glory that was Greece', with their spectacular discovery of an even older culture or civilization now commonly referred to as 'Minoan'.

We do not know the name(s) that the pre-Hellenic inhabitants of Crete used to call themselves, but many scholars believe that the Egyptians of the second millennium BC referred to them as the people of 'Keftiu'. In the early twentieth century, Evans suggested using the existing label 'Minoan' (after the mythical figure of King Minos) as a convenient term for this newly rediscovered culture of the Aegean Bronze Age (third and second millennia BC: see Table 0.1). Ever since, 'Minoan' Crete and its corollary 'Minoans' have captured the imagination of archaeologists, Classicists, Ancient historians, and a much wider public alike. For example, Minoan Crete appears in the scholarly works of the famous archaeologist Gordon Childe, the historian Arnold J. Toynbee, the historian-philosophers Oswald Spengler and R. G. Collingwood, in the pages of novels such as Marcel Proust's *In Search of Lost Time*, Ford Madox Ford's *The Good Soldier* and Don DeLillo's *The Names*, and in poems by Cecil Day Lewis, D. H. Lawrence, Nikos Kazantzakis, and Salvatore Quasimodo, to name but a few. The Minoans have also been the subject of numerous TV programmes (e.g. the recent *Atlantis: End of a World, Birth of a Legend*, BBC, 2011), while allusions to famous Minoan artefacts (e.g. the 'Bull-leaping fresco' and the 'Snake Goddess') can be found in countless works by famous and not so famous artists: from sketches by Marc Chagall and Sir Harrison Birtwistle's opera *The Minotaur* (2008) to textiles, paintings, and ceramics by British and Cretan artists such as Lilah Clarke (granddaughter of Theodor Fyfe, the first architect employed by Evans at Knossos), Florentini Kaloutsi, and Roussetos Panagiotakis. Replicas of Minoan objects appear in well-know TV series, from *Doctor Who* to *Games of Throne* and the 2018 BBC/Netflix production *Troy: Fall of a City*, while even Linear A is referred to in *Stargate*.

Table 0.1 Chronological table for relative and approximate absolute chronology used in this volume.

Relative chronology		Approximate absolute chronology (BC)
Aceramic Neolithic	Neolithic	7000–6500
Neolithic		6500–3000
Early Minoan I	Prepalatial	3000–2650
Early Minoan IIa		2650–2450
Early Minoan IIb		2450–2200
Early Minoan III		2200–2050
Middle Minoan Ia		2050–1900
Middle Minoan Ib	Protopalatial/Old Palace/ First Palace Period	1900–1800
Middle Minoan IIa		1800–1750
Middle Minoan IIb		1750–1700
Middle Minoan IIIa		1700–1650
Middle Minoan IIIb	Neopalatial/ New Palace/Second Palace period	1650–1600
Late Minoan Ia		1600–1500
Late Minoan Ib		1500–1450
Late Minoan II	Final palatial	1450–1400
Late Minoan IIIa		1400–1350
Late Minoan IIIb	Postpalatial	1350–1200
Late Minoan IIIc		1200–1100
Sub-Minoan		1100–1000
Early Iron Age		1000–750

This book aims to combine a history of Minoan archaeology with a history of modern responses to its major discoveries. By situating the Minoan discoveries in their broader historical and intellectual contexts, and by using elements of reception studies, I suggest that the Minoan past is not merely what happened in Crete in the third and second millennia BC, but the product of centuries of scholarship, interpretations, and responses to it, and that it is precisely this chain of interpretations and receptions, often beyond recondite archaeological research, which constitutes the main cultural legacy of Minoan Crete.

The materials treated in this book are broad and heterogeneous, and I am fully aware of the hazards involved in any interdisciplinary study of this kind, and of my own limitations. Nevertheless, I hope that, despite its faults, this work provides a substantial amount of new or little-known materials for people interested in the Minoan past, its modern receptions, uses, and appropriations, and that it will stimulate the research of others.

Many people have helped me over the years, and I have endeavoured to record all of them below (or in the relevant notes and captions). If I have unwittingly forgotten some,

I can assure the omitted that my oversight will upset me more than it will displease them. Also, if I record many people without mentioning the specific reasons for my gratitude, this is not because I have forgotten their good deeds, but for brevity's sake.

First of all, I would like to thank all the friends and colleagues who contributed to two volumes: *Archaeology and European Modernity: Producing and Consuming the 'Minoan'* (2006), which I co-edited with Yannis Hamilakis, and *Cretomania: Modern Desires For the Minoan Past* (2017), which I co-edited with Alexandre Farnoux. In addition to my co-editors, I particularly thank Roderick Beaton, Fritz Blakolmer, Cathy Gere, Pietro Militello, Christine Morris, Anna Simandiraki, Lena Sjögren and Esther Solomon, who continued to help my Minoan obsession (i.e. Cretomania) also beyond those volumes. I learnt a great deal from all of them. The same applies to all the friends and colleagues who contributed to the volume *Hellenomania* (2018), especially Katherine Harloe and Artemis Leontis, who also helped me with the present book.

Other people who have provided support over the years are Ellen Adams, Katerina Athanassaki, Robin Barber, Anna Bastaki, Lisa Bendall, John Bennet, Helen Brock, Gerald Cadogan, Kostis Christakis, Margarita Díaz-Andreu, Oliver Dickinson, Ermioni Dova, Jan Driessen, Lesley Fitton, Vasso Fotou, Katerina Frenzou, Lilah Fyfe, Yannis Galanakis, Lynn Garafola, Kostas Georgakopoulos, Despoina Hatzi-Vallianou, Giorgos Kaloutsis, Nektarios Karadimas, David Konstan, Tobias Korpf, Dag Kronlund, Olga Krzyszkowska, Alexandra Livarda, Colin Macdonald, Afroditi Mitsotaki, Glenn Most, Lucia Nixon, Kostas Paschalides, John Penney, Sir Adam Ridley, Andrew Shapland, Simon Shaw-Miller, the late Jon Stallworthy, Agata Ulanowska, and Anja Ulbrich. Members of the Minoan Brotherhood (Steven Bragg), Minoan Sisterhood (Lady Rhea and Lady Asteria) and Modern Minoan Paganism (Laura Perry) kindly provided information on their Neo-Pagan groups. I also thank all my former and present colleagues in the Department of Classics and Ancient History and at the Institute of Greece, Rome, and the Classical Tradition at the University of Bristol, especially Richard Buxton, Gillian Clark, Robert Fowler, Duncan Kennedy, Charles Martindale, and Elizabeth Prettejohn.

I am particularly grateful to the friends and colleagues who read and commented on drafts of this book and, above all, the three anonymous reviewers who read the manuscript I submitted to Bloomsbury Academic in September 2019. I also extend my warmest thanks to all the writers and artists (or their descendants) who allowed me to reproduce their works; and all the writers, musicians, and artists who patiently answered my questions about the Minoan elements in their works, especially Sir Harrison Birtwistle, Don DeLillo, Aaron Gregory, Céline Murphy, Roussetos Panagiotakis, and Stavros Platsis. Birtwistle and Panagiotakis generously welcomed me into their homes, and I shall always cherish my memories of the afternoons I spent in their invigorating company.

Thanks are also due to all the people who organized and attended my lectures on Cretomanic topics in Dublin, London, Nottingham, Oxford, Reading, Sweden (Universities of Stockholm, Uppsala, Gothenburg, and Lund), and Voroi (Mesara, Crete); and to all the students who over the years studied the Minoans with me at the University of Bristol, especially Jack Fuller and Robert Beavis (the latter organized an archaeological-poetical meeting on the Minoans, and got himself a Minoan tattoo).

The British School at Athens, the Institute of Greece, Rome, and the Classical Tradition of the University of Bristol helped in indirect but useful ways.

Alex Wright, formerly of I.B. Tauris, first persuaded me to write this book, while Ronnie Hanna, Merv Honeywood, Georgina Leighton, Lily Mac Mahon, and Alice Wright at Bloomsbury Academic were instrumental in getting this work to the press.

Last but not least, I thank my husband Roger Lonsdale for his help in finding some obscure Cretomanic poems and books, and above all for his forbearance and humour.

Introduction: Desperately Seeking Ariadne – the Cultural Legacy of Minoan Crete[1]

The Minoan civilization has been brought across the threshold of the western modern imagination, to become part of the familiar landscape of our minds, like the Hellenic and the Roman, only still with that mysterious and monstrous strangeness which lends to pre-Hellenic ages something of the dissolving, uneven quality of dreams. It is almost too much to take.

Rose Macaulay (1953: 112)

Kunst gibt nicht das Sichtbare wieder, sondern macht sichtbar.
Art does not reproduce the visible; rather, it makes visible.

Paul Klee (1920: 28)

On 1 March 1933 a new patient knocked on Sigmund Freud's door at Berggasse 19 in Vienna: the bisexual imagist poet Hilda Doolittle, a.k.a. H.D.[2] This former fiancée of Ezra Pound, and wife of Richard Aldington, was about to start a course of treatment for her neurosis, in which Minoan Crete played no small part. After one of her sessions with Freud, H.D. wrote to her lover Bryher (the nom de plume of author and heiress Annie Winifred Ellerman):

> We got to Crete yesterday. I went off the deep end, and we sobbed together over Greece in general. He [Freud] hasn't one of the little Crete snake goddesses. I said 'I will get you one.' He said 'ah . . . I doubt if even YOU could do that.' Now my object in life will be to starve in an attic and get him a little goddess for his collection. He loves Crete almost more than anything and I had to tell him how we balanced there in rainbows last spring and I felt it was a promise and I would return. We are terribly en rapport and happy together. Do you happen to know how one would go about finding him a goddess? Would there be one in a private collection or are they very, very rare? Please let me know. Would you write Evans for me, he might like to know Freud has all his books, he might help one get one for Freud.[3]

H.D. never managed to present Freud with a Minoan 'snake goddess' (see Fig. 1.1).[4] The Viennese psychoanalyst, however, provided his patient with a Minoan diagnosis. As

FIG. 63.—SHRINE OF SNAKE GODDESS WITH MARBLE CROSS AS CENTRAL CULT
OBJECT. CONJECTURAL ARRANGEMENT.

Fig. 1.1 Knossos, 'The Snake Goddess and her votaries': Evans's conjectural arrangement of her shrine (after Evans, 1903: fig. 63).

shown by Cathy Gere, according to Freud's controversial notion of inherited memory, H.D.'s neurosis, poetic obsession with Greek islands, Minoan Crete, and bisexuality were clear symptoms of her regression to a pre-Oedipal, mother-fixated stratum in her psyche, which, in turn, was linked to the Mother Goddess–matriarchal–Minoan stratum in the evolution of human psychic layers.[5]

This Viennese episode is just one of numerous examples illustrating the considerable fascination that 'Bronze Age' or 'Minoan' Crete has exercised among a wide public since its discovery in the early twentieth century, in the wake of the spectacular excavations by Sir Arthur Evans and other archaeologists at sites such as Knossos and Phaistos. The French author Paul Morand, writing in the early 1960s, described this fascination as an obsession – a 'Cretomania' – that swept European cultural capitals, such as Vienna, Munich, and Paris: 'Cretan and Mycenaean arts and all their decorative elements came to shake Viennese art, to animate the official art of Munich in 1905, and also the art of the first painters who worked for Diaghilev [Ballets Russes] . . . This Cretomania was to last until 1914.'[6] One might even adapt Rose Macaulay's words quoted in this chapter's epigraph, and suggest that Cretomania was part and parcel of the Minoans' becoming 'part of the familiar landscapes of our minds', while also representing something strange, disturbing, and 'almost too much to take'.

The period 1900–14 – Morand's age of Cretomania – coincides with the latter part of what Lesley Fitton has aptly called the 'Heroic Age of Excavation' of the Aegean

Bronze Age, starting with Heinrich Schliemann's discoveries at Troy in 1870 and ending with the First World War.[7] The years 1900–14 could be seen as the 'Heroic Age' of Cretomania too, but as I illustrate in this work some obsessions with the Minoan past can be found even in antiquity, while Morand's Cretomania arguably increased after the First World War, has lasted into our present, and is not limited to the fine arts, as it occurs in a wide variety of different cultural forms and practices.

The persistence of Cretomania after the Belle Époque is partly due to new spectacular discoveries in the field that captured the public imagination, such as the new series of excavations conducted by Evans and others on Crete in the 1920s and 1930s; the decipherment of Linear B by Michael Ventris and John Chadwick in the early 1950s; the spectacular finds by Spyridon Marinatos at Akrotiri on Thera (Santorini), the Pompeii of the Aegean, in the late 1960s and early 1970s; and the gruesome discoveries by Efi and Yannis Sakellarakis at Anemospilia, and by Peter Warren at Knossos, in 1979, hinting at Minoan human sacrifice and ritual cannibalism. But the continuing fascination with Minoan Crete is also due to the desire that every generation has to rewrite history, to provide new meanings and responses to the Minoan past, and to find in it the cultural legacy it looks for.

This legacy is not limited to what the inhabitants of Bronze Age Crete left to Mycenaean Greece and, via Mycenaean Greece, to Classical Greece and hence Europe in terms of material and non-material culture, from religion to language. This legacy also includes the dreams, desires, and creativity that the Minoan past has inspired since antiquity, and especially since the early twentieth century AD. In fact, I should like to suggest that the most significant and enduring Minoan cultural legacy largely rests upon the long chain of its interpretations and receptions, both within and beyond recondite archaeological research.[8] After all, the label 'Minoan Crete' does not simply refer to what happened on that island in the third and second millennia BC – the current canonical chronology of its 'Bronze' or 'Minoan Age'. Minoan Crete is largely a modern construct – the product of centuries of scholarship, interpretations, reconstructions, and modern responses to this Bronze Age past. These are all steeped in interpretative traditions, which are not exclusively related to archaeology and its practice, but encompass other fields, from anthropology to sociology, gender studies, and art history. Whether it is the iconic 'snake goddess' figurines or the amazing 'Palace of Minos' at Knossos with its famous Minoan frescoes, these material remains are the products of Minoan or Bronze Age Crete, but have also acquired multiple layers of meaning throughout their life.[9] They were produced in the past, but are also simultaneously part of our present, and are understood within it: to recognize this constant, two-directional, and ever-changing dialogue between past and present is a first step towards a deeper understanding of both.[10] It is often impossible to create a clear-cut distinction between ancient objects on the one hand and people's ideas about them on the other, and least of all in connection with the place of Minoan Crete in the modern imagination – both are products of complex webs of entanglements.[11] For example, the faience statuettes of the 'snake goddess' and her votaries from the Temple Repositories at Knossos (see Fig. 1.1), which for Evans were symbols of the Great Minoan Mother Goddess and precursors of the Virgin Mary,[12] in other contexts have represented the Oriental and alluring nature of Minoan culture, full of sexual promise, or the simultaneous antiquity and modernity of Minoan culture, its feminine or even matriarchal/matrilineal character, symbolic of a happier past and hope for a happier future, especially for women (see Fig. 1.2). Similarly, the Knossos 'palace', from a possible ceremonial centre or 'temple-palace',[13] has become the labyrinth of King Minos of Classical sources, a *lieu de mémoire* (realm of memory) for both ancient and modern societies,[14] a Cretan 'Acropolis',[15] and something resembling what the French philosopher Michel Foucalt has called a 'heterotopia': a place that, unlike utopias and dystopias, has a physical presence and reflects but also distorts reality.[16] In fact, one might argue that Minoan Crete (and, by extension, the Minoans and their legacy) can be seen as a heterotopia: a real place that has been used as a mirror for modern societies and individuals, linking past, present, and future.

As will be clear from the above discussion, this book is not intended for the reader who wishes to learn what amazing inventions we have ultimately inherited from the Minoans, since I believe that the most significant cultural legacy of Minoan Crete consists of both the spectacular remains of the third and second millennia BC and the accumulated layers of responses to and interpretations of this material culture, i.e. how and why they have captured the scholarly and public imagination alike. To give a concrete example, the fact that generations have believed in a Minoan matriarchy or matrilineal succession is as important and interesting as whether or not this form of social organization actually existed in Bronze Age Crete. In addition, as I have also argued elsewhere, there is much one can learn from various responses to the Minoan

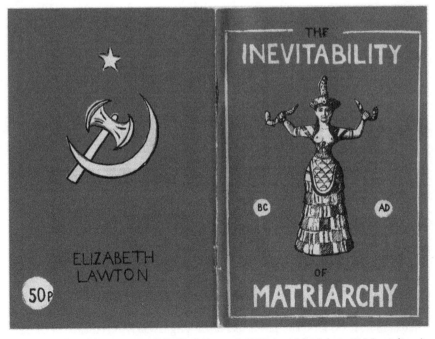

Fig. 1.2 Back and front cover of Elizabeth Lawton's 1977 pamphlet (photo N. Momigliano).

past beyond archaeology.[17] Although each response can be seen as subjective and historically contingent, it is not arbitrary, since it does pertain to specific features of Minoan culture. For example, numerous writers (e.g. Dmitry Merezhkovsky, André Gide), artists (e.g. Marc Chagall, Roussetos Panagiotakis), and even followers of Neo-Pagan movements (e.g. members of the Minoan Brotherhood) have responded to gender-ambiguous human representations in Minoan iconography, such as those in the Toreador Fresco from Knossos (cf. also below). Each response can be historicized and evaluated in its own terms, but can also be compared and studied alongside specialist literature to encourage reflection on representations of sex and gender, and on how some assumptions regarding iconography have been employed to extrapolate generalizations about social organization and gender relations both in antiquity and today. Thus, in this book I offer some ideas on the Minoan cultural legacy by presenting a history of the rediscovery of Minoan Crete and its reception, both within and beyond archaeology.

The story of the main excavations on the island of Crete since 1900, especially for the early twentieth century, is relatively well known and has been recounted many times, whereas it is only in recent years that scholars have developed an interest in the uses of Minoan Crete in modern cultural practices.[18] Here, I attempt a more integrated discussion of both: as suggested above, if Minoan Crete mattered to a wide public in the last two decades of the Belle Époque, and has continued to matter to the present day, it is precisely because its discoveries have been incorporated into contemporary narratives and debates on a wide variety of topics, from developments in social organization to art history, sexuality, gender relations, and the construction of different types of identities. To give some examples, Minoan Crete is regularly cited in discussions about the history of matriarchy (e.g. Fig. 1.2), it has also been involved in debates about early modernist art (e.g. Art Nouveau, Art Deco),[19] and has inspired Neo-Pagan and LGBT groups, such as the Minoan Brotherhood, the Minoan Sisterhood, and Modern Minoan Paganism.[20] Furthermore, Minoan Crete has played an important role in discourses relating to regional (Cretan), national (Hellenic), and even transnational (European) identities. Thus, the Minoan past is a common source of pride among modern Cretans, and its images are frequently used in both official and unofficial art, from official stamps to local crafts;[21] the Minoans were the first tableau in the parade of Hellenic history at the opening ceremony of the 2004 Olympic games in Athens;[22] and Minoan Crete, since Evans's times, has often been invoked as the fountainhead of European civilization.[23] Minoan elements have not only been incorporated into numerous discourses on topics that range from matriarchy to Cretan, Hellenic, and European identities, but also figure in a wide variety of modern cultural practices, from the visual arts to literature (see Figs. 1.2–1.3), modern fashion, television programmes, movies, graphic novels, comics, and even music, as illustrated by the gigantic Minoan snake goddess in Harrison Birtwistle's 2008 opera *Minotaur* and the 2014 album *Minoans* by the post-metal, progressive-rock band Giant Squid.

In this book, besides providing an outline of Minoan discoveries and their uses in different cultural practices, I wish to highlight (or, at least, begin to explore) some topics pertaining to the reception of the Minoans that have not attracted much attention so far, such as the role of Minoan material culture as a catalyst for new creativity; the role of modern artists and writers in the diffusion of knowledge about the Minoan past, beyond the narrow boundaries of specialist disciplines; and, last but not least, the potential influence of artists and writers on archaeological and historical enquiry, its reception and interpretation.

With regard to the last point, we take almost for granted that archaeological discoveries have been used in, and therefore have affected, modern cultural practices. But what is the influence that, in turn, literary and artistic works have exercised upon archaeological interpretations and practices? As recent works on Pompeii have shown, scholarship on this famous site has 'porous boundaries' and 'is deeply susceptible to the workings of the public imagination', whether one is dealing with the history of the Gabinetto Segreto (Secret Cabinet) of Roman erotica or the delayed application of scientific archaeological techniques to the bodies discovered there, to mention a couple of examples.[24] How has the public imagination interacted with Minoan Crete? What are the dynamics between scholarly (e.g. archaeological or linguistic) views of the Minoans and the uses of Minoan elements in modern literary works, paintings or other artefacts? Paul Klee's famous words – 'Art does not reproduce the visible; rather, it makes visible' – are a good reminder that modern responses to Minoan Crete have the potential to stimulate different ways of seeing it and offer opportunities to reflect on its past, present, and future significance.

Thus, as illustrated in the following chapters, artistic movements, such as Art Nouveau, which partly preceded but also coincided with the archaeological discoveries on Crete, paved the way for the enthusiastic reception of the vivid imagery of Minoan Crete. In addition, while sometimes artists and writers have reaffirmed dominant scholarly narratives and orthodoxies about the Minoans, at other times they appear to have significantly modified or questioned them, in ways that intriguingly intersect with and anticipate later scholarly debates. For example, Marc Chagall's *L'écuyère*, an irreverent take on the famous Toreador Fresco from Knossos (see Figs. 1.3 and 1.4), in which all genders are transformed or reversed (the bull becomes a gelding or a mare, the bull-leaper a woman, and the attendants are male), seems to foreshadow modern scholarly debates on gender representation and ambiguity in Minoan iconography, since, at that time, no scholar had seriously challenged Evans's interpretation of the two white-skinned figures in the Toreador fresco as female.[25] Similarly, Mary Renault's hybrid Graeco-Minoan Knossian elite of her *The King Must Die* (1958) finds an echo in more recent discussions of the hybridity of the Knossian Throne Room imagery in its latest stages, while some of Don DeLillo's works, especially his 1988 short story 'The Ivory Acrobat', which is partly inspired by a well-known Minoan object (see Fig. 1.5), intersects with more recent scholarly discussions about materiality and agency, including such issues as the relationship between archaeology and the senses, and how material culture affects our own identities and self-awareness.[26]

Although I focus on the relatively recent discovery and reception of Minoan Crete from *c.* 1900 onwards, my story starts much earlier, since evidence of fascination with things Minoan and some uses of Minoan material culture as catalyst for further creativity are found already in antiquity. The chain of discoveries, interpretations, and responses to what we now call Minoan Crete can be seen already in the use of Minoan elements by other groups in the second millennium BC, including the Mycenaeans, the

Fig. 1.3 Marc Chagall, *L'écuyère* (1925), Private Collection, North California (photo courtesy of the current owner).

Fig. 1.4 Knossos, the Toreador fresco (after Evans, 1930: fig. 144).

Fig. 1.5 Knossos, The Ivory Acrobat (photo: Wolfang Moroder, https://commons.
wikimedia.org/wiki/File:Bull-leaper_ivory_figurine_from_the_palace_of_Knossos.JPG).

Egyptians, and perhaps even the Hittites. This pattern is evident in later periods of
Greek antiquity too. For example, in the Greek Early Iron Age (tenth–eighth centuries
BC) one can see a conscious manipulation of surviving Minoan monuments and local
memories in the form of burial and cultic activities. These activities involved the reuse
of Minoan tombs and decorative motifs on funerary pottery as well as depositions of
votive offerings by the monumental ruins of Minoan buildings. Indeed, scholars have
traced a variety of responses to the remains of a Minoan past even in later Hellenistic
and Roman times (cf. Chapter 2). To take one example, it has been suggested that
Hellenistic uses of older Minoan sites and even Minoan scripts are indicative of
communities exploiting their own local traditions for their own specific purposes. In
the Roman period, however, the uses of the Minoan past seem to have been based more
on literary sources (including local mythographical traditions) than actual physical
remains, and they present a more pan-Cretan and pan-Hellenic character, which could
be linked to Roman genealogies and imperial legitimation.

This shift towards literary sources is a reminder that, for centuries, a great deal of
what people knew about what we now call Minoan Crete was largely textual – from
Homeric poems to Attic tragedies, accounts by ancient historians such as Herodotus
and Thucydides, and later elaborations in Hellenistic and Roman mythography –
although material culture also played a part (see Fig. 1.6). Some of these later Greek

Fig. 1.6 Black-figure Attic vase with Minotaur image (photo: Marie-Lan Nguyen, at https://commons.wikimedia.org/wiki/File:Tondo_Minotaur_London_E4_MAN.jpg).

stories about Crete in the period before and around the time of the Trojan War, often referred to as 'myths', could be considered as early examples of Cretomania, as they indicate a fascination with and use of the Minoan past to create something new. These stories illustrate how later Greeks attempted to make sense of their surrounding world –a world that included their Minoan forebears in the form of remains of buildings, artefacts, words, landscapes, and rather distant memories.[27] Thus, Evans may have been right in his suggestion that representations of bulls, especially frescoes illustrating bull-leaping (e.g. Fig. 1.4), 'go far to explain the myth [of the Minotaur]'.[28] He may have been right in the sense that later Greek mythological narratives were to some degree creative responses to the ruins of an older Minoan world, which remained highly visible for some considerable time after the final destruction and abandonment of Bronze Age Knossos. These stories were an attempt to explain, within the Greek Iron Age present, these Minoan remnants, whose meaning was no longer part of living memory. But I think he was probably wrong in suggesting that 'it may even be that the captive children of both sexes were trained to take part in the dangerous circus sport portrayed on the Palace walls',[29] because this implies that later Greek stories can be used, without further scrutiny, as evidence for some kind of historical or folk memory of Minoan practices involving captive youths trained in bull-leaping. But how could Greeks of the first millennium BC accurately know and remember that remote past? At the risk of sounding arrogant, there are times when I think that modern archaeologists may have a fuller understanding of some of the activities that occurred in Crete during earlier millennia.

The fact that material remains of the Minoan past remained highly visible in antiquity, especially in the early first millennium BC, and acted as catalysts for remarkable creativity, leads me to suggest that the Minoan and Mycenaean past acted on later generations of Aegean inhabitants in a way comparable to that in which the Classical past, especially fifth–fourth-century BC Athens, has done on subsequent generations: as a reality but also as an ideal, a source of nostalgia, a past of unattainable splendour that could be weighty, even oppressive, but at the same time empowering – something to be emulated, celebrated, and imaginatively used. Just as the Classical past inspired the European Renaissance, *mutatis mutandis* the Aegean Bronze Age, including Minoan Crete, acted, I suggest, as a 'classical' past and inspiration for later Greeks.[30]

The literary and visual depictions of King Minos and his dysfunctional family in Classical sources are one of the earliest responses to the Minoan past and one of the most consequential links in the complex chain of Minoan receptions. After Minoan remains became less visible, and before modern archaeology rediscovered them, Classical sources were effectively the only evidence from which some knowledge of Bronze Age Crete was derived. These sources, especially texts, also formed the basis of Western education for many centuries: their authority and the fact that they were often the locus of one's first encounter with the distant Minoan past have had far-reaching consequences. When excavations made the material culture of Bronze Age Crete visible once again, later Greek narratives became inextricably linked with the ways in which these remains were interpreted. The very fact that Minoan civilization is named after King Minos is eloquent testimony of this tendency. And yet, there are significant and important mismatches between later Greek sources and Minoan ruins – not surprisingly, since, as argued above, these narratives were largely imaginative responses to material remains, rather than accurate remembrances of the Cretan Bronze Age past. Many modern visitors to the archaeological site of Knossos expect to see the Greek myths 'inscribed in the ground',[31] and can be disappointed by the lack of a more labyrinthine experience, with accompanying Minotaur. Some would be astonished to realize that, despite the abundance of bull imagery in Minoan Crete, representations of bull-headed men are extremely rare and also quite late, i.e. dating to a period when, according to many scholars, Crete was ruled by a Greek-speaking Mycenaean elite. It is also possible that some bull-man images could be interpreted as schematic renderings of bull-leapers on tiny seal-stones. In addition, many so-called Minotaur images show representations of monkeys (see Fig. 1.7), dog-, bird-, and goat-human hybrids more often than bovine-human creatures; and some of the bovine-human hybrids appear to be female, as shown by their prominent breasts.[32] Many people interested in Crete may also be disappointed to learn that the palace of Knossos and Minoan civilization generally were not wiped out by a colossal tsunami linked to an eruption of the Santorini volcano, echoing Plato's myth of Atlantis. More baffling than disappointing, perhaps, is the fact that there are competing candidates for the location of the Homeric dancing ground built by Daedalus for Ariadne.[33]

24a 24b 24c

Fig. 1.7 Three different drawings of the same clay seal impression from Knossos, reproduced at different times, which according to Evans showed a seated young Minotaur, but in fact represents a monkey (after Krzyszkowska, 2005: figs. 24a–c reproduced with the author's permission; 24a, after Evans, 1901a: 18 fig. 7a; 24b, after Evans, 1928: 763 fig. 491; and 24c: more recent drawing produced for the *Corpus der minoischen und mykenischen Siegel CMS*, II.8 no. 262: https://www.uni-heidelberg.de/fakultaeten/philosophie/zaw/cms/).

Even if Bronze Age archaeological realities do not match neatly ancient Greek narratives (and imagery), our first encounters with the latter linger in our individual and collective memory. In other words, conscious or unconscious remembrance of powerful Greek myths continues to colour our perceptions of the Minoan past.[34] After all, if Macaulay qualifies the 'strangeness' of Minoan civilization as 'monstrous', it is probably because Greek stories about Pasiphae's bestiality and the resulting Minotaur are lurking in the back of her mind. Indeed, these literary, mythological connections were often the very motive behind some early archaeological endeavours. There can be little doubt that the first modern excavations at Knossos conducted by Minos Kalokairinos in 1878 were a search for the palace and labyrinth of his famous namesake,[35] since they were conducted only two years after Heinrich Schliemann had discovered the famous Shaft Graves at Mycenae, and had written to the King of Greece: 'Your Majesty, it is with great pleasure that I inform you that I have discovered the tombs which, according to Pausanias' account, belong to Agamemnon, Cassandra, and their comrades who were murdered by Clytemnestra and her paramour, Aegisthus, during a feast.'[36]

The connections between later Greek myths and Bronze Age Cretan remains also helped to make the Minoans somewhat more familiar, and even to 'Hellenize' them, to some extent. This and the close relationship between the Minoans and the Greek-speaking Mycenaeans can also partly explain the inclusion of the Aegean Bronze Age within the discipline of Classics, albeit in a marginal position. Often construed as the background of 'the glory that was Greece',[37] the Aegean Bronze Age is usually taught in departments concerned with Classics and Ancient History in Europe and elsewhere. And yet, as I discuss in later chapters, the Aegean Bronze Age, and Minoan Crete in particular, remains for many not 'classical' enough.[38] The Mycenaeans at least had the decency of speaking and writing in a form of ancient Greek, as Michael Ventris's decipherment of Linear B has shown. The Minoans did not, at least for most of their history. Even worse, they have not shown the courtesy of allowing us to decipher their other scripts – Cretan Pictographic (a.k.a. Cretan Hieroglyphic), Linear A, and the signs on the enigmatic Phaistos disk – despite endless attempts. Thus, one could almost say of the Minoans that they 'went out from us but they were not of us', in the sense that they are too alien and different, or simply too anti-Classical.[39] They are at the same time a reminder that what constitutes ancient Greece contains much that many would regard as 'un-Greek' – and if some people find this mixture of the familiar and the strange stimulating, others find it disturbing. The Minoans appear as marginal also geographically, culturally, and academically vis-à-vis other great ancient cultures of the Ancient Near East, such as the Hittite, Egyptian, Sumerian, Akkadian, and Babylonian, as well as the cultures of continental Europe. Geographically and culturally, they are often seen as being suspended between Africa, Asia, and Europe, between East and West, however these are defined. For many scholars and laypeople alike, this very ambiguity is one of the Minoans' most attractive features, together with their perceived mixture of strangeness and familiarity, primitivism and modernity, barbarity and refinement. Being strange, mysterious or even 'desperately foreign' is not necessarily always a bad thing.[40]

In the remaining pages of this Introduction, I outline the main chapters in my journey into the Minoan cultural legacy. Before I do so, however, I must clarify a methodological point related to the contents of this book. The crucial criterion for the selection of material has been the evidence of actual engagement with the material culture of Minoan Crete in the creation of something new. Consequently, even if I do consider some Greek narratives as the first important link in a long chain of responses to the Bronze Age material culture of Crete, I do not necessarily include as part of the *Minoan* cultural legacy every work of the twentieth and twenty-first centuries that was inspired by later Greek narratives pertaining to the island, unless it also engages with Minoan archaeology. As already suggested by Farnoux and Ziolkowsky, there is no doubt that the archaeological discoveries on Crete in the early twentieth century stimulated a considerable revival of interest in Greek myths related to Crete among writers and artists.[41] This revival is in itself part of the Minoan cultural legacy. Yet, it is clear that not every modern novel or artwork dealing with Minos, Pasiphae, Ariadne, Phaedra, the labyrinth, and the Minotaur was necessarily inspired by Minoan material culture in any significant way. Examples of this are Picasso's female matadors and Minotaur images, which make no significant allusion to the imagery of Minoan Crete and are more closely inspired by classical iconography and literature, especially Ovid's *Metamorphoses*.[42] Similarly, I see no clear evidence that De Chirico's *Ariadne* (1913) and other paintings were inspired by Minoan archaeological discoveries – despite the fact that De Chirico was briefly taught by Émile Gilliéron, one of the artists who worked for Evans at Knossos.[43] Even some modern works that appear, at first sight, to show quintessential Minoan features, such as bare-breasted snake-handling women, do not necessarily allude to the material culture of Bronze Age Crete. An example is Gustav Klimt's representation of Hygeia, which was part of his larger composition titled *Medicine*, the second of his University of Vienna ceiling paintings, commissioned in 1894 and presented in March 1901 at the tenth Secession Exhibition. Here, the personification of the Greek goddess of health is portrayed with a snake twisted around her arm, in a manner reminiscent of the famous 'snake goddesses' from Knossos (see Fig. 1.8a–b; cf. Fig. 1.1). The latter, however, were not discovered until 1903, so Klimt evidently drew on classical and even modern representations of Asclepius's staff, not on Minoan Crete.[44] Similarly, Klimt's representation of bare-breasted women with slithering snakes in their hair in his 1902 Beethoven Frieze precedes the Minoan discoveries, and is related to classical imagery of the snake-haired gorgons. Yet, Klimt's works are significant for Minoan Crete because they help to explain why the material culture of this island was so enthusiastically received in the early twentieth century, especially among some avant-garde artists. By contrast, my survey of examples of Minoan cultural legacy includes works that seem to all appearances unrelated to Bronze Age Crete, but actually refer to specific Minoan finds. An example of this is Paul Klee's sketch reproduced in Fig. 1.9. This work betrays its Minoan inspiration mostly through its title – *The Snake Goddess and her Foe* – but also through other elements, such as the fact that the enemy appears to be modelled on a sign from the Phaistos disk (cf. also Chapter 4).

My journey into the Minoan cultural legacy starts with Chapter 2, where I present a sketch of ancient responses to Minoan Crete and outline the body of knowledge about what we now call 'Minoan' Crete that existed before 1900. More specifically,

a　　　　　　　　　　　　　　b

Fig. 1.8a–b Gustav Klimt, *Medicine*, and detail of Hygieia, University of Vienna ceiling paintings (presented in March 1901 at the tenth Secession Exhibition) (photo: https://en.wikipedia.org/wiki/Klimt_University_of_Vienna_Ceiling_Paintings and https://commons.wikimedia.org/wiki/File:Hku_Klimt_Hygieia.jpg).

Fig. 1.9 Paul Klee, *The Snake Goddess and her Foe* (1940) (after Klee and Read, 1948: 52).

Chapter 2 offers a brief overview of Bronze Age Crete in contemporary sources of the second millennium BC; the mythological cycles connected with Crete found in Classical sources; and views of the distant, pre-Classical history of Crete as it was conceived from the Middle Ages down to the mid-nineteenth century, including the invention of a 'Minoan Age', modelled on the 'Homeric Age', by a group of German scholars linked to the University of Göttingen.

Chapter 3 covers the period from *c.* 1870 to the First World War, i.e. from Schliemann's excavations at Troy, Mycenae, and elsewhere to the main discoveries made on Crete by Evans and others up to *c.* 1914. I focus on Evans's work, especially his allegedly peaceful vision of the Minoans as non-Aryan devotees of a Great Mother Goddess, and on the early rapturous reception of the Minoans, i.e. the 'Cretomania' of the final decades of the Belle Époque as exemplified in the works of Léon Bakst, Mariano Fortuny, Henri Antoine Jules Bois, František Kupka, and many others. I also examine the dynamics and tensions between local, national, and transnational uses and appropriations of Minoan Crete that are visible in various processes of familiarization, Europeanization, and Hellenization of the Minoans before the First World War.

Chapter 4 examines the main archaeological developments in Crete and their reception in the period framed by the First World War and the Greek Civil War. Here I discuss relevant discoveries and influential archaeological publications, such as Evans's *The Palace of Minos* and Gordon Childe's *The Dawn of European Civilization*, as well as contemporary responses to Minoan Crete in a wide variety of works, including novels (e.g. Merezhkovsky's *The Birth of the Gods*), universal histories (e.g. Oswald Spengler's

Decline of the West), poems (e.g. by D. H. Lawrence and Nikos Kazantzakis), the visual arts (e.g. works by Massimo Campigli), architecture and textile productions (e.g. by Florentini Kaloutsi and Josef Frank), among other examples. My discussion highlights how the Minoans in this period began to elicit contradictory interpretations and responses, from Evans's grandiose imperialist vision to Spengler's notion of the Minoans as decadent and Oriental. I also discuss how the rise of Aryanism contributed to the polarization of the Minoan and Mycenaean worlds as feminine and pacifist vs. patriarchal and warlike, respectively. Yet, as the otherization and feminization of the Minoans gained more currency, at the same time processes of familiarization, Hellenization and Europeanization continued in this period, especially in Greek contexts.

Chapter 5 presents the main archaeological discoveries of the third quarter of the twentieth century (from the aftermath of the Greek Civil War to the end of the Colonels' dictatorship), which include, among others, the decipherment of Linear B and its implications for the Minoans; the discovery of new Minoan palaces; and the excavations of Akrotiri on Thera. In this chapter I discuss the resurgence of Minoan Crete as a feminine, and feminist, peaceful paradise, which was partly stimulated by second wave feminism and anti-war movements. I show how archaeological discoveries and developments interacted with modern receptions of the Minoans, and often continued to polarize Minoans and Mycenaeans/Greeks, as illustrated in numerous 'Cretomanic' works of this period, such as Mary Renault's historical novels, the poetry of Salvatore Quasimodo, and travel writings. I also examine further examples of the uses and appropriations of Minoan Crete in the visual arts, cinema and television productions, and even comics and advertising.

Chapter 6 deals with the archaeological discoveries made in the last quarter of the twentieth century, including the evidence for ritual cannibalism at Knossos and for human sacrifice at Anemospilia near Archanes, and further develops the idea of Minoan Crete as a paradise lost, but also regained – a useful utopia or Foucauldian heterotopia – as illustrated in many cultural products of this period, especially those that present strong feminist and pacifist messages, such as Christa Wolf's *Cassandra: A Novel and Four Essays*. I also discuss works that explore the darker sides of the Minoans and open a new dialogue between the distant Minoan past and the postmodern self, such as Don DeLillo's novel *The Names* and his short story 'The Ivory Acrobat', Dorothy Porter's quirky and sensuous poems from her collection titled *Crete*, and Rhea Galanaki's historical novels.

In Chapter 7 I summarize my journey into the Minoan cultural legacy from antiquity to the end of the last millennium, and discuss some recent trends and examples of Cretomania in the twenty-first century, from opera and rock music to Olympic parades and sensory experiences of the Minoan past.

It has not been feasible (or desirable) to include in the present volume every single painting, building, object, novel, poem, fashion item and other cultural product that expresses some form of Cretomania. This would have been especially difficult, if not impossible, for the first two decades of the twenty-first century, which have seen a multiplication of the use of the Minoan past in an ever wider variety of cultural practices. My choice has been, at times, serendipitous, and influenced by the help of friends and colleagues, who have kindly brought some material to my attention. Some readers may find puzzling my inclusion of rather obscure and not exactly high-quality materials, but these too are interesting and have a function, since both famous and not so famous artists and writers have responded to the same materials and ideas, and all their works help to elucidate patterns and broader trends: Elisabeth Lawton (see Fig. 1.2) is not as famous as Sigmund Freud, but her work is a response to the same Minoan iconography and persistent notion that Minoan Crete was a society in which women played an important role, and even maintained some vestiges of matriarchy. At any rate, the examples discussed in the following chapters should amply illustrate the remarkable and fascinating variety of materials that are available for understanding ancient and modern responses to Minoan Crete. I also hope that these examples will suffice to show how the study of Cretomania can be good to think with, in an attempt to understand the Minoan cultural legacy and our changing relationship with the intriguing past of this Mediterranean island. Above all, I hope that this work will stimulate others to conduct further research with different approaches and in more depth than I was able to pursue in this broad survey.

Sons of Europa: From Medical Remedies for Constipation to Bestiality, Sexually Transmitted Death, and the Dawn of the 'Minoan Age' (from Antiquity to the Mid-Nineteenth Century)

Another [remedy] for defecation: 6 grains of gngnt. It is like the bean of the land of Keftiu.

> Papyrus Ebers: cf. Jean Vercoutter (1956: 39–40); Eric Cline (1994: 109 A.9)

Mythisch ist durch und durch die Minoische Zeit . . . Alles bedeutsame mehrerer Jahrhunderte ward an jenen Namen (Minos) angereiht.
The Minoan Period is mythic through and through . . . everything of some significance [that happened] over several centuries was linked to that name (Minos).

> Karl Hoeck (1828: vi and xxxi)

Most works on Minoan Crete begin with Sir Arthur Evans's epoch-making excavations of the 'Palace of Minos', and may briefly refer to the short-lived, but significant, excavations conducted in 1878 by the suitably named Minos Kalokairinos as well as the failed attempt to continue them by William J. Stillman, since both were contributing factors in Evans's later decision to dig at Knossos.[1] Evans first visited Crete in 1894, but only started his series of excavation campaigns six years later, on 23 March 1900, because of the turbulent political situation on the island, which engaged in its last rebellion against Ottoman rule in the final years of the nineteenth century.[2] Evans's excavations were followed by Federico Halbherr's at Phaistos only a few weeks later, and soon afterwards by the work of other archaeologists, such as D. G. Hogarth, Harriet Boyd, Richard Seager, and R. C. Bosanquet at the sites of Psychro, Kato Zakro, Gournia, Vasiliki, Mochlos, Pseira, and Palaikastro.

The spectacular excavations conducted by Evans and others in the early twentieth century arguably represent the most significant watershed in our modern understanding of what we now call Minoan Crete, especially in regard to the quantities of material remains that were unearthed and revealed to global audiences. Nevertheless, these explorations did not start from a *tabula rasa*, especially in terms of interpretative frameworks and theories. An appreciable body of knowledge concerning the distant past of Crete existed already, and this included not only literary but also archaeological and linguistic data, all of which influenced later discoveries and interpretations of the Minoans to a considerable extent. In addition, intriguing and important responses to what we nowadays call the Minoan past started in antiquity, and some deeply affected modern responses to the Cretan Bronze Age. Thus, this chapter attempts to provide a snapshot of previous perceptions and receptions of Minoan Crete, starting from contemporary Near Eastern sources of the third–second millennia B C and ending with Federico Halbherr's epigraphic and archaeological explorations in the 1880s and 1890s, before the start of excavations at Knossos and Phaistos in 1900.

Ancient responses to Minoan Crete

Ancient responses 1: Minoans 'under Near Eastern eyes'[3]

Minoan Crete interacted with major civilizations of the ancient Near East, Egypt in particular, from the late fourth and especially during the second millennium B C. This is shown by the discovery of numerous Minoan artefacts in Near Eastern regions and, vice-versa, of Near Eastern artefacts at various Minoan sites. These archaeological finds are sometimes accompanied by textual and pictorial evidence, which, according to most scholars, allude to Minoan Crete.[4] Although useful for illustrating ancient responses to Minoan Crete, one should also bear in mind that these objects and texts were not available to scholars (and the wider public) until the nineteenth and early twentieth century A D. Thus, to a large extent, the ancient Near Eastern responses to Minoan Crete are mediated through modern scholarship of the last three centuries, and did not influence modern responses to Bronze Age Crete as much as the ancient Greek responses discussed later.

Minoan artefacts, ranging from high-quality pottery and stone vases to more humble items (such as loom-weights), were exported to Near Eastern sites and, in some cases, locally produced, as indicated by analyses of raw materials, such as their clay. Some Near Eastern sites have also yielded frescoes and painted plaster floors in Minoan style and *buon fresco* technique (e.g. at Avaris, Tell Kabri, and Alalakh).[5] All this suggests esteem for Minoan products and also movements of people originating from Crete, or trained by Cretans, to the lands surrounding the Aegean and Eastern Mediterranean seas.

The textual evidence is the most intriguing, and largely relies on connecting some place names with Crete. Texts that may refer to what we now call the 'Minoans' have been discovered in various Near Eastern regions: at various sites in Egypt, where one also finds pictorial representations and plenty of other archaeological evidence; at Ugarit (Syria–Palestine), where texts are also accompanied by other archaeological evidence; as far as Mari on the Euphrates, although no accompanying Minoan artefacts have been found to date in Mesopotamia; and, finally, it has been recently suggested that references to the Minoan world appear in contemporary Hittite documents. In none of these written documents, however, are there references to the word Minos (and derivatives), or even to the word Crete (and derivatives), although the latter already appears in the Linear B tablets of the late second millennium BC. What one finds, instead, are other terms that in the nineteenth and twentieth centuries have been correlated with Crete by many if not all scholars.

Egyptian texts

Egyptian texts with likely Minoan connections span chronologically the nineteenth through to the twelfth century BC, i.e. from the times of Sesostris I in the twelfth dynasty down to Ramesses VI. They range from topographical lists to medicinal remedies, including one for constipation through the use of beans (cf. epigraph).

Two Egyptian words in these texts have been associated with Minoan Crete: the first is *Kft(j)w*, vocalized as 'Keftiu', the other is *Iww hryw-ib nw W3-wr*, usually translated as 'People from the Isles in the Middle of the Great Green' or 'from the islands in the midst of the Sea'.[6] Particularly important for this association are some Theban tombs of the 18th Dynasty (*c.* fifteenth century BC), which depict and mention in their accompanying inscriptions people from Keftiu and from the Isles in the Middle of the Great Green, who are carrying objects brought to Egypt as either 'tribute' or 'gifts', depending on one's translation of related terms. The objects that are being carried are clearly recognizable as Aegean and ultimately Minoan (see Fig. 2.1).

One should also note that some of this evidence, such as the Theban tombs and later documents, date from a period of growing Mycenaean influence in the Aegean,

Fig. 2.1 Detail from a scene depicting foreigners bringing gifts in the tomb of Rekhmire (TT 100) at Thebes, Egypt: facsimile painting by Nina de Garis Davies (in the public domain: https://www.metmuseum.org/art/collection/search/544609).

and that it is therefore possible that Keftiu and People from the Isles in the Middle of the Great Green may, at different times, have been used to refer to both what we now call Minoans and Mycenaeans.

Mesopotamian and Ugaritic texts

Most scholars believe that the term Keftiu can be related to the toponym Kaphtor/Caphtor (Hebrew כפתור) found in the Bible and in other sources, and that Kaphtor, in turn, can be identified with Crete.[7] Assuming that this identification is correct, there is an interesting text from Assur, dating to the late eighth or seventh century BC but possibly referring to some earlier tradition, which makes the rather unlikely claim that Kaphtor/Crete was part of Sargon's Akkadian Empire of the third millennium BC. One stands on firmer ground with the texts related to King Zimri-Lim of the city of Mari on the Euphrates, dating to the eighteenth century BC. These mention the trade of tin with people from Kaphtor as well as people and objects from Kaphtor being present at Mari. There are also fourteenth–mid-thirteenth-century Ugaritic texts mentioning tax arrangements for shipments arriving from Kaphtor at this important Levantine port.

Minoan–Anatolian–Hittite relations

That some level of interactions existed between the ancient cultures of what is now modern Turkey and Minoan Crete during the third and especially second millennium BC is attested by a large number of archaeological finds, ranging from obsidian blades of Anatolian provenance in Crete to second-millennium Minoan vases found in Turkey, and stylistic similarities among seal impressions from Cretan Phaistos and Anatolian Karahöyük.[8] Relationships were especially close with Aegean Turkey, but there are also a few Hittite (central Anatolian) finds attested in Minoan Crete, which probably reached the island indirectly, via other coastal sites and Aegean islands. One should also mention a remarkable (Anatolian) ceramic vase found at Hüseyindede Tepe in central Turkey and dated to the reign of the Hittite ruler Hattusili I (late seventeenth century BC), which depicts a scene of bull-leaping in relief.[9] Although bull-leaping is now considered one of the most emblematic motifs in Minoan iconography, this is not uncommon in other contemporary Near Eastern cultures, and for this reason its usefulness as evidence of direct Minoan–Hittite influences remains uncertain.

In regard to written evidence for Minoan–Anatolian relations, in the late 1990s Eric Cline wrote that 'at the moment there are no recognized references to Minoans or to Crete in the texts of the Hittites or other people in second-millennium Anatolia, despite the numerous mentions of the Ahhiyawa, accepted by many scholars as Hittite references to the Mycenaeans . . . So far, there are no explanations for such an absence.'[10] This continues to be the case, even if, more recently, there has been a suggestion that the term Ahhiyawa, which first appear in Hittite documents usually dated from the late fifteenth to mid-fourteenth century BC, may have been used by Hittite scribes to describe people from the Aegean in different periods, including both what we now call Minoans and Mycenaeans, like the term Keftiu discussed above.[11] This speculative suggestion, however, has not found wide acceptance, largely because it requires a higher date for the Hittite documents and a lower date for the Mycenaean takeover of Crete than currently accepted by most scholars (and not everybody agrees that the term Ahhiyawa does refer to Mycenaean Greeks in any case).[12]

At any rate, and despite all the uncertainties, the evidence reviewed above suggests that, on the one hand, Minoan Crete enjoyed close interaction with Egypt and at least most coastal areas of the Eastern Mediterranean: Minoan artisans and their products were widely appreciated and had a degree of mobility. On the other hand, Minoan Crete does not seem to have been a full member of the exclusive 'Great Powers Club' of Near Eastern kingdoms, such as those found in Egypt, Anatolia, and Mesopotamia.[13] Egyptian texts and pictures even suggest a kind of vassal status for Keftiu, although it is not clear whether this reflects the wishful thinking of Egyptian pharaohs or historical reality.

Ancient responses 2: Minoans under northern (Greek) eyes (Mycenaean–Classical)

Mycenaean Greece and the Aegean islands

The close relationship between the Minoans and the Greek-speaking Mycenaeans was briefly mentioned in the introductory chapter, in connection with the inclusion and yet marginal position of the Aegean Bronze Age, and the Minoans in particular, within the discipline of Classics. This close relationship is attested above all by archaeological evidence, which includes a considerable amount of Minoan and Minoanizing objects found on mainland Greece, especially in the centuries around the middle of the second millennium BC, as well as the adoption by the Mycenaeans of various Minoan cultural practices, especially elements of palatial culture, such as the use of wall paintings and Minoan iconography (e.g. depictions of women in typical Minoan ceremonial dress and bull-leaping scenes) and bureaucracy, from the use of seals to the employment of the Linear B script, which is a development of Linear A to express a different language, i.e. Greek.

Extensive adoption of Minoan material culture and practices can also be observed on many Aegean islands, such as Thera (Santorini), Melos, Kea, Naxos, Rhodes, and Kos, to name a few, and even extends to some sites on the Aegean coast of Turkey. This phenomenon was particularly evident in the century or so before the eruption of the Santorini volcano in LM IA, but in some cases, i.e. Kythera, it started as early as the end of the third millennium BC.[14]

The discovery of material culture traits and practices that originated, directly or indirectly, from Crete is often referred to as 'Minoanization' in the relevant archaeological literature.[15] Interpretations of its causes range from military conquest and colonization to commerce, gift-exchanges, emulation, and acculturation processes. As discussed further in the next chapter, Evans had no doubts that the adoption of Minoan features on the Greek mainland, and in many other areas of the Aegean, was ultimately the result of Minoan military action to gain control of trade routes, starting in the Middle Minoan period and leading to conquest and domination of mainland Greece as well as much of the Aegean Sea and even beyond. This view was influenced by the testimony of later Classical sources (cf. below), which described the establishment of a Minoan *thalassocracy* (sea empire) some generations before the Trojan War, as much as it was affected by the imperialist environment of Evans's own time. It still attracts some strong support, but was already contested in the 1910s by scholars such as Carl Blegen and Alan Wace, who maintained that

> The glory of Tiryns and Mycenae was the climax of prehistoric art on the mainland of Greece and, as shown conclusively by Sir Arthur Evans . . . is derived from Crete. Yet though Minoan in origin, the Mycenaean civilisation is not merely transplanted from Crete, but it is the fruit of the cultivated Cretan graft set on the wild stock of the mainland.[16]

Nowadays, most scholars eschew mono-causal interpretations of the Minoanization of the Aegean, whether these follow colonialist/imperialist narratives or other models, if only because this phenomenon is too varied and extended, both geographically and chronologically, to be accounted for through a single explanation. Almost every site tells a different story, and the complexity of comparable and better-documented phenomena, such as the so-called Hellenization and Romanization (to remain within the ancient world), provide sufficient warning against oversimplification. But the occurrence of Minoanization, whatever processes underlie it, is incontrovertible and so is the existence of some form of Minoan cultural prestige in the Aegean, especially in the first half of the second millennium BC, whether accompanied or not by military and political hegemony. Also incontrovertible is that 'Mycenaeanization' replaced 'Minoanization' in the Aegean, especially after the Santorini eruption (see Fig. 2.2). One of the most intriguing facets of this development is that, towards the end of the Aegean Bronze Age (*c.* 1400–1200 BC), the Cretan ruling elite employed a new language (a form of ancient Greek) for its own bureaucratic records, as shown by the Linear B tablets from Knossos and other Cretan sites. This is usually interpreted as a Mycenaean takeover of the island, even if this did not imply a massive migration from the Greek mainland and the obliteration of the non-Greek speaking Minoan population. In fact, inscriptions dating to the seventh–third centuries BC found in east Crete show that a non-Greek language continued to be used on the island as late as the Classical period (cf. also below).

Yet, one should not underestimate the significance of the switch from the language(s) behind the yet to be deciphered Cretan Hieroglyphic and Linear A scripts to the Greek language expressed in Linear B. One may even wonder whether some strange stories regarding the Minoans started in this period, with some elements of their culture getting somewhat lost in translation. Interestingly, as Linear B started being used on Crete, one finds the first, and very rare, representations of a bull-headed man or 'Minotaur' on some seals (cf. Chapter 1) – an image that will become commonly associated with Crete and the story of Theseus in late Geometric–Archaic Greece, especially in Attica.

The end of the period of Mycenaean administration on Crete eventually coincided with the upheavals that occurred in much of the eastern Mediterranean at the end of the Bronze Age (thirteenth–twelfth centuries BC) and are usually referred to as the

Fig. 2.2 Cartoon of Santorini eruption as Mycenaean plot (from A. G. Fawkes, *Cartoons of Cyprus*, 2001, reproduced with the author's permission).

collapse of Bronze Age civilization.[17] Despite some degree of cultural continuity (e.g. languages), these upheavals led to a series of important transformations, which heralded the emergence of new social, political, and economic systems in the period conventionally labelled as the Early Iron Age.

Early Iron Age (Sub-Minoan–Late Geometric, eleventh–eighth centuries BC)

Together with the rediscovery of Minoan culture in the early twentieth century, this period is probably one of the most significant in the complex chain of Minoan receptions. It is likely that during this phase many of the famous Greek stories surrounding King Minos and his family started to emerge. These narratives can be seen as an attempt to make sense of an existing world, which included prominent ruins of buildings and strange artefacts brought to light by the reuse of old tombs, ploughing, digging for wells, and other similar activities. It was also a world that included a somewhat distant, imperfectly remembered past, but also something perceived as splendid, and offering exciting possibilities for reinvention in the process of creating new social identities – a transformation from *milieux* to *lieu de mémoire* (i.e. from living memory to memory crystallized by a will to remember).[18]

During the Early Iron Age, and especially in the late ninth and eighth centuries BC, there is considerable evidence for what Nicolas Coldstream has referred to as a kind of nostalgia for a Minoan past and Mieke Prent as a conscious manipulation of local

Minoan realities.[19] At Knossos, for example, in the late ninth century BC, after a break in the use of traditional burial grounds (since no tomb in the Knossos region appears to show continuous use from LM III to sub-Minoan), there is evidence for reuse of older Minoan tombs and *larnakes* (clay coffins), especially for child burials.[20] The reuse of tombs brought to light older Minoan objects and these encounters with Minoan material culture at times acted as catalysts for new artistic creativity. Examples of this are some Early Iron Age vases that appear to draw inspiration directly from Neopalatial motifs, such as some Geometric domed lids found in Knossian tombs decorated with an octopus motif, in which the position of the octopus's head above its tentacles and the number of tentacles indicate that it derived from Marine Style pottery of the Late Minoan IB period, and not from later examples (where the position of the head is inverted and the number of tentacles reduced).[21]

Further encounters with the physical remains of the Minoan past, and active engagement with them, are attested among the ruins of various Minoan settlements, which remained highly visible for some centuries, especially in the Early Iron Age. The evidence suggests both deliberate avoidance and veneration. The former is demonstrated by the fact that some areas among the Bronze Age settlements, especially those linked with the former Minoan palaces or other significant buildings, were not employed for habitation purposes.[22] The latter is indicated by the Early Iron Age votive offerings that are often found near impressive Minoan ashlar walls, showing that these ruins were used for repeated cultic activities. This has led some scholars to speak of 'ruin cults', examples of which have been found at sites such as Knossos, Amnisos, Tylissos, Phaistos, Hagia Triada, Kommos, and Palaikastro.[23] In other words, these Minoan ruins, especially ashlar walls, become foci of rituals and *lieux de mémoire* inspiring stories similar to those found in the Homeric poems and other Classical sources about the walls of Troy, Mycenae, Tiryns, and Athens, which were said to have been built by gods (Poseidon and Apollo), Cyclopes instructed by Zeus, and the Pelasgians.[24]

As shown in the preceding chapter, Evans suggested that the imposing wall paintings still visible after the Bronze Age may have inspired later Greek myths, such as that of Theseus and the Minotaur. He even proposed, perhaps less reasonably, that these myths could have preserved some (folk?) memory of the Minoan practice of training captive youths (male and female) to take part in the bull-leaping activities portrayed in Knossian frescoes. More recently, Sarah Morris has suggested that the Minotaur story (including related human offerings) may have been inspired, instead, by misunderstood images of Late Bronze Age–Early Iron Age Canaanite/Cypriot horned gods and the Semitic custom of human sacrifice, which were widely spread around the Mediterranean – a custom later rejected in Greece, but remembered in mythology.[25] Her suggestion is strengthened by the fact that Crete has offered plenty of evidence for contacts with the Levant and the Near East in the Late Bronze Age–Early Iron Age, and was one of the first regions in Greece to adopt Orientalizing fashions. Yet, the potential agency of Minoan ruins and artefacts in the creation of Greek mythological narratives about Crete should not be underestimated either. Seal-stones and other finds in reused tombs as well as imposing ruins and frescoes served as one of the catalysts in the creation of new stories. It is unlikely that these stories reflected accurately Bronze Age activities and events, but had resonance in new Iron Age realities and social identities. In this period Crete started developing the Dorian character that came to dominate the island in its Archaic–Classical phases, and in the competitive context of the emerging Greek poleis, perhaps it is not fortuitous that some of the earliest surviving representations of the Minotaur (as bull-headed man) in the Late Geometric period (eighth century BC) come from Ionian Attica, the home of mythical Theseus.[26] It is also in Attic literary works that one can find many stories related to Crete, as discussed in the next section.

A girl and bull story: The creation of Cretan literary topoi

As mentioned above, before the excavations of the twentieth century, knowledge of the Bronze Age Cretan past derived almost exclusively from Classical texts that contained mythological narratives, such as those of Europa and the Bull, the labyrinth of King Minos, and Theseus and the Minotaur.[27] These texts and the stories that they relate are not only powerful, authoritative, 'good to think with' narratives,[28] but also often represent people's first encounter with the pre-Classical Cretan past. For all these reasons – especially as 'first impressions' – Greek myths about Crete have continued to colour our perceptions of this island and its Minoan past.[29]

In this section, I provide a brief overview of the main Greek myths linked with Crete and set in that period that we now call the Bronze Age. Most of these narratives are somehow connected to the figure of King Minos, and portray Crete as a strange and contradictory place. This was a land where immortal Zeus (Minos's father) was nurtured, but also died and was buried; a land ruled by law-giving Minos – a Cretan Moses – who conversed with and was wisely guided by Zeus, but also rife with extreme sexual desires, adultery, bestiality (mostly involving women and bulls), pederasty, human sacrifice, magic, murder, and betrayal.

As in the case of the Trojan War, the main sequence of events for the story of the House of Minos can be reconstructed from a variety of sources of different periods, which present intriguing and often contradictory variants. A useful outline of the main elements of the Minoan saga, albeit in a late and systematized form, appears in the compilation of Greek myths known as *The Library/Bibliotheca*, traditionally attributed to Apollodorus and generally believed to be a second-century AD work based on earlier sources.[30] *The Library* recounts how Zeus became enamoured of Europa, a princess from Phoenicia, who was a sister of Cadmus, Phoenix, and Cilix as well as descendent of Poseidon. Zeus, as was his custom when seducing mortals, performed one of his metamorphoses, on this occasion turning himself into a tame bull. After enticing Europa to sit on his back, he jumped into the sea and transported her all the way to Crete, where he ravished her. This text does not tell us why Zeus chose Crete, but perhaps this is not surprising, since we know from other ancient Greek sources (such as Hesiod) that this island was quite important to him: it was here that his mother Rhea hid him in a cave to save him from being devoured by his father Kronos. After Europa's seduction, Apollodorus's story continues by informing us that the union between her and Zeus resulted in the birth of Minos, Sarpedon, and Rhadamanthys.

His lust satisfied, Zeus palmed Europa off on a Cretan prince called Asterios. Since the latter died childless, his kingdom passed on to Minos, who, meanwhile, had previously gone to war with his siblings over the favours of a young boy called Miletus.

Minos prevailed, but Miletus did not reciprocate his love, and left Crete for Asia Minor. Sarpedon and Rhadamanthys also emigrated: the former became king of Lycia, and the latter, after a spell as lawgiver, settled in Boeotia.[31] Minos then married a Cretan demigoddess, Pasiphae, daughter of the god Helios. Their children were Catreus, Deucalion, Glaucus (who drowned in a jar of honey but was resuscitated thanks to herbal remedies), Androgeus, Acalle, Xenodice, Ariadne, and Phaedra. In addition, Minos had Eurymedon, Nephalion, Chryses, and Philolaus by the nymph Paria as well as Euxanthius by the Kean princess Dexithea, whereas no offspring seem to have emerged from his affair with Procris, daughter of the Athenian king Erechtheus (according to Callimachus, Minos even lost his head for the nymph Britomartis).[32] Pasiphae, perhaps tired of her husband's escapades, put a spell on him: if he took another woman to his bed he would ejaculate, lethally and embarrassingly, wild beasts (snakes, scorpions, and millipedes according to Antoninus Liberalis).[33]

Despite prevailing upon his brothers, Minos's claim to his stepfather's kingdom was challenged. To overcome this problem, he maintained that he had received it from the gods, as shown by the fact that whatever he prayed them for would be granted. To prove this, during a sacrifice to Poseidon, he asked for a bull to be sent from the sea and promised to sacrifice it. Poseidon obliged and Minos got his kingdom. Minos, however, did not keep his promise, and sacrificed another bull. This was a big mistake, and Minos's undoing: in revenge, Poseidon made Pasiphae conceive a great passion for the bull. This was not Platonic love: with the help of that *über* craftsman, Daedalus, she satisfied her lust by camouflaging herself as a heifer. The result of this bestial intercourse was a bull-headed boy named Asterios (after his stepgrandfather), a.k.a. the Minotaur, who was concealed in a labyrinth built by Daedalus (see Fig. 1.6).

The Minotaur later became an instrument of Minos's revenge. Minos's son Androgeos had died in Athens in suspicious circumstances, and his father besieged the city, after sailing across the Aegean with his powerful navy (Herodotus and Thucydides also famously refer to Minos's mastery of the Aegean isles). Athens was eventually forced to accept Minos's demand for an annual tribute consisting of seven youths and seven maidens to be fed to his Minotaur. Theseus, the son of the king of Athens, Aegeus, volunteered to be one of the sacrificial victims and promised to liberate his city from this burdensome levy by slaying the Minotaur. He travels to Knossos and achieves his goal with the help of one of Minos's daughters, Ariadne. He then escapes with her, stopping at Naxos where, according to *The Library*, Dionysus abducts Ariadne (one of the many versions of the Ariadne–Theseus–Dionysus triangle).[34] *The Library* then reports how angry Minos took it out on Daedalus by incarcerating the craftsman and his son Icarus in the recently vacated labyrinth. Daedalus and Icarus managed to escape thanks to wings made of feathers and wax, which allowed them to fly. Icarus's flight ended badly, but Daedalus reached Sicily. Minos followed him in hot pursuit with his navy, but met his death while at the court of the Sicilian king Kokalos.

The connection between Theseus and Crete continued after these events: after the death of her father, Phaedra is given in marriage to Theseus. After giving birth to two sons, however, she falls hopelessly in love with Hippolytus, her chaste and misogynist stepson, with disastrous consequences. Equally unfortunate is the story linked to

Aerope (Catreus's daughter and Phaedra's niece), which perpetuates the theme of Cretan sexual extravagance: married to Mycenaean Atreus, she has an affair with his brother Thyestes. This sets in motion a series of horrific events, starting with Atreus's revenge on Thyestes (feeding him his own children), continuing with the adultery between Agamemnon's wife Clytemnestra and Thyestes's son Aegisthus, and ending with Clytemnestra's murder by her own son Orestes. There is no happy ending in the story of Idomeneus either. Another grandchild of Minos and king of Crete, Idomeneus led the Cretan forces in the Trojan War. He commanded forty ships according to *The Library* and eighty according to the *Iliad* (2.645ff.), which makes it one of the largest contingents after that of Agamemnon. He survived the Trojan War, but his journey home was ill-fated, as it involved offering his own son in sacrifice, a plague, and his subsequent exile from Crete.

As indicated above, *The Library* is a late source which presents a simplified version of numerous, contradictory variants of the Minoan saga known from earlier sources. But many characters and elements must be at least as early as the Early Iron Age, since they are attested in the Homeric poems and in Hesiod, and Minotaur images appear in Greek figurative art in the mid eighth-century BC (cf. above). But how far back do elements of this story go? We know that some forms of storytelling and even poetry existed in the Aegean Bronze Age and even earlier times.[35] On the basis of the evidence currently available, however, one cannot establish whether Bronze Age narratives contained specific elements of Minos's story as we know it, *pace* Evans, who believed that Homer had merely translated original Minoan epics.[36] It seems likely that a crucial period for the invention or radical transformation of any narratives set in what we now call Minoan Crete must have been the Early Iron Age, especially the ninth–eighth centuries BC. It is also clear that some elements and variants in the stories were introduced at later stages. For example, the Athenian origins of Daedalus mentioned in *The Library* do not seem to go back much earlier than the fifth century BC: there is no suggestion in the Homeric poems that this ingenious craftsman is not Cretan (in fact, Linear B tablets from Knossos show the existence of a related Cretan toponym).[37] Even the story of a Minoan *thalassocracy* appears undisputedly only in fifth-century Athenian texts, such as those of Herodotus and Thucydides, although some scholars have maintained that there are hints of this in Hesiod and, one might add, that the François Vase (mid-sixth century BC) already depicts Theseus leading the Athenian human tribute to Crete.[38]

In surviving Attic tragedy and comedy, Cretan subjects do not loom large, apart from the sad story of Phaedra in Euripides' *Hippolytus*. This prompted Ziolkowski to suggest that 'it was not thanks to the Athenians, but only to later Alexandrine Greeks and the Romans that Cretan myths . . . were passed along to posterity'.[39] Undoubtedly, the popularity of Cretan myths owes a great deal to Ovid, Virgil, and other Roman poets, but fifth-century Attic works, which have reached us only as titles and meagre fragments, show that Aeschylus, Sophocles, Euripides, and even Aristophanes did not neglect the house of Minos, and this contributed in no small measure towards its survival among later generations.[40]

The Attic narratives about Minos contained many inventions, which were prompted by Crete's Dorian make-up, its peripheral position in both the Persian and Peloponnesian wars,[41] its perception as 'foreign' and 'oriental',[42] and the desire to enhance the exploits of the Athenian hero *par excellence*, Theseus. By the time of Plato, who admired the conservative Cretan society, the Athenian bias against the Minoan family was already recognized.[43] Despite this, and the fact that these Attic narratives usually tell us more about the Greeks than the Minoans, many scholars and non-scholars alike have chosen to believe that they retain some real memory (or at least folk memory) of Bronze Age Crete. This has helped to create a vision of that distant past in which the ancient narratives have been conflated with archaeological remains and this, in turn, has contributed to the incorporation of Bronze Age Crete into the long continuum of the Classical tradition and to its Hellenization in some twentieth-century contexts, as I discuss further in later chapters.

Ancient responses 3: Hellenistic and Roman Minoans

A relatively small amount of research has been conducted so far on Hellenistic and Roman attitudes to the material remains of the Minoan past, but this has revealed intriguing and significant differences.[44] For the former period, scholars have suggested a deliberate use of older Minoan sites and material culture, i.e. a physical and direct engagement with Minoan realities, which seems to indicate local Cretan communities and their strategies. In the latter period, although the Minoan past is by no means ignored, the engagement seems to focus on Greek literary traditions and to be part of wider imperial strategies, to the actual detriment of local pride.

Hellenistic engagements with the Minoan remains

In the Hellenistic period, Crete remained politically fragmented, since none of the major potentates, such as the Ptolemaic dynasty of Egypt, dominated the island, although treaties were agreed with individual Cretan cities. Crete also seems to have enjoyed some prosperity, despite the pretty constant state of warfare among its city-states, of which Knossos, Lyttos, and Gortyn were the main contenders for supremacy.[45]

The fluctuating politics of Hellenistic Crete are seemingly reflected in some ritual and commemorative practices. These included a return to old Minoan grounds as a way to lay claim to disputed boundaries: as Alcock has shown, new Hellenistic shrines were often established in the countryside at sites that would have been recognizably 'old'.[46] Examples include a shrine at Hagia Triada, which seems to have received votive offerings from Minoan times to the seventh century BC, followed by an apparent hiatus until the Hellenistic period; the site of the Minoan tomb of Kamilari, which saw the foundation of a shrine to Demeter in this period; and the Minoan Villa at Pyrgos, which appears to have been barely visited after its Late Minoan IB destruction, but saw the foundation of a shrine in the Hellenistic period. Most intriguing of all, perhaps, is what appears to be the use of Linear A signs on an inscription from Psychro: its date is uncertain, but it seems likely to be Hellenistic.[47]

This direct engagement with Minoan remains in the Hellenistic period seems to be on a small, local scale, performed by people living close by, and perhaps celebrating local memories. What these memories might have been is not clear, but these practices shrank drastically in the Roman period.

Roman engagements with Minoan remains

Rome conquered mainland Greece in the mid-second century BC, and consequently became more involved with Cretan affairs. After some earlier Roman interventions, Quintus Caecilius Metellus 'Creticus' subjugated the island in his 69–67 BC campaign. In 27 BC Crete was combined with Cyrenaica as a Roman province: Gortyn was the capital, an arrangement that lasted until Diocletian (third century AD), while Knossos became the Colonia Iulia Nobilis Cnossus.[48] In 395 AD, with the division of the Roman Empire, Crete was included in its Eastern part, usually called the Byzantine Empire from *c.* 330 AD, and shared its fortunes until Arab forces conquered the island in the ninth century

In the Roman period, uses of the Minoan past seem to focus more on literary traditions than physical remains, and one can infer that a dynamic local mythographic tradition was still active in the first century BC from Diodorus Siculus's glowing account of Crete, which attributed to the island considerable pre-eminence in human and divine matters.[49] In terms of direct engagement with Minoan physical remains, Mount Juktas, the site of one of the most famous Minoan cult places, and generally associated in later times with the tomb of Zeus, is provided with an altar in this period.[50] Knossos also attracts visitors, but more as a tourist site and because of its links with stories of King Minos and his labyrinth (see, e.g., Philostratus, *Life of Apollonius of Tyana*, 4.34), even if this is no longer visible, as one can gather from Diodorus (I.61) and Pliny (XXXVI, 19), who report that the Knossian labyrinth had vanished long before their times (first century BC and AD respectively). Other sites were visited too, but once again more because of their literary associations than the visible presence of old Minoan remains – a pattern that will continue in later centuries. One of these sites is the Idaean cave, which was linked to the birth of Zeus and became one of the major cult places on Crete in Roman times.[51]

Roman coins make little reference to local myths, apart from the Knossian labyrinth, which appears on the reverse of some issues, but Tiberius used the image of Zeus Cretagenos to convey a parallel or assimilation between himself and the god, thus linking this myth to imperial legitimization.[52] Intriguingly, in Roman Crete even the use of the double-axe or labrys – which is nowadays considered one of the most iconic Minoan symbols – does not seem to represent a link with the Minoan past of the island, but is the result of shifting Roman perceptions of it as a symbol of good fortune.[53]

Yet, in Roman times one finds an intriguing story of what seems to be an encounter with Minoan objects. This appears in a Latin text of the fourth century AD, which was based on an earlier Greek version, surviving on fragmentary papyri of the second or third centuries AD, and may have been originally composed in the first century AD.[54] This text purports to be Lucius Septimius's translation of a Greek chronicle of the Trojan War by Dictys of Crete (an otherwise unknown personage, said to be a companion of Idomeneus). It narrates how, in the thirteenth year of Nero's reign (66 AD), there was an earthquake at Knossos, which exposed the tomb of Dictys. This contained a tin chest full of lime-wood tablets inscribed in strange letters, which were presented to Nero. The Roman emperor believed them to be written in the Phoenician script, and called experts to decipher them, who reported that they contained the memoirs of one of the ancients who had been present at the siege of Troy. The remaining text presents this Trojan account.

Arthur Evans ingeniously suggested that this could be the description of the accidental discovery, during the historically recorded 66 A D earthquake, of clay tablets inscribed in one of the Minoan scripts within a tin-lined cist, like those he had found in the store rooms of Knossos.[55] At any rate, the identification of the script as 'Phoenician' is also interesting, since this could show that the foreign characterization of Crete was still lingering and/or reflected the oscillating Roman perceptions of the island, which was sometimes seen as the birthplace of Hellenic culture and sometimes as barbarian and Oriental.[56]

From Arab to Ottoman: Responses to Minoan material culture *c.* 824–1860, and the dawn of the 'Minoan Age'

This long and fascinating period in the history of Crete, lasting over 1,000 years, is rich in vicissitudes and cultural developments, but is also, by contrast, quite obscure regarding our understanding of people's engagement with and responses to the physical remains of Bronze Age Crete.[57]

Ninth–late eighteenth century A D

In 824, Crete fell into the hands of a group of Arabs based in Alexandria, but originally from Spain, led by Abu-Hafs-Umar. They set up camp in what is now Heraklion, and surrounded it with a huge ditch, *el-Khandak* in Arabic, from which the name Candia derived and was often applied to both the town and the whole island. In 961, Crete was recaptured by the Byzantines and remained in their hands till the 1204 sack of Constantinople by the Crusaders, after which the Venetians gained control. Between 1204 and 1669, Crete remained under Venetian administration despite numerous rebellions, the most famous of which resulted in the creation of the short-lived republic of St Titus in 1363. After Ottoman forces captured Constantinople in 1453, Crete became a mecca for Greek refugees, often on their way to the West, and witnessed a kind of Renaissance. In this period, monasteries such as Arkadi, Gonia, and Hagia Aikaterini became important centres for the collection and copying of manuscripts. It is in this environment that the painter Domenikos Theotokopoulos (a.k.a. El Greco) was born and where Vincenzo Kornaros wrote his epic, the *Erotokritos* (first published in Venice in 1715, but dating to the mid-seventeenth century).

In 1669, Crete succumbed to the Ottoman forces of Sultan Mehmet IV and remained under the rule of the Sublime Porte until 1898 – much later than mainland Greece, which gained independence in 1832. Like the Venetian, Ottoman rule on Crete was punctuated by insurrections, such as that of 1866, which saw the blowing up of the Arkadi monastery; that of 1878, which inspired a 1953 novel by Nikos Kazantzakis

(Ο Καπετάν Μιχάλης, translated in English as *Freedom and Death*); and the last insurrection of 1896–8, which led to a period of autonomy, the *Kritiki Politeia* (1898–1913), and the first major excavations on the island. Crete became part of the Greek kingdom in 1913, shortly before the start of the First World War.

Despite the length of the period discussed in this section (*c.* 824–1800) and the relative abundance of historical records, there is very little information about people's responses to the material remains of Bronze Age Crete. There is no doubt that accidental discoveries and other encounters with Minoan remnants continued to occur, since Minoan objects must have come up through building and agricultural activities, while shepherds must have continued to visit caves that had been important Minoan cult places and were rich in offerings such as clay figurines, pottery, and other objects. One can also assume that Minoan stonework was continuously reused for new structures over the centuries.[58] It is also possible that some Minoan objects were collected, as is amply documented from the early nineteenth century (cf. below). Yet, so far, modern scholars scouring local and non-local archives as well as printed sources regarding the ninth–eighteenth century AD do not seem to have found and/or published much evidence of direct engagement with Bronze Age materials. In addition to official and non-official reports by Venetian and Ottoman bureaucrats, there are numerous fascinating accounts by foreign visitors to Crete, such as the botanist Simone di Cordo (a.k.a Simone di Genova or Simone Ianuense) in the thirteenth century; Cristoforo Buondelmonti, Ciriaco D'Ancona, and Piero Tafur in the fifteenth century; Francesco Barozzi and Onorio Belli in the sixteenth century; Marco Boschini, William Lithgow, and George Sandys in the seventeenth century; and J. Pitton de Tournefort and Richard Pococke in the eighteenth century.[59] These travellers and officers at times deal with questions of ancient mythology and topography as well as archaeological matters, especially when they are describing their visits to archaeological sites such as Knossos, Gortyn, and the Idaean cave. In all their reports, however, there is precious little, if anything at all, that clearly refers to Minoan material culture. It is likely that some thirteenth–eighteenth century travellers and officials, on their visits to Knossos, ventured further south, beyond the visible remains of the Hellenistic and Roman town, in the area of the Minoan palace that would be excavated by Kalokairinos, Evans, and others in years to come. It is also possible that their eyes gazed upon some Minoan potsherd or masonry protruding from the ground. Yet, whenever some descriptions or drawings appear in their accounts, it is clear that they are not dealing with Minoan remains, but with those from the Graeco-Roman or even later periods.[60] It is as if the literary *topos* had become far more important than the actual physical place. The general location of Knossos becomes an excuse for displaying knowledge of Classical sources, the hallmark of a good education. But in some cases even the location of ancient Knossos and its mythical labyrinth appears to have been mistaken, since some of these accounts locate the labyrinth by an impressive Roman quarry near Gortyn, *pace* Strabo and other sources.[61] These erroneous identifications are a good reminder of the irrepressible human desire to find tangible proof of what is described in texts and help to illustrate Anthony Snodgrass's 'positivist fallacy' of archaeology, namely the belief that 'archaeological prominence and historical importance are much the same thing; that the observable phenomena are by definition the significant phenomena ... This is the tub in which Telemachus took the bath described in the Odyssey.[62] This can lead to the creation of false correspondences between prominent and visible archaeological remains and written sources, even if the location of prominent ruins does not quite match the information in the texts.

Not only do clear descriptions of actual Minoan antiquities appear to be missing in thirteenth–eighteenth-century travellers' accounts, but also Minoan objects seem to be absent from sixteenth–eighteenth-century *Wunderkammer* (Cabinets of curiosities) and other collections. By contrast, travellers and members of the Cretan intelligentsia actively collected Classical objects from the island, especially statues and inscriptions, from at least the fifteenth century AD onwards.[63] Moreover, we have evidence of Aegean Bronze Age artefacts in other regions being acquired and excavated in the eighteenth century: for example, in this period the Comte de Caylus published a Mycenaean gold figurine believed to be of 'Scythian' craftsmanship and from Amyclae, but perhaps originally from the nearby Mycenaean tholos tomb of Vapheio, while Count Pasch van Krienen excavated an Early Bronze Age cemetery in the Cyclades.[64] So far, the earliest evidence for the collecting of Minoan objects that I was able to find is illustrated by the splendid gold signet ring, now in the British Museum, acquired by Thomas Burgon probably in the early 1800s (see Fig. 2.3).[65] One reason for this relatively late start may be the predominant interest in other types of artefacts, such as manuscripts, inscriptions, statues, and botanical specimens amid Humanist, Renaissance, and Enlightenment scholars. Another reason may be aesthetic: Aegean Bronze Age seals, which ended up in private or public collections in the late eighteenth and early nineteenth century, were often regarded as 'crude and primitive' and described as 'Persepolitan, Persian or Pehlevi' or even 'Indian',[66] thus showing the prevailing classicizing taste (and lack of real understanding of what these objects were). Yet, these factors could have hampered but not completely prevented the collection of Bronze Age artefacts from Crete (as indeed the examples of Calylus on mainland Greece and van Krienen in the Cyclades suggest). I suspect this may be a case of absence of evidence not being necessarily evidence of absence: it is possible that some Minoan objects did find their way into local and

Fig. 2.3 The Burgon ring (© Trustees of the British Museum).

foreign collections (especially via Venice) before the nineteenth century; it is also possible that the Cretan women's custom of keeping Minoan seals as charms 'of great virtue especially in time of child-bearing',[67] which is well documented in the late nineteenth century, may have earlier origins. Only further research can clarify this.

The dawn of the 'Minoan Age': Early–mid-nineteenth century

From the early nineteenth century, an interest in and responses to the material culture of Minoan Crete are clearly attested by documented collections of Minoan artefacts and descriptions of Minoan ruins in works such as Robert Pashley's *Travels in Crete* (1837) and Thomas Spratt's *Travels and Researches in Crete* (1865).

Pashley, who visited Crete in the early 1830s, on many occasions mentions masonry 'of Cyclopean style'. For example, during his visit to the 'tomb of Zeus' on Mt Juktas, south of Knossos, he refers to walls of the 'first Cyclopean style' on what seems to be its northern peak (now an excavated Minoan peak sanctuary), while on his visit to Aptera he compared some of its walls to those of Tiryns.[68] Most of Pashley's 'Cyclopean' walls turned out to be Classical or later (except, perhaps, those on Juktas), but the deliberate search for pre-Classical remains and the use of the term 'first Cyclopean' are significant. As shown by Karadimas, 'first Cyclopean' is a reference to Richard Hamilton's 1806 article, titled 'Remarks on the fortresses of ancient Greece', which attempted a systematic typological and chronological classification of ancient masonry, based on comparative studies and observations in situ, using the Bronze Age walls of Mycenaean citadels in the Argolid to illustrate his 'first Cyclopean' type.[69]

Thomas Spratt visited Crete in the 1850s, and in his *Travels and Researches in Crete* he remarked that most visible remains at Knossos were Roman. He noted, however, 'Cyclopean walls' at other sites, such as Malia and Goulas (i.e. Lato), even if the latter turned out not to be Minoan – a mistake repeated later by Evans and others in the early stages of their researches on the island.[70] Spratt also described a Minoan clay larnax in connection with his visit to the site of Palaikastro.[71] In addition, he bought Minoan seals during his travels, especially in the eastern part of Crete, although he published them only in 1879, after Schliemann's excavations at Mycenae (1874 and 1876) finally impressed upon scholars and general public alike the significance of these finds.[72]

This emerging curiosity about pre-classical Cretan remains in the early–mid-nineteenth century can be contextualized within other developments, which, at the risk of oversimplification, may be conveniently summarized as follows.

First, there was the fascination with the origins and early stages of human culture, which soared after Darwin's publication of *On the Origin of Species* (1859), but was in the air well before the 'Darwinian Revolution' as shown, among other things, by Christian Jürgensen Thomsen's innovative classification of artefacts according to his Three-Age system of Stone, Bronze, and Iron, which was devised in the 1810s and was later followed by Sir John Lubbock's subdivision of the Stone Age into Palaeolithic and Neolithic.[73] The effects of evolutionism are particularly clear on mainland Greece in the two decades before Schliemann's excavations at Troy and Mycenae of the 1870s, as shown by a number of archaeological activities recently discussed by Mihalis Fotiadis and, in a Cretan context, by the work of Spratt, who corresponded with the geologist

Charles Lyell and Charles Darwin.[74] Second, there was the growing fascination with the ancient Greek past, as opposed to an interest in a generic Classical, Graeco-Roman antiquity, and this occasionally involved Pre-Classical Greece. The interest in things Greek has been variously labelled as Hellenism, Romantic Hellenism, Philhellenism, Graecophilia, and Hellenomania, and took a particularly strong turn in German lands – hence the title *The Tyranny of Greece over Germany* of Eliza Marian Butler's classic volume on the subject.[75] It is beyond the scope of my work to examine the different uses and nuanced meanings of these terms.[76] Here it suffices to remember that this Germanic fascination with ancient Greece acquired momentum through the work of Johann Joachim Winckelmann in the mid-eighteenth century and increased after the Napoleonic military campaigns of the 1790s–1800s, since Hellas was now seen as symbolic not only of a particular kind of beauty and originality, but also of anti-French sentiments, in opposition to the well-established Napoleonic–Roman connections.[77] Also, in a more practical way, the Napoleonic Wars made travel to parts of Europe, including Italy, more difficult for Europeans engaged in their Grand Tour, while making journeys to Greece more attractive because of its relative security. The passion for and idealization of ancient Greece were by no means an exclusively German phenomenon. Winckelmann's ideas spread to other countries, and other influential publications – together with the arrival in European museums of original Greek statues in the first decades of the nineteenth century (e.g. the Parthenon marbles in London, the Aeginaetan pedimental sculptures in Munich) – contributed to this growing 'Hellenomania' and to the creation of what Artemis Leontis has aptly called the 'Heterotopia of Hellenism'.[78] Among the influential publications that reflected and stimulated further this Hellenic passion were *The Antiquities of Athens Measured and Delineated* by 'Athenian' James Stuart and Nicolas Revett; the *Voyage pittoresque de la Grèce* by Choiseul-Gouffier; the volumes published in the 1830s by Guillaume-Abel Blouet and others after the *Expédition scientifique de Morée*; and, last but not least, Jean-Jacques Barthélemy's popular historical novel *Voyage du jeune Anacharsis en Grèce dans le milieu du IVe siècle*, which went through forty editions and was translated into all major European languages.[79] These publications focused on the Classical period, but also included references to the more nebulous 'Heroic' past of Greece (i.e. the Aegean Bronze Age). For example, the introduction to the *Voyage du jeune Anacharsis* contained almost 100 pages of 'mythical' history, while other works mentioned above all included descriptions and illustrations of Bronze Age monuments. Although these publications did not include Crete, they constitute an important part of the background that made Cretan travellers, like Pashley and Spratt, pay more attention to materials belonging to pre-Classical Greece.

A third element that contributed to an interest in pre-Classical Greece and influenced later interpretations and receptions of the Minoans is represented by the developments in the field of philology during the late eighteenth–early nineteenth century. Besides the advances that many scholars made in the study of various Indo-European languages and of 'Proto-Indo-European', in this period Friedrich Augustus Wolf introduced his *Altertumswissenschaft* or Science of Antiquity, partly by applying the lessons learnt from biblical philological exegesis to the Homeric epics.[80] His approach – a product of the Enlightenment's application of reason to myth – denied the existence of Homer as a historical figure and championed a more rational, rigorous study of philology and etymology as well as mythology and physical remains. Some works by Karl Hoeck and Karl Otfried Müller offer good examples of this new approach and had significant influence on Minoan research, as discussed below. In addition, Müller's publications illustrate the emerging Romantic fascination with the character of specific ethnic groups.

Hoeck's three-volume *Kreta*, on the history of the island from the most distant times to the Roman Empire, was published between 1823 and 1829. Building on the work of previous scholars, such as Karl Friedrich Neumann, Hoeck distinguished four periods in the history of the island.[81] The first 'pre-Minoan period' (*vorminoische Zeit*) represented the times before Minos's kingship. The second, the 'Minoan Age' (*minoische Zeit*), spanned the two centuries before the Trojan War (*c.* 1400–1200 BC). This was followed by his 'post-Minoan' period, which saw the beginning of the Trojan War (dated to around 1200 BC) and represented a Hellenized phase of decline in the history of the island. Minos's descendants continued to rule, but only for a brief period. The Dorian invasion, dated by Hoeck at around 1040 BC, heralded his fourth period, the Dorian Age. Hoeck explained his use of the term 'Minoan' by maintaining that the name Minos was a dynastic term used by a series of priest-kings. This name did not represent an historical figure, but encapsulated a whole period – a notion that appears to have been formulated by analogy with that of the 'Homeric Age', already established by the early nineteenth century. Hoeck's 'Minoan Age' was the most brilliant in the island's history: during this period, a non-Hellenic people (equated with the Homeric 'Eteocretans') had created a splendid civilization, rich in monuments such as the famous labyrinth built by Daedalus. Hoeck's Minoan Age also included the Minoan *thalassocracy* referred to by many ancient sources, which had ended around 1250 BC.

Among Müller's numerous publications, *Geschichten hellenischer Stämme und Städte: Die Dorier* (1824), *Prolegomena zu einer wissenschaftlichen Mythologie* (1825), *Handbuch der Archäologie der Kunst* (1830), and *Denkmäler der alten Kunst* (1832–35) (all translated into various European languages), are especially important in an Aegean Bronze Age and Minoan context. *Handbuch* and *Denkmäler*, although largely based on written evidence, paid close attention also to material culture and included drawings of Bronze Age monuments, such as the Lion Gate at Mycenae. *Prolegomena* was a programmatic text explaining that ancient Greek myths contained a kernel of historical truth (an idea that in fact goes back at least to Plutarch): they represented memories of historical events that had occurred in the distant Greek past, before the introduction of writing. *Die Dorier*, in particular, presented a history of Crete that had points of similarity with Hoeck's *Kreta*, such as the notion of a splendid Minoan Age dating to *c.* 1400–1200 BC, but differed in one fundamental respect: for Müller the inhabitants of pre-Classical Crete largely belonged to the Hellenic Doric race from at least the first half of the second millennium BC. Müller subdivided his history of Crete into three main phases. The first embraced the initial and very early Dorian migration to Crete from their original homeland in Thessaly, and saw the foundation of temples of Apollo at Delphi, Delos, and Crete (his chronology is a bit vague, but a *terminus ante quem* of 1400 BC is implicit). The second represented the zenith of Minoan civilization (*c.* 1400–1200 BC): in this phase, the Dorian Cretans took control of the Aegean Sea

(Minoan *thalassocracy*) and spread their cult of Apollo to the whole region. Two or three generations before the Trojan War, however, a period of decline started. This was soon followed by Müller's third main phase, characterized by the main Dorian migration after the Trojan War.

As further discussed in the next chapter, the volumes published by various travellers, such as Pashley and Spratt, as well as Hoeck's and Müller's works (Hoeck's *Kreta* in particular), had considerable influence on Evans's choice of the label 'Minoan' and other aspects of his interpretation of Bronze Age Crete, such as the dynastic use of this word by a series of priest-kings. Hoeck's and Müller's works also offer a useful background for Schliemann's own remarkable exploits, which provided such an important stimulus for later researches on Crete. Schliemann has often been portrayed as a romantic, revolutionary Hellenist, who proved the scholars wrong because he believed, and demonstrated with his spade, that behind ancient Greek myths stood historical realities: in other words, he took a stance against prevailing sceptical attitudes, such as that illustrated by George Grote's *History of* Greece (1846), with its description of Greek myths as portraying 'a past which was never present' and as a curtain behind which stood nothing.[82] But many others had already excavated Bronze Age sites in the Aegean,[83] guided more often than not by the testimony of the ancient sources, and it was Grote who, arguably, was more revolutionary with his rejection of Greek myths and his breaking 'with K.O. Müller and his English admirers'.[84]

The search for *realia* behind Greek myths has enjoyed a very long tradition, persisting to the present. If Schliemann's claims found considerable resistance at first, especially in his native Germany, it was not because he dared to believe in the historicity behind the Homeric epics, but for a number of reasons, discussed in the following chapter, which included his lack of professional credentials and unsophisticated interpretation of the Homeric texts, which ran counter to the increasing professionalization and scientific turn of various academic disciplines in this period, including archaeology.

Rediscovering European Origins:
Ariadne as the Great Mother Goddess
(Mid-Nineteenth Century–First World War)

*One fact at least, and one of capital importance, we have learnt from the discovery
of the archaeologists, and that is that it is impossible to regard Greek civilization as a
thing sui generis, an isolated phenomenon which sprang from the brain of the
Hellene complete in itself, like Athene [sic] from the brain of Zeus.*

H. R. Hall (1901: 20)

*[The] legendary cycle seemed to point to Crete, and in particular to Knossos, as the
centre of the earliest civilisation of Greece and, with it, of the whole European world.*

From the brochure accompanying the 1903
Cretan exhibition at the Royal Academy, London

*It is a Darwinian age, when the search for origins seems to fascinate men more than
the search for what is good in itself: and the fact is that our eyes are somewhat
dazzled by the brilliant discoveries of Schliemann, Dörpfeld and Evans. Of these we
have heard much, but strange to say, there is no book which gives a comprehensive
account of the epoch-making discoveries at Olympia.*

Percy Gardner, preface to Michaelis (1908)

*This [Knossos] palace is, one would say, a modern building . . . In comparison . . . the
palaces of Egyptian Pharaohs were but elaborate hovels of painted mud. Only the
sculptured corridors of Ashurbanipal's Nineveh probably surpassed it in splendour;
but Assyrian splendour was after all as old, cold and lifeless as that of Egyptian
temples, while Knossos seems to be eloquent of the teeming life and energy of a
young and beauty-loving people for the first time feeling its creative power and
exulting with the pure joie de vivre . . . The Minoan Court must have resembled the
joyous surrounding of an [sic] European prince of the thirteenth and fourteenth
centuries with a touch here and there of the Tuileries and the Second Empire.*

H. R. Hall (1913: 47)

In this chapter, I resume my story with a brief discussion of Schliemann's own work,
the subsequent 'Heroic' period of excavations on Crete and 'Cretomania', up to the First

World War. Unlike Schliemann's Mycenaean finds a generation earlier, in the early twentieth century Minoan Crete received an immediate enthusiastic reception from specialists and general public alike. This was partly because its world was made to resonate with contemporary discourses on gender and races, and partly because modernist movements, such as Art Nouveau, paved the way for the aesthetic appreciation of Minoan imagery. By the early twentieth century, fashions and tastes had changed to the extent that the un-Hellenic Minoans struck a chord in a new cultural environment, which reacted against Classicism and was fascinated by nature, the primitive, and the exotic, whereas a generation earlier the Mycenaean finds had often provoked lukewarm responses and even rejection because they did not look sufficiently 'Greek'.

The Schliemann factor

In the new kingdom of Greece that emerged from the Greek War of Independence (1821–32), and after Jakob Philipp Fallmerayer's controversial publications on the racial and cultural discontinuity between ancient and modern Greeks, most archaeological efforts focused on the Classical period and on Byzantium, since these two eras, especially the former, played a crucial role in the construction of a modern Greek national identity and its Europeanization.[1] Despite the emphasis on the Classical and Byzantine heritage, some interest in pre-Classical remains is documented from the late eighteenth–mid-nineteenth century in Greece generally, and at least from the early nineteenth century in Crete more specifically, as discussed in Chapter 2. Indeed, by the late 1860s a significant amount of collecting of prehistoric materials (from Palaeolithic to Bronze Age) and excavations of Aegean Bronze Age sites had already taken place.[2] Even if these archaeological activities were often little more than despoliation, illicit grabs, and accidental discoveries, the number of Bronze Age sites explored in this period amounted to several dozen and included Hissarlik (Troy), Mycenae, the Vaphio tholos tomb, the Mycenaean acropolis in Athens, Ialysos on Rhodes, Kalathiana on Crete, and, last but not least, various locations on Thera (Santorini), to mention some notable examples.[3] In fact, the investigations carried out by French and Greek scholars on Thera between 1866 and 1870 have been considered to represent the first systematic prehistoric excavations in the Aegean.[4] Schliemann's work on Ithaka in the 1860s and his excavations at Troy, Mycenae, Tiryns, and other 'Homeric' sites in the 1870s–1880s (see Figs. 3.1–3.2) are a continuation of these activities.[5] In 1870, before going to Troy, Schliemann visited the excavations on Thera.[6] But this volcanic island had no Homeric aura, and scholars had not made, as yet, the alluring connection between, on the one hand, Plato's Atlantis and, on the other hand, Thera's Bronze Age remains, its Bronze Age volcanic eruption, and the decline and fall of Minoan Crete.

Schliemann's archaeological explorations and his claims to have found Homeric Troy, King Priam's treasure, and the grave of Agamemnon represent both a moment of continuity and a watershed in the study of Greek history, Homeric studies, and archaeology more generally. Schliemann was by no means the first to excavate Aegean Bronze Age remains and to succumb to the irresistible desire to link the literary and

Fig. 3.1 Bust of Heinrich Schliemann in the Neues Museum, Berlin (photo: Marcus Cyron, https://commons.wikimedia.org/wiki/File:Bust_of_Heinrich_Schliemann_(1822-1890),_Neues_Museum,_Berlin_(8169157750).jpg).

Fig. 3.2 The so-called Treasure of Priam (after Schliemann 1875: pl. II).

physical *topoi* of Homeric Greece. In fact, some of his initial work may be regarded more as a return to old-fashioned antiquarianism than a step towards modern professional archaeology and liberation from the tyranny of the written word.[7] Furthermore, the works by Hoeck and others, discussed in the previous chapter, do not support the oft-repeated claim that before Schliemann nobody had even dreamed of a sophisticated civilization flourishing in Greek lands before the Archaic–Classical periods.[8] Many scholars had conjectured the existence of a splendid pre-Classical civilization, mostly on the basis of ancient literary sources, and well before Schliemann was even born. But the German businessman-turned-archaeologist provided tangible evidence for this remote past in spades. In other words, Schliemann's originality and his debt to previous scholars have often been overrated and understated, respectively, and not least by Schliemann himself. Nowadays scholars examine his work more critically and even question his entitlement to labels such as the 'Father of Mycenaean Archaeology', but his pioneering role and the epoch-making effects of his discoveries are widely acknowledged.[9] Schliemann trod in the path of many previous scholars, but the magnificence and amount of his finds as well as the controversy over his interpretations were of a different magnitude. His excavations literally dazzled the world with hundreds of splendid objects, many made of gold and other precious materials, the like of which had rarely or never been seen before. In addition, even if some impressive tholos tombs (e.g. the so-called Treasury of Atreus) and the fortifications of Tiryns and Mycenae had always remained visible, the mighty walls of Troy had not, and even the location of the site that had inspired the Homeric saga was disputed; nor had anybody set eyes on any Bronze Age palace, such as that excavated by Schliemann at Tiryns.

The quantity and quality of his finds, his rash but crowd-pleasing interpretations, astonishing drive and knack for publicity allowed Schliemann to focus scholarly and public attention alike on pre-Classical, Heroic Greece in an unprecedented way. They also turned him into what many regard as the most famous archaeologist of all time.[10] To paraphrase Mark Twain, Schliemann's life and work are stranger than fiction: his rags-to-riches romantic story and his archaeological discoveries are arguably more intriguing than those of imaginary archaeologists such as Indiana Jones and Lara Croft. Which other archaeologist has been so widely recognized, and has become the subject of several novels and even an opera?[11] More importantly, although initially ridiculed by many scholars, Schliemann was pivotal in revealing tangible remains of what, for many people, had largely remained a 'lost world'.[12] His work, as argued by Suzanne Marchand, showed quite dramatically that archaeology was more useful in providing information about certain periods and aspects of Greek history than the study of ancient sources, thus undermining the privileged position of text-based studies within Classics.[13] His finds also undermined the popular idea of a 'Greek Miracle', i.e. the notion that Greece's golden Classical age had been created by a few generations of supermen almost out of nothing and in splendid isolation, as reflected in Hall's epigraph above (1901), and perhaps most famously illustrated by Ernest Renan's *Prière sur l'Acropole* (Prayer on the Acropolis).[14] As Cathy Gere has suggested, besides adding prehistoric Hellenic examples to Nietzsche's 'blond beast', Schliemann provided a solid materiality for some of the most cherished myths of Western literature: 'His excavations of the great sites of pagan legend elevated the Homeric epics to the status of a non-Christian origin for Western civilization, a pagan prehistory for a secular modernity.'[15]

The significance of Schliemann's finds, however, was not immediately accepted by much of the classical establishment, especially in Germany, for a variety of reasons ranging from the scholarly to the institutional, personal, aesthetic, and even ethnic. In regard to scholarly motivations, the rejection of Schliemann's claims about his finds was not caused by his attempt to find a kernel of historical reality behind the Homeric epics, but by his unsophisticated and literal attitude towards the ancient sources, which seemed rather quaint and out of date in comparison to more erudite theories current at the time, such as Max Müller's interpretation of Greek mythology as reflecting a hypothetical solar religion, and Grote's sceptical stance.[16] From an institutional point of view, Schliemann was distrusted because of his amateurish ways and lack of proper academic credentials, and also because, as mentioned above, his archaeological work threatened the dominance of philology within Classics. At a personal level, his arrogance, self-promotion, tendency to embellish his stories, and academic rivalries played a considerable part. The famous classical archaeologist Ernst Curtius called Schliemann a swindler and bungler.[17] Curtius had nourished the hope of excavating Olympia since the 1850s, but had to wait until 1875 to accomplish his goal.[18] Schliemann, largely thanks to his personal wealth, never had to delay the fulfilment of his archaeological dreams – only Knossos escaped him, and probably only because death intervened (cf. below). Besides, the publicity gathered around Schliemann's work at Troy, Mycenae, and other sites, as well as his prompt publications, must have often overshadowed the contemporary discoveries made at Olympia (cf. Gardner's epigraph above). Last but not least, in terms of aesthetic perceptions and ethnic reasons, many scholars resisted, at first, Schliemann's interpretations of his finds because they did not conform to expected canons of what constituted ancient Greece – hence their characterization as Phoenician, Celtic, Scythian or even Byzantine.[19] It is almost as if, before they could be accorded serious scholarly attention, Schliemann's finds (and Bronze Age finds more generally) had to be properly Hellenized and incorporated into contemporary discourses of national (Hellenic) and transnational (Aryan, European) identity.[20]

One of the most obvious and effective strategies that could help to Hellenize (and, consequently, Aryanize and Europeanize) the Bronze Age finds was to reinforce their links with Classical texts. Schliemann, followed by many others, eagerly and successfully pursued this tactic, especially after Flinders Petrie's discoveries of Aegean Bronze Age finds in Egypt, in well-dated Pharaonic contexts, provided irrefutable evidence that the Mycenaean finds were not Phoenicians, let alone Byzantine, but dated to the second millennium BC, thus broadly fitting with what was known about the Greek 'Heroic' period, since most ancient authors dated the fall of Troy to *c*.1200 BC, leave or add a few generations. Another effective strategy involved the use of images, namely the integration of Aegean Bronze Age elements within Neoclassical art and architecture. In this way, the Aegean Bronze Age was incorporated not only into the long continuum of Hellenic history, but also of the European Classical Tradition. An example of this is Schliemann's Athenian mansion, the Iliou Melathron, built by the German architect Ernst Ziller between 1878 and 1880, where Bronze Age elements are embedded in larger Neoclassical compositions, like the mansion itself.[21] For instance, one of the many frescoes (by the Slovenian painter Jurij Subic) that decorate the mansion depicts a group of putti, one of whom is holding a classical Greek theatrical mask and another a gold mask like those found by Schliemann in the Shaft Graves, while the classicizing mosaics that adorn the floors include Trojan swastikas and Mycenaean butterflies as decorative motifs. Similarly, Cyclopean walls such as those of Mycenae and Tiryns decorate Schliemann's Neoclassical mausoleum in the First Cemetery in Athens (also designed by Ziller).[22] A further example is Franz von Matsch's painting *The Triumph of Achilles* (c. 1892) in the Achilleion, a Neoclassical palace built by the Austro-Hungarian empress Elisabeth II on Corfu around 1889–92.[23] The painting includes references to the Bronze Age walls of Troy, the Lion Gate of Mycenae, and objects from Schliemann's excavations of the Shaft Graves, all within a broadly classicizing imagery.[24]

Despite many initial detractors, Schliemann's work did enlist the early support of some notable Homeric scholars, such as the British Prime Minister William Gladstone, who contributed a preface to the English version of Schliemann's Mycenae volume.[25] Nevertheless, it took almost a decade for a widespread appreciation and acceptance of Schliemann's discoveries to emerge, and this involved the collaboration of a respected insider, Wilhelm Dörpfeld, who had previously worked at Olympia, as well as the efforts of other scholars, such as Christos Tsountas in Greece and Petrie in Egypt. As mentioned above, Petrie's work, in particular, proved that Schliemann's finds broadly fitted with ancient chronologies about the Heroic period of Greece, even if it undermined some of Schliemann's more exuberant claims, such as that he had found the treasure of Priam and the tomb of Agamemnon, since these finds were centuries earlier than the supposed date of the Trojan War. Nevertheless, the work of Tsountas and later scholars valiantly continued the processes of Hellenization, Aryanization, and Europeanization of the Aegean Bronze Age.[26] By the late nineteenth century, much of the Bronze Age/Heroic material culture of Greece was labelled 'Mycenaean', and the corollary 'Mycenaean' people were usually equated with Homer's Achaeans.[27] Yet, it was only after major excavations took place on Crete in the 1900s that a fuller contextualization of Schliemann's discoveries was achieved, since the Cretan finds revealed that, in turn, the ultimate origin of many Mycenaean traits was the island of King Minos, as discussed below.

From the tomb of Agamemnon to the palace of Minos

In December 1878, just over two years after Schliemann's discoveries at Mycenae, Minos Kalokairinos – a Cretan merchant, dragoman (interpreter), lawyer, and antiquarian – sought to unearth the Knossian abode of his mythical namesake, and conducted the first, albeit brief, modern excavations of the 'Palace of Minos'. This archaeological work too, like the reception of Schliemann's finds, can be appreciated in the context of contemporary Hellenism as well as national (Hellenic) and transnational (European) discourses on identity. Under Ottoman rule, the majority Christian population of Crete enjoyed some power and autonomy, especially after the signing of the Pact of Chalepa (October 1878), but aspired to *enosis* (union) with the Kingdom of Greece. Kalokairinos's excavations, by revealing a new Bronze Age 'Mycenaean' palace, was used as symbolic capital, i.e. as another illustration of the long continuum of Crete's Hellenic and European past, stretching back to Idomeneus's forebears.

Kalokairinos seems to have been the first to record that the area of ancient Knossos called 'Kephala tou Tselevi' (a.k.a. 'Tou Tselevi i Kephala', meaning 'the gentleman's head' or 'the squire's knoll') was the likely location of the 'ancient palace [*anaktoro*] of King Minos', because it looked quite different from other parts of the site, which were covered with Roman remains.[28] His excavations took place in the winter of 1878-9 (December 1878–April 1879), and were supervised by a schoolteacher, Christos Papaoulakis, who would become one of the main characters in the 2002 novel *O αιώνας των λαβυρίνθων* (*The Century of Labyrinths*) by the acclaimed contemporary Greek author Rhea Galanaki.[29] His excavation brought to light the remains of a substantial structure built with ashlar blocks, some bearing masons' marks, and numerous other finds, which resembled those from Mycenae and other Aegean Bronze Age/Heroic sites previously investigated. But the local authorities soon stopped his work, partly because most Cretans opposed excavations at that time, fearing that the best finds would be taken to Istanbul to increase the Ottoman imperial collections.[30] Kalokairinos's finds included potsherds, possibly Linear B tablets[31] and about a dozen large *pithoi* (storage jars), of which he donated examples to the Crown Prince (later King) Constantine of Greece and to several European museums, including the Louvre and the British Museum – a gesture that stressed, once again, Crete's Greek and European ties and anticipated the Greek government's gift, in 1913, of a marble replica of the Knossian throne to the International Court of Justice (Peace Palace) in The Hague.[32] Besides the name of the first modern excavator of Knossos, by another amusing twist of fate, the *pithos* sent to the British Museum (see Fig. 3.3) was shipped by HMS *Minotaur*, the flagship of HRH the Duke of Edinburgh, Queen Victoria's son Prince Alfred.[33]

Fig. 3.3 Pithos from Minos Kalokairinos's 1878 excavations at Knossos donated to the British Museum (© The Trustees of the British Museum).

Sadly, with the exception of the storage jars donated to various museums, Kalokairinos's collection of antiquities was destroyed in 1898, during the last Cretan insurrection against the Ottomans. Various scholars, however, including Schliemann and Evans, who visited to the island in the 1880s and 1890s, respectively, were able to see Kalokairinos's 'Mycenaean' building and finds. They immediately realized their importance and tried to excavate the site. For example, in 1879 Thomas B. Sandwith (British Consul on Crete from 1870 to 1885) tried to persuade the Keeper of Greek and Roman Antiquities in the British Museum, Charles T. Newton, to take over the excavations at Knossos, but to no avail.[34] A year later, William James Stillman – a journalist, photographer, and diplomat (American Consul at Chania from 1866 to 1869), whose second wife was the Pre-Rapahelite artist Marie Spartali – tried but also failed to continue Kolokairinos's work. Nevertheless, he published interesting reports and stressed that this could be the true location of the Minoan labyrinth.[35] In 1885, the Italian epigraphist and archaeologist Federico Halbherr, an important figure in the development of archaeological research in Crete (cf. below), was able to conduct a small test, thanks to his excellent relationship with the local (Christian) Greeks authorities, especially the influential Iosif Chatzidakis (whose name is also often transliterated as Hazzidakis).[36] The area he investigated, however, was not the Kephala, but a site a few hundred metres to the north, at 'sto Katsouni' near Makryteichos, where he found Roman remains – a choice that perhaps reflects his classical and especially epigraphic interests.[37] Schliemann too had plans to dig the 'Mycenaean' site at Knossos as early as January 1883.[38] He visited Crete more than once in the mid–late 1880s and tried to acquire the land. His interest in Knossos must have been sparked by various reports on Kalokairinos's excavations; by the numerous archaeological investigations undertaken especially by Italian archaeologists in Crete in the 1880s, including their excavations of the Idean cave (cf. below); and last but not least by Arthur Milchhöfer's volume *Die Anfänge der Kunst in Griechenland* (*The Beginning of Art in Greece*), which suggested that Crete was the commercial and intellectual centre of the Aegean in pre-Homeric times, and that the origins of Mycenaean art, and Greek art generally, should be sought on that island – an idea largely based on textual evidence, but also on Bronze Age seal-stones, many of Cretan provenance, that were becoming more and more visible in various publications and in the antiquarian market.[39]

Schliemann did not come to an agreement with the landowners of the Kephala, and died suddenly in Naples in 1890.[40] But his failed attempt to continue Kalokairinos's excavations stirred even further the interest of others. For example, in 1891 André Joubin started negotiations to acquire Knossos on behalf of the French School in Athens, but his efforts were unsuccessful, partly because his close cooperation with the Ottomans, and his work for the Imperial Museum in Constantinople, made him *persona non grata* among the influential Christian population of the island.[41] In 1893 the British archaeologist John L. Myres also toyed with the idea of continuing Kalokairinos's heroic pursuits.[42] It was Evans who eventually won the battle for Knossos: he bought one quarter of the Kephala in 1894, during his very first visit to Crete, and completed the acquisition in February 1900, about one month before the start of his momentous excavations.[43] This delay was caused by uprisings on the island and difficulties encountered by Evans in his dealings with the several Muslim co-owners of the land, to whom he paid the 'highest tribute' for their 'almost inexhaustible powers of obstruction'.[44] But how and why did Arthur Evans come to excavate at Knossos, and exercise such influence on Minoan studies?

'Little Evans – son of John Evans the Great' and the road to Knossos[45]

Evans may not be as colourful a character as Schliemann, and his life certainly lacks the romantic rags-to-riches and outsider elements associated with the German archaeologist. Yet, in many other ways, he is as intriguing, charismatic, and even controversial. If Schliemann has been called a 'hero for the age of Wagner and Nietzsche, a pagan industrialist, a colossal braggart, a self-made superman',[46] Evans may perhaps be described as a hero of both Victorian and Freudian times – a man steeped in racist and imperialist nineteenth-century ideas, and yet a liberal proto-feminist, who provided a springboard for modernist paradises. His half-sister Joan described him as a genius and a man of paradox, who could be generous and egotistical, flamboyant and modest, short-tempered and incredibly gentle – a picture very close to that presented by other people who knew him well, such as his excavation field director at Knossos, Duncan Mackenzie.[47] Complexity and contradiction emerge also from his writings, where contrasting methodologies and ideas can be found side by side: to use Isaiah Berlin's categorization of scholars, Evans was probably more of a fox than a hedgehog, as he did not always obey to a single, universal, organizing principle, but was an intellectual magpie.[48] A strong evolutionary streak does underlie all his works, together with what nowadays are considered racist notions – for he did believe in the existence of inferior ethnic groups – but Evans was also open to other ideas to explain cultural change, such as diffusionism and migrations.[49] Above all, he had a great flair for linking the past with the present, for making the Minoans appear relevant to the modern world.[50]

Arthur Evans, the eldest of Sir John Evans's six children, was born in 1851 at Nash Mills in Hertfordshire, into an upper middle-class, intellectual English family of distant Welsh and Huguenot origins (see Fig. 3.4). His father had made a considerable fortune after joining his uncle John Dickinson's papermaking business and marrying the latter's daughter, Harriet, with whom he had five children.[51] A man of remarkable intellectual qualities and vigour, John Evans became a renowned numismatist, archaeologist, and geologist, who played a crucial role in paving the way for the acceptance of the great antiquity of mankind and the theory of evolutionism in mid-nineteenth-century Britain and Europe. Thus, Arthur Evans effectively grew up in a home imbued with Darwinism, and among rich collections of coins and other archaeological artefacts, acquiring a 'knowledge of prehistory and numismatics learned so gradually and so easily that it had become unconscious'.[52] Arthur Evans lost his mother in 1858, and a year later John Evans married another cousin, Fanny (Frances) Phelps, with whom he had no children. She predeceased him in 1890, and two years later John Evans married Maria Millington Lathbury, a Classical scholar, with whom he had a daughter in 1883, Joan Evans, who became a notable art historian. Her *Time and Chance: The Story of*

Fig. 3.4 Sir Arthur Evans at Knossos (after Evans 1935: vii).

Arthur Evans and his Forebears (1943) remains a fundamental source on the history of her distinguished family.

Unlike his father, who was unable to study at university, Arthur Evans enjoyed a privileged education and could be said to be a typical product of the English educational establishment. After primary school at Callipers, he was educated at Harrow, where his studies were mostly devoted to Classical subjects. At university, as a student at Brasenose College, Oxford, he graduated with a first-class degree in Modern History in 1874. His early academic career, however, was not particularly distinguished. He appears to have applied for, but failed to obtain, a number of scholarships, travel bursaries, and fellowships at Oxford. After graduating, he attended a summer term at the University of Göttingen, where he continued his studies of history (with Reinhold Pauli and Ernst Winkel), but soon found a more congenial occupation: travelling in Bosnia and Herzegovina. The latter was in revolt against Ottoman rule, and Evans became correspondent for the *Manchester Guardian* from 1877 to 1882, reporting on the natives' rebellions against Ottoman and, later, Austrian rule – an activity that he interspersed with antiquarian research. Not that he needed to work, given that his father provided him with a generous yearly allowance of £250, and further help in case of emergencies.[53] In 1878 he married Margaret, the daughter of the historian Edward Augustus Freeman, and set up house in the city of Ragusa (modern Dubrovnik). The marriage did not produce any children, and Margaret died of tuberculosis in the spring of 1893.

While based in Ragusa, Evans's articles for the *Guardian* made him *persona non grata* to the Austrian authorities, with the result that he was imprisoned and later expelled from the Croatian city. He then settled in Oxford, where he was appointed Keeper (Director) of the Ashmolean Museum in 1884. Museum life did not entirely suit his exuberant character and love for travelling, but he fully embraced the challenge of transforming the then neglected Ashmolean into a proper home for archaeology in Oxford. Evans's transformation of this venerable institution was an achievement sufficient to ensure honour and lasting reputation, but during his tenure as Keeper he developed an interest in the Aegean, which eventually led to his excavations at Knossos and even greater fame.

Joan Evans wrote of her half-brother that in 1894, 'Time and Chance were now to guide him to a land that for the rest of his life was to be the kingdom of his mind'.[54] The factors that led Evans to Crete and Knossos can be seen as mixture of *histoire événementielle* and *conjonctures* (after Fernand Braudel) or 'internalist' and 'externalist' factors.[55] Among internalist/*événementielle* factors (in the sense of immediate developments within the more limited field of the disciplinary history, i.e. Aegean prehistory) one can consider the stimulus provided by Schliemann's and Kalokairinos's discoveries, Evans's meeting with Federico Halbherr, as well as the influence of his own father. Amongst the 'externalist' factors/*conjonctures*, one could enlist the impact of evolutionary and racial theories, Eurocentrism, and growing anti-German feelings in Britain.

Before the 1880s, Evans showed no particular interest in the Aegean, let alone in Homeric studies. His research mostly focused on numismatic as well as Illyrian and Celtic antiquities. Like most scholars and non-scholars alike, however, he had been intrigued by Schliemann's finds. In 1878 he saw the exhibition of Schliemann's Trojan discoveries held in London together with his then fiancée Margaret Freeman, and in 1883 he visited the German archaeologist in Athens.[56] In the same year Evans also published a slightly sceptical review of Schliemann's volume *Troja*, in which he kept referring to the archaeological site as 'Hissarlik' and even suggested that 'archaeology has perhaps little call to concern itself . . . with poetical topography'.[57] But Schliemann's finds posed questions that could be viewed within the prism of the most fashionable macro-idea of the time, evolutionism, and which intrigued Evans: what were the origins of 'Mycenaean' civilization? How did this civilization compare to others in terms of cultural evolution? Regarding the latter question, Evans was particularly struck by the lack of clear evidence for the existence of an established system of writing in Mycenaean Greece, and found it difficult to accept that the Mycenaeans could be so below the level of contemporary Egypt and other Near Eastern civilizations with regard to literacy, especially in view of the fact that they had regular contact with them.[58] Similarly influenced by evolutionary ideas was Evans's belief that the first step in what he considered to be the natural development of writing was a simple pictographic or hieroglyphic stage, as it was possible to observe, for example, in Egypt, and amongst the surviving 'primitive races of mankind'.[59]

That the son of 'John Evans the Great' had inherited an interest in evolutionism is unsurprising. But it seems that his father also influenced his specific curiosity about early forms of writings, since John Evans gave lectures on this very topic in the 1870s.[60]

Arthur Evans's desire to discover evidence of early writing systems in Europe was also stimulated by Salomon Reinach's ideas expressed in the article 'Le mirage oriental' (1893), where the French scholar had denied that civilization spread from the Near East and advocated European cultural independence. Indeed, even before he started digging at Knossos, at the time of his very first visit to Crete in 1894, Evans had already characterized the island's prehistoric population as 'European' and as relatively 'advanced'.[61]

Evans's interest in and search for a system of writing in Bronze Age Greece developed in the 1880s and culminated with the excavations at Knossos in 1900. The main stages of this search were as follows. In 1883, as reported above, Evans met Schliemann. In 1884, Evans was appointed Keeper of the Ashmolean Museum, and in 1889 the museum was presented with a four-sided seal-stone engraved with strange signs, which came from Greece, and which Evans immediately recognized as representing a pictographic script (see Fig. 3.5).[62] In 1892, Evans met in Rome the Italian epigraphist and archaeologist Federico Halbherr, the 'Patriarch of Cretan excavation' (as Evans dubbed him).[63] By that time, Halbherr had already been exploring Crete for almost a decade and had made remarkable discoveries (briefly discussed below). It is possible that during this meeting, or soon afterwards, Halberr discussed with Evans the important archaeological assemblage accidentally discovered at Hagios Onuphrios near Phaistos in 1887, and eventually published by Evans, which included seal-stones and scarabs.[64] In 1893, Evans visited Athens, where he saw and acquired other similar seal-stones, whose provenance was Crete. In 1894, Evans visited the island for the first time, acquired more seal-stones, visited Knossos, and started the acquisition of the site.

The 1892 meeting with Halbherr is an important link in the chain of events leading Evans to Knossos and the start of an important archaeological friendship.[65] Sent by his teacher, the Italian Classical scholar and epigraphist Domenico Comparetti, Halbherr had landed on Crete in June 1884 in search of inscriptions – a pursuit that he shared with other scholars, such as Bernard Hassoulier and Ernst Fabricius, and offers a good illustration of the German positivistic imprint and considerable influence on Classical scholarship, best exemplified by the establishment of great epigraphic corpora in the nineteenth century. The year 1884 proved to be an *annus mirabilis* for Cretan epigraphy,

Fig. 3.5 Seal-stone with pictographic signs donated to the Ashmolean Museum in 1889 (after Evans 1909: 8, fig. 4).

and for Halbherr, since only a month after his arrival on Crete he found the famous fifth-century BC inscription of the laws of ancient Gortyna. In that year, Halbherr also discovered the 'Eteocretan' inscriptions at Praisos.[66] These were written in the Greek alphabet, but expressed a non-Hellenic language. This suggested to scholars a link with the 'Eteocretans' mentioned in a famous passage of the *Odyssey* (XIX, 172-7) and, subsequently, the idea that the Eteocretans were descendants of the Minoans.[67] In 1884-5, Halbherr, Paolo Orsi, and Giorgos Pasparakes explored the Idean cave and discovered rich votive materials dating to the Geometric and Orientalizing periods, especially some spectacular bronze shields.[68] In 1886-7, Halbherr excavated the Pythion at Gortyna, with its many Archaic inscriptions, and in the 1890s, helped by a group of younger colleagues (such as Lucio Mariani, Luigi Savignoni, Antonio Taramelli, and Gaetano de Sanctis), he embarked on a systematic exploration of the island of Minos. By 1899 the research activities led by Halbherr had become officially the 'Italian Archaeological Mission in Crete'.

Halbherr's own main passion was and always remained Greek epigraphy, but he and his colleagues did not neglect prehistoric research. Their discoveries in the 1890s of many archaeological sites dating from the Neolithic to historical periods, together with Flinders Petrie's findings of Aegean Bronze Age objects (including Minoan products) in Egypt, highlighted the archaeological potential of Crete.[69] By the time Evans started his own researches in 1894, a considerable number of Bronze Age–Early Iron Age sites had been located, and some had even been partly excavated (e.g. Ergano, Kourtes, and the Kamares, Psychro, and Miamou caves).[70] In fact, and despite having started the acquisition of Knossos in 1894, before 1900 Evans toyed with the idea of digging other sites, especially Goulas (ancient Lato), which he mistook for a prehistoric settlement: he may well have opted to excavate this site instead of Knossos had he not been gazumped by the French, who started excavations at Goulas in 1899.[71] In any case, the work of Kalokairinos at Knossos, the site's huge potential, its literary links, and the fierce competition for securing the excavation rights eventually focused Evans's attention on the Kephala and the 'Palace of Minos'.

From the Palace of Minos to the Palace of Ariadne: Κρητική Πολιτεία (Cretan State) (1898–1913) and the Heroic Age of Cretan excavations

The Cretan State: Archaeology and crypto-colonial regimes

Evans's visits to Crete continued throughout the period 1894-9, but his excavations at Knossos did not start until the spring of 1900 because of the volatile political situation.[72] Particularly violent insurrections in 1896-8, with mutual massacres of Christian and Muslim populations, led to the intervention of a number of European states. In 1898, Crete was granted autonomous status within the Ottoman Empire, but was ruled by a High Commissioner, Prince George of Greece, appointed by four European powers that effectively supervised the island, which was divided into four sectors or districts: Heraklion, under the British; Sitia, under the French; Sfakia and Apokorona under the

Italians; and Rethymnon, under the Russians. All four powers had headquarters and diplomatic representation in Chania – the capital of the island at that time. This new regime, the Κρητική Πολιτεία or Cretan State, lasted from 1898 until the official union of Crete with Greece in 1913.[73] Its establishment greatly facilitated the start of archaeological investigations, since the best finds had to remain on the island, especially after the Cretan Assembly approved a new archaeological law in 1899 preventing the export of antiquities.[74] In the words of D. G. Hogarth and R. C. Bosanquet, during the Cretan State the island effectively became a 'Promised Land' of archaeological research.[75] Many important excavations took place, which were almost exclusively led by foreign archaeologists, who had the economic power to carry out such enterprises, unlike the destitute Cretans. This situation, closely reminiscent of 'crypto-colonial' or 'quasi-colonial' regimes, in which military, political, economic and cultural hegemony go hand in hand, caused occasional friction with the locals.[76] This is indicated, for example, by the 'Kalyvia affair'. In the late summer of 1901, after Halbherr had returned to Italy from his excavations at Phaistos, peasants had accidentally discovered some Bronze Age tombs on the nearby hill of Kalyvia. Stephanos Xanthoudidis, one of the official archaeological superintendents appointed by the Cretan State, was alerted to the discoveries: he inspected the site and decided to complete the excavations of the tombs that had been exposed (a sensible decision, likely taken, at least in part, to avoid further looting and loss of information). Halbherr, however, was incensed, because he considered this as poaching in Italian territory. Even Prince George became embroiled in this quarrel, which concluded in rather humiliating fashion for Xanthoudidis, who had to provide a justification for his actions, was not allowed to publish his finds and felt that Cretans had been 'enslaved'.[77]

Of the four European powers that policed the island, France, Italy, and Britain accompanied their military and political presence with a number of archaeological and other scientific expeditions. This produced a kind of 'archaeological colonisation' of Crete, the legacy of which is still felt today.[78] Besides the French excavations at Goulas (Lato) and the already active Italian Archaeological Mission, a Cretan Exploration Fund was established in 1899 to support the work of British archaeology on the island. Prince George was the patron and Evans one of the three directors, the other two being D. G. Hogarth and R. C. Bosanquet, who at the time were the current director and the director elect of the British School at Athens, respectively; George Macmillan (the philhellenic scion of the Macmillan publishing dynasty, who eventually published Evans's magnum opus, *The Palace of Minos*) was the treasurer; and the archaeologist and ancient historian John L. Myres the secretary.[79] During the Cretan State regime, the exciting new discoveries did capture the interest of Russian intellectuals, but no Russian scholar appears to have engaged directly in archaeological expeditions.[80] Instead, American archaeologists became very active, especially in east Crete. Germans archaeologists also showed an interest in Crete, but this did not materialize in any excavation during the period of the Cretan State: Wilhelm Dörpfeld had some claims on the site of Palaikastro, which he relinquished in 1902 to the British School in Athens.[81] One should also note that the 'archaeological colonisation' of Crete did not exactly match the administrative districts of the European powers: the choice of sites was more influenced by previous researches – from Pashley's and Spratt's travel accounts, to the recent systematic explorations initiated by Halbherr, and his discovery of inscriptions at Praisos, which sparked a noticeable interest in the 'Eteocretans' and their origins. Other factors that affected the archaeologists' choice of sites were, naturally, their own explorations and information received from locals.

After the establishment of the Cretan State, much diplomatic activity took place between foreign archaeologists and the Cretan authorities to obtain permissions to excavate the most promising sites. This was accompanied by some skulduggery, as suggested, among other things, by the surviving correspondence between Halbherr and Evans.[82] From the spring of 1900, Crete saw a veritable boom in archaeological excavations at some of the most important Minoan sites, many of which continue to be excavated to the present day: Evans's on the Kephala at Knossos (on 23 March; with Hogarth's tests around the site in search of cemeteries starting about a week earlier); Halbherr's (and Luigi Pernier's) at Phaistos (on 2 June); D. G. Hogarth's at Psychro (Dictaean Cave) (June); and Harriett Boyd's (later Boyd Hawes) at Kavousi (June). These were soon followed by excavations at many other sites, such as Praisos (to search for 'Eteocretans'), Petras, Gournia, and Kato Zakros in 1901; Hagia Triada and Palaikastro in 1902; Vasiliki and Mouliana in 1904; Koumasa in 1905–6; Pseira and Mochlos in 1907–8; Tylissos in 1909; Sphoungaras in 1910; Archalokori in 1912; and Pacheia Ammos in 1914, to mention some notable examples.[83]

From Mycenaean to Minoan

Although other sites, such as Phaistos, Hagia Triada, Palaikastro, and Gournia, attracted considerable attention, of the excavations that took place between 1900 and the start of the First World War, those by Evans at Knossos captured both scholarly and public imagination above all.[84] This was for very good reasons. First, there was the richness of the finds from Knossos, which also turned out to be the oldest and most extensive prehistoric settlement on the island, provided with the largest 'palatial' building, the richest archives of written documents, rich tombs, and the only site with a beautifully carved stone seat, interpreted as a 'throne' set in a 'council chamber' (see Figs. 3.6–3.7).[85] Second, there were Evans's journalistic flair and remarkable ability to provide interpretations of his finds that situated them in broader contemporary debates, from evolutionism to issues of racial identities and even gender. Last but not least, as at Troy and Mycenae, the site's association with well-known ancient Greek myths provided the perfect match between the literary and the physical *topoi*, and gave free rein to the irresistible yearning for associating tangible remains with familiar ancient narratives.

Evans's excavations at Knossos started on 23 March 1900 and continued until 1931, albeit with some interruptions. With Mackenzie as his field director, Evans dug every spring from 1900 until 1910, except for 1906, when his funds were devoted to the construction of his own Knossian home and excavation headquarters, the Villa Ariadne; there was no work at Knossos in 1911 and 1912 largely because Mackenzie had been appointed 'Explorer' of the Palestine Exploration Fund, and was then directing his own excavations at Ain Shems (biblical Beth Shemesh); Evans conducted a short season by himself in 1913, while Mackenzie was digging in the Sudan for Henry

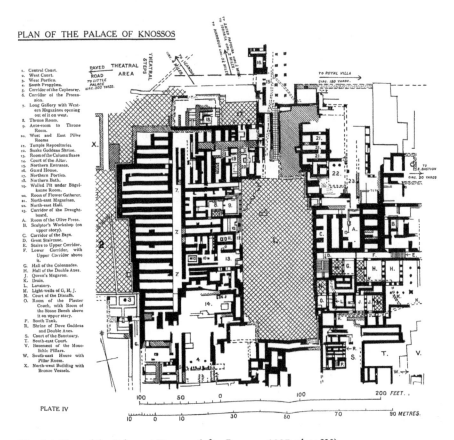

PLAN OF THE PALACE OF KNOSSOS

1. Central Court.
2. West Court.
3. West Portico.
4. South Propylaea.
5. Corridor of the Cupbearer.
6. Corridor of the Procession.
7. Long Gallery with Western Magazines opening out of it on west.
8. Throne Room.
9. Ante-room to Throne Room.
10. West and East Pillar Rooms
11. Temple Repositories.
12. Snake Goddess Shrine.
13. Room of the Column Bases
14. Court of the Altar.
15. Northern Entrance.
16. Guard House.
17. Northern Portico.
18. Northern Bath.
19. Walled Pit under Bogelkamme Room.
20. Room of Flower Gatherer.
21. North-east Magazines.
22. North-east Hall.
23. Corridor of the Draughtboard.

A. Room of the Olive Press.
B. Sculptor's Workshop (on upper story).
C. Corridor of the Bays.
D. Great Staircase.
E. Stairs to Upper Corridor.
F. Lower Corridor, with Upper Corridor above it.
G. Hall of the Colonnades.
H. Hall of the Double Axes.
J. Queen's Megaron.
K. Drain.
L. Lavatory.
M. Light-wells of G, H, J.
N. Court of the Distaffs.
O. Room of the Plaster Couch, with Room of the Stone Bench above it on upper story.
P. South Tank.
R. Shrine of Dove Goddess and Double Axes.
S. Court of the Sanctuary.
T. South-east Court.
V. Basement of the Monolithic Pillars.
W. South-east House with Pillar Room.
X. North-west Building with Bronze Vessels.

PLATE IV

Fig. 3.6 Plan of the Palace at Knossos (after Burrows 1907: plate IV).

Wellcome; in 1914 work was interrupted by the First World War, and resumed in 1920, with major campaigns from 1922 to 1931.[86] By the end of the first week of excavation in the spring of 1900, Evans had already brought to light hoards of clay tablets inscribed in a script later labelled Linear B, thus providing even more evidence for the existence of writing in the Aegean during the second millennium BC. Indeed, in very little time the excavations on Crete, and at Knossos in particular, showed that, besides the unique and undeciphered Phaistos disk, three main scripts had been used on the island during the Bronze Age – scripts that Evans labelled Cretan Pictographic (a.k.a. Cretan Hieroglyphic), Linear A, and Linear B (see Fig. 3.8).[87] The scripts shared a number of signs and appeared to evolve from each other, with Linear B being the last, and this led Evans and others to suppose (erroneously) that all three were used to express the same, non-Hellenic, Cretan language.

Clear evidence of literacy was only one of the major discoveries made in just a few weeks of excavation at Knossos. Scholars already knew from Kalokairinos's limited tests that an impressive Bronze Age building stood on the Kephala hill, but Evans's work soon revealed its elaborate and monumental architecture, which was in fact older and

Fig. 3.7 The Throne Room at Knossos (after Evans 1935: fig. 895).

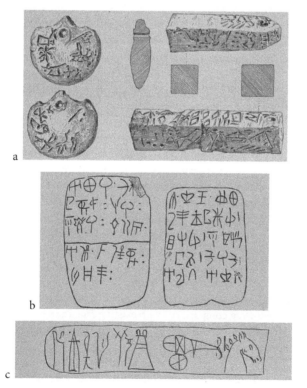

Fig. 3.8a–c Examples of Pictographic, Linear A, and Linear B scripts (after Evans 1909: figs. 10, 13, and 19).

quite unlike that of the Mycenaean palaces on the Greek mainland. Evans also explored part of the large town that surrounded this palace, including some of its cemeteries. In a nutshell, in less than a fortnight Evans had discovered a new culture or 'civilization', older than the Mycenaean and shedding considerable light on the latter's origins. This Cretan civilization was not only older, but also quite different from the Mycenaean in many respects. For these reasons, Evans proposed to give it a different name, and opted for the memorable 'Minoan'. This was not a neologism, since this word (and its counterparts in other European languages) had existed in English for centuries, often as a poetic equivalent of 'Cretan'.[88] In fact, Evans's choice was largely inspired by the work of German scholars such as Hoeck and Müller, whose idea of a brilliant 'Minoische Zeit' (Minoan Age), covering several centuries during the second millennium BC, had already influenced many others, from Gladstone to Milchhöfer (cf. Chapter 2). Evans applied an existing label and concept to the material culture that emerged from the Cretan excavations and extended its chronological meaning. In other words, the new excavations on Crete provided masses of tangible evidence for the already established 'Minoan Age', as Schliemann's excavations had done for the 'Homeric Age'.

In only a few years, Evans's excavations at Knossos, together with those by Halbherr's at Phaistos and Hagia Triada, Hogarth's at Kato Zakros and Psychro, Boyd's at Gournia, and Bosanquet's at Palaikastro, to mention a few, showed that Crete in the third and second millennia BC had produced a sophisticated culture, with numerous settlements ranging from large urban centres with monumental palaces to small villages with narrow cobbled lanes reminiscent of contemporary rural communities, and fascinating burial sites. All had produced exquisite artefacts, such as beautifully carved stone vases and seals, faience and ivory figurines, and decorated ceramics that were often likened to Japanese porcelain (cf. also below). Most of the attention was devoted to the Minoan palaces – multi-storey buildings that were older and larger than those found on the Greek mainland and presented a different layout. In terms of their history, these Minoan palaces, and the settlements in which they were located, partly mapped that of the familiar Egyptian periodization of Old, Middle, and New Kingdom, while Knossos also showed evidence of a long Neolithic occupation.[89] In terms of layout, Minoan palaces were organized through wings built around an open space, a central court (see Fig. 3.6), and were provided with western paved courts, extensive storage facilities as well as idiosyncratic Minoan features, such as *polythira* (rooms with a row of double doors, i.e. a system of pier-and-door partitions) and the so-called lustral basins (sunken rooms reached via a flight of steps, reminiscent of a Jewish *mikveh*).[90] Some rooms were decorated with colourful frescoes (see Figs. 3.9–3.10), which were often compared to those of Pompeii and of Etruscan tombs. Some of these wall paintings provided an immediate and vivid picture of the men and women who had lived in Crete thousands of years previously, allowing comparisons with existing racial and physiognomic types – something of considerable interest in this period, in which phrenology and physiognomy enjoyed considerable popularity.

Besides complex buildings, written documents, frescoes, and beautiful artefacts, three specific aspects of the new Cretan discoveries were perceived as particularly striking. The first was the absence of fortifications, in contrast with Mycenaean settlements on the Greek mainland: in the words of the Classical scholar Adolf

Fig. 3.9 Knossos, The Cup Bearer fresco (after Evans 1928: plate XII).

Fig. 3.10 Knossos, Dancing Lady fresco (photo: https://commons.wikimedia.org/wiki/File:AMI_-_T%C3%A4nzerin.jpg).

Michaelis, 'the great Palace of Knossos, situated in the open county and undefended by walls, compares with the small walled fortress-palaces of Tiryns and Mycenae as the palace of Versailles compares with the Wartburg'.[91] The second was the evidence for good sanitation, namely drainage systems and flushing toilets.[92] Last but not least was the intriguing, and abundant, representation of women in frescoes and other media (cf. below). Most important, however, was the overall picture emerging from Evans's pen and from that of other scholars as well as journalists, which captivated the scholarly and public imagination alike. The rediscovery of Minoan Crete reinforced the notion that Greek myths reflected some historical reality, but also went beyond this: it undermined the notion of a 'Greek miracle' even more than the discovery of 'Mycenaean' Greece, since Minoan Crete was largely considered as non-Hellenic. It appeared even more exotic and mysterious than Mycenaean Greece, and had an immediately enthusiastic reception, since the Minoan artistic language appeared to strike a familiar chord among early twentieth-century avant-gardes. Above all, the Cretan discoveries were made to resonate with many of the contradictions, tensions, and paradoxes of the late nineteenth and early twentieth centuries, such as the 'Eastern Question', the 'Woman Question', and notions of racial supremacy. Minoan Crete was often portrayed as a unique and captivating mixture of primitive and advanced, ancient and surprisingly modern, European and Oriental, imperialistic and peaceful, feminine and masculine, familiar and unfamiliar, comfortable and uncomfortable. This sense of duality and contradiction, the notion of a culture that straddles contrasting or even opposite camps, and yet maintains its own distinctiveness, are significant aspects in the perception of Minoan Crete, which have persisted to the present day, with different generations and individuals emphasizing different elements.

An early example of the contrasting and even contradictory ways in which Minoan Crete was portrayed, sometimes even within a single work, is the article published by Evans in the March 1901 issue of the *Monthly Review*, a London magazine on literary and art criticism as well as a commentary on current affairs. Here Evans presents the women depicted on Knossian frescoes as having a pale complexion because of their seclusion in some kind of Oriental harem, whereas only a few lines later he shows that they intermingled freely with the other sex, and compares them to modern Parisian women because of their dress and coiffeur.[93] Similarly, in this article one can find a description of the 'oldest throne in Europe' (see Fig. 3.7) as very modern, because it shows 'an extraordinary anticipation' of the Gothic style.[94] Another early example of Minoan Crete being presented as an intriguing mixture of old and new, familiar and exotic, Western and Oriental appears in an article written by D. G. Hogarth for the literary and cultural periodical *The Cornhill Magazine*, reporting on the exhibition of drawings, photographs, plans, and casts (mostly taken from Evans's 1900–2 excavation), which was held at the Royal Academy in 1903. This highlights the primitive, naturalistic, and even idealistic aspects of Minoan art; it also notes points of contact with Egyptian, Babylonian, Greek, and even Renaissance art, while remarking on its idiosyncratic strangeness:

> Visitors passing directly from Wilsons, De Wints, Constables, and Calcotts have found it difficult to adjust their mental vision. At the first glance they think they have left art for sheer antiquarianism: at the second, if they know art at all, they

realise that here, too, it is, and that true art, based on conscientious study of nature and inspired by the conception of an ideal. The Cretan exhibition needs close attention, and is worth it. To distinguish the artistic achievement in such primitive effort is not easy; but once the mind is attuned to the primitive key, the admirable character not only of the effort, but the achievement, reveals itself on all sides. Perhaps, however, to the end the exhibition leaves the most discerning spectator a little uncomfortable. He hankers after a point of repose in the familiar. At one point memories of Egyptian art seem to promise him the pleasure of recognition; at another Babylonian, at another Greek, characteristics raise his hope. But presently he must always see that, much as there is of Egyptian, Babylonian, Greek, even Renaissance character in these Cretan representations of human, animal and vegetable forms, there is something besides, new, individual, and strange; and he ends by wondering less why such things appear in an exhibition of old masters at Burlington House than why a fuller commentary has not been supplied to help him over the gulf of three thousand years.[95]

The above passage also hints at one of the rhetorical ploys used consciously and/or unconsciously by Evans and others in their narratives about Minoan civilization, namely the introduction of elements that would cause a 'pleasure of recognition' in their readers, in the sense of the reassuring discovery of the familiar in an unfamiliar world, the recognizable paving the way for the new and strange.[96] Thus, Evans used liberally Greek myths and parallels with well-known arts in his publications, and, in doing so, he continued to some extent the processes of Hellenization and Europeanization of the Aegean Bronze Age started in the previous generation. But he also added some fascinating twists in the tale ending, and the shift from Minos to Ariadne alluded to in the title of this section, as discussed in more detail below.

Although Evans, in the 1880s, had been very sceptical of Schliemann's reliance on ancient Greek mythological narratives, by the time he started digging at Knossos his attitude had somewhat changed. Evans's use of Greek myths is generally subtler than Schliemann's, but he too made extensive references to familiar stories and tried to identify in them a kernel of truth. For example, Evans presented the large structure he excavated as the real Cretan 'labyrinth', by connecting this word with *labrys* (a term used in later Greek texts for 'double-axe') and suggesting that 'labyrinth' meant the 'House of the Double Axe', noting that many mason's marks found at Knossos in prominent locations had the shape of this object (see Fig. 3.11).[97] One should note, however, that the connection between labyrinth and *labrys* appears to be more tenuous than Evans suggested: apart from the linguistic difficulties in relating the two words pointed out by several philologists, one may also observe that, while masons' marks in the shape of a double-axe do appear most frequently at Knossos, they are not exclusive to this site, and other signs are also very common.[98]

Other intriguing examples of Evans's use of Greek myth at Knossos include his interpretations of the 'Dancing Lady fresco' (see Fig. 3.10) and the 'Theatral Area' (see Fig. 3.12), which, according to him, demonstrated the reality behind the Homeric *choros* (dancing floor) of Ariadne.[99] Similarly, a number of seal impressions with bulls helped to explain the historical origins of the story of Theseus and the Minotaur,[100]

Fig. 3.11 Knossos, mason's marks in the shape of double-axes (after Evans 1921: supplementary plate X).

Fig. 3.12 Knossos, the Theatral Area (photo N. Momigliano).

while images of bull-leaping, such as the famous 'Toreador fresco' (see Fig. 1.4), showed that 'the legends of Athenian prisoners devoured by the Minotaur preserve a real tradition of these cruel sports'.[101] In fact, Evans may have been almost too keen, at times, to find connections between Bronze Age archaeological materials and later Greek narratives: for example, many of his 'Minotaur' images (see Fig. 1.7), including his 'Young Minotaur', turned out to be monkeys, or goats, or possibly goat-human hybrids.[102] Even the so-called 'Early Keep', i.e. the deep walled pits in the north-west wing of the palace, became entangled in a mythological web: Evans interpreted this structure as the Knossian gaol, and suggested that 'the groans of these Minoan dungeons may well have found an echo in the tale of Theseus',[103] an interpretation that nowadays seems as hyperbolic and as unfounded as some of Schliemann's previous claims, even assuming that Evans may have made it with tongue in cheek.

This blending of a new material culture with familiar Greek myths increased the aura of Evans's Knossian discoveries, provided some 'pleasure of recognition', and also continued the processes of Hellenization and Europeanization of the Aegean Bronze Age that had started with Schliemann. In Evans's writings, however, these processes took intriguing turns, especially with regard to topics related to gender and racial issues, perhaps because Evans used Greek myths more as a comparative anthropologist-archaeologist than as a Hellenist.[104] Thus, although Evans chose to name the newly discovered culture after King Minos, he was partial to Ariadne and matriarchal heritage (as seen especially in his notion of a Great Minoan Mother Goddess); and although he considered his Minoans to be European, he distanced them from any notion of Aryan and Greek racial purity, preferring the superiority of the Mediterranean race and the idea that Minoan Crete (like the contemporary British Empire) included a mixture of different people.[105]

From King Minos to 'Queen Ariadne', and back to King Minos – and from Greek to European via the 'Mediterranean race'

Evans, following in the footsteps of previous scholars, considered the name Minos to be a dynastic title (like Pharaoh, Caesar, and Tzar) used by a series of priest-kings whose palaces combined royal and religious functions.[106] But who was (or were) the object of their piety? Evans proposed that the Minoans venerated essentially one divinity, a Great Mother Goddess, accompanied by her son/consort – a belief system labelled by D. G. Hogarth with the oxymoron 'dual monotheism'.[107] Evans's Great Mother Goddess represented an early evolutionary stage of later goddesses, such as Rhea, and was a precursor even of the Virgin Mary: she was a single female deity, worshipped under many different aspects, who later developed into separate goddesses.[108] According to Evans, this female-centred, quasi-monotheistic religion represented the vestiges of an earlier matriarchal system of social organization on Crete (how much earlier, though, is not entirely clear), which had later been supplanted by patriarchy and, later still, by the male-dominated pantheon of Greek religion.[109]

In this reconstruction of Minoan religion and society, Evans was taking the cue from his Knossian finds, in particular the prevalent and remarkable female iconography, from signet rings to wall paintings, including the 'Toreador Fresco' (see Fig. 1.3), which was interpreted, until the 1980s, as representing two intrepid, androgynous, cross-dressing female 'cowgirls' taking part in dangerous bull-games performed in honour of the Goddess.[110] This Minoan female empowerment resonated with topical debates related to the 'Woman Question',[111] as also illustrated in some Cretomanic works of the 1900s, such as Jules Bois's *La Furie* (cf. below).

Besides cues in the Knossian finds, Evans's ideas about a supreme female divinity in Minoan religion owed a great deal to scholarship on early societies and religions, which was fashionable at the time, especially the work of scholars such as James Frazer, William Robertson Smith, and the so-called Cambridge Ritualists, including Jane Harrison. These scholars, in turn, were building on previous works on mother goddesses, matrilineal societies, and matriarchy such as E. Gerhard's *Über das Metroon zu Athen und über die Göttermutter der griechische Mythologie* (1849) and J. J. Bachofen's *Das Mutterrecht* (1861), where many pages were devoted specifically to the existence of an early Cretan matriarchy as evidenced in ancient Greek sources, such as Herodotus on Lycian and Cretan matrilineality. Other significant works on these topics include L. H. Morgan's *Ancient Society* (1877), which also influenced F. Engels's *Origin of the Family, Private Property and the State* (1884) and E. B. Tylor's 1896 article on the matriarchal family system.[112] As Walter Burkert has remarked:

> [T]he discovery of Minoan civilization coincided with the period of the Cambridge [Ritualists] School's greatest influence. Attempts had long been made to search out the original forebears of Greek religion, and now, it seemed, they had come to light, the pre-Greek religion had been uncovered. The antithesis of the Olympian, anthropomorphic and polytheistic world of Homer's gods was no sooner sought than found: a predominance of chthonic powers, matriarchy, and non-anthropomorphic deities, or a single divine figure [i.e. the Great Mother Goddess] in place of a pantheon.[113]

As persuasively argued by Christine Morris, by highlighting the mother-centred aspect of Minoan spiritual life, Evans was also tapping into the Victorian idealization of motherhood, which partly coincided with the 'Marian Age', a term referring to the period from *c.* 1850–1950 that saw an increase in devotion towards the Virgin Mary, accompanied by the Catholic Church's recognition of many Marian apparitions (e.g. at Lourdes and Fatima) and of the dogmas of her Immaculate Conception and Assumption.[114] Indeed, Evans's Minoan monotheism could also appeal to many elements of modern European society, who were searching for a new religiosity, partly as a reaction to the increasing secularization of early twentieth-century society (cf. also Chapter 4). At the same time, and by contrast, Evans's emphasis on the purely nurturing, non-sexual, and even virginal aspects of his Minoan Mother Goddess seem less attuned to the emerging interest in sexuality, especially female, partly stimulated by the works of individuals such as the famous French neurologist Jean-Martin Chacot and his even more renowned pupil, Sigmund Freud.

As discussed above, the importance of female figures in Minoan religion was regarded in evolutionary terms as an indication of early matriarchy, later replaced by patriarchy. In this context, it is interesting to see how the struggle between male and female as well as the latter's dethronement were also enacted in some of Evans's own writings. In an article published with D. G. Hogarth in *The Times* of 31 October 1900, Evans suggested that the Knossian 'throne' he had discovered was that 'on which (if so much faith be permitted to us) Minos may have declared the law' (see Fig. 3.7). But from remarks in his excavation notebooks and accounts by early visitors to the site, Evans at times envisaged the 'Throne of Minos' as being occupied by a 'Queen Ariadne'.[115] This is also apparent in some of Evans's early publications on Knossos, such as the already mentioned article in the the *Monthly Review*. Here Evans describes a 'procession of painted life-size figures, in the centre of which was a female personage, probably a queen in magnificent apparel', while a few pages later, the 'female personage' becomes 'Queen Ariadne herself', and the room where the 'throne' was found is referred to as 'the council chamber of a Mycenaean King or Sovereign Lady'.[116] The references to a Queen Ariadne and Sovereign Lady in this article, published in March 1901, could be partly a homage to the British queen and empress Victoria, who had died on 22 January of that year. But many of Evans's earlier and later remarks on Minoan religion as being dominated by a female deity are influenced, above all, by the scholarship on social and religious evolution mentioned above. One of Evans's clearest allusions to this can perhaps be seen in his discussion of the Knossian 'Theatral Area' (see Fig. 3.12) discovered in 1903:

> We see then here a theatral building ... containing what seems to have been an orchestra. On the other hand we possess independent evidence of ceremonial dances in honour of the great native Goddess of whom Aphroditê Ariadnê is a later transformation. In view of these facts it is difficult to refuse the conclusion that this first of theatres, the Stepped Area with its dancing ground, supplies a material foundation for the Homeric tradition of the famous 'choros' ... It is symptomatic of the increased importance attached to male divinities in the later religion of Greece that 'choros' and theatre should pass from the Goddess to the God. In the more recent cult the 'choros' of Ariadnê is superseded by that of her Consort Dionysos.[117]

This passage identifies the 'Theatral Area' as one of the physical realities behind the Homeric description of Ariadne's dancing floor and as symbolic of the evolution from a female-dominated Minoan monotheism to a male-dominated Greek polytheism. One can see here clear reflections of ideas supported by the 'Cambridge Ritualists' (a.k.a the 'Classical Anthropologists', a small group of Classical scholars with an interest in ritual as the origin of myths) and especially by Jane Harrison, even if Evans does not refer to her works explicitly. Her influential *Prolegomena to the Study of Greek Religion* was published after these discoveries, in November 1903, but in 1898 Harrison had already given a series of lectures (on Delphi), reported in *The Times* for February–March 1898, in which she had argued for an evolutionary development from a primitive matriarchal order, and a goddess as the focus of worship, to the later patriarchy personified in Apollo.[118] Moreover, Harrison and Evans were personally acquainted: they were both members of the managing committee of the British School at Athens in the early 1900s, and she had visited Knossos in 1901.[119] Yet, despite the importance of women in Evans's vision of Minoan religion and society, it was his priest-kings who ruled the island and the Aegean waves under the benevolent gaze of a Great Mother Goddess.

The above passage on the Theatral Area is also interesting for another reason: it reinforced the notion that the 'Greek miracle' was a renaissance, by suggesting that even a famous Greek institution such as the theatre had a precursor in Minoan Crete. Schliemann's work had already started the process of undermining the 'Greek miracle' by showing the great achievements of Bronze Age Greece, but Evans went even further by substituting his non-Hellenic, non-Aryan Minoans as the origins of Greek and European culture. In other words, Evans raised the issue of what was 'Greek' in Greek art, in a manner that was more radical than the way in which Schliemann's discoveries in the late nineteenth century had problematized the origins of Greek art, and the arrival of the Parthenon marbles in early nineteenth-century London had problematized the Winckelmannian Greek ideal.

Evans's ideas regarding the ethnic affiliations of Minoan Crete were largely based upon the evidence found in Classical sources, Halbherr's discoveries of the 'Eteocretan' inscriptions, and the anthropological work of the Italian polymath Giuseppe Sergi. Sergi's work, now largely forgotten, was quite influential in the late nineteenth and early twentieth centuries, and represented a contrasting voice against emerging Aryanism.[120] According to Sergi, a significant component of the European population belonged to his 'stirpe Mediterranea' (Mediterranean stock), which was the ultimate source of all that was civilized in Europe. This population was different from, and intellectually superior to, the Aryans of Asian (or Germanic) origins. It was the product of the intermingling of many related people that shared a common African origin and was characterized by small stature, oval face, long head, brown wavy hair, dark eyes, and brunette complexion (i.e. white-skinned, but with a dark olive tone).

Sergi's anti-Aryan stance (like that of other scholars before and after him) partly represents a reaction against contemporary Germanic racial theories, according to which European civilization, the pinnacle of human development, was linked to the tall, dolichocephalic, blond, and blue-eyed Aryans. This, in turn, concurred with the increasing anti-German feelings, nurtured by fear of German military power, which emerged after the German unification and Franco-Prussian war in the 1870s, and eventually produced the French–British *Entente Cordial* of 1904.[121] Anti-German attitudes are also illustrated by the glee with which some authors of popular books on the Minoans highlighted the superiority of Evans's work in comparison to Schliemann's, and how the German 'solar myths' constructed to explain the Minotaur and his labyrinth had been 'demolished' by the (British) 'excavator's spade'.[122] In the case of Evans, personal factors may have also played a part in his rejection of Aryan superiority, since his own appearance did not fit the northern ideal. As he humorously commented, 'The ancient Greek might not have accepted kinship even with the "blameless Ethiopian," but those of us who may happen to combine a British origin with a Mediterranean complexion may derive a certain ancestral pride from remote consanguinity with Pharaoh.'[123] Evans's (anti-Aryan) notion of Minoan/Mediterranean racial-cultural superiority and primacy of attainment in most fields can be found in many of his publications, but is nowhere expressed more vividly, and ironically, than in his presidential address to the Society for the Promotion of Hellenic Studies of 1912, in which he argued that the study of the origins of Greek civilization had demonstrated that, during the Bronze Age, a non-Hellenic people had anticipated on Greek soil all the great inventions attributed to Classical Greece.[124] Among these inventions, Evans included epic poetry. In a letter to a colleague, in which he commented on his presidential address, Evans wrote that '*Pour épater MM. les Héllénistes*, I told them with pious unction that Homer, properly speaking, was a translator, and that part of an illustrated edition of his original had lately come up in Crete and Mycenae. In short, he worked up an older Minoan Epic, and was after all somewhat of a "literary dog."'[125] Adding insult to injury, Evans suggested that the Greek genius had nothing to do with Aryan descent, but to their mixing with the superior Mediterranean race: '[C]an it be doubted that the artistic genius of the later Hellenes was largely the continuous outcome of that inherent in the earlier race in which they had been merged? Of that earlier "Greece before the Greeks" it may be said, as of the later Greece, *capta ferum victorem cepit.*'[126]

Evans's writings on the 'Cup Bearer' fresco (see Fig. 3.9) provide further illustration of Evans's racial views, his use of familiarization, and wavering between male and female elements. In the notes that Evans took during the excavations in 1900, he remarked upon the resemblance to Etruscan paintings and Egyptian representations of the 'Keftiu' people; he also expressed the view that this fresco represented a woman, naming her 'Ariadne', despite the fact that his right-hand man, Duncan Mackenzie, had immediately (and correctly) identified this image as male.[127] In an article published in 1901, however, Evans interpreted this figure as male and emphasized his 'European' characteristics:

> The profile of the face is pure and almost classically Greek. This, with the dark curly hair and high brachycephalic head, recalls an indigenous type well represented still in the glens of Ida and the White Mountains – a type which brings with it many reminiscences from the Albanian highlands and the neighbouring regions of Montenegro and Herzegovina. The lips are somewhat full, but the physiognomy has certainly no Semitic cast. The profile rendering of the eye shows an advance in human portraiture foreign to Egyptian art, and only achieved by artists of classical Greece in the early fine-art period of the fifth century B.C. – after some eight centuries, that is, of barbaric decadence and a slow revival.[128]

This passage should also be seen in the context of Evans's anti-Ottoman stance, the recent Cretan struggle for liberation from Ottoman rule and union with Greece, and the archaeological colonization of Crete by European (and American) archaeologists. Evans's views on the 'Mediterranean' ethnic component among the Minoans, as mentioned above, were largely adopted from Sergi. But the Mediterranean race was not the only element constituting Evans's Minoans. He also envisaged Knossos to have been ruled by an early dynasty of 'Armenoid-Anatolian' type, later supplanted by people of Mediterranean race; furthermore, in his Minoan realm he also envisaged the presence of Greeks and 'negro' elements, the latter as mercenaries among Minoan troops fighting on the Greek mainland.[129]

One can speculate as to whether this multi-ethnic view of the Minoan world was partly influenced by Evans's first-hand knowledge of British and Ottoman imperialism and multi-ethnic realities, including on Crete itself. Many visitors to the island commented on its varied and colourful ethnic composition as well as exotic Oriental feel, which were much more prevalent in the early twentieth century than after Crete's unification with Greece in 1913, and especially after the 1923 population exchange between Greece and Turkey. For example, Gaetano De Sanctis and his wife Emilia, in their memoirs and travel notes of the early 1910s, described the Oriental atmosphere as well as the cosmopolitan, multicoloured population of Crete, including Turks, Greeks, Arabs, Africans, and people from almost every European country.[130] At any rate, Evans's multi-ethnic views of Minoan Crete were based on a variety of factors, such as Sergi's racial theories, the linguistic admixture described in later Greek sources (such as *Odyssey* 19, 164ff.), the skull measurements taken by various scholars,[131] and his vision of Minoan Crete as an imperial power.

With regards to Evans's views on the Minoans and their empire, it should be noted that they were much more warlike than is nowadays commonly believed. In Evans's writings, the Minoans do often appear as highly civilized, young, long-haired, bejewelled lovers of flowers and nature (see Fig. 3.13), but they were also accomplished warriors and even had a darker, bloodthirsty side: Evans's bull-leaping was a 'cruel sport in which barbarians were "butchered to make a Roman holiday"'.[132] In other words, Evans's Minoans loved flowers and nature, but had little time for Flower Power. Yet, he has often been accused of creating the myth of the pacifist Minoans, as discussed below.

Fig. 3.13 Knossos, The Priest King or Prince of Lilies fresco (after Evans 1928: plate XIV).

Evans's Minoans: Pacifist 'flower lovers' or warlike imperialists?

In a 1982 conference paper, published in 1984 with the catchy title 'Minoan Flower Lovers', the historian Chester G. Starr discussed the evidence for Minoan love of flowers and alleged pacifism, effectively pointing the finger at Evans for the origins of this idyllic view. Remarkably, however, and quite significantly, Starr derived all his quotations in support of Minoan pacifism not from Evans's publications, but from those of later scholars, such as Jacquetta Hawkes and R. F. Willetts.[133] Likewise, the archaeologist Stylianos Alexiou, in an earlier article on Minoan fortifications and the myth of the *Pax Minoica*, provided a list of quotations about the peaceful Minoans, of which not a single one derived from Evans's numerous publications, whereas references to the excavator of Knossos pertain to his observations about defensive walls, refuge settlements, and other warlike themes.[134] Alexiou seems, therefore, not to hold Evans responsible for Minoan pacifism, unlike Starr and later scholars, such as Castleden, who accused Evans of showing the Minoans as 'milk-and-water', 'languid flower- and peace-lovers' – phrases that must have made Evans turn in his grave.[135] Sandy MacGillivray, in his 2000 biography of Evans, similarly blamed his subject for creating the enduring 'myth of peace-loving and seafaring Minoans',[136] and Cathy Gere perpetuated this notion in her *Knossos and the Prophets of Modernism* (2009), by suggesting that Evans suppressed the evidence for warlike Minoans as a reaction to his horrifying first-hand experience of the last insurrection on Crete against Ottoman rule.[137]

The idea that Evans should be blamed for the notion of Minoan pacifism is, however, a modern myth: unquestionably, Evans's Minoans often appear too good to be true, but he does not deserve to be criticized for this. The notion of the pacifist Minoans seems to have arisen from superficial reading of his writings and, above all, from the works of others. Evans's own views of the Minoans involved a Golden Age accompanied by a period of '*Pax Minoica*'.[138] This Golden Age/*Pax Minoica*, however, just like the Augustan Golden Age and *Pax Romana*, to which Evans compared it, was a relatively short episode in the long Minoan era. In addition, Evans believed that this Golden Age followed, and was even accompanied by, military conquests and colonization. In other words, Evans's concept of a *Pax Minoica* was closely connected with that of the Minoan *thalassocracy* – war and peace being two sides of the same Minoan imperialist coin.[139]

First, Evans did not eschew Minoan militaristic traits: mentions of battle scenes, Minoan warriors, weapons, and even slaves (including those acquired in military excursions) abound in all his writings, from popularizing articles to his annual archaeological reports and the later *The Palace of Minos* (1921–35).[140] Second, Evans believed in a kernel of historical truth regarding later Greek traditions on the Minoan *thalassocracy*, which was further corroborated, in his view, by archaeological discoveries all over the Aegean and even beyond;[141] more importantly, his Minoans had not acquired their overseas dominions through a Bronze Age equivalent of passive resistance, by chanting slogans of 'Flower Power' and 'Make Love Not War'.

So, how, when, and why did Evans's Minoans acquire their sea empire? Did they conquer much of the Aegean, like the British, 'in a fit of absence of mind'?[142] And was it a kind of 'defensive imperialism'?[143] The answer to the last two questions is probably 'no'. Evans's writings are not explicit on these last two points, but it is abundantly clear that Evans's Minoan Sea Empire involved a series of military conquests and settlement abroad, and, at times, this could be a burdensome yoke on its subjects.[144] Evans's Minoan military expeditions and colonization started in the Middle Minoan period and were principally motivated by the need to control trade routes, particularly in connection with the supply of metals and other precious substances.[145] Minoan conquest was not limited to the islands and coastal zones of the Aegean (as suggested, e.g., by Herodotus and Thucydides),[146] but extended all over the Aegean, including mainland Greece, and went even beyond, e.g. to Cyprus and Libya.[147] After an earthquake on Crete in Late Minoan IA, Minoan colonization abroad intensified, especially on mainland Greece, and this overstretched the stability of the Minoan Empire and caused disruptions at home: 'Overseas conquest and migration to Mainland sites may also have caused an unfavourable reaction in Crete itself.'[148] Nevertheless, the Minoan Empire marched on, albeit in a degenerated form, until, like the Roman Empire, it was eventually taken over by barbarians (i.e. Greeks) coming from the north, around 1200 BC.[149] Yet, the civilizing force of the Minoans of Mediterranean race continued, since Crete *capta ferum victorem cepit* (cf. above).

Despite these colonialist and imperialist views, some scholars, as illustrated above, have suggested that Evans is responsible for the myth of the peaceful Minoans. This can, perhaps, be explained by his dominant position in the field of Minoan studies, which, in turn, leads to the idea that he must be responsible for most views on the Minoans that are currently popular. It seems to be the result also of a few of his phrases taken out of context. For example, some scholars have suggested that Evans's stress on the lack of fortifications around the site of Knossos created the myth of pacifist Minoans,[150] forgetting, however, that for Evans there were walls, albeit of another kind, i.e. a strong navy, as in imperial Britain: 'Why is Paris strongly fortified and London practically an open town? The city of Minos . . . was the centre of a great sea-power, and it was in its "wooden walls" that its rulers must have put their trust.'[151] Similarly, some scholars have quoted a passage concerning Evans's description of Knossos as the 'peaceful abode of priest-kings, in some respect more modern in its equipments than anything produced by classical Greece', which appears on the very first page of the introduction of his *The Palace of Minos*. But only a few lines later, Evans refers to the Minoan *thalassocracy* and to the idea that 'Minos "the destroyer" may certainly have existed and that the yoke of the more civilized ruler should at times have weighed heavily on subject people is probable enough'.[152]

His writings also show that the 'abode' of his priest-kings may have been 'peaceful', but only for a relatively short period, during 'The Golden Age of Minoan Crete' (Middle Minoan III–Late Minoan I) – a period that Evans compared to the 'Pax Romana in the best days of the Empire'.[153] In fact, Evans even remarked that this *Pax Minoica* of 'later days' led to the neglect of defensive works, constructed in earlier and less peaceful periods of Minoan history.[154]

Evans's comparison between his Minoan 'Golden Age' and the *Pax Romana* also recalls the very title of the introduction to the first volume of *The Palace of Minos*, 'The Minoan Age: magnus ab integro saeclorum nascitur ordo' (a reference to Virgil's fourth Eclogue), as well as other Roman parallels favoured by Evans. This is also significant, since the Roman peace was, in any case, only internal, relative, and short-lived, and

Evans could hardly have conceived it as the result of peaceful processes. In other words, *pace* Gere and other scholars mentioned above, Evans never set out to 'suppress' the evidence for warlike Minoans, because he never thought they were always peaceful in the first place. He believed in a Minoan Empire that emerged from acts of conquest and colonization, which, like Augustan Rome, led to a Golden Age – a period of remarkable prosperity and relative internal peace. Evans's Minoans did not succumb to northern invading barbarians because they were not bellicose, but because, like living organisms, they had reached by then a period of decline, and this made them vulnerable to the attacks of barbarians on the rise.

One additional piece of evidence, which suggests that Evans should not be blamed for creating the myth of Minoan pacifism, is the fact that there is also hardly any mention of it in many publications by other scholars, especially before the First World War. These include scholarly and popularizing volumes as well as articles in high-brow literary magazines and daily newspapers. Had Evans been so keen on Minoan pacifism, one might have expected to find traces of it in relevant literature. Instead, Minoan warriors, imperialism, and even civil wars are alive and well. Even the famous 'Harvester Vase' from Hagia Triada (see Fig. 3.14) was also known as the 'Warrior Vase' in the first decade of the twentieth century, and even later.[155] Unlike in more recent narratives on the Minoans (cf. Chapters 4 and 5), pacifism is not conspicuous, whereas other aspects of Minoan civilization captured people's imagination, such as the remarkable intellectual, artistic, and military achievements of Minoan Crete, and its contribution to the later splendour of Hellas; the linguistic and racial associations of the Minoans; the relationship between Crete, Egypt, and other 'Oriental' civilizations; and the position of women in Minoan religion and society (cf. also below). If a state of peace on Crete or in the Aegean is mentioned, it is only as a temporary state of affairs, and obtained through a powerful navy.[156]

Fig. 3.14 The Harvester Vase from Hagia Triada (photo: Zde, https://commons. wikimedia.org/wiki/File:Harvester_Vase,_steatite,_Agia_Triada,_1450_BC,_AMH).

A popular work by Angelo Mosso, published in 1907, offers a good example of this and of the author's dislike for contemporary socialist pacifism.[157] Mosso, an Italian physiologist, senator, and amateur archaeologist, was keenly aware of Minoan militarism, since he had studied and illustrated weapons from various Minoan tombs in his publications.[158] He believed that Minoan Crete had enjoyed a period of peace under a 'democratic' government and the 'guidance of princes' in the Neopalatial period, but that this was brought to an end by a 'socialist revolution'; this Minoan socialism, however, 'was very different from that of to-day, in that the laws were chiefly designed with the object of preparing the nation for war'.[159] This was an invective against socialist opposition to war in the period of the Second International. At any rate, according to Mosso, whether ancient or modern, pacifist or militarist, socialism was not a good thing: the Minoan socialist revolution merely led to a period of decline.

In this period, one significant exception to the prevailing imperialist and militarist views of the Minoans is the popularizing volume by Harriet Boyd Hawes and her husband Charles Henry Hawes, *Crete: The Forerunner of Greece* (1909). Here one finds several sentences extolling Minoan pacifism, such as: 'In direct contrast to such peoples as the Assyrians, whose story is one long series of wars and plundering expeditions, the ancient Cretans, unlike their modern representatives, were a peaceful people, and made their conquests in arts, industries, and commerce.'[160] Even Evans's conquests and colonization of mainland Greece become a 'peaceful invasion' by artists and craftsmen.[161] According to these two scholars, the Aryan Achaeans (who created Mycenaean culture through intermingling with non-Hellenic populations) were a 'pastoral fighting folk', while the non-Aryan Minoans had maintained traces of matriarchy, as shown by the pre-eminence of the Mother Goddess in their religion, and by the prominent place of women in their society, as evidenced by iconography.[162] Yet, like Evans, they believed that male leaders ('princes') ultimately ruled on Crete, at least in the period of the Minoan palaces.[163]

Might it be fairer, then, to trace some of the origins of Minoan pacifism not to Evans, but to the pen of Harriet Boyd Hawes, an intrepid humanitarian and devout Christian? I attribute these pacifist views above all to her, rather than her husband, because, unlike him, she had a considerable knowledge of both Crete and mainland Greece, and much of the text of *Crete: The Forerunner of Greece* often repeats, word for word, what she wrote in the introductory chapters of her famous book on Gournia.[164] If so, one may also wonder whether Boyd Hawes's stress on pacifism is connected with her first-hand experience of the human sufferings caused by conflicts, through her relief work in Greece and Florida in 1897–8, i.e. during the Graeco-Turkish War (especially her work with the Red Cross in Volos) and the Spanish–American war over Cuba.[165] Also worth noting is the fact that *Crete: The Forerunner of Greece* went through several further reprints (1911, 1916, and 1922), was regularly cited in the bibliographies of many scholarly and popular works and has even been republished in recent years.[166]

In any case, in the context of Evans's and of other scholars' contribution to Minoan studies, and without detracting from the former's dominant position, it is time to recognize not only that Evans's vision of Minoan Crete owes much to previous scholarship, but also that other people influenced considerably the production and the diffusion of knowledge about Minoan Crete, both within and without academia, and in doing so affected the reception and cultural legacy of the Minoans, as discussed in more detail in the following sections.[167]

All aboard! The Minoans in the late Belle Époque

In the article on 'Minoan Flower Lovers' mentioned above, C. G. Starr wrote that 'Minoan civilization is the only great civilization created in the twentieth century'.[168] This alluded to the relatively recent discovery of the Minoan world in the early 1900s (in comparison with earlier discoveries of Egyptian, Mesopotamian, and even Mayan antiquities) and the creative flair that Evans displayed in presenting his findings. More recently, other scholars have suggested in a similar vein that Evans 'invented' the Minoans (and not just in the sense of creating or starting something new), by means of both his publications and his reconstructions at Knossos.[169] Yet, other people contributed significantly to this creative process. Especially important was the intellectual atmosphere of some European cities, such as London (where the first exhibition on Minoan finds took place in 1903), Vienna, Berlin, Venice, and Paris, which enabled Minoan Crete to reach European and non-European audiences well beyond the narrow disciplinary boundaries of archaeology and Classical studies. Early twentieth-century Paris, in particular, became almost like a European capital of Minoan culture, and it is largely through the fulcrum of this city that a wide public, including artists, writers and couturiers, were introduced to Minoan Crete and used it in works that, in turn, reached even wider audiences, as illustrated in the following pages.

The crucial role of Paris in the diffusion and reception of things Minoan can be explained by two interconnected factors: first, the almost missionary zeal in publicizing the new Cretan discoveries shown by Parisian scholars such as the archaeologists and art historians Salomon Reinach and Edmond Pottier;[170] and, second, the unique intellectual atmosphere of the French capital from the Belle Époque to the Second World War, which attracted artists and writers from all over the world, and where cross-fertilization of ideas in different arts ruled supreme – from poetry to music, from dance to painting, and from archaeology to haute-couture.

Minoan missionaries in Paris: Salomon Reinach (1852–1932) and Edmond Pottier (1855–1934)

In the first decade and a half of the twentieth century, Reinach and his friend and colleague Pottier are among the most important individuals in spreading the Minoan gospel to *Tout Paris*, and from *Tout Paris* to other audiences. Both wrote many articles on Minoan Crete in a number of prominent literary and art-historical magazines that had a wide circulation, and where Minoan artefacts were discussed alongside articles on a variety of current literary, historical, and artistic matters, often penned by famous writers, such as Anatole France and Gustave Flaubert.[171] For example, between 1900 and 1901, Reinach published at least a dozen articles on prehistoric Crete in *Le Petit Temps* and *La Chronique des arts et de la curiosité*, a supplement of the *Gazette des beaux-arts*, while Pottier published two articles on Knossos in 1902, one in *La Revue de*

Paris (the main rival of *La Revue de Deux Mondes*) and the other in *La Revue de l'Art ancient et moderne*.[172] The latter article celebrates the affinity of Minoan art and modernity, draws parallels between Minoan and Parisian women, and shows a modernist and sexualized interpretation of a famous Knossian fresco (see Fig. 3.15), which contrasts with Evans's motherly and prudish vision of Minoan female imagery but is very much in tune with contemporary Parisian sensibilities:

> Even more modern and unpredictable are the representations of women. One can judge from the example reproduced here. Which poet or artist with a wandering imagination could have dared to envisage that Cretan women in the palace of Minos would have such aspect? What would Racine have said, what would Euripides himself have said, had he been presented with an authentic image of a relative of Phaedra in such guise? As always, reality transcends and disconcerts what poetic invention has created. This ruffled hair, this provocative 'kiss-curl' on the forehead, this huge eye and sensual mouth, which on the original is stained with a violent red hue, this tunic with blue, red and black stripes, this stream of ribbons thrown back in the fashion of 'follow me, young man', this mixture of naïve archaism and spicy modernism, this *pochade* paintbrushed on a wall of Knossos more than 3,000 years ago, to give us the feeling of a Daumier or a Degas, this Pasiphaë who looks like an habitué of Parisian bars, everything here contributes to surprise us, and in truth, there is something in the discovery of this incredible art that amazes and even scandalises us.[173]

Fig. 3.15 Knossos, La Parisienne fresco (after Evans 1921: 433, fig. 311).

Reinach, besides publicizing the Minoan discoveries in the Parisian press, wrote many scholarly articles about them and a chapter on 'Aegean, Minoan and Mycenaean Art' in his influential *Apollo* (1904), which became a standard handbook on the history of art, going through numerous editions and translations in all major European languages.[174] In this chapter Reinach expressed many ideas that became often-repeated clichés in later years. For example, he extolled the modernity and refinement of 'Minoan art' (*c.* 2000–1500 BC), especially its naturalism and love for movement, whereas he defined his 'Aegean art' (*c.* 3000–2000 BC) and 'Mycenaean art' (*c.* 1500–1100 BC) as 'rude' and 'decadent', respectively.[175] For Reinach, Minoan art was not as accomplished as that of Classical Greece, but compared favourably vis-à-vis the 'cold elegance' of Egyptian art, and fared even better in comparison with Assyria: 'Assyrian art expresses the idea of strength, Minoan art may be said to embody that of life.'[176] Following Evans, Reinach described the Minoan palaces as fulfilling the function of temples as well as royal residences of priest-kings, and saw the end of the Bronze Age as a catastrophe caused by barbarian invasions and comparable to the fall of the Roman Empire. According to Reinach, the fugitive Aegean people moved east (Anatolia, Levant) and, eventually, re-educated barbaric Greece in a process reminiscent of the way by which learned men from Constantinople, the distant heirs of Roman civilization, paved the way for the Italian Renaissance.

Other works disseminating the Minoans

Besides Reinach's chapter in *Apollo*, many works in English, French, German, Greek, Italian, Polish, Russian, Spanish, and Swedish helped to disseminate the new Minoan discoveries around the world in the period before the First World War.[177] Like Reinach's *Apollo*, some dealt with broader subjects but included sections on Crete, such as Adolf Michaelis's influential *Die archäologischen Entdeckungen des neunzehnten Jahrhunderts* (1906), translated into English as *A Century of Archaeological Discoveries* (1908), which had a chapter on 'Prehistory and Primitive Greece'.[178] Other publications, from essays to entire books, dealt exclusively with the Aegean Bronze Age, Crete in particular, such as Marie Joseph Lagrange's *La Crète ancienne* (1908) and René Dussaud's *Les civilisations préhelléniques dans le bassin de la mer égée* (1910; 2nd edition 1914).[179] Because French was the *langue de culture* in the early twentieth century, it was largely thanks to French publications that many people were first introduced to the Minoan world. For example, the 1913 essay 'The Stratification of Aegean Culture' by the Russian intellectual Pavel Florensky derived most of its information and illustrations not directly from Evans's publications, but from Reinach's *Apollo* and Lagrange's *La Crète ancienne*.[180]

Among popularizing volumes, the melodramatic and popular *The Sea Kings of Crete*,[181] by the prolific writer James Baikie, is worthy of note because of his discussion of T. K. Frost's idea that Plato's Atlantis retained some memory of Minoan Crete as well as his amalgamation of archaeological reports and extrapolations from influential works by the 'Cambridge Ritualists', such as Jane Harrison's *Prolegomena to the Study of Greek Religion* (1903) and Gilbert Murray's *Rise of the Greek Epic* (1907).[182] In *Prolegomena* and in her later *Themis* (1912), Harrison made extensive use of Minoan material culture to illustrate her views on the Minoan origins of Orphism, Dionysian bull-rituals, omophagy, sacred marriages, ritual regicide, and other types of human sacrifice.[183] Her ideas, either directly or through other authors, such as Baikie, found fertile grounds in many Cretomanic works discussed in later chapters. In *Rise of the Greek Epic*, Murray (the Regius Professor of Greek at Oxford) presented the view that, despite some remnants of this earlier world in later Greece, the 'pre-Hellenic Aegean societies were in some ways highly developed, in others a mere welter of savagery' and had 'few or none of the special marks that we associate with Hellenism'.[184] Consequently, even if Murray (like Harrison) accepted that Dionysus was not a late Oriental import, but the offspring of Minoan Crete, he believed that the real 'beginning of Greece' was to be found in the so-called Greek Dark Ages (Early Iron Age).[185] Similar views on the 'totally un-Hellenic' character of the Aegean Bronze Age are present in J. L. Myres's *The Dawn of History* (1911), which included two chapters relevant to Minoan matters.[186]

These non-Hellenic characterizations of the Aegean Bronze Age chime with a curious episode in the life of the Spanish archaeologist Pere (Pedro) Bosch-Gimpera. Minoan Crete, and Aegean prehistory generally, sparked relatively little interest in the Iberian Peninsula before the First World War.[187] In this period, only José Ramón Mélida published a note on Mycenaean and Iberian architecture (1905), and Bosch Gimpera a longer essay on the Minoan–Mycenaean civilization (1912).[188] In his later autobiography, Bosch Gimpera explained that this publication was inspired by a course of lectures given by August Frickenhaus that he had attended when he was a student in Berlin; he also recalled that, on his return to Spain, he almost failed an exam because he mentioned Crete and Mycenae in his answer to a question about the origins of Greek art.[189]

As mentioned above, among the publications on Aegean Bronze Age subjects of the period before the First World War, Minoan pacifism is noticeable only in *Crete: The Forerunner of Greece*, and even in this volume it is not a central topic. Other questions were at the forefront of scholarly and public curiosity alike. One of the most intriguing was the relationship between Greek myths, history, and archaeological realities, especially the identification of Knossos with the labyrinth of King Minos and tangible evidence for a Minoan Sea Empire. In the words of Baikie, many believed that 'one of the most remarkable results of the explorations has been the disclosure of the solid basis of historical fact on which they [i.e. the Greek myths] rested'.[190] Other topics that attracted attention were Minoan religious iconography and beliefs, including how these could represent the origins of later aspects of Greek religion. Also important was the role of women in Minoan religion and society, and how this could be mapped onto the evolutionary orthodoxy of the times, which predicated a development from primitive matriarchy to patriarchy. After Evans, most people accepted the idea of a main female deity in Minoan religion and the existence of some form of matriarchical and/or matrilineal society in some ill-defined early stage of Cretan development (possibly Neolithic and Early Minoan). Most people, however, also accepted that by the second millennium B C, and perhaps earlier, it was priest-kings and princes who ruled Minoan palaces, sat on the Knossian throne, and created a Minoan Empire, even if women continued to fare better than in Aryan Greece.[191]

Another topic that attracted attention was the relationship between the Aegean and other ancient civilizations, especially Egypt, in terms of artistic developments, political and trade relations, broad evolutionary sequences, and racial–linguistic affinities. The racial attribution of the now 'decadent' Mycenaeans became or remained ambiguous: some people continued to believe, with Schliemann and Tsountas, that they could be equated with the Homeric Achaeans, or that they included at least some Aryan elements, whereas others thought that they were largely non-Hellenic and non-Aryan. Regarding the Minoans, almost everybody believed that they largely belonged to the 'Mediterranean race', and pondered over the contribution of this non-Hellenic race to later (Aryan) Hellas. In other words, the relevant questions posed were: when and how did Minoan art develop? Should one consider the Minoans and their art as Western (European) or Oriental? And how did Minoan art compare with contemporary and later achievements?

With regard to the first question, effectively all writers followed Evans's memorable tripartite chronological scheme (and mostly also his dates),[192] which embodied a well-established model of the birth–growth–maturity–decline of culture and the evolutionary Zeitgeist of the period, even if his label 'Minoan' found some resistance in some quarters (cf. Chapter 4).

In relation to the second question, most acknowledged some Egyptian influence, but stressed the independence, originality, and superiority of the Minoans. In fact, most scholars, starting with Evans, embraced the newly discovered Minoans as firmly European, if only for Eurocentric, anti-Ottoman, and even anti-Semitic reasons. Thus, for example, the incorporation of Crete into the long continuum of Western (Hellenic-European) history is self-evident in the very title of *Crete: The Forerunner of Greece*, and is reinforced by many passages in this work, such as the following, which compares the Cup Bearer (see Fig. 3.9) with later Greek sculpture: 'No one who has seen this portrait of a youth will doubt that the Minoan artist was on the right path, the path followed later by Polygnotus and by all artists filled with the Greek love of beauty and distinction.'[193] A few scholars, however, offered more ambivalent positions, allowing Minoan Crete to partake of both East and West. Examples of this are Dussaud's *Les civilisations préhelléniques dans le bassin de la mer égée* and H. R. Hall's *Ancient History of the Near East*.[194] The subtitle of Dussaud's volume, *Études de Protohistoire Orientale* (Studies of Oriental Proto-history), suggests that Minoan Crete is part of the East, but in the introduction, titled 'From History to Proto-history' ('De l'histoire à la protohistoire'), Dussaud places the discoveries by Schliemann, Evans, and others within a familiar European narrative of Classical art history, which starts with Winckelmann's work, continues with the excavations of Pompeii (after a small detour on the Napoleonic expeditions in Egypt), carries on with the arrival of the Elgin Marbles in London, and concludes with the discovery of Archaic Greek art thanks to various excavations in Sicily, Aegina, and Athens.[195] Hall's *Ancient History of the Near East* was intended almost as a companion to Herodotus for students of Classics, to help them appreciate that Greece was 'as much or as little oriental as originally was Egypt, with whose culture hers may have had, at the beginning, direct affinity. Later she was westernized, but in the fifth century she was not more distinct from the more oriental nations of the Near East than she is now. She called them "barbarian": that only meant that they did not talk Greek. Greece respected Persia while she fought it.'[196] And yet, even Hall presented Minoan art almost as the antithesis of the Near East, and closer to a modern European spirit (cf. epigraph).

With regard to the third question, three main attitudes can be discerned. For some, such as Evans, the Minoans belonged to a gifted race that had invented everything for which later Hellas was praised: the Aryan Greeks were unoriginal parvenus. Other scholars offered a compromise: they continued to regard Classical Greece as the unsurpassed pinnacle of civilization but not a miracle: rather, it was the fruit of the magical combination of two gifted races (Mediterranean and Aryan) with complementary traits.[197] Others still, while fascinated by Minoan Crete, continued to prefer the fruits of Classical Greece and felt that the latter, and the essence of Greece generally, was something quite distinct, despite Minoan–Mycenaean survivals. At any rate, most scholars marvelled at the modernity of the primitive Minoans, which was perceived, above all, in sanitary installations, women's demeanour, and artistic language. The latter was almost consistently described as expressing remarkable élan, love of nature, verve, sense of movement, and bold colours. Also widely appreciated was the idea of a Minoan sense of beauty that extended to the 'minor' arts, as in the modern Arts and Crafts Movement.[198] Minoan 'naturalism' was often compared to that of Classical Greece, the Renaissance, and more recent trends, but equally admired was the presence of abstract tendencies and of other artistic traits, which were reminiscent of the exotic arts of Japan and Polynesia, thus suspending Crete, once again, between East and West, ancient and modern.[199] This chimed with many trends of early modernism, which paved the way for the enthusiastic reception of Minoan imagery among contemporary artists and the general public alike. Dussaud's remarks on the discovery of Greek Archaic sculpture in the previous century equally apply to Minoan Crete: '[It] was all the more sensational because it seemed to have chosen its right time, when the educated taste could appreciate the intimate appeal of a style less severe than the purely Classical.'[200] Early twentieth-century taste was ready for the Minoans, as shown by the work of avant-garde artists, such as Léon Bakst, who enthused about Minoan Crete because it looked 'close' and 'familiar', as discussed in the next section.

Cretomania in the late Belle Époque: The Minoans in modern cultural practices *c*. 1900–1918 – Neo-Minoans from Crete to Paris and beyond

In 1953, Rose Maucaulay wrote that the Minoans had 'become part of the familiar landscape of our minds' (cf. epigraph to Chapter 1), and numerous works of art and literature of the early twentieth century offer apt illustrations of this process. A good case in point is the very casualness with which Ford Madox Ford mentions the Cretan discoveries in his novel *The Good Soldier* (1915): 'my whole endeavours were to keep poor dear Florence on topics like the finds at Gnossos and the mental spirituality of Walter Pater'.[201] The same applies to Marcel Proust's allusions to Evans's discoveries at Knossos in some of the volumes of his masterpiece, *À la recherche du temps perdu*. In *À l'ombre des jeunes filles en fleurs*, for instance, Proust observes, with a tinge of regret, that scholars who discovered Calypso's island and excavated the Palace of Minos turned the nymph into a mere a woman and Minos into a king with no semblance of divinity, but at the same time first impressions and mythological imaginations continue to add something supernatural and wondrous even to everyday banality.[202] This idea is also illustrated in another reference to Minoan Crete from a passage in *Le Côté de Guermantes*, where Proust recounts how a walled orchard of pear trees in white blossoms looked like roofless rooms that, in turn, reminded him of a Palace of the Sun, such as those discovered on Crete. In other words, with a few lines from his pen, Proust conjures up intriguing and memorable links between archaeology, French royalty, and Greek mythology – between excavated ruins (roofless rooms) of Minoan palaces and Versailles, as the palace of the Sun King, and perhaps between Louis XIV and King Minos, whose wife Pasiphae in some traditions was the daughter of the sun-god Helios.

The passages in Ford and Proust illustrate how Minoan Crete was becoming familiar in the intellectual landscape of the European cultured classes before the First World War. But the closeness and familiarity implied by the artist Léon Bakst was of a different order. It was more like the pleasure of recognition discussed above, since it refers to the realization that some characteristics of Minoan imagery showed affinity with the ideals of emerging artistic canons linked to early modernism.[203] Bakst's own written words, paintings, and theatrical works provide ample illustrations. For example, in his 1909 article 'The Paths of Classicism in Art', Bakst discussed the history of classicism in European art and analysed aspects of contemporary artistic developments in painting, praising in particular the works of Gauguin, Matisse, and Minoan art.[204] According to his vision for a future classical art, Bakst suggested that artists should pay more attention to simplicity and the human body as well as worship nudity and the beauty of the human form. In establishing new artistic canons, modern artists could take some lessons from the Greek past, but their models should not be ancient sculptors such as Phidias or Praxiteles. Instead, both primitive and children's works were more suited to modern tastes and a future classical art because of three main qualities that characterized them and all great art: sincerity or lapidary style (i.e. a focus on essential lines), movement, and bright, clean colours. Minoan Crete, with its archaic look, love of movement, attention to the human form, and bold colours was a particularly inspiring model:

> We also know of the clamorous success enjoyed now in Europe by the Cretan culture newly uncovered by Evans and Halbherr. Yesterday it was virtually unknown, but today it constitutes a new order of antique art, one that is so close and familiar to us! This art evolved independently of the Egyptians and the Chaldeans, full of unexpected audacity, of unreasoned, impudent solutions and of light, shining victories. It trembles with the life of its own style. Cretan art is bold and dazzling, like the mad, courageous gallop of nude youths, who clutch the wild and acrid manes of their overheated steeds … In this art, which is so close to us, the arresting perfection of Praxiteles is not etched; the almost absolute beauty of the Parthenon is not to be found. Cretan culture never attained the extraordinary heights beyond which lie abstraction or effeminacy. For this reason, it is more closely related to our new art, with its half-perfection: it smiles and breathes with human efforts. Naturally, involuntarily, the contemporary artist fixes an attentive gaze on Cretan culture, not without hope of scaling the inaccessible summits of

perfection. Out from behind the unfettered ornamentation and the turbulent frescoes peers the keen eye of the Cretan artist, an eternally smiling child. From such an art it would be possible to cut a shoot and to graft it onto our own art.[205]

Bakst was true to his words: he did graft Minoan shoots into his own art, as illustrated below. But he was neither the first nor indeed the only one to use Minoan imagery as a catalyst for innovation and a springboard towards modernism in the period 1900–14.

The earliest example of Cretomania that I was able to find is Nea Skini's 1901 staging of *Alcestis*, which was described as pioneering because of its 'Minoan look'.[206] This Athenian production of Euripides' tragedy illustrates the use of Aegean Bronze Age material culture as a catalyst for artistic creativity and is an attempt towards authenticity or historical accuracy, because it employs sets, props, and costumes evocative of the period in which the Greek tragedy was set (second millennium BC, before the Trojan War), instead of the period in which it was created (fifth century BC). This is a practice that will be employed by several other artists and, indeed, continues to the present day.[207]

Another early example of the use of Minoan elements in innovative design is the Neo-Minoan suburban villa built on the outskirts of Herakleion by a Turkish Cretan, Bahaettin Rahmi Bediz, a.k.a Rahmizade Behaeddin. Bahaettin was an Istanbul-born professional photographer, who called his studio 'Photographie Minos', sold postcards that included Minoan antiquities, and worked for R. M. Dawkins on the 1913 excavation at the Kamares cave.[208] His villa, constructed in *c.* 1905, was designed a year earlier by the Danish artist Halvor Bagge, who was working for Evans at Knossos at that time. Unfortunately, this remarkable building, probably the very first example of Neo-Minoan architecture, has disappeared and only photographs by Behaeaddin and a sketch by Bagge have survived.[209] But why did this Istanbul-born lover of Crete choose a Minoan style for his villa? Was it the non-Hellenic character of the Minoans suggested in most scholarly narratives? Was his villa built in a spirit of resistance against the prevailing Greek nationalist aspirations? Was it a suggestion that the Cretan (and Greek) past and present incorporated significant non-Hellenic elements? Or was he celebrating a kind of *genius loci*, an exquisitely Cretan identity? Or was he attracted by the novelty and aesthetics of Minoan designs, and did he build his villa as a statement about his own education, modernity, and sophistication? These, for the time being, remain unanswered questions, and a reminder of how little we still know about modern responses to the Minoan discoveries by some groups (e.g. Muslim Greeks, Turks, Armenians, and Jews), who formed a significant proportion of the island's population at the time.

We are better informed about the dominant Christian Cretans, especially the members of the educated classes, for whom the Minoan discoveries were a source of great pride and symbolic capital. During the period of the Cretan State, and in their struggle for unification with Greece, Christian Cretans started using the Minoan discoveries for their agendas in complex narratives of local, national, and transnational character. We can see this, for example, in the novel by Nikos Kazantzakis, *Freedom and Death*. Although first published in 1953, the novel attempts to reconstruct the atmosphere of the late nineteenth century, during one of the Cretan rebellions against Ottoman rule. One of its main characters is the erudite antiquarian Hadjisàva, who is clearly based on the archaeologist Iosif Chatzidakis. Hadjisàva believes that liberation would come from the rediscovery of the Cretan cultural heritage, as seen, for example, in a passage in which he addresses the Orthodox Church metropolitan: 'Your Reverence expects freedom from Moscow, the people expect it from guns, and I from this ring, which you, Bishop, despise.'[210] Significantly, the ring in the novel is partly modelled on some well-known Minoan gold signet rings, such as the 'Ring of Minos'.[211] Even more concrete uses of Minoan motifs for symbolic capital are illustrated in the official media of the Cretan State. Examples are the stamps of the early 1900s, which showed the archaeological site of Knossos and some Minoan finds, and the official press reports on the Minoan discoveries, which exploited the Eurocentric and anti-Ottoman visions of Minoan Crete produced by foreign archaeologists, since these showed some convergence of interests between Westerners and Cretans.[212] Despite the fact that it was essentially British, Italian, French, and American archaeologists who rediscovered the Minoan past in a crypto- or quasi-colonial environment, everybody could claim that they were acting in the name of the Cretan government and were seeking to uncover and understand a common European heritage, not appropriating an alien culture, thus reinforcing the claims of independence from Ottoman rule on cultural grounds.[213] Even if dominant narratives portrayed the Minoans as non-Hellenic, they still characterized them as European, and tended to incorporate them into the long continuum of Hellenic history by stressing elements of continuity and the debt owed by later Hellas to Crete. Moreover, by substituting the Minoans for the Greeks as the origin of European culture, these narratives also contributed to the creation of a strong local Cretan identity and notions of Cretan exceptionalism, which continue to the present day.[214]

Despite the early Cretan examples and Nea Skini's *Alcestis* discussed above, it is in Paris or among artists closely connected with the French capital that one can find many instances of Paul Morand's Cretomania. Among the most appealing and innovative uses of Minoan motifs are the textiles of the Spanish-Venetian artist Mariano Fortuny y Madrazo, who started making his 'Knossos scarves' and other Minoan-inspired outfits (see Fig. 3.16) at least as early as 1906, the year in which the scarves made their first public appearance in Paris.[215] Since that time, in the years before and after the First World War, many Parisian celebrities donned Fortuny's garments, which Proust famously immortalized in many passages of his fifth volume of *À la recherche du temps perdu* (*La Prisonnière*), such as the following:

> Like the theatrical designs of Sert, Bakst and Benoit, who at that moment were recreating in the Russian Ballets the most cherished periods of art – with the aid of works of art impregnated with their spirit and yet original – these Fortuny gowns, faithfully antique but markedly original, brought before the eye like a stage setting, with an even greater suggestiveness than a setting, since the setting was left to the imagination, that Venice loaded with the gorgeous East from which they had been taken, of which they were, even more than a relic in the shrine of Saint Mark suggesting the sun and a group of turbaned heads, the fragmentary, mysterious and complementary colour.[216]

The 'faithfully antique but markedly original' character that Proust attributed to Fortuny's garments (and theatrical designs by Sert, Bakst, and Benois) arguably derived

Fig. 3.16 Mariano Fortuny's 1935 portrait of his wife, wearing dress and scarf with Minoan motifs, in the Fortuny Museum, Venice (photo: N. Momigliano).

from the fact that in some cases they were decorated with Aegean Bronze Age motifs, especially Minoan. Fortuny, apparently, never visited the Aegean, and it seems therefore likely that it was in the French capital that he first encountered Aegean art through newspapers and literary-artistic magazines. Although Venice had become his home by 1889, Fortuny had previously lived in Paris and his close connection with the French capital persisted throughout his life, as illustrated by the fact that he continued to work there on various theatrical projects, opened ateliers and boutiques for his textile productions near the Champs Elysées, and patented there many of his inventions between 1901 and 1934.[217] Another possibility is that he was introduced to Aegean Bronze Age art in Berlin, through his contacts with the theatre and film director Max Reinhardt, the poet and dramatist Hugo von Hofmannsthal, and the dancer Isadora Duncan.[218] In the early 1900s, Reinhardt and Hofmannsthal were involved in theatrical productions of *Elektra*, which included an Aegean Bronze Age setting (cf. below), while Isadora Duncan visited Knossos and performed an *impromptu* dance at the Grand Staircase, shocking Sir Arthur Evans's field director, Duncan Mackenzie.[219]

Fortuny used abstract, floral, and marine motifs from the Minoan repertoire, which found favour also among other artists, such as Bakst. As Caloi has illustrated, the use of these motifs, especially the octopus, chimed with the *Japonisme* of the Belle Époque.[220] This and other aspects of Fortuny's use of Minoan imagery suggest that, to a large extent, he perceived Bronze Age Crete as exotic and Oriental, and its women as alluring and sensual (like the Parisian archaeologist Pottier and unlike Evans).

Another exotic, Oriental, and sensual perception of the Minoan world is attested in some early works by František Kupka.[221] This Czech symbolist-abstract painter and graphic artist, who settled in Paris in the 1890s, made extensive use of Minoan–Mycenaean motifs while working on book illustrations between 1906 and 1909. The best examples are his engravings for the 1908 edition of Leconte de Lisle's tragedy *Erinnyes* (The Furies). Given the drama's subject (Agamemnon's and Clytemnestra's murders) and Argolic setting, Kupka naturally derived most of his inspiration from Schliemann's Mycenaean discoveries, as also indicated in a letter of October 1906: 'The costumes are the same as those worn at Mycenae in the 13th century and the Acropolis has been reconstructed after Schliemann, Dörpfeld, and others.'[222] Nevertheless, distinctly Minoan elements are easily discernible in the exposed breasts and colourful flounced skirts of his female figures, both in the watercolours that he prepared as a study for his engraved illustrations and in the resulting illustrations (see Fig. 3.17).[223]

In the spring of 1907, the already mentioned Russian artist Léon Bakst visited Crete and was immediately smitten by the Minoan discoveries.[224] He soon started practising what he preached, namely that 'from such an art it would be possible to cut a shoot and to graft it onto our own art' (cf. above), as one can see, for example, in the Minoan

Fig. 3.17 One of F. Kupka's Minoan-inspired illustrations for the 1908 edition of Leconte de Lisle's tragedy *Erinnyes* (photo: courtesy of the Bibliothèque Nationale de France; © ADAGP, Paris and DACS, London 2019).

elements used in his 1908 painting *Terror Antiquus* (Knossos Town Mosaic); in his 1909 illustrations for the Russian magazine *Apollon* (Minoan columns and horns of consecration); and in his designs for the Ballets Russes and other theatrical productions, such as his sets and costumes for Emil Verhaeren's drama *Hélène de Sparte*, which were all performed in Paris between 1911 and 1912, where Bakst himself had settled in 1910 (see Fig. 3.18). In many of these 1911–12 stage productions, Bakst took inspiration from both Minoan Crete and Archaic–Classical Greece. In fact, the Minoan features are sometimes discernible, like the devil, only in the detail. For example, in *L'Après-midi d'un Faune*, which might be seen as the first in a lineage of Minoan ballets,[225] the overall appearance of the nymphs show strong links with the Archaic Greek world of the seventh–sixth century BC. Yet, there are specific Minoan features, such as the decorative elements in the nymphs' costumes (e.g. spirals and wavy lines), their very long locks of hair (much longer than in Greek archaic statues, but matched by Minoan hairstyle), and possibly even some of their gestures, which recall those of Knossian frescoes that Bakst had sketched. In fact, Bakst seems to have fused, in a modernist eclectic manner, elements from Archaic Greece and Minoan Crete in an attempt to create a more archaic, primitive, and, at the same time, more modern look for this ballet, in accordance with his artistic manifesto. The result, perhaps, was not entirely successful, at least in terms of very avant-garde modernism, since there is much that still presents a classicizing look in Bakst's work for this and other ballets. Nijinsky, the choreographer and leading dancer of *L'Après-midi d'un Faune*, found the sets and costumes insufficiently austere for his tastes.[226] Nevertheless, one might argue that Bakst's archaic but still recognizably Greek look works well for the ballet from a '*Gesamtkunstwerk*' (total artwork) point of

Fig. 3.18 L. Bakst, sketch of costume for Ida Rubinstein as Helen in the drama *Hélène de Sparte* (1912), showing Minoan sacral ivy combined with crocus motif (photo: http://commons.wikimedia.org/wiki/File:Helene_de_Sparte_ballet_by_L._Bakst_03.jpg).

view, given the music by Debussy and its ultimate inspiration from Mallarmé's poem (which would have also been very familiar to Parisian audiences and were composed well before the rediscovery of Minoan Crete). At any rate, Bakst's designs for this and other stage productions were considered very innovative and caused a real sensation at the time, influencing new fashions in dress and interior decoration, as also indicated by Bakst's collaboration with the Parisian couturier Jeanne Paquin.

Besides a marked sensuality, one of the modern elements in Bakst's works was his use of bright, vivid colours, which he also associated with Archaic Greece and especially with Minoan Crete:

> In my sets I have tried to show the Homeric world as I see it. I did my research on Crete, in the labyrinth of Minos. And I must admit that I found what I hoped for there. In fact, I have always thought that early Greek art, which corresponds to the same Egyptian period, did not have that lack of colour which is generally ascribed to the classical period. Statues and monuments were all multi-hued and I have used traces of those vivid, even brutal colours.[227]

Bakst did attain a more Minoan and modernist look after the First World War, in his work for Ida Rubinstein's multi-media production of *Phèdre* at the Paris Opera in 1923 (based on Gabriele D'Annunzio's 1909 tragedy *Fedra* and music by Ildebrando Pizzetti). In this work there is no need to look for the devil in the detail: Bakst's use of Minoan elements is pervasive and spectacular, as one can see from many of his sketches for both sets and costumes (see Fig. 3.19).

Fig. 3.19 L. Bakst, set design for Ida Rubinstein's 1923 production of D'Annunzio's tragedy *Phédre* (*Fedra*), Thyssen-Bornemisza Museum (image available from http://commons.wikimedia.org/wiki/File:Phaedra_%28Bakst%29_01.jpg).

Another intriguing Parisian work of the early twentieth century, which shows symptoms of Cretomania, is the psychological-esoteric drama *La Furie* (loosely inspired by Euripides' *The Madness of Heracles*), in which the hero loses his mind after being hypnotized by an Egyptian priest. The author was the occultist-feminist Henri Antoine Jules Bois, who, by a strange coincidence, visited Crete almost at the same time as Bakst, in the spring of 1907, and was guided among the Minoan ruins by Angelo Mosso.[228] Jules Bois explained that he chose a Minoan setting for his violent, gory drama because he wanted to bring the new Minoan discoveries to a wider public, since he felt that this world was savage but also civilized, and close to his own.[229] Particularly interesting were his ideas regarding the position of women in Minoan society. This appears to be a concoction of his own personal (and very different!) interpretation of Mosso's socialist revolution, with a feminist twist: according to Jules Bois, the Minoans had established a form of collectivism and feminism, showing more social advancement than contemporary Europeans.[230] First performed at the Comédie-Française in February 1909, *La Furie* presented a remarkable mixture of Near Eastern, Mycenaean, and especially Minoan sets and costumes, created by Désiré Chaineux (see Fig. 3.20a–c), a designer at the Comédie-Française, who was in touch with archaeological circles and an expert in historical attires.[231] Her Minoan designs had a positive reception, to judge from contemporary reports in the press, which praised them for their novelty, authenticity, primitive barbarism, and curious modernity, whereas Jules Bois was criticized for imbuing his characters with the feelings of twentieth-century Parisians.[232] Compared to Kupka's and Bakst's, Chaineux's Minoan costume designs are less original and vibrant, but they are more historically accurate, except for her décolletages, which are less risqué than the Minoan originals.

a   b   c

Fig. 3.20a–c D. Chaineaux's sketches for costumes in Jules Bois's *La Furie* (1909), on display at the 2014 exhibition *La Grèce des origins: entre rêve et archéologie*, Musée d'Archéologie Nationale, Châteu Saint-Germain-en-Laye, Paris (photo: N. Momigliano).

Jules Bois' interest in hypnotism, madness, and the psychopathology of sexual desire suggests the influence of the Parisian neurologist Jean-Martin Chacot, who worked and taught at the famous Pitié-Salpêtrière Hospital, and perhaps of one of Charcot's most famous pupils, Sigmund Freud, another Cretomania sufferer (cf. Chapters 1 and 4). At any rate, clear Freudian effects have been detected in other early twentieth-century theatrical performances based on Greek dramas that, like *La Furie*, combined a fascination with psychology and the use of Minoan material culture for sets and costumes. In 1903, Hugo von Hofmannsthal's version of Sophocles' *Elektra* premiered in Berlin under the direction of another charismatic Viennese Jew, Max Reinhardt, starring Gertrud Eysoldt in the title role.[233] This eventually led to Hofmannsthal's collaboration with Richard Strauss for the opera *Elektra*, premiered in Dresden in 1909.[234] Because of the story's Mycenaean setting, much inspiration came from the monuments of Agamemnon's citadel and Schliemann's discoveries. Yet, even in this opera Minoan material culture made an appearance: British newspapers, reporting on the 1910 London performance, described how the sets and costumes were explicitly based on the recent excavations of Schliemann at Mycenae and Evans at Knossos, and the illustrations accompanying one of these reports show costumes alongside the ancient originals, which include the Knossos snake votary and a figure from the Hagia Triada sarcophagus (see Fig. 3.21).[235] As in the case of *La Furie*, the costumes apparently did not cause negative responses, probably because they were considered to be an attempt at authenticity, albeit one that did not offend public modesty (since no naked female breasts were actually in sight), whereas Von Hofmannsthal was criticized for projecting hysterical emotions of twentieth-century Paris and Vienna onto a Mycenaean setting.[236]

Minoan costumes, however, caused offence in the case of a performance of *Oedipus Rex*. In 1910, Reinhardt directed the first large-scale production of Hofmannsthal's version of this Sophoclean tragedy at the Munich Musikfesthalle, which later travelled throughout Europe, including London, where it was performed in the English translation by Gilbert Murray.[237] In London, as in Munich, the 'Pre-Hellenic ... partly Cretan and Mycenaean, partly Oriental, partly ... merely savage' *Oedipus Rex* reportedly shocked audiences, and not least because of the half-naked torchbearers wearing Minoan loincloths.[238] Murray defended Reinhardt on the grounds of historical accuracy: the Bronze Age elements were most suited to the actual date of the Oedipus story, which belonged to the 'dark regions of pre-Hellenic barbarism', not to Classical Athens.[239] To use Rose Macaulay's words once again, the Minoans were becoming part of the familiar landscape of our minds, but were almost too much to take, especially for those who had been nourished with Hellenic ideals of Winckelmann's 'noble simplicity and quiet grandeur' and Arnold's 'sweetness and light'.

My final example of Cretomania of the late Belle Époque is provided by two paintings of Clytemnestra by the Victorian artist John Collier (see Fig. 3.22). The first was created in 1882, after Schliemann's excavations at Troy and Mycenae, but before the rediscovery of Minoan Crete: it makes use of isolated Bronze Age elements within a classicizing atmosphere, such as one of the famous gold diadems from Troy, and a column reminiscent of those decorating the Treasure of Atreus, now housed in the British Museum. The second, created in 1914, has a strong Bronze Age and Minoan flavour, shown by a number of architectural motifs and, above all, by the fact that

DRESSES FOR "ELEKTRA."

CHRYSOTHEMIS. The model is a female figure in gold-leaf from a Mycenæan grave.

A TORCH-BEARER. The model is taken from a stone sarcophagus from Phaistos.

SERVING-MAID. Design from a statuette at Knossus, in Crete.

ANOTHER SERVING-MAID. The model was found in Tyrins, near Mycene.

Some of the costumes which will be worn in Mr. Thomas Beecham's production of " Elektra " on Saturday evening are illustrated above. The Mycenæan relics from which the designs were adapted by Mr. Attilio Comelli are also shown. A portrait of Miss Frances Rose, who will take the part of Chrysothemis, appears in the centre.

Fig. 3.21 Illustration of some costumes used in Richard Strauss's *Elektra*, based on Minoan and Mycenaean artefacts (after *Daily Express*, 17 February 1910).

Fig. 3.22 John Collier (1850–1934), *Clytemnestra* 1884 and 1914 (photo: https://www. reddit.com/r/Art/comments/692e8j/clytemnestra_john_collier_18501934_oil_on_ canvas/).

Clytemnestra, while still wearing the Trojan diadem, is now dressed in Minoan fashion. Not only are her breasts exposed, but her long skirt is modelled on two specific finds from Evans's 1903 excavations at Knossos: a votive robe in faience found together with the famous snake-goddess figurines in the Temple Repositories, and a polychrome ceramic bridge-spouted jar, which also inspired one of the costumes produced by Bakst for the 1912 drama *Hélène de Sparte*.[240]

Conclusions: The romance and triumph of Minoan Crete, the decadence of Mycenaean Greece

In this chapter I have illustrated how the notion of a splendid 'Minoan Age' had emerged even before the extensive and systematic excavations of Bronze Age sites on Crete, which followed the establishment of the Cretan State. The existence of a brilliant Minoan civilization in the second millennium BC, and the likely origins of Greek art from Crete, had already appeared in various nineteenth-century works by German scholars (e.g. Hoeck, O. K. Müller, Milchhöfer), which were mostly based on ancient texts, but also included some archaeological evidence. In the last quarter of the nineteenth century, Schliemann dazzled the world with his finds at Troy and Mycenae, and provided tangible realities behind many Greek myths and the 'Homeric Age'. But what was the origin of the Mycenaean culture that he had discovered? The excavations on Crete helped to answer this question and, in turn, provided tangible realities for the 'Minoan Age' of earlier nineteenth-century German scholarship.

Despite the fact that Minoan material culture looked, in many respects, even more distant from classical Greece than the Mycenaean, the encounter between Minoan Crete and the late Belle Époque was like love at first sight: the Minoans were immediately accepted as desirable European ancestors. This romance and triumph of Minoan Crete was largely due to the construction of Minoan civilization as primitive and modern, exotic and familiar, and above all highly relevant to contemporary concerns, from Cretan *enosis* with Greece to the 'Woman Question'.

The depiction of the Minoans as Europeans, and of Crete as the cradle of European civilization, chimed with contemporary Eurocentric, colonialist, nationalist, and Cretan politics (and their related anti-Ottoman discourses). Indeed, for many 'The glory that was Greece' was no longer a 'miracle' but a renaissance, and the outcome of racial mixing between artistically gifted Mediterranean people and vigorous Aryans. Even Mycenaean culture fell from its Heroic splendour, as it was now usually perceived as a late, decadent offshoot of the brilliant Minoan culture. Besides, the great Minoan Empire was portrayed as a society in which women enjoyed a high status, and must have been a matriarchy at some earlier developmental stages – a feature that was particularly significant in a period of high activity by the suffragette movement, and of interest in the Woman Question more generally.

The romance and triumph of Minoan Crete was also due to the establishment of modernist trends in the visual arts, which paved the way for the appreciation of the artistic language of Minoan Crete. Within a generation since Schliemann's discoveries, aesthetic sensibilities had changed considerably, as attested by the emergence of Art Nouveau and other early modernist trends, whereas Winckelmannian ideals and Neo-classicism were on the wane: to use Ezra Pound's words, Classical Greece and its imitations came to be regarded in some quarters as 'cake-icing and plaster of Paris' suitable only for 'super-aesthetes and matinee girls'.[241] Artists such as Bakst, Kupka, and Fortuny found in Minoan Crete new inspiration to forge new artistic creations. Their use of Minoan motifs occurred, above all, because they felt considerable affinity between the Minoan artistic language and their own aesthetics, but also because they believed that Minoan features could lend historical colour and even an aura of authenticity to works that were set in mythological Greece. The dynamics between scholarly narratives and other cultural products, however, show that dramatists and artists suffering from Cretomania often perceived and portrayed Minoan Crete as more Oriental, sensual, and feminist than in specialist works. This seems to foreshadow later archaeological debates and other modern responses to Minoan Crete, as discussed in subsequent chapters.

As I mentioned in my Introduction, according to Morand, Cretomania lasted only until 1914. But the First World War did not extirpate this disease: on the contrary, as shown in the following chapter, in the aftermath of this conflict the fascination with the Minoan past increased and developed along many new paths.

4

Minoans and the World Wars (*c.* 1915–49): The Aryan Revenge

A Mycenaean palace is a promise, a Minoan something that is ending.

Oswald Spengler ([1922] 1927: 88)

The oldest civilisation in Europe is set before us in a strangely vivid fashion by the author's discoveries. This work is literally 'epoch-making', because Sir Arthur has supplied the epochs for European prehistory; but he has done more, because he has made the Minoan Cretans live for us. He has pictured a race bound to sacerdotalism and haunted by the supernatural, a people whose art like their culture was sometimes superficial. Yet they prepared the way for the civilisation of the Greeks and consequently for our own. We can look back and say that poetry, history, philosophy and science might not have arisen in the world but for those early and successful attempts of the Minoans to build an ordered and civilised society.

Charles Seltman (1935: 202)

Cette villa d'Haghia Triada m'apparaît comme le terme de la civilisation crétoise, l'Alhambra où le Prince aux fleurs de lys ressemble à Boabdil. [This villa of Hagia Triada appears to me as the end of Cretan civilisation, the Alhambra where the Prince of Lilies resembles Boabdil.]

Jacques de Lacretelle (1931: 189)

Creta . . . gentis cunabula nostrae says Virgil;[1] the same thing might be said of Crete as the holy cradle of Christianity.

Dmitry Merezhkovsky ([1930] 1933: 237)

Crete is the land of the Androgynes.

Dmitry Merezhkovsky ([1930] 1933: 319)

I am mad to get to Knossos and examine the traces of a Minoan civilisation, of which by this time I'm quite sure my ancestors were a part. Do you know that the average height of the race was five four? Think it over. They were sturdy and lustful and had a vital art of their own, which owes practically nothing to the huge contemporary civilizations around it. Only one more discovery will complete my certainty &

happiness: did they wear silver candle-snuffers upon their most wholesome privities?
I pray hourly that they did.

Letter from Lawrence Durrell to George Wilkinson of
c. 1934, in Durrell (1969: 29)

We can be certain that after the great catastrophe the majority of the inhabitants
fled in terror from the island. They thought that the mother-goddess had turned
against her island and cursed it.

Spyridon Marinatos (1939: 437)

Important and contrasting developments in the study and reception of the Minoans occurred in the eventful period covered in this chapter, which is framed by the unification of Crete with Greece (1913) and the Greek Civil War (1947–9). Besides important archaeological research within and outside Crete, these decades saw the publication of major works of synthesis, such as Evans's *Palace of Minos* (1921–35), which offered a vision of an Aegean Sea as a Minoan *mare nostrum* and a Minoan Empire as essentially non-Hellenic. Evans's views attained considerable prominence, but a growing number of scholars argued for a sharp distinction between Minoans and Mycenaeans and opposed Evans's pan-Minoan model. In fact, *pace* Evans, the notion that the Mycenaeans were Greeks and had conquered Crete gained (or regained) considerable ground, and by the early 1920s had become mainstream, partly thanks to growing Aryanism.

Processes of familiarization, Hellenization, and Europeanization of the Minoans continue in the period, partly because of the persisting association between later Greek myths and Bronze Age Aegean culture, as encapsulated in a 1924 Cretomanic novel: 'even such a seemingly improbable story as that of the Minotaur and the Labyrinth has been provided with a reasonable interpretation.'[2] By contrast, some interpretations of, and responses to, the Minoans now stressed their distance, Oriental character, and significant otherness. These conflicting attitudes appear in both archaeological-historical writings and in works by artists and writers that drew inspiration from the material culture of Minoan Crete. Despite Morand's statement that 'Cretomania' ended with the Belle Époque, this illness continued well after 1914. In fact, one might argue that it became more contagious, as the Cretomanic virus and its mutations spread to many new genres, such as universal history, poetry, historical novels, children's books, travel writing, films, detective stories, fantasy fiction, and even Mills & Boon escapist romances. All of these show intriguing responses to the Minoans, which sometimes appear to anticipate later scholarly discourses, especially regarding gender issues.

Crete from the *Kritiki Politeia* to the Second World War and its aftermath

After two previous unilateral declarations of unification with Greece in 1905 and 1908 (by Cretans and Greeks, respectively), in the aftermath of the Balkan Wars (1912–13)

Crete officially became part of the Greek kingdom with the 1913 Treaty of London.[3] This encouraged more sustained Greek–Cretan involvement in archaeological research on the island, even if Minoan palaces and many other important sites continued to be explored by foreign archaeologists. For the first two years of the First World War, Greece maintained neutrality, but was torn by internal discord and political instability caused by clashes between two opposing factions: one anti-war, led by King Constantine I, and the other pro-war (on the side of the Triple Entente of Britain, France, and Russia), led by the Cretan-born prime minister Eleftherios Venizelos. Greece entered the war in 1917, after foreign intervention helped the Venizelist cause, but the island of Crete escaped much of the fighting, which took place mostly in northern Greece, on the Macedonian front.

More significant for Crete were other developments in the aftermath of the First World War. The diminishing power of the Ottoman Empire gave further encouragement to Greek irredentist claims and the *Megali Idea* (Great Idea), namely the notion of a Greater Greece nation state that would encompass all territories inhabited by ethnic Greeks. In 1921, with the encouragement of the British prime minister Lloyd George, Greece sent troops to Asia Minor, to occupy areas with substantial Greek populations that remained under Ottoman rule. The *Megali Idea*, however, turned into a great Greek catastrophe and a momentous military opportunity for the Turkish leader General Mustafa Kemal (Ataturk), which eventually led to the creation of the modern Turkish state. The 1923 treaty signed in Lausanne stipulated an exchange of Christian and Muslim populations between Greece and Turkey (Η Ἀνταλλαγή in Greek, and *Mübadele* in Turkish). Although many Greeks, especially in Istanbul, were allowed to stay, approximately 1 million people moved from Turkey to Greece, a figure that makes current problems of migration into Europe and the UK from Syria and other war zones look rather petty, especially if one considers that the Greek population at that time was about 5 million. On Crete, the Muslim population had steadily decreased since the establishment of the *Kritiki Politeia*, but still represented a substantial presence, especially in urban areas.[4] After 1923, however, c. 30,000 Muslim Cretans (mostly Greek-speaking) left the island.[5] Among those who stayed was Ali Baritakis, one of the foremen employed by Evans on his excavations at Knossos: in 1927 he was buried in a (now vanished) Muslim cemetery close to the archaeological site where he had worked for much of his life.[6]

In the period between the exchange of populations and the Second World War, Greece continued to be dogged by institutional and economic problems. In 1924 a republic was proclaimed, but its governments were unstable and the economy in poor condition, despite loans from the US and other powers. Friction with neighbouring countries further compounded this difficult situation. Monarchy was restored in 1935, but this did not bring more stability. This situation eventually led to the so-called 4th of August Regime, the dictatorship of General Ioannis Metaxas, who ruled from 1936 until his death in January 1941, a few months after Greece had entered the Second World War (on 28 October 1940), following the Italian invasion of Albania. Greek forces repelled Mussolini's advance, forcing Hitler to intervene. The German invasion of Greece was completed with the Battle of Crete in May 1941 and was followed by German–Italian occupation of the island. The Italians were mostly based in east Crete, but only until Badoglio's armistice of September 1943.

After liberation from German occupation and the end of the Second World War, in a referendum held in 1946, Greece voted in favour of retaining the monarchy, but until 1949 the country was engulfed in a bitter civil war between the forces that had been at the forefront of Greek resistance against the Axis powers: those linked to the left-wing National Liberation Front (EAM) and its military arm (ELAS) against the anti-communist groups supported by Britain and the US, such as EDES.[7] In other words, in the aftermath of the Second World War, Greece became one of the first battlegrounds of the Cold War. Crete did suffer from the effects of the civil war, but not as much as other parts of Greece, partly because, although active on Crete, EAM/ELAS never got a strong foothold on the island, where the resistance was also organized under another alliance of non-communist groups (EOK) supported by the British.[8]

From pan-Minoan Aegean to 'Minoans go home!' – the return of the Aryans and the decline and fall of the Minoan Empire

In terms of archaeological developments in Crete, the period between the *Kritiki Politeia* and the Greek Civil War saw the start of new important excavations and the resumption of old ones. Among the latter, Evans's new excavations at Knossos of the 1920s attracted considerable public attention, as did his work of reconstruction or 'reconstitution', to use his term, which was facilitated by the employment of a new material: ferro-concrete.[9] Union with Greece gave considerable impetus to Greek–Cretan archaeological explorations on the island. Scholars already active before and during the First World War, such as Chatzidakis and Xanthoudides, together with those from a younger generation, such as Spyridon Marinatos (active from the mid-1920s), conducted dozen of excavations at various sites, from caves (e.g. Pyrgos) to cemeteries (e.g. Gournes, Messara tombs), and from Minoan 'villas' (e.g. Amnisos and Nirou Chani) to the newly discovered palace at Malia, where Chatzidakis carried out some work in 1915. By coincidence, in the spring of that year, a young postgraduate student at the university of Oxford, Vere Gordon Childe, who later became one of the most famous archaeologists of the twentieth century, visited Crete and soon after produced his very first archaeological publication (cf. below).

Archaeological explorations of the palace at Malia stopped during the First World War, and when they resumed in the 1920s, they were under the aegis of the French School in Athens. Indeed Greek, French, Italian, and British archaeologists seem to have been the most active in the period between the two World Wars, whereas the Americans, so involved in Cretan prehistoric explorations during the *Kritiki Politeia*, now focused their efforts on other Aegean regions.[10] Several short-lived German-led archaeological investigations took place during the island's occupation in the Second World War, for example at the Minoan sites of Monastiraki in the Amari valley and Apesokari in the Messara.[11] Besides excavations, scholars such as John Pendlebury explored Crete on foot, identifying more sites and continuing similar investigations by the Italian Archaeological Mission before the First World War.[12]

This archaeological research enhanced the achievements of Minoan Crete, by producing a fuller picture of its internal and external networks, its complex settlement patterns, road networks, the variety of its material culture and its relations with other Mediterranean regions. It also sowed the seeds of significant future explorations, such as the famous excavations by Spyridon Marinatos at Akrotiri on Thera of the 1960s, since it was during his Cretan excavations of the 1920s and 1930s, such as those at Amnisos, that this Greek archaeologist conceived the idea that Minoan Crete had been destroyed not by human agency, but by the Bronze Age eruption of the Santorini volcano, of which he believed memories were preserved in Plato's myth of Atlantis and other sources.[13]

Equally important for the Minoans and their reception were the archaeological studies and discoveries made in other Aegean, Mediterranean, and Near Eastern regions. These included Hrozný's decipherment of Hittite, Gerhard Rodenwaldt's publications of frescoes from Tiryns, Georg Karo's full publications of the Shaft Graves at Mycenae, and the archaeological investigations conducted by Alan Wace and Carl Blegen at various Bronze Age sites on the mainland, such as Korakou, Zygouries, Prosymna, Mycenae, and Pylos.[14] This work produced considerable evidence that challenged Evans's dating of some mainland finds and his pan-Minoan theories. The Aryan-Greeks began exacting their revenge, both within and beyond specialist academic circles.

Minoan elements attested on mainland Greece were now seen by more and more scholars as a veneer on a strong, indigenous 'Helladic' culture, as local elites' acquisition of cultural traits from Minoan Crete, not as the result of a Minoan conquest, even if many (e.g. Pendlebury) continued to followed Evans's more imperialistic line for several decades.[15] In this period, Mycenaean culture was no longer seen as the late, decadent emanation of Minoan civilization, but as the ascending power in the Aegean during the fifteenth–thirteenth centuries BC. Mycenaean art, on the whole, continued to be perceived as derivative and not on a par with the best Minoan period, but its grandeur found new appreciation. The imposing walls of the Mycenaean citadels and the astonishing Mycenaean tombs (such as the Treasury of Atreus) were now more securely dated to *c.* 1400–1250 BC, and not to the period of acme of the Minoan Palaces (*c.* 1700–1400 BC), as Evans believed.[16] Last but not least, the Mycenaeans were seen, once again, as Aryans/Greeks: by the late 1920s, Blegen's and other scholars' suggestion that a Greek-speaking population had arrived in Greece as early as *c.* 2000 BC (at the start of the Middle Helladic Period), if not before, had become the new orthodoxy.[17]

The idea that an Aryan, Indo-European, and more specifically Greek-speaking population had lived in Greece during Bronze Age, and even in the Neolithic period, was not new. As discussed in Chapter 3, Schliemann and Tsountas, for example, had already supported this notion. But the close equation between Achaeans and Mycenaeans had somewhat waned, after close observations of the discrepancies between the Homeric texts and Mycenaean realities, coupled with Evans's discoveries and dominance in the field of Aegean prehistory (especially his suggestion that the Mycenaeans were decadent Minoans).[18] In the period after the First World War, however, more and more scholars embraced the suggestion that Hellenic people had entered Greece much earlier than Evans and other scholars had envisaged. This Greek–Aryan revival was partly helped by linguistic investigations, including the discovery that the Hittites spoke an Indo-European language.[19] The fact that the Hittites ruled much of Asia Minor by the middle of the second millennium BC bolstered the idea that Indo-European people were established on mainland Greece by that time. Blegen and others, in fact, went even further in their opposition to Evans's pan-Minoan vision, by suggesting that Greek was spoken by the ruling classes on Crete from Late Minoan II, and by the early second millennium B C on mainland Greece.[20]

This view turned out to be prophetic, but was fully validated, and almost unanimously accepted, only several decades later, with Ventris's decipherment of Linear B in 1952. In 1939, when Blegen started finding Linear B tablets on his excavations at Bronze Age Pylos (Ano Englianos), many people who favoured Evans's interpretation saw this discovery as slightly problematic, because these tablets dated *c.* 200 years later than those found by Evans at Knossos, and belonged to a period of supposed decline. But they also saw this as a confirmation of a Minoan conquest of mainland Greece, since only a few suspected that the Linear B script, which had clearly developed from Linear A, could represent a non-Minoan language (and hardly anybody believed that the Minoans spoke Greek, because of racial theories and the evidence of the Eteo-Cretan inscriptions from Praisos). It was the common mistake of confusing and conflating language with script: the continuity/evolution of writing systems was equated with continuity of the language that they represented. It was only the decipherment of Linear B that eventually undermined Evans's pan-Minoan theories.[21]

In the three decades after the 'Heroic Age of Excavation' on Crete, archaeological explorations created a fuller and more complex picture, and this accumulation of data required significant works of categorization and synthesis. To paraphrase A. N. Whitehead's tripartite classification of the 'rhythms of education' and apply it to Minoan studies, if the period before the First World War is the 'stage of romance', when a subject matter has the vividness of novelty, the decades examined in this chapter represent the 'stage of precision', when acquisition of knowledge is systematized through the application of the 'grammar of science', while later periods, discussed in Chapter 5, may be regarded as the a 'stage of generalization', comparable to a Fichtean-Hegelian concept of synthesis.[22]

A Minoan *mare nostrum*

Few would disagree that the most fascinating and influential narrative emerging from this 'stage of precision' was Evans's four-volume *The Palace of Minos: A Comparative Account of the Successive Stages of the Early Cretan Civilization as Illustrated by the Discoveries at Knossos* (1921–35). Yet, one should remember that this publication was beyond the means of many people, and that other more affordable (and portable) works played an important role in the diffusion and reception of the Minoans, especially beyond academic circles, disseminating views that at times differed from Evans's.

Evans's first volume of his *magnum opus* was published in 1921, and the other three followed in 1928, 1930, and 1935, respectively; the index, compiled by his half-sister Joan, came out in 1936. The work had a long and complex gestation: its original title was *The Nine Minoan Periods: A Classification and Illustrative Sketch of the Successive Phases of Early Cretan Civilization from the Neolithic to the Beginning of the Iron Age*; its initial aim was *not* to embark on a comparative study of Minoan civilization, but to expand and provide ample illustration for Evans's classification of the Minoan Age in various phases and sub-phases, first expounded in his *Essai de classification des époques de la civilisation minoenne* (1906); it was supposed to comprise either one large volume or two, of which almost 500 pages of text were already typeset between January 1914 and July 1917; but by February 1919 Evans had delivered the preface of a much revised and enlarged publication, with the more catchy (final) title: *The Palace of Minos*.[23]

This four-volume work added a considerable amount of new evidence, especially regarding archaeological explorations that had taken place in 1907–13 and in the 1920s, since Evans had published very little on these activities in comparison to the early years of the excavations, when substantial annual reports by his pen had appeared in the *Annual of the British School at Athens* up to 1905. The amount of details and, above all, the comparative material presented in *The Palace of Minos* are so abundant that its characterization as an encyclopaedia of Minoan Crete appears justified.[24] Evans's evolutionary outlook, however, his use of cyclic stages of growth, maturity, and decline, combined with some diffusionist ideas, and many of his other main tenets can be traced back to his earlier publications. For example, the old idea of Crete as the cradle of European civilization appears now an established cliché, and so are Evans's priest-kings and his Minoan Mother Goddess. Regarding the latter, in *The Palace of Minos* Evans reinforced his suggestion of Minoan religious monotheism, based on a dominant female divinity and her younger son-consort, albeit often through finds that turned out to be fakes, such as the 'Boston Goddess' and the 'Boy-god'.[25] Evans also continued to regard women as important in Minoan society, able to mix freely and perform in the important bull-leaping religious ceremonies; at the same time he maintained that they were partly segregated in areas of the palace and that the real power rested in the hands of priest kings.[26] Also reinforced and fleshed out is his vision of a Minoan sea empire. Despite the evidence emerging from mainland Greece,[27] Evans's views regarding Minoan hegemony and subordinate position of mainland Greece became more entrenched. He now considered the term 'Mycenaean' as superfluous, since he considered mainland Greece to be effectively a Minoan colony, and Mycenaean culture a late Minoan offshoot, even if he conceded that, after Late Minoan II, the Minoan 'seat of government' had probably moved to Mycenae.[28] Evans also repeated the idea that the end of Minoan civilization was partly caused by northern barbarians (the Aryan Greeks) towards the end of the Bronze Age (*c.* 1200 BC or slightly later), even if in *The Palace of Minos* he gave more significance to earthquakes as agents of destruction, especially after he had experienced one in 1926.[29]

In other words, in Evans's biological-evolutionary-cyclic scheme, the Minoan empire had become vulnerable to barbarian conquest towards the end of the Bronze Age as the result of earthquakes, overexpansion, and the inevitable decline that follows the acme or maturity of a civilization.[30] It was not a foreign revolt and invasion in *c.* 1450–1400 BC that put an end to the Minoan empire. Evans continued to entertain the idea that Minoan civilization, including Mycenaean Greece, was largely non-Hellenic, and predominantly belonged to Sergi's Mediterranean race, with some Armenoid/Anatolian input and other admixtures: a mixed race, but essentially non-Aryan/Greek.[31] Perhaps one might also see traces of Evans's anti-Hellenic stance in the fact that Minoan Crete and its *thalassocracy* seem to be modelled more closely on the multi-ethnic Roman and British empires than the Athenian-led Delian League with its stress on Ionian ethnicity.[32]

Evans's Minoans may, at times, appear too idealistic, partly because he focused on what he (and others) perceived as the most appealing aspects of their culture (e.g. love of nature) and on what he considered to be their Golden Age. His rosy vision was not due to suppression of Minoan militaristic aspects, as an emotional response against war atrocities, whether in late nineteenth-century Crete or the First World War. Evans's Minoan Golden Age and *Pax Minoica*, like the Augustan Golden Age and *Pax Romana*, were relatively short and went hand in hand with military conquests and empire-building (cf. Chapter 3). The notion that the Minoans were a peaceful people for much of their history largely emerged from the works of other scholars after the First World War, as a consequence of the polarization between Aryan Mycenaeans and non-Aryan Minoans and beliefs in their alleged essential characteristics. Renewed appreciation of Mycenaean power and Aryan character, in turn, fostered decadent views of the Minoans and prepared the ground for their decline and fall, as discussed in the following sections.

Peaceful Minoans and warlike Mycenaeans: the Aryan resurgence

The same year in which the first volume of Evans's *Palace of Minos* appeared also saw the publication of three archaeological monographs that help to illustrate the points made above: Carl Blegen's *Korakou*, Diedrich Fimmen's *Die Kretisch-mykenische Kultur*, and Helmut Theodor Bossert's *Alt Kreta*.

In *Korakou: A Prehistoric Settlement near Corinth*, Blegen acknowledged the stimulus provided by Crete on Mycenaean Greece but, echoing Harriet Boyd Hawes, suggested that this was due to 'peaceful penetration, chiefly of Minoan commerce and Minoan standards, and perhaps of colonies of Minoan artisans, among a people ready and eager to seize upon new ideas', a people of 'a mainland race which had a vigorous spirit of progress', clearly identified with the Homeric Achaeans.[33] This 'vigorous spirit of progress' was one of the features that Blegen attributed to the Greek *Volkgeist* and reflects racial ideas common at the time. The son of a professor of Greek and German, Blegen is usually regarded as a master of understatement, a calm, sober, empirical archaeologist piecing facts together.[34] Yet, he was also influenced by contemporary views on the physical-intellectual attributes of the Indo-European Greeks, which affected his archaeological interpretations just as ideas about the 'Mediterranean race' affected Evans's. According to Blegen, the Greeks of Classical times were a blend of different people and races, comparable to a metallic alloy: the 'peculiar Hellenic alloy is a complex blend of metal fused together from many elements', to which the Neolithic people contributed 'superstition, coarseness ... unbridled passion and cruelty'; the Early Bronze Age people, and especially the Minoans, added 'delicacy of feeling, freedom of imagination, sobriety of judgment, and love of beauty'; and the 'Aryan lineage', who had reached Greek lands by the Middle Helladic period, gave 'physical and mental vigour, directness of view, and that epic spirit of adventure in games, in the chase, and in war, which so deeply permeate Hellenic life'.[35]

Another interesting illustration of Blegen's views on racial traits, and Greek superiority, appears in a seminal article on the date of the Linear B tablets, published after the decipherment: after remarking on the close similarity between the Knossos tablets, dated by Evans to *c.* 1400 BC, and those found on the mainland, dated to *c.* 1200 BC, he suggested a re-examination of the date and stratigraphy of the Knossos tablets for a variety of reasons, of which the very first was that 'we are dealing with Greeks and their works', with a people so interested in change and so inventive (unlike cuneiform-using Near Eastern groups) that could not have left a script unchanged for two centuries.[36]

Fimmen's 1921 volume was published posthumously, under Georg Karo's supervision (the author having died in combat in 1916). It greatly expanded on Fimmen's earlier work on the subject,[37] included many illustrations, and clearly benefited from the author's long sojourn in Greece in the years before the First World War. It is a meticulous but rather dry, descriptive piece of work, which often employs the term 'Mycenaean' in a rather quaint, old-fashioned way (almost as a synonym for Aegean Bronze Age), and adopts the term 'Minoan' only as a chronological label for Crete. Fimmen generally eschews political, ethnic and even religious questions. The Achaeans, the Mediterranean race, and Indo-Europeans are barely mentioned,[38] while Evans's Minoan Great Mother Goddess (especially in her famous incarnation as 'snake goddess') is conspicuous by her absence. *Die Kretisch-mykenische Kultur* is essentially a presentation of the Aegean Bronze Age through exhaustive lists and descriptions of settlements (including settlements beyond the Aegean, where 'Mycenaean' finds were discovered); main types of architecture, graves, cult-places, and ceramics; relationships with other regions (especially Egypt); and absolute chronology. Yet, even this descriptive work illustrates an emerging appreciation of Mycenaean culture as a distinct, individual entity. It shows mainland Greece, the Cyclades, and Crete as fundamentally separate cultures (and people), brought under the Cretan sphere of influence in the Middle Minoan period, but by the end of the fifteenth century BC (Fimmen's Late Mycenaean period) the centre of power had shifted to the mainland, and (*pace* Evans) the Aegean was a Mycenaean *koine*.

Bossert's *Alt Kreta* could not be more different in aims and tone from Fimmen's *Die Kretisch-mykenische Kultur*. Yet, like Fimmen's, this work snubs Evans's 'Minoan' terminology for the entire Aegean, preferring 'kretisch-mykenisch(en)' instead, and highlights some differences between mainland Greece and Crete. Bossert's main goal was to make a large corpus of illustrations readily available to educated laymen, teachers, and students. His book went through three editions (in 1921, 1923, and 1937), of which the last was also translated into English.[39] With each subsequent edition the number of illustrations increased, while some objects, such as the notorious chryselephantine 'Boston Goddess', were removed because too many scholars (unlike Evans) considered them to be fakes.[40] The first edition presented a slightly different title, but the most significant variation is a twenty-one-page introduction, with illustrations by the archaeologist Fritz Krischen, which was eliminated in subsequent editions.[41] Krischen's illustrations were not meant to be accurate reconstructions of Aegean life, but to represent the 'spirit' of Aegean culture as well as the 'impulsive' interpretations of a 'modern man' (see Fig. 4.1 a–b).[42] They also match the flowery prose of Bossert's introduction, in which he highlights differences and tensions

a   b

Fig. 4.1a–b Examples of Fritz Krischen's illustrations for Bossert (1921).

between Minoan and Mycenaean material culture and wonders whether the 'Achaean–
Greek spirit' is already visible even in the Late Mycenaean period (*c.* 1400–1200 BC).[43]
Divergences also appear in his discussion of women in the Aegean Bronze Age.
Although Bossert does not regard Minoan Crete as a quasi-socialist matriarchy (unlike
Jules Bois), he suggests that women played an important role in society, as among the
Etruscans (to whom Bossert often compares the Minoans), adding that they may have
even occasionally ruled on Crete, while this would have been impossible on the Greek
mainland.[44] He also remarks that, to the superficial modern viewer, Minoan women
may appear like courtesans, even if he is quick to explain that the Minoans were in fact
a highly moral people, as demonstrated by the absence of obscene representations in
their imagery, and that the greatness of their art is linked to the profound religious
sentiments that inspired it.[45]

   Despite acknowledging significant differences between Bronze Age Crete and
mainland Greece, for Bossert Minoan and Mycenaean art could be treated essentially
as one, given the impact of the former on the latter, which could be considered both
Oriental and European, because 'European' is, in any case, a mixture of East and West,
North and South, and the constantly evolving heritage of different races and elements:
'Cretan–Mycenaean art can be described as non-European only if we consider stylistic
origins. But if we look forward instead of backwards, we must recognise that what can
be related to us is precisely the old inheritance that these pre-Indo-European peoples
gave to their successors. This inheritance truly continues to the present day.'[46] Bossert
describes Minoan art through a number of established clichés, such as playful, carefree,
almost childlike, full of joie de vivre and love of nature. Unlike earlier authors, however,
he praises it for its expressionism rather than naturalism, an idea derived from
contemporary artistic developments in Germany.[47] Probably under the influence of
Boyd Hawes and/or established racial characterizations, and post-First World War
pacifist sentiments, in Bossert's volume Evans's Minoan Empire, which involved
military conquest, becomes a 'commercial monopoly', which entailed colonies, a strong

navy, and even some attacks on coastal areas, but these merely 'paved the way for peaceful expansion'.[48]

Neither Fimmen's nor Bossert's 1921 editions could have taken into account Evans's first volume of *The Palace of Minos*, unlike the more substantial and significant monograph by the French ancient historian Gustave Glotz, *La civilisation égéenne*, published in 1923, the same year in which the first volume of J. B. Bury's first edition of the *Cambridge Ancient History* appeared, with several relevant chapters by John L. Myres and Alan B. Wace. Glotz's book was soon translated into English as *The Aegean Civilization* (1925) and in several other languages.[49] It was one of the sources used by writers such as André Gide (for his *Thésée*) and Robert Graves (for his *White Goddess*) (cf. below). One may even wonder whether Glotz's description of the Minoan double-axe as a 'bisexual fetish',[50] together with the Minoan imagery and Greek myths, may have helped even further the association between Minoan civilization and complex, adventurous, unconventional sexuality, which is so clearly visible in the work of many artists and writers of this and later periods.

Although Glotz's work shows more evidence of Evans's influence, like Blegen, Fimmen, Bossert, Wace, and others, he opposed the term Minoan for the entire Aegean, continued to stress the differences between Cretan (Minoan/non-Indo-European) and Mycenaean (Achaean/Indo-European) cultures and made a vigorous plea for the arrival of Indo-European people from the Caspian region to other areas, including Greece, as early as the beginning of the second millennium BC.[51] As an ancient historian, Glotz was predisposed to use archaeological evidence as the handmaiden of ancient Greek sources and to construct a grand narrative, especially for the later part of second millennium BC, which was made to chime with the literary evidence. By the time the English translation was published, his belief in the historical kernel of Greek sources was further enhanced by the publication of the Hittite 'Ahhijawa texts', which, according to many scholars, refer to Greek 'Achaeans'.[52] Thus, Glotz conceived the main developments in the history of the Aegean as a succession of three Bronze Age hegemonies, brought to an end by the Dorian invasion, which heralded a period of great decline. The First Cretan Hegemony (*c.* 2000–1750 BC), equivalent to the period of the first palaces, ended with earthquakes, internecine war, and possibly a dynastic change. The Second Cretan Hegemony (*c.* 1700–1400), equivalent to the even more beautiful and brilliant period of the new palaces, saw the emergence of Knossos as the major power (and the only palace in 1450–1400 BC), which was eventually destroyed by Mycenaean Greeks because they 'grew tired of paying tribute to the Cretan thalassocracy', with some memories of this liberation from Minoan commercial interference being reflected in the Greek myth of Theseus and the Minotaur.[53] The third or Mycenaean Hegemony (*c.* 1400–1200 BC) ended with the Dorian invasion, because the Mycenaeans had overextended themselves all over the Mediterranean: 'They tried to take in too much; by scattering itself about the circumference the race weakened itself at the centre.'[54] In this reconstruction of Aegean developments, the Mycenaeans appear as more powerful but not as artistically gifted as the Cretans, while the Dorians are just hopeless barbarians. Echoing Evans's ideas, but allowing for a Mycenaean–Achaean conquest of Crete in *c.* 1400, Glotz wrote that the 'beautiful bronze civilization went under when iron appeared. The submission of Crete to the

Achaians was the conquest of Greece by Rome – *capta ferum victorem cepit*; the advent of the Dorians was the barbarian invasions, the Middle Ages, to be followed by the Renaissance.'[55]

But did the more artistic and civilized Minoans conquer and rule the Mycenaeans, or did they simply impose some heavy taxes? Glotz's picture is perhaps slightly more pacifist than Evans's, but not entirely: his Minoan hegemony is the 'result of sporadic and *peaceful* colonization' (my italics) and of the natives' acceptance of 'the blessings of a superior civilization'.[56] Following Evans, Glotz portrays the Minoan rulers as commanding a powerful army, installing themselves 'as masters and impos[ing] their dominion' even beyond the Aegean, as far as the Levant and the West.[57] Yet, despite the notion that in the Argolid 'everything became Cretanized', from fashion to religion, Glotz does not attribute this phenomenon to wholesale invasion and Minoan dominance: according to the French scholar, the main population remained Greek, their rulers maintained their bearded appearance, rude way of life, and preference for war and the chase, while their women kept a subordinate position in society, which improved, but only slightly, after contacts with Crete.[58] Glotz admired the grandeur of Mycenaean civilization, but for him the later phases of the Aegean Bronze Age, as for Evans, still represented a period of artistic decadence. Mycenaeans may have been more powerful and rich, but this could not make up for 'the lack of inspiration', since the 'Cretanized Achaians were after all not Cretans. From one civilization to the other there was no break in the curve, but it was a descending curve', and their material culture became 'vulgar and degenerate'.[59] Unlike the Minoans, the Mycenaeans could never be considered as 'truly the Japanese of Mediterranean'.[60]

Even Evans's potential *dauphin*, the archaeologist John Pendlebury (who died prematurely during the battle for Crete in the Second World War), in his influential *The Archaeology of Crete* (1939), accepted the 'Helladic' terminology for mainland Greece and presented a vision of Aegean developments (and use of later Greek sources) that is not too far from that of Glotz, reflecting common racial characterizations of the Minoans as peaceful and Greek-Aryans as warlike, already present in earlier works by Boyd Hawes (cf. Chapter 3).[61] Pendlebury believed in a Minoan conquest of the Aegean that occurred 'gradually and probably peacefully', because 'on the whole the Minoans seem to have been a peaceful folk', and suggested that Minoan rulers continued to use local princes as vassals, as the British did in India.[62] In Pendlebury's view, the Minoan *thalassocracy* and its Golden Age were brought to an end by external human agency (instead of Evans's earthquakes and internecine strife): like Glotz, he envisaged a Mycenaean revolt against Minoan domination, of which memories were preserved in the myth of Theseus and the Minotaur. This conflict did not involve an immediate Mycenaean colonization of Crete, but broke the Minoan spirit, possibly wiped out the Cretan ruling caste, and eventually led to Cretan absorption into an 'Achaean Empire'.[63]

From Minoan vitality to Minoan decadence

Most works on the Aegean Bronze Age of the period discussed in this chapter continued to extol the artistic superiority of Minoan Crete, while stressing the differences between

Minoans and Mycenaeans, especially in terms of attitudes to war and women as well as physical appearance.[64] The Minoans were perceived as modern primitives, a civilizing force, original and creative, full of joie de vivre, vitality, gracefulness, and love of nature; and they were often compared to children, Etruscans, and Japanese, even if, as discussed above, Evans favoured analogies with the Romans (at least regarding his *Pax Minoica*).[65] Yet, some uneasiness was beginning to emerge. This was sometimes expressed in terms of coexisting opposite traits, such as beauty and ugliness, civility and cruelty. For example, Pendlebury described the fall of Knossos, 'on a wild spring day at the beginning of the fourteenth century B.C.', as the end of something 'which the world will never see again; something grotesque perhaps, something fantastic and cruel, but something also very lovely'.[66] Above all, in a period of growing Aryanism and preoccupation with decline, some of the very characteristics for which the Minoans were often admired sowed the seeds of their downfall: they were civilized, artistic, and graceful, but they were also beginning to be perceived as over-refined and decadent, unlike the taller, more vigorous, and warlike northern Mycenaeans/Aryans, who eventually defeated them.

Two rather different works by the famous author H. G. Wells may serve to illustrate this point: his novel *The Time Machine* (1895) and his *Outline of History* (1920). Both are symptomatic of the *fin de siècle*'s preoccupation with decadence that continued after the First World War, while the latter also illustrates a revived interest in universal histories that emerged in the interwar period.[67] *The Time Machine* was published before the discoveries on Crete, but Well's description of the Eloi, one of the people he encounters in his journey into the future, is curiously reminiscent of the Minoans: they are small, graceful, childlike, beautiful creatures, curly-haired and beardless, large-eyed and red-lipped, lovers of flowers and dance, living in a Golden Age and in (apparent) peace. But something rather unpleasant lurks behind this beautiful façade: the Eloi live in the ruins of once splendid palaces and in fear of the Morlocks, the people that they had previously subjugated, who extract their revenge under the darkness of night. Above all, the Eloi are a spent force: they 'had decayed to a mere beautiful futility', their peaceful (and false) security had set 'a premium on feebleness', which was the result of their mastering of 'nature and also fellow-man'.[68] For Wells, intelligence, strength, and vigour were the outcome of freedom as well as need and hardship, and in his *The War of the Worlds* (1898) he even suggested that invasions and conflicts did provide some benefits, since they undermined 'that serene confidence in the future which is the most fruitful source of decadence'.[69] Thus, unsurprisingly, the Minoans do not fare well in his *Outline of History*. For Wells, Minoan achievements and uniqueness have been exaggerated, while their peace (which he envisaged as lasting much longer than Evans's *Pax Minoica*) did not give them an advantage over the 'healthy barbaric' Aryans, who rebelled against Minoan violence. The end of the Minoans was well deserved:

> It is the custom nowadays to make a sort of wonder of these achievements of the Cretans, as though they were a people of incredible artistic ability living in the dawn of civilization. But their great time was long past that dawn; as late as 2000 B.C. It took them many centuries to reach their best in art and skill, and their art

and luxury are by no means so great a wonder if we reflect that for 3000 years they were immune from invasion, that for a thousand years they were at peace ... The palace at Cnossos was destroyed, and never rebuilt nor reinhabited. Possibly this was done by ... those newcomers into the Mediterranean, the barbaric Greeks, a group of Aryan tribes ... The legend of Theseus tells of such a raid. ... The Homeric Greeks were a healthy barbaric Aryan people ... It is fairly clear from the Minos legend and from the evidence of the Cnossos remains, that the Cretans kidnapped or stole youths and maidens to be slaves, bull-fighters, athletes, and perhaps sacrifices. They traded fairly with the Egyptians, but it may be they did not realize the gathering strength of the Greek barbarians; they 'traded' violently with them, and so brought sword and flame upon themselves.[70]

In the context of universal history, preoccupation with social degeneration, and decadent views of the Minoans, arguably the best example is Oswald Spengler's *Der Untergang des Abendlandes* (*The Decline of the West*), published in two volumes (1918, 1922).[71] This controversial and influential work presented a universal history that was not Eurocentric and did not follow a linear trajectory of continuous progress. History was seen through the emergence and decline of eight high cultures or civilizations: Indian, Babylonian, Egyptian, Chinese, Mexican, Arabian, Classical, and European/Western. Spengler's civilizations had a soul, a notion indebted to Herder's idea of *Volksgeist*, but were also treated like biological organisms, which went through cyclic developments of peaks and troughs, and biological stages of infancy, youth, virility, decline, death, and rebirth in another individual form.[72] It is in the second volume of *The Decline of the West* that both Minoans and Mycenaeans make a fascinating appearance, in a section titled 'The soul of the City', which is well worth quoting at length, since many of the ideas expressed here found an echo in later archaeological narratives and Cretomanic works. In Spengler's long passage, the traditional narrative is turned upside down. The Mycenaeans are not the late, derivative, and degenerate stage of Minoan culture, but the beginning of a new and vigorous future, whereas the Minoans are decadent, pampered Orientals, whose art is 'clever and empty' and whose decline was already palpable even by the time of Evans's Golden Age:

> About the middle of the second millennium before Christ, two worlds lay over against one another on the Aegean Sea. The one, darkly groping, big with hopes, drowsy with the intoxication of deeds and sufferings, ripening quietly towards its future, was the Mycenaean. The other, gay and satisfied, snugly ensconced in the treasures of an ancient Culture, elegant, light, with all its great problems far behind it, was the Minoan of Crete. We shall never really comprehend this phenomenon, which in these days is becoming the centre of research-interest, unless we appreciate the abyss of opposition that separates the two souls. The man of those days must have felt it deeply, but hardly 'cognised' it. I see it before me: the humility of the inhabitant of Tiryns and Mycenae before the unattainable esprit of life in Cnossus, the contempt of the well-bred of Cnossus for the petty chiefs and their followers, and withal a secret feeling of superiority in the healthy barbarians, like that of the German soldier in the presence of the elderly Roman dignitary. How are we in a

position to know this? There are several such moments in which the men of two Cultures have looked into one another's eyes. We know more than one 'Inter-Culture' in which some of the most significant tendencies of the human soul have disclosed themselves. As it was (we may confidently say) between Cnossus and Mycenae, so it was between the Byzantine court and the German chieftains who, like Otto II, married into it – undisguised wonder on the part of the knights and counts, answered by the contemptuous astonishment of a refined, somewhat pale and tired Civilization at that bearish morning vigour of the German lands which Scheffel has described in Ekkehard ... That which stands on the hills of Tiryns and Mycenae is *Pfalz* and *Burg* of root-Germanic type. The palaces of Crete – which are not kings' castles, but huge cult-buildings for a crowd of priests and priestesses – are equipped with megalopolitan – nay, Late-Roman – luxury. At the foot of those hills were crowded the huts of yeoman and vassals, but in Crete (Gournia, Hagia Triada) the excavation of towns and villas has shown that the requirements were those of high civilization, and the building-technique that of a long experience, accustomed to catering for the most pampered taste in furniture and wall-decoration, and familiar with lighting, water-circulation, staircases, and suchlike problems. In the one, the plan of the house is a strict life-symbol; in the other, the expression of a refined utilitarianism. Compare the Kamares vases and the frescoes of smooth stucco with everything that is genuinely Mycenaean – they are, through and through, the product of an industrial art, clever and empty, and not of any grand and deep art of heavy, clumsy, but forceful symbolism like that which in Mycenae was ripening towards: the geometric style. It is, in a word, not a style but a taste. In Mycenae was housed a primitive race which chose its sites according to soil-value and facilities for defence, whereas the Minoan population settled in business foci, as may be observed very clearly in the case of Philakopi [sic] on Melos which was established for the export trade in obsidian. A Mycenaean palace is a promise, a Minoan something that is ending. But it was just the same in the West about 800 – the Frankish and Visigothic farms and manor-houses stretched from the Loire to the Ebro, while south of them lay the Moorish castles, villas, and mosques of Cordova and Granada. It is surely no accident that the peak of this Minoan luxury coincides with the period of the great Egyptian revolution, and particularly the Hyksos time (1780–1580 B.C.). The Egyptian craftsmen may well have fled in those days to the peaceful islands and even as far as the strongholds of the mainland, as in a later instance the Byzantine scholars fled to Italy. For it is axiomatic that the Minoan Culture is a part of the Egyptian ...[73]

A rehabilitation of the Mycenaeans also appears in some publications by the great Marxist archaeologist Gordon Childe. Besides Marxism, he was influenced by the strong Germanic tradition of culture-historical archaeology, best exemplified by the work of Gustaf Kossinna, with its emphasis on migrations as agents of change as well as the idea of a close relationship between material culture, race, and language – notions partly inspired by Herder's *Volkgeist*, like Spengler's.[74] Childe's views on the Minoans, however, are more positive than Spengler's (and Well's), since they also owe a great deal to his Oxford mentors, Evans and Myres.

While a graduate student at Oxford, in the spring of 1915 Childe travelled to Greece and Crete, and soon after he produced his first publication, the article 'On the date and origin of Minyan Ware', which included references to Minoan Crete and discussed the arrival of the Indo-Europeans in Greece.[75] This topic was developed in his 1916 B.Litt. dissertation, titled 'The Influence of Indo-Europeans in Prehistoric Greece', of which no copy appears to have survived.[76] One can assume, however, that it formed the basis of chapters appearing in later works, such as *The Dawn of European Civilization* (1925, with a sixth and final edition in 1957) and especially *The Aryans* (1926).

Childe's Minoans generally appear to be suspended between East and West, Oriental and European at the same time. In *The Aryans*, Childe argued that, while the Mycenaeans could not be equated with the Homeric Achaeans (except from *c.* 1250 BC), Indo-European/Hellenic, patriarchal elements were already present in Greece by the early second millennium BC, as shown by the Minyans, whom he considered to be the early second millennium forefathers of the Mycenaeans.[77] Childe acknowledged a Minoan conquest of Greece in *c.* 1600 BC, but maintained that this involved a small number of Cretans, who probably adopted the Greek language already spoken by the Mycenaeans.[78] Following Evans and Myres, Childe stated that the Minoans were clearly 'un-Aryan' devotees of a 'Mother Goddess', in contrast to the Aryans, who had a pantheon based on 'a patriarchal earthly society'.[79] In *The Dawn* he treats the Minoans as effectively part of the Near East, acknowledging their considerable debt to Egypt and Mesopotamia. Unlike Spengler, however, and like most other scholars, he maintains the cliché that the Minoan spirit was 'thoroughly European', since the Minoans' 'modern naturalism' demonstrated 'a truly occidental feeling for life and nature'.[80] But Childe's Minoans are also described in terms that recall those of H. G. Wells and Spengler: they were merchantmen, who lacked 'vigour for expansion', unlike the warlike Aryan-Achaeans; they had reached a stage of decadence in the Late Minoan III period; their art had a whiff of Oriental 'luxury and exuberance', whereas Aryan-Achaean 'decorative principles' and humanism were the true harbinger of the Greek Renaissance:

> The Minoans had created a civilization which was truly European and an art which, at its best, surpassed any contemporary product of the East. But that civilization seems to have lacked the vigour for expansion; it was already in its decline when the Achaeans overthrew it. To Egypt the Minoans brought tribute or gifts; the Achaeans slashing swords. Minoan merchantmen reached the Delta and the Levant; men of war were captained by the Hellenes. Minoan art reached its zenith by 1600 B.C.; in the Second Late Minoan Age conventionalization had set in to lead to decadence in the Third. That decadence was not arrested by the infiltration of Achaean dynasts, but they at least inspired new decorative principles which bore abundant fruit in the VIth [sic] century. The metopic style in ceramic art provided a corrective to the luxury and exuberance of Minoan decoration which still retained something Oriental. The Aryan interest in humanity provided the potter with a theme in which, after the rude attempts of the warrior-vase and the Dipylon, his classical successors were to achieve supremacy.[81]

As remarked by Sherratt, this 'Aryan period' was one that Childe, later in life, 'increasingly sought to play down or even forget (the fact that no copy of his B.Litt thesis survives may be a symptom of this).[82] One can easily see why Childe would distance himself from any form of racial stereotyping, especially after the Second World War. But some of his observations about the Minoans are slightly puzzling even for the early–mid-1920s, especially in view of Childe's well-known pacifism and being a conscientious objector during the First World War.[83] At any rate, *The Aryans* exemplifies how long-held notions of Indo-European physical and intellectual superiority (as well as belligerent and patriarchal character) had become commonplace in the interwar period, and to the extent that some scholars, such as the archaeologist Gustaf Kossinna and the Orientalist L. A. Waddell, felt able to retain the Minoans as illustrious European ancestors only by turning them into Indo-Europeans.[84]

To summarize, many archaeological-historical works produced in the period examined in this chapter presented rather contrasting views of the Minoans and showed an increasing interest in cultural and racial distinctions, especially in the opposition between Aryans and non-Aryans. Other themes that emerge (or reoccur) in these works are a preoccupation with Minoan imperialism and decadence as well as a strong sense of Minoan duality. The latter could take various forms, such as the notion that the Minoans embodied elements of both primitiveness and modernity, of Europe and the Orient, of vitality and decadence, of civility and cruelty.[85] These themes, as illustrated in the following section, also loom large in works that make use of the Minoans beyond history and archaeology and that, in addition, explore subjects such as non-conformist sexuality and gender representation, in ways that intersect with and, at times, seem to anticipate later scholarly discourses.

Cretomania amidst World and Civil Wars: The Minoans in modern cultural practices *c.* 1918–1949 – from decadence to hope for the future

After the Belle Époque, uses of the Minoan past extended to a variety of new literary genres and other cultural practices, such as poetry, historical novels, crime fiction, children's literature, travel writing, films, official parades, and even furnishings, as spectacularly illustrated by the French ocean liner *Aramis* (see Fig. 4.2).[86] The increase in academic and non-academic publications, exhibitions (such as those organized by Evans in 1926 and 1936, in Youlbury near Oxford and London, respectively), and cruise travelling made encounters with the Minoan world easier and in part explain the flourishing of Cretomania after the First World War.[87] The work of intellectuals such as the art historian Christian Zervos, who founded the *Cahiers d'Art* in 1926, a name that refers to a gallery, a publishing house, and a magazine, continued Salomon Reinach's and Edmond Pottier's proselytizing work. His magazine *Cahiers d'Art* was published, albeit irregularly, until the 1960s and was mostly devoted to the artistic and literary avant-gardes, but included ancient art and the new problems it raised, especially regarding its relationship with the present. In the period between the two World Wars, *Cahiers d'Art* included many articles and pictures about Minoan Crete,[88] unlike the surrealist magazine *Minotaure*, published by Albert Skira between 1933 and 1939, with fascinating covers by artists such as Picasso, Dali, and Magritte. Despite its promising

Fig. 4.2 Ocean liner *Aramis*: grand staircase of the first-class dining room (after Boucher 2017: fig. 7.4; © Collection French Lines, DR, reproduced by permission of French Lines).

title, in *Minotaure* a direct engagement with Minoan archaeology is conspicuous by its absence.[89] Readers of *Minotaure* can find plenty of references to Ovid and other Classical materials in its pages, but will look in vain for articles and illustrations of works of art directly inspired by Minoan Crete: the island appears only in advertisements for cruises to Greece organized by the company Neptos.[90] It is, nevertheless, possible that the renewed excavations on Crete, as well as the publication of *The Palace of Minos* and other works discussed above, may have helped to revive an interest in later Greek myths related to Crete.

Among the new literary genres that make use of the Minoans, one of the most interesting is the historical novel.[91] Here, the fascination with Minoan–Greek encounters, the otherness of the Minoans, and especially their decadence are often highlighted by the fact that many are set during the last days of Knossos, and often describe its decline and fall as modern reimaginings of the myth of Theseus's slaying of the Minotaur, as discussed in the following section.

Decadence and sex: The last days of Knossos in historical novels, epic poetry, and other literary genres

One of earliest and most interesting historical novels set in Minoan Crete is Dmitry Merezhkovsky's *The Birth of the Gods* (1925), which is provided with a sequel set in Egypt, *Akhnaton: King of Egypt*, and an accompanying historical–philosophical–religious treatise, *The Secret of the West: Atlantis–Europe*.[92] This Russian author completed these works during his Parisian exile, and reportedly escaped to France (via Poland) in 1919, on the pretext of giving lectures to soldiers stationed in southern Russia, with the manuscript of *The Birth of the Gods* disguised under a cover showing the title 'Materials for lectures to Red Army units'.[93]

The Birth of the Gods offers a picture of Minoan society in the late fifteenth century BC, shortly before its conquest by hordes of northern barbarians, as seen through the eyes of Tutankhamon, the ambassador to Crete of the Egyptian pharaoh Akhenaton.[94] Albeit sprinkled with some liberties and anachronisms, the novel is full of specific and precise allusions to Minoan material culture, which provide historical and local colour. The novel reflects, above all, the author's long-held preoccupation with sexuality and religion. Merezhkovsky could be described as a self-styled prophet of a new Christianity, which would provide salvation for humanity by reconciling Christian spirituality with Pagan love for beauty and appreciation of the human body. He was particularly attracted by androgyny (cf. chapter's epigraph), because he believed that humans had both male and female elements within themselves, and this, in turn, reflected a divinity that was also both male and female. He was also convinced that all ancient cults foreshadowed the notion of a sacred trinity, usually composed of a Mother, Father, and Son – with the Mother (as Mother Earth) often holding priority.[95] Christianity, he believed, was the revelation of the Son, but it had largely forgotten the importance of the Mother, and the stress on the masculine had led to wars, which threatened humanity. His new Christianity would reaffirm the importance of the feminine, peaceful elements within the divinity, and save the world.

Merezhkovsky's fascination with Minoan Crete is therefore unsurprising, since several aspects of its culture resonated with his ideas. In particular, he connected the androgynous, cross-dressing Minoan representations (e.g. the alleged female bull-leapers in the Toreador fresco) and the use of double-axes with his own belief in divine bisexuality. Also, he regarded the Knossian marble cross, found by Evans in the Temple Repositories (see Fig. 1.1), as a symbol of the sun and a foreshadower of Christ. Yet, despite some positive elements of Cretan religion, which prefigured his new Christianity, the picture of Minoan Crete that emerges from *The Birth of the Gods* is somewhat ambiguous: Crete is wonderful and monstrous, seductive and decadent at the same time. Merezhkovsky is fascinated by Minoan art, and describes its aim as 'to destroy the eternal, to perpetuate the momentary, to arrest the flying', a phrase that seems to anticipate Henriette Groenewegen-Frankfort's well-known definition of Minoan art (in her 1951 book *Arrest and Movement*) in terms of disregard for timelessness and acceptance of 'the grace of life' as movement.[96] Merezhkovsky's Minoans are very artistic and 'very charming ... [but] they are devils all the same',[97] largely because they practice human sacrifice in their bull-rings, and have reached a period of decadence. They are long past their Golden Age, when men were peaceful, worshipped a Mother Goddess above all, and did not know the 'god of war and slaughter'.[98] A disquieting mixture of eunuchs, cross-dressing priestesses and priests, sexually forward women, and androgynous youths populates the Knossian palace, the Labyrinth, adding to a feeling of decay. This is perhaps best encapsulated in Merezhkovsky's description of King Idominin: he overturned the matriarchy, killing his own mother, after conspiring 'with the leaders of the people who had grown tired of women's rule'; he is addressed as both King and Queen and wears a bull mask to covers his face, which is 'as flabby and womanish as the faces of the eunuchs by the walls, only it looked still more dead'.[99]

A sense of decline and depravity also appeared a few years later in *The Double Axe: A Romance of Ancient Crete* (1929) by the little-known author Audrey Haggard.[100] In this novel the fall of Knossos is the result of an unholy alliance of petty and often corrupt Cretan kings, devious snake priestesses, and northerners (the Dorians), who revolt against the equally unsavoury King Minos of Knossos. More than a romance, this is a cloak-and-dagger novel, with a sprinkling of interracial love between the hero and heroine: a Minoan youth from Palaikastro and a blonde Dorian princess, who had been enslaved. After a series of adventurous deeds, the Palaikastrian and his beloved eventually escape from Crete, where the conquering Dorians established an even harsher regime: they reach Philistia and start a new, simpler life. There is no Minoan Golden Age in this novel: the only gold is the precious metal with which King Minos is obsessed. Cretans are still worshipping their Great Mother Goddess, but Minoan women (except for priestesses) do not seem to be very relevant. Although the romance between the dark Minoan Palaikastrian and his blonde Dorian has a happy ending, this is only at the cost of becoming exiles.

Also set at a time of Minoan decline, but more romantic and sexually titillating than Haggard's volume, is the 1930 novel *Son of Minos*, by the equally little-known author David Cheney.[101] This novel shares with Merezhkovsky's *The Birth of the Gods* and other works discussed below a keen interest in gender ambiguity and homosexuality, ultimately inspired by Minoan iconography, and anticipates the more daring use of twins in André Gide's *Thésée* (cf. below). The foreword, by the journalist Burton Rascoe, informs the reader (alas, erroneously) that this is 'the first work of fiction to treat at any length of life as it may have been lived in the ancient Minoan civilization – a civilization which, archaeologists tell us, surpassed in grandeur that of Babylon, Nineveh, and Tyre, and may possibly have surpassed in some phases, the civilization we know'; it also remarks that the author 'sustained throughout his narrative a mood and cadence in consonance with the epic nature of his theme'.[102] An epic feel is indeed attained through both style and content, especially with the deliberate admixture of archaeological references with elements of exaggeration and sheer invention.

The story takes place during the Trojan War, and recounts the adventures of the Prince of Taras, from the Italian tribe of the Celeboni. These are distant relations of the Minoans who, in previous generations, had settled in many trading posts all over Italy, as part of a Mediterranean-wide Minoan trade network. The current Cretan 'Minos' (the dynastic title used for the island's kings), during one of his commercial journeys to Italy, chooses the Prince of Taras as his successor, as he has no sons. This causes the displeasure of Minos's brother, Archites of Phaistos, who wants his son Tictys, the effeminate identical twin of his daughter Ariadne, to accede to the Cretan throne. Archites hatches various plots to eliminate the Prince of Taras, which are often foiled by Tictys himself, who has fallen in love with his rival. The Prince of Taras, in turn, feels an increasing guilty attraction towards the girlish Minoan boy.

The novel follows Minos, Archites, the Prince of Taras, and Tictys in their travels from Apulia to Crete, via Venice, Sicily, mainland Greece, and even Troy, where a mighty battle takes place: the Greeks are helped by the Minoans, who are led by Minos, Idomeneus, and the Prince of Taras (who is complimented by Achilles on his fighting prowess).[103] On their final return to Crete, it is revealed that Archites had only one daughter, Ariadne, whom he had forced to impersonate an identical male twin so that she could inherit the Knossian throne, since the Minoan law of succession forbids women from sitting 'upon the Sun-Throne of Crete'.[104] The novel ends with the Prince of Taras becoming the new Minos, marrying Ariadne, and making her 'Queen of Minoa'.[105] One assumes that they will live together happily ever after, but despite the absence of explicit references to nasty barbarians on the horizon, all educated readers will know that this can only be the Minoan swan song.

Overall, Cheney's Minoan Crete is not as decadent as in other works discussed in this chapter: it is a still a strong sea power, with trading posts scattered all over the Mediterranean, technically and artistically more advanced than its neighbours; and the Minoans are 'war-like men, short yet lithe and strong', 'glorious conquerors of the wide Mid Sea, builders of the glory of Labyrinth'.[106] Yet, even in this novel there are some unfavourable signs: some members of the Minoan elite are described as 'milk-sop' youths, wearing strange hairdos and 'peacock clothes';[107] Cheney often underlines that the Minoans are shorter and less vigorous than other people;[108] and the choice of the Prince of Taras as *dauphin* is welcomed in some quarters as an injection of 'new life' in Minoan veins that have become 'cold'.[109] Interestingly, the novel reaches its happy ending by almost inverting contemporary scholarly orthodoxy and general perceptions of Minoan women, who play a minimalist part. There are no references to the famous cowgirls of the Toreador fresco and even to Evans's Great Mother Goddess, who is replaced by a variety of divinities, especially a Bull God. In fact, far from presenting Minoan Crete as a paragon of gender equality, let alone as the proto-feminist paradise envisaged by Jules Bois two decades earlier, perhaps the clearest message that emerges from the novel is that women are unhappy when forced to take on male roles.

By contrast, a feminist stance appears in *The Winged Girl of Knossos* (1933), a children's novel written and illustrated by Erick Berry (nom de plume of Allena Champlin), which received the Newbery Honor award in 1934.[110] The novel was partly inspired by Greek myths about Crete, visits to the Metropolitan Museum in New York, Evans's publications, and other works discussed above.[111] Like many others, it is set in a period of Minoan decadence vs. Aryan/Greek ascendancy, since it is a modern reimagining of the traditional myth of Theseus's Cretan adventure, but with a happy ending for the female characters. The novel uses allusion to Minoan material culture for historical colour, and many of the illustrations are representations of well-known Minoan artefacts, especially frescoes, while others are Berry's own imaginative creations (see Fig. 4.3a–b). Minoan illustrations in children books of this period are rather uncommon, but Louise Lamprey's *Children of Ancient Greece* (1928) and Naomi Mitchison's *Boys and Girls and Gods* (1931) offer two other rare examples (see Figs. 4.4 and 4.5), which can be compared with Berry's.[112]

In *The Winged Girl of Knossos* the main protagonist is Inas, who replaces the traditional Icarus of Greek mythology. She is the feisty, tomboy, proto-feminist daughter of a Greek slave woman and the local genius, Daidalos, a name that, according to Berry, was transmitted along generations of craftsmen, together with their skills, in a manner reminiscent of the dynastic interpretation of the word Minos. Crete has been a peaceful

Fig. 4.3a–b Two illustrations from Berry's *The Winged Girl of Knossos* (1933), one (a) modelled on the well-known Knossian fresco 'Ladies in Blue' (after Evans 1921: fig. 397), the other (b) using Minoan elements and Berry's imagination.

land for almost two millennia, and this is perceived as something negative: à la H. G. Wells, Berry shows that this peace helped to create wonderful art, but also a dangerous sense of security, which enfeebled its elite and encouraged bigotry. Minoan courtiers are precious and effete. Minos is a wizened, jaundiced old man, wearing a feathered crown: a decrepit version of the Prince of Lilies fresco. More and more mercenaries are used as troops, and war is effectively practised only as ritual, at the Bull Festivals; slaves perform the bull-leaping, instead of youths from the Minoan elite as in older times.

Only Daidalos seems alert to the growing menace from other countries and wants to fortify Crete, since he believes that its 'wooden walls' no longer provide adequate defence. Minos, however, is unsupportive. Thus, the frustrated Daidalos, helped by his daughter, turns his efforts to a new enterprise: flying.[113] Their experiments, however, must be kept secret, since the devitalized and narrow-minded Cretans would consider flying as sacrilegious sorcery. As Daidalos exclaims, 'Witchcraft! How could the people, common, ignorant, sunk in nearly twenty centuries of peace and ease, forgive a man

Fig. 4.4 Detail of one illustration by Edna F. Hart-Hubon in Lamprey's *Children of Ancient Greece* (1928).

Fig. 4.5 Detail of illustration from Mitchison's *Boys and Girls and Gods* (1931).

who dared defy the laws of the gods and become a bird?'[114] Meanwhile Theseus arrives in Crete for the Bull-Festivals. He is rather uncouth, but his forceful manliness arouses Ariadne. Thus, the rest of the story follows the main lines of the traditional myth, but there are some intriguing variants. Theseus kills a bull (instead of a Minotaur) and elopes with Ariadne, thanks to Inas's help; Inas escapes from Crete using the flying device created by her father to reach a nearby boat, which will eventually lead her to Athens, where she finds Ariadne living in a blissfully happy marriage with Theseus.

Minoan decadence and Aryan vigour loom large also in the slightly later novel by the Icelandic author Kristmann Guðmundsson, *Gyðjan og uxinn: skáldsaga* ('The Goddess and the Bull: a novel', 1937), translated into English as *Winged Citadel* (1940), which also contains explicit references to homosexuality. Set in the final days of Knossos, the story is narrated by a young Macedonian immigrant to Crete, who eventually becomes the 'Minos' as consort of the Minoan queen. At first, he admires the Minoans' peaceful, egalitarian, matrilineal, sexually liberated society, and especially their desire to attain freedom and equality for all humankind. With time, however, he questions the Minoans' peaceful liberalism and over-refined civilization. They have allowed the rise of extremist factions and paved the way for the inevitable Mycenaean conquest of Crete: they were 'a gentle and decadent race, bred in a humane, civilized atmosphere', and too vulnerable to military attacks.[115]

A comparable ambivalence about Minoan Crete appears in the much more famous novel *Sinuhe egyptiläinen* (1945) by the Finnish author Mika Waltari, translated into English as *Sinuhe the Egyptian* (1949). A bestseller that was even made into a Hollywood film,[116] this historical novel tells the adventures of Sinuhe, an Egyptian physician at the time of Akhenaton, who travels to the Levant, Babylon, the Hittite kingdom, and Minoan Crete.[117] Sinuhe's first impression of Crete is that of a sophisticated and happy land, its people unencumbered by thought of death and sexual conventions: 'Nowhere in the world, then, have I beheld anything so strange and fair as Crete, though I have journeyed in all known lands … No one acts but by the impulse of the moment, and the minds of the people veer from hour to hour … death is not acknowledged among them, nor do I believe they have named it.'[118] Minoan Crete is also a paradise for sexual swingers (Sinuhe is particularly impressed by female boldness). Eventually, however, he comes to regard Minoan sexual freedom as 'wantonness' and 'immoderate lechery'.[119] This is a land of 'ease and gaiety',[120] which has a darker side: the Minoans practice human sacrifice as offering to a live bull-god, who ensures the island's prosperity and whose death, according to a prophecy, will cause its decline. Minea, a Cretan woman with whom Sinuhe has fallen in love, becomes one of the sacrificial victims, and he discover that the bull-god has, in fact, been dead for months: the Minoan high priest (whose hereditary title is 'Minotaur') has kept the secret and killed the victims himself in a desperate effort to maintain his people's belief in Cretan power and avert its prophesized end. Sinuhe recalls that, on leaving the island, he even rejoiced at the thought of the disappearance of this strange civilization:

> I reflected that the god of Crete was dead and that the might of Crete would now
> decline according to the prophecy. I was in no way cast down by this although the
> Cretans had shown me kindness, and their mirth sparkled like sea spray on the

shore. When I came near the city, I was glad to think that those airy, delicate buildings would one day be in flames and that the lecherous cries of women would turn into mortal shrieks, that Minotauros' mask of gold would be beaten flat and divided among the rest of the spoils and that nothing would remain of the splendid majesty of Crete. The very island would sink again into the sea from which, with other marvels of the deep, it had once arisen.[121]

In the period encompassed by the two World Wars, Minoan Crete fared no better even among Cretan writers, as some of Nikos Kazantzakis's works illustrate, especially his monumental epic poem *The Odyssey: A Modern Sequel* (1938). This vies with Merezhkovsky's earlier *Birth of the Gods*, Waltari's *Sinuhe*, and Gide's later *Thésée* for the most debauched and oversexualized portrayal of the Minoans. Kazantzakis's *Odyssey*, a modernist epic comprising 33,333 verses, picks up the story of Odysseus from book 22 of the Homeric *Odyssey* (the massacre of the suitors) and follows the hero's story until his death. Soon after returning to Ithaka, Odysseus gets rather bored. Spurred by a wanderer's lust, he travels to Crete, Egypt, the head of the river Nile, the southern tip of Africa and reaches Antarctica, where he dies. On the first leg his journey, he is accompanied by Helen, who willingly leaves Menelaus and Sparta once again. The twilight of Bronze Age Crete is described especially in books V and VI. Kazantzakis's verses provide plenty of allusions to bare-breasted females, bull-leaping action, double-axes, and other Minoan niceties. As observed by Roderick Beaton, the Minoan elite appears as 'an out-and-out bad lot' and prefigures the decadence of contemporary Western bourgeoisie.[122] Minoan Crete is an oppressive and depraved society, addicted to blood sports, sexually extravagant and excessive. The elite oppresses the common people and thrives on slavery. The senile King Idomeneus harbours incestuous passions for one of his own daughters, and is keen on 'blood to flow' and on 'lewd erotic rites'.[123] The reader is regaled with descriptions of bull-leaping rituals carried out by young lesbian virgins, who end up gored to death; of priestesses, called the 'Holy Harlots', spreading lust among the crowds; and of ritual copulation between Idomeneus, impersonating the Bull-God, and his chosen bride (Helen), impersonating Mother Earth, in a bronze bed made in the shape of a cow. The bull-leaping and sacred-marriage rituals are followed by frenzied orgies, fuelled by the consumption of raw flesh from a sacrificed bull. But the end is nigh, as foreigners (the Dorians) have discovered a new secret weapon: iron. They join the oppressed slaves (led by one of Idomeneus's own daughters) and storm the palace, which is engulfed in a fire. The only positive characters emerging from this work are the poor peasants, the Cretan salt of the earth, who are reminiscent of their contemporary counterpart, and perhaps offer some element of continuity from the distant Minoan past to Kazantzakis's present.[124]

Decadent Minoans also appear in two other works by Kazantzakis: the children's novel *At the Palace of Knossos*, published in the 1980s but written in 1940, and his play *Kouros*, written in 1949.[125] Despite their considerable differences, both offer modern retellings of the myth of Theseus and the Minotaur and an overall vision of Minoan Crete comparable, in some respects, to that found in *The Odyssey*: a spent force, enervated by peaceful Oriental luxury, oppressive and cruel, dominated by femininity, whose conquest by more masculine, dynamic northern Hellenic tribes is a well-deserved outcome. In *Kouros* this change is presented as a quasi-homoerotic encounter between Theseus and the Minotaur, which recalls Gide's later treatment of the subject (cf. below), but with a rather different symbolism: in Kazantzakis's play the monster emerges from this encounter transformed into the statue of a Kouros as an emblem of the triumph of the Hellenic over the Minoan or, at least, of the transformation of the Minoan into the Hellenic; in Gide's novel the homoeroticism is more marked and related to the idea of individual identity (including sexuality) and self-discovery, as discussed below.

In *The Odyssey*, *At the Palace of Knossos*, and *Kouros* the decadent view of the Minoans, and their elites in particular, owes much to the author's well-known fascination with Lenin and Spengler, which is expressed in his choice of physical and chronological setting (the Knossian palace, the period of Achaean conquest) as well as the dramatic portrayal of Minoan and Aryan/Mycenaean worlds as antithetical. As Beaton has observed, however, the Minoans that emerge from these works (and also in *Zorba the Greek*) could be seen as 'a doomed digression from an eternal and unchanging Cretan spirit which is older still'.[126] This older Cretan spirit is a form of *Weltanschauung* encapsulated in Kazantzakis's phrase 'the Cretan glance', which could be traced back to Minoan times, as Kazantzakis explained in a letter to a friend of May 1943, discussing his *Odyssey*:

> Neither Greece nor the East, but Crete, is the key enabling one to enter the *Odyssey*. If that is satisfactorily explained, the *Odyssey* becomes simple, totally illuminated. Minoan Crete expresses what I want to say – Minoan Crete with its frightful earthquakes symbolized by the bull, and the game that the Cretans played *precisely with the bull*. To regard the abyss without fear; on the contrary, to wrestle with it, play with it comfortably – that's what I call the Cretan glance. It explains, I believe, how my soul was perfectly illuminated for the first time, continuing an age-old impetus that emerged originally in Crete and still exists. This is how Crete is perfectly distinguished from the East and from Greece, just as it is geographically. For me, Crete constitutes Synthesis.[127]

As discussed in the next chapter, despite tracing the origins of the special 'Cretan glance' to Minoan Crete in some of his 1930s–1940s writings, Kazantzakis presented a positive overview of Bronze Age Crete only in his later autobiographical *Report to Greco*.

My last example in this section on Minoan decadence and problematic sexuality is André Gide's already mentioned last novel, *Thésée*, published in 1946 but conceived at least a decade earlier.[128] This recounts the famous Cretan episode of Theseus and the Minotaur, which occupies most of the book, and the founding of a new Athens. It presents an ironic version of the myth, as a springboard from which the French author considers modern issues ranging from personal freedom and fulfilment to the conscious and the unconscious, the function of art and poetry, interpersonal relationships, one's legacy, and, last but not least, sexuality, identity, and spirituality. Gide's main sources are the stories about Theseus transmitted in various classical authors, especially Plutarch, Strabo, Sophocles, and Euripides, as well as more recent versions, such as Racine's *Phèdre*. Numerous passages in the novel, however, indicate that he engaged with Minoan archaeology (for which the volume by Glotz discussed above was Gide's main source).[129] For example, Gide's Minos wears a necklace with fleurs-de-lys and a feathered crown, as in Evans's famous reconstruction of the 'Priest-King' or 'Prince of Lilies' fresco (see Fig. 3.13), while bare-breasted women wear flounced skirts. Similarly, Gide's descriptions of the Minoan acrobatic 'corrida' and of the large Knossian courtyards, monumental balustraded staircase, and winding corridors show familiarity with the archaeological discoveries. This direct engagement with the material culture of Minoan Crete is further reflected in Massimo Campigli's illustrations for the 1949 English edition of the book (see Figs. 4.6 and 4.7),[130] some of which play on the androgynous, cross-dressing representations in Minoan iconography, as indeed does Gide's text (cf. below).

From this melange of archaeological and literary sources, Gide's Minoan Crete emerges as utterly exotic, alien, and sophisticated but also quite decadent. Theseus's encounter with this 'other' helps him to discover his Greek identity, and he eventually overcomes his initial feelings of inferiority. In a passage that recalls Spengler's encounter between Minoans and Mycenaeans, Theseus recalls: 'I cannot describe how foreign the Cretans appeared to me to be ... At the court of Minos I realized for the first time that I was a Hellene, and I felt very far from home. All unfamiliar things took me by surprise – dress, customs, ways of behaving ... household objects and the manner of their use. Among so much that was exquisite, I felt like a savage.'[131] Crete's cultural sophistication is accompanied by sexual complexity and diversity: pederasty is widespread; women are very forward, taking the initiative in seduction; and some women take a mystic

Fig. 4.6 One of Massimo Campigli's illustration for Gide's *Theseus* (1949), showing the twins Phaedra and Glaucus exchanging their clothes (reproduced by courtesy of Massimo Campigli Archives; photo N. Momigliano).

Fig. 4.7 Massimo Campigli, test lithography for Gide's *Theseus*: cf. Fig. 4.6 (work in possession of N. Momigliano, reproduced by courtesy of Massimo Campigli Archives; photo: N. Momigliano).

view of sex as union with the divine. The androgynous representations of youths in Minoan Crete, especially the cross-dressing young 'girls' in the Toreador fresco (see Fig. 1.4), which captured so many people's imagination, struck a chord in Gide too. Gide's Theseus does not find mature and voluptuous Ariadne attractive, unlike her younger, *gamine* sister Phaedra, who is the 'absolute double' of her twin brother Glaucus.[132] After his encounter with the Minotaur, Theseus escapes with both sisters: he persuades Phaedra to dress up like her twin Glaucus and pretends that he wants to make him his boy-lover, since this would be perfectly understandable on Crete (see Figs. 4.6–4.7). Moreover, Gide's labyrinth, anticipating later psychedelic interpretations, is a place where one can 'satisfy every kind of appetite', including the use of narcotics.[133] In other words, Gide's Minoan labyrinth is a place where people could escape from, but do not want to, and the Minotaur is not a monster, but a young beautiful male creature, a 'harmonious blending of human and animal elements', whom Theseus discovers in a meadow of flowers (perhaps recalling Evans's flowery background in the 'Prince of Lilies' fresco, Fig. 3.13).[134] Theseus's memory of how he killed the Minotaur is blurred but 'voluptuous'.[135]

The high attainments but also decadence, strangeness, and otherness of Minoan Crete, exemplified in the works discussed above, find a match in other genres, in which this ambivalence can be expressed as disappointment and even out-and-out dislike. These perceptions often emerge through comparisons between Minoan Crete and Classical Greece, in which the former is found wanting. This is particularly well illustrated in travel writing (including travel diaries), as discussed in the next section.

Minoan otherness as decadence in travel writing between the wars

Disappointment in and even dislike for things Minoan can be found in many accounts of Cretan journeys made in the 1920s and early 1930s that were penned by well-known authors, such as Evelyn Waugh, Mario Praz, Jacques de Lacretelle, and Camille Mauclair (nom de plume of Séverin Faust), and by the philosopher-historian R. G. Collingwood.[136] Given their negative responses, it is probably just as well that their journeys did not involve that paragon of Neo-Minoan–Art Deco style, the ocean liner *Aramis* (see Fig. 4.2), which, ironically, never travelled to Crete on its route from Marseilles to China.[137]

Waugh's entertaining *Labels: A Mediterranean Journal* (1930) describes his one-day visit to the Heraklion Museum and the site of Knossos. His reaction to 'the barbarities of Minoan culture' was that they showed 'nothing to suggest any genuine aesthetic feeling at all'.[138] He was more charitable regarding the artistic merits of Minoan frescoes, but suspected that the artists-restorers 'tempered their zeal for accurate reconstruction with a somewhat inappropriate predilection for the covers of *Vogue*,'[139] an observation that intersects and even anticipates subsequent interpretations of the supposed impact of Art Nouveau on Minoan restorations.[140] Waugh's comments on Knossos and Evans's reconstructions are withering: 'if our English Lord Evans ever finishes even a part of his vast undertaking, it will be a place of oppressive wickedness', while the original ruins emanate something 'fearful and malignant', and even the so-called throne of King Minos (see Fig. 3.7) is a 'squat little throne . . . not the seat of a lawgiver nor a divan for the recreation of a soldier; here an aging despot might crouch and have borne to him, along the walls of a whispering gallery, barely audible intimations of his own murder'.[141]

De Lacretelle's slightly longer visit to Crete (about six days), described in his *Le demi-dieu ou le Voyage de Grèce* (1931), was similarly unsatisfactory, despite his claim that he did not leave the island disappointed.[142] Even if he was escorted around Knossos by Sir Arthur Evans himself on the first of several visits he made to the site, the French novelist (who later became a member of the Académie française) was unimpressed, as shown by his remarks on the uninspiring location as well as on the lack of architectural symmetry and grandiosity, even in comparison with Mycenaean monuments (let alone Greek ones). He acknowledges that there is comfort, colour, and attention to detail in Minoan ruins, but his overall impression is simply underwhelming. His views on Evans's reconstructions are not entirely negative, but only because he considers them as a revenge of the senses over the spiritual speculations, because before one can imagine, one must see.[143] Yet, these reconstructions contribute to the sense of otherness, since they make Knossos look so different from other Greek archaeological sites. He is more effusive in his descriptions of frescoes and objects in the Heraklion Museum, but even these elicit only partial admiration and an overall impression of decadence: they bring to mind the collection of an aesthete. He muses on how the writer and art critic Edmond de Goncourt would have been infatuated with Minoan art, because it is so reminiscent of Japan, and on how D'Annunzio and Montesquieu might have admired the Prince of Lilies, had they set their eyes on it. The site of Hagia Triada prompts similar impressions of decadence, since it reminds de Lacretelle of Granada and Boabdil, and the latter of the Knossian 'Prince of Lilies' (cf. chapter's epigraph). De Lacretelle even admits that the more he spends time on Crete familiarizing himself with Minoan sites and museum collections, the more he craves for the temples of Attica. The treasures of Mycenae, which he had visited earlier, had already made him dream of the achievements that came afterward, and his visit to Crete merely reinforced his negative response to the Aegean Bronze Age generally. For de Lacretelle, the main problem with Minoan (and Mycenaean) art is that it lacked grand themes, symbolism, and ideas.

Camille Mauclair, a prolific French poet, novelist, and literary and art critic, was possibly even more disappointed by Minoan Crete than de Lacretelle. In his *Le pur visage de la Grèce* (1934), he describes his first impression of Knossos as a place that is dead and does not inspire emotions.[144] Even if Mauclair does not dare to criticize Evans's aims, scientific accuracy, and use of ferro-concrete, he thinks that the British archaeologist tried too hard. Mauclair finds the reconstructions disagreeable and more evocative of modern garages than a 4,000-year-old culture. His overall impression of Knossos is one of artificiality, and the site reminds him of pavilions in colonial exhibitions (a likely reference to the *Exposition Coloniale Internationale* held in Paris in 1931). He leaves the site with feelings of discontent and irritation. His visit to the Heraklion Museum produces more positive reactions, but still far from enthusiastic: he is effusive about the modernity of Minoan frescoes and writes admiringly of some well-known carved stone-vases from Hagia Triada and Knossos, which he compares to works by Antoine Bourdelle and Antoine-Louis Barye. Yet, he finds the famous faience figurines of the snake goddess and her votary (see Fig. 1.1) disquieting and comic at the same time. His overall conclusion is that Minoan art is far too distant to provoke emotions: like de Lacretelle, he is happy to return to more familiar Athens and its Acropolis.[145] Unlike de Lacretelle, however, who was unimpressed by the Mycenaean ruins because they reminded him of Cretan decadence, Mauclair includes them among his discussion of 'true Greece': he finds them majestic and fascinating, expressing an intriguing savage barbarity, evocative of the Vandals and medieval times,[146] thus echoing, once again, Spengler's comments on Mycenae vs. Knossos.

Mario Praz's visit to Crete (c. 1931) lasted several days and included excursions to the Heraklion Museum and the archaeological sites of Knossos, Phaistos, Hagia Triada, and the recently excavated palace at Malia.[147] The impressions of this anglophile Italian writer are more positive than de Lacretelle's and Mauclair's, but still present the hallmarks of high expectation followed by disappointment. On his arrival, he greets Crete as one of the noblest Mediterranean islands, the cradle of Western civilization and the homeland of 'thalassocrats' – a term that he cherishes, for it has a flavour of D'Annunzio and evokes an impressive series of sea powers: Crete, Corinth, Athens, Venice, and England. He also perceives Minoan Crete as the link in the chain between two civilizations, Egypt and Greece, whose artistic expressions are solid and static, whereas Minoan art is eminently dynamic, almost impressionistic, and reminiscent of Gothic and Japanese art. The account of his visit to the Heraklion Museum provides some lively and appreciative descriptions of Minoan finds, especially regarding seductive ladies and athletic women dressed as men found in Minoan frescoes. Some iconic Minoan finds, however, appear to him as unappealing and inspire a sense of decadence. For example, Praz describes the snake goddess figurines as having staring eyes, a yellowish jaundiced complexion, and overflowing breasts: after initial surprise, they do not invite further scrutiny. He finds that the Prince of Lilies would be perfect as the frontispiece illustration of the super-decadent *Princes de Nacre et de Caresse* by Jean Lorrain. Praz's overall impression of Minoan Crete, after his museum visit, is one of superficial closeness and profound distance, otherness, a different 'rhythm'.[148]

His visit to the archaeological site of Knossos is even more disappointing. Praz found the site garish, while the reproductions of frescoes, such as the charging bull at the north entrance, reminded him of the Bovril billboards that dominated English cities (see Fig. 4.8a–b) – an image that will be ironically evoked some decades later in some adverts for the Liebig Extract of Meat Company (cf. Chapter 5: 183–4). A reconstructed small building in the palace (probably the 'North Lustral Basin', Fig. 4.9) brings to his mind memories as unpoetic as the public lavatories in some Italian train stations.[149] Although other Minoan sites such as Phaistos, Hagia Triada, and Malia elicit more positive reactions, for Praz Crete remains strange, distant, and ultimately Oriental. Like his French colleagues, he is glad to return to Athens, to see again the Parthenon and enjoy its serenity, measure, and perfection.[150]

The British philosopher-archaeologist-historian R. G. Collinwood, on his visit to Knossos (7–12 April 1932), was similarly reminded of public toilets and longed for the balanced perfection of Classical Greece. He recorded his reactions to Knossos in a travel diary, from which Sinclair Hood has published the relevant excerpts.[151] Collingwood starts his account by stating that 'The first impression on the mind of a

a   b

Fig. 4.8a–b (a) Knossos, the North Entrance, with replica of charging bull fresco (photo N. Momigliano). (b) This replica reminded Mario Praz of Bovril posters, such as the one illustrated here (photo: Victoria and Albert Museum; © Univiler).

Fig. 4.9 Knossos, west view of the North Lustral Basin, which reminded Mario Praz of public lavatories (photo: N. Momigliano).

visitor is that Knossian architecture consists of garages and public lavatories.'[152] He reflects that his negative perception is partly due to Evans's reconstructions and matters of detail, such as 'flat-roofed shed-like buildings', and partly to his feeling that Minoan buildings 'are designed with no reference to sound canons of proportions, and are therefore undignified and mean ... no taste, no elegance, no sense of proportion'.[153] In short, Collingwood concludes that, from an aesthetic point of view, Minoan Crete is the antithesis of Greece: the secret of the former's modernity is its barbarous utilitarianism, in contrast to the latter's endeavour to express an ideal and attain beauty (ideas that remind one closely of de Lacretelle's earlier writings).

But, as the saying goes, beauty is in the eye of the beholder: the Minoans continued to find enthusiastic supporters in the periods framed by the two World Wars as much as they had done in the late Belle Époque, and often precisely because of their non-Hellenic, primitive, exotic, and sensual otherness, as illustrated in some of the works discussed in the following section.

Minoan otherness as hope: Minoan Crete as sexual promise and feminine Garden of Eden

A slightly ambiguous, yet quite appreciative, response to Minoan distance and otherness appears in Marcel Brion's popular *La résurrection des villes mortes*, first published in 1937. This author, historian, and member of the Académie française wrote effusively about Minoan civilization, which he regarded as perfect in all respects.[154] At the same time, comparisons of Minoan and recent European styles, previously employed by many authors to familiarize, domesticate, and Europeanize Crete (cf. Chapter 3), for Brion reveal profound differences. His parallels range from Jean-Antoine Watteau and French Rococo to Constantin Guys. Yet, he concludes that, even if Minoan art shares a 'hyperaesthesia' of taste with more recent artistic trends, these analogies are superficial and, in fact, expose notions of space and time that are quite different from what one finds in later European art.[155]

A strong sense of otherness and opposition to Classical Greece in terms of art, architecture, and religion, but without negative connotations, also recurs in another French work published in 1937 – the article on Minoan Crete, titled 'Jeux d'ombre sur l'Hellade. Style de vie du monde minoen', by the French intellectual and member of the Académie française Roger Caillois. First published in the magazine *Le Voyage en Grèce*,[156] this essay underlines the extreme elegance of Minoan civilization and its fundamental dualism, illustrated by its art, which for Caillois is at the service of something mysterious and earthy ('des plus nocturne réactions vitales').[157] His interpretation of the Minoan world as full of Dionysian impulses probably owes more to later Greek myths about Crete (and scholars such as Jane Harrison) than the material culture of Bronze Age Crete (and Evans). Nevertheless, he makes interesting observations on Minoan archaeology, e.g. on the theatricality of Knossian architecture and its sacred as well as temporal uses.

In other authors the feelings of Minoan distance and otherness are transformed into a sense of mysterious, Oriental, and earthy sexual promise, albeit of a more conformist, heterosexual kind than that portrayed by Merezhkovsky, Kazantzakis or

Gide. An early example of this is the poem 'Minoan Porcelain' (*c.* 1917) by Aldous Huxley, later of *Brave New World* fame, which appears to address one of the replicas of the faience figurines of the 'snake goddesses' from Knossos (see Fig. 1.1). The poem was probably inspired by a visit to the Ashmolean museum in Oxford, where Huxley read English at Balliol College between 1913 and 1916. By that time, the Ashmolean had on display numerous Minoan finds as well as replicas, including those of the 'snake goddesses'.[158] Huxley's poem hails the woman as a priestess of an unknown, distant 'strange cult', whose attire and exposed breasts excite desire and promises erotic fulfilment:

> Her eyes of bright unwinking glaze
> All imperturbable do not
> Even make pretences to regard
> The justing absence of her stays,
> Where many a Tyrian gallipot
> Excites desire with spilth of nard.
> The bistred rims above the fard
> Of cheeks as red as bergamot
> Attest that no shamefaced delays
> Will clog fulfilment, nor retard
> Full payment of the Cyprian's praise
> Down to the last remorseful jot.
> Hail priestess of we know not what
> Strange cult of Mycenean days![159]

About three decades later, Cecil Day-Lewis, another Oxford alumnus and a future poet laureate, wrote a poem on the same subject, 'Statuette-Late Minoan', which is also likely to have been inspired by a visit to the Ashmolean museum during his time at Wadham College, where he read Classics and studied under Maurice Bowra.[160] The poem expresses feelings of distance and mystery ('I seem to be peering at you through the wrong end of time'), and the poet does not know whether the statuette represents a goddess or a woman, nor can he imagine the religion behind her image. Yet, despite the sense of distance, she continues to 'warm us today' and exert an earthy sexual promise ('you are earth . . . the offered breast'):

> Girl of the musing mouth,
> The mid archaic air,
> For whom do you subtly smile?
> Yield to what power or prayer
> Breasts vernally bare?
>
> I seem to be peering at you through the wrong end of time
> That shrinks to a bright, far image
> Great Mother of earth's prime–
> A stature sublime.

So many golden ages
Of sunshine steeped your clay
So dear did the maker cherish
In you life's fostering ray,
That you warm us today

Goddess or girl, you are earth.
The smile, the offered breast –
They were the dream of one
Thirsting as I for rest,
As I, unblest.

D. H. Lawrence, a friend of Aldous Huxley, also composed a Minoan-themed poem that, albeit not inspired by the 'snake goddess', evokes a sense of remoteness but also promise, like those of Huxley and Day-Lewis. This is titled 'The Middle of the World', was written in 1929, not long before Lawrence's death in March 1930, and was published posthumously.[161] Ocean liners and 'other stinkers', he writes, cross 'the Minoan distance', but even if modern devices can bring people to Crete more easily, 'the distance never changes'. For Lawrence the Minoans speak 'the music of lost languages', and yet are also the future, since the 'slim naked men from Cnossos ... will without fail come back again':

This sea will never die, neither will it grow old,
nor cease to be blue, nor in the dawn
cease to lift up its hills
and let the slim black ship of Dionysos come sailing in
with grape-vines up the mast, and dolphins leaping.
What do I care if the smoking ships
of the P. & O. and the Orient Line and all the other stinkers
cross like clock-work the Minoan distance!
They only cross, the distance never changes.
And now that the moon who gives men glistening bodies
is in her exaltation, and can look down on the sun,
I see descending from the ships at dawn
slim naked men from Cnossos, smiling the archaic smile
of those that will without fail come back again,
and kindling little fires upon the shores
and crouching, and speaking the music of lost languages.
And the Minoan Gods and the Gods of Tiryns
are heard softly laughing and chatting, as ever;
and Dionysos, young, and a stranger
leans listening on the gate, in all respect.

Lawrence never visited Crete, but in 1922 he saw at least its snow-capped mountains from the boat on which he was sailing towards the Suez Canal, on his way to Ceylon.[162]

His interest in the Minoans, as shown by this poem, letters, and other writings, seems to have been sparked by a feeling of affinity between them and his beloved Etruscans, whom he described in his *Etruscan Places* as mysterious, earthy, full of vitality, lustful, and carefree.[163] His Minoans partake of these Etruscan qualities, representing a distant, primitive past, but also an idealized golden age that offers hope for a better future.[164]

The notion of artistic and possibly ethnic affinities between Minoans and Etruscans was not new: it had been noted by many others, including Evans, by the early 1900s.[165] But these earlier Minoan–Etruscan comparisons did not extend to sexual vitality and erotic promise, which make an appearance also in the work of the Italian literary critic, art-historian, and author Emilio Cecchi, who visited Crete in the early 1930s. In his *Et in Arcadia Ego* (1936), which describes his travels in Greece of *c.* 1934, Cecchi remarks that entering Greece from Crete is like entering Italy from Etruria.[166] He also comments on the Oriental character of ancient Crete, albeit touched by something more personal, prefiguring Homer.[167] The Minoan ruins of Knossos appear to him as remarkable, but also as disappointing and distant.[168] Besides, he finds the admixture of ancient remains and Evans's restorations, including replicas of frescoes, rather disturbing.[169] Nevertheless, Greek myths and beautiful Minoan artefacts in the Heraklion Museum allow Cecchi to populate the Knossian ruins with graceful ghosts and to convince himself that he would have liked living at Knossos immensely (Minoan cruelty was merely Athenian propaganda to inflate Theseus's glory).[170] Cecchi dreams of meeting Ariadne, the woman 'who opens a path to knowledge through love': he feels she is close and yet unattainable, because he missed his rendezvous by 'three thousand and five-hundred years'.[171] He is glad to catch a few glimpses of Ariadne also on mainland Greece, as he sees Mycenaean art as a continuation of the Minoan.[172] Yet, like most authors discussed so far, Cecchi underlines the dichotomy between Minoans and the Mycenaeans: Minoan Crete is carefree, airy, light-hearted, feminine, a magic of spring, with a whiff of the Orient; Mycenaean Greece emanates egoism, tyranny, and feudalism: it is a 'masterpiece of bullying, of individual violence'.[173]

Idealized, utopian, joyful, earthy, peaceful, feminine Minoans and, by contrast, ponderous, cruel, barbarous, and oppressive Mycenaeans reappear in the pages of Henry Miller's *The Colossus of Maroussi* (1941), a book that has been described as the 'most nakedly pacifist response to Knossos', and its American author as 'the man most responsible for uncovering these libidinal Minoans from the ruins of Knossos'.[174]

Miller visited Crete in 1939, after the start of the Second World War. Before his Greek journey, he had been working on a never-completed book on D. H. Lawrence, with whom he shared the view of the Minoans as a wonderful archaic world, close to that of the Etruscans.[175] He had been dreaming of visiting Knossos for many years, after reading works by Evans, as he mentions in his *The Colossus of Maroussi* and correspondence with his friend,[176] the British author Lawrence Durrell, who jokingly claimed descent from the Minoans (cf. chapter's epigraph) – a shared admiration for the Cretan past rooted in their invention of a Greek 'paradise' that would 'keep the war at a safe distance and give both of them, at least for a while, all the new life they longed for'.[177]

Miller's Cretan sojourn lasted several days and involved visits to the Heraklion Museum, Knossos, Gortyn, and Phaistos. Despite his high expectations, he was not disappointed. On the contrary, Miller's views of the Minoans are arguably more idealistic than Evans's, and he even appreciated the reconstructions at Knossos.[178] Miller's Minoan Crete, as encapsulated by Knossos, is opulent, sophisticated, powerful yet peaceful, joyful, salubrious, egalitarian, feminist, and reminiscent of all that was positive not only among the Etruscans, but also the Incas, Chinese, and French:

> There has been much controversy about the aesthetics of Sir Arthur Evans' work of restoration. I found myself unable to come to any conclusion about it; I accepted it as fact. However Knossos may have looked in the past, however it may look in the future, this one which Evans has created is the only one I shall ever know. I am grateful to him for what he did ... Knossos in all its manifestations suggests the splendor and sanity and opulence of a powerful and peaceful people. It is gay – gay, healthful, sanitary, salubrious. The common people played a great role, that is evident. It has been said that throughout its long history every form of government known to man was tested out; in many ways it is far closer in spirit to modern times, to the twentieth century, I might say, than other later epochs of the Hellenic world. One feels the influence of Egypt, the homely human immediacy of the Etruscan world, the wise communal organizing spirit of Inca days. I do not pretend to know, but I felt, as I have seldom felt before the ruins of the past, that here throughout long centuries there reigned an era of peace. There is something down to earth about Knossus, the sort of atmosphere which is evoked when one says Chinese or French. The religious note seems to be graciously diminished; women played an important, equal role in the affairs of this people; a spirit of play is markedly noticeable. In short, the prevailing note is one of joy. One feels that man lived to live, that he was not plagued by thoughts of a life beyond, that he was not smothered and restricted by undue reverence for the ancestral spirits, that he was religious in the only way which is becoming to man, by making the most of everything that comes to hand, by extracting the utmost of life from every passing minute. Knossos was worldly in the best sense of the word.[179]

Unlike Waugh, who referred to it as a 'squat little throne' unsuitable for a lawgiver, Miller's first impression was that the 'great throne chair of Minos – in itself speaks volumes. One did not sit down in this seat as one now takes a chair. One lowered the full, majestic body to make a magical contact with the earth ... It was a seat of justice, everything carefully weighed, carefully deliberated. In the legend one thinks of Minos as a monster exacting tribute. When one descends to the seat one feels that he was a great legislator.'[180] Miller bestowed similar praise on Phaistos, describing it as a serene Garden of Eden – a place that contained 'all the element of the heart' and was 'feminine through and through',[181] unlike Tiryns and Mycenae. Minoan Crete 'stands for a culture based upon peace: Tiryns smells of cruelty, barbarism, suspicion, isolation. It is like an H. G. Wells setting for a prehistoric drama, for a thousand years' war between one-eyed giants and blunder-footed dinosaurs', while Mycenae is similarly reminiscent of 'a cruel and intelligent monster which had been bled to death'.[182] At Mycenae 'gods once walked the earth', but 'everything about the place is contradictory ... grim, lovely, seductive and repellent'.[183]

The powerful theme of a Minoan feminine Garden of Eden overpowered by patriarchal Aryans appears in other literary works of the 1940s, such as Robert Graves's essay on the nature of poetic myth-making, *The White Goddess: A Historical Grammar of Poetic Myth* (1948), and his futuristic novel *Seven Days in New Crete* (1949), which encapsulate ideas that also underpinned Grave's later, popular, and influential *Greek Myths* (1955).[184] For example, in *The White Goddess*, Graves maintained that the language of poetic myth found in the ancient Mediterranean and northern Europe was originally a magical language (a 'true' poetic language) linked with religious ceremonies in honour of a moon goddess, who acted as a kind of muse; this language, however, had been 'tampered with in late Minoan times' by Aryan invaders from Central Asia, who introduced patriarchy and remodelled the myths 'to justify the social changes'.[185] In *Seven Days in New Crete*, Graves presents a futuristic utopian world partly inspired by Minoan Crete. Despite Graves's admiration for goddess-centred, magical poetry, and women as muses, his assessment of New Crete is rather ambivalent, as illustrated below.

Seven Days in New Crete is set in a future Golden Age, in which the demise of Christian civilization, through extended warfare, has led to a revival of Minoan culture as reimagined by Graves. The narrator, the poet Edward Venn-Thomas, has been magically transported into New Crete from his post-Second World War present. He describes New Crete as an ideal, peaceful society devoted to a supreme goddess and ruled by her earthly incarnation, a powerful Queen supported by a yearly Priest-King. Almost everybody is good-looking and happy; poet-magicians are the legislators; women are recognized as the superior sex; violence is limited and highly regulated. Indeed, warfare is practised only as a ritual game (cf. *Winged Girl of Knossos*) and homicide occurs only in the annual ritual of the Priest-King sacrifice. The Queen, whose attire is modelled on that of the Knossian snake goddess figurines, leads this yearly ceremony, which includes a 'Dance of the Holy Perverts' and involves cross-dressing participants (perhaps an allusion to Evans's cross-dressing Minoan 'cowgirls' of the Toreador fresco).[186] The dance is followed by the death of the Priest-King, and this, in turn, by the birth of an infant, while women feast on the flesh of the sacrificed Priest-King in the background.[187] This repast truly shocks the narrator: despite all its disgusting aspects, his own era had at least drawn a line at cannibalism.[188]

Cannibalism, however, is not the main problem with New Crete. As it turns out, the Goddess herself had summoned Venn-Thomas to create discord in her idyllic but also incredibly dull society. New Crete does not produce good art, especially poetry, because it lacks the ingredients that arouse the strong emotions and passions necessary for true artistic achievements. Venn-Thomas quickly accomplishes his task: partly by means of his sexual attraction, he creates tensions, especially among the women, which reintroduce jealously, deceit, murder, and even suicide. After blowing away the insipid security and dullness of New Crete, Venn-Thomas is transported back to his own time. Thus, in a manner reminiscent of H. G. Well's *The Time Machine*, Graves's utopian-dystopian novel explores the snares of a Golden Age, and in particular the issue of 'how much evil is needed to sustain "the good life"'.[189] By taking direct inspiration from Minoan Crete, it offers at the same time a critique of the idealized views presented by various scholars, Evans above all, who was one of Graves's distinguished neighbours, when this writer went up to Oxford after the First World War, and lived on Boar's Hill for a brief period.[190]

The notion of Minoan Crete as a Golden Age, lost Garden of Eden, and hope for the future, even if turns out not to be as idyllic as wished for, also appears in Nigel Worth's *The Arms of Phaedra: A Tale of Wonder and Adventure* (1924).[191] This work illustrates not only how Cretomania, after the Belle Époque, extended even to the genre of Mills & Boons escapist romances, but also how ideas about Minoan religion, proto-feminism, and female forward sexuality had reached a wide public.[192] The novel is set in a contemporary, post-First World War world, in which direct descendants of the Minoans have survived in an impenetrable location in the White Mountains of west Crete, almost entirely forgotten by humanity. Only a few people know about their existence and secret: a magical pool of water situated in a labyrinth of caves, between the arms of a gigantic statue of Phaedra, the supreme Minoan goddess. This pool has properties similar to those of Lethe, the river of forgetfulness in Greek mythology, with the difference being that it obliterates only memories of traumatic experiences. The hero in the novel is the British Hugh Carslake, a fluent Modern Greek speaker, who spent the First World War in Greece. He is hired by a rich American of Greek origins to accompany him, his only daughter (and heiress), and a few other travellers on an expedition to reach the Minoan enclave, so that they can partake in the century-old Minoan ritual and forget the horrors of war and other traumas that continue to haunt them. They reach the Minoan enclave and encounter a people who are Semitic-looking, semi-vegetarian, happy, and quite peaceful; they worship a Goddess above all deities, women are the stronger sex, and are also sexually forward – in fact too forward for the taste of the British hero: when the Minoan high priestess-cum-queen tries to seduce him, Carslake informs her that women who take such initiative are not appreciated in his country. Undeterred, she continues to pursue him. After considerable efforts, he escapes from her amorous Minoan clutches, returns to his own world, and becomes engaged to the young American heiress. She is much more demure, and yet after their engagement and her sexual awakening, Carslake begins to see in her 'a look of quiet content and happiness' that reminds him 'irresistibly of the Great Goddess of the Minoans'.[193]

Minoan femininity and peace beyond literature

The connection between Minoan Crete and femaleness finds intriguing illustrations also beyond the literary domain, ranging from the visual and performing arts to psychoanalysis – the last as exemplified by Freud's use of Minoan Crete in his treatment of the poet H.D. in the early 1930s (cf. Chapter 1). In regards to the visual arts, the 1940 painting *Crete* (see Fig. 4.10) by the Australian artist Norman Lindsay offers an opulent vision of Minoan assertive female sexuality, which has also a strong whiff of the Orient and decadence: it might have served as illustration for several of the literary works discussed above. Another instance of the connection between the Minoans and femininity (and perhaps pacifism) is Paul Klee's *Die Schlangengöttin und ihr Feind* (The Snake Goddess and her foe) (see Fig. 1.9), also created in 1940, when Europe was in the grips of the Second World War – a work that, in turn, inspired Variation no. 26 of

Fig. 4.10 Norman Lindsay, *Crete*, 1940 (©: H. C. & A. Glad; photo: Potter Museum of Art, University of Melbourne).

the 2009 *Symphony no. 2: Kleetüden; Variationen Für Orchester Nach Paul Klee* by the American composer Jason Wright Wingate.[194] Klee's snake goddess appears to be a stylized version of one of the Knossian figurines from the Temple Repositories, while her enemy looks remarkably like sign 24 on the Phaistos disk, the so-called Lycian wooden hut or granary.[195] The sign is made more menacing, and reminiscent of a tank, by being turned on its side and provided with an elongated prong; a snake occupies a prominent position, separating and perhaps even shielding the goddess from her foe.

It is not clear whether Klee actually saw the original snake goddess figurines and Phaistos disk, but he might have done so during his trip to Egypt of 1928, since his boat seems to have made brief stops in Heraklion on the outward and return journeys.[196] At any rate, he certainly had at least a glimpse of Crete from his boat, like D. H. Lawrence some years earlier. This, combined with his well-known fascination with the Mediterranean and its civilizations as well as with signs and symbols, may have resurfaced and found expression in some of his very last works, since, in his own words 'all art is a memory of age-old things, dark things, whose fragments live on in the artists'.[197] Whether inspired by direct visual memories, illustrations in publications, or both, in the last year of his life Klee produced not only *Schlangengöttin und ihr Feind* but also *Stadtbild Knossos* (View of Knossos),[198] which appears to be typical of Klee's explorations of cities and buildings based on chessboard patterns.[199]

Among the performing arts, a reference to the perceived Minoan gynocentrism appears in Ted Shawn's dance *Gnossienne* (1919), as illustrated by Christine Morris.[200] This work represents a Minoan priest performing a ritual at the altar of the snake goddess. Throughout the performance, both the altar and the goddess are imagined offstage, and only a single male dancer in the priest's role appears to the audience. His movements suggest submission to the goddess, but also some pride and resistance. As argued by Morris, this dance reflects received views about Minoan religion and society, but also mirrors Shawn's desire to emerge from the shadow of his wife, Ruth St Denis, one of the most famous dancers at that time, and establish a more distinct male role in a dance world dominated by female performers.

The ballet *The Minotaur*, premiered in 1947, also connected Minoan Crete with femininity, and at the same time highlighted the differences between Greeks and Minoans.[201] The choreography was by John Taras, the music by Elliot Carter, and the Minoan-looking costumes by Joan Junyer – a Catalonian painter and friend of Robert Graves, who also worked with the Ballets Russes de Monte Carlo, the company created by Léonide Massine after the demise of Diaghilev and the original Ballets Russes. The ballet presented in uncompromising modernist terms the well-known story of Ariadne, Theseus, and the Minotaur, with Junyer's costumes adding a considerable touch of both archaism and modernity. His sketches for these provide powerful and sensual depictions of Ariadne and other female figures, dressed in the typical Minoan flounced skirts and also as bull-leapers (see Fig. 4.11a–b). Junyer himself commented that the colours of the costumes – red, tan, and white for the Cretans, yellow and grey for the Greeks – were chosen to stress the distinction between the two cultures.[202]

Ours once more: Further Hellenization and Europeanization of the Minoans, from local pride and nationalism to individual eclecticism

Most Cretomanic works discussed so far in this chapter highlight Minoan femininity, distance, and otherness as well as the difference between Minoans and Mycenaeans. At the same time, however, the use of Minoan material culture to illustrate works linked with later Greek myths, such as Gide's *Theseus* and Junyer's *The Minotaur*, helped to perpetuate processes of familiarization and incorporation of the Minoans into Greek and European history as well as the Classical Tradition, which had started before the First World War (cf. Chapter 3). For example, in addition to works discussed in previous sections, Minoan elements continued to be used in performances of Greek dramas (or works inspired by them), such as Ida Rubinstein's 1923 production of *Phèdre* at the Paris Opera, with sets and costumes by Bakst (cf. Chapter 3, Fig. 3.19); the modernist production of Euripides' *Medea* at the Royal Dramatic Theatre in Stockholm in 1934, with Swedish translation by Hjalmar Gullberg and Minoan-style costumes by Otte Sköld (see Fig. 4.12 a–b); and the staging of Racine's *Phèdre* by Jean-Louis Barrault at the Comédie Française in 1942, with Jean Hugo's classicizing sets juxtaposed to costumes based on Minoan attires.[203] Further instances of the Minoans' incorporation into the long continuum of Hellenic–European history are provided by the use of Minoan material culture in silent films of this period, which are also interesting in that they foreshadow the more extensive Minoanization of the Trojans in later cinematic

a

b

Fig. 4.11a–b Joan Junyer, two designs (screenprints) for the ballet *Minotaur* (1947); (a) Handmaidens. (b) Ariadne (photos: Detroit Institute of Arts, USA; gifts of John S. Newberry / Bridgeman Images).

Fig. 4.12a–b Photograph from the 1934 production of the drama *Medea*, designed by Otte Sköld and cartoon from *Stockholms-Tidningen* (23 February 1934) (reproduced by kind permission of the Archive of the Royal Dramatic Theatre in Stockholm).

productions.[204] One example is *Helena* (1924), directed by Manfred Noa, which used a replica of the Knossian throne as the symbol of Priam's royalty and power.[205] Another example is *The Private Life of Helen of Troy* (1927), directed by Alexander Korda, in which one of Helen's alluring dresses is embroidered with Minoan sprays of lilies (see Fig. 4.13 a–b).[206]

The most emphatic incorporation of the Minoans into the long continuum of Greek and European history in the period covered by this chapter appears in Greek public pageants commemorating the 1821 Greek Revolution, which were delayed for some years because of the 1922 catastrophe in Asia Minor.[207] Typical examples are two events organized by the still active Lyceum of Greek Women, an organization founded in 1911 to preserve and promote Greek cultural heritage and help the training and education of women.[208] The first event, held in 1926 in the Athenian Panathenaic Stadium, included a parade of women in Minoan costumes, some of which are demure versions of the dresses worn by the Knossian snake goddesses, while others are modelled on garments depicted on the Hagia Triada sarcophagus.[209] The second event, held in 1929 at the same venue, presented a 'blood-less sacrifice from the Minoan period'.[210] According to Dora Markatou, the inclusion of the Minoan past in these patriotic celebrations occurred at the instigation of Ioannis Damvergis, a Cretan man of letters (and friend of Venizelos), who was the General Secretary of the Central Committee for the 1821 commemorations and as early as 1910 had suggested that an athletic event called the 'Cretan leap' should be included in the Pan-Hellenic Games.[211] One may add that the founder of the Lyceum of Greek Women, Kalliroi Parren, and the archaeologist who created the 1926 Minoan costumes, Anna Apostolaki, were also of Cretan extraction and probably played a significant role in the inclusion of the Minoans in such events.[212]

Pageants that incorporated Minoan Crete into the long continuum of Greek history were also held in the 1930s. One was the Flag Ceremony held in Athens in 1930, which was a re-enactment of the ancient Panathenaic procession, with the Greek national flag substituting for the Athenian *peplos*. This included features inspired by classical antiquity, Byzantium, and the War of Independence as well as 'two rows of "five Minoan maidens"', but omitted the Roman, Frankish and, Ottoman periods (an omission that has continued among such pageants well into the twenty-first century).[213] Minoan elements were also part of the 1936 ceremony that took place, once again, in the Panathenaic Stadium, on the occasion of the celebration of 40th anniversary of the Olympics revival.[214] In addition, the Metaxas regime, established by a coup on 4 August 1936, used a double-axe among its emblems: although it is unclear whether this choice was prompted by its Bronze Age Cretan association, many would have perceived it as Minoan.[215]

In addition to pageantries, some Neo-Minoan public architecture was commissioned in connection with the centenary of Greek independence. The best-known example is Dimitrios Kyriakos's Heroon in Heraklion, built in 1930 (see Fig. 4.14a–b). Its Minoan style appears to have been chosen at the instigation of Spyridon Marinatos, the then Director of Heraklion Archaeological Museum, who was particularly keen to stress the modernity and universality of Minoan art.[216] The universal appeal of the art of Bronze Age Crete is indeed illustrated by the fact that Minoan features also appear in official

a

b

Fig. 4.13a–b (a) Still from the silent film *The Private life of Helen of Troy* (First National Pictures, 1927), directed by Alexander Korda, showing Maria Corda as Helen wearing a Minoan-inspired dress decorated with sprays of lilies (photo: © Getty images / General Photographic Agency / Stringer). (b) Jars decorated with lilies from Knossos (after Evans 1921: 603, fig. 443).

Fig. 4.14a–b Dimitrios Kyriakos's Heroon building in Heraklion (1930), including detail of Minoanizing iron gate (photo: N. Momigliano). For a picture of the Heroon in its prime, see cover of Momigliano and Farnoux (2017).

Fig. 4.15 Octopus vase by Charles Catteau (1932), on display at the 2014 exhibition *La Grèce des origins: entre rêve et archéologie*, Musée d'Archéologie Nationale, Châteu Saint-Germain-en-Laye, Paris (photo: N. Momigliano).

buildings of the 1920s–1930s outside Greece, such as the Chamber of Commerce, Work and Industry in Ljubljana and the Bull Staircase in the Prague Castle.[217] In these cases, the use of Minoan elements are related to the personal aesthetic preferences and eclectic passion for antiquity of Jože Plečnik, the Slovenian architect who designed these buildings, rather than the desire to express ideological messages of ethnic affiliations and Minoan originality. Personal and aesthetic reasons also appear to underline the choice of a Minoan model for the octopus vases produced by the French Art Deco ceramic master Charles Catteau in 1932 (see Fig. 4.15).[218] The same applies to the Minoanizing textile design 'Anakreon' (see Fig. 4.16a–b) created by the influential Austrian-born architect and designer Josef Frank for Svenskt Tenn in 1938, at the suggestion of Estrid Ericson, the company's founder.[219] Although the design is named after the Greek lyric poet of the Archaic period, it is modelled on the 'Blue Bird' fresco discovered during the excavations of the House of the Frescoes at Knossos in 1923.[220]

   Uses of Minoan material culture that are personal, almost intimate, but could also become intertwined with wider issues of Cretan, Hellenic, and European identity find illustration in the Athenian home of the architect Nikolaos Zoumboulides (1934), which Osbert Lancaster referred to as 'that okapi among architectural modes, Minoan Revival',[221] and especially in the Minoan textiles created by the Cretan artist Florentini Kaloutsi (see Fig. 4.17). According to a recent study by Philippides and Sgouros, Zoumboulides's employment of Minoan motifs was essentially inspired by his own eclecticism and search for novelty.[222] In the case of Kaloutsi, the reasons appear more complex. This Cretan artist, who studied in London between 1906 and 1911 and had links with the Arts and Crafts movement, opened a painting atelier in Chania in 1914.[223] Later, she extended her talents to handicrafts, weaving in particular, and this was partly connected with the existence, in her neighbourhood, of an institute that helped poor women, directed by her own mother.[224] With the growing success of her craft, in *c.* 1920 she established the firm Dyplous Pelekys (Double Axe): her Minoan-inspired, handwoven, and naturally dyed textiles – ranging from handbags to curtains,

a

b

Fig. 4.16a–b (a) Samples of black and white versions of Josef Frank's fabric 'Anakreon' created for Svenskt Tenn in 1938, in possession of the author (fabric copyright: Svenskt Tenn, Stockholm; photo of samples: N. Momigliano). (b) Knossos, 'Blue Bird Fresco' (after Evans 1928: 454, colour plate XI).

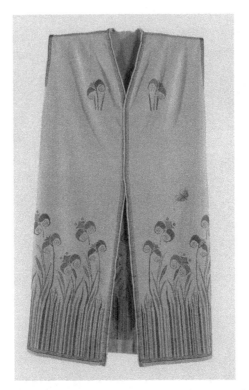

Fig. 4.17 Woven gown by Florentini Kaloutsi, alluding to the Prince of Lilies fresco from Knossos (after Mitsotaki 1999: illustration on page 69, reproduced by kind permission of G. Kaloutsis and A. Mitsotaki).

tablecloths, cushions, and gowns – were exhibited at various locations in Greece (Crete, Athens, Delphi, Thessaloniki), the UK (London), Germany, and the United States.[225] Her textiles present lively and original combinations of Minoan motifs with traditional Cretan weaving techniques and, more significantly, embody her resistance to Western fashions and desire to improve working conditions for Cretan women.[226] This recalls the unconventional 'anadromic' Hellenism of her friend Eva Palmer-Sikelianos, which, as Artemis Leontis has shown, found expression in, among other things, her weaving and wearing Greek-inspired garments as an act of resistance against crypto-colonialism and as a contribution towards a future that reanimated the ancient Greek past.[227]

Conclusions: The Minoans in an age of extremes and catastrophes

In an age of extremes and catastrophes, to borrow Eric Hobsbawm's phrases,[228] it is perhaps unsurprising that the Minoans elicited the gamut of interpretations and responses – from Evans's imperialist conquerors of Mediterranean race, to Spengler's notion of decadent, spent force, steeped in pampered luxury, reminiscent of the late

Roman Empire; and from Merezhkovsky's androgynous, bisexual, and pre-Christian Minoans, to Mauclair's disappointment in Minoan Crete and Miller's idealization of it as a feminine Garden of Eden.

Despite Evans's prestige and dominance in the field of Aegean studies, by the time the first volume of *The Palace of Minos* was published (1921), many scholars had rejected his pan-Minoan view of the Aegean. Instead, they supported the idea that Indo-European tribes had settled in mainland Greece by the early second millennium B C and had replaced the Minoans as the dominant force in the Aegean by the end of the fifteenth century B C. Above all, the growing concern with ethnic-linguistic groups in archaeology and the rise of Aryanism in interwar Europe furthered the polarization between Minoans and Mycenaeans. This, in turn, opened that path to the idea of Minoan Crete as the opposite rather than the precursor of Hellas. On the one hand, the Mycenaeans were seen as possessing traits that scholars and laymen alike had associated with the Indo-Europeans: they were warlike, patriarchal, physically and intellectually superior to the earlier Mediterranean people(s) that they eventually conquered; on the other hand, the Minoans assumed more peaceful, feminine, Oriental, and decadent characteristics. The myth of Theseus and the Minotaur came to be seen as symbolic not only of a Mycenaean–Greek rebellion against the Minoan *thalassocracy*, but also of the clash between two different worlds – Spengler's 'abyss of opposition that separates the two souls', the 'healthy' and vigorous northern barbarians vs. an over-refined, woman-centred, and Oriental south.

The decline and fall of the Minoans was frequently perceived in the interwar period as the direct outcome of their alleged peacefulness. Evans's relatively short Minoan Golden Age and *Pax Minoica* were often portrayed, in the works of others, as extending over the whole of the Minoan Age. Pacifism became an innate racial trait of the Minoans as well as their Achilles' heel. In addition, the Minoan decline was associated in some literary and artistic works with their perceived extravagant sexuality, especially female. Evans's notion of a supreme Minoan Mother Goddess and its implications for Minoan society, despite some scholars' resistance, effectively acquired canonical status in this period: together with Evans's ferro-concrete reconstitutions at Knossos, it is this reconstruction of the Minoan past – the narrative about a supreme Mother Goddess and the importance of Minoan women – that may be regarded as one of the most significant and enduring cultural legacies of Minoan Crete. This narrative was exploited and transformed in many specialist publications, popularizing works, novels, visual art, and even psychoanalysis. In other words, a mixture of bare-breasted iconography, Evans's Mother Goddess, the perceived importance of women in Minoan society, their cross-dressing, and memories of later Greek myths (e.g. Pasiphae and the bull) stimulated endless fantasies about the Minoans' sexual mores, which further contributed to their doom, since sexual indulgence and non-conformity have long been associated with decay and corruption in people's minds.[229]

Besides the idea of Minoan over-refinement and decadence, this period witnessed the emergence of notions of Minoan otherness and distance. These provoked, in turn, a wide range of negative, neutral, and positive responses. Negative attitudes are especially visible in pro-Aryan narratives, such as Spengler's *Decline of the West*. Neutral reactions are illustrated, for example, by Brion's appreciation that temporal and spatial conceptualizations in Minoan art are different from those of the traditional European canon. The Minoan distance and otherness, however, could also be perceived as a positive alternative to the war-ravaged present, and as a hope for a different future, especially in writers and artists, such as Lawrence and Miller, representing a strand of modernism that revels in primitivist utopias, earthy sexuality, and more pacifist attitudes.

Despite emerging perceptions of the Minoans as the 'other' and even the opposite of Hellas, during the period marked by the two World Wars, processes of familiarization, Hellenization, and Europeanization also continued unabated in some cultural practices. This is illustrated, for example, by the sustained use of later Greek mythological narratives to interpret the material culture of Bronze Age Crete (and vice-versa), and through other media, such as dramas, ballets, and novels based on Greek mythological themes (from the story of Theseus and the Minotaur to that of Medea and even the Trojan War saga) that incorporate elements from Minoan archaeology. It is also illustrated in the pageantries that accompanied the celebrations of the centenary of Greek independence. In this instance, the inclusion of the Minoan Age in the long continuum of Greek history, alongside the exclusion of other periods (such as the Roman, Frankish, and Ottoman), suggests a process of Hellenization of the Minoans rather than an attempt to present a more subversive, inclusive, multicultural interpretation of Greek history (and Greekness), which, by contrast, will be found in more recent uses of the Minoan past, as illustrated in subsequent chapters.[230]

The Minoans in the Cold War and Swinging Sixties: From the End of the Greek Civil War to the End of the Colonels' Dictatorship (*c.* 1949–74)

Of course, all this stuff is queer to me – that's half the fascination. The men's waists are too small, and the women's breasts are too big, and they have hair like live snakes, and they all look as if they were doing some fantastic ballet and their life depended on doing it right – and yet no one seems to have quite discovered what they were doing . . .
Katharine Farrer ([1954] 2004: 26)

If the palace in whose ruins the Linear B documents were found was destroyed in 1425 (the usually accepted date) it could be said that the Achaeans had occupied Knossos soon after the great disaster caused by the eruption of Thera. The sacking of a country already overwhelmed by such a catastrophe would not seem inappropriate to their warlike and adventurous character. But we may also entertain the possibility of a peaceful change of dynasty brought about by the marriage of a Knossian queen to an Achaean prince.
Spyridon Marinatos and Max Hirmer (1960: 26)

The Cretans seem to have reduced and diverted their aggressiveness through a free and well-balanced sexual life, and through their enthusiasm for sports, games and dancing.
Jacquetta Hawkes (1968: 156)

The peaceful transfer of power in Crete from the Minoans to the Mycenaeans is difficult to explain. Since all other hypotheses do violence to the archaeological evidence in one way or another, we may be justified in suggesting that a passive renunciation of power was in accord with Minoan character, just as the skill of the Mycenaeans in usurping the position of their Minoan predecessors in the overseas markets was typical of their energy and thrust.
Friedrich Matz (1973b: 580)

Within the discipline of Aegean archaeology and the period treated in this chapter, many would regard Michael Ventris's 1952 decipherment of Linear B as the most significant achievement, closely followed by the excavations of a new Minoan palace at

Kato Zakros, the settlement of Akrotiri on Thera (Santorini), and the second Shaft Graves circle at Mycenae. These attainments were spectacular and momentous, but in terms of overall perceptions of the Minoans more specifically they often reinforced ideas already developed in the interwar period (or even before): as I argue in this chapter, in a climate of Cold War, gender tensions emerging from the Second World War, and second wave feminism, the Minoan–Mycenaean dichotomy simply became even more entrenched. This opposition was often portrayed as a conflict between two powers encroaching on the same territory and especially as a clash of worldviews, most commonly expressed in terms of femininity/matriarchy vs. masculinity/patriarchy, since the Minoan Great Mother Goddess, despite serious doubts expressed about her reality, dies hard. This enhanced polarization between Minoans and Mycenaeans sometimes helped to underline the former's links to the Near East or their uniqueness. Nonetheless, in this period one continues to find instances of the Minoans' incorporation into the long continuum of Hellenism and European history, especially in Greek–Cretan contexts. One significant new trend, especially after the Vietnam War, is that Minoan pacifism, sometimes linked to gynocentrism and even proto-communism, came to be regarded as a positive trait, whereas in the interwar period it was frequently portrayed as a weakness leading to an inevitable and almost well deserved defeat. At the same time, the belief in a Minoan Sea Empire started to decline, despite the increasing evidence of Minoanization brought to light by new excavations on various Aegean islands and the western coast of Asia Minor. Overall, as the 'age of extremes' continued, so did the gamut of contrasting responses to the Minoans, which are attested in an ever-wider variety of genres – from scholarly works to novels, poetry, movies, and even in the advertisements of international brands: Minoan Crete could be regarded as a distant, alien culture, and a quaint episode in the march of Hellenism; or it could be experienced as a lost paradise – a nostalgic antidote to the present and blueprint for a better future.

Crete: From civil war to military junta and tourist boom

In the aftermath of the Second World War, Greece opted to remain a monarchy in the referendum held in 1946. The country also became one of the first battlegrounds of the Cold War, engulfed in a bitter civil war between communist and non-communist factions until 1949. Although Crete was spared the worst of this internecine conflict, clashes between government forces and communist EAM/ELAS groups did occur, especially in the Cretan mountains. After fierce fighting in the Samaria Gorge in 1948, the EAM/ELAS forces rapidly dwindled, and by the early months of 1949 only a few dozen individuals were still holding out in their mountain refuges. Over the years they were all killed, captured, or gave themselves up after taking advantage of amnesties. The last two guerrilla fighters (nicknamed the Eagles of Crete) emerged from their hideouts in the White Mountains only in 1975, the year in which the Vietnam war ended, and a year after the fall of the Regime of the Colonels in Greece.[1] The Truman Doctrine and Marshall Plan, announced in 1947, increased US involvement in Greece, which became part of NATO in 1949. A period of relative stability and reconstruction followed, but political squabbles and fear of growing communist influence led to a military dictatorship that ruled Greece from 1967 to 1974. Constantine II, the last king of Greece, originally supported the military coup, but was forced to flee his country in 1967. He officially remained king of Greece until the junta held a referendum to abolish the monarchy in 1973. The republican choice was later confirmed by another referendum held in 1974, after the collapse of the Regime of the Colonels, in the aftermath of their coup against Archbishop Makarios III and the Turkish invasion of Cyprus. In the late 1950s and 1960s, the economic aid and relative peace in Greece led to a tourist boom on Crete, which gained pace especially under the dictatorship.[2] This was accompanied by urban expansion of Cretan towns, particularly Heraklion, with implications for archaeological finds, as discussed below.

New discoveries: From the decipherment of Linear B to volcanic catastrophes

In the period covered by this chapter, many fresh archaeological discoveries occurred on Crete, from the uncovering of a new palace at Kato Zakros in the far east of the island, to hundreds of other less spectacular findings that were due, at times, to the increasing building activities (including road-building) linked to post-war regeneration. Many significant archaeological excavations also took place outside Crete, such as those at Akrotiri on Thera and other Minoanized sites all over the Aegean, from Miletus and Iasos on the western coast of Turkey to the island of Kythera in the west,[3] and the discovery of the second Shaft Grave Circle at Mycenae (a.k.a. Circle B), to name but a few. A most remarkable and far-reaching discovery, dubbed the 'Everest of Greek Archaeology',[4] occurred in 1952: Michael Ventris's decipherment of Linear B as Greek. This also had substantial implications beyond archaeology. One can speculate that Evans, who had been dead for a decade, would have been rather shocked and sceptical, at least at first. His older colleagues Schliemann and Tsountas, however, would have rejoiced, while younger ones, such as Blegen, Childe, and Wace felt that they had been completely vindicated, since the decipherment supported their belief that Greek-speaking people had entered Greece well before the end of the Bronze Age. Accordingly, the seminal volume *Documents in Mycenaean Greek*, published by Ventris and Chadwick only a few weeks after Ventris's death in a car accident in September 1956, was dedicated to the Hellenophile Schliemann as the 'Father of Mycenaean Archaeology', and not to Evans, the main discoverer of the Aegean Bronze Age scripts, and despite the fact that it was a 1936 lecture by the doyen of Minoan archaeology, attended by the fourteen-year-old Ventris, which spurred the latter's interest in Linear B.[5]

The decipherment of Linear B and the Minoans

Evans's failure to produce a systematic publication of the Linear B tablets from Knossos, Minoan supremacy theories, and dominance in the field of Aegean archaeology have all been blamed for the delay in the decipherment and its surprise effect,[6] although one might add that the influential opinion of other scholars, such as John Myres and

Gilbert Murray, contributed to this, since they considered the Mycenaeans as largely 'un-Hellenic' (cf. Chapter 3). Thus, it is often reported that the decipherment of Linear B as Greek came as a shock, including to Ventris himself, who originally thought that the script expressed a language related to Etruscan.[7]

As argued by Sinclair Hood, however, this element of surprise is largely a modern myth.[8] As shown in the previous chapter, many scholars had long been convinced that Greek-speaking populations had reached Greece by the late third or early second millennium BC; that the Mycenaeans were identifiable with Homer's Achaeans or were at least their direct forebears; and that they were the rising and dominating power in the Aegean from about the mid–late fifteenth to the twelfth century BC and had conquered Crete. Moreover, Haley, Blegen, Childe, and others had suggested that Greek was the language used by the ruling classes on Crete from Late Minoan II-III and by the Minoan invaders on mainland Greece even earlier. Their views had gained considerable ground and, indeed, had become the new orthodoxy, even if other scholars, following Evans, continued to believe that the Minoans conquered mainland Greece and the Mycenaeans adopted the non-Hellenic Cretan tongue as their court language.[9] The decipherment of Linear B supported this new orthodoxy and challenged Evans's vision of the dynamics of power in the Aegean: it provided the strongest evidence for a Mycenaean takeover of Minoan Crete (or at least much of it), probably in the late fifteenth century BC, not long after the Late Minoan IB destructions that occurred on the island, or by the Late Minoan III period at the very latest. The decipherment also had other implications for the understanding of the Aegean Bronze Age, including perceptions of the Minoans more specifically, as discussed below.

The decipherment provided indisputable evidence that the Mycenaeans spoke Greek, while the Minoans did not, and this, in turn, had repercussions on their categorization in terms of Greek and European history. Thus, for example, the decipherment could facilitate the incorporation of Mycenaean Greece into Hellenism, at least if one followed the eloquent exhortations of scholars such as Wace:

> The true student of Greek art must begin his studies with the Middle Bronze Age at least … The importance of Mr Ventris' decipherment can hardly be over-estimated, for it inaugurates a new phase in our study of the beginnings of classical Hellas. We must recognise Mycenaean culture as Greek, and as one of the first stages in the advance of the Hellenes towards the brilliance of their later amazing achievements. In culture, in history and in language we must regard prehistoric and historic Greece as one indivisible whole.[10]

But what were the implications for the Minoans? Despite some attempts to link the idiom expressed by Linear A with that of the (Indo-European) Luwian language of ancient Anatolia (and even with Greek), the persisting elusiveness of both Linear A and Cretan Pictographic helped to underline the Minoans' non-Hellenic character and Oriental affinities.[11] At other times, however, the Minoans continued to be incorporated into the long continuum of Hellenic and/or European history because of their influence on the Mycenaeans and, via the Mycenaeans, on later Greek culture, and also because the rhetoric of Crete as 'the cradle of European civilization/the first civilization in

Europe' could be usefully redeployed in other contexts, such as that of the emerging European Union.[12]

Yet, if the Mycenaeans' cultural debt to the Minoans could facilitate, at times, the latter's incorporation into a Hellenic–European continuum, at other times it could Orientalize the former and bar them from exclusive membership of the 'ancient Greece club'. For Greekness, like beauty, appears to be in the eye of the beholder and also ever changing: whether any part of the Aegean Bronze Age is considered Greek or not is contingent on modern desires, individual preferences, and contexts. In other words, it depends on how one chooses to define and essentialize (or not essentialize) Greekness as well as Europeanness and Orientalness – something that also brings to mind the answer that John Myres gave to the question 'Who were the Greeks?' in 1930, namely that they were always in the 'process of becoming', also recently readapted by the British archaeologist and Conservative life peer Colin Renfrew.[13]

Within a scholarly context, an example of the ambivalent perception of both Minoans and Mycenaeans as Greek, European, or Oriental is the French series 'Collection Les Grandes Civilisations', of which over a dozen volumes were published between the early 1960s and mid-1970s under the general editorship of Raymond Bloch. The Mycenaean Aegean is included in François Chamoux's 1963 volume on Greece (*La civilisation grecque, à l'époque archaïque et classique*), while Minoan Crete appears in J. Deshayes's 1969 volume on the ancient Near East (*Les civilisations de l'Orient ancien*). Both inclusions, however, were made somewhat reluctantly. Chamoux accepted that Ventris and Chadwick had demonstrated that the Mycenaeans were Greeks or, rather, that at least they spoke Greek, something that he considered as fundamental, because being part of Hellenism in his opinion was demonstrated above all through language; yet, he thought that, strictly speaking, the Greek world started only with Homer.[14] Deshayes considered Bronze Age Crete as part of an Oriental rather than a Greek *koine*, while stressing many Minoan peculiarities in terms of socio-political organization and artistic features, which set Crete apart from other Oriental cultures. He expressed this Minoan uniqueness by using familiar ideas, such as the alleged lack of militarism and of clear-cut separation between rulers and subjects, the importance of women, the Minoan joie de vivre, love of nature and sense of movement, and a 'Cretan humanism' ('humanisme crétoise', meaning an interest in the individual and humanity).[15] Deshayes even suggested that the transmission of this Minoan humanism to the Hellenic people could explain the superior achievements of ancient Greek art. At the same time he characterized Minoan art as decorative, lacking a profundity of ideas and the Mycenaean–Greek logical spirit, echoing de Lacretelle's earlier comments on its dearth of symbolism and ideas.[16]

Further evidence of Orientalization of the Minoans and Hellenization of the Mycenaeans is illustrated by the University of Chicago Press's decision to publish two separate books on the Aegean Bronze Age: one on the Minoans, assigned to Machteld J. Mellink, and the other on the Mycenaeans, assigned to Emily Vermeule, of which only the latter, titled *Greece in the Bronze Age*, was published, in 1964. As one gathers from Vermeule's introduction, this division allowed Mellink to 'deal more extensively' with the Near Eastern and Anatolian history and influences to which Crete responded'.[17] Above all, it was an attempt to avoid 'disturbing comparisons of worth' often encountered in works that discussed both Minoans and Mycenaeans, in which the usual outcome was that either the Mycenaeans were presented as 'rough tectonic imitators of a Crete delicately refined in art and cult, with few authoritative developments of their own apart from some architectural and military habits' or Minoan Crete appeared as 'a refined and pastel brothel where the sturdy mainlanders found experience and sophistication which they put to more manly uses after destroying the corrupters of their adolescence',[18] words that equally apply to specialist works and Cretomanic novels, and indeed might have been influenced by the latter (e.g. Mary Renault's famous *The King Must Die* and *The Bull from the Sea*, discussed below).

To some extent, the issue of whether one should incorporate the Minoans either into a Greek or Oriental *koine* did not arise with the *Cambridge Ancient History* series, because this started from the premise that 'the history of Europe begins outside Europe', and considered the early history of Egyptian and Mesopotamian civilization more important than 'the barbarous life' of Germans and Celts.[19] Yet, one might be forgiven for deriving an Oriental impression of the Aegean Bronze Age generally, and of Minoan Crete particularly, if only because all the chapters on this topic are surrounded by others on canonical Near Eastern civilizations, such as those of Egypt, Anatolia, and Mesopotamia. In addition, although Friedrich Matz's chapters on Minoan Crete differentiate it from other Near Eastern cultures and make it a case *sui generis* (often by repeating long-established clichés, such as those regarding the Minoan Mother Goddess, Minoan pacifism, the naturalism and love of nature in Minoan art, its lack of concern with immortality), they also stress commonplace views regarding some alleged racial traits of Hellenic and non-Hellenic people, in which Minoan passivity is contrasted with Mycenaean dynamism (cf. epigraph above), two characteristics that have long been associated with the Orient and Europe, respectively.[20]

An example of the Orientalization of both Minoans and Mycenaeans, after the decipherment of Linear B, appears in C. G. Starr's *The Origins of Greek Civilization, 1100–650 B.C.* (1961), which starts precisely with a discussion of why Minoans and Mycenaeans should not be considered as part of Greek civilization. This and other works that emerged after Moses Finley's influential *The World of Odysseus* (1954) focus on the fact that, despite linguistic and other elements of continuity, the Linear B tablets illustrated very profound differences in the social organization and economy of Minoan–Mycenaean palaces on the one hand, and Homeric society on the other. Starr regarded Minoan civilization as 'one of the most extraordinary achievements of mankind' and acknowledged its crucial role in understanding the culture of the Greek-speaking Mycenaeans, but in his opinion Minoan art lacked the main elements that characterized later Greece, such as 'innate love of balanced order, the feeling of structural symmetry'.[21] Above all, according to Starr the Linear B tablets showed that the organization of Minoan–Mycenaean palaces resembled that of their Oriental counterparts and 'aspects of the social and political superstructure ... connected with the ever increasing power of the kings, vigorous in war and in trade, were to be unique to this [Bronze Age] era'.[22] In other words, despite acknowledging many elements of continuity between Bronze Age and Iron Age Greece, for Starr the Minoan and Mycenaean palaces were too despotic to be regarded as the true origins of Greece, unlike the so-called Greek Dark Ages, which reflected the establishment of a broader social base more relevant to the development of the Greek *poleis* and, ultimately, Greek democracy.[23]

Another consequence of the decipherment of Linear B was that it unveiled the close similarity between the Knossos tablets, dated by Evans to *c.* 1400 BC, and those found on the mainland, dated approximately two centuries later. This, in turn, prompted a re-examination of the chronology/stratigraphy of the Knossian documents, which sparked an acrimonious controversy in the early 1960s, and even called into question Evans's integrity as a scholar.[24] Research on the date of the Linear B tablets from Knossos was still topical among specialists in the 1990s, but the dispute was mercifully conducted more politely than when it first erupted.[25] It is only in the late twentieth-early twenty-first century that the debate petered out, with most scholars reaching some kind of consensus on the idea that the Linear B tablets from Knossos do not necessarily belong to a single archive and destruction horizon, but could date to different phases, and also that conservative scribal traditions may show relatively little change over a number of generations.[26]

A further consequence of the decipherment of Linear B, which was not, however, widely appreciated at the time, concerns Minoan religion and, by implication, the role of women in Cretan society. As noted in Chapter 4, *pace* Evans and well before the decipherment, some scholars, such as Martin Nilsson, had suggested that Minoans and Mycenaeans worshipped a polytheistic pantheon instead of a supreme Mother Goddess. In their seminal *Documents in Mycenaean Greek*, Ventris and Chadwick provided further evidence that undermined Evans's monotheistic theory. This included the presence in the Knossos tablets of several non-Greek theonyms (seemingly male and female) and of frequent dedications to 'all the gods', which could suggest a Minoan practice inherited by Mycenaean rulers.[27] And yet, the idea of a Great Minoan Mother Goddess and related matriarchy or matrilineality, so enthusiastically produced and consumed since the early1900s, persists in both specialist and non-specialist literature. For example, among the latter, Mary Renault (pen name of Eileen Mary Challans), in her bestseller historical novels about Theseus, *The King Must Die* (1958) and *The Bull from The Sea* (1962), paid close attention to the decipherment of Linear B and other historical-archaeological niceties, but retained the Minoan Mother Goddess, since the tension between two worldviews – a conquering patriarchy and a defeated but still powerful matriarchy – was crucial to her narrative (cf. also below). Evans's Minoan Mother Goddess also looms large among specialist publications, such as E. Neumann's *The Great Mother: An Analysis of the Archetype* (1955), O. G. S. Crawford's *The Eye Goddess* (1957), and E. O. James's *The Cult of The Mother-Goddess* (1959), which provide overviews of Mother Goddess cults from the Palaeolithic to Christianity, but overlook the Linear B evidence.[28]

Even scholars who paid more attention to Linear B in this period were still reluctant to accept its implications for Minoan religion. For example, W. K. C. Guthrie (Laurence Professor of Ancient Philosophy at Cambridge from 1952 to 1973) admitted that before the decipherment of Linear B he preferred to believe in a 'ubiquitous mother-goddess' with a male consort-son and was surprised to see the extent of individual divinities in the tablets; yet, he concluded that these sources showed a 'transitional stage' from monotheism to polytheism.[29] Similarly, in the late 1950s–early 1960s,

Spyridon Marinatos observed that most respected scholars were inclined to believe in a Minoan polytheism, but his own view was more ambivalent. He suggested that there were 'very few individual male deities in Crete, if indeed there were any at all, but there was a whole, distinctive series of goddesses'.[30] He mentioned some of the (non-Greek) names of individual female divinities in the tablets, such as Kupanatuna, Pipituna, and Asasara, and yet wondered whether these and the varied iconographic representations could still refer to a single female deity.[31] Even if, by the late 1960s, a tide against 'The Myth of the Mother Goddess' was beginning to rise among archaeologists,[32] in the mid-1970s and in the 1980s the efforts of European archaeologist Marija Gimbutas and others gave new impetus to this myth, by offering Minoan Crete as a last bastion of a matriarchal, Mother Goddess paradise against Aryan hordes of warlike patriarchs.[33] Even nowadays the idea of a supreme female deity finds acceptance among some renowned scholars of Minoan religion.[34]

Go west (and east) young man! New archaeological discoveries on Crete

The relative political stability after the civil war and the accompanying urban expansion as well as construction and agricultural activities (including road-building) widely intensified archaeological explorations on the island, which ranged from salvage operations to the continuation of long-standing projects at 'palatial' sites such as Knossos, Phaistos, and Malia. In fact, a quick comparison between the number of sites explored in the two decades comprising the 1920s and 1930s on the one hand, and in the 1950s and 1960s on the other, shows that the figures are approximately 150 and more than 300, respectively.[35] The latter figure includes many sites located in western and eastern districts of the island, which had been relatively neglected in previous decades. Italian, French, and British archaeologists continued to be active at major palatial sites such as Phaistos, Malia, and Knossos, respectively, but the lion's share of the new explorations goes to Greek archaeologists such as Spyridon Marinatos, Nikolaos Platon, Stylianos Alexiou, Kostis Davaras, Yannis Tzedakis, and Yannis Sakellarakis, who excavated dozens of new sites, from new Minoan palaces to Minoan 'villas',[36] peak sanctuaries, and cemeteries, while working for the Greek Archaeological Service (Αρχαιολογική Υπηρεσία) or the Athens Archaeological Society (Η Εν Αθήναις Αρχαιολογική Εταιρεία).

At the sites of Phaistos and Malia, the former in particular, excavations that resumed in the late 1940s or early 1950s have continued almost without interruption to the present day, and have greatly contributed to a better understanding of the history of these settlements, especially of the Old Palace structures, which are better preserved than at Knossos. Work at Phaistos was conducted under the directorship of Doro Levi, who started a diatribe against Evans's chronological and ceramic phases. Levi's excavations provided a wealth of new data on the Protopalatial period, but his stratigraphic and chronological interpretations turned out to be less reliable than Evans's.[37]

Explorations at Knossos and Palaikastro have been more intermittent, but some important work took place from the 1950s to the early 1970s. Between 1957 and 1961, Sinclair Hood carried out numerous soundings within the palace and along the Royal

Road at Knossos, which elucidated the site's stratigraphy and history, especially for its earlier phases.[38] At Hood's invitation, John Evans (no relation of Sir Arthur) directed important excavations of the Neolithic and Early Minoan strata between 1958 and 1972. These showed that settlers from the Fertile Crescent (probably from southern Anatolia) inhabited Knossos already in the Neolithic Aceramic period, and radiocarbon dating revealed that this occupation went back to the seventh millennium BC, earlier than previously known.[39] Between 1967 and 1972, Mervyn Popham and Hugh Sackett extended our knowledge of Knossos beyond the palace, by exploring a fine mansion located in the west side of the town.[40] A few years earlier (1962–3) they had conducted some soundings at Palaikastro to elucidate the topography and long history of this site, which has not yet revealed a palatial structure, despite its considerable size and complexity.[41]

Two new palaces were discovered in the 1950s and 1960s respectively: one in the west, at Chania, ancient Kydonia, even if it was not recognized immediately as a palatial building; the other on the far eastern shores of the island, at Kato Zakros, which was missed by only a few metres by D. G. Hogarth in the early 1900s.[42] The excavations at Kato Zakros, directed by Nikolaos Platon, produced some remarkable finds, which highlight the important maritime connections of this site with the Near East and Levant, such as hoards of elephant tusks and copper ingots, which were abandoned, together with many other exquisite objects, when the site was destroyed in Late Minoan IB, like many other settlements on the island. Minoan palaces have long dominated Minoan archaeology and the public's imagination, but one should not overlook the scientific importance of the cumulative knowledge provided by the discoveries made at many other sites in these years. To use Whitehead's terminology once again (cf. Chapter 4), the period from the 1950s to the mid-1970s, like the decades between the two World Wars, could be regarded as part of a 'stage of precision' that follows the whirlwind 'stage of romance', when acquisition of new knowledge is systematized through the application of the 'grammar of science'. But it could also be regarded as the beginning of Whitehead's third stage, the 'stage of generalisation', in which scholars attempt to reach a new synthesis of romance and theory, of classified data and powerful analytical/theoretical techniques. In this context, since the other Cretan excavations are too many to be discussed here in any detail, and even if it is invidious to single out one example, I should like to mention Peter Warren's uncovering of the Early Minoan settlement at Myrtos (Fournou Koryfi) in 1967–8, promptly published in 1972.[43] This is because this site offers a link to wider debates about the development of complex or state societies, which were thriving at that time among the so-called New Archaeology, and it played an important part in some seminal works of synthesis published in this period, such as Colin Renfrew's *The Emergence of Civilisation*, discussed below.

Even during the period covered in this chapter (c. 1949–74), there were moments that recall the 'stage of romance', capturing the scholarly and public imagination alike, and indeed continue to do so nowadays. This was no more so than in some of the archaeological explorations that, although conducted beyond Crete, were crucial to new perceptions of the Minoans and their history, as discussed in the next section.

Akrotiri, the Pompeii of the Aegean and other discoveries outside Crete

By coincidence, between 1952 and 1954, as the decipherment of Linear B was making headway, George Mylonas and Yannis Papadimitriou revealed a second group of Shaft Graves at Mycenae (Circle B), which was slightly earlier than that excavated by Schliemann seven decades earlier.[44] This discovery, among others, helped scholars to appreciate that the tombs found by the German archaeologist in 1876 were a more elaborate development of earlier types. It also helped to polarize Minoans and Mycenaeans even further. In the words of Mary Renault, both Linear B and the new tombs of Mycenae seemed to offer a view of 'a mainland culture different from the mannered elegance of the Minoan ... a warlike society, well organised, aristocratic and art-loving, but primitive and barbaric by the standards of Crete's millennial sophistication'.[45] Even the physical appearance of the Mycenaeans, described by some scholars as 'big, tall men, quite different from the smaller, lithe, beardless Minoans,'[46] served to underline this divide.

By another coincidence, while some ancient historians were beginning to view more critically the Greek sources on the Minoan *thalassocracy*,[47] the evidence of Minoanization and even Minoan settlements abroad increased, especially in the 1960s, and involved sites that spanned the entire Aegean: from Akrotiri on Thera (Santorini) and Aghia Irini on Kea (Keos) in the Cyclades, to Miletus and Iasos on the Aegean coast of Turkey, and Kastri on Kythera at the western end.

The most spectacular finds were made at Akrotiri on Thera, which was first explored in the nineteenth century (cf. Chapter 3), but only in this period became closely linked to mythological narratives. As mentioned in Chapter 4, by the late 1930s the Greek archaeologist Spyridon Marinatos, spurred by archaeological discoveries that he had made on Crete, had already conceived the idea that the decline and fall of Minoan Crete was not caused by human agency (e.g. Mycenaean/Achaean conquest), but natural causes, namely the Bronze Age eruption of the Santorini volcano, which, by the 1950s, he had firmly linked to the Platonic myth of Atlantis.[48] To corroborate his theory, in 1967 Marinatos started a series of excavation campaigns, which have continued to this time under the directorship of Christos Doumas, after Marinatos's untimely death in 1974.[49]

Marinatos's excavations, however, did not entirely confirm his hypothesis that the eruption was the direct cause of the fall of Minoan Crete. By the late 1960s–early 1970s, scholars had already realized that the evidence produced by his work, combined with other finds on Crete, pointed to a more complex series of events: the eruption occurred in the Late Minoan IA phase in the Minoan relative chronology (the extensive debate on the absolute or calendar date of this event is not relevant in this context).[50] Undoubtedly, the eruption had an impact on Crete and other adjacent areas in the Aegean, and this may have even involved some social and psychological disturbances.[51] But despite the significant effects, these were not as immediate and direct as Marinatos had originally envisaged. After the eruption, life on Crete went on and for many scholars the Late Minoan IB phase actually represents the acme (or swansong) of Minoan civilization.[52] In other words, many scholars now believe that the eruption and its aftermath weakened the Minoans, but the 'Minoan Golden Age' ended in a mature phase of Late Minoan IB, with a series of destructions, often accompanied by fire and a subsequent abandonment of many sites, with human hands delivering the coup de grâce. Whether these human hands belonged to Mycenaeans (perhaps symbolized by the mythological Theseus) or locals is a matter of interesting speculation, although the adoption of Greek as the language used for administrative purposes in Late Minoan II (or Late Minoan IIIA at the latest) appears to many like the proverbial smoking gun (cf. also Fig. 2.2).

But why should a complicated and uncertain reconstruction of events get in the way of a good, simple, and dramatic narrative of natural catastrophes? And especially when this narrative involves, once again, a link between Greek myths and archaeological realities, between literary and physical *topoi*? The catastrophe theory became extremely popular and rekindled the notion that Plato's myth of Atlantis did contain some memory of Bronze Age events, as already proposed by T. K. Frost in 1909 (cf. Chapter 3).[53] The difference now was that both the Theran eruption and Minoan decline were linked to the Platonic narrative. The idea that Plato's narrative contains some remembrance of the Bronze Age is still very popular today. Yet, although one cannot exclude the possibility that oral tradition may have preserved across many centuries some memory of the Theran eruption and Minoan decline, the Platonic myth of Atlantis is more likely to be inspired by events closer to the philosopher's time, from the Persian and Peloponnesian Wars, to the establishment of the Second Athenian League, and even the fate of Helike, a town located on the Corinthian gulf, which was submerged by an earthquake-related tsunami in 373 BC (i.e. a quarter of a century before Plato's death). Perhaps, as suggested by Vidal Naquet, the identification of Atlantis with Akrotiri is to some extent 'as absurd as all the others' that preceded it over the centuries and 'owes much to the patriotism of . . . Marinatos and his disciples, and it has continued to be exploited for patriotic ends'.[54]

At any rate, because Akrotiri was buried under metres of ash and pumice from the Santorini Bronze Age eruption, it has been dubbed the Pompeii of the Aegean and has yielded the best-preserved settlement in the whole of the Aegean. Many of its buildings survive almost to their roof, and the frescoes that decorated them are so stunning that they have even inspired the 1994 spring–summer collection designed by the famous couturier Karl Lagerfeld for the Chloé fashion house.[55] Even objects made of organic materials, which would normally perish in the Aegean climate, could be reconstructed through the impressions left in the ash that engulfed the settlement. Unlike the victims of Vesuvius, however, the inhabitants of Akrotiri seem to have been able to escape, perhaps because the earth tremors that preceded the eruption gave them sufficient warning to evacuate the island; further explorations may change this picture but, so far, no human remains have been found at this Aegean site.

The finds from Akrotiri attest to very close contacts between Thera and Minoan Crete, as illustrated, for example, by architecture that comprises Minoan features, such as ashlar masonry, mason's marks, lustral basins, and polythira (cf. Chapter 3); frescoes in Minoan style and depicting women in typical Minoan dress as well as other Minoan elements; and Minoan objects, such as pots and loom-weights. This, together with the abundance of Minoan and Minoanizing finds discovered at other Aegean sites excavated in the 1950s–1970s, rekindled the issue of the relationship between archaeological realities and other ancient narratives concerning the so-called Minoan *thalassocracy*, while some scholars were beginning to approach these ancient sources more critically and to provide less imperialistic explanations for the Minoanization of the Aegean than Evans's. By the late 1970s, scholarly views appeared to have crystallized into two broad camps. The first, which one might perhaps call the 'colonialist', supported the idea of some form of Minoan settlements abroad, albeit with different degrees of hegemony, ranging from military expeditions and conquest, to more peaceful establishment of emporia or trading posts.[56] The second, which one might call 'emulative', sought to explain the Minoanization of the Aegean largely through emulation strategies deployed by local elites.[57] These views recall, to some extent, Evans's pan-Minoan imperialistic view of the Aegean, Hawes's peaceful invasion, and Wace's and Blegen's notion of local elites adopting a Minoan veneer (cf. Chapters 3 and 4). The ideas expressed by the 'emulative' camp also illustrate a reaction against grand narratives of great powers carrying the torch of civilization to less advanced regions, which owes much to the emergence of post-colonialism, with its emphasis on the agency of indigenous people, and of the New Archaeology (a.k.a. Processual Archaeology). The New Archaeology focused on processes instead of invasions and migrations to explain cultural changes, and rejected the simplistic correlation between material culture and people, which were the cornerstones of culture-historical approaches in archaeology, as discussed further in the next section.[58]

Minoan archaeological-historical narratives in a Cold War and post-colonial world: From culture-historical to processual approaches

In the late 1960s and early 1970s, the influence of the New Archaeology on Aegean Bronze Age studies, comparable to Whitehead's 'stage of generalisation', became more visible. Before, and often even after, this period, many scholarly publications on Minoan Crete did not differ in many respects from works produced before the Second World War, since they were still largely influenced by Hellenism (in the sense of an idealization of ancient Greece) and informed by a culture-historical approach, in which material culture was closely linked to race, language, and *Volkgeist*. Thus, issues such as the relationship between Bronze Age archaeological evidence and later Greek literary sources, between Minoans and Mycenaeans, and between Minoan–Mycenaean cultures and Europe (via Classical Greece) continued to attract scholarly attention. The use of later Greek mythology to interpret archaeological finds and, vice-versa, of archaeological discoveries to extract a grain of historical truth from the mythological narratives persist in many seminal publications: the Aegean Bronze Age appears as a succession of *thalassocracies* and destructions caused by invasions, with some variations in their dates, agents, and nature. In a Cold War environment, in particular, narratives that discussed clashes between opposite hegemonies, worldviews, and mindsets resonated among readers and lent the Aegean Bronze Age more topicality: Minoans and Mycenaeans continued to function as a foil to each other, often through a series of well-rehearsed binary oppositions, such as un-Hellenic/Oriental/Southern vs. Hellenic/Aryan/Northern; pacifist vs. warlike; feminine vs. masculine; movement and disorder vs. symmetry and rationality; inventiveness vs. imitation; decadent over-refinement vs. vigorous barbarism.

An example of these continuing trends among scholarly works of the early 1950s, and preceding the decipherment of Linear B, is Arne Furumark's seminal article 'The settlement at Ialysos and Aegean history c. 1550–1400 B.C.' (1950). This publication deploys a subtle stylistic analysis of material culture to distinguish between the successive arrivals of Minoan and Mycenaean colonists at this settlement on the island of Rhodes. This succession of colonizations is the starting-point for Furumark's overview of the Late Bronze Age Aegean, where the crucial phenomenon was the confrontation (*Auseinandersetzung*) between two contrasting worlds – Helladic and Minoan, northern and southern – in which the former triumphed. The Minoans are peaceful tradesmen, more interested in commerce than war: their colonization of some Aegean islands was a non-violent 'trade before the flag' progression; the relationship between the 'kings' of Mycenae and Knossos was 'peaceful' and deteriorated only when their spheres of interest began to overlap, and the belligerent Mycenaeans emerged victorious.[59] Most significantly, Minoan Crete is reduced to a 'picturesque episode' in the long continuum of Hellenic–European history, only useful to stimulate the Greeks and connect them with the great civilizations of the ancient Near East.[60]

A similar approach, which differentiated the Minoans and Mycenaean peoples through stylistic analysis of their material culture, appears in Henriette Groenewegen-Frankfort's volume *Arrest and Movement*, published a year after Furumark's article.[61] But this Dutch archaeologist and art historian (wife of the distinguished archaeologist Henri Frankfort) did not share Furumark's idea that Minoan Crete was merely a 'picturesque' chapter in the long march of Hellenic glory. On the contrary, she teased Hellenophiles, for whom Greece had acquired a 'transcendent significance', and their perceptions of Crete through Hellenic lenses:

> The memory of Cretan culture survives in classical times only in the form of myths and it is remarkable that the ambivalent attitude towards Crete which marks them is also noticeable in those scholars for whom the Greek world has in turn acquired a transcendent significance. The phenomenon of Cretan art has baffled, enchanted, and irritated in turn because it seemed preposterous that it should be the historical antecedent and yet the absolute antithesis of what is most valued in classical art. Hence a certain self-consciousness in the scholarly ... efforts either to overpraise Cretan 'naturalism' and to link it with something similar in Greek art or to overemphasize its undisciplined waywardness and thereby to prove its utterly alien character. In fact, the only comfort for the harassed Grecophile has been throughout that this strange island culture, so uncomfortably close, so mysteriously linked with the mainland, was not 'oriental'.[62]

Groenewegen-Frankfort's aim was not to judge Minoan Crete from a Hellenic viewpoint, nor to define it as either 'European' or 'Oriental'. Instead, she stressed its delightful individuality. Minoan art stood apart from any other ancient culture, because of its distinctive characteristics:

Cretan art ignored the terrifying distance between the human and the transcendent which may tempt man to seek a refuge in abstraction and to create a form for the significant remote from space and time; it equally ignored the glory and futility of single human acts, time-bound, space-bound. In Crete artists did not give substance to the world of the dead through an abstract of the world of the living nor did they immortalize proud deeds or state a humble claim for divine attention in the temples of the gods. Here and here alone the human bid for timelessness was disregarded in the most complete acceptance of the grace of life the world has ever known. For life means movement and the beauty of movement was woven in the intricate web of living forms which we call 'scenes of nature'; was revealed in human bodies acting their serious games inspired by a transcendent presence, acting in freedom and restraint, unpurposeful as cyclic time itself.[63]

These ideas, albeit not so articulately expressed, were anticipated by earlier scholars and writers, such as Merezhkovsky (cf. Chapter 4), since they are based on similar observations, responses, and interpretations of specific elements of Minoan material culture and iconography noted since the early 1900s, such as the sense of movement, interest in the natural world, and relative infrequency of hunting and battle scenes (often exaggerated to suit peaceful views of the Minoans).

As pointed out by Gere, Groenewegen-Frankfort's enchanted view of Minoan Crete and Jungian psychology influenced even more pacifist and hippie interpretations that emerged in the 1960s.[64] Examples of this are Károly Kerenyi's ecstatic, opium-eater Minoans in his *Dionysos: Archetypal Image of Indestructible Life* and Jacquetta Hawkes's peaceful, feminine, and drug-fuelled Minoan paradise in her *Dawn of the Gods*.[65] Hawkes even suggests that plenty of sport, dancing, and well-balanced sex ensured a peaceful and enjoyable life for the Bronze Age inhabitants of Crete (cf. epigraph above).

Whether influenced by Groenewegen-Frankfort or not, pacifist views of the Minoans, which had originated in the first half of the twentieth century, occur in many historical-archaeological publications of the period examined in this chapter, ranging from popularizing volumes, such as Cottrell's *The Bull of Minos* (1955) and Alsop's *From the Silent Earth* (1962), to more specialized publications, such as Ronald Willetts's *Cretan Cults and Festivals* (1962), *Everyday Life in Ancient Crete* (1969), and *Ancient Crete* (1977).[66] Minoan pacifism continues to be associated with essentialist perceptions of the Minoans as feminine, matriarchal, pre-Hellenic opposites of the warlike, patriarchal Aryan Mycenaeans.[67] More interestingly, however, and also predictably in the context of the Cold War and Vietnam War, views on Minoan pacifism started to change: it was no longer regarded as necessarily a negative trait leading to well-deserved defeat (cf. Chapter 4), but as symptomatic of positive aspects of Minoan civilization and explicable through socio-economic materialist analysis. Willetts's monographs offer good illustrations of these points. According to this scholar, who was a member of the British Communist Party for part of his life[68] and whose works betray the influence of the Marxist archaeologist Gordon Childe, the Minoans were pacifists because their environment, egalitarian society, and long-lived collective habits created favourable economic and social conditions that eliminated strife, not because of some innate racial attributes: '[A]ggressive instincts were channelled into the conquest of the environment, in which indeed the Cretans early outdistanced the other Aegean people. The co-operative settlement at Early Minoan Myrtos, the long-continued practice of communal burial, the apparently even development of the several palace regions, combine with a general, though not total, absence of fortifications to indicate at least a high degree of mutual tolerance.[69] In addition, the agglutinative character of Minoan architecture reflected 'the continuing influence of a collective form of social organisation' and the Minoan palaces were 'symbolic of a large, close-knit household'.[70] Even the Minoan priest-kings appear like altruistic managers, servants of the people, rather than despotic Oriental rulers: '[T]he priest-king of the Cretan town-palace . . . is intermediary as priest, as he is intermediary as merchant. And he is one among many. His fellow-merchants are his social peers, his counterparts in the other palaces are his religious peers.'[71] Yet, the Minoans too, in the course of their history, started displaying an increased militarism, and before their conquest by the warlike Mycenaeans, when changing economic conditions brought an increase of social inequality.[72] If Willets had a fondness for Minoan collectivism, other scholars preferred to link Minoan pacifism more decidedly with the feminine–matriarchal element of this culture, usually deduced from a combination of evidence from Minoan iconography (the prominence of female imagery), Classical sources (such as Herodotus), and socio-anthropological theories, from Bachofen to Engels, as in previous decades. Examples are Schachermeyer's *Die minoische Kultur des alten Kreta* (1964) and Hawkes's *Dawn of the Gods* (1968).[73] Hawkes, in particular, suggested that the importance of the feminine element is one of Minoan Crete's main legacies to European civilization (via Greece), but wavered as to whether or not this actually implied female temporal power. According to this feminist archaeologist, the 'genesis' of the great achievements of Classical Greece occurred when the 'predominantly feminine force' of the southern, Mediterranean Minoans united with the 'predominantly masculine one' of the northern and more barbaric Mycenaeans, something that recalls earlier ideas in which the greatness of Greece was sought in the union of two gifted races, one more artistic and the other more virile.[74] While she recognized that a feminine principle would not necessary result in matriarchy, she suggested the probability of matrilineality on Crete and female temporal power, albeit only during the Old Palace period. By the New Palace period, this power had greatly diminished and suffered a major setback with the Mycenaean conquest of Crete: the role of the Minoan queen became limited to being a high priestess, even if she continued to sit on the throne at Knossos to enact the epiphany of the goddess.[75]

Even scholars who were more reluctant than Hawkes to accept the idea of a Minoan matriarchy, such as Hutchinson and Matz, still supported the idea that women on Crete enjoyed more social freedom than in other ancient societies and played an important role, especially in religious affairs,[76] while according to others the 'assured' place that women also held in Mycenaean society was probably due to the influence of 'the polished culture of Minoan courts'.[77]

Among so many publications offering an idyllic picture of a peaceful Minoan commercial *thalassocracy*, quasi-communist feminine harmony, mystical union with nature and the transcendent, brought to an end by patriarchal, warlike Mycenaeans taking advantage of the Santorini eruption, Sinclair Hood's *Home of the Heroes* (1967) and *The Minoans: Crete in the Bronze Age* (1971) stand out as both more old-fashioned and attuned to ideas of realpolitik. Hood's volumes mark a return to Evans's idea of the Greeks as the destroyers of Aegean palatial societies in *c.* 1200 BC, and the Minoans as the (not so peaceful) conquerors of parts of the Aegean, hence also his tenacious rejection of Ventris's decipherment of Linear B.[78] Hood, who was a pupil of Gordon Childe, also deployed a typical culture-historical approach, as illustrated by his use of invasions, migrations, and technological advances in the Near East as catalysts for innovation in the Aegean. Hood acknowledged the uniqueness and originality of Minoan Crete, its ecstatic religion, the importance of women in the religious sphere, and even the likelihood of matrilineality; at the same time, he appears to be sceptical regarding the actual extent of freedom for women.[79] Hood's use of analogies with the Near East, in particular, avoided the impression that Minoan Crete was an isolated, feminine, semi-communist paradise: instead, it is presented as a society ruled by kings, affected by wars of conquest and invasions in the Near East, and comparable to other cultures of this region, for which textual and archaeological evidence is more abundant.

If Hood's volumes stood out as nostalgic revivals of Evans's ideas, even more distinctive was Colin Renfrew's seminal *The Emergence of Civilisation: The Cyclades and the Aegean in the Third Millennium BC* (1972) because of its more radical novelty and New Archaeology flavour.[80] In the words of John Cherry:

> ... [T]his was a volume that not only deployed concepts and terminology radical in an Aegean setting – systems theory, cybernetics, locational analysis, statistics and quantification, and so on – but one that displayed a refreshing awareness of the wider world of archaeology, especially Mesopotamia, Mesoamerica and Europe, as well as a warm sympathy for at least some tenets of the New Archaeology ... Unlike then-recently published textbooks, such as Emily Vermeule's *Greece in the Bronze Age* (1964), organized in terms of lively descriptions of pseudo-historical, narrative structure, *Emergence* placed culture process and the explanation of culture change unabashedly front and centre. By proposing causal, system-based models, it seemed to provide, for the first time, a coherent over-arching framework for trying to understand how and why palace-based state polities emerged where and when they did in the Aegean Bronze Age.[81]

A detailed analysis of *The Emergence of Civilisation*, which largely focuses on the Cyclades and on the period before the great Minoan palaces, is beyond the scope of the present volume. Here it will suffice to point out Renfrew's general aims and approach as well as some of his specific views regarding the Minoans, especially in comparison with other works discussed above. This work grew out of Renfrew's dissatisfaction with Childe's diffusionist view that the Minoan and Mycenaean civilizations were 'an offshoot of Oriental civilisation, by which they were inspired and without which they would not have existed' and 'that Aegean civilisation was something borrowed by Europe from the Orient'.[82] In Renfrew's opinion, there were many developments that occurred in the Aegean during the third millennium BC, from agriculture to religion, which owed little to Oriental inspiration, but were crucial for understanding the emergence of 'civilization'. This was equated with the presence of writing, large urban settlements, and monumental ceremonial centres, which, in turn, were symptomatic of other transformations in the 'culture system' of a human group and were typical of the palatial societies of second-millennium Crete and mainland Greece.[83] Moreover, the endogenous processes leading to 'civilization' could benefit from cross-cultural comparisons.[84] The focus, thus, was not on invasions and migrations, and contacts between different people as an explanation for change, but on processes of adaptation and manipulation of the environment, changes in the various 'subsystems' of society, ranging from subsistence and settlement patterns to settlement sizes, population growth, and social organization, which could be examined through the analysis of quantitative data, not vague impressions and qualitative judgements.

This approach also offered more analytical explanations for the emergence of complex societies and cultural change than the inevitability of increasing complexity derived from evolutionary biology or recourse to alleged racial traits. Renfrew did not attempt to differentiate neatly between Minoans and Mycenaeans, but focused, instead, on their common features, since his main purpose was to understand the factors that led to the emergence of palatial centres on both Crete and mainland Greece. Similarly, he did not explain the lack of fortification on Crete in terms of some innate pacific characteristic of the Minoan people, but of the emergence of a systematic hierarchical organization.[85] In fact, he considered the lack of fortification as paradoxical, in view of the large quantity of weapons found on the island: this was linked with metallurgical development in the Aegean, in which Crete played an important role, which, in turn, was 'largely the consequence of military requirements'.[86] Furthermore, Renfrew did not attribute the collapse of Minoan and Mycenaean palaces to specific catastrophes caused by natural or human agency (or a combination of both), let alone by 'passive renunciation of power' (cf. epigraph). Instead, he explained this phenomenon through the vulnerability of the overextended palatial system and its inability to react against triggers that undermined its artificial 'equilibrium'.[87] Finally, in Renfrew's narrative there was no room for the Minoan Mother Goddess (nor, indeed, for matriarchy), but some sympathy for a polytheistic system: 'Nothing is gained by over-simplifying, by lumping all religious and funerary observances together as directed towards a single "Great Earth Mother", since more can achieved by observing the differences.'[88]

Despite being one of the most significant works on Aegean prehistory, and not just for the period examined in this chapter, Renfrew's book appears to have had relatively little impact beyond scholarly circles, especially when compared with, for example, Graves's *Greek Myths* or Chadwick's *The Decipherment of Linear B*. This can perhaps be ascribed to two main factors: its use of jargon, and the substitution of processes and more abstract ideas for people and individuals. As mentioned by Cherry (cf. above), one of the novelties in Renfrew's *The Emergence of Civilisation* was its terminology, and one notorious and oft-derided trait of the New Archaeology was its impenetrable prose. Suffice here to mention one of the reactions to an article by David Clarke, 'Archaeology: the loss of innocence', which is generally regarded as the leading manifesto of the New Archaeology in the UK.[89] For Clarke, the loss of innocence meant that archaeologists had lost the theoretical-methodological naivety of their forebears, and had become more self-aware, self-critical, and explicit about interpretative approaches. As J. N. L. Myres (the son of John Myres) humorously pointed out, however, 'If David Clarke and his New Archaeologists are no longer Innocent, it follows that they must be Guilty. Guilty of what? Well, clearly of at least one unpardonable sin, an outrageous misuse of their mother tongue.'[90] Although Renfrew's prose is far more readable than that of other exponents of the New Archaeology, it was not entirely immune from jargon and other sins against language.[91] This made the volume less appealing to many readers, non-specialists in particular, than the more accessible writings of other scholars, such as the dedicatee of Renfrew's book, Gordon Childe. The use of concepts, such as 'homeostatic control' and 'negative-feedback', despite their merits, did not have the same immediacy of more familiar ideas, such as conflicts between different nations, classes, and genders; similarly unappealing was the substitution of processes and more abstract ideas for the actions of ethnic groups and individuals. The famous 'Ode to Man' from Sophocles' *Antigone* is the epigraph to *The Emergence of Civilisation*, but human beings, as specific groups of people let alone as persons, are hard to find in its pages. Yet, even if this innovative work may not have had much immediate influence beyond academia, connections between specialist publications and Cretomanic novels and other cultural products continued unabated in this period, as discussed in the following section.

Cretomania in the Cold War: The Minoans in modern cultural practices *c.* 1949–1974 – from 'The mother strikes back' to the Minoans as Trojans

The increased polarization of Minoans and Mycenaean, in the wake of the decipherment of Linear B and other discoveries, is illustrated also in Cretomanic works of the 1950s–1970s, ranging from poetry to films and travel writings. This is especially evident in novels that offer new reimaginings of the myth of Theseus and Ariadne and connect it with the idea of Aryan patriarchal conquest of older matriarchal/matrilineal societies. But despite the Mycenaean/Aryan takeover of Crete, the Minoan Mother Goddess, in Mary Renault's words (cf. below), did strike back, and not only because of the growing influence of feminist and pacifist movements, as shown below.

'The mother strikes back' in historical and other novels

Mary Renault's *The King Must Die* (see Fig. 5.1) and *The Bull from the Sea* (1958 and 1962) are the most famous novels of this period that illustrate the confrontation between patriarchal and matriarchal belief systems. But this motif also appears in earlier works, such as the 1954 novel *Atlantis* by the British author, literary critic, and poet John Cowper Powys. In *Atlantis*, which is set after the Trojan War, Odysseus sails away from Ithaca once again, reaches America and explores, on his way, the recently submerged city of Atlantis, where he witnesses a tremendous battle between Olympians and older gods. This is the culmination of an attempted 'revolution of the older gods against the newer gods, of the great old giant-gods, animal-gods, dragon-gods, serpent-gods, and, above all, women-gods, for the older times were *matriarchal times*, and women, *not* men, however heroic such men might be, ruled Heaven and Earth, since at

Fig. 5.1 Dust jacket of Mary Renault's 1958 edition of the *King Must Die* (photo: N. Momigliano).

the beginning of things it was Gaia, our real old mother the earth'.[92] The novel contains only a few allusions to the material culture of Bronze Age Crete, but significantly refers to an earlier '"Minoan" or "Cretan" revolution', which preceded the conflict between Olympians and older gods.[93] Cowper Powys, who was an older contemporary of Robert Graves, shared his belief that ancient, prehistoric poetry and mythology were connected with the cult of a powerful female divinity (cf. Chapter 4). He also believed in strong connections between the ancient Welsh and the Minoans, via their common worship of a Mother Goddess, as indicated in some of his earlier novels and writings: 'one cannot help suspecting that a race as ancient as this – whose ways and customs still retain memories of the Golden Age when Saturn, or some megalithic philosopher under that name, ruled in Crete, and the Great Mother was worshipped without the shedding of blood – must have some secret clues to the mystery of life ...'.[94]

Cowper Powys's views on Minoan–Cymric affinities may have been mocked in a Cretomanic work first published, like his *Atlantis*, in 1954: *The Cretan Counterfeit* by Katharine Farrer – the wife of Austin Farrer, who was a close friend of C. S. Lewis and member of the Oxford 'Inklings'. This is an amusing detective story set in England and Greece in the year 1953, in which the Minoan Mother Goddess looms large, albeit in an ambivalent light.[95] Richard Ringwood, an Oxford-educated inspector at Scotland Yard, helped by his wife Claire (also an Oxford alumna), uncovers a gang of Cretan forgers while unravelling three mysteries. The first is the sudden and suspicious death of the fictional Minoan archaeologist, Sir Alban Worrall, in a London restaurant called 'Minos', which is run by a colourful Cretan and is suitably decorated with 'bad copies' of Minoan frescoes that, nevertheless, still show a 'typical feeling of primitive passion expressed in the style of a Diaghilev ballet – violence enacted in plasticity'.[96] The other mysteries are the attempted murder of one of Worrall's assistants and the earlier death of a young

Cretan workman on Worrall's excavation on Corfu. The solution of the case is partly assisted by some knowledge of Minoan archaeology, which Inspector Ringwood acquired while a student at Oxford. In the novel, Minoan Crete appears in an ambivalent light, as a remote, strange, and fascinating culture, which produced exquisite art, but also practised human sacrifice and was too dominated by a voluptuous Mother Goddess:

> ... [T]he great labyrinthine palaces they had discovered in Crete, their frescoes with groups of crinolined, big-breasted women, snaky-locked, postured like dancers; the slender youths vaulting unarmed between the fierce bulls' horns; the animals so spontaneous in movement and feeling, the humans so hieratic and remote. The many inscriptions written in letters no one could yet interpret. And, above all, the jewels, the rings and seals engraved with tiny, perfect pictures, some as flawless as if they had been carved yesterday; nearly all depicting the rites of their religion – virtually unknown except through their art. At the centre, clearly, stood the Mother Goddess, voluptuous and sovereign. A stripling god or king attended on her ways like a shadow. Was he son, mate, or victim, or all in turn, during the sacred dance of his ambiguous reign? His choreography was set for nine years, but hers went on forever. Presented with such beauty of form, and so far distant in time, even that cruel cult had a strange fascination; deep down, we all had it in us. If we went among modern savages the blood and stench and howling would revolt us; here, it was disguised in formal beauty, and we could still exclaim 'What pipes and timbrels! What Wild ecstasy!'[97]

Other passages illustrate a similar response, by describing Minoan Crete as 'queer' and fascinating at the same time, because of its strangeness and mystery (cf. chapter's epigraph). Farrer writes eloquently on the beauty of Minoan objects, but also refers to 'secret and nasty' games that involve human sacrifice,[98] and caricatures Minoan female empowerment and sensuality as well as Welsh–Minoan matriarchic affinities. For example, the architect and photographer in Worrall's team is a Welsh nationalist who fervently believes (like Cowper Powys) in the close connection between Wales and Crete: '[W]omen have access to a deeper kind of knowledge than we have ... It's the Life Principle, you see – they're so much closer to it. Women are surely part of the great Rhythm of Nature. And that's the reason why ancient Crete – yes, and ancient Wales, too; they're not so different as people think – were in a sense matriarchal.'[99] But the Welshman is also the cuckold husband of Zoe, an assertive Cretan woman who looks like a living replica of the Knossian snake goddess and satisfies her sexual appetites with a younger Minoan-looking Cretan waiter. Zoe, one of the ringleaders in the gang responsible for the Minoan forgeries, is domineering, insatiable, manipulative, and a foil to Farrer's real heroine: Clare, the demure wife of Inspector Ringwood, who finds fulfilment in her life by being her husband's helpmate. Vying with Zoe as the most wicked character in Farrer's story is the archaeologist Sir Alban Worrall, a selfish and exploitative man: besides other misdeeds, he adulterates an original artefact to suit a cherished theory and gain everlasting fame – the cherished theory being that 'Corfu is Homeric Scherie, last and latest outpost of the great Minoan culture',[100] something that could be read as an indirect criticism of Evans's use of fakes to support of his ideas, such as the chryselephantine figurines of the 'Boston Goddess', the 'Boy-god', and 'Our Lady of the Sports', as well as other artefacts (such as seals and gold signet rings).[101]

Another ambivalent view of the Minoan Mother Goddess and Crete appears in Mary Renault's famous *The King Must Die* and *The Bull from the Sea*. This dyad, which has been aptly described as a *Bildungsroman* for the Athenian hero Theseus,[102] explores Theseus's deeds and reactions at a juncture in history when significant shifts are taking place in society, from politics to religion and gender relations (i.e. the change from matriarchy to patriarchy). As Renault explained, a passage in a dialogue from her earlier novel, *The Charioteer* (1953), provided the starting-point for her very first historical novel, *The Last of the Wine* (1956), and a passage in the latter, in turn, gave her a cue for the *King Must Die*.[103] Also crucial were the discovery of the new Shaft Grave circle at Mycenae, the decipherment of Linear B, and her reading of Robert Graves's *Greek Myths* (published in 1955), especially his ideas on royal sacrifice.[104] For Renault, royal sacrifice seemed to have been at times enforced and at other times voluntary, prompting her to make further conjectures about its relationship to the 'tensions between victorious patriarchy and lately defeated, still powerful matriarchy' of the Aegean Late Bronze Age.[105] Besides, although Renault first visited Greece and Crete in 1954,[106] she had earlier and very personal connections with the Aegean Bronze Age: in 1926, as a second-year undergraduate at St Hugh's College, Oxford, she lived at 82 Woodstock Road in a house that Joan Evans, Sir Arthur Evans's half-sister, had recently donated to the college; this provided another stimulus for Renault's visits to the Ashmolean Museum and appreciation of Minoan art, and perhaps also for her interest in Gilbert Murray's investigations in the 'primitive' elements of Greek civilization.[107]

Unsurprisingly, in Renault's novels patriarchy is associated with the tall, blond, sky-god worshipping, vigorous Hellenic people of mainland Greece, and matriarchy with the small, dark, chthonic, and rather decadent pre-Hellenic Minoans of Crete. More surprisingly (and *pace* Childe, Blegen, Wace, and others), matriarchy is also associated with her 'Minyans' (also referred to as Shore-People and Pelasgians), who live in mainland Greece and the Cyclades.[108] The Minyans, however, kill the king ritually every year, whereas the Minoans, for the last couple of centuries, after a conquest by a Hellenic dynasty, replaced human sacrifice with the custom of hanging dolls on trees.[109] In any case, matriarchy is cast in a bad light, since for Renault no system in which one gender has overbearing power, and individuals are cast in strict binary roles, can be a good thing: the most admirable characters in her two Bronze Age novels are Theseus and Hippolyta, who are both unusual in their disregard for customary gender, class, and even racial conventions.[110]

The King Must Die and *The Bull from the Sea* represent a fascinating archaeological, anthropological, and psychological reimagining of the life of Theseus, from his childhood in Troizen to his death on the island of Skyros, which Renault portrays as suicide (i.e. voluntary royal sacrifice). His Cretan adventure – from his time as an accomplished 'bull-dancer' to his escape with Ariadne to the island of Naxos – is described in book four of *The King Must Die*, but references to the Minoans, their appearance, their material culture, and their customs are found throughout the two volumes. Renault's Minoans are small, slender, wasp-waisted, dainty, effeminate (wearing flowers in their hair), as well as proud and condescending (at least as far as members of the ruling classes are concerned).[111] They have an Oriental, rather than European, feel: for example, Minos, with his bull mask and hieratic pose on his throne, reminds Theseus of Egyptian gods; the Minoans had 'learned civility from Egypt, and from the men of Atlantis who came flying eastwards from Poseidon's anger'; and, in turn, like the Phoenicians centuries later, they had taught the Greeks how to write.[112] The widespread literacy on Crete and the Minoan crafts and architecture are highly admired: for example, Theseus is thunder-struck by his first sight of the 'House of the Axe' at Knossos, and feels 'like a goatherd who comes from the back hills and sees his first city'.[113] In addition, the Minoan potters 'lead the world', and it is a 'pleasure only to take their pots in your hand, to feel the shape and the glaze', even if the ceramic designs were beginning to show signs of decline, like many other aspects of their culture.[114]

Renault enthuses about Minoan arts and crafts but, like many other authors before and after her, she presents, beneath the beauty, an undercurrent of primitive, barbaric, and violent passions as well as decadence and corruption. Theseus abandons Ariadne on Naxos because she took to the island's annual ritual of killing and devouring the king 'like a fish to the sea, though she had been reared softly, knowing nothing of such things. There is rotten blood in the House of Minos'.[115] When Theseus makes a stop-over at Delos, on his way back to Athens, he feels only relief, and his words underline the dichotomy between the darkness, secrecy, and decadence of Minoan Crete and the light and openness of Hellas: 'the sharp white sunlight' of Delos washes away from him both 'the earth-darkness' of Naxos and 'the rotten glow of Crete'; everything on Delos is 'lucid, shining, and clear; even the awe of the god, the secret of his mystery, hidden not in shadows but in a light too dazzling for human eyes'.[116] The Minoans are not only 'rotten', but 'in second childhood; fruit for the plucking; finished, played out'.[117]

The Minoans are portrayed as decadent because of Renault's Hellenism, but also because of the chronological setting of her story. Many scholars and non-scholars alike had previously rationalized the traditional myth of Theseus's slaying of the Minotaur as commemorating the Minoan decline and correlated Mycenaean ascendancy in Late Minoan IB/II (late fifteenth century BC). Renault too, like Schliemann and others, did find 'the smell of truth' in Greek myths,[118] but her rationalization takes into account the decipherment of Linear B and the fact that, according to Greek tradition, Theseus lived only one generation earlier than the Trojan War (his son Akamas takes part in the Trojan War),[119] which is usually situated chronologically in the mid–late thirteenth century BC. Thus, in her story, Theseus's Cretan adventure occurs when Knossos had already been in the hands of a Mycenaean Greek dynasty for generations. Furthermore, partly because the actual date of the Theran eruption was only elucidated after Marinatos's excavations of the late 1960s, and partly to make the story more dramatic, Renaults conflates the final days of Knossos with the eruption of Thera and related earthquake and tsunami.[120]

The decline and fall of Knossos, however, are not ultimately attributed to natural disasters or events triggered by them; nor are they ascribed to some inevitable evolutionary-cum-cyclic development of birth–maturity–decline or to some innate racial trait, such as pacifism, which made the Minoans easy prey to Aryan/Greek conquest. One might almost say that Renault's reconstruction anticipates a New Archaeology approach: the main cause of the Minoan decline and collapse is the inability of the Minoan system to withstand adversity. In other words, the vulnerability of Crete in the face of adversity is caused by a rotten government system: the Mycenaean Greeks, who had conquered Crete many generations earlier, have turned out to be unscrupulous and impious; their elite is a strange Graeco-Minoan hybrid still following matrilineal customs merely to hold on to power; they despise the native Cretans unjustly, tax them harshly, and have lost respect for true religion and its significance. It is no wonder that the oppressed Cretan subjects are more than ready to revolt against their hated masters, with the help of Theseus.[121]

Theseus liberates the lowly Cretans from this rotten dynasty and fake, empty Minoan rituals, but the Mother Goddess strikes back. In *The Bull from the Sea*, she exacts her revenge in several ways: through Theseus's son Hippolytus, the 'Kouros of the Maiden',[122] who worships above all a female deity; through Phaedra's attempt to persuade Hippolytus to commit parricide, marry her, and restore the cult of a Mother, with its fatal consequences; and, perhaps above all, through Theseus's final suicide, which returns to one of the main themes of *The King Must Die* – the involuntary vs. voluntary king sacrifice. In the words employed by Renault in her own, Jungian analysis of her story, 'What is Theseus, after all, but primitive man struggling to defend his new-found ego against the surrounding jungle of the unconscious; his kingship resulting from his first success and in its turn demanding greater efforts towards evolution? Of course by the end of the book he has not reached the point of reconciliation with his anima, and of course the tragedy before him is inevitable; you could call the rest of the tale THE MOTHER STRIKES BACK'.[123]

And the mother did strike back, albeit in more benign ways, also among other authors (and artists) of this period. Two intriguing examples can be found in the works of a married couple: the Cambridge graduate, novelist, poet, and cookery writer Elisabeth Ayrton and her second husband, the writer, painter, and sculptor Michael Ayrton, who travelled extensively in Greece and Crete in the late 1950s and early 1960s.[124]

Elisabeth Ayrton's 1963 novel *The Cretan*, which reminded me of an Indiana Jones film, is a story of archaeological adventures, the power of female love, therapeutic psychoanalysis, and the tensions between local and global interests in the Minoan past. Well-known real archaeologists, such as Sir Arthur Evans, Duncan Mackenzie, John Pendlebury, R. W. Hutchinson, and Stylianos Alexiou make cameo appearances among its pages, together with Michael Ventris, and even Sigmund Freud and Carl Jung. The novel focuses on the illicit excavations of a new palatial site in east Crete (partly modelled on Kato Zakros), which has been discovered by Arkas, a fictional hero of the Cretan resistance in the Second World War. Before the war, Arkas had visited Evans's excavations and worked with R. W. Hutchinson at Knossos, but is now a bit of a misfit because of his total deafness, caused by an explosion in a cave while he was fighting the Germans.[125] The arrival of a Greek-American dealer, acting on behalf of a rich American collector, causes Arkas to quarrel with his accomplices in crime. This eventually leads to the intervention of the authorities and eventual redemption of Arkas, but not before a murder is committed and the dealer escapes with some choice finds. Besides loving descriptions of Minoan objects (especially Pyrgos, Kamares, and Marine style ceramics)[126] as well as commonplace allusions to the Minoans' love of nature, beauty, peace, and the Great Mother Goddess,[127] the novel contains some intriguing reflections on the Minoan past, its meaning for modern inhabitants, and female power – ancient and modern. Thus, for example, Arkas reflects that, when working for R.W. Hutchinson, he

> … began to learn about those who first lived a civilised life on this island, who were probably not, in any direct sense, our ancestors, but the remnants of whose culture seem … to be our heritage, part of Crete for the Cretans. One does not grudge the world the knowledge of the deep past which palaces and tombs of the Minoans can give when they are excavated, but should the things themselves belong to the Greek Government, even though Crete is part of Greece, and not to those who dig the ground and find them?[128]

Powerful women and deities play an important role in Arkas's life. One is Koryne, a young woman he is in love with and who looks, not fortuitously, 'like the accepted image of the Minoan Snake Goddess'.[129] Another is his educated sister, who helps him to communicate with the rest of the world. A third is an old woman who rescues him from his enemies, and is also connected with archaeology, since she worked on Evans's excavations at Knossos and leads Arkas to a sacred cave near the palatial site that he has discovered, where she performs a 'pre-Christian ritual' to honour her dead, using Minoan pottery as offering.[130] Even the Minoan Mother Goddess intervenes in Arkas's life: on one occasion, while tunnelling in a cultic area at the site, he feels a sense of dread, which soon dissipates, but makes him wonder whether this had 'come in some way from the earth goddess whose place it was and who did not wish to be disturbed again after so long, who had perhaps had the intention, but no longer the power, to bring the great stones down above us'.[131] Yet, the power of the goddess may not have vanished after all. On discovering an amazing chryselephantine statuette of the goddess, a likely allusion to the infamous 'Boston Goddess', Arkas admits, 'I felt, truly, though I may be laughed at for this, that she and her place had a good deal of magic left, a good deal of power'.[132] In fact, the discovery of this exceptional find will eventually lead to the murder of one of the bad guys in the story, the intervention of the Greek authorities, and Arkas's final redemption through therapy and his reciprocated love of Koryne, the living image of the snake goddess. The goddess in the novel, however, seems powerless against American money, since the dealer escapes justice, and with the chryselephantine statuette in his pocket to boot. Yet, one might say that, albeit unbeknown to the author, the goddess did show her undiminished potency and strike back, since the chryselephantine 'Boston Goddess' turned out to be a fake.[133]

Michael Ayrton's artistic and literary works also show some evidence of Minoan influence and involve the Minoan Mother Goddess, albeit in a very different way. Among his artistic output, one of his bronze works and two of his paintings are titled *Minoan landscape*, and various drawings that he produced in the 1960s depict Minoan archaeological sites, such Amnisos, Malia, Gournia, Zakros, and Phaistos.[134] None of these works, however, betray a strong, real Cretomania, in the sense of incorporation of Minoan material culture and stylistic traits. In fact, real Minoan elements in his artistic output are very few: possible examples are his use of a double-axe in his collages *Night*

Labrys (1962) and *Labrys* (1963);[135] in his 1970 bronze sculpture *Point of Departure*;[136] and in his 1971 etching *Minotaur as calf*.[137] His limited engagement with Minoan archaeology can be explained by the fact that, although his works shows a fascination with Daedalus, Icarus, and the Labyrinth, his inspiration comes above all from Classical authors and his appreciation of later Greek sculpture, whereas he had considerable reservations about Minoan art, as attested in his writings, especially his novel *The Maze Maker* (1967). This is a reimagining of the life of Daedalus, who is firmly Athenian in this version,[138] presented as an introspective autobiography, in which Daedalus examines his feelings, thought-processes, and relationship with other people as well as materials (especially metals). Although it shows some points of contact with Mary Renault's Theseus dyad (e.g. the period in which Daedalus lived is a time of transition from 'Cretan mother' to 'sky-gods'),[139] *The Maze Maker* is more reminiscent of Gide's *Thésée*, since Daedalus's labyrinth is the very life of the artist/craftsman and his fight with his own self.[140]

The novel includes many references to Minoan material culture, and Minoan art is portrayed as widely admired everywhere in the Greek world.[141] Daedalus commends some of its aspects, but his praise is mingled with criticism, and his overall view is ultimately negative, because Minoan art lacks vigorous large-scale sculpture, is effeminate, imitative, rigid, and above all decadent: 'Cretans are skilled beyond measure in the art of inlaying bronze with other metals, but remarkably inept in the craft of working bronze itself. Their sculpture in this metal is as abject as their large stone images of the goddess. Their genius lies in the perfection of small and precious objects,'[142] and even if they 'are the most accomplished craftsmen, the most skilled architects ... more inventive than the Egyptians',[143] they only excel in 'an effeminate delicacy of execution', whereas 'the male vigour of bronze sculpture defeats them and their votive bronzes lack all tension; they look as soft or as stringy as vegetables; nor can the Cretans make large sculpture in wood or stone.'[144] The Minoans are good at imitating and transforming foreign objects 'into something instantly recognizable as Cretan', but for Daedalus this is not 'an adequate way of spending a lifetime'.[145] Furthermore, they are 'rigid in their acceptance of convention', whereas Daedalus is proud of surpassing them in 'inventiveness and flexibility'.[146] The worst feature of Minoan art, however, is its decadence: 'Their arts hang overripe from their minds or go dry like pomegranates whose skins in time reach the brittleness of fine Cretan pottery and crack untouched. The gods will burst out through Crete and spill their red pomegranate seeds on Knossos and Knossos will rot under this autumn weight.'[147]

In *The Maze Maker* the Mycenaeans have not yet conquered Minoan Crete, but will soon do so, as suggested, for example, by allusions to increasing use of the Greek language (and Linear B).[148] More importantly, Hellas will eventually prevail over Minoan Crete in other, artistic ways: in a scene reminiscent of Kazantzakis's homoerotic encounter between Theseus and the Minotaur in *Kouros* (cf. Chapter 4), Daedalus fights with the monster, whose face changes during the contest so that it bears 'no longer the stupid and yet familiar countenance of a bull but that of a kouros carved from marble'.[149] Yet, despite the final Hellenic triumph, the Minoan Mother Goddess 'strikes back' during Daedalus's lifetime: when he and his pupils, Dipoinos and Skyllis, create 'the first Cretan monumental sculpture', this is 'a figure of Brito holding twin serpents', a clear reference to the Knossian snake goddess.[150] This work impresses Pasiphae so much that she entrusts Daedalus with building the contraption that will famously enable her to mate with Poseidon's bull, thus setting in motion a series of events that will lead to Daedalus's imprisonment and exile.[151]

Other curious examples of the Minoan Goddess getting her revenge, albeit in more benign ways, are two very different works: Thomas Burnett Swann's Minotaur trilogy – *Day of the Minotaur* (1966), *The Forest Forever* (1971), and *Cry Silver Bells* (published posthumously in 1977) – and the science-fiction novel *The Dancer from Atlantis* (1971) by the prolific award-winning author Poul Anderson. Both the trilogy and *Dancer from Atlantis* are also slightly unusual for this period, because they present a positive, non-decadent picture of the Minoans, even if their narrative is set in the last phases of the Minoan *thalassocracy*, close to the eruption of Thera and its aftermath.

Swann's trilogy portrays a fantasy world partly based on Minoan Crete, Greek mythology, and the author's humorous imagination. The story is told in reverse chronological order: *Day of the Minotaur* tells the adult adventures of the Minotaur Eunostos, and is set at the time of Achaean raids on Crete after the eruption of Thera; *The Forest Forever* and *Cry Silver Bells* are prequels that recount events in his adolescence and childhood, respectively. Eunostos is the last surviving Minotaur and one of the 'Beasts', namely centaurs, dryads, thriae, panisci, bears of Artemis, and other such beings (but not the griffin, which is 'the awesome but docile beast which the early Cretans had kept as pets in their palaces'),[152] who had migrated to Crete from their original homeland, the Isle of the Blest, before humans reached the Mediterranean island. The Cretans/Minoans, who arrived from the East, pushed the Beasts into a forest in the mountains. The two communities live together peacefully but on the whole separately, each within their respective territories. There are only some fateful exceptions to this rule, such as a Minoan prince's three-year sojourn in the land of the Beasts and his affair with a dryad, which produced two children: Thea and Icarus.

Eunostos, like his forebears, is not a monster: he does have pointed ears, a small tail, and voluminous red hair, which resembles a mane and partly hides his short horns, but he is 'far more human than bovine'.[153] He is keen on poetry, flowers, and gardening, and is an accomplished artisan, who produces artefacts, such as signet rings that are clear allusions to the material culture of Minoan Crete, as are the references in all three novels to other Minoan elements, such as frescoes, Kamares pottery, seal-stones, writing, bare-breasted women, bull-leapers, and figure-of-eight shields.

Day of the Minotaur purports to be the full publication of an ancient manuscript written by Eunostos on a scroll of papyrus, which the archaeologist T. I. Montasque (Ph.D, Sc. D, LL.D of Florida Midland University) discovered during his excavations in a Cretan cave near Phaistos. Poking fun at those scholars who are eager to find elements of historicity in ancient mythological tales, Swann describes the disappointment caused by the fact that the decipherment of Linear B revealed mere palatial inventories, instead of a Cretan *Iliad*, whereas Eunostos's manuscript contains a proper narrative. This text, which was initially described as the world's 'earliest novel, the fanciful story of a war between men and monsters', is in fact one of the world's 'first histories, an authentic record of several months in the late Minoan Period soon after 1500 B.C', as demonstrated by the discovery in the same cave of a 'seal ring of lapis lazuli which depicted a field of crocuses, a blue monkey, and a young girl of grave and delicate beauty' matching exactly the description of such a ring in the papyrus, thus showing that 'many of our so-called "myths" may in fact be sober history'.[154] The fictional papyrus tells the story of the victorious alliance of Beasts and Minoans that repelled one of the many Achaean attacks on Crete, which had increased after the Theran eruption. Despite their victory, many realize that the island will eventually fall to the Achaeans, whose power is on the rise: thus, Eunostos and other Beasts decide to return to their original homeland. Icarus and Thea, the adolescent children born of the affair between a Minoan prince and a dryad, decide to join them: Icarus has always been closer to nature than civilization, unlike Thea; but over time she has come to terms with her sexuality and love for Eunostos, and chooses the 'beastly' side inherited from her mother. Thus, 'the mother strikes back' in *Day of the Minotaur* too, but in a gentle and utopian way.

In all three novels the Minoans are portrayed according to well-established characterizations. They are a peaceful trading nation, fighting only against pirates or invaders, unlike the warlike Achaeans/Mycenaeans. They are very civilized, and worship above all a Great Mother Goddess, whose cult rituals include bull-leaping, drugs, and ecstatic dancing.[155] They are sensual people, who 'enjoy a considerable versatility in sexual practices'.[156] Women often held the Cretan throne, and are as equally regarded and 'as bold and as amorous as the men'.[157] Knossos is 'not a virtuous city by any means: its consumption of beer and wine was legendary, its sexual practices imaginative and prodigious; but its sins (said the Egyptians), or rather its pleasures (said the Knossians), lay in partaking, not in taking'.[158] The Minoans are a joyous people living for the present, unlike the Egyptians, who 'live in the past ... and yearn for departed majesties', and unlike the Achaeans, who 'live in the future ... and yearn for tomorrow's battle'.[159] The Minoans may appear 'light and fickle, incapable of deep, enduring love, because their funerals resembled festivities ... to a Cretan, however, death was not oblivion but another country, where all that one loved, all those one loved, were restored and immortalized beneath the radiant smiles of the Great Mother and her Griffin Judge'.[160] In *The Forest Forever*, in particular, a sense of love and justice pervades Knossos. Swann's description of the city and the ruling Minos is full of admiration.[161] The Minoans have a good relationship with animals: men and bulls perform together, and the latter are not killed in the arenas (as Kazantakis and others had already suggested).[162] When Eunostos visits Knossos, people stare at him in awe, but not in fear.[163] Animals, especially snakes, are believed to be reincarnated ancestors and friends.[164] Beasts and Minoans share some characteristics, yet to the former 'Nature is sometimes irascible, sometimes unpredictable, but still – a friend', while for the latter 'in spite of all their talk of worshiping the Great Mother, she is either a slave or a Master. They fear her unless they can put her in chains,'[165] a view that contrasts, to some extent, with other perceptions of the Minoan as a people living in empathy and great harmony with nature.

Only in *Cry Silver Bell* does one find a more ambivalent picture of Minoan Crete. As mentioned above, in *The Forest Forever*, the Bull Games are portrayed as a joint human–animal performance where no blood is spilt, whereas in *Cry Silver Bell* they are rather bloody affairs, in which 'the bull and the dancer stab each other to death, the one with the horns, the other with a short-sword or knife',[166] partly to satisfy certain urges created by the relative peace on the island: 'The Cretans ... not having fought a land war in several centuries ... relish the sight of blood.'[167] The Bull Games could be particularly 'barbarous' at Phaistos, since this town, contrary to Miller's and Lacarrière's feminine and Edenic visions (cf. Chapter 4 and below, respectively), was 'not so civilized as larger, northern Knossos'.[168] There is the recognition that the Bull Games may have degenerated in more recent times, following a shift from matriarchy to patriarchy: 'Perhaps, in earlier ages, when Woman instead of Man had ruled on Crete, such games had been a genuine ritual; no more ... Bigger ships and smaller hearts; thus, the Cretans of now.'[169] Yet, even in *Cry Silver Bell* the Minoans are 'brilliant artists ... Consummate merchants and seamen', who 'never even make war except against pirates', employ 'spears and axes in rituals, not in combat', and whose cruelty reminds one of that of children.[170]

A favourable and sensuous perception of the Minoans appears also in Anderson's *The Dancer from Atlantis*. This science-fiction novel starts with an accident that has struck the crew of a time machine on an expedition into the past. The machine and crew perish, but not before they have collected four people from distant ages, who survive the crash and are the main characters of the novel: Duncan Reid, an American architect and narrator of their adventurous tale, who, at the time of his abduction in 1970, was travelling with his unhappy and distant wife on a ship heading for Japan; Oleg, a Russian from the times of Yaroslav the Wise (early eleventh century AD); Uldin, a Hun from the fourth century AD; and Erissa, a Minoan/Keftiu wise-woman and former bull-leaper (or bull-dancer, as the author prefers to call her), who had survived the Santorini eruption. Just before the accident, the expedition had travelled back in time to a period preceding the eruption by a few months. The story thus covers the adventures of these odd four musketeers from that moment until the eruption and subsequent fall of Knossos, two events that are telescoped in the narrative and dated to *c.* 1400 BC.

The action takes place mostly in Athens, Knossos, and Santorini, which is identified with Atlantis. Like Renault's novels and many other works, *The Dancer from Atlantis* is largely a retelling of the myth of Theseus and the Minotaur, interpreted as a folk memory of the fall of the Minoan *thalassocracy* at the hands of conquering Achaeans–Mycenaeans. Anderson, however, takes issue with Renault (and Classical sources): his version presents an unsympathetic portrait of Theseus and a rosy view of Minoan Crete.[171] The Minoans are described as worshippers of a supreme goddess, whose high priestess is called 'the Ariadne' and is based on the sacred island of Santorini/Atlantis, whereas the ruler called 'the Minos' and based at Knossos governs in temporal matters. They are a strange but highly admirable people. Their women rank high in society (including those who perform the sacred 'bull-dancing'), and fare much better than their Mycenaean counterparts and those living in the 'purdah of Classical Greece'.[172] The Minoans are extremely hard-working and prosperous, and enjoy 'more leisure and probably more individual liberty than Americans, 1970 A.D.'.[173] Indeed, Reid 'wondered how the Keftiu, preservers of law and peace, carriers of a trade that brought prosperity to every realm it touched, clean, friendly, mannerly, learned, gifted, totally human, would come to be remembered for a man-devouring monster in horrible corridors'.[174]

Reid's own experience of the Minoan/Keftiu people, compared with his memories of Greek myths and other stories (like the novels by Renault!), allows him to unmask the truth behind the victor's stories. Theseus and his Achaeans–Mycenaeans merely desired to increase their commercial gains, envied Minoan prosperity, and resented the Minoans and their goddess.[175] In Anderson's version there is no monstrous Minotaur, and no human tribute either: instead, youths at a 'most impressionable age' are taken from the noblest families in Athens to be raised at Knossos, so that, on their return home and when they become leaders of their society, they will be more sympathetic to and malleable by the Minoan regime.[176]

Reid's admiration for the Minoans is such that he attempts to change the course of history by delaying the fall of Crete, even if for just one generation, to ensure that more of the Minoan heritage might survive. Although he does not accomplish his mission, he reflects that all was not lost: Theseus's abandoned Ariadne and the goddess may have gone, but the legacy of the Minoans lived on nevertheless, because 'when Achaeans, Argives, Danaans, Dorians have become Greeks ... the blood of the old Keftiu seafarers runs all in their vein'.[177] Theseus eventually becomes a good king, and Mycenaean civilization 'a worthy child of the Minoan'.[178] Even magnificent Classical Athens owed its 'secret seed' to a Minoan heritage.[179] Thus, although the narrator acknowledges that victors write history, thanks to archaeologists (or the right novelist?), modern people can still find out the truth about the Minoans and learn from them, as indeed he does from his comrade and lover Erissa. She gives him his best sex ever and teaches him 'what it is to be a woman, and so what it is to be a man ... the spirit that does not surrender, the courage to be joyful'.[180] After being rescued by another expedition and returned with his three companions to the times of their original abductions, Reid is keen to apply what he learnt from the past and restore a meaningful relationship with his wife. In other words, despite some touches of male condescension, *The Dancer from Atlantis* makes a nod to the emerging second wave feminism of the 1960s and in some ways anticipates the more radical reimagining of Greek myths, and revenge exacted by the Minoan Mother Goddess, illustrated in the works discussed in Chapter 6.

The opposition between Minoan Crete and the Mycenaean–Classical Greek world is also explored in other genres, in which, once again, archaeology and Greek mythology are intertwined.[181] In the cases discussed in the following section, however, the focus is on individual responses to the otherness of Minoan Crete and familiarity of Mycenaean Greece, now speaking in a well-known tongue, rather than on matriarchal–patriarchal conflicts.

The otherness of Crete and Hellas über alles

Examples of this are two poems by Salvatore Quasimodo, the winner of the Nobel Prize for Literature in 1959, who was also a translator of ancient Greek poetry and tragedy. The poems are 'Minotauro a Cnosso' and 'Micene', which were inspired by Quasimodo's journey to Greece in the 1950s.[182] In the former, Minoan Crete appears as a very refined culture, unencumbered by the idea of death, but also with undercurrents of bestial passions and very distant from the present:

I giovani di Creta avevano vita
sottile e fianchi rotondi. Il Minotauro
mugghiava nel Labirinto anche per loro.
Sapienza, Arianna, dei sensi di Pasifae
che schiumò immagini bestiali col toro
scattato come Venere dal mare.
Ma l'arte, gli arnesi dell'uomo, i segni
raffinati d'una vita civile
sono vostri, cretesi, non c'è morte.
Ma non c'è più nessuno che accoltella
il mostro a Cnosso, e nel mercato
d'Hiràklion confuso e sporco d'Oriente
non c'è nulla che assomigli
alla Grecia di prima della Grecia.
[The young Cretans had slim / waists and rounded flanks. The Minotaur / bellowed in the Labyrinth for them too. / Knowledge, Ariadne, of Pasiphaë's lusts / who foamed out bestial likenesses with the bull / sprung up like Venus from the sea. / But art, the trappings of man, the finer / signs of a cultured living / are yours, Cretans; there is no death. / But no one is left to knife / the monster at Knossos, and at Heraklion / in the market's oriental dirt and disorder / there is nothing that resembles / the Greece that was before Greece.]

Mycenae, by contrast, feels closer. There's something familiar about the ewe's cheese and resinated wine that Quasimodo finds at the tavern Belle Hélène near the famous archaeological site, as there is about the Greek heroes who populate its ruins, from Agamemnon to Electra and Orestes. Most significant for the poet, however, is a shared sense of Greekness. In the final verses of 'Micene', Quasimodo offers his Sicilian Greek greeting to the Lion Gate and other remains that the archaeologists (the philologists of the stones) have restored:

Ai Leoni della porta,
agli scheletri dell'armonia scenica
rialzati dai filologi delle pietre,
il mio saluto di siculo greco.
[To the Lions of the gate / to the skeletons of the scenic harmony / re-erected by the philologists of the stones / my Sicilian Greek greeting.]

Feelings of distance and familiarity elicited, respectively, by encounters with Minoan and Mycenaean archaeology, also appear in the poems 'Knossos' and 'Coming to Mycenae' by the American writer Lawrence Lee, who lived and travelled in Greece for five months in 1960.[183] In 'Knossos', there are allusion to Minoan elegance, and famous artefacts such as frescoes (showing slender youths, bulls, the Prince of Lilies, and saffron gatherers), Minoan stone vases, and the throne upon which a 'princess' sat. But all is remote, part of a 'drowned' past of 'dark blue depths we do not understand':

Forever Minos sleeps, and his tall queen.
The silence is a lonely bellowing
Of bulls, between each sharp
And golden horn
Of which is hung a harp
Where sea winds sing
Their questioning
While shadows reach forlorn
Through story meadows that were green:
Forever? . . . When such elegance has been?

Evening, like ocean, flows upon the land
And in that sea are more than dolphins drowned;
Young girls, slender boys,
A Flower Prince –
Where music gives them poise
With unheard sound
As from underground –
Have, smiling, drowned long since
With lilies for a necklace band
In dark blue depths we do not understand

'No more . . .' The saffron gatherer no more
Bends in the field to pluck the purple blooms
Nor hears the hoopoes cry
Among the wheat.
Noon is a stifled sigh
From empty rooms
In which nothing looms
Except a royal seat
Where a princess sat before
And hear outside the red bull's angry roar

The joy is solemn – that we can create:
Lift this libation vessel made of gold,
Jasper, and steatite –
A bull's head for a son of Zeus –
Into the cloudless light.
Its shape is old
And will unfold
Its sacred use,
The love the maker spent to celebrate
All that is proud and undefeated in our fate.

In 'Coming to Mycenae', by contrast, the poet has 'come home':

The way rose north of Argos from the plain
To the ruined walls of Cyclopean stones
And earth that held the bones
Of Agamemnon slain;
by presences invisible
Beneath the unresounding dome
I knew the tomb
And by the silences which fell
That I had come,
After much wandering, home.
Where they who had engendered me must wait
Impalpable, in pride and passion, beyond the Lion Gate.

To return to an Italian context, one can also compare Quasimodo's and Lee's responses to Minoan and Mycenaean material culture with those of the art historian (and Director of the Istituto Centrale del Restauro) Cesare Brandi and the writer Riccardo Bacchelli, who visited Knossos and Mycenae in the 1950s and 1960s, respectively. Their reactions suggest a feeling of recognition and admiration for the Mycenaean remains, and perceived strangeness (even dislike) for Minoan Crete, in a manner that closely recalls the earlier negative impressions of their compatriot Mario Praz as well as French writers de Lacretelle and Mauclair, discussed in the previous chapter.

Brandi, in the pages of his *Viaggio nella Grecia Antica* (1954), claimed that Crete found a way to his heart ('Creta, mi sei rimasta nel cuore').[184] If this was the case, however, it was not through the island's Minoan past, but rather through its landscape, Byzantine churches, and picturesque market of Heraklion. Brandi described his visit to the Palace of Minos at Knossos as a black day ('giornata nera'): his artistic and historic sensibilities were profoundly shocked by Evans's restorations, which made even the 'venerable' throne of Knossos look 'pretentious and ridiculous'.[185] Although Brandi was more favourably impressed by Phaistos, Hagia Triada, and some of the finds from the latter in the Heraklion Museum, such as the famous steatite vases and frescoes, he concluded that Minoan art was not really art and that the Minoans were a rather peculiar Mediterranean people, since they tightly swaddled infants' waists, cruelly forced women to bare their breasts, and could not be a matriarchy, despite some notable feminine traits in their iconography.[186] By contrast, Brandi's report on his later visit to Mycenae is peppered with literary allusions and enthusiastic terms: not only does he prefer the nudity of the remains of the Mycenaean palace to Evans's reconstitutions, but the Lion Gate lives up to its fame; the roughly hewn blocks of the citadel's walls are magnificent; the Shaft Grave circle excavated by Schliemann is magical; and even the postern gate reminds him of barbaric grandiosity.[187]

Bacchelli visited Mycenae and Tiryns for the first time in the spring of 1958, and found these sites fascinating, surprising, provocative, and a 'must see', the former in particular.[188] He described the ruins of Mycenae as powerful, grandiose, and astonishing: they reminded him of the cruel deeds linked to the site in Greek epics and Attic tragedies, of Machiavellian ferocious and terrible virtue, of Homeric vigour and Vichian barbaric heroism. Mycenaean tombs, in particular, exemplify for him elegant perfection and exquisite architectonic beauty. In other words, for him Mycenaean ruins evoke powerful literary memories and the archaeological discoveries add to the ancient myths something real, credible, and significant.

By contrast, his encounter with the physical remains of the Minoans, during a visit to Crete in September 1962, leaves a sense of disappointment.[189] His impression is that whatever was original and peculiar in Minoan civilization did not leave much trace in the Hellenic. The stories about Minos, Pasiphae, the Minotaur, and Theseus for Bacchelli are only fairy tales, which reflect the wonder and fear of the unknown, and something that is misunderstood and distorted. This does create a sense of mystery – but for Bacchelli the mystery turns out to be, mostly, the unexpected discovery of a new civilization, which is not that special and original after all: it is a surprise that disappoints. He finds Minoan architecture much inferior to the Mesopotamian and Egyptian, and considers Evans's reconstructions as fake antiques, which interfere with both scientific undertakings and poetic reimaginings. Even the famous Minoan frescoes are a mere expression of barbaric taste: opulent and destitute, refined and coarse at the same time. This is not a salubrious, vigorous barbarism, but a decadent and artificial one, corrupted before maturity. Only the actual choice of the physical setting of the Minoan palaces and the minor arts elicit some praise, especially the representations of marine life in ceramic productions. Bacchelli concludes his Cretan musing by wondering whether the irretrievable Minoan music and poetry may have been among this civilization's most interesting aspects – an idea that echoes earlier suggestions by Evans and Glotz about the existence of Minoan music and poetry.[190] In sum, for Bacchelli the only fascinating mystery about Crete is not the discovery of a disappointing new civilization, but that created by the later Greek myths, which turned a banal building into a wondrous labyrinth, and the bull-ceremonies into absorbing stories about monstrous beings and sexual desires.

Neither Crete nor Mycenae elicited a sense of recognition and even curiosity in Martin Heidegger, as illustrated in his brief memoir of his first journey to Greece, which took place in 1962.[191] For the German philosopher, who was travelling with his wife, things started to go wrong on their arrival at Corinth: 'A day of painful conflict began. We were about to visit Mycenae. I felt a resistance against the pre-Hellenic world, although it was the critical exchange with it that first helped the Greeks to grasp their proper element.'[192] Such was his 'resistance' that he recorded not a single sentence about the citadel of Agamemnon. Soon afterwards, following an 'uneasy nightly crossing from Nauplia', he reached Crete, and encountered 'a strange, pre-Greek world'.[193] After visiting Knossos and the Heraklion Museum, he recorded his reactions:

> ... the labyrinthal Palace bears witness to a nonwarrior [sic!], rural and commercial Dasein dedicated to the joys of life, although highly stylized and refined. A feminine divinity is supposed to have been the center of all the worship. What comes in view is something of an Egyptian-oriental essence. Enigmatic as the whole is also the sign of the double axe that keeps occurring. Everything is focused on the luxurious, on adornment and embellishment, from the large frescoes to the insignificant utensils of everyday life ... the abundance of objects and forms, the impressive glimmer and the luxurious shine beg the question: what is this that shines in things and hides itself in the shine?[194]

Heidegger further elaborates that the Minoan 'shine ... once belonged to a vigorous Dasein, strange, but all the same enchanting for the Greeks', and yet he also wonders whether 'what shines in the shine is only the shine itself, and therefore neither can conceal nor hide anything', an observation that recalls Spengler's and de Lacretelle's idea that Minoan Crete lacked profound symbolism.[195] Even if the Minoan 'shine' enchanted the Greeks, it had no attraction for the philosopher: most telling of all, perhaps, is the fact that Heidegger and his wife relieved themselves 'from the burdensome expedition to Phaistos, on the south of the island', preferring to stay on their boat.[196] Heidegger felt that he had found the Greece he was looking for only once he arrived on Delos.[197]

Minoan Crete as feminine lost paradise and unembarrassed monument to the pleasures of the flesh

Minoan otherness and opposition to Mycenaean–Classical Greece appear in the pages of other travellers to Greece in this period, but in the cases examined in this section these features are perceived as admirable. For example, the French poet and writer André De Richaud regarded Crete (ancient and modern) as Oriental and completely different from Mycenaean and Classical Greece, but while Mycenae is a place haunted by ghosts, Knossos is the wonder of wonders ('la merveille des merveilles') and is populated with human beings who are still alive.[198] The flawless Parthenon conveys Winckelmannian calm and serenity, but Knossian architecture reaches tranquillity and perfection too in its disorder.[199] The golden whiteness of the Athenian temple produces a feeling of reason, but Minoan Crete provides a sense of emotion and colour, which touches the most intimate recesses of one's being.[200]

A similarly enthusiastic response to the otherness of Minoan Crete appears in the work of another prominent French writer and critic, Jacques Lacarrière, who visited the island twice in the 1950s.[201] In his popular *L'été grec* (1975), Lacarrière recounts that, when he first visited Crete, he had little knowledge of Minoan civilization: he spent a few days at Knossos and let the Knossian ruins and frescoes appear to him unmediated by historical and literary baggage, as if he were leafing through a book which offered something attractive and unusual on every page, and was so different from Greece.[202] He felt that nothing of the famous later Greek myths really transpired from the Knossian ruins but, unlike Bacchelli, he was not disappointed by the disjuncture between physical and literary *topoi*. Instead, Minoan Crete reminded him of Occitania, another lost civilization full of the sweetness of life ('douceur de vivre'), and left him with a taste of paradise lost ('un goût de paradis perdu').[203] For Lacarrière, the ruins of Knossos emanate a sense of freedom and osmosis between palace and town, those of Mycenae one of oppression and isolation.[204] If Minoan Crete is feminine and full of joy, Mycenae is steeped in death and matricide: the Greeks needed to kill the mother (the *genos*) to create the brotherhood of the polis – something vaguely reminiscent of Renault's *The King Must Die* and *The Bull from the Sea*.[205] His feminine, innocent, and joyous impression of Minoan Crete is also partly created by the contrast between this lost world and the recent history of the island – the centuries of foreign occupation, war, vendettas, and the very masculinity that modern Cretans convey through discourses of *andreia* (manliness), *levendia* (male bravery), and *philotimo* (love of honour).[206]

When Lacarrière, years after his visit to Crete, read Miller's *The Colossus of Maroussi*, he was much surprised to discover that they had coincidentally shared the strong feeling of femininity elicited by Phaistos.[207] Neither surprising nor coincidental is that Lawrence Durrell shared with his friend Miller some impressions about Minoan Crete and Mycenae in some of his writings of the 1960s and 1970s. For example, Durrell's description of Agamemnon's citadel as 'ominous and grim', 'a place of tragedy and blood', 'transgression, tears and insanity', which appears in *Spirit of Place* (1969), recalls Miller's similar feelings in *The Colossus of Maroussi* and even uses some of the same terms.[208] In *The Greek Islands* (1978), Durrell writes appreciatively of Minoan civilization, which he believes was destroyed by the eruption of Santorini, even if the encounter with some Minoan artefacts, such as the 'snake goddesses', conjures lukewarm reactions.[209] In words reminiscent of Miller's earlier impressions, Durrell describes the ruins of Knossos as emanating from the presence of a civilization that was 'gay' but also 'thoughtful', mysterious, 'faraway', sometimes reminiscent 'of China and sometimes of Polynesia'.[210] Like Miller, Durrell was also much impressed by Phaistos but, unlike his friend, was not grateful to Evans for his restorations at Knossos, which he found 'insipid and in poor taste'.[211]

Neither in *Spirit of Place* or in *The Greek Islands* did Durrell return to the topic of the earthy and lustful Minoans of the period before the Second World War, which was also shared by many other writers and poets (cf. Chapter 4). This theme, however, appears in the 1961 novel *The Gold-Hatted Lover* by the American prize-winning novelist, translator, essayist, and poet Edmund Keeley. In this work, one finds the most peculiar reactions to Minoan antiquities and Evans's reconstructions, in which the distant past, recent past, and present are mingled in a strange erotic fantasy and the palace of Knossos becomes 'an unembarrassed monument to the pleasures of the flesh', but also a *memento mori*.[212] The novel tells the story of a holiday in Athens and on Crete, which the narrator, Tom Macpherson, the thirty-year-old American vice-consul in Thessaloniki, spends with his old college friend Bradley Cole, Bradley's wife Gloria, the writer and poet Patrick Lanahan, and Vera Karras, a beautiful, sexy young Greek woman of Cretan birth, who acts as their guide. Bradley soon embarks on an affair with Vera, and his wife eventually turns her attention to Tom, who struggles between his (unfulfilled) erotic impulses and moral qualms. Alcohol, a holiday atmosphere, and the sexual chemistry between Bradley and Vera provide stimuli to Tom's own sensual feelings, imagination, and misgivings. A visit to Knossos creates a heady mix of archaeology, libidinal fantasies, self-analysis, and reflections about the recent and distant past. On their way to Knossos, Tom and his companions witness the aftermath of the explosion of a Second World War mine, which had killed a local. During the visit to Knossos, despite using the *Blue Guide*, Tom and his companions soon find out 'why they called this palace a labyrinth'.[213] He gets separated from the others, after lingering over 'one of those frescoes [in fact a replica] of black-tressed women lavishly clothed except for their gorgeous breasts'.[214] He continues his visit alone, moving aimlessly through the rooms and corridors of the palace, marvelling at the tapering Minoan columns, giant *pithoi*, lustral basins, and other spaces 'too dark and secret to have been useful for anything but sin'.[215] The (reconstructed) ruins and frescoes set his fantasy alight, and mingle with other memories:

> My eyes settled on the fresco opposite me, a fresco of dark-skinned vase-bearers in a stylized procession, and that made my imagination leap again. I began to see that palace as an unembarrassed monument to the pleasures of the flesh. I saw lovers offering libations to bull-headed gods in order to prolong their virility, then bearing wine to banquet tables full of Keatsean delights, filling themselves not quite to satiety in order to be light for further gratification, descending to bathe in vast pools of perfumed oil so that their sunbaked skins would soften and their mind relax, retiring eventually to those secret rooms for an orgy whose only limit would be the final exhaustion of the senses, certainly never caring for a second that those same rooms would one day be filled not with the cries of their pleasures but the stillness of their death.
>
> I must have began to suffer some kind of hang-over from our experience on the road earlier that afternoon, because this thought, and the fresco opposite, and the weight of history in that place started to oppress me; the beautiful ghosts that I had raised suddenly vanished and I began to see new images that almost made me sick: bodies turning white and rotting, the flesh falling away from the bones, and too much else that I can't describe with comfort. The whole place turned as cold as a tomb. I stood up abruptly and moved into the sunlight beyond the colonnade, where the walls in front of me became piles of stone again, and the columns, the roof, the whole portico behind me merely a reconstruction of contemporary cement. Then I heard voices on the level below me – loud American voices – and I took a long breath.
>
> – 'Where the hell have you been?' Patrick yelled. 'We'd given you up to the Minotaur'.[216]

As Tom rejoins his group, Bradley and Vera go missing, and so, together with Patrick and Gloria, he sets out to find them. Despite some initial misgivings, Tom finds himself more and more on the side of the amorous couple. He delays the search to give them as much time as possible together, hoping that 'they were linked in some kind of embrace at the end of one of those dark corridors, making a gesture (even if they didn't know it was a gesture) against the history of death around them to please my ghosts – that is, doing exactly what I would do if I had the courage and the chance'.[217] His wish is fulfilled, although not quite in the way that he had hoped for. He finds them in the Throne Room, which Tom describes as the most beautiful room he has seen on that day. They are sitting side by side on one of the ancient stone benches flanking the throne, and their figures are described against the bright background of the room's frescoes (or, rather, their replicas), almost as if they were part of them. They are holding hands and do not react to Tom's presence: they are immersed in a contemplative reverie, 'gazing straight ahead between those tapering columns at the wall opposite in an attitude of suspended motion, like dancers in a momentary trance',[218] an image also evocative of some Minoan frescoes. Thus, although not linked in a carnal embrace, the couple seems to make more than a gesture against the history of death, as they appear to achieve a deep, sensory, and serene connection with the Minoan surroundings (and Evans's reconstructions).

Minoans in Greek–Cretan contexts after the decipherment of Linear B: Between Hellenization of the Minoans, Minoanization of the Greeks, and universal history

From the 1950s to the early 1970s, equally intriguing responses to Minoan Crete as a sensuous place and lost paradise appear in the works of Greek authors of Cretan birth who continue to incorporate the Minoans into the long continuum of Hellenism in many imaginative ways, even after the decipherment of Linear B. An example of this is Kazantzakis's romanticized autobiography, *Report to Greco*, written between 1955 and 1957 (the year of his death) and first published posthumously in 1961. As shown by Beaton and discussed in Chapter 4, Kazantzakis's works of the 1930s and 1940s presented a view of the Minoans, or at least of their palatial elites, as decadent, debauched, oppressive, and the very antithesis of Hellenism. Even if he considered the 'Cretan glance' to have Minoan origins, a favourable appreciation of the Minoans and their place in Hellenism only emerged clearly in his *Report to Greco* in a chapter titled 'Return to Crete', which describes a visit to Knossos that he probably made in the mid-1920s.[219] His narrative repeats some established ideas, such as the contrast between the 'balanced geometric architecture of Greece' and the more imaginative and free-flowing layout of the Knossian palace, which expresses 'imagination, grace, and the free play of man's creative power' and grows 'like a living organism, a tree'.[220] In a similar vein, he suggests that 'landscape, palace, paintings, and sea' show 'faultless harmony and unity' because the Minoans worship a divinity that was 'as nimble and playful as the sea which embraces the island'.[221] Kazantzakis does not seem to be bothered by Evans's reconstructions, and describes in warm, sensuous terms the replicas of Knossian wall paintings interspersed in the ruins (whose originals he would have seen in the Heraklion Museum):

> ...large almond-shaped eyes, cascades of black tresses, imposing matrons with bare breasts and thick voluptuous lips, birds – pheasant and partridge – blue monkeys, princes with peacock feathers in their hair, fierce holy bulls, tender-aged priestesses with sacred snakes wrapped around their arms, blue boys in flowering gardens [see Fig. 5.2]. Joy, strength, great wealth; a world full of mystery, an Atlantis which had issued from the depths of the Cretan soil. This world looked at us with immense black eyes, but its lips were still sealed.[222]

Kazantzakis asks what kind of world this was, and what feats it accomplished. His answer combine long-lived ideas, such as Minoan Crete as a bridge between different continents and the spark that ignites Europe; the contrast between Near Eastern and Minoan art, illustrated by the latter's gracefulness and appreciation of the human scale, the human body, and movement. But it also contains some more intriguing elements, which mark a departure from his previous views of the Minoans:

Fig. 5.2 Knossos, Saffron Gatherer fresco, as originally restored by Evans, with blue boy instead of a monkey (after Evans 1921: colour plate IV between pp. 264 and 265).

> Crete served as the first bridge between Europe, Asia, and Africa. Crete was the first place in a then totally dark Europe to become enlightened. And it was here too that the Greek soul accomplished its destined mission: it reduced God to the scale of man. Here in Crete the monstrous immovable statues of Egypt or Assyria became small and graceful, with bodies that moved, mouths that smiled; the features and stature of God took on the features and stature of man. A new, original humanity full of agility, grace, and oriental luxury lived and played on the Cretan soil, a humanity which differed from the subsequent Greeks.[223]

Minoan Crete and its 'humanity' are still portrayed here as different from later Greece, but thanks to the 'Greek soul' or, rather, the 'soul of Greece', as I would prefer to translate the original 'η ψυχή της Ελλάδας' (for reasons that will become apparent later), one can find on this island the first step in making the divine more human and graceful – something that is reminiscent of Groenewegen-Frankfort's Minoan 'grace of life' and Deshayes's 'Cretan humanism' (cf. above). As Beaton has observed, this represents a remarkable change not only because in *Report to Greco* Kazantzakis expresses a more positive view of the Minoans in general, but also because he acknowledged that they had developed a form of humanism thanks to 'the soul of Greece', whereas in earlier works, such as *Kouros*, it was Theseus's encounter with the Minotaur that transformed something monstrous into something humane, a Greek *kouros*.[224]

Beaton has also suggested that in *Report to Greco* Kazantzakis 'allowed himself to do something that Evans had always stood against: he has domesticated the "exotic", "alien" Minoans as *Greeks*', weaving them 'into an imagined diachronic synthesis of Hellenism'.[225] There is much to be commended in Beaton's analysis, but Kazantzakis's position has some points of contact with Evans's vision: even if the Cretan author crucially allows a spirit of place ('the soul of Greece') to inspire his Minoans, instead of Evans's innate superiority of the Mediterranean–Minoan race, he still describes them as different from the Greeks, and he implicitly expresses the idea, already championed by Evans and many others, that later Greece is culturally indebted to Minoan Crete. I suggest that Kazantzakis is foreshadowing what Hamilakis has described, for later periods, as the 'ambivalent incorporation' of the (local) Cretan identity and Minoan past into (national) Hellenic narratives.[226] In other words, I would suggest that, while Hellenizing the Minoans, Kazantzakis is also Minoanizing the Greeks: he is creating a broader Hellenism, which valorizes the Minoan contribution, is partly rooted in a spirit of place, and is based on shared ideas rather than essentialist notions of race.[227]

According to Beaton the decipherment of Linear B in 1952 could have contributed to Kazantzakis's change of perspective and Hellenization of the Minoans, since it showed that, in its final phases, the rulers of Knossos used Greek, the language still spoken today on Crete, and that their transactions involved 'such still-familiar commodities as sheep and wine', thus making the Minoans 'much less formidably "other" than their discoverer, Arthur Evans, had been determined that they should be'.[228] This is a valid point, but other factors also explain the negative portrait of the Minoans in Kazantzakis's earlier works, such as their chronological and elitist settings (end of the Bronze Age; palace of Knossos); the more dramatic effect created by a Spenglerian clash between two opposite worlds; and the desire to present the outcome of this conflict as the victory of a more dynamic, democratic, Hellenic order.[229] In addition, if the decipherment of Linear B familiarized the last rulers of Knossos, it could also underline Minoan otherness and opposition to the Mycenaeans/Greeks, especially if one considers that language has been a significant marker of Greek identity at least since Herodotus's times. The decipherment could have stimulated further the desire to valorize the Minoan past and incorporate it into the long continuum of Hellenic history, especially among Cretans authors who took pride in both their Hellenic and Cretan identity, as did those who were involved in earlier incorporations of Minoan Crete into Greek history, such as the 1920s pageants discussed in Chapter 4. Indeed, one may wonder how much these pageants and other earlier incorporations of the Minoans into Hellenic history may have influenced Greek works published in the 1950s–1970s, such as Kazantzakis's *Report To Greco* and others by Odysseus Elytis, Aris Diktaios, and Demetrios Michalaros, discussed below.[230]

The Heraklion-born poet and Nobel Prize winner Odysseus Elytis included his sensuous and creative Minoans in a wider Hellenism in his famous poem *To Axion Esti* (first published in 1959), which has been described as 'a spiritual autobiography' offering 'a contemporary Greek consciousness through the developing perspective of a first-person persona who is at once the poet himself and the voice of his country', an effect created partly by constant 'allusion to the historical and literary tradition of Greece'.[231] In the poem, the creativity of the poet vanquishes the forces of oppression, destruction, and evil by promoting Eros, the first creative power, especially through an empathy with the natural world and the long literary-historical tradition.[232] It is therefore quite significant that, towards the climax of this work, one finds the following allusion to Minoan frescoes, especially the 'Prince of Lilies' (see Fig. 3.13) as a symbol of the poet himself and of a '"new order" that is prophesized as emerging out of the violence and destruction of World War II':[233]

> He, the conqueror of Hades and the savior of Eros
> he is the Prince of Lilies.
> And I saw myself painted for a moment
> by those same Cretan breaths,
> So that the crocus might be vindicated by the skies.[234]

The reference to the poet as 'Prince of Lilies' (see Fig. 3.13) probably alludes to Elytis's Cretan birth; his description as 'conqueror of Hades and saviour of Eros' may also partly refer to the oft-repeated notions of Minoan creativity and lack of concern for the afterlife, while the 'crocus that might be vindicated' may refer to the Knossian images of crocus-gatherers (see Fig. 5.2) and reflect ideas of Minoan love for and empathy with nature.

The lesser known Cretan poet Aris Diktaios also paid homage to his nature-loving Minoan ancestors in two of his poems, one titled 'Keftiu' (the term used by the Egyptians to indicate people usually identified as the Minoans: cf. Chapter 2) and the other 'A Minoan – Reading the clay disk of Phaistos'.[235] The former was written in 1938, but was first published in the 1950s and republished in 1974. As Beaton has remarked, the poem recalls Elytis's appropriation of the 'Prince of Lilies' and has an elegiac feel as it suggests that 'the passing of the "Keftiu/Minoans" was also the end of an Edenic, golden age, of a time of heroes when man and nature were not yet fully separated'.[236] The poem describes a youth who wrestles with sounds, and with sounds tries to save his race, and feels that inside his blood there is a meeting point of all his ancestors. His upbringing alludes to his Cretan roots: as a young man, he was suckled from a she-goat and learned from bees, bulls, and the Mother Goddess Diktynna. He is a youth in harmony with nature, and Spring herself has called him her king. He is the last hero of his tribe. The illustration accompanying the poem shows Spring and the youth surrounded by butterflies and lilies, and recalls Evans's reconstruction of the 'Prince of Lilies' (see Fig. 5.3; cf. Fig. 3.13). A similar enchantment and sensuous engagement appears in his poem on the Phaistos disk, first published in 1965 and probably composed around that time. In an accompanying note, Diktaios explains that he was attracted by the pattern of repetition of certain signs on the disk, and that he had become convinced that the artefact recorded Minoan poetry.[237] He first had the idea to compose a poem 'à forme fixe' based on the disk after reading about the 1908 discovery of an inscription recording the Hymn of the Kouretes to Diktean Zeus at Palaikastro.[238] He later composed 'A Minoan – Reading the clay disk of Phaistos' by equating his own line of Greek verse to each of the signs found on the disk. The result is a rather peculiar hymn to nature, sung by a youth, with refrain and stanzas full of sensual imagery, from flowering crocuses to budding green branches on trees, a breeze singing among leaves, and an erotic sun the colour of desire. Diktaios himself commented on the coherent but also surrealistic results of his experiment, while Beaton, who translated into English the first few verses of the poem, reported below, has remarked upon its 'incantatory quality', due to its obscure meaning and repetitive nature:

The saffron-crocuses at Phaistos will be flowering now
and green branches will be sprouting
on the new plane-trees that follow the stream.

My day was all of light the colour of honey, and it was,
this light, a single song made up of colours.[239]

Diktaios further explains that he wanted to produce an archaic poem similar to a
Sumerian story of the goddess Inanna, but in the end he was left only with his Greekness
and his modern psychological insights, which he loaded, anachronistically, upon the
shoulders of an old Minoan, in a way reminiscent of how Cranach painted Paris as a
medieval knight, Goethe gave his Iphigenia an awareness of Christian morality, and
Stratis Tsirkas saw Cavafy as a communist.[240] Thus, perhaps partly as a consequence of
the decipherment of Linear B (and in the context of Minoan incorporation into
Hellenism), this poem embraces the distance and otherness of Minoan Crete while
expressing a nostalgic desire for this lost paradise, which can only be mediated through
the poet's own Greekness.[241]

A different stance appears in the ambitious epic poem *The Minoan* (1958) composed
in English by the Greek-American poet, journalist, and magazine editor Demetrios
Michalaros. Here Minoan Crete can live again and be incorporated not only into the

Fig. 5.3 Detail of illustration accompanying the poem 'Keftiu' by Aris Diktaios (Diktaios
1974), showing Spring naming the youth/poet her king (by kind permission of Dodoni
publications; photo: N. Momigliano).

long continuum of Hellenism, but into a global history, in which the main theme is the fight for equality and freedom against any form of repression.[242] *The Minoan* interweaves references to Minoan material culture (such as 'ring-waisted youths', bull-games in which girls take part, and double-axes) with mythological themes from ancient Greece, Asia, and America.[243] Above all, the poem expresses the notion of an original, egalitarian, and freedom-loving Minoan ideal that survives in the New World. It tells the story of Antalos, a young Knossian prince, who embarks on a voyage to find Rhea, the legendary early queen of the Minoans who, according to a prophecy, can save the Cretans from the tyranny of the Minotaur. Rhea knew the secret of immortality, but chose exile in an unknown, distant land in the west rather than reveal it to mankind. Only former slaves offer to accompany Antalos in his perilous journey, which includes a stopover in a strange half-sunk island in the Atlantic Ocean, whence the Minoans originally came (i.e. Atlantis). Antalos and his crew eventually arrive in South America at the city of Selene, the capital of the Atlan people. They discover that this was originally founded by Rhea and her followers, and is presently ruled by one of her descendants, the young queen Merope. Selene is threatened by an evil Asian invader, Ghundu-Zhan, who has conquered almost all of the Americas. Antalos and Merope, after recognizing their common origins, join forces against the enemy. The poem ends with Antalos emerging victorious from an epic combat with Ghundu-Zhan, and proclaiming that in this new land, where men do not live in fear but holy brotherhood, he has found what he was looking for:

> And so Antalos the magnanimous youth
> Proclaims all men free to live in the land
> For he has found the elixir
> Of life he was dispatched to seek!
> For this is the legendary land
> This is Merope's own kingdom fair,
> This is the dynasty enthroned in love!
> Enthroned in Selene this April morn.
> Let bells proclaim the joyous news
> Of a world that's new, of a life reborn![244]

From local to global Minoans, from the sublime to the banal, and the Minoans as Trojans

In the early decades of the Cold War, the Minoan past, whether incorporated or not into the long continuum of Hellenism and universal history, continued to inspire Cretans and non-Cretans alike. Moreover, with the increase in tourism after the Second World War, the Minoans reached even wider audiences. This is attested by the extensive use of Minoan-related themes not only in literature, as discussed in previous sections, but also in many other cultural practices, such as architecture, the visual and performing arts (paintings, drawings, cinema), and also new media such as television (which became common in the 1950s), radio documentaries, and even cartoons and adverts for international brands.

In architecture, for example, as recorded by Cadogan, travellers who flew to Heraklion Airport were greeted, until the early 1960s, by a Neo-Minoan terminal building.[245] This terminal, which was probably constructed after the Second World War in connection with the emerging tourist expansion under the Colonels, has now vanished, but visitors to the old Dimarchio (City Hall) in the southern town of Ierapetra, built in the 1960s, can still admire its Minoan façade (see Fig. 5.4).[246] Minoan Crete also attracted the attention of Le Corbusier, who sketched the Prince of Lilies and the Cup Bearer frescoes in one of his notebooks, and of other architects and designers, as shown by Donald Preziosi's reminiscences of his time at Harvard.[247] The art historian and scholar of American architecture Vincent Scully was particularly keen on finding affinities between the architecture of Minoan Crete and the famous American architect, interior designer, and city-planner Frank Lloyd Wright, but the idea that the former influenced the latter appears to be a modern myth, as recently argued by Preziosi.[248]

The decipherment of Linear B could not fail to capture the imagination of various artists, as illustrated, for example, by Gastone Novelli's painting *Tavola degli ornamenti* (1965) and Antonino Nacci's untitled work (1973), which include not only signs from Linear B but also from Linear A, Cretan Hieroglyphic, the Phaistos disk and other writing systems, and are indicative of a general interest in the relationship between artwork and writing typical of that period.[249] Other interesting examples of artistic works inspired by Minoan Crete are the abstract painting *Knossos* (1956) by the German-French artist Jean (Hans) Arp[250] and the Knossian snake figurine with *banderillas* instead of serpents (*c.* 1963), which the French writer, poet, artist, and filmmaker Jean Cocteau created for Jean-Marie Magnan's 1965 volume *Taureaux*.[251]

Fig. 5.4 Dimarchio (City Hall) of Ierapetra, Crete (photo: Vasso Fotou).

Cocteau's illustration was probably inspired by a visit to Knossos in the early 1950s, which he briefly describes in a couple of passages in his 1953 volume, *Journal d'un inconnu* (*Diary of an Unknown*): '[W]e were nearly lost in the open labyrinth of Knossos, that conceals ideas of red bulls and bees, to which the hillside hives, and the waists of princes and princesses, mercilessly crushed against the walls and bloody columns, bear witness.'[252] He was particularly attracted by Minoan frescoes showing 'wasp-waisted people going from flower to flower, making perhaps that golden honey of which the pendant in the Candia museum – the one on which two bees face each other – is made.'[253] Despite being 'crushed against the walls', the frescoes depict people who still projected a sense of life: 'Destroy my paintings and you destroy me. Our visible forms can be destroyed. Our perspective on time and space prevents the destruction of their invisibility. For a work overflows its own existence. It projects itself even when destroyed. The ruins of Knossos are scented by such works.'[254]

Illustrations inspired by Minoan Crete also appear in children's literature, usually in books of stories about Greek heroes, especially Theseus. Although already attested by the 1920s (cf. Chapter 4), this practice was not very common. It seems that it was only thanks to the publication of Mary Renault's bestselling novels on Theseus that Minoan elements were eventually employed in the 1960s in the illustration of a classic of this genre, Charles Kingsley's *The Heroes, or Greek Fairy Tales for My Children*, first published in 1856 and still in print.[255] Most, if not all, of the illustrated editions of this well-known work exhibit images largely inspired by Classical Greece, except for the 1964 volume, which uses only Kingsley's text on Theseus's adventures, has an afterword by Mary Renault, and illustrations by the Spanish-American artist Federico Castellon. In this work one finds women wearing a demure version of the Minoan dress with flounced skirt and open bodice, the Pallantides using Minoan crockery at a banquet, King Minos sitting on the famous throne found by Evans, and other nice allusions to the material culture and architecture of Bronze Age Crete.[256]

With regard to cinema, as far as I am able to ascertain, there are no films entirely devoted to a recreation of life in Minoan Crete for this period or, indeed, of any other period, with the exception of docudramas. Nevertheless, Minoan elements appear in many films of the 1950s–1960s which deal not only with subjects such as the myth of Theseus and the Minotaur, but also with Troy, Ulysses, Sappho, the Titans, the Queen of Sheba, Samson and Delilah, and even Christian gladiators.[257] One of these films, *The Egyptian* (1954), directed by Michael Curtis, is a Hollywood adaptation of Waltari's 1945 bestselling novel *Sinuhe egyptiläinen* (*Sinuhe the Egyptian*), discussed in Chapter 4. The film offers, among other things Minoan, a reproduction of the Knossian Toreador fresco in one of the scenes portraying Sinhue's visit to Crete.[258] The most extensive cinematic use of Minoan elements, however, appears in *Helen of Troy* (1956), directed by Robert Wise (best known for *West Side Story*, *The Sound of Music*, and *The Sand Pebbles*), in which the Trojans are the heroes, the Achaeans are a pretty unsavoury lot, and Troy looks like a reconstruction of the palace of Minos at Knossos.[259] Minoan tapering columns, horns of consecration, and frescoes are ubiquitous, albeit often mingled with more classicizing elements (see Fig. 5.5). But why did Wise make Troy look like Knossos? I have not been able to find an explanation provided by any of the people involved with the film, but several possible reasons spring to mind. To begin

Fig. 5.5 Screenshots from *Helen of Troy* (Warner Bros., 1956), directed by Robert Wise (after https://www.youtube.com/watch?v=bd5Sq225JTE).

with, since Wise identified Homer's Achaeans with the Mycenaeans, he was probably looking for a built environment based on a culture contemporary with and linked to them, and yet somewhat different. The archaeological site of Troy, however, unlike Knossos and despite Schliemann's, Doerpfeld's, and Blegen's excavations of the late nineteenth century and the 1930s, did not yet offer appealing reconstructions of its architecture (whether on paper or on the ground) which could spark the imagination and facilitate the work for a set design. Moreover, as illustrated in previous chapters, since the Cretomania of the late Belle Époque, Minoan features had been frequently employed in theatrical productions, such as ballet, dramas, silent films, and other genres to convey an impression of pre-Classical Greece. It is also possible that Wise made other connections between Minoans and Trojans. First, they both succumbed to Achaean–Mycenaean forces, and the fall of Knossos could be seen as a prefiguration of the fall of Troy (as the Trojan War had been used as a prefiguration of the Persian Wars, and other wars, since the fifth century BC).[260] Second, the fate of both Minoans and Trojans was closely linked to a female goddess: Evans's Mother Goddess for the former, and Aphrodite for the latter. Thus, perhaps it is not a coincidence that Wise's romantic hero, Paris, is portrayed as worshipping Aphrodite to the exclusion of all other deities, as shown in the following lines, pronounced by one of the Trojan priests: 'The virgin Cassandra does make one point that causes me much concern. Prince Paris, it appears, gives all his worship to one goddess alone, Aphrodite.'[261] Finally it is conceivable that, by portraying the Trojans as the heroes and associating them with the peaceful and feminine Minoans, Wise was trying to project an anti-war and feminist message.[262]

The extensive use of Minoan elements in Wise's *Helen of Troy* may have influenced not only some later films about the Trojan War, discussed in the next chapter, but also television series, such as *Doctor Who*, the British science-fiction television programme produced by the BBC since the early 1960s and still very popular today.[263] *Doctor Who* employed a wooden replica of the 'Throne of Minos' in its very first episode (see Fig. 5.6), broadcast in November 1963, and this replica continued to be used as one of

Fig. 5.6 Wooden replica of the throne in the Throne Room at Knossos in Doctor Who's TARDIS: still from first episode, 23 November 1963 (after https://ancworlds.wordpress.com/2017/09/25/a-visual-guide-to-the-aegean-bronze-age-in-doctor-who/).

the chairs inside the TARDIS (the time machine and spacecraft employed in the series) for over a decade. Furthermore, in the episode 'The Myth Makers' (broadcast in November 1965), which is set in Troy, a replica of the Griffin fresco from the Knossos Throne Room decorates the palace of Priam, while in the episode 'The Time Monster' (broadcast in June 1972), which is partly set on Santorini/Atlantis, one finds more props and frescoes based on Minoan Crete, especially the Hagia Triada sarcophagus.[264]

Knossos and the 'peaceful' Minoan civilization are the subjects of the prize-winning radio documentary *Notturno a Cnosso*, created for the national Italian broadcasting corporation RAI (Radio Audizioni Italiane) by Giovanni Battista Angioletti and Sergio Zavoli in 1953.[265] This documentary takes the listeners on a magical night visit to Knossos and Minoan Crete, the 'homeland of our civilization' ('l'antica patria della nostra civiltà'), in which a local boy-shepherd guides the Italian narrator. Together, they explore the palace of Minos under a full moon, and marvel at the sight of the ancient ruins and reconstructions (which are treated indiscriminately). Greek myths and archaeology are intermingled in a magical narrative, conducted in modern Greek and Italian, in which the Minotaur symbolizes the war brought to the peaceful Minoans by warlike (Greek-Mycenaean) conquerors, and Evans is presented as the visionary archaeologist who resurrects the 'happy royal palace' ('la reggia felice'), so that 'genius and love can triumph again' ('il genio e l'amore vinsero ancora').

Finally, the Minoans appear also in the 1950s comics *L'Enigme de l'Atlantide* in the series *Blake and Mortimer*, created by the Belgian author Edgar P. Jacobs,[266] and in the advertisements of international brands, such as the Liebig Extract of Meat Company, which had a series of trading cards created in the 1950s to promote their product. These included vignettes of Minoan life, from bull-leaping to a procession of men and women bearing gifts to King Minos in the Throne Room, and a sacred dance on the shore with a woman brandishing snakes (see Fig. 5.7).[267] This seems almost an ironic materialization of Mario Praz's comment that the garish replica of the charging bull relief fresco at Knossos reminded him of the Bovril posters that dominated English cities (cf. Chapter 4 and Fig. 4.8).

Conclusions: The Minoans in the Cold War and swinging sixties

The considerable variation in the interpretations of, and responses to, Minoan Crete which appeared in the interwar period continued into the first decades of the Cold War, as examined in this chapter. Some trends, however, became more entrenched and new ones emerged in response to socio-political developments and new discoveries in the field of Aegean studies, such as the decipherment of Linear B. The decipherment, in particular, enhanced the polarization between Minoans and Mycenaean, already noticeable after the First World War. For many scholars and non-scholars alike, this confirmed the idea that an Indo-European (Greek)-speaking population had already settled in Greece by the early second millennium BC; that the Mycenaeans were the model of Homer's Achaeans; and that they were an integral part of *Greek* history. The ability to understand the Linear B documents, and their use of common Greek words and names, including those of Olympian divinities, helped to create a feeling of

Fig. 5.7 Trading cards with Minoan images created for the Liebig Extract of Meat Company in the 1950s, on display in the Virtual Museum Vallée (http://www.vmv.it/), which includes the Museo della Mucca (Cow Museum): http://www.vmv.it/toro+storia+antica+architettura_1-2-85-3591-4.aspx?ric=0-liebig.

familiarity, a pleasure of recognition, which extended to Mycenaean material culture, as exemplified even in some poetic responses, such as those of Quasimodo, even if for some scholars (such as Starr and Heidegger) Mycenaean Greece remained hopelessly un-Hellenic and closer to the Orient. For the Minoans the situation was equally if not more ambiguous: on the whole, the decipherment, combined with the continuing obscurity of the language(s) expressed by the earlier Cretan scripts, underlined their mystery, distance, and otherness. Nevertheless, at times the Minoans continued to be incorporated into wider Hellenic and European discourses, largely because of their influence on Mycenaean Greece, their distinctiveness in relation to Near Eastern cultures, and the convenience of perpetuating the idea of Crete as the cradle of European civilization in a variety of contexts, including that of the emerging European Union.

The relationship between the testimony of later Greek sources and the archaeological remains of Bronze Age Crete continued to exercise considerable fascination. Many works, such as those by Spyridon Marinatos in relation to Plato's myth of Atlantis, Arne Furumark in relation to the Minoan thalassocracy, and Mary Renault in relation to the heroic figure of Theseus, illustrate the persisting conviction that the narratives found in Greek sources contained a kernel of historical truth regarding Aegean Bronze Age events, and could be combined with the archaeology to create a more rational history. But another interesting and different trend also begins to appear, which is connected with the increasing sense of Minoan otherness and distance and emphasizes the disjuncture between Greek narratives and archaeological realities. Examples of this are Bacchelli's and Lacarrière's responses to Knossos, as they describe an incongruity between Greek narratives and the material culture of Minoan Crete, as does Anderson's fantasy fiction to some extent. This new trend could be seen as a prelude to later interpretations, uses, and appropriation of Minoan Crete discussed in later chapters, which show a greater focus on archaeological remains and more radical reimaginings of ancient Greek mythological stories, or even dispense with them altogether.

Another new trend that emerged in the period discussed in this chapter concerns the idea of Minoan pacifism, which came to be generally perceived as a positive trait, unlike in the interwar period. In fact, the idea of Minoan Crete as a feminine, peaceful society, in which people lived in harmony with nature and with each other, and led very interesting and well-balanced sexual lives, now reached new heights. As anticipated by Henry Miller, and in the words of Lacarrière, Minoan Crete acquired even more 'a taste of lost paradise', which was lost not because its people had sinned, but because it was destroyed by external forces and had vanished in the course of time, until archaeologists resurrected it. In the following chapter, however, I shall examine how, in some people's eyes, Minoan Crete did become a paradise lost through the abhorrent transgressions of its inhabitants, and how this paradise was regained.

Minoan Paradises Lost and Regained: From Cannibalism to Postmodernism (*c.* 1975–99)

Recent discoveries suggesting human sacrifice if not cannibalism at Knossos in the heyday of the Minoan civilisation make the epithet 'barbarous' which Collingwood applies to it not wholly inappropriate.

Sinclair Hood (1995: 179)

It may seem surprising that this romantic and idealistic vision of an innocent, strifeless, fair [Minoan] society, survived to form a controlling model for my generation, but we have to recall the 1960s rejection of the Materialist, Consumer ethos of the 1950s symbolized by Flower Power and the fascination with alternative worlds such as Eastern Mysticism, the Commune, Pot, and Lewis Binford. The collapse of this 1960s to early '70s renewed optimism in the perfectability or regeneration of modern society, is reflected in the surge of archaeological research from the 1970s into the origins of inequality, the rise of elites and modes of coercion, the 'punch behind the priest', and so on.

John Bintliff (1984: 36)

King Minos the mafia boss tallies with the evidence of the archives, and perhaps with realistic assumptions about human nature, more readily than does Minos the voluntary social worker . . .

Paul Halstead (1988: 523)

To speak of 'models' in relation to many of the traditional accounts of Minoan society is, quite simply, farcical. Rather, these accounts often represent the thinly-disguised libidinal fantasies of repressed athletes and nature-lovers, seeking to find in the 'perfectible' world of the past a utopia surpassing their wildest dreams. In contrast, the 'modern' approaches, which attempt a more 'scientific' rational analysis, are unsatisfactory precisely because of their complete rejection of all that is lyrical in favour of the coldly compartmentalized, separatist outlook. It is conceivably possible to see societies as a collection of different spheres of activity (such as The Economic, The Functional, The Symbolic, The Political, etc.) . . . but it is not a view I find attractive, helpful, or tenable in trying to understand human social behaviour, whether in past or present societies.

Sheena Crawford (1983: 47)

The Old European mythical imagery and religious practices were continued in
Minoan Crete. The Minoan culture mirrors the same values, the same manual
aptitude in artistic endeavour, the same glorification of the virgin beauty of life. The
Old Europeans had taste and style – whimsical, imaginative and sophisticated; their
culture was a worthy parent of the Minoan civilization ... The teaching of Western
civilization starts with the Greeks ... but European civilization was not created in
the space of a few centuries; the roots are deeper – by six thousand years.

Marija Gimbutas (1974: 238; 1982: 238)

I told her how the world had been in Crete before the consorts gained power, how it
had been in the time of Phaedra's grandmothers, how the Goddess had been revered
by men as well as women for thousands of years, and there had been no violence, no
warriors, only a joyous celebration of sea and earth and sky and all the living things
born of the Mother's love. So that it had existed before, such a world, and could come
again if we work and have faith and endure.

June R. Brindel (1985: 226)

The last quarter of the twentieth century saw some fascinating changes in the interpretation, reception, and uses of the Minoan past. This was an eventful period framed by the re-establishment of democracy in Greece and the conclusion of the Vietnam War in the mid-1970s, and by the end of the Cold War in the 1990s, in the aftermath of the collapse of the Soviet Union. In this period the Minoans lost the paradise that had been created by the scholarly and public imagination, but also regained it, as illustrated in a variety of specialist and popularizing archaeological publications and other cultural practices, from the writings of the controversial German author Christa Wolf, to those of the acclaimed American novelist Don DeLillo, and from the spiritual journeys in search of the Goddess organized by Carol P. Christ, to the paintings by the Cretan artist Roussetos Panagiotakis, among many others. Two discoveries made in the late 1970s at Knossos and Archanes-Anemospilia revealed some of the sins that caused the Minoans' exit from paradise (at least in the view of some people: cf. Hood's epigraph above). But other trends too, especially more reflexive and postmodern moods, helped to introduce less rosy views (cf. Halstead's, Bintliff's, and Crawford's epigraphs above), even if they were counterbalanced by the growth of second wave feminism, the Goddess Movement (Thealogy), and the search for alternative female-voiced narratives, which helped the Minoans to regain (or maintain) their taste of paradise both in archaeological literature and beyond (cf. Gimbutas's and Brindel's epigraphs above).

Greece and Crete from the fall of the Junta to the new millennium

In 1974, after the collapse of the military dictatorship, the former prime minister Konstantinos Karamanlis was recalled from exile and led an interim government that oversaw the legalization of communist parties and the first democratic elections after the Regime of the Colonels. Karamanlis's newly founded centre-right party, Nea

Demokratia (New Democracy), won the 1977 elections by a landslide and remained in power until 1981. Karamanlis was also largely responsible for Greece's entry into the European Union in 1981, after submitting a successful application in 1976. This move was strongly opposed by PASOK (Πανελλήνιο Σοσιαλιστικό Κίνημα, Panhellenic Socialist Movement), the centre-left party founded by Andreas Papandreou in 1974, on the grounds that membership of the EU would enhance Greece's marginality within a capitalist system.[1] Despite his original opposition, Papandreou kept Greece within the EU after PASOK won the 1981 elections and came to dominate Greek politics for the next two decades. He managed to do so without losing face, thanks to a great deal of political manoeuvring and clever rhetoric. In fact, under Papandreou, Greece became more and more reliant on EU funding. This gave Greece some economic prosperity, albeit built on shaky foundations, and financed a considerable increase in state sector employment, which included the Greek archaeological services.

The reopening of Greece to more foreign influence after the fall of the junta, its incorporation into the EU, and Papandreou's populist, anti-elitist, anti-capitalist, and anti-Western rhetoric created some intriguing tension and paradoxical situations, which extended to the field of archaeology. Thus, the new political situation facilitated the increase in archaeological projects carried out as 'collaboration' (συνεργασία/*synergasia*) between Greek and foreign institutions, but this was accompanied by a tightening of archaeological legislation and limitations regarding foreign archaeological activities in Greece.[2] In addition, although clashes between Greek and foreign archaeologists have always punctuated Greece's archaeological history,[3] in the last quarter of the twentieth century Papandreou's rhetoric contributed further to this conflict and especially to the growing tension with some powerful nations, such as the UK and the USA (some Greeks already mistrusted these nations because of their significant interference during the Civil War and/or because they had inadequately supported the democratic forces during the Regime of the Colonels).

In an archaeological context, the most famous materialization of PASOK's populist and anti-Western narrative is Melina Mercouri's vocal campaign for the return of the Elgin/Parthenon Marbles, which started in 1981, after Greece had safely secured its EU membership and she had become Minister for Culture, a post that she held until 1989. A Cretan example is the 1979 demonstration in Heraklion to prevent the loan of Minoan objects to an exhibition on Aegean Culture in Paris and New York.[4] Although this demonstration predates PASOK's 1981 election to government, and cannot be explained only in terms of political activism, Crete had been a PASOK stronghold from its foundation, and politics did play an important part in the protests, since these included an element of resistance to the US military presence on the island.[5] In addition, PASOK's political dominance may have influenced the creation of more egalitarian narratives about the Minoans or, at least, may have facilitated their acceptance in Greek–Cretan contexts (cf., e.g., the discussion about Nikolaos Platon, below).

Three years after the demonstrations in Heraklion, a wealthy US citizen, Malcolm H. Wiener, founded INSTAP (Institute for Aegean Prehistory) – a non-profit organization that, over the last four decades, has supported research in the Aegean, including archaeological fieldwork, from the Palaeolithic through to the eighth century BC, and has so far awarded over 3,000 grants to individual scholars and organizations from more than a dozen countries.[6] The impact of this institution on Greek and Minoan archaeology can hardly be overestimated. At the time of writing, no statistical studies were publicly available on how the grants have been awarded according to country, region, institutions, and other criteria, but it is not too far-fetched to suggest that INSTAP has been of particular benefit to Greek archaeologists, who were liberated from their dependence on their relatively limited public resources. Minoan archaeology, in particular, has benefited from INSTAP, and from Wiener's personal generosity, not only through the funding of many archaeological projects, but also thanks to the establishment of the INSTAP Study Center for East Crete (1997) and the special funds assigned to research at Knossos. Thus, Minoan archaeology continued to flourish in the last quarter of the twentieth century, and even more so than in the two decades after the Second World War. The number of archaeological investigations carried out on Crete over the period 1975–99 amounts to approximately 850, i.e. an average of over thirty archaeological projects per year, including excavation campaigns at well-known palatial centres, rescue operations at new sites, and other field projects, such as surveys.[7] To this figure one should add numerous discoveries outside Crete that had considerable implications for Minoan archaeology, such as those made in various Aegean islands, Egypt, Israel, and Turkey. All these activities have greatly increased our understanding of Minoan culture, from settlement patterns to international relations and religion, even if questions regarding Minoan language(s), socio-political organization, and gender roles continue to be hotly debated.

Crete of the hundred palaces, human sacrifice, and cannibalism: Archaeological discoveries on Crete and elsewhere (*c.* 1975–1999)

Archaeological excavations on Crete continued unabated, but a novelty of this period is the popularity of regional 'intensive' surveys, a.k.a. 'New Wave' surveys.[8] The main aim of earlier archaeological surveys was usually to locate sites worthy of excavation or to discover particular types of sites, whereas the main aim of intensive surveys is to establish changing settlement patterns over long periods of time, and to shift the attention from important sites, such as palaces, to a more comprehensive understanding of human interaction with the environment. Intensive surveys were largely influenced by the 'New Archaeology' (cf. Chapter 5), as evidenced, among other things, by their focus on systematic use of quantitative data, sampling, and, since the 1990s, GIS (Geographical Information System) to understand the processes of cultural change through time. 'New Wave' surveys started on Crete in the early 1970s, but became a significant component of archaeological research in the Aegean and Crete especially from the end of that decade. Their growing popularity to the present day is due to both scholarly and practical reasons, namely the considerable range of information that these surveys can produce and the fact that they are generally less expensive to run than excavations.

The main intensive surveys of the 1970s–1990s on Crete were carried out in the following areas (listed in alphabetical order): Chania, Gournia, Kavousi, Lassithi, Pseira, Sphakia, Vrokastro, Western Mesara (Phaistos), and Ziros.[9] Despite interpretative issues (e.g. the comparability of data from one survey to another, how to establish the size and function of site from surface data alone, and even the definition of a 'site'), these surveys have highlighted important aspects of Cretan culture, such as the size, variety, density of, and relationship between settlements (i.e. population distribution and land use). They have also generated new data relevant to the interpretation of socio-political factors, such as the emergence of Minoan palaces in the late second millennium BC and the possible Knossian dominance over much of Crete in the Neopalatial period.[10] Another archaeological venture that started in the mid-1980s and shares elements of survey work (such as a focus on landscape, territories, and connections between different sites) is the 'Minoan Roads' project, which also questioned the idea of Minoan pacifism through its interpretation of some sites as guard posts with a military function.[11]

In addition to surveys, archaeological work took place at major palace sites, such as Knossos and Malia, and at other substantial settlements, such as Haghia Triada, Palaikastro, and Kommos. Although these sites had been known and explored since the early 1900s, the last quarter of the twentieth century saw new excavation campaigns. For example, in 1978 archaeologists undertook the excavation of an important Iron Age cemetery located north of the Bronze Age palace at Knossos.[12] This discovery is also particularly interesting for the Minoan period, because the cemetery reused earlier Minoan tombs, and some of its Iron Age finds seem to represent a genuine form of ancient 'Cretomania' – an early link in the long history of Minoan receptions (cf. Chapter 2). New excavations at Palaikastro from the mid-1980s brought to light new impressive structures and finds, but the discovery of a palatial building eluded excavators once again, whereas the excavators of Kommos from the late 1970s were rewarded by the discovery not only of the first ship-sheds in the Bronze Age Aegean, dating to Late Minoan IIIA, but also of a Neopalatial building with wings surrounding a central rectangular court.[13]

There were also important new excavations at significant Cretan cult places, such as those carried out at the peak sanctuary on Mount Juktas,[14] at the Idean cave,[15] and at the sanctuary of Hermes and Aphrodite at Kato Symi Viannou,[16] with the latter showing an impressive continuity of cultic use from Minoan times to the Roman period (third century AD). In addition, Minoan cult places were investigated beyond Crete, most notably at Ayios Giorgos on Kythera, which is the first unmistakable Minoan peak sanctuary excavated outside Crete.[17] Excavations on Crete also brought to light new villas, such as that at Nerokourou in the western regions of the island and at Zominthos on the slopes of Mount Ida, one of the highest – if not the highest – Minoan settlement and villa discovered so far, with an impressive ceramic workshop.[18]

Another important aspect of Cretan archaeology in the last quarter of the twentieth century is the excavation of 'mini-palaces', such as those at Kommos, Petras near Sitia, and Galatas (Pediados), as well as other substantial buildings at settlements such as Mochlos and Palaikastro. These new discoveries, in addition to previously known mini-palaces (e.g. at Gournia), prompted the research group Topography of Power, established in 1999, to give the title 'Crete of the hundred palaces' to a workshop they held in 2001.[19] As the editors of the workshop proceedings suggested, these discoveries (and, I might add, the number, density, and variety of sites revealed by surveys) made the 'Minoan Neopalatial socio-political landscape' look 'considerably different' from what was previously known a generation earlier.[20] The density and proximity of sites, including those provided with a special building, attested to the high level of human settlement and territorial exploitation on Crete, especially in the Neopalatial period. This, together with the ongoing study of the Linear B tablets, renewed questions about the socio-political nature and function of the palaces and other administrative buildings. With regards to function, Halstead memorably and humorously described Minoan palaces as 'combining under one roof the equivalent of Buckingham Palace, Whitehall, Westminster Abbey and, perhaps, even Wembley Stadium' (the latter referring to Minoan bull-leaping and other rituals).[21] But other views emerging in this period include the idea that the palaces were occupied by the winning side among competing heterarchical factions; or that, as in the Near East, political and religious power might have become more separate, with the former residing outside the main large Minoan palaces, and the palaces functioning essentially as ceremonial, religious centres used by different groups.[22] Nevertheless, Evans's idea that the Minoan palaces, especially those of Knossos, Phaistos, Malia, Zakros, and Chania, were palace-temples, i.e. seats of both religious and temporal power, seems to retain considerable support, even if the character and gender of their ruler(s) remains a matter of great debate, as illustrated in the following sections.

Important Minoan discoveries also continued to occur outside Crete. Besides the already mentioned excavations on Kythera, the work at Akrotiri on Thera (under the direction of Christos Doumas) continued to reveal exceptional new finds, from remarkable frescoes to more humble artefacts. In addition, Thera became central to some fierce debates about the absolute chronology (calendar date) of its Bronze Age eruption and related phases in the chronological scheme created by Evans and elaborated by other scholars over the years. As explained in the previous chapter, in terms of relative chronology, a date for the Santorini Bronze Age eruption during a mature phase of Late Minoan IA was clarified within a few years of the start of Marinatos's excavation. This meant that the eruption had occurred in the late sixteenth century BC (*c.* 1500 BC) in the chronology obtained through traditional archaeological methods. These involved matching Minoan phases with the already established Egyptian and Near Eastern chronologies by means of cross-finds (i.e. the discovery of Minoan finds in Near Eastern contexts and vice-versa). Many scholars, however, also tried to obtain a date for the eruption through an array of scientific analyses (e.g. radiocarbon dating, tree-ring records, and ice-core studies). A considerable number of these analyses suggested that the Santorini eruption had taken place in the mid–late seventeenth century BC, a discrepancy of over a century vis-à-vis the date obtained by traditional methods.[23] No solution to these chronological disputes seems in sight as yet.[24] But even if these disputes have engaged specialists and have attracted the curiosity of the general public, as part of the overall fascination with the Theran eruption, they have not influenced in a significant way interpretations and reception of the Minoans.

In the 1980s and 1990s, excavations took place at Avaris (Tell el-Dab'a) in Egypt, Tel Kabri in Israel, and Miletus in Turkey, which brought to light considerable new evidence for Minoan international relations, especially thanks to the discoveries of Minoan-style frescoes at these sites.[25] The wall paintings from Avaris prompted the excavator, Manfred Bietak, to make the romantic suggestion that they are the tangible remains of a political marriage between pharaoh Thutmose III and a Minoan princess.[26]

Other scholars, however, have preferred different explanations for the presence of Minoan-style frescoes at this and other sites in the Eastern Mediterranean – from itinerant to refugee craftsmen, or exchanges of craftsmen between rich patrons.[27] At any rate, whether the result of dynastic marriages or other factors, the finds from Avaris, Tel Kabri, Miletus, and other sites in the Eastern Mediterranean convey the international spirit of the mid-second millennium BC and appreciation of Minoan craftsmanship in other contemporary cultures, and also suggest the sharing of some symbolic iconography among their elites.

No major breakthrough has yet been made with regard to the language(s) used by the Minoans. Despite the discovery of more Cretan Pictographic/Hieroglyphic and Linear A tablets, the establishment of corpora of Hieroglyphic and Linear A inscriptions, and the valuable suggestions made by various scholars, a conclusive and widely accepted decipherment of these two scripts (and the Phaistos disk) remains elusive. Nevertheless, the acronyms by which the corpora of inscriptions are commonly referred to – GORILA and CHIC – show that Aegean linguists have at least maintained a sense of humour.[28] In terms of suggestions, by the 1960s, scholars such as Leonard Palmer and George Huxley had proposed that Linear A expressed a language related to Anatolian Luwian (cf. Chapter 5). In 1987, Colin Renfrew lent further support to this idea, or at least to the notion that the Minoan language(s) may be related to the Indo-European family, by arguing that the diffusion of Proto-Indo-European was related to the spread of farming in the Neolithic period.[29] In a later work, Renfrew discussed the likely Minoan linguistic legacy to Mycenaean and later Greek, and suggested that Minoan palatial language constituted a significant linguistic ad-stratum of Mycenaean Greek, rather than a sub-stratum, especially through the loan of Minoan words relevant in palatial contexts, such as *basileus* (the title of a relatively low-ranking officer in the Linear B tablets) and *wanax* (the title of the supreme ruler), among many others.[30] These linguistic borrowings, according to Renfrew, were part and parcel of the Minoan influence in fashions, customs, beliefs, and other cultural practices, a 'Versailles' effect that could result even without recourse to political control (*thalassocracy*).[31]

The two discoveries that attracted most publicity in this period were those made during the excavations at Knossos and nearby Archanes-Anemospilia in the summer of 1979.[32] These investigations yielded many other finds of archaeological and scholarly significance,[33] but it was the evidence suggesting human sacrifice and ritual cannibalism that created quite a stir, especially thanks to some vivid accounts in the popular press (e.g. in *National Geographic*),[34] and at a time when views on the Minoans had started to oscillate from the idyllic to the cynical.

At Anemospilia, on the north slope of Mount Juktas, the excavators Yannis and Efi Sakellarakis discovered a unique stand-alone building, which was destroyed by an earthquake around 1700 BC (Middle Minoan IIIA). Trapped within its walls were the skeletal remains of four people. Three (one male aged about thirty-seven, one female aged about twenty-eight years, and one too poorly preserved for sexing and aging) were found on the floors of two rooms, in positions suggesting that they had died while trying to escape and protect themselves from the falling roof and masonry that crushed them. The fourth skeleton belonged to a young male aged about eighteen years. It was found on a low-built platform, possibly some kind of altar. His skeletal remains suggested that he may have already been dead when the earthquake struck and that he may have been tied: he was lying on his side, his knees were not bent in the foetal position typical of some burials, but in unnatural manner, and his jawbones appeared to have been clenched together. In addition, a bronze spearhead rested on his skeleton. For the excavators this suggested human sacrifice: it was, perhaps, the ultimate, if vain, attempt to placate a divinity and avert a more severe earthquake.

In the same summer, Peter Warren discovered the bones of two children (aged about eight and eleven) that bore unmistakable marks of butchery. These were found in an assemblage datable to the Late Minoan IB phase (end of the Neopalatial period), inside the basement of a building located to the west of the palace at Knossos. Knife marks on human bones recovered from Minoan cemeteries are quite common, and indicate secondary burial practices and associated rituals, which involved de-fleshing and other manipulation of skeletal materials. The children's bones, however, were not found in a burial context, but in a building within the settlement. Moreover, the other finds included edible snails, the bones of butchered sheep, and some pottery often associated with ritual assemblages. The excavator, somewhat reluctantly, dismissed other possibilities, such as an undiscovered crime and secondary burial rituals, and suggested that the children's bones were evidence of Minoan ritual cannibalism.

Both claims of human sacrifice and cannibalism were met with considerable surprise and scepticism in some circles, as illustrated, for example, by the 1982 article published by the archaeologist Keith Branigan in *Nature* and by a recent (2017) interview given by the excavator of Anemospilia, Efi Sakellarakis.[35] The very title of Branigan's article ('The unacceptable face of Minoan Crete?'); his suggestions that, until that point, only the legend of the Minotaur had cast a shadow on the otherwise civilized Minoans; his argument for alternative interpretations; and his conclusion that both cases for Minoan human sacrifice and ritual cannibalism were not proven, all suggest a desire to maintain the Minoan taste of paradise. In a similar vein, Efi Sakellaraki recalled that, at the time, some English archaeologists were reluctant to divulge their gruesome discoveries, as they feared an angry reaction.[36]

Equally revealing is how these finds were dealt with in two significant works of synthesis on Aegean civilizations published in the 1980s and in a novel of the 1990s. Platon's *La Civilisation égéenne* (1981) does not mention the Anemospilia and Knossos discoveries, and while this omission could be due to the fact that relevant publications on them appeared too late to be included in the volume, it is also significant that Platon argued that the Minoans showed moral superiority over other civilizations because they had replaced human sacrifice with other offerings.[37] *Les civilisations égéennes* (1989) by Rene Treuil and others devoted a few lines to the Anemospilia and Knossos finds, in which human sacrifice and ritual cannibalism are accepted, but explained as the result of exceptional circumstances.[38] Finally, Roderick Beaton's 1995 novel, *Ariadne's Children* (see further discussion below), fictionalized these discoveries and presented the refusal vs. acceptance of Minoan human sacrifice and cannibalism as symbolic of a change of the guard between different generations of archaeologists: one older and more romantic, the other younger and more scientific.

For scholars and members of the general public alike, who had come to idealize Minoan Crete as a highly civilized and gentle society, the idea of human sacrifice and eating children was difficult to accept, especially after the Summer of Love, Flower Power, and the emergence of the Goddess Movement (cf. Bintliff's epigraph, above). But it is unlikely that the discoveries at Anemospilia and Knossos would have raised eyebrows in the first half of the twentieth century, since the notion that the Minoans practised human sacrifice (in the bull ceremonies) goes back to Sir Arthur Evans's early excavation reports, while Jane Harrison, in her *Prolegomena to the Study of Greek Religion* and *Themis*, had suggested Minoan origins for Dionysian cannibalism and omophagy (cf. Chapter 3). Some or all of these gruesome practices were attributed to the Minoans in the Cretomanic works of Baikie, Merezhkovsky, Kazantzakis, Graves, Mary Renault, and other authors discussed in previous chapters.

The evidence for human sacrifice and cannibalism from Knossos and Archanes-Anemospilia could be rebutted or explained, if accepted, as the outcome of extraordinary situations, thus allowing the Minoans to regain, or rather, maintain their idealized status. But in the materialistic world of the 1980s and 1990s, so well encapsulated by Madonna's song 'Material Girl' (released in 1985), it became more difficult to shake off the emergence of more self-interested, hard-nosed, and even militaristic interpretations of the Minoans. This also partly coincided with the waning positivism of the New (Processual) Archaeology and waxing of postmodernist approaches in many disciplines, including archaeology, as illustrated in the Postprocessual (a.ka. Interpretative) Archaeology spearheaded by scholars such as Ian Hodder and Christopher Tilley (cf. Bintliff's, Halstead's, and Crawford's epigraphs).

As explained in Chapter 5, many saw the New Archaeology as an important development in the history of the discipline in terms of a 'loss of innocence', in the sense of a loss of theoretical-methodological naivety. Arguably, Postprocessual Archaeology represents an equally significant development and an even greater loss of innocence, because of its awareness of how social biases and other influences affect our interpretations of the past. Yet, in the last quarter of the twentieth century, the Minoans managed to regain (or maintain) their paradisiac status, thanks to feminist archaeologists, such as Marija Gimbutas, who were instrumental in perpetuating and bringing to even wider audiences the idea of Minoan Crete as the last bastion of gender equality and pacifism against warlike Aryan invaders.

All the ideas and trends mentioned above – from idyllic, to barbaric, and even military Minoans, and from Processual to Postprocessual interpretations – found new expressions in archaeological writings and Cretomanic works, as illustrated in the following sections.

Minoans in archaeological narratives of the last quarter of the twentieth century: From priest-kings to Buddhism and matriarchal theocracies

Important works of syntheses on the Minoans published in this period show innovation but also the remarkable persistence of many ideas formulated by earlier generations.

Although one might trace a tendency from idealism to realism, utopian beliefs die hard, and the Minoan 'mother strikes back' once again.[39]

From ideal to real?

One might conveniently start with the overview of the Minoans presented by one of the archaeologists who revealed their sins, Peter Warren, in his popular *The Aegean Civilizations*, first published in 1975, with a second edition in 1989. The only significant difference in the latter is an expanded introduction, which discusses major discoveries that had occurred in the Aegean since 1975, including those relevant to human sacrifice and cannibalism. Nevertheless, both editions offer an enthusiastic, celebratory, and quite idealistic portrayal of Minoan civilization. Warren's volume shows the innovative influence of the New Archaeology, as indicated, for example, by his discussion of 'living systems', agricultural, industrial, trading, and religious 'subsystems', the 'multiplier effect', and by his general restrain from using invasions and migrations as explanatory tools.[40] At the same time, Warren's lively portray of the Minoans presents many old favourites. For example, the emergence of Minoan civilization appears as largely explicable through essentialist reasons: the Minoans are an exceptionally gifted people, with 'extraordinary individual and collective human abilities' – something that is almost reminiscent of Evans's idea of their racial superiority.[41] For Warren the Mycenaeans' rise to civilization was due to 'initial stimulation ... from the Minoans', but the latter 'developed their civilization with extraordinarily little dependence on external abilities', thanks to their innate originality and brilliance.[42]

In Warren's narrative, further explanations of the remarkable achievements of the Minoans in every field similarly recall traditional ideas. For example, their gradual evolution was free from strife and foreign invasions for most of their history: it was a 'peaceful rise to civilisation' that went on for 'some 15 centuries' (which is in fact six time longer than Evans's *Pax Minoica*). It was disturbed only by natural disasters, such as earthquakes, and was finally brought to an end by the Santorini volcanic eruption and its aftermath.[43] Minoan religion appears as a form of polytheism, but 'dominated by a female divinity intimately connected with the natural world',[44] with rituals involving orgiastic dances and other ceremonies. Minoan society is 'hierarchical', but also relatively egalitarian, since it presents 'no great distinction of class', at least up to the end of the Protopalatial period, whereas in the period of the New Palaces social differences seem to intensify, suggesting 'a ruler at the top', who lived in the palaces and fulfilled religious functions, like Evans's priest-king.[45] Furthermore, according to Warren, the Neopalatial period witnessed the intensification of Minoan settlement abroad, remembered as the Minoan *thalassocracy* in ancient Greek sources. This also could be seen as harking back to more imperialistic and culture-historical views, given Warren's checklist approach to determine the presence of Minoan settlers outside Crete.[46]

Minoan art is described in familiar terms too: it expresses 'intense delight in the natural world' and the ability to 'capture fleeting movement'[47] – phrases that recall earlier characterizations. In a later article for the popular magazine *Scientific American*, Warren similarly reiterates ideas about Minoan art that emerged in the first decades of the twentieth century, such as the notion that it has a certain 'vitality' and even 'humanism', which distinguished it from the Orient and made it part of a 'European tradition of humanism and individualism'.[48] In *The Aegean Civilizations*, however, 'individualism' was precisely the element lacking in Minoan art, and the main heritage that the Bronze Age people left to the later Greeks was not in artistic and material terms, but through language, poetry, and, above all, religion, since the art of wall-painting and most other aspects of Minoan–Mycenaean material culture were either lost or thoroughly transformed after the onset of the so-called Greek Dark Ages.[49]

An even more traditional and eirenic view of Minoan Crete appears in the already mentioned synthesis by Platon, *La civilisation égéenne* (1981), which aimed at replacing Glotz's influential volume of the same title, first published in 1923 (cf. Chapter 4). Like Glotz's and many other works (including Warren's *The Aegean Civilizations*), Platon's synthesis is organized largely in chronological order (Neolithic, Early Bronze Age, Middle Bronze Age, etc.) and geographical areas (Crete, Greece, other Aegean islands, Troy), with further subdivisions such as architecture, arts and crafts, social-political life, and religion. Platon's volume starts with the idea of Minoan Crete as the first great civilization in Europe and the beginning of European civilization – an old cliché suitably redeployed at a time that coincided with Greece's entry into the European Union.[50] His references to Sergi's racial groups, to the 'dynamic character of new racial elements',[51] his reliance on later Greek mythological traditions as containing a kernel of historical truth, and other features discussed below, further contribute to the old-fashioned flavour of this work.

For Platon, the Minoan is a 'happy civilisation', relatively egalitarian and peaceful: Evans's relatively short, Neopalatial *Pax Minoica* is extended to the whole of the Protopalatial period, and the Minoan *thalassocracy* is seen as a peaceful enterprise.[52] A variety of factors contribute to this harmonious state of affairs: the racial characteristics of the Minoans; the high status of women; the absence of marked social divisions (including a hypothesized lack of slavery); the benevolent and enlightened rule of the elites; and the great importance of religion in Minoan life, which not only helped social cohesion, but also the emergence, in the late Prepalatial period, of a powerful priesthood that eventually led to the kingship of later phases.[53]

Platon characterizes Minoan religion as a polytheistic, but with a rather limited pantheon dominated by a supreme goddess, who represents the deification of nature as 'mother'.[54] The Minoan palaces are dwellings of Minoan divinities and their representatives on earth, comparable to the palace-monastery of the Tibetan Lamas.[55] Yet, despite the importance of women (especially as priestesses) and of the Minoan Mother Goddess in his narrative, Platon seems untouched by more feminist trends, and believes that, from the Old Palace period, the Minoan rulers were kings with supreme religious powers – a picture of theocratic kingship not so different, after all, from Evans's.[56] Platon's discussion of Minoan art and imagery also recalls views circulating since the first decades of the twentieth century, such as the predominance of religious scenes; the delight in nature (and special character of Minoan 'naturalism'); the lack of individuality and historical sense (i.e. the absence of a glorification of individuals and human actions, such as the defeat of enemies); and the childlike joyfulness, dreamlike quality, and affinity with Japanese art.[57]

Although published only eight years after Platon's *La civilisation égéenne*, and in the same year as Warren's second edition of *The Aegean Civilizations*, the previously mentioned *Les civilisations égéennes* by René Treuil, Pascal Darcque, Jean-Claude Poursat, and others presents a less idealized picture and has generally a more modern feel. For example, in contrast to Platon and Warren, Treuil and his colleagues make more extensive use of modern scientific techniques (from radiocarbon dating to palaeo-environmental data), settlement patterns, modes of subsistence and production, stratigraphic sequences, demography, and even models derived from social anthropology. In addition, they pay limited attention to racial affiliations, and none at all to supposedly associated character traits (such as peaceful Minoans vs. warlike Mycenaeans). They also offer far more cautious hypotheses regarding the type of socio-political organization correlated with the Minoan palaces and the identity of the Minoan rulers, especially before the Neopalatial period. In homage to their distinguished French colleague Henri Van Effenterre, they include a brief discussion of his Minoan 'primitive democracy', curbing the power of the palatial elites in the Protopalatial period but followed by a strengthening of royal power and reinforcement of ritual in the Neopalatial period.[58] In this synthesis, readers will look in vain for an endorsement of theocratic kingship, let alone of matriarchy and matrilineality. But if their ideas on the nature and identity of the elites are more circumspect, Treuil and his colleagues are more forward regarding the alleged peaceful nature of Minoan society and the 'punch behind the priest' (cf. Bintliff's epigraph above). Thus, for example, the widespread destruction horizon at the end of the Old Palace period, often accompanied by fire, is no longer attributed to earthquakes, but to conflicts among palaces, which are presented as the main administrative centres of independent and rival territories.[59] For the Neopalatial period, however, one finds the likely (but admittedly unproven) hypothesis that Knossos may have extended its power to other regions, and may have been ruled by a king – a suggestion partly based on the evidence provided by an Egyptian text of the time of Thutmosis III (fifteenth century BC), which mentions a king of the Keftiu lands.[60] Also less idealistic than Platon's are their views on the Minoan establishment of colonies, which is seen as dictated by commercial reasons, demographic expansion on Crete, and the desire to create a buffer zone around the island, linked to the increasing palatial power and land exploitation, especially by Knossos.[61]

An innovative approach also appears in Oliver Dickinson's *The Aegean Bronze Age* (1994), which was described by one reviewer as 'the first survey of the Aegean Bronze Age written by a scholar cognizant of some of the theoretical advances in anthropological archaeology since the 1960s ... by far the most intelligent and up-to-date survey of the Aegean Bronze Age in print'.[62] Unlike previous syntheses, this volume was arranged thematically through eight chapters encompassing terminology and chronology; natural environment and resources; the first human populations; settlement and economy; arts and crafts; burial customs; trade, exchange, and overseas contact; and religion. Also refreshing, compared to some previous scholarship, is the author's forthright dismissal of craniology and the relevance of race in the analysis and attribution of artefacts to either Minoans or Mycenaeans.[63] Dickinson does not romanticize the Minoans, and shows more awareness of the 'danger ... of succumbing to the recurrent temptation to create an ideal Minoan society in terms that reflect modern preoccupations'.[64] He regards human sacrifice and ritual cannibalism as plausible, and makes relevant observations on Minoan weapons, on the likelihood of internecine conflicts among Protopalatial polities, and on the presence of Minoan fortifications.[65] He further suggests that, if the Minoans appear peaceful, it is merely because the absence of a clear iconography of rulers, unlike in other cultures (such as the Egyptian and Mesopotamian) suggests that Crete was not governed by 'anything resembling a Near Eastern monarch', but by an elite class, including both men and women, who preferred to present their power as deriving from religious status rather than military exploits.[66] Dickinson is also highly sceptical about a supreme Mother Goddess, and favours some form of Minoan polytheism, while acknowledging the importance on Crete of both male and female priesthood, unlike in other Near Eastern religions, where priests are usually male, although women could hold important positions too.[67]

Women on top? Feminist Minoans

If Platon preferred the idea of priest-kings, and Dickinson an elite class with gender equality, in the last quarter of the twentieth century other scholars followed more feminist avenues. Hesitant steps towards this path appear, for example, in Gerald Cadogan's *Palaces of Minoan Crete* (1976), where he admits that he was 'much less certain that the rulers of Minoan Crete until 1450 were men, whether kings, priests or gods, or any or all combined, rather than women', and wonders whether the Priest-King a.k.a. the Prince of Lilies fresco (see Fig. 3.13) might represents a priestess.[68] By contrast, no hesitation appears in the works of the Lithuanian-American archaeologist Marija Gimbutas, who gave considerable new impetus to the long-lived idea that in the Bronze Age hordes of patriarchal Aryan populations conquered earlier matriarchal societies in much of Eurasia, and that Minoan Crete was one of the last bastions against this advance, until the island succumbed to Mycenaean Greeks in the fifteenth century BC.[69] Unlike the archaeologists discussed so far, Gimbutas was not an Aegean specialist, but an expert in Baltic and other East European cultures, and indeed her work rarely figures in specialists works by Aegeanists. Nevertheless, she enlisted the Minoans in her powerful narratives of the prehistoric migrations of the Indo-European people, which had considerable influence beyond archaeological circles.

According to Gimbutas, from the Neolithic period (*c.* seventh millennium BC) European–Anatolian societies were characterized by the dominance of women and the worship of a goddess representing the creative principle. This 'Old European' and Anatolian cultures were pre-Indo-European, matrifocal and probably matrilineal, agricultural and sedentary, egalitarian and peaceful. Between *c.* 4500 and 2500 BC, however, patriarchal, hierarchical, pastoral, and warlike Indo-European groups, originating from the Russian steppe (her 'Kurgan hypothesis') conquered most of Europe and also parts of Anatolia, with Crete and a few other areas resisting into the second millennium. In this vast area, a masculine world was superimposed upon a feminine one. The feminine element was not entirely vanquished, but it was deeply transformed and distorted. According to Gimbutas, this was particularly evident in

Greek mythology, where strong goddesses survived, thanks to the deep influence of Minoan Crete on Mycenaean Greece; this allowed a goddess element also to linger, via Classical Greece, into modern European culture,[70] an idea that echoes Jacquetta Hawkes's earlier suggestion that the feminine element is one of the Minoans' main legacies, via the Greeks, to European civilization (cf. Chapter 5).

Echoes of both Hawkes and Gimbutas abound in some popular and popularizing archaeological volumes on the Minoans of the last quarter of the twentieth century, such as Rodney Castleden's *The Knossos Labyrinth* (1989) and *Minoans: Life in Bronze Age Crete* (1990). Castleden, a prolific author, who has published dozens of book on topics ranging from the Aegean Bronze Age to Neolithic Britain and criminology, in his Minoan volumes makes no direct references to Gimbutas, and appears to have been more inspired by Hawkes, with whom he shares a predilection for Jungian psychology. This is indicated by his idea that a particular 'ideology . . . held the Minoans in its grasp', which may have 'released an archetype' that possessed them – an idea modelled on Jung's analysis of the Germans as possessed by the archetypal figure of Wotan (or Dionysos) unleashing a *furor teutonicus* during the 1930s–1940s.[71] Since, according to Castleden, the Minoans had a polytheistic religion, which of their many deities was their archetype that unleashed their '*euphoria minoica*'?[72] Castleden does not provide a direct answer in his *Minoans*, but he implies that this was a female deity, since he suggests that 'we should see the Minoan civilization as a whole symbolized in the Isopata Ring: a group of opulently dressed and bejewelled priestesses dancing ecstatically to produce an epiphany, willing themselves to be possessed by the goddess who hovers in the air among them' (see Fig. 6.1).[73] But he is more explicit in his foreword to Susan Evasdaughter's *Crete Reclaimed* (cf. below), where he suggests that the Minoans 'were possessed by their Great Goddess' and that their priestesses reinforced this possession by means of elaborate rituals unleashing a *euphoria minoica*.[74]

Jungian analysis aside, Castleden's *Knossos Labyrinth* and *Minoans* are attempts to critique what he considers traditional and outdated views of the Bronze Age inhabitants of Crete, which he summarized as follows: the Minoans are elegant, refined, and feminine; a people interested in physical beauty and nature, but uninterested in individual ambition; they are peaceful and carefree, but also very religious, and especially devoted to a Mother Goddess, or practising a form of polytheism, in which goddesses predominate; they may have had a matrilineal organization, and yet were also ruled by powerful kings (as suggested by later traditions about Minos), who resided in palaces; they possessed a strong fleet and colonies abroad, but were weakened by the Theran eruption, and eventually conquered by the Mycenaeans.[75]

Castleden's own vision of the Minoans is that they 'were sensual aesthetes and visionaries with bloodstained hands, and possessed a much fiercer, darker, grimmer and more exotic beauty than we hitherto imagined'.[76] This seems, however, more of a return to earlier, less peaceful, and more multifaceted visions of the Minoans, such as those of Arthur Evans and Jane Harrison, and also illustrated in some early Cretomanic works, such as Merezhkovsky's novel *The Birth of the Gods* (cf. Chapter 4). The latter, in fact, even anticipates Castleden's suggestion that the Minoans had an order of transvestite priests, who 'were probably eunuchs'.[77] Castleden rejects the 'traditional'

Fig. 6.1 The Isopata Ring (photo: Oltau, https://commons.wikimedia.org/wiki/File:Minoischer_Siegelring_03a.jpg).

notion that the Minoans were peaceful, and also doubts that they possessed a matrilineal organization.[78] But many of his own characterizations of Minoan Crete sound very traditional, such as his description of the 'childlike freshness' of Minoan culture, its pervasive 'religious zeal', its 'delight in the sheer physical beauty of the human body', and the importance of women, especially in the religious sphere.[79]

More original, but rather eccentric, is Castleden's suggestion that the Minoan palaces were not palace-temples but merely temples ruled by a powerful elite of priestesses, whose religious significance led to considerable temporal powers, which were shared with the *lawagetas* known from the Linear B tablets, while the *wanax* fulfilled merely a ceremonial role.[80] This unorthodox interpretation is partly based on Castleden's equally unorthodox conviction that a Greek-speaking Mycenaean elite did not take over the administration of Crete after the Theran eruption and that the Minoans simply adopted Greek as their administrative language, since this had become the new *lingua franca*.[81]

If Gimbutas only lurks, implicitly, in the distant background of Castleden's works, she looms large in *Crete Reclaimed: A Feminist Exploration of Bronze Age Crete* (1996), written by the appropriately named Susan Evasdaughter, for which Castleden, as mentioned above, provided the foreword. *Crete Reclaimed* vies with H. G. Wunderlich's interpretation of Knossos as a giant necropolis, in his *The Secret of Crete*,[82] as the most heterodox vision of Minoan Crete in a non-fictional work published in the last three decades of the twentieth century, and perhaps ever since the rediscovery of Minoan Crete. Evasdaughter avoids the term 'Minoan', because this indicates a form of kingship for which the evidence is 'less than there is for there being a minotaur'.[83] Instead, she presents Crete in the Bronze Age as a feminist–communist paradise: a society that is largely egalitarian and ruled by an elite of priestess-queens, whose 'Temple Palaces' were constructed for the worship of their Great Goddess, a peaceful force of creation. The temple-palaces' topography indicates that they signify the 'vulva of the Goddess', the conical hills nearby represent '[h]er pregnant abdomen', and 'double peaked mountains' stand for her breasts.[84] Unsurprisingly, Knossian cannibalism and the Archanes-Anemospilia human sacrifice cannot find a place in this quixotic reconstruction: the former is described as 'unexplained', and the latter, albeit accepted, is considered as an activity conducted 'by people with ideas at variance with those of mainstream Cretan culture'.[85] The *pièce de résistance* in Evasdaughter's vision, however, is her interpretation of the final destruction of the Minoan temple-palaces. This happened at the hand of the priestess-queens themselves: it was a ritual of obliteration to make them 'unseen and unusable by the patriarchal tribes' and to protect their sanctity from the 'barbaric Indo-European forces'.[86] Even if one assumed that this unusual suggestion is correct, this act of pious obliteration does not seem to have been carried out very effectively, given the archaeological evidence for both Late Bronze Age (Late Minoan III) and Early Iron Age use of the palaces.

Cretomania in a postmodern world: The Minoans in modern cultural practices *c.* 1975–1999 – from New Age Minoans to postmodern critiques of Greek history

The discoveries at Anemospilia and Knossos, the never-ending fascination with the Theran eruption, processual, postprocessual, and feminist interpretations of Minoan Crete find echoes in many Cretomanic works of the last quarter of the twentieth century. These further illustrate how the Minoan past never ceases to inspire artists and writers, by acting as an arena for the discussion of modern concerns, ranging from New Age Spiritualism to postmodern critiques of traditional Minoan archaeology and Greek history. Some of these works focus on the darker side of the Minoans, while others present alternative versions of the Minoan past, often presented through female voices.[87]

'New Age' Minoans

Two novels published in the 1970s, *The Sea King's Daughter* (1975) and *The Lily and the Bull* (1979), offer an intriguing combination of New Age spiritualism and Minoan archaeology. They predate the Minoan fall from paradise caused by the discoveries at Knossos and Archanes-Anemospilia – in fact, *The Sea King's Daughter* presents human sacrifice as part and parcel of Minoan civilization. Nevertheless, their uses of the

Minoan past could also be linked to the idea of paradise lost and regained, but in the context of religious conflicts, renewed spirituality, and belief in reincarnation.

The Sea King's Daughter by Barbara Michaels (one of the pen names used by award-winning American author, and Egyptology graduate, Barbara Louise Mertz) is a romantic thriller set in the early 1970s, recounting a summer of Greek adventures experienced by Ariadne Frederick – a young sporty woman from Florida. Her estranged father is a cantankerous archaeology professor – remote, cold, and obsessed with his work. He re-establishes contact with his daughter after two decades only because he wants to exploit her scuba-diving skills in a dangerous and illicit enterprise on the island of Santorini. Despite lacking a permit for underwater research, with his daughter's help he attempts to locate the lost fleet of King Minos, which sank in one of the Santorini bays during the Bronze Age eruption of *c.* 1500 BC.[88] Remains of the fleet were discovered just before the start of the Second World War, but were largely kept secret by his British colleague, Vincent Durkheim, whom Frederick had befriended while they were studying at Oxford in the 1930s – a friendship further cemented by their involvement with the Cretan guerrillas against the Germans during the war. Durkheim was captured and killed by the Germans, but managed to reveal his discovery to Frederick, who is now keen to locate it, since technical developments in diving have made the task more feasible.[89]

Before joining her father on Santorini, Ariadne travels around Greece. She is left cold and unimpressed by the Athenian Acropolis, whereas she has the most peculiar reaction in the Heraklion Museum and in Knossos. While visiting the former, she 'recognises' the objects in the cases, especially the 'gaming board', feeling that she 'knew how to play the game', although the object 'that shook [her] most was the clew box' because, once again, she felt that she knew exactly what it was used for.[90] At Knossos, she admires Evans's reconstructions and experiences the same feeling of *déjà vu*: 'It was as if I were two people in the same body. The real me ... But down underneath, in the dark places of my mind, someone else was waking up from a long, long sleep ... she knew this place, and she had known the gaming board and the clewbox [sic].'[91]

On Thera, Ariadne joins her father's archaeological endeavours and meets several intriguing characters: the English archaeologist Sir Christopher Penrose, a friend of her father in their Oxford and Cretan days, but now a rival; the reclusive German colonel Jürgen Keller and his Greek lover, the flamboyant Madame Kore, who wears snake-shaped gold bracelets coiled around her arms and is engaged in resurrecting ancient cults and rituals with the help of the local women; and last but not least Sir Christopher's assistant, the young and beautiful archaeologist Jim Sanchez, with whom Ariadne becomes romantically entangled. The still active volcano provides a rumbling and unsettling backdrop to the story, which contains a heady mixture of Minoan archaeology, Greek mythology, modern Greek folklore (there are even references to *vrykolakes*, i.e. vampires), the survival and transformation of ancient beliefs into modern Greek rituals (e.g. the cult of the Virgin Mary as a reincarnation of a much older cult of Mother Earth), the 1941 Battle of Crete, Freudian dreams, and Jungian archetypes. The novel delves, in particular, into the influence of the past into the present, into ideas of birth–death–rebirth, and reincarnation.[92] As Madame Kore explains to Ariadne, there was nothing strange about her feeling of *déjà vu*, because she already had and will live 'many lives', of which one was in ancient Crete.[93]

The novel also alludes to the non-Hellenic character of the Minoans, including Ariadne's mythological namesake and the practice of human sacrifice. In Ariadne Frederick's words, 'Medea wasn't Greek, though, any more than Theseus and Ariadne were. They came from further back in time, back in the dark abysses of prehistory when people still believed in human sacrifice and killed the king every nine years and sprinkled his blood around to bring back the spring.'[94] But Madame Kore explains to Ariadne Frederick that after the eruption of Santorini, 'the Greeks came from the mainland and made a new palace and a new dynasty in the ruins. What you see now in Knossos is the remains of this dynasty – all Greek.'[95] This is partly reinforced by her father's belief that 'The Mycenaeans were certainly Greek, but they derived a certain amount of their culture from the Minoans. After Knossos and the other Cretan centers were destroyed by the explosion of Thera, a Mycenaean dynasty ruled at Knossos for a time. The last Minos – the word is a title, like the Egyptian Pharaoh, not a name – was a Greek. Like his predecessors he worshiped the mother goddess, and his daughter – your namesake – was priestess of the goddess.'[96]

An even stronger flavour of New Age spiritualism pervades Moyra Caldecott's *The Lily and the Bull* – and not surprisingly, given the well-known interest in the subject of this this South African-born British novelist.[97] Like most other historical novels on Minoan Crete, this is set in a period of Minoan decline, but, instead of the usual Knossian location, the action takes place in and around Ma-ii, a town in northern Crete inspired by the palace of Malia, where Caldecott experienced feelings of *déjà vu* reminiscent of those felt by the fictional Ariadne Frederick in *The Sea King's Daughter*. Caldecott visited Crete in April–May 1977 to celebrate both the publication of two of her books on Bronze Age Britain (part of her popular 'Sacred Stone Trilogy') and her miraculous liberation from angina after consulting a 'spirit healer'.[98] While wandering around the palace at Malia, Caldecott sensed that she had been there before, 'knew how it had looked when it was inhabited in Minoan times . . . saw the wall paintings, the garden, the furniture, the people . . . felt the life all around'.[99]

In *The Lily and the Bull*, abundant allusions to Minoan material culture, customs, and history are combined with meditation, the use of crystals, alternative medicine, other cosmic dimensions, the need for inclusiveness, a touch of feminism, and, above all, love of nature.[100] Ma-ii is a town in which women are extremely important, especially in religious matters, and is ruled by a supreme Queen, whose succession is matrilineal. Ma-ii and the whole of Crete, however, are undergoing a period of instability, which recalls the matriarchy–patriarchy struggle in Renault's and other novels, but with a difference and a New Age twist: no Mycenaean invasion is in sight and there is almost a complete lack of allusion to ancient Greek myths.[101] The struggle, instead, is between two Cretan religious factions: many Cretans still worship the Mother Goddess, the Lady of the Groves and the Lilies, who represents the creative force as manifested, for example, in vegetation. The official religion led by the Queen, however, for some time has been shifting the emphasis to the Cult of the Bull, which represents the destructive force, as manifested, for example, in earthquakes.

The crucial issue is that, over time, the Minoans have come to believe that the Lady of the Lily and the Bull cults embody separate irreconcilable forces, and tend to support either one or the other, with the latter now prevailing on Crete. The Minoans have lost the sense of wholeness, have forgotten that 'Life depended on the fusion of the two opposing forces by the mysterious, violent, beautiful energy of Love.'[102] The situation is exacerbated by the fact that the Queen of Ma-ii is mad with grief because of the death of her son and is manipulated by a group of snake priestesses linked to the Bull cult. She has given pre-eminence to this cult and is set to change elements of the bull-leaping performances, which are funerary rituals symbolizing the human attempt to defy death through reincarnation.[103] The Queen, however, wishes to change these rituals to make her son immortal through deification, in a manner reminiscent of the Egyptian apotheosis of the pharaoh. Her impious attempts are thwarted by an earthquake, which heralds the more severe cataclysm of the Santorini eruption.

Against this background, Caldecott develops a love story between Ierii, the daughter of the chief gardener of the Knossos palace, and Thyloss, the son of Quilla, a former female bull-leaper, who has become a 'Seer, in touch with the Spirit Realms and with the earth forces'.[104] Thanks to her prophetic powers, Quilla warns the inhabitants of Ma-ii of the impending volcanic catastrophe: those who heed her premonition flee to the mountains and escape the second earthquake, tidal wave, and toxic ash. Ma-ii and most of its inhabitants are utterly destroyed, but the novel ends with a sense of hope. What the Minoans had in Ma-ii is finished, but the survivors will carry 'the seed to a new place and start again'.[105] The plain of Ma-ii is all destruction and death, but on the mountains the plants are still alive – and a 'small white lily', the symbol of the Goddess, shines from a cleft in the rocks.[106] Thus, *The Lily and the Bull* presents Minoan Crete as a kind of paradise that has gone wrong, but can be regained, if people go back to some good old Minoan principles: belief in rebirth and regeneration (instead of seeking immortality); respect for the creative forces of the natural world; and also respect, but no glorification, of the forces of violence and destruction.

Besides literature, a connection between New Age spiritualism and the Minoans appears in modern pagan groups founded by Edmund ('Eddie') Buczynski in the mid-1970s: the Minoan Brotherhood and Minoan Sisterhood.[107] These groups, which are still very active (see Fig. 6.2), were established as a response to the predominant 'heterosexist' culture of most witchcraft organizations at the time, rooted in the idea that, given 'the inherent polarity of nature, magic must be performed between a man and a woman, and any groups that work without this balance are doomed to failure'.[108] The Minoan Brotherhood is a male 'initiatory tradition of the Craft celebrating Life, Men Loving Men, and Magic in a primarily Cretan context, also including some Aegean and Ancient Near Eastern mythology', while the Minoan Sisterhood provides a similar framework for women to practise in all-female settings.[109] Although very different in origins, aims, and outlook, they may be seen as distant precursors of more recent Neo-Pagan groups that either use some Minoan elements or are entirely inspired by Minoan Crete, such as the Greek group Labrys, founded in 2008, and Laura Perry's Modern Minoan Paganism, founded in 2014.[110]

Fig. 6.2 Minoan Brotherhood shrine for the grove Temenos ta Theia of Minos Hermes, Chicago, IL, 2018 (photo reproduced by kind permission of Steven Bragg; see https://www.facebook.com/minoanbrotherhoodchicago/).

Minoan paradises lost and regained in feminist novels and other works

Since the early twentieth century, Minoan Crete has been associated with femininity and power conflicts that are performed along racial and gender lines, such as the supposed struggle between (Minoan/non-Aryan) matriarchal/matrilineal vs. (Mycenaean/Aryan) patriarchal societies. In the last quarter of the twentieth century, largely thanks to Gimbutas, these themes became the focus of a considerable number of Cretomanic works, from novels to a wide variety of other genres. A few examples of the latter are Elizabeth Lawton's obscure political pamphlet, *The Inevitability of Matriarchy* (1977) (see Fig. 1.2); Judy Chicago's installation *The Dinner Party* (1974–9), which has been described as 'the most famous feminist artwork of all time';[111] Riane Eisler's sociological-historical essay and international bestseller, *The Chalice and The Blade: Our History, Our Future* (1987), which presented Crete as a gender egalitarian society or 'gylany'; Marilyn Coffey's collection of poems, *A Cretan Cycle: Fragments Unearthed from Knossos* (1991); and Carol P. Christ's autobiographical essay, *Odyssey with the Goddess* (1995), and her creation of organized Goddess pilgrimage tours.[112] Above all, the feminist theme and matriarchy–patriarchy struggle loom large in many Cretomanic novels written by both men and women, and for both adult and younger readers. Among those authored by women, interesting examples are June Rachuy Brindel's *Ariadne* (1980) and *Phaedra* (1985), which read like a bloodbath worthy of a Greek tragedy, since the myth of Theseus and the Cretan sisters is reimagined as a killing spree to suppress the Goddess cult and the power of women (cf. chapter's epigraph). Other examples are Brigitte Riebe's *Palast der blauen Delphine* (1994); Jyotna Sreevivasan's children's book, *The Moon Over Crete* (1994); Theresa Dintino's *Ode to Minoa* (1999); Judith Hand's *Voice of the Goddess* (1999); and Christa Wolf's *Kassandra* (1983).[113]

Hand's *Voice of the Goddess* is quite typical of its genre. In a manner reminiscent of Caldecott's *The Lily and the Bull*, Hand presents Crete around the time of the Theran eruption as a society troubled by two opposing religious factions: one is devoted to the traditional cult of the Mother Goddess, which fosters harmony and eschews war; the other, the Poseidonist faction, is devoted to a male, earth-shaker divinity, and consists mostly of Mycenaeans and Cretans under their growing influence. Crete appears as a deeply religious and peaceful society, very advanced in the arts and commerce, organized into various classes and clans, but largely egalitarian (and with no slavery): instead of a supreme Priest-King, one finds a High Priestess guided by a council of elderly women. Minoan sexuality is also presented in a flattering light: children receive sex education at school, which includes information about foreplay and oral sex. It is no wonder that 'Keftian men are the finest lovers in the world'.[114] The only blemishes among Hand's Minoans are a superiority complex and a dogmatic conservatism: they frown on mixed race marriages and many of them show an inflexible devotion to religious laws and traditions, even when faced with exceptional circumstances in a changing world. Their conservatism (which includes pacifism) has disastrous consequences, since it makes them vulnerable to the Mycenaean conquerors. Despite these flaws, Hand's Minoan Crete is a unique and exceptional society: 'elegant and peaceful' and 'a source of great hope for humanity'.[115]

Wolf's novel *Kassandra*, together with the four essays that accompany many of its editions, is arguably the most intriguing of the works mentioned above, and one of the most interesting Cretomanic works of the late twentieth century because of its narrative power, complexity of ideas, and intriguing reception of the Minoans.[116] It also offers another example of the Minoanization of the Trojans (cf. Chapters 4 and 5), hence the Minoan images employed on the covers of some of its editions (see Fig. 6.3).[117] *Kassandra* is not a historical novel about Troy, let alone about Minoan Crete, but a deconstruction of the traditional portrayals of the Trojan heroine by male authors, especially Aeschylus's *Agamemnon*, with strong anti-war and anti-patriarchal undertones. It offers an introspective autobiography of the Trojan heroine, narrated as a flashback, after she has just arrived at Mycenae in the full knowledge that she is about to die: it is a lucid and bitter reflection on war and its effects on society, on the condition of women past and present, and presents parallels to Wolf's own story of growing up in Nazi Germany and living in the German Democratic Republic – a female voice that struggles to be heard and believed.

In the novel, the Trojans have curiously acquired a number of elements usually associated with the Minoans. For example, Trojan society appears as fairly egalitarian in terms of gender: as (allegedly) in Minoan Crete, and in contrast to Mycenaean Greece, fathers and brothers do not dominate women. But the conditions of war alter this and make the Trojans more and more similar to patriarchal Greeks. Besides, Hecuba is presented as the 'ideal queen', who sits on a wooden chair that resembles a

Fig. 6.3 Cover of English paperback edition of Wolf's *Kassandra* (1984) (photo: N. Momigliano).

throne and discusses political matters with her husband.[118] Significantly, one of Hecuba's dreams is interpreted in the novel as showing Paris as the restorer of 'her rights to the snake goddess as guardian of the hearth fire in every home'.[119]

The four essays reveal how Minoan Crete acted as a catalyst in Wolf's creative journey towards writing *Kassandra* – a journey that was both literal and metaphorical. Wolf wrote the novel after she visited Greece in the spring of 1980, and the first two essays are partly a travel diary of this sojourn. From the first essay we learn that, the day before Wolf flew to Athens, she started reading the *Oresteia* trilogy, was immediately captured by the character of Cassandra, and began questioning the way in which Aeschylus portrayed the Trojan heroine. Wolf wanted to find an answer to the question 'Who was Cassandra before anyone wrote about her?'[120] Her search for an answer continued throughout her Greek visit, which included an excursion to Crete, before she visited Argos and Mycenae.[121]

On Crete she was enthused by the Minoan culture, which inspired elements of her novel. In her own words, the encounter with Minoan ruins and with Evans's reconstructions 'induced in me an excitement which has continued until today, virtually unabated by my later reading of commentaries, objections, and rejections of Evans's method of reconstruction, and doubts about its results'.[122] Wolf was captivated by Minoan frescoes showing 'fantastic plant and animal shapes' and 'so sparkling with life and glowing with color'.[123] She recalled that 'the first glimpse of the Minoan paintings (of their reconstructions) is a joyful shock', but also a 'recognition'.[124] Wolf vividly describes the Toreador fresco (see Fig. 1.4) and remarks that 'my confrontation with this painting, with the Palace of Knossos and, one day later, the Palace at Phaestos, remains one of the rare cases when follow up reading has not diminished, but rather enhanced, the luster of the first meeting'.[125] Small Minoan terracotta figurines in the Heraklion Museum convey to her a feeling of shared humanity 'far more powerfully than any Apollo of Belvedere'.[126] She gazes 'hypnotized into the wide-open, staring eyes of the snake-goddess from the Palace of Knossos'.[127] For Wolf, above all, part of the 'magic' of Minoan culture is its 'ambiguity', stating that 'no later monument could surpass it ... the Minoans with their "palaces" had aroused our imagination and, even at a deeper levels, our buried hope for a "Promised Land"'.[128] Yet, she admits that this 'promised land' is a constructed utopia. The visions of Minoan Crete created by Evans and others 'reflect the unconscious desires of the interpreters, desires whose effects are all the more powerful for being unrecognized', especially in the case of Evans's views, which later 'less imaginative ... scholars find hard to resist'.[129]

Wolf knows about the human sacrifice and cannibalism of Anemospilia and Knossos, and she compares them to the theme of the 'the corpse in the cellar' in Western culture; she shows awareness of recent debates about the functions of the Minoan palace; she even questions the existence of a *Pax Minoica* and the alleged egalitarianism of Minoan Crete: 'there was probably slave labor, radical contrasts of wealth and poverty; an increasing trend towards centralisation'.[130] Thus, unlike other authors, such as Hand, who take the peaceful, matriarchal, egalitarian character of the Minoans as established, uncontroversial historical facts, Wolf is more sceptical: '[T]hroughout Western civilization Crete was being turned into the Promised Land of those who looked to the past to satisfy their longings – namely feminists, women committed to the women's movement, who ... saw in the Minoan kingdoms *the* social bodies to which they could concretely attach their utopian speculations and yearnings.'[131] Wolf seems to accept the idea of a change from matriarchy to patriarchy in prehistoric times (and the related displacement of a supreme female divinity).[132] But she muses as to 'why women today feel they must derive part of their self esteem and justification of their claims from the fact that civilisation begins with the worship of a woman', and pointedly asks, 'How does it help us to know that the ancient Greeks gradually replaced "mother right" with "father right"? ... Doesn't this harking back to an irretrievable ancient past reveal more clearly than anything else the desperate plight in which women see themselves today?'[133] Thus, Wolf consciously presents *Kassandra* 'not as a description of bygone days, but a model for a kind of utopia'[134] that shares some characteristics traditionally associated with an idealized Aegean Bronze Age culture: Minoan Crete.

In her four essays, Wolf describes how she came to give Minoan attributes to her Trojans. She reveals that, after wandering among the ruins of Knossos, she became 'infected with a pathogenic organism which triggered a slight but persistent fever; the fever continued to rise when I got back home in Germany. (You might call it the Crete and Troy syndrome ... I was prepared for it by my obsession with the name Cassandra ...)'[135] During her visit to Crete she was partly 'seeking the comparative time scale of the battle for Troy and the destruction of Minoan culture ... both of which, if scholarly dating is accurate, took place around the thirteenth century B.C. – Crete having been destroyed before Troy'.[136] She even wonders whether she should 'picture King Priam's fortress as a palace similar to the Palace of Knossos',[137] and describes how her notion of the port of Troy, of the sea that Cassandra would have looked at, was formed during a visit to Matala, a village and archaeological site on the south coast of Crete near Phaistos.[138] For Wolf, 'Troy belonged, in the widest sense, to the Mycenaean culture sphere, which … was modified by features of the culture of Asia Minor (the Hittites) and no doubt the powerful influences of Minoan–Cretan culture, which, as it petered out, passed major influences not only to the Greek mainland but also to the islands and the coast of Asia Minor; "permeated them". To what extent? What were the specifically "Minoan" traits of Troy?'[139] Wolf further reflects on the relatively close chronology of the Achaean destruction of both Knossos and Troy, effectively considering the fall of Knossos as a prefiguration of the fall of Troy, as others have done, and envisages Ionian bards being 'schooled by Minoan culture'.[140]

To sum up, a number of recurrent themes appear in Wolf's *Kassandra* and the other feminist novels mentioned in this section: the idea of Minoan Crete and Mycenaean Greece as symbols of the struggle between matriarchy and patriarchy and/or between a gender-egalitarian gylany and a male-dominated society; the use of Minoan Crete as a past that can inspire the future; and the desire to give space to alternative, mostly female, voices that have been silenced by the accounts of male victors, voices that no longer wish to celebrate violence – be it rape or war – but expose its disastrous effect on society.[141] There are also, however, some intriguing differences: for example, Greek literature provides the initial stimulus for some authors (e.g. Wolf, Brindel, and Riebe), whereas the material culture of Minoan Crete and feminist narratives take centre stage in the works of others (e.g. Hand, Dintino). Also, for most of these authors the notion of Minoan Crete as a peaceful, mostly egalitarian, matriarchal or matrilineal society tends to appear as an assured historical fact.[142] By contrast, Wolf shows a more reflective awareness of how modern desires have been projected onto the Minoan past. Wolf's critical stance, her reflectivity, and also her appreciation of the enigmatic character of the Minoans give *Kassandra* and its accompanying essays a postmodern flavour, which links it to the Cretomanic works discussed in the next section. These works share a sense of mystery, of deconstruction of romantic views of the Minoans, and of reflection on archaeology and its interpretative processes, and often present very personal, intimate uses of the Minoan past to explore issues of selfhood and identity.

Darker sides of the Minoans and the (postmodern) self[143]

Two works, almost contemporary with Wolf's *Kassandra*, which explore the darker sides of the Minoans, their otherness, and use Minoan material culture as a cue for introspection, are the novel *The Names* (1982) and the short story 'The Ivory Acrobat' (1988) by the acclaimed American author Don DeLillo.

In *The Names*, which is set in Greece, the Middle East, and India, the main character and narrator is the American James Axton, a risk analyst for a multinational corporation (but effectively working for the CIA). He has moved to Athens to be close to his young son and estranged wife, who are living on an obscure Cycladic island, where she is taking part in her first archaeological excavation. After the strange murder of one of the islanders, Axton becomes involved in the investigation of a mysterious sect obsessed with ancient scripts, languages, and names, and linked to this and similar murders. The novel offers several observations on the Athenian acropolis, archaeology, and ancient objects in general, and on the Minoans in particular. For example, Axton and his wife engage in a dialogue that encapsulates most of the typical commonplaces about the Minoans, but also questions them, while referring to the Archanes-Anemospilia human sacrifice:

'How would your Minoans have handled a situation like this?'
'A quickie divorce probably.'
'Sophisticated people.'
'Certainly the frescoes make them out to be. Grand ladies. Slim-waisted and graceful. Utterly European. And those lively colors. So different from Egypt and all that frowning sandstone and granite. Perpetual ego.'
'They didn't think in massive terms.'
'They decorated household things. They saw the beauty in this. Plain objects. They weren't all games and clothes and gossip.'
'I think I'd feel at home with the Minoans.'
'Gorgeous plumbing.'
'They weren't subject to overwhelming awe. They didn't take things that seriously.'
'Don't go too far,' she said. 'There's the Minotaur, the labyrinth. Darker things. Beneath the lilies and antelopes and blue monkeys.'
'I don't see it at all.'
'Where have you looked?'
'Only at the frescoes in Athens. Reproductions in books. Nature was a delight to them, not an angry or godlike force.'
'A dig in north-central Crete has turned up signs of human sacrifice. No one's saying much. I think a chemical analysis of the bones is under way.'
'A Minoan site?'
'All the usual signs.'
'How was the victim killed?'
'A bronze knife was found. Sixteen inches long. Human sacrifice isn't new in Greece.'
'But not Minoans.'
'Not Minoans. They'll be arguing for years.'
'Are the facts that easy to determine? What, thirty-five hundred years ago?'
'Thirty-seven,' she said.[144]

Axton is somehow reassured by the gruesome discoveries: 'It did not take me long to see how shallow my resistance was to this disclosure. *Eager to believe the worst.* Even as she was talking I felt the first wavelets break on the beach. Satisfaction. The cinnamon boys, boxing, the women white and proud in skirts like pleated belts. Always the self finds a place for its fulfilments, even in the Cretan wild, outside time and light.'[145] The director of the excavations where Axton's wife works also offers an unflattering picture of the Minoans: '. . . he's weary of the Minoans, it seems. He says the whole tremendous theme of bulls and bull's horns is based on cuckoldry. All those elegant women were sneaking into the labyrinth to screw some Libyan deckhand.'[146] In addition, Axton's wife wonders whether the strange ritual killings carried out by the sect are a 'latter-day version' of the human sacrifice of Anemospilia, a 'latter-day plea to the gods', and recalls the Linear B tablets listing offerings that include humans (and could represent more evidence of human sacrifice).[147]

In *The Names*, DeLillo remarks upon ancient objects, their otherness, materiality, agency, entanglements with humans, and relationship to selfhood, in a manner that seems to intersect and contrast with more recent debates relevant to 'the material turn' and even 'the sensory turn' in many fields, including Minoan archaeology: 'Maybe objects are consoling. Old ones in particular, earth-textured, made by other-minded men. Objects are what we aren't, what we can't extend ourselves to be. Do people make things to define the boundaries of the self? Objects are the limits we desperately need. They show us where we end. They dispel our sadness, temporarily.'[148] These ideas are further elaborated in relationship to a specific Minoan object in DeLillo's short story 'The Ivory Acrobat', which takes its title from a well-known bull-leaper figurine from Knossos (see Fig. 1.5) and recounts how Kyle, a young American schoolteacher, experienced an earthquake while living in Athens in the early 1980s.[149] Kyle is given a replica of a bull-leaper figurine by one of her colleagues, Edmund, to replace her ornamental terra-cotta head of Hermes that had been shattered by the seismic shocks. Unlike the original 'Ivory Acrobat', however, the replica is female.[150] Edmund chose this particular object for Kyle to remind her of her 'hidden litheness', of the fact that she is 'lean and supple and young . . . throbbing with inner life'.[151] But Kyle does not see this connection: for her the figurine represents something strange, distant, and mysterious, unlike the 'knowable past' represented by the Hermes (cf. passage below).[152] These are feelings that match DeLillo's own impressions of the Minoan world: at Mycenae, he felt he was dealing with 'an historical landscape', but when visiting 'sites associated with the Minoans' he 'sensed a kind of unknowableness . . . a culture of sheer imagination'.[153] Yet, the gracefulness, tactility, materiality, and otherness of the Minoan replica are a catalyst for Kyle's self-awareness, for defining her selfhood, and she ends up carrying it with her everywhere, like a talisman or even relic.[154] In DeLillo's words:

> Edmund had said the figure was like her. She studied it, trying to extract the sparest recognition. A girl in a loincloth and wristband, double-necklaced, suspended over the horns of a running bull. The act, the leap itself, might be vaudeville or sacred terror. There were themes and secrets and storied lore in this six-inch figure that Kyle could not begin to guess at. She turned the object in her hand. All the facile parallels fell away. Lithe, young, buoyant, modern; rumbling bulls and quaking earth. There was nothing that might connect her to the mind inside the work, an ivory carver, 1600 BC, moved by forces remote from her. She remembered the old earthen Hermes, flower-crowned, looking out at her from a knowable past, some shared theater of being. The Minoans were outside all this. Narrow-waisted, graceful, other-minded – lost across vales of language and magic, across dream cosmologies. This was the piece's little mystery. It was a thing in opposition,

defining what she was not, marking the limits of the self. She closed her fist around it firmly and thought she could feel it beat against her skin with a soft and periodic pulse, an earthliness.

She was motionless, with tilted head, listening. Buses rolled past, sending diesel fumes through seams in the window frame. She looked toward a corner of the room, concentrating tightly. She listened and waited.

Her self-awareness ended where the acrobat began. Once she realized this, she put the object in her pocket and took it everywhere.[155]

Minoan archaeology as exploration of the self plays an even larger role in *Prince of the Lilies* (1991) by the Australian writer Rod Jones – best known for his award-winning *Julia Paradise* (1986) and *Billy Sunday* (1995). *Prince of the Lilies* illustrates the fall from grace of the Minoans and the postprocessual (and sensory) turn in archaeology, in a Minoan context. It is like a fictional embodiment of Sheena Crawford's critique of earlier approaches to Minoan archaeology, especially her comments on libidinal fantasies (cf. chapter's epigraph), and even of her abandoned research on Minoan society, because she felt 'unable to marry successfully ideas for a new approach and the available data'.[156] In the novel, not only does the main character, an archaeologist, asserts that 'in one sense the entire enterprise of Minoan archaeology was a kind of libidinal fantasy', but also gives up his research project and the teaching of Minoan Crete, preferring to focus, instead, on a deconstruction of Evans's vision.[157]

Prince of the Lilies tells the story of archaeologist Charles Saracen, an Australian Rhodes scholar at Oxford, his German wife Magda, and their young son Dylan, who move from England to eastern Crete in the mid-1970s in search of a new life closer to nature, and for Charles to work on his project: '"The Golden Age", which was to be a scholarly exposition of Sir Arthur Evans' Minoans as well as a celebration of that gentle civilization'.[158] Both Charles and Magda 'had fallen in love with that innocent, less spoiled age, when human beings of original grace and beauty had wandered in peace upon the earth'.[159] At first their Cretan sojourn mirrors the Minoan paradise: they make friends with a Californian couple, Tasma and Nicholas, who live in a house that for Charles 'stood out like a beacon, pointing the way to a future, and for a moment they were again living on the island in its Golden Age. They faced the future in a kind of innocence shared with those figures from the [Minoan] frescoes'.[160]

Tasma and Nicholas are interested in arts and crafts, astrology, herbalism, metaphysics, yoga, mysticism, reincarnation, promiscuous sex, marijuana, and Minoan Crete. Their passion for the Minoans, however, is aesthetic, sensory, even mystical, and reminiscent of New Age spiritualism. Charles's approach, at least at first, is more intellectual and pedantic, but on Crete his 'intellectual grip on Minoan archaeology' starts disintegrating.[161] He is fascinated by Tasma's interest in archaeology as a 'sensuous experience of the past', by her wish 'to connect with the mysteries, the ecstasies, the powerful myth residing in the unconscious'.[162] Indeed Charles's entire Cretan sojourn becomes a new sensory experience, especially when he and his family move in with the Californians, and after Tasma starts decorating one of the rooms with Minoan-inspired frescoes, including the Prince of Lilies. Looking at her frescoes, Charles experiences new feelings, such as the 'dark smell . . . of Minoa',[163] which he compares to 'the dark wet of a woman'.[164] Charles realizes that 'the meaning of the Minoans could now be found only in sensations – the compelling dark smell, a feeling of speeding when he looked at the clean line of the Prince's thigh against the ochre-coloured earth, the pounding of feet, a suffocating sensation as dark as the embrace of the earth, which brought on in him the rushing return of past moments and the kind of uncertainty which seemed to belong to the nocturnal world'.[165] As archaeologists bring to light evidence of ritual cannibalism and human sacrifice, and start questioning many assumptions about ancient Crete, Charles becomes disillusioned with Evans's 'sunny view of the Minoans'.[166] And as the happy Minoan edifice disintegrates, so does Charles's personal life. His relationships with his wife, son, and Californian friends fall apart, and he returns to England, alone. Nevertheless, the novel ends on a positive, sensory note. Fifteen years later, Charles returns to Crete to confront his past. As he starts enjoying again the simple pleasures of nature, friendship, and banausic work, he understands that he will soon also resume his archaeological research.

Jones's *Prince of the Lilies* was 'the inspirational trigger' for the poetry volume *Crete* (1996) by fellow Australian writer Dorothy Porter, which contains over forty poems inspired by the island and the Minoan past.[167] Porter uses Minoan material culture, and later Greek myths pertaining to Crete, in sensuous but also critical and subversive ways to explore a wide variety of subjects, which range from the timeless to the contemporary and the most intimate, such as the crafts of the poet and the archaeologist, vivisection, her own sexuality, and the Minoans themselves. For example, in the poem 'Bull-leaping' Porter wonders whether 'poetry is a strange left over' of the dexterous, and dangerous, Minoan practice or is more like 'a forgotten fresco crumbling under a mound of prose', while in 'Gorgeous breasts' she relates bull-leaping to the first kiss she exchanged with a lover.[168] In the poem 'Archaeology', she compares Evans's excavations and restorations at Knossos to her own poetry, as excavation and reconstruction of her own self, in a way that recalls the way in which Minoan archaeology is juxtaposed with the exploration of the self in other works discussed in this section:

> Am I the Arthur Evans
> of my own lost city?
> Excavated
> with shovelling obsession
> Restored
> with wishful thinking?[169]

In her poem 'Linear A',[170] the undeciphered Minoan script is related to her youthful naivety, her lack of understanding, and 'becomes an analogue for the narrator's as-yet unreadable world and her untried, individual desires'.[171] With regards to current issues, and taking her cue from the sacrificial bull on the famous Hagia Triada sarcophagus (see Fig. 6.4), in the poem 'Altars' Porter compares and contrasts ancient animal sacrifices with the experiments carried out on live animals in modern laboratories.[172] Overall, Minoan Crete emerges from Porter's poems as a contradictory place: 'the wind the Goddess brings / is both wonderful and vicious'.[173] It is mysterious, sensuous, wondrous, 'volatilely feminine', a place where 'the breast' appears to have been 'mightier

Fig. 6.4 The Hagia Triada sarcophagus, detail of side showing bull sacrifice (photo: Zde, https://commons.wikimedia.org/wiki/File:Agia_Triada,_sarcophagus,_long_side_1,_limestone,_fresco,_1370-1320_BC,_AMH,_145305.jpg).

than the sword'.[174] For Porter, 'nothing is more passionate than a Minoan octopus', Minoan paintings are 'mischievously lovely . . . their landscapes / like nothing on earth', and the blue monkeys are 'lighter than life'.[175] Yet, she does not idealize Minoan Crete: instead, she juxtaposes these luminous images with others that are impregnated with blood, terror, violence, and sheer brutality. For example, in the already mentioned poem 'Altar', Porter imagines that 'Every altar in Crete / must have reeked / of the fluids of terror – / diarrhoea and fresh blood'. Similarly, the poems 'Exuberance with bloody hands', 'Atlantis', 'The body', 'Lost civilisation', and 'Triumph of the Will' allude to darker things – human sacrifice, cannibalism, bull-leaping as a dangerous blood-lusty spectacle – while the Minoans are compared to Lithuanians, who clapped every time the victim of a pogrom was beaten to death, and even to Nazis: in short, despite all the Minoan wonders, not all was 'glorious among the slithering lilies'.[176]

The darker side of the Minoans, and archaeology as excavation and reconstruction of identity, also appear in Beaton's *Ariadne's Children* (1995), among a myriad of other interesting themes (from opera to psychoanalysis). The narrative is framed by events in Sarajevo that started the First World War in 1914 and the Bosnian War in 1992, and tells the story of three generations of an English family, the Robertsons, and their involvement with the fictional Minoan site of Ano Meri. At the beginning of the book, the reader finds Lionel Robertson, a character that has touches of both Sir Arthur Evans and Heinrich Schliemann, witnessing the assassination of Archduke Franz Ferdinand. He later travels to Crete where, in the interwar period, he carries out excavations at Ano Meri, dubbed 'Ariadne's Summer Palace', a site that yields spectacular and exquisite finds, such as a fresco representing the myth of Europa and the Bull.[177] His son Daniel, who shares some elements with Evans's dauphin, the archaeologist John Pendlebury (they both die on Crete while fighting against the Germans in the Second World War), also works on the excavations, with his wife Laura. In 1990, their son Dan, also an archaeologist specializing in scientific analyses, becomes involved in new investigations at Ano Meri. The story concludes two years later, with Dan in Sarajevo, at the time of the Bosnian independence referendum, which was soon followed by the 1992–5 Bosnian War.

Lionel, Daniel, and Dan Robertson appear to represent, to some extent, stages in the history of Minoan archaeology, from a romantic and imaginative pursuit to a more scientific enterprise. This is shown, for example, through various allusions to Minoan archaeology, such as changing views about the functions of the Minoan palaces, from the residence of peaceful priest-kings where the ancient Greek myths become 'true' (as in the discovery of the fresco of Europa and the Bull) to dwellings of decadent rulers exploiting a Minoan *lumpenproletariat*, ceremonial centres where strange rituals took place, and hubs for storage and redistribution systems run by an elite of priests and priestesses acting as 'managers of a rural economy'.[178]

The intergenerational differences come especially to the fore in Beaton's description of the reactions of Lionel, Daniel, and Dan to a particularly gruesome discovery. Taking his cue from the 1979 finds at Knossos and Anemospilia, Beaton imagines that in 1939, at the start of the Second World War, the Ano Meri excavations yielded indisputable evidence of human sacrifice and cannibalism. This, however, is concealed at the time, because Lionel, the patriarchal old guard, cannot accept this. Lionel believes that the bones have been planted, and orders for them to be destroyed, whereas his son Daniel accuses him of refusing to face the evidence and of creating a too civilized vision of Ano Meri and the Minoans, in his own image. But, as Daniel puts it, it turns out that the Minoans 'weren't such lovable people after all'[179] or, in the words of Daniel's wife, Minoan human sacrifice-cum-cannibalism 'in its way . . . is just as beastly as Hitler and this whole beastly war'.[180]

Although the discovery is suppressed at the time, Daniel partly disobeys his father's orders. Instead of destroying the bones, he reburies them in another part of the site, as Dan discovers while reading his mother's diaries three decades later. Dan, the youngest archaeologist in the family, conceived and born during the Second World War, effectively carries out double, parallel excavations, and in more than one sense. He excavates both within the family papers and Ariadne's Summer Palace to find out the truth about a civilization 'hailed as the oldest in Europe',[181] but in this process he also digs up his family history and the shocking truth about his own conception on the island of Crete – something reminiscent of Freud's use of archaeological metaphors in explaining his psychoanalytical methods: 'This procedure was one of clearing away the pathogenic psychical material layer by layer, and we like to compare it with the technique of excavating a buried city'.[182]

Some of the themes discussed above – such as family history, different identities, Minoan antiquities, and the complex history of Crete – are also intertwined in the volume *Summer Snow* (1990) by award-winning British poet and prose writer Ruth

Padel, who enjoyed the first-hand, sensory experience of digging up the Minoans when she took part in excavations at Knossos in the 1970s.[183] For example, in her poem 'Deus absconditus' she compares her baby daughter to the Ivory Acrobat (see Fig. 1.5) and refers to the island's rich past, including the undeciphered Phaistos Disk, waiting 'in the museum, identity's absent script'.[184] In 'South Wind', the sirocco blowing from the Sahara, during one of her stays on Crete, reminds Padel of the destruction of 'the plundered faked-up palace' at Knossos, visited by 'a million foreigners each year, / shattered on a day in spring / when the wind blew from the south', and where her child is learning how to climb on the steps of the Theatral Area.[185] In 'Royal Road', Padel reminisces on her experience of digging at Knossos, 'Europe's labyrinthine vulva on the medieval map', muses about well-known Minoan finds, such as the Prince of Lilies, and seems to mourn a past that cannot be relived ('you can't remake what's gone').[186] Her poem 'Shards' evokes the numerous destructions revealed in the superimposed layers found in excavations at Knossos, from Minoan to Arab.[187] 'Orgeat' focuses on the archaeologist Alan Peatfield, a former Curator at Knossos, and his dissatisfaction with previous interpretations of Minoan Peak sanctuaries; the poem also alludes to the island's Turkish past and how its influence on present Cretan–Greek customs must often go unmentioned.[188] Indeed, the whole collection, in Padel's own words, is about 'the pressure of past relationships on the present, of different peoples who have inhabited the same ground – Minoans, Greeks, Venetians, Turks', and how this past 'undermines any modern traveller's escapist desire to forget home pain in a glittering elsewhere'.[189]

Minoans and the Cretan–Greek postmodern self

The entanglement between Cretan past and present as well as the idea of a heritage that can be painful, but should not be forgotten, similarly enrich the writings of the acclaimed Cretan novelist Rhea Galanaki, such as her *The Life of Ismail Ferik Pasha: Spina nel Cuore* (1989; English translation 1996), a work that 'has become the focus of debates about the relationship of Modern Greek literature to postcolonialism and postmodernism'.[190] Layers of the Minoan, Greek, Roman, Arab, Byzantine, Venetian, and Ottoman pasts help to create complex palimpsests in Galanaki's works, which often focus on conflicting identities (and countries) and, at times, offer multiple versions of the narrated events, as in the three different accounts of the death of the protagonist with which *The Life of Ismail Ferik Pasha* ends. Although references to the Minoan past are more prominent in later works by Galanaki, such as *The Century of Labyrinths* (2002) or 'Growing up next door to Knossos and "The other Ariadne"' (2017),[191] they also make a brief, yet significant, appearance in *The Life of Ismail Ferik Pasha*, even if this novel is set well before the rediscovery of Minoan Crete.

The Life of Ismail Ferik Pasha presents the fictional story of a real nineteenth-century historical character, Ismail Selim, an Egyptian-Ottoman general of Cretan origin, whose Greek name was Emmanuel Papadakis. In the novel, during the suppression of the 1821 Cretan revolt, the five-year-old Emmanuel is captured by Ottoman forces and taken to Egypt, where he is brought up as an Ottoman Muslim. After a successful military career, in 1866 he returns to his native island as commander of an Ottoman army to quell another rebellion, and there he dies a year later. In 1821, the protagonist is captured when he emerges from a cave where the rebellious inhabitants of his native Lasithi plateau have taken refuge. This is none other than the Psychro or Dictean cave, a major cult place in Minoan and later periods, associated with the birth of Zeus in later Greek tradition, where archaeologists conducted investigations in the late nineteenth–early twentieth century (cf. Chapter 3). While hiding in the cave, Emmanuel/Ismail finds a bronze blade among the stalagmites and stalactites: although this is not stated explicitly, an educated reader would recognize in this object one of the many Minoan (or possibly later) votive offerings found by archaeologists at Psychro. In the years to come, Emmanuel/Ismail 'was never to remove the blade from under the embroidered costume he wore as an Ottoman pasha, preferring to believe that it was the sword of some creedless angel who had ordained that his life should revolve within the orbit of knives'.[192] The blade thus becomes a constant reminder of his conflicting double identity as Cretan (Christian-Greek) and Egyptian (Muslim-Ottoman), but Ferik always resists choosing between the two. As Beaton has remarked, by allowing her hero not to renounce either his Cretan or Ottoman self, Galanaki implicitly suggests that, likewise, the Ottoman period should not be overlooked as an integral part of Cretan (and Greek) history and identity, and in doing so she 'places in doubt the established historiography of the entire nation to which that hero belongs'.[193] In other words, Galanaki undermines the traditional opposition of Greek–Turk and Christian–Muslim: she embraces a difficult past and the hybridity of Cretan (and Greek) identity.

The Minoan past is also an integral part of the complex Cretan identity but, unlike the Ottoman, this is not a painful, difficult heritage either in this or later works by Galanaki. Is this because, as Beaton has remarked, the non-Hellenic character and, one might add, the Anatolian/Levantine origins of the Minoans are 'never tackled head on' by Galanaki and other Greek-Cretan writers in general?[194] This seems to be the case. In fact, as discussed in previous chapters, since its rediscovery in 1900, the inclusion of the Minoan heritage in the long continuum of Hellenic and European history has been, on the whole, unproblematic, especially for Greeks. The political situation on Crete in the late nineteenth and early twentieth century, which Europeanized the Minoans for anti-Ottoman purposes, greatly contributed to this process (cf. Chapter 3). But there is another important factor that has facilitated the Greeks' incorporation of the Minoans into Hellenism, namely the idea that Greek-speaking populations had eventually prevailed over the Bronze Age inhabitants of Crete: *Creta capta ferum victorem cepit.* In other words, the non-Hellenic Minoan heritage, unlike the Ottoman, can be construed as the result of Greek military victory and colonization, instead of a painful defeat and long foreign occupation.

The smooth incorporation of the Minoans into the long continuum of Hellenic history is also evident in some of the works of the Cretan artist Roussetos Panagiotakis.[195] His engagement with and deployment of Minoan material culture dates from the 1950s and continues to the present day (cf. Chapter 7), but a substantial number of his Cretomanic paintings date to the 1990s.[196] In these works, Panagiotakis often uses Minoan elements to illustrate Greek myths related to Crete and sometimes also alludes to Cretan customs of more recent periods. For example, his painting *Zeus and Europa*

(1997), which shows Europa in typical Minoan ceremonial dress, is also known as 'The abduction', an allusion to the custom of marriage by bride-kidnapping that was still in vogue on Crete in the early–mid-twentieth century.[197] The painting *Ariadne, wife of Dionysus* (1997) likewise shows the heroine dressed in Minoan fashion. A similar conflation of Greek mythology and Minoan archaeology also appears in *The Upbringing of Zeus* (1997), which represents the Greek god as a child dressed in Minoanizing attire, surrounded by nymphs in Minoan dress and Kouretes wielding spears and figure-of-eight shields (see Fig. 6.5).

Many other works by Panagiotakis, however, focus purely on Cretan Bronze Age elements, such as his *Theophaneia* (1996), which is an ambitious and imaginative representation of Minoan rituals in the palace of Malia (see Fig. 6.6). Other examples are his *The wine-press of Vathypetro* and *Throne Room* (both 1999) (see Fig. 6.7), where the architectural elements follow fairly closely the archaeological finds. These paintings illustrate that Panagiotakis's broader vision of Minoan Crete largely aligns with canonical interpretations, but also shows some differences. For example, he portrays

Fig. 6.5 Roussetos Panagiotakis, *The Upbringing of Zeus* (1997) (© Roussetos Panagiotakis).

Fig. 6.6 Roussetos Panagiotakis, *Theophania* (1996) (© Roussetos Panagiotakis).

men and women as ruddy and white-skinned respectively, following the usual Egyptian–Minoan convention. Both genders, however, especially men and female bull-leapers, tend to appear rather muscular, sturdy, and more reminiscent of some square-built statues of Archaic *kouroi* or modern bodybuilders than the lithe, wasp-waisted figures one usually finds in Minoan iconography. In terms of Minoan social organization, Panagiotakis also appears to accept the high status of women, especially in the religious sphere, as well as Evans's notion of a supreme goddess and son, as indicated, for example, in both his *Theophania* and *The Great Mother* (see Fig. 6.8). Yet,

Fig. 6.7 Roussetos Panagiotakis, *Throne Room* (1999) (© Roussetos Panagiotakis).

Fig. 6.8 Roussetos Panagiotakis, *The Great Mother* (1997) (© Roussetos Panagiotakis).

against more contemporary trends, he is far from presenting Minoan Crete as a feminist utopia, since his *Throne Room* shows a male figure (Minos as Priest-King) wearing a bull-mask and surrounded by other men standing in front of him or sitting on the benches flanking the throne.[198]

Fashionable Minoans in other media: From high art and *haute couture* to popular culture and erotica

In the last quarter of the twentieth century, Minoan material culture continued to inspire the visual arts and other cultural practices at local, national, and international levels. Besides the various works discussed above, a recent exhibition at the British Museum on *Charmed lives in Greece: Ghika, Craxton, Leigh Fermor* (2018) featured the painting *Voskos* (1984), by the British artist John Craxton, which appears to have been partly inspired by Minoan Crete.[199] According to the explanatory panel, *Voskos* is the 'portrait of a Cretan Shepherd inspired by a Greek Bronze Age gold cup that John had admired in the National Archaeological Museum in Athens', probably a reference to one of the Vaphio cups, usually attributed to Minoan workmanship, which show the capture of a bull.

In the performing arts, the renowned American dancer and choreographer Paul Taylor premiered a Minoan ballet in 1977, titled *Images*, choreographed to music by Debussy (piano pieces from *Images* and *Children's Corner*), with 'Minoan' costume by Gene Moore, which are slightly more discreet versions of the Minoan breast-baring bodices and loincloths.[200] With its Minoan-inspired costumes, music by Debussy, and the angular two-dimensional movements of the dancers, as in a frieze, Taylor's *Images* seems to pay homage not only to the distant Minoan past but also to other ballets with Minoan connections, such as Nijinsky's *L'Après-Midi d'un Faune* (also choreographed to Debussy's music) and Ted Shawn's *Gnossienne* (cf. Chapters 3 and 4).

Haute couture also continued to succumb to Minoan charm. As shown in previous chapters, Fortuny, Bakst, and Kaloutsi created many garments inspired by Minoan Crete in the early decades of the twentieth century. In the last quarter of the twentieth century, Karl Lagerfeld followed in their footsteps with his 1994 spring–summer collection for the French fashion house Chloé, which took its cue from the Minoan-style frescoes from Akrotiri and presented light, sensuous dresses in cotton tulle fabric. Some of these dresses were on display twenty years later in an archaeological exhibition held in Paris.[201]

The Minoans continue to be attested in popular culture too. For example, Minoan Crete appears in several comics aimed at children or young adults, such as the Italian *Topolino e il Disco di Festòs* (Micky Mouse and the Phaistos Disk), released by Panini Comics in November 1988 and translated into many languages;[202] and the *La Galère d'Obélix* (1996) in the famous Asterix series created by René Goscinny and Albert Uderzo.[203] *La Galère d'Obélix* traces the journey made by Asterix, Panoramix, and Obelix to Atlantis, a land partly based on Minoan Crete, as illustrated by its architecture rich in tapering columns and horns of consecration, the presence of a 'Grand-Prêtre' (cf. Evans's priest-king), and the fact that the inhabitants are presented as eternal children, a likely reference to common descriptions of the Minoans as childlike (e.g. by Bossert and Platon). Instead of griffins, however, this Atlantis is provided with centaurs and flying bovids. Asterix is impressed by 'la vache qui vole!' – a cheeky allusion to the importance of bulls in Minoan iconography and also to a well-known French processed cheese, 'La vache qui rit', produced since the 1920s.[204] Even erotic comics for adults draw inspiration from Crete. Examples include *El Toro Blanco* (1989) by Laura (Perez-Vernetti) and Lo Duca, which juxtaposes the end of Minoan civilization with Pasiphae's bestial desires;[205] and Ugolino Cossu's *Le Ninfe* (1989), which tells the Cretan adventures of American journalist/photographer Dan Morrison, who works for a multinational organization called CippaCola. *Le Ninfe* is the tale of an encounter between modern consumerism and a Minoan lost paradise, and curiously foreshadows a much more recent and real encounter between Minoan Crete and one of the most famous global brands. Sent to report on the natural beauty of the Samaria Gorge in Crete, Morrison finds a secret cave that leads him to a part of the island where an ancient civilization, based on a mixture of Minoan Crete and Greek mythology, has somehow survived untouched by modernity. This appears as an earthly paradise, populated by nymphs with considerable sexual appetites. Besides nymphs and satyrs, Morrison meets a lusty King Minos and his ingenious craftsman Daedalus. Although the royal abode is not as magnificent as the palace of Knossos, it is still replete with Minoan architectural features (such as horns of consecration and inverted columns) and objects (such as ceramic pithoi and rhyta, stone vases, the Phaistos disk, and even pieces from the Town House Mosaic faience), while its wall are richly decorated with frescoes (among others, the Blue Bird fresco: cf. Fig. 4.17). All is going well until Morrison takes part in Dionysian rites and defiles the rituals when he starts taking pictures and brings out a can of CippaCola, whose content spills on the face of a nymph. As punishment, Morrison is to be sacrificed, but he manages to escape, and on his return home one of his Minoan photographs appears on a gigantic billboard, showing a satyr surrounded by nymphs and holding a can of CippaCola (see Fig. 6.9). This is not a particularly edifying story for modernity, Minoan Crete, and profit-minded encounters between the two.

By coincidence, almost three decades later, in the summer of 2017, a Greek design agency created a seasonal, limited edition Coca-Cola bottle (and other related merchandise, such as drink mats) illustrating the history and culture of Crete (see Fig. 6.10a–b) and, in later years, produced bottles for other regions of the Greek world that similarly 'highlight their rich history and heritage'.[206] As Christine Morris has commented, this is a nice illustration of the global going local.[207] The Cretan Coca-Cola bottle, like many other Cretomanic works, combines Minoan archaeology and Greek mythology, since it shows elements inspired by several well-known Minoan wall paintings, such as the Toreador and Ladies in Blue frescoes, and allusions to the myth of Theseus, Ariadne, and the Minotaur, as suggested, for example, by the ball of thread held by the female figure and the labyrinth pattern of the bull's body. The larger size of the female figure may also be an allusion to Minoan iconography (e.g. the Grand Stand fresco). The commendable creative idea behind the bottle in Fig. 6.10a–b is to celebrate the rich local heritage and history of Crete. But could one also deduce from this image that, if you drink Coca-Cola, you can perform like a Minoan bull-leaper (and impress your girl)? And can one also perceive the message that one must be careful about some women who show their breasts, because they could make you act rather dangerously?

Fig. 6.9 Vignette from U. Cossu's *Le Ninfe* (1989) showing CippaCola billboard (reproduced by kind permission of U. Cossu; photo: N. Momigliano).

a

b

Fig. 6.10a–b Coca-Cola seasonal limited edition bottle dedicated to Crete, inspired by Minoan decorations and Greek mythology, created by Asterias Creative Design, and acquired by the author in the summer of 2017 (photo: N. Momigliano).

Finally, uses of the Minoans in popular culture during the last decades of the twentieth century include the science-fiction franchise *Stargate*, which has attracted global interest. For example, the episode 'The Broca Divide' in the television series titled *Stargate SG-1* (season 1) shows the SG1 team (the flagship team of the Stargate Command) heading for planet P3X-797, which is divided into two opposite sides: the Land of Light, inhabited by civilized people, who are descendants of the Minoans, and the Land of Dark, inhabited by banished citizens of the Land of Light, who have contracted a mysterious disease that leads them to savagery – perhaps an allusion to the often remarked upon dual character of Minoan civilization.[208]

Conclusions: The Minoans in postmodern times – between paradises lost and regained

The last quarter of the twentieth century saw a remarkable increase in Minoan archaeological research, from new excavations within and beyond Crete to 'New Wave' surveys. New and contrasting interpretations of the Minoans and responses to their material culture emerged in this period, as illustrated in specialist syntheses on Aegean civilizations and a variety of Cretomanic works, which ranged from novels and poetry by acclaimed writers to paintings, ballets, fashion collections, television programmes, and even erotica.

The archaeological activity of this period contributed, in particular, to a deeper understanding of the complexity and diversity of Minoan settlements, and highlighted the extensive interaction between Minoan Crete and other Mediterranean cultures. This helped the development of new interpretations regarding the evolution and organization of Minoan palatial society: although Evans's priest-kings (sometimes turned into queens) continued to loom large in specialist and non-specialist works (e.g. those by Platon, Warren, Michaels, and Caldecott), corporate elites started to replace kingship (e.g. Dickinson), and some authors even tried to evict Minos and his relatives from their palaces, by interpreting these structures as purely ceremonial centres (temples) effectively run by groups of priestesses (e.g. Castleden, Evasdaughter). In addition, many archaeologists and Cretomanic authors were beginning to find peaceful Minoan sophistication and feminine equality rather too sugary. The much-publicized discoveries of human sacrifice and cannibalism at Archanes-Anemospilia and Knossos came as a shock to many, but also added grist to the mill of those who considered some Minoan visions as too biased by the desires of earlier periods, and also too unappealing in the materialist and postmodern world of the 1980s and 1990s. But Minoan Crete as a peaceful feminine bastion against Aryan patriarchal hordes, like the Minoan Mother Goddess, dies hard: if the last quarter of the twentieth century witnessed a Minoan fall from paradise, it also represents the apogee of Minoan Crete as a feminist Garden of Eden.

Many archaeologists and writers continued to incorporate the Minoans into the long continuum of Hellenic and European history, and many Cretomanic works used Minoan material culture to give colour, material setting, and almost a veneer of historicity to Greek legends about Theseus, Ariadne, and Platonic Atlantis. Nonetheless, the perceived disjuncture between Greek narratives and Minoan archaeological realities, discussed in the previous chapter, became more established and gave way to new trends. The Minoan past now acted as an inspiration for more radical reimaginings of the traditional Greek myths than those seen, for example, in Mary Renault's novel, and for narratives that expressed alternative perspectives, often female (e.g. Brindel). At the same time, one can observe that some publications (including some archaeological syntheses) simply paid little or no attention to the relationship between Classical texts and Bronze Age archaeology: the focus shifted to archaeology and its combination with more modern concerns. Thus, for example, in some Cretomanic works the Minoan past is used to explore ideas such as reincarnation (e.g. Michaels), the complex hybridity of Cretan and Hellenic history and identity (e.g. Galanaki, Padel), individual sexual identity (e.g. Porter), materiality and selfhood (e.g. DeLillo), the senses and archaeology (e.g. DeLillo, Jones), and at times this appears to closely intersect, contrast, and even anticipate material and sensory turns in Minoan archaeology. Some of these trends continue in the new millennium, as discussed in the final chapter.

Minoan Cultural Legacies: Every Age Has the Minoans It Deserves and Desires

And indeed archaeology is only really delightful when transfused into some form of art . . . who does not feel that the chief glory of Piranesi's book on Vases is that it gave Keats the suggestion for his 'Ode on a Grecian Urn'? Art, and art only, can make archaeology beautiful . . .

Oscar Wilde ([1891] 1913: 239)

But who would be content with a barrowload of painted plaster when he could make a prince out of it? . . . [Evans's reconstruction of the Prince of Lilies fresco] may not amount to fraud, but it is certainly a long-sustained deception. Does it really matter? In the course of the century since he was put together, the prince has taken on symbolic force. The fresco is a false image that exposure to millions of people has made true, embedded in the popular imagination as the essential expression of Minoan elegance and vivacity of spirit. The original is still on display, among the most treasured possessions of the museum; and a copy still stands under the portico of the south entrance to the palace of Knossos where Evans placed it in 1901, a potent proof – if we needed another – of the power of the image to transcend objective categories of truth and falsehood.

Barry Unsworth (2004: 139–41)

A chapter devoted to the principal archaeological discoveries, interpretations, and uses of the Minoans in the first two decades of the twenty-first century could easily be almost as long as several of the preceding chapters put together, since the amount of available archaeological information and Cretomanic works produced in this period has increased exponentially, and in no small measure thanks to the growth of the Internet and World Wide Web. Minoan archaeological research has continued apace, even in times of global economic crisis and shifts in the political landscape of Greece. Many important archaeological projects have been carried out in this period (e.g. KULP, the Knossos Urban Landscape Project), but have not been completed and/or fully published as yet. Consequently, the full implications of their findings, both within and beyond academia, are difficult to assess. The number of Cretomanic works has grown so dramatically that many pages could be devoted to a basic list of novels, new artistic genres, and media. For these reasons, in this final chapter I present an overview of how ideas about the Minoans and their cultural legacy developed over the ages treated in previous chapters, followed by a brief discussion of several uses of the Minoans since 2000 and some concluding remarks.

Every age has the Minoans it deserves and desires

In 1967, echoing de Maistre's well-known dictum that 'every nation has the government it deserves', Jaquetta Hawkes wrote that 'Every age has the Stonehenge it deserves – or desires', a phrase that could be applied to many ancient monuments, the people who produced them, and their cultural legacy.[1] Indeed, the present volume could be seen as an illustration of this idea, taking the Minoans as a case study, but also as an example of a Foucauldian heterotopia, since Minoan Crete is both a real and unreal place, and a mirror to the yearnings of different ages. As I attempt to summarize below, some predominant trends can indeed illustrate that each age has the Minoans it deserves and desires, but one should also recognize that, on the one hand, within one age different Minoans have emerged according to the particular wishes of groups and individuals while, on the other hand, some common threads have appeared across the ages.

Starting with the period from the Bronze Age up to 1900, the evidence for the desires that created different perceptions of the Minoans throughout this long era is relatively limited and patchy, especially for some phases (e.g. from Late Antiquity to the Enlightenment). Something more substantial, however, can be gleaned from Classical authors and the works of nineteenth-century Classical scholars, for whom Classical texts were the principal sources. Ancient Greek narratives were partly inspired by the impressive Minoan ruins, which remained highly visible for centuries, especially in the Early Iron Age. These narratives, on the whole, show Minoan Crete as a paradoxical and strange place: it is a civilized, powerful sea empire (and the home of an early legislative system), but the House of Minos also vies with the House of Atreus as one of the most unhappy families in Greek mythology, given its more than fair share of extravagant sexual activities, human sacrifice, murder, betrayal, and other such pursuits. Even if the Platonic dialogue titled after King Minos praises this ancient foe of Athens, the perceived Minoan–Athenian antagonism and Athenian chauvinism (together with the fact that in the Homeric epics the Cretans were sometimes confused with the Phoenicians) helped to create a rather ambivalent portrait of the Minoans, which has had a lingering influence on some modern responses.

Nineteenth-century scholars such as Hoeck, Müller, and Milchhöfer, whose work was heavily reliant on the testimony of Classical texts, often provided a more positive spin. Within their own 'Minoan Age', both Hoeck and Müller presented the period *c.* 1400–1200 as particularly luminous, while providing contrasting views on the ethnic identity of Minos and his subjects: the former considered them to be non-Hellenic, whereas the latter fervently believed that they were part of his beloved Dorians. Milchhöfer sought in Minoan Crete the beginnings of the Mycenaean culture that Heinrich Schliemann had so spectacularly revealed: his work prompted Schliemann to seek more glory at Knossos, but time and chance left this prize to Evans.

The period from 1900 to the First World War can be regarded as the heroic period of Cretan excavations, coinciding with Paul Morand's Cretomania of the late Belle Époque, and provides much more abundant evidence for the Minoans and the cultural legacy that this age desired. The antagonism between European powers and the declining Ottoman Empire, the related situation on Crete (still under Ottoman suzerainty, but aspiring to *enosis* with Greece), and the fascination with origins in the wake of evolutionism are among the most significant elements that contributed to an identification of the Minoans as Europeans, i.e. as ancestors that Europeans deserved and desired. Schliemann and Tsountas had shown that ancient Greece, long regarded as the fountainhead of European civilization, had a forerunner in the Mycenaean period. But what was the origin of Mycenaean civilization? Evans and other excavators provided a clear answer: Minoan Crete, an earlier civilization that had flourished on a contested European–Ottoman island, which was appropriated by Europeans both physically and intellectually during the *Kritiki Politeia*.

Although the Minoans were not usually considered as Greeks (or Aryans), they steered clear of any Oriental (and Semitic) taint, since they were presented as belonging to a mixed Mediterranean race, which some regarded as the true origin of European civilization. Also significant was the fact that Knossos and other Cretan sites rich in Bronze Age ruins loomed large in Classical sources – the staple of the educated European elites. As Schliemann populated his excavations with Homeric heroes, so Evans and others populated the Minoan ruins with well-known figures and events from Greek mythology, rationalized the word Minos as the title of a dynasty of priest-kings, and found proofs for the Herodotean and Thucydidean sea empire of Minos in the archaeological evidence. These connections between Classical sources and new archaeological discoveries helped to familiarize and Europeanize the unfamiliar material culture of Minoan Crete, and gave a further boost to the perception that archaeology could expose the kernel of truth behind Greek mythology, as Schliemann had done a generation earlier.

Other factors that, in the late stages of the Belle Époque, turned the Minoans into desirable European ancestors were their perceived primitivism and modernity, as expressed, for example, in their (alleged) social organization and artistic language. The rich and often startling female iconography of Minoan Crete was thought to represent a quasi-monotheistic religion focused on a Mother Goddess, which was, in turn, associated with the importance of women in Minoan society, even if the temporal-religious rulers were usually believed to have been priest-kings. It seems that, in this period, only the dramatist Jules Bois dared to think that the Minoans had established some form of feminist collectivism, anticipating later scholarly views. This Minoan monotheism and proto-feminism echoed contemporary theories on religious and social evolution as well as the aims of the suffragette movement, which was particularly active at this time. Similarly, the imagery and style of Minoan art chimed with the desires and aspirations of early modernism, as encapsulated by Bakst's remark that Minoan art appeared close and familiar, and artists could graft shoots from it onto their own art. Minoan art appeared primitive but also close to modern sensibilities in the simplicity of its lines, sense of colour and movement, and attention to nature and the human body. It was often seen as anticipating the naturalism and humanism of

Classical Greek and Renaissance art, but also as reminiscent of the exoticism and sensuality of the Orient. Perhaps one might summarize the encounter between the late Belle Époque and the Minoans as a romantic *coup de foudre* combined with the pleasure of recognition: scholars and non-scholars alike fell in love with this new and strange civilization which, however, had to be familiarized and domesticated first, in order to be made intelligible and possessed.

Rather different Minoans emerged from the desires of the period encompassing the two World Wars and the Greek Civil War. This age saw the publication of Evans's seminal *The Palace of Minos* (1921–35) and other important works of synthesis (such as Glotz's *La Civilisation Égéenne*), which continued to extoll the Minoan virtues, especially in artistic terms. But some of Evans's cherished ideas had already lost considerable ground by the early 1920s, such as his view that Mycenaean Greece was a late, decadent offshoot of a great Minoan Empire, which Greek-Aryan barbarian invaders conquered in *c.* 1200 BC. With Aryanism on the rise, and a growing interest within archaeology in the relationship between material culture and ethnic-linguistic groups, this period witnessed a polarization between Minoans and Mycenaeans. As the latter regained admirers (qua descendants of Indo-Europeans who had settled in Greece by the early second millennium BC), the former lost some lustre. On the one hand, the Mycenaeans became more closely associated with racial traits long perceived as Aryan, such as masculinity, belligerence, rationality, linguistic-intellectual superiority, and vigour. On the other hand, the Minoans were connected with opposite characteristics, such as femininity, pacifism, commerce, artistic flair, but also, at times, utilitarianism and lack of profound symbolism, Oriental over-refinement, and decadence (including sexual extravagance). Indeed, in some quarters, Minoan Crete came to be seen more as a distant, strange culture and the antithesis rather than the forerunner of Greece. Yet, despite the emerging otherization of the Minoans, elsewhere they continued to be regarded as worthy European-Greek ancestors and even as a blueprint for the future. For example, unlike the Romans and Ottomans, they were incorporated into the long continuum of Greek history in pageants that celebrated the centenary of Greek independence, while their perceived distance, femininity, sexuality, and pacifism became inspiring traits for writers (e.g. Lawrence, Miller, and Day-Lewis), artists (e.g. Klee), and dancer-choreographers (e.g. Shawn). In short, the contrasting desires of the early decades of Hobsbawm's age of extremes (and catastrophes) produced suitably contrasting Minoans – from imperialist, military conquerors, and first Europeans (e.g. Evans), to peaceful merchants and colonizers (e.g. Bossert, Glotz), decadent bourgeois elite (Kazantzakis), over-refined decadent Orientals (Spengler, Praz), over-refined decadent pre-Christians (Merezhkovsy), and sophisticated inhabitants of a peaceful, feminine Garden of Eden (e.g. Miller).

Later decades (*c.* 1949–74) in Hobsbawm's age of extremes, which saw the acme of the Cold War as well as the swinging sixties, continued to present contrasting visions of the Minoans and offered some intriguing new developments. The decipherment of Linear B in 1952 confirmed prevailing theories concerning the arrival of Greek-speaking populations in Greece by the late third millennium BC and a Mycenaean conquest of Crete in the mid–late fifteenth century BC. The decipherment also served to emphasize the opposition between Minoans and Mycenaeans, Mycenaean familiarity and Minoan otherness, even if, occasionally, it helped to Orientalize the Mycenaeans and separate them from the supposedly real Greeks, because the importance of the supreme ruler (*wanax*) and the organization of the Aegean Bronze Age palaces resembled that of their Oriental counterparts rather than the broader social base one could see in some later Greek poleis (e.g. Starr).

Attempts to reduce the Minoan cultural legacy to no more than a picturesque, minor stage in the development of Hellenism, *pace* Evans and other Minoan aficionados, existed even before the decipherment, but after it the Minoans came to be associated even more closely with a matriarchal, feminine, Oriental, or quasi-Oriental stage that, brilliant as it may have been, needed to be overcome for real Greece to emerge (e.g. Starr, Renault, Lacarrière). Yet, the Minoans and their otherness continued to fascinate scholars, writers, and artists, who appreciated them precisely because of their perceived femininity, pacifism, and even proto-communism. In the interwar period, pacifism was often considered a negative trait and the Minoans' Achilles's heel, but this changed in the wake of the Second World War. The growth of pacifist movements (especially with the US involvement in the Vietnam War), second wave feminism, and support for socialist-communist ideals prompted a nostalgia for distant, peaceful, egalitarian worlds, attuned with nature, and this turned Minoan Crete into a lost paradise, an antidote to the present, and a hope for the future (e.g. Hawkes, Willetts, Lacarrière, Andersen).

Another dichotomy detectable in this post- Second World War age regards changing perceptions of the relationship between ancient Greek sources and Minoan archaeology. On the one hand, there is a continuation of earlier euhemeristic approaches, which used archaeology to rationalize Greek myths and show that they contained a kernel of historical truth. On the other hand, there is an emerging sensitivity to a disjuncture between textual and archaeological evidence, as well as a realization that Greek narratives distorted the ancient reality both wittingly and unwittingly, as histories written by victors and as narratives in which much got lost in translation (e.g. Bacchelli, Lacarrière, Anderson).

The last quarter of the twentieth century also presents contrasting visions of Minoan Crete. On the one hand, the growth of neoliberalism and materialism in the Thatcher–Reagan years as well as the emergence of postmodernist trends (also reflected in archaeology) created a reaction against some over-idealized and romanticized portrayals of the Minoans – a reaction that was also promoted by archaeological discoveries of possible human sacrifice and ritual cannibalism (e.g. Treuil et al., Dickinson). On the other hand, more traditional, idealized views persisted (e.g. Platon) and coexisted with new feminist constructions of Minoan Crete (e.g. Eisler, Gimbutas, Castleden, Wolf). In fact, the notion of Minoan Crete as a last bastion of matriarchal societies (or of Eisler's more gender-egalitarian gylany) against invading swarms of patriarchal, warlike Aryans reached its zenith in the final decades of the last century. This, combined with the perceived disjuncture between the ancient Greek (and male) narratives and Minoan archaeological remains, already observed in the previous age, helped to give voice to more radical reinterpretations of Greek myths in some Cretomanic works, and to perpetuate the dichotomy between Minoans and Mycenaeans (e.g. Brindel, Wolf).

As can be gleaned from the above summary, despite all the differences, some common threads can be detected across the ages. One may conveniently start with the persistent influence of Classical texts in the construction of the Minoans. Although there are examples of scholarly and Cretomanic works in which Greek myths played an insignificant part or even no part at all (especially in the last few decades of the twentieth century and in the twenty-first century), more often than not Classical narratives and archaeological evidence have been closely intertwined since the early twentieth century, even if with contrasting approaches and results. These range from those scholars who maintained the idea that Greek mythological narratives have 'the smell of truth', in Renault's words, to those who believed that they were merely economical with the truth. The former usually produced multifaceted or even ambivalent visions of the Minoans, in conformity with the contradictory picture that emerges from Classical texts, while the latter could produce visions that are arguably even more idealistic than Evans's Minoan Golden Age.

Another common motif is the repeated use of the Minoans as a mirror for concerns related to different types and levels of identity, which may be subdivided into ethnic-cultural, socio-political, artistic, and personal (but other categorizations are, of course, possible).

The ethnic-cultural identity of the Minoans could be exploited at local, national, and transnational levels (e.g. Cretan, Hellenic, Mediterranean, European), and the differing perceptions have often depended on how Greekness, Europeanness, and indeed the Orient were defined (e.g. Evans, Heidegger, Starr). Interestingly, despite the fact that the Minoans did not speak Greek and that this language has been a significant element in Hellenic self-definition since antiquity, for many if not most (modern) Greeks the incorporation of the Minoans into the long continuum of Hellenism has seemed unproblematic. The reason for this, as I suggested in Chapter 6, is probably the fact that the Minoan legacy, unlike the Roman and Ottoman, could be construed as the result of interactions between Greek and non-Greek peoples in which the former emerged victorious. This Minoan incorporation into the long continuum of Hellenism has more often than not assumed the form of a Hellenization of the Minoans, rather than a more hybrid perception or Minoanization of the Hellenes, although examples of the latter occur too, especially in the work of some Cretan authors (e.g. Kazantzakis, Diktaios, and Galanaki).

Contrasting views of the Minoan socio-political identity are often one of the best indicators of the kind of Minoans and Minoan cultural legacy that each age, group, and individual wished for. Kingship, queenship, corporate priesthoods, imperial power (which made use of slavery), proto-communism (with no slavery), matriarchy, patriarchy, and gylany have all been imagined at one time or another as characterizing ancient Minoan society. Despite these variations, almost without exception all interpretation accepted the significant social identity of women, even if opinions on the nature and amount of their power have varied.[2] The main evidence for the importance of women is found in the abundant and striking Minoan iconography, which was interpreted according to different theories and approaches, from evolutionism to feminism. The idea that women had a considerable role in Minoan society is one of the most significant Minoan cultural legacies. It emerged at a time of intense debates on the Woman Question and suffragette activism, and since then has provided inspiration for subsequent generations of feminist thought. This partly explains why the suggestions that the bull-leapers in the Knossian Toreador fresco do not include female participants (which have found wide acceptance among specialists over the last three decades) have made little or no headway among wider circles, whereas the belief in a Minoan Queen-High Priestess is quite popular.[3]

Another common thread across the ages concerns Minoan artistic identity, especially the notion of Minoan Crete as a precursor (or not) of later artistic movements. In the first two decades of the twentieth century, Minoan art could be incorporated into both the long continuum of Classicism and into early modernism. Many regarded the sophistication and naturalism of Minoan art as a forerunner of later Greece and Renaissance Italy, but parallels with more exotic, Oriental, and modern artistic idioms, such as those of Polynesia, Japan, and European Art Nouveau, were common too. In later periods, Minoan art was interpreted as being eidetic or closer to expressionism (e.g. Snijder and Bossert), while some scholars stressed its difference from any European tradition (e.g. Praz, Brion). Indeed, some well-known art critics and writers even questioned whether Minoan art could be considered as art at all, and found it wanting in terms of symbolism and ideals (e.g. Brandi, de Lacretelle). Such negative appreciations of the Minoans and their material culture often emerged from individual perceptions of what was essential and admirable in Greek art, just as the incorporation (or not) of Minoan Crete into the long continuum of Hellenism and Europeanism depended on conceptions of what constitutes Greekness and Europeanness.

Minoans through the ages have also been used to explore more personal types of identity, and this approach at times involved the analysis of individual social roles, such as writer, artist, poet, and archaeologist (e.g. Gide, Michael Ayrton, Elytis, Porter). In the case of individuals of Cretan birth, the use of the Minoans in their works was often intertwined with their sense of a hybrid Cretan–Hellenic ethnic identity (e.g. Kazantzakis, Diktaios, Galanaki), while for others it encompassed more intimate and existential aspects of individuality, such as sexuality (e.g. Gide, Porter) and sense of selfhood (e.g. DeLillo).

Into the new millennium: Minoans in post-postmodern and post-humanist times[4]

Many of the threads and topics summarized above continue into the twenty-first century, which has seen a resurgence of Cretomania in a remarkable variety of genres, including, among other cultural practices (and in no particular order), novels, poetry, music, paintings, pageants, stage and other performances (including culinary events),[5] amusement parks,[6] sculpture,[7] murals (see Fig. 7.1a–c), video installations,[8] jewellery and fashion,[9] websites,[10] radio plays,[11] books and play scripts for children,[12] comics,[13] Neo-Pagan groups,[14] cinematic productions,[15] and advertisements for global brands, such as Coca-Cola (as curiously anticipated in an erotic comic of the 1980s (cf. Chapter 6, with Figs. 6.9 and 6.10).

The first two decades of the new millennium saw the appearance of dozens of novels inspired by Minoan Crete.[16] Many, such as Peter Huby's *Pasiphae* (2000),

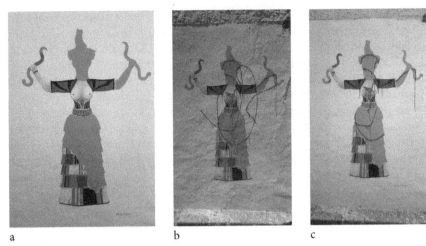

a   b   c

Fig. 7.1a–c (a) Céline Murphy's mural before defacement (April 2018); (b) after defacement (July 2018); and (c) after retouch by the artist (July 2018). Murphy's work indicates how this image, which has become like a poster-girl for Minoan Crete, has been heavily reconstructed (photos: C. Murphy, reproduced with kind permission of the artist; see also https://celine-murphy.com/projects/the-minoan-snake-goddess-faience-figurine/).

continue the pattern of interweaving Greek myths and archaeological finds, since they are reimaginings of famous Cretan stories that make more or less frequent use of Minoan material culture to give historical and local colour, while others draw inspiration from Minoan material culture alone (with very little or no help from Greek myths), such as W. Sheppard Baird's *The Minoan Psychopath* (2007), which tells the story of a Knossian warrior-cum-detective who leads an expedition to Avaris and investigates the murder of four children near Knossos.[17]

This interweaving of Greek myths with Minoan archaeology is also attested in many other media, as illustrated, for instance, by amusement parks recently opened on Crete,[18] and further recent paintings by Roussetos Panagiotakis, such as his *Minotaur* (2014; see Fig. 7.2) and *Atlantis* (2019; see this book cover). In the amusement parks, Greek Minoan material culture is often used merely to provide some local colour to later Greek myth. By contrast, Panagiotakis's *Minotaur* presents an interesting and disturbing image, which suggests that the Hellenic is a superficial narrative superimposed on Minoan material culture (in our discussion of this work he even used the phrase 'Greek lies').

The poems 'The Minotaur Speaks' and 'Swimming with the Bull' in Claire Williamson's collection *Visiting the Minotaur* (2018) also illustrates this archaeological-mythological interweaving. In the former poem, the monster does not devour the seven youths sent to him or even 'touch a hair on their Minoan heads'; the children simply 'eat each other in the end'. 'Swimming with the Bull' is an emotional exploration of the Knossian Toreador fresco, in which the poet evokes 'the rising myth of Atlantis' and finds herself 'swimming next to bovine hide / pulled through the labyrinth's two thousand rooms / . . . all stamped with the sign of the bull'.[19]

Fig. 7.2 Roussetos Panagiotakis, *Minotaur* (2014). The setting recalls the lustral basin area in the Throne Room at Knossos (© Roussetos Panagiotakis).

Operas, such Sir Harrison Birtwistle's *The Minotaur* (2008) and the 2011 production of Mozart's *Idomeneo* by Opera San Jose, provide other examples of this thread uniting Greek mythology and Minoan material culture. The latter employed quite faithful reproductions of Knossian and Theran frescoes, Knossian architectural elements, and other features, such as the so-called Throne of Minos, thus giving a very Minoan colour to this work by Mozart, which had its premiere in 1781, almost a century before Minos Kalokairinos's fateful excavations at Knossos.[20] The Minoan settings of this opera could nicely illustrate Oscar Wilde's idea that 'archaeology is only really delightful when transfused into some form of art' (cf. chapter's epigraph), but Birtwistle's use of the Minoan past is more intriguing, since he transformed, rather than reproduced, the Minoan imagery, as illustrated below.

Birtwistle's *The Minotaur* is an opera in two acts and thirteen scenes, with libretto by David Harsent, which was commissioned by the Royal Opera House and premiered on 15 April 2008 at Covent Garden. The work is a modern retelling of Theseus's slaying of the Minotaur, in which the Minotaur is presented as the victim and the half-brother not only of Ariadne but also of the Athenian hero (since Poseidon is their common father). The inspiration comes mostly from Greek mythology and modern works, such as Friedrich Dürrenmatt's *Minotaurus: Eine Ballade*,[21] but an allusion to Evans's Minoan snake goddess and her votaries appears in Scene 10, 'The Oracle at Psychro'. The oracle, consulted by Ariadne, is a gigantic bare-breasted 'Snake Priestess' (see Fig. 7.3). While in a trance, she utters unintelligible sentences, which are translated by a male priest.[22] The part of the Snake Priestess is sung, if one can use this term for her utterances, by a countertenor (Andrew Watts in the original production).

Fig. 7.3 Snake Priestess in Harrison Birtwistle's *Minotaur* (2008): screenshot from DVD published by Opus Arte (Catalogue no. OA 1000D; photo: Bill Cooper).

In November 2015, I interviewed Birtwistle and asked him about his use of this Minoan image, especially his choice of an imposing size for the priestess and a countertenor to sing the part. The composer, who visited Crete in the mid-1970s, commented that these choices were guided, above all, by his desire to create a wondrous theatrical effect and reflected his interest in theatrical devices as well as the aura of magic; but they were also related, to some extent, to the appearance of the Knossian figurines, which Birtwistle perceived as showing an unrealistic exaggeration of the female body, with preposterously long legs and unrealistic breasts. Thus, for theatricality's sake, Birtwistle made his Snake Priestess larger than life, but he also matched the perceived exaggerated femininity of the Knossian figurine with his use of a countertenor, because he considers this type of voice as womanlier than a woman's.[23] Thus, Birtwistle's use and perception of the Knossian snake figurine seem to reflect the sense of power that emerges from this Minoan object, but are also reminiscent of female sexual objectification. This raises questions about different users and viewers of this figurine, and whether notions of the male/female gaze might be usefully employed (or not) to explore Minoan iconography.[24]

Another thread that persists in the new millennium regards the Minoan ethnic-cultural identity, especially its incorporation into the long continuum of Hellenic and European history. In this context, the opening ceremony of the 2004 Athens Olympics offers an excellent example of a twenty-first-century Hellenization of the Minoans.[25]

This ceremony, titled 'Clepsydra' (water-clock) in reference to the passing of time, opens with numerous Minoan tableaux full of colour and sensuous movement, especially that representing Evans's snake votary, whose breasts were blurred through pixelation in some but not all television broadcasts.[26] Some of the tableaux also portrayed Minoan bull-leaping and boxing, implicitly suggesting that they are the forerunners of the Olympic Games. The Clepsydra was a worthy descendant of the 1920s pageantries that celebrated the centenary of Greek independence: it included the Minoans, but omitted entire periods of Greek history, such as the Roman, Frankish, and Ottoman (since the ceremony jumped from the tableaux with the Macedonian Alexander and the Hellenistic Tanagra figurines to Byzantium, and from Byzantium to the Greek War of Independence). It was a missed opportunity not only to embrace all periods of Greek history, but also to question other stereotypes, such as the idea of the colourfulness (and sensuality) of Minoan Crete vs. the whiteness (and purity) of Classical Greece, since all the tableaux symbolizing the latter used the imagery of statues in white, pure marble, instead of acknowledging that these were originally painted in vivid colours.

This Hellenization of the Minoans can have serious consequences, as illustrated by a rather disturbing episode in the history of Minoan archaeology that took place in 2009 and involved two distinguished archaeologists: Metaxia Tsipopoulou and Kostis Christakis. During the public launch of a book by the latter, they discussed the idea that the Minoans were of Middle Eastern origins, i.e. from the Fertile Crescent, and non-Greek. This caused a furore: hostile reports appeared in the press, Christakis was subjected to verbal abuse and threats of physical violence, and questions on the Greek vs. non-Greek ethnicity of the Minoans were asked in parliament.[27]

Works such as Dintino's *Stories They Told Me* (2003), the sequel to her *Ode to Minoa* (1999), continue to explore other established trends and topics, such as Minoan gylany and sexual mores, while the exhibition 'Contemporary Minoans' and related conference, held in May 2018 at the Archaeological Museum in Heraklion, addressed the influence of Minoan Crete on contemporary fashions created by Greek designers.[28]

'Contemporary Minoans' was held in the European Year of Cultural Heritage under the aegis of Branding Heritage and other organizations. It focused on the dynamic dialogue between the Minoan legacy and individual, personal artistic identities, which help to transform and translate Minoan motifs into modern idioms. Besides exhibiting numerous Neo-Minoan creations (especially dresses and jewellery), the designers offered some interesting personal reflections on their work and Minoan Crete.[29] For example, the fashion designer Faye Chatzi talked about her perception of Minoan dress, especially female, as modern and symbolic of female freedom; her and Alexandra Theochari's use of traditional weaving techniques and local weavers to revive the Greek economy is also reminiscent of the earlier efforts of Florentini Kaloutsi and Eva Palmer Sikelianos (cf. Chapter 4). The co-founder of the company Ancient Greek Sandals, Christina Martini, explained how some of her products included elements inspired by specific Minoan artefacts from Knossos, such as the steatite bull-head rhyton from the Little Palace, the Prince of Lilies fresco, and the snake goddess/votaries figurines from the Temple Repositories, which she applied to classical-looking sandals. Similarly, the jewellery and fashion designer Sophia Kokosalaki spoke eloquently of her first encounter with the snake goddess/votary figurines when she was an eight–nine-year-old girl, and of Minoan Crete as a rich and inexhaustible source of inspiration for her work, especially as a Greek designer of Cretan descent. One should note, however, that the Minoan elements for these designers are usually part of a broader Hellenic heritage that they strive to valorize, and as such this can be seen as another example of the unproblematic incorporation of the Minoans into the long continuum of Hellenism (as discussed above and in previous chapters). Also noticeable is how the inspiration provided by Minoan material culture is usually linked to long-established ideas that go back to the first decade of the twentieth century, such as Crete as the first European civilization (especially important in the context of the European Year of Cultural Heritage), the modernity of the Minoans, and, last but not least, the importance of women in Minoan society.

Different and more novel trends have also emerged in the twenty-first century, as illustrated, for example, by the album *Minoan* (2014), produced by the post-metal, progressive-rock band Giant Squid.[30] This uses the Minoan past to reflect on topical issues such as global warming, rising sea levels, and environmental disasters. In the words of Aaron John Gregory, one of the band's founders, the album was a 'love letter to the Mediterranean and specifically Bronze-age Greece . . . which I feel mirrors these heartbreakingly brutal, turbulent times we live in today'.[31] The picture of Minoan Crete that emerges from the lyrics (and from interviews given by Gregory) follows quite traditional lines: the Minoans are a people suspended between East and West, who live in harmony with nature, especially with the sea; they are a naval power, but they are quite peaceful; though now largely forgotten, they represent the origins of European civilization because of the legacy they passed on to the Mycenaeans and, through them, to the Greeks; they practised cannibalism, but this, as explained, for example, in the song 'Mycenaeans', was the result of the dire circumstances in the aftermath of the Theran eruption, which eventually led to the Mycenaean conquest: 'What will the Greeks think when they see what we've become? / Delusion, chaos, and cannibalism'. The song 'Palace of Knossos', in particular, describes the feeling of obliteration, fragility, and impermanence experienced by its inhabitants after the catastrophe: 'We will be forgotten, we will be lost / A sunken island, legend to none'. The effects of the tsunamis connected with the Theran eruption are evoked in 'Sixty Foot Waves', which, according to Gregory, besides its historical reference, can also be interpreted metaphorically as a prophecy of what might happen to our contemporary coastal towns if hit by tsunamis, especially in the light of rising ocean levels and the Fukushima Daiichi nuclear disaster of March 2011.[32] The song 'Phaistos Disk' presents this artefact as the record of a great catastrophe caused by the sea and a warning for future generations, while seemingly alluding, once again, to Minoan cannibalism (i.e. to the children's bones with butchery marks found at Knossos): 'Let the disc illustrate, / why our children's bones are flayed . . . Let the disc serve as warning / Never unearth these graves'. In fact the whole album can be understood literally and figuratively as an elegy to the downfall of the Minoans but also to the timeless feelings of impermanence and loss that can be experienced at any time when humanity confronts natural and man-made disasters.[33]

Another growing trend of the twenty-first century is the desire to have more spiritual as well as sensory Minoan experiences: to commune with Minoan divinities, immerse oneself in Minoan practices, perform the Minoans, dress like a Minoan, and even eat the Minoan past. This is well illustrated, for example, by the flourishing of long-established Neo-Pagan groups, such as the Minoan Brotherhood and Minoan Sisterhood, which now also have branches in Europe, as well as the recent Modern Minoan Paganism founded by Laura Perry in 2014 (cf. Chapter 6 and Fig. 6.2). Perry has authored books that offer practical advice on how to set up sacred spaces in your home and perform rituals, and include prayers (daily devotionals) that one may recite.[34] A more sensory turn, in particular, is exemplified by Jerolyn Morrison's Minoan Tastes and Anna Bastaki's Minoan Theater. The former enterprise, founded in 2012, started as an academic pursuit in experimental archaeology to recreate authentic Minoan meals, prepared with modern replicas of Minoan cooking pots; it now provides 'Minoan Experiences' to the public, involving Minoan cooking classes, Minoan catering for receptions and other events, as well as walking tours of the town of Ierapetra.[35] The latter is a cultural events centre that similarly offers a 'Minoan Experience' (see Fig. 7.4).[36] Visitors are invited to immerse themselves in a journey that leads them from the Minoan past to the Cretan present, by watching acrobatics alluding to Minoan bull-leaping performed by men dressed in Minoan kilts, and dances by women dressed in a demure version of the well-known Minoan attire (i.e. with breasts modestly covered). They 'dance to honour the Goddess along with the men' as a 'symbol of equality and love in honour of the Great Mother'.[37] After these spectacles, visitors can enjoy a meal that includes 'both Minoan and traditional Cretan delicacies of the modern era', and listen to 'music played with ancient and modern Greek instruments, moving towards a more traditional Greek fiesta with dancing'.[38] Another example of sensory 'Minoan' activities is the appearance, in the summer of 2019, of a young actress/street-performer in the main square of Heraklion, who impersonated the snake-brandishing 'votary' figurine from Knossos (see Fig. 7.5). Unlike other imitations, her dress presents a full décolleté, even if the breasts on display, like the serpents, are not real.

Fig. 7.4 Minoan Theater, Crete: performance inspired by the Minoan past (photo N. Momigliano, September 2019).

Fig. 7.5 Ermioni Dova impersonating the Knossos 'Snake Goddess' in the main square of Heraklion, summer 2019 (photo: Kostas Georgakopoulos).

The examples discussed above suffice to show that Cretomania is alive and well in the new millennium, and provide further illustrations of how the study of modern responses to Minoan Crete in different cultural contexts is relevant not only to scholars whose research focuses on the reception of the Minoans but also to wider audiences. Indeed, I hope that I have shown throughout this book that these representations of Minoan Crete are worth studying because they are an intrinsic part of its history, since the Minoan past and its cultural legacies are not reducible to what happened in the second and third millennium BC and the possible material, iconographic, linguistic, or even spiritual legacy transmitted to us via Mycenaean and Classical Greece. Minoan Crete is also the product of interpretations, reconstructions, and complex entanglements between objects and ideas about them, which are influenced by a wide array of interpretative traditions. As Barry Unsworth's comments on the Prince of Lilies remind us (cf. epigraph and Fig. 3.13), the most emblematic images of Minoan Crete are almost without exception modern reconstructions. These include much of the site of Knossos (e.g. Figs. 3.7, 4.8, and 4.9) and even Evans's snake 'votary', whose powerful snake-brandishing image has effectively replaced Evans's less fragmentary snake 'goddess' as the symbol of the Minoan supreme deity and Minoan female power, and has become a kind of poster girl for Minoan Crete (see Figs. 1.1, 1.2, and 7.1).[39]

Minoan specialists may also wish to reflect on whether their own works are immune to Cretomania. After all, a Regius Professor of Greek at Oxford recommended reading Mary Renault's novels for an insight into the Greek past.[40] These novels inspired a passion for the Aegean Bronze Age in a doyen of Aegean prehistory, Oliver Dickinson, when he read them as an adolescent,[41] and I suspect they also influenced many others. Indeed, I wonder whether Emily Vermeule's criticism of the notion of Minoan Crete as 'a brothel where the sturdy mainlanders found experience and sophistication', which appears in one of her scholarly works, alluded not only to the works of other academics, but also to such Cretomanic novels (cf. Chapter 5). I should also like to suggest that Minoan specialists ignore at their peril how various media help to disseminate their favourite subject to wider audiences and give it new vitality as well as relevance to the present. To paraphrase Wilde, art can make the Minoans even more delightful and beautiful. But it can also do much more than that: Cretomanic works can pose serious questions of historical and social importance, and can stimulate different ways of looking at Minoan Crete. They offer new provocations and opportunities to reflect on the Minoan past and its significance for past, present, and future generations.

Notes

Chapter 1

1 With apologies to Susan Seidelman, Rosanne Arquette, and Madonna.
2 Gere (2006a and 2009: 153–71).
3 Cited in Gere (2006a: 215; 2009: 168–9). Despite H.D's request, there appear to be no surviving letters from Bryher/Ellerman to Evans on this subject in the Evans archive of the Ashmolean Museum, Oxford.
4 For Freud's collection of antiquities, and the absence of Minoan finds, see D'Agata (1994).
5 Gere (2006a: 213; 2009: 169–71). For allusions to Minoan Crete in H.D's works, see Gere (2009: 177–94). See also Gere (2002) for Freud's use of archaeology, and archaeological metaphors in particular, in his writings.
6 Morand (2011 (1960–1): 121–3): 'L'art crétois, mycénien, et toute leur décoration . . . vinrent bouleverser l'art viennois, animer l'art officiel munichois de 1905, puis les premiers peintres qui travaillèrent pour Diaghilev . . . Cette "crétomanie" devait durer jusqu'en 1914.' Morand gives many examples of this 1900–14 Cretomania, but some of his details seem rather hazy, which is unsurprising, given that he was writing this piece in the early 1960s and probably relying on memory instead of checking facts in a library. For example, he cites the ballets *Le Dieu Bleu* and *Schéhérazade* as examples of Cretomania, even if these do not appear to have Minoan elements, unlike others that the artist Léon Bakst produced for Diaghilev's company; moreover, Morand seems to forget that Bakst's most Minoan work was, in fact, created in the early 1920s: cf. Chapter 3 and Momigliano (2013 and 2017a). Morand also cites the influence of the Knossian 'Blue Bird' fresco in this period, but this was not discovered until 1923 (cf. Chapter 4). Finally, despite Morand's statement, I was unable to find Cretomanic elements in the 'official art of Munich' of c. 1905.
7 Fitton (1995: 5 and 47).
8 Cf. Jauss (1982: 20).
9 On the importance of the cultural biography of objects, see Kopytoff (1988: 66–8).
10 Cf. also Olivier (2011: xvi): 'Once exhumed, artifacts, some of which may come from a very distant past, are with us in the here and now, where we attempt to decipher them and reconstruct the history of which they are part. Thus, what the archaeologist brings to the surface is not so much an object recalling some clearly delimited time period of the past, as the evolving memory of that past, whose meaning can be determined only by and in the present.' This echoes the notion in literary reception theory that 'meaning is always realised at the point of reception' (Martindale 1993: 3; cf. also Murnaghan 2007).
11 On entanglements between objects and people, see Hodder (2012).
12 Evans (1903: 62–94, esp. 86).
13 For changing interpretations of the function of Knossos as 'palace' or 'temple-palace', see Schoep (2010, with earlier bibliography) and further discussions in the present

volume. While I am perfectly aware of the controversy surrounding the term 'palace' and of the attempts to replace it with other words, I will continue to use it to avoid confusion: as Fitton (2002: 72) has observed, even if the term 'palace' may not be entirely adequate, the 'expression "Minoan palace" defines a specific phenomenon'. Moreover, I disagree with the idea that this term is inapt because it is too closely linked with the idea of royalty: whether in English or in other languages, the meaning and use of the term 'palace' is not restricted to a residence of royalty (see, e.g., Lambeth Palace and the Italian Renaissance 'palazzi').

14 On the concept of *lieu de mémoire*, see Nora (1996). For Bronze Age ruins used as *lieux de mémoire*, see Alcock and Cherry (2006).

15 For Knossos as a Cretan acropolis, see Galanaki (2017: 191): 'Knossos was our Acropolis, the great past of Crete.'

16 Cf. Foucault (1984). For Knossos as a Foucauldian heterotopia, see also Solomon (2006).

17 Cf. Momigliano (2017b: 5).

18 The history of Minoan archaeological discoveries is already outlined, for example, by Michaelis (1905 and 1908), Burrows (1907), and Lagrange (1908). See also the perceptive retrospective on Cretan research by Myres (1933), with further bibliography. More recent overviews are available in McDonald and Thomas (1990) and Fitton (1995 and 2002). For illustrations of the more recent scholarly interest in the uses of Minoan Crete in modern cultural practices, see, e.g., Farnoux (1993 and 1996), Fitton (2002, the chapter on 'The mythological legacy and the reception of Minoan Crete'), Hamilakis and Momigliano (2006), and Momigliano and Farnoux (2017).

19 For Minoan Crete, Art Nouveau, and Art Deco, see, e.g., Blakolmer (2006 and 2017, with further references).

20 Cf. Chapters 5 and 6. It is not clear as to whether or not the LGBT Labrys group of Kyrgystan (http://www.labrys.kg/en/) was influenced by Minoan Crete in their choice of name.

21 See, e.g., Hamilakis (2006) and Solomon (2006) and discussions in later chapters of this book.

22 Cf. Chapter 7. For earlier incorporations of the Minoans into the Hellenic past in state-sponsored pageants, see Chapter 4.

23 See, e.g., letter to *The Times* (31 October 1900) by Evans and D. G. Hogarth, cited in Momigliano (2002: 270) and referring to Crete as the 'fountain-head of our own civilization'; see also further examples discussed in later chapters, and Davies (1996: 81): '... it is now generally accepted that Minoan culture on Crete, and [the later] Mycenaean culture on Mainland Greece, formed the twin peaks of Europe's first civilization'.

24 Hales and Paul (2011: 4, with further references).

25 On Minoan gender ambiguity, see, e.g., Hitchcock (2000), Alberti (2002), Alexandri (2009), McGowan (2011, esp. 28–32). On interpretations of the Toreador fresco as presenting only male figures, see Damiani Indelicato (1988), Marinatos (1989 and 1994), Shaw (2004), Shapland (2013). Chagall's *L'écuyère* also recalls the fascination with Minoan gender ambiguity found in other Cretomanic works discussed in later chapters, such as those of Merezhkovsky and Gide (cf. Chapters 3 and 4). I wonder whether *L'écuyère* is partly a tribute to the Cretomania of his former teacher and fellow-Russian émigré in Paris, Léon Bakst, who had died in 1924 and a year earlier had produced the remarkable Minoanizing sets and costumes for *Phèdre* (cf. Chapter 3). For Chagall as a pupil of Bakst, see Momigliano (2017a: 86, with further references).

26 On the hybridity of the Knossos Throne room, see Galanakis et al. (2017); for earlier discussion of Minoan-Helladic hybridity at Knossos, see also, e.g., Vermeule (1964: 137–48); for further discussion of how Renault's work anticipates other archaeological developments, see Chapter 5; on materiality, agency, bodily senses, and archaeology, with special reference to Minoan Crete, see Hamilakis (2013).

27 Cf. Boardman (2002: 15): 'a major source for Greek myths was also the result of Greeks' imaginative response to the natural world around them and to the artefacts of their predecessors'.

28 Evans (1921: 2).

29 Evans (1921: 2).

30 I elaborate here on the idea that Classical Greece was an empowering but also weighty past for modern Greeks as expressed, e.g., by Yalouri (2001: 187–8) and Lambropoulos (2010), as well as on ideas about what is 'classical' about Classical antiquity discussed by Porter (2005 and 2006) and Alcock and Cherry (2006).

31 Solomon (2006: 173).

32 For 'Minotaur images' generally, including the fact that they often show monkeys and other animals, see Krzyszkowska (2005: 8–9 with figs. 24a–c and 201, 207 with figs. 395–400). Such was the desire to find the Minotaur in Bronze Age Crete that one German scholar saw a 'Minotaur' in an image that shows a human figure and goat in the background, and dubbed as 'Female Minotaur' a hybrid bird-female image from Zakro (Tittel 1903: figs. 1 and 8).

33 Momigliano (2006), with further references.

34 Cf. Momigliano (2019).

35 On Kalokairinos's excavations, see Chapter 3.

36 Original in Greek – English translation taken from http://www.hellenicaworld.com/ Greece/Museum/NationalMuseumAthens/en/NAMAMLSchliemann.html. Other versions are cited in many books and articles, e.g. in Bryce (2006: 36).

37 E. A. Poe, 'To Helen' (1845 version: see https://www.poetryfoundation.org/ poems/44888/to-helen and https://www.poets.org/poetsorg/poem/helen-0).

38 Cf. also Porter (2005: 29) and repeated in Porter (2006: 5–6), who refers to the Aegean Bronze Age as one of those periods usually regarded as 'losers or non-starter' among the contenders for a 'classical' status.

39 Cf. Sherratt (1996). The New Testament quotation 'went out from us but they were not of us' is from 1 John 2.19.

40 'Desperately foreign' refers to the title of Finley's essay on Greek Attic tragedy in his 1968 collection of works, not to the essay on the 'Rediscovery of [Minoan] Crete', which happens to be the next in his volume. Some of Finley's observations on Attic tragedy, nevertheless, could be applied to Minoan Crete, such as the idea that 'the more precisely we listen and the more we become aware of its pastness, even of its near-inaccessibility, the more meaningful the dialogue becomes. In the end, it can only be a dialogue in the present about the present' (Finlay 1968: 7).

41 Farnoux (1993:118–19); Ziolkowski (2008:10–11); see also Momigliano (2010).

42 *Pace* Gere (2009: 151–3). See further discussion of Picasso and Minoan Crete in Chapter 4 (especially note 90).

43 *Pace* Gere (2009: 98–104); regarding De Chirico's lack of (or extremely tenuous) connection with Minoan Crete, see also La Rosa and Militello (2006: 249) and Barber (2008).

44 On Klimt and Minoan Crete, cf. also Bammer (1990).

Chapter 2

1 See, e.g., Cottrell (1955), Warren (1975), Fitton (1995), McDonald and Thomas (1990); see also Chapter 3.

2 His excavations were preceded by a series of tests started ten days earlier by D. G. Hogarth in the area around the palace: see Hood and Smyth (1981: 1–2).

3 With apologies to Joseph Conrad.

4 For summaries of Egyptian and Near Eastern evidence, see Cline (1994 and 1999), with further bibliographical references. For recent suggestions about Minoan–Hittite relations, see Georgakopoulos (2012a and 2012b), also with further references.

5 See, e.g., Niemeier and Niemeier (1998 and 2000, with earlier references); Bietak at al. (2007).

6 Cf. Cline (1994 and 1999), Panagiotopoulos (2001), all with further references. Most scholars accept the equation Keftiu = Minoans, but see *contra* Vandersleyen (2003).

7 On identification of Caphtor with Crete, see Cline (1994 and 1999).

8 See Cline (1991 and 1994), Georgakopoulos (2009 and 2012a).

9 Georgakopoulos (2012b, with earlier references).

10 Cline (1999: 125).

11 Georgakopoulos (2009 and 2012a).

12 Dickinson (1994: 253 and 2009); see also review of scholarship on the subject in Beckman et al. (2011).

13 For the 'Great Powers Club', see Van De Mieroop (2016: 137).

14 See, e.g., Coldstream and Huxley (1972).

15 For early uses of the term 'Minoanization', see Anonymous (1932: 213) and Pendlebury (1939: 230). For overviews, see Broodbank (2004) and Niemeier (2009); see also Gorogianni et al. (2016).

16 Wace and Blegen (1918: 188).

17 E.g. Cline (2014) and Van De Mieroop (2016: 201–20).

18 Nora (1989 and 1996).

19 Coldstream (1998), Prent (2003).

20 Coldstream (1998).

21 Coldstream (1988: 28–9 with fig 2.3, and also discussing other examples of Iron Age pottery drawing inspiration from Minoan motifs, such as goats, birds, fish, and goddesses.

22 This taboo did not extend necessarily to the wider palatial area, such as the Theatral Area at Knossos, but, as Coldstream has proposed (2000: 298), this suggests that the palace walls stood high and provided a clear demarcation.

23 For 'ruin cults', see, e.g., Prent (2003) and McEnroe (2010: 158–9). The phenomenon of votive depositions near impressive Bronze Age ruins is not, of course, limited to Minoan Crete: see, e.g., references in Coldstream (2000: 296, n. 87). For Iron Age cultic activities near the Bronze Age walls of Troy, see Basedow (2007) and Aslan and Rose (2013). For Knossos, see also Popham (1978) and Coldstream (2000), with further references. At Knossos a temple was eventually built on the ruins of the palace, but probably not before the fifth century BC: Evans (1928: 6–7, 344) identified this with the 'house of Rhea' mentioned by Diodorus (5.66.1).

24 Troy: *Iliad* book 7.452–3 and book 21.441–57; Mycenae and Tiryns, Pausanias 2.16.5 and 2.25.8; Tiryns: Bacchylides, *Ode* 11.72–80; Athens: Herodotus 6.137.

25 Morris (1992: 113, 165, and esp. 184: 'The sources of this "bull of Minos", a term only compounded as "Minotaur" after 400 B.C., is probably a misunderstanding of images

of gods in the shape of bulls or men wearing bull's masks in ritual, attested in Cyprus and the Near East but imported into Aegean ritual'). For eastern elements in the Homeric epic, see especially West (1997).

26 Hurwit (1999: 93, fig. 65); see also figurine in the Louvre, found at Olympia but of Attic provenance: http://www.louvre.fr/en/oeuvre-notices/minotaur.

27 On Greek myths relevant to Crete, see Morris (1992) and Ganz (1993, esp. Chapter 8, 'Minos and Krete'). Although focusing on three Cretan women in Latin poetry, Armstrong (2006) also offers a useful account of various stories about Crete in Greek sources.

28 Lévi-Strauss (1963: 89), Culler (2013).

29 Momigliano (2019).

30 For the story of Minos and his family, see especially Book III and the Epitome.

31 For other versions of Miletos's and Sarpedon's migrations to Asia Minor, and the role of Crete in mythological narratives regarding the Carian region, see Unwin (2017: 66–90).

32 Callimachus, *Hymn* 3 (to Artemis).

33 Antoninus Liberalis, *Metamorphoses* (The Fox of Procris): see Antoninus (1992: 101).

34 In the Homeric version, Artemis kills Ariadne on the island of Dia (*Odyssey* xi, 322), usually identified with Naxos, but this is also the name of an islet just north of the Cretan coastal town of Amnissos near Heraklion. According to W. S. Barrett, the Homeric version suggests that this was the punishment for Ariadne's abandoning Dionysus for Theseus (see Barrett (1964: 222–3), referring to verse 339 in *Hippolytos*). Diodorus Siculus (iv.61.5) follows a version in which Ariadne is abducted by Dionysus, and suggests that Dia is an old name for Naxos; Plutarch (*Theseus*, 20) presents a version in which Theseus abandons Ariadne.

35 Bennet (1997), West (2007).

36 Evans (1943: 365); see also Chapter 3.

37 Morris (1992: 73–7, 216–19, 257–8, 336).

38 For Hesiod and the Minoan *thalassocracy*, see Huxley (1961 and 1968) and Niemeier (2009). For the François Vase, see http://www.beazley.ox.ac.uk/tools/pottery/painters/keypieces/blackfigure/francois.htm.

39 Ziolkowski (2008: 8).

40 Morris (1992: 215–17).

41 Huxley (1994).

42 A shown, e.g. by Sherratt (1996: 91), in Archaic–Classical times the Cretans were often confused with the Phoenicians. On Phoenicians in Crete, see also Stampolidis and Kotsonas (2006). In this context, one may note that, after the disappearance of writing in the Aegean, following the collapse of the palatial system, one of the earliest inscriptions found in Greece so far has come from Crete and is in Phoenician.

43 For Attic inventions concerning Crete, see the pseudo Platonic dialogue *Minos* (318d). For Plato's admiration for Crete, see, e.g., *Laws* I.624b.

44 See especially Alcock (2002), Romeo (2010), and Kouremenos (2016), all with further references.

45 Alcock (2002: 102–3), Paton (1994).

46 Alcock (2002: 108–21).

47 Alcock (2002: fig. 3.9).

48 Paton (1994 and 2000), Alcock (2002: 104–5).

49 Alcock (2002: 121–31) and esp. Romeo (2010: 71 and passim).

50 For this and other examples discussed below, see Alcock (2002).

51 Alcock (2002) suggests that this Idaean cave renaissance appears to be connected with a boom in the use of caves generally in this period, unconnected as to whether or not their use went back to Minoan time, but possibly linked to the cultural atmosphere of the Second Sophistic.

52 Romeo (2010).

53 Kouremenos (2016).

54 Frazer (1966: 3–15).

55 Evans (1909: 108–10, and 1935: 672–3).

56 For oscillating perception of Crete in Roman times, see Romeo (2010); for earlier perceptions of Crete as 'oriental' and Phoenician, see discussion above, with n. 42.

57 For a potted history of Crete from prehistoric to modern times, see, e.g., Momigliano (2000a) and Cameron (2003), with further references.

58 See, e.g., Karadimas (2009: 64, with n. 171, and 366–9), citing nineteenth-century accounts of visits to Crete by E. Falkener, C. E. Savary, R. Pashley and T. A. B. Spratt, which record the reuse of ancient materials for building Candia, and the sending of ancient statues to Venice.

59 On Simone di Cordo, see De Renzi (1845: 167). On various travellers to Crete, and especially to Knossos and the Minoan labyrinth, see Beschi (1984), Farnoux (1993), Warren (2000), Kopaka (2004), Karadimas (2009: 63–8), D'Agata (2010) – all with further bibliography.

60 See, e.g., Onorio Belli's description of the Knossian Basilica in Kopaka (2004: 502, fig. 47.2).

61 Kopaka (2004), Karadimas (2009: 63–8), D'Agata (2010: 62–3).

62 Snodgrass (1983: 142 and 145).

63 See, e.g., Beschi (1984).

64 For the publication of an Aegean object by Caylus in the mid-eighteenth century and the 1771 excavations by Van Krienen, see Karadimas (2009: 79–80 and fig. 3.20, with further references).

65 See Krzyszkowska (2000: 151–5), who suggests that the Burgon gold ring is the earliest clearly documented Minoan object to reach the West, in the first decade of the nineteenth century; she also discusses an Aegean Bronze Age seal in a catalogue published in 1791, probably acquired in the 1770s in Italy, but this could be a Mycenaean rather than a Minoan object and is of uncertain Late Bronze Age date (pers. comm.: email of 14 July 2016). See also Krzyszkowska (2005: 311–16).

66 See Krzyszkowska (2005: 31). On nineteenth-century views of Aegean Bronze Age seals generally, see Krzyszkowska (2000).

67 Evans (1895: 6; 1909: 10; 1921: 673).

68 Visit to Aptera: Pashley (1837: 38), also cited in Moore (2013: 64); visit to Juktas: Pashley (1837: 220), also cited in Moore (2013: 70). See also Karadimas (2009: 240–1 with n. 569), reporting that the existence of Cyclopean remains on Crete had already been mentioned by authors who had not travelled to Crete, such as Walpole (in 1818) and Hoeck (in 1823).

69 Karadimas (2009: 136). For descriptions and drawings of 'Cyclopean walls' at Tiryns and Mycenae, see Karadimas (2009: 21 and esp. 136ff.).

70 Brown (1993: 51).

71 Spratt (1865, vol. 1: 210).

72 Spratt (1879); see also Karadimas (2009: 241–5) and Moore (2013: 94–6). Despite the incipient interest in pre-Classical finds, even after Spratt many travellers to Crete did

not visit Knossos, or commented on the complete lack of remains at the site: see Kopaka (2004: 508–9).

73 On evolutionism before Darwin, see, e.g., Gregory (2008); see also Burrow (1982); for the term 'Darwinian Revolution' see, e.g., Ruse (1979); on Jurgen Thomsen's Three-Age system and later subdivision of the Stone Age into Neolithic and Palaeolithic, see Lubbock (1865) and Trigger (1989).

74 On prehistoric archaeological activities in Greece before Schliemann, see Fotiadis (2016) and also the next chapter; on Spratt's correspondence with Lyell and Darwin, see Moore (2013: 1, 91–2).

75 Butler (1935).

76 For a brief overview, see Harloe and Momigliano (2018). See also Jenkyns (1980), Tsigakou (1981), Leontis (1995), Marchand (1996), Stoneman (2010).

77 Marchand (1996).

78 Leontis (1995). For various European and non-European Hellenisms see, e.g., Jenkyns (1980), Tsigakou (1981), Dyson (1998), Stoneman (2010), Harloe and Momigliano (2018).

79 See also Tsigakou (1981: 20).

80 On Wolf's work and its relation to biblical exegesis, see Grafton (1981); on Wolf and *Altertumswissenchaft*, see Bernal (1987: 280–316), Marchand (1996: 17–24), and Morris (1994), all with earlier bibliographies. Wolf's *Altertumswissenschaft* focused on Greeks and Romans, especially the former, at the expense of Egyptians, Persians, Jews, and other cultures that he considered more barbaric.

81 For the 'Minoan' work of Neumann, Hoeck, and Müller, see Karadimas and Momigliano (2004), Karadimas (2009: 32–48, and 2015), with further references.

82 For Schliemann as romantic revolutionary see, e.g., Ceram (1999: 34) and McDonald and Thomas (1990: 3–4, 10). For Grote's views on myths as a curtain that conceals nothing behind and as a past that never was present, see Grote (1846: viii and 41).

83 See Chapter 3.

84 Momigliano (1966: 63).

Chapter 3

1 For the emphasis on Classical archaeology, see, e.g., Leontis (1995), Jusdanis (2004), Tzachili (2005: 233–4), and Hamilakis (2007: 57–123, including discussion of Fallmerayer's controversial views on the racial and cultural discontinuity between ancient and modern Greeks).

2 For the prehistoric collections and archaeological activities in Greece in the decades before the arrival of Schliemann on the Aegean scene, see, most recently, Fotiadis (2016), with further bibliography.

3 For various prehistoric excavations that took place between 1771 and 1875, see Karadimas (2009: 349–54, Appendix 8.5).

4 Tzachili (2005).

5 The bibliography on Schliemann and his work is vast: for useful overviews in English, see McDonald and Thomas (1990: 9–82), Fitton (1995: 53–103), Traill (1995 and 2014), and Runnels (2007).

6 Bloedow (1999: 315–16), with further bibliography.

7 On antiquarianism and its impasse caused by reliance on written evidence (especially Biblical), see Trigger (1989: 70–2).

8　See, e.g., Traill (1995: 2).
9　On Schliemann as 'father' of Mycenaean archaeology, see Dickinson (2012). For descriptions of Schliemann as founder of Aegean archaeology, see also, e.g., Runnels (2007: 2–4) and Traill (1995: 1–2).
10　See, e.g., Runnels (2007).
11　See, e.g., Akroyd (2006) and Betsy Jolas's *Schliemann*, an opera in three acts, with libretto by Bruno Bayen and Betsy Jolas, premiered in 1990 (https://musicalics.com/en/composer/Betsy-Jolas/Schliemann, http://operadata.stanford.edu/catalog/19962230, and http://brahms.ircam.fr/works/work/13376/). The much less famous Minos Kalokairinos, however, has also been portrayed in a novel and an opera, as discussed below (n. 29).
12　Michaelis (1908: 216).
13　On Schliemann and archaeology generally as a threat to philological establishment, see Marchand (1996: xx, 17, 117ff.).
14　First published in *La Revue des Deux Mondes* in 1876, and with many subsequent editions (see, e.g., Renan 1899).
15　Gere (2009: 25; see also 35, 36, 41, and 229). For Schliemann and Nietzsche, see also Porter (2004: 331).
16　On Müller, see Chauduri (1974), Van den Bosch (2002), and Stone (2002); on Grote, see Chapter 2.
17　Marchand (1996: 120), Calder (1999). For other German rejections of Schliemann, see also Traill (1995: 178) and Gere (2009: 39).
18　For the excavations at Olympia, see Michaelis (1908: 125ff.).
19　For interpretations of Schliemann's finds as Phoenician etc., see, e.g., Milchhöfer (1883: 103), Myres (1933: 274 and 281), Vermeule (1975: 4), and Fitton (1995: 182).
20　The importance of Hellenizing not only the Aegean Bronze Age but also earlier periods of Greece is evident in Christos Tsountas's work: see Voutsaki (2002 and 2003).
21　Darling (2004: 155–8), Burns (2010: 59–61).
22　Gere (2006b: 60–2).
23　Blakolmer (2006: 231, fig. 14.12; and 2010), Kardamitzi-Adami (2009: 247–65, fig. 338).
24　The Lion Gate of Mycenae always remained visible and is therefore incorporated into the long continuum of Greek history and the Classical Tradition even before Schliemann. An example of this is Frederic Leighton's *Electra at the Tomb of Agamemnon* (1868), where the relieving triangle of the Lion Gate of Mycenae is set in a typical Neoclassical context (cf. Gere 2006b: illustration 21). On nineteenth-century illustrations of the Lion Gate, see Blakolmer (2010).
25　On Gladstone and the reception of Schliemann in England in the late nineteenth century, see Vaio (1990).
26　See n. 20 above.
27　See, e.g., Hall (1901: 77): 'the current hypothesis assumes that the "Mycenaeans" were Achaian Greeks'.
28　Kopaka (2004: 509–10). On Kalokairinos and his excavations at Knossos, see also Hood (1987), Kopaka (1989–90 and 2015, with earlier references), Driessen (1990: 14–31), Brown and Bennett (2001: 389–90). Tselevi is a transliteration of the Greek pronunciation of the Turkish word and surname 'çelebi', meaning gentleman or squire.
29　On this novel, see also Chapter 6, Beaton (2017) and Kopaka (2017). Besides appearing in Galanaki's novel, Kalokairinos and his work at Knossos have been celebrated in the opera *Minos* composed by his great-granddaughter, Marielli Sfakianaki, in 1989: see Kopaka (2017: 185–6), who mentions 2006 and 2012 performances in Athens and

Bari; another performance took place in the central court of Knossos in 2017: https://
news.gtp.gr/2017/08/10/knossos-host-minos-opera-tribute-cretan-explorer-
kalokairinos/; http://www.amna.gr/articlep/177722/Proti-parousiasi-tis-operas-
Minos-sto-Anaktoro-tis-Knosou; http://www.grecehebdo.gr/index.php/actualites/
culture/2276-l%E2%80%99histoire-m%C3%A9connue-de-
l%E2%80%99arch%C3%A9ologue-minos-kalokairinos-au-palais-de-cnossos.

30 On the fear of finds being taken to Istanbul, which hampered excavations in this
period, see Momigliano (2002: 267 and esp. n. 22), with further references.

31 On Linear B tablets from Kalokairinos's excavations, see Driessen (1990: 40–3).

32 On the throne replica in The Hague, see http://www.kulturstiftung-des-bundes.de/
cms/en/programme/fellowship_internationales_museum/die_thronfolger.html and
http://www.icj-cij.org/files/press-releases/6/19046.pdf.

33 Fordsdyke (1925: 123–4, donated in 1884, accession no. A 739). Hood (1987: 91)
reports that Kalokairinos donated one pithos to the Crown Prince (later King) of
Greece (now in the National Museum in Athens); one to a museum in Rome (it is now
in the Museo Pigorini); two to the Louvre; and three to the collection of the Cretan
Philekpaideutikos Syllogos (Society for the Promotion of Education) in Candia.

34 Hood (1987).

35 As reported in Myres (1933: 288) and Brown and Bennet (2001: 394). On Stillman, see
also Dyson (2014).

36 Chatzidakis was, at the time, the President of the Philekpaideutikos Syllogos (Society
for the Promotion of Education), which effectively acted as guardian of the island's
archaeological heritage and had established a collection of ancient artefacts, which
formed the nucleus of what is now the Archaeological Museum in Herakleion: see
Chatzidakes (1931: 9), La Rosa (2000: 91–2), Carabott (2006).

37 Rizzo (1984, 61 fig. 21), Hood and Smyth (1981: 42, no. 111), Hood (1987: 94).

38 Brown and Bennett (2001: xxi, n. iv).

39 Michaelis (1908: 226–9).

40 Myres (1933: 288 and 308), Hood (1987: 93).

41 Brown and Bennett (2001: 389), Driessen (1990: 26–7).

42 Brown (1986).

43 Panagiotaki (2004).

44 Evans (1901b: 5).

45 For quotation, see Evans (1943: 163, citing a 1875 letter by the historian J. R. Green to a
friend).

46 Gere (2006b: 64).

47 Evans (1943: 350–1), Momigliano (1999a: 201–3).

48 Berlin (1953).

49 Since Bruce Trigger's influential volume *A History of Archaeological Thought* (1989), it
has been fashionable to see evolutionism and diffusionism (or culture-history
approach) as successive and almost incompatible paradigms or archaeological
approaches to cultural change; see also McEnroe (1995), who argued that in Evans's
writing the two paradigms succeeded one another. In fact both paradigms can often
appear in the same publication by Evans, especially in *The Palace of Minos*.

50 This knack for making the past relevant to the present is already visible in Evans's
writings before his Minoan career: see, e.g., Evans (1896), where the contemporary
'Oriental Question' and the 'Sick Man of Europe' were linked to the past, especially to
the notion of *Mirage orientale* a.k.a. *Ex-Oriente lux*, namely the idea that civilization
has spread to Europe from the Near East.

51 On John Evans, see Evans (1943) and MacGregor (2008, with further bibliography).

52 Evans (1943: 163).

53 Evans (1943: 163). Different systems provide widely divergent estimates of today's equivalent, varying between *c.* £12,000 and £220,000, but a common estimate is *c.* £30,000. Useful comparisons are the £60 salary that Evans offered Mackenzie to cover four months of work at Knossos (plus expenses) and the £150 yearly salary of the Carnegie Fellowship, which Mackenzie obtained in 1906 (Momigliano 1999a: 34 and 70).

54 Evans (1943: 308 and 350: 'He had set out to find a script; he had found four and could read none of them. But Time and Chance had made him the discoverer of a new civilization, and he had to make it intelligible to other men. Fortunately it was exactly to his tastes: set in beautiful Mediterranean country, aristocratic and humane in feeling . . .').

55 Cf. Abadía (2009), with further bibliography.

56 Evans (1943: 207 and 263), Brown and Bennett (2001: xxi).

57 Evans (1883). See also MacGillivray (2000: 65).

58 See, e.g., Evans (1909: 1–8), Evans (1943: 308–9).

59 Evans (1894: 270).

60 For example, see lecture by John Evans 'On the Alphabet and its Origin' delivered to Royal Institution of Great Britain on 15 March 1872, which included a discussion of the pictorial origins of the Phoenician or Hebrew alphabet (http://discovery. nationalarchives.gov.uk/details/rd/54d3abad-c026-43b0-b0c3-4c8f95ce5e2e); see also John Evans's (and Arthur Evans's) ideas on the topic referred to in Peters (1901: 184).

61 Evans (1894: 333): 'It stands to reason that the indigenous European culture represented by the primitive Cretan population must have reached a comparatively advanced stage before it could have placed itself in direct contact with the higher Egyptian civilisation.'

62 Evans (1909: 8).

63 Evans 'gratefully and affectionately' dedicated the fourth and last volume of his *Palace of Minos* (1935) to the memory of Federico Halbherr, and in the preface referred to the Italian archaeologist as 'the Patriarch of Cretan excavation'.

64 Evans (1895); cf. also La Rosa (1984: 35).

65 See Momigliano (2002), with further bibliography.

66 The Eteocretan inscriptions were published by Comparetti a few years later: see, e.g., Duhoux (1982: 12–13), with further bibliography.

67 See, e.g., Whitley (2006). Besides the Homeric verse cited above, see also Herodotus (I.173), who reports that the Cretans in ancient times were not Greek (i.e. did not speak Greek); Diodorus Siculus (V. 64.1); and Strabo (10, 475).

68 Michaelis (1908: 228–9), Di Vita (1984: 17).

69 Momigliano (2000b: 102). By 1895 the connexion between Bronze Age pottery found in the Kamares cave and Egyptian Middle Kingdom dynasties had already been made.

70 Scuola Archeologica Italiana di Atene (1984: 59–61).

71 Momigliano (2002).

72 Brown and Bennett (2001).

73 Unofficial union with Greece was also announced in March 1905 (Theriso revolt) and again in October 1908 (Zaimis's declaration): see Detorakis (1990: 445–53).

74 Momigliano (2002).

75 Hogarth and Bosanquet (1899: 321).

76　On the economic state of the island in this period, see Carabott (2006); for notions of 'crypto' and 'quasi-colonialism', see Herzfeld (2002), Holland and Makrides (2006), Beaton (2009).

77　Momigliano (2002).

78　On the 'archaeological colonisation' of Crete and its consequences, and on the link between political hegemony and scholarship, see, e.g., Momigliano (2002).

79　Myres (1901).

80　On the interest shown by Russian artists and intellectuals in Minoan Crete and the lack of Russian 'archaeological colonisation' on the island, see Momigliano (2017a).

81　Bosanquet (1902: 286).

82　Momigliano (2002). See also Morris (2007: 120–2), for political interventions on Evans's behalf.

83　Glotz (1925: 12–20), La Rosa (1984), Momigliano (1999a: 37), Gesell (2004).

84　For press coverage, see, e.g., Farnoux (1996: esp.113–14) and Sherratt (2009); for other types of publications, see below.

85　For the early idea that this was a 'council chamber', see Evans (1901a: 124).

86　See Momigliano (1999a).

87　See, e.g., Evans (1909).

88　Karadimas and Momigliano (2004).

89　Evans's field director, Mackenzie, had already worked out the basic phases in the history of the Knossos palace by the end of the first season: see Momigliano (1996).

90　Kriga (2011).

91　Michaelis (1908: 230).

92　On sanitation and flushing toilets, see, e.g., Baikie (1910: 99), Bury (1913: 14), Hall (1913: 47), Papadopoulos (2005: 126), Sherratt (2009: 637–8).

93　Evans (1901a: 125–6).

94　Evans (1901a: 124).

95　Hogarth (1903: 319).

96　On the importance, reassurance and pleasure of finding the familiar in the unfamiliar, see also, e.g., Freud (1916), Nencioni (1967), and Ricoeur (1990: 49).

97　See, e.g., Evans (1901a: 131).

98　On linguistic difficulties, see, e.g., Rouse (1901), Gallavotti (1957: 162–3), Obsomer (2003: 107–8), Walde (2005: 139), Beekes (2010: 819). On mason's marks at Knossos and elsewhere in the Aegean, see Hood (2020: especially Chapter 5, Category V, type 9a – double-axe).

99　Evans (1903: 111). Cf. also below.

100　Evans (1901b: 18–19).

101　Evans (1901b: 96).

102　Evans (1901b: 18–19, figs. 7a–7b): cf. Krzyszkowska (2005: 8–9, figs. 24a–24c) and Chapter 1.

103　Evans (1901b: 37). For various interpretations of the function of the Early Keep, including Evans's alternating views, see Branigan (1992).

104　Cf. also similar views in Marinatos (2015: 10–20).

105　In the context of discourses on ethnic purity and Aryan superiority, it is interesting to note that Hall (1901: 77) was already arguing against the identification of the label 'Mycenaean' with a single ethnic group (whether Homeric Achaeans or mythical Pelasgians), and argued that by the modern term 'Mycenaeans' one should allow the inclusion of both Hellenic and non-Hellenic (and non-Aryan) populations. Hall reiterated similar views in subsequent publications (e.g. Hall 1915: 256–60).

106 Karadimas and Momigliano (2004), with further references.
107 Hogarth (1908: 143).
108 See, e.g., Evans (1900: 32–3 and 64; 1901b: 29; 1902: 102; 1903: 86).
109 See, e.g., Evans (1900: 42–3, n. 1): 'The leading part played by Goddesses and female votaries in the cult-scenes may have been due to the longer survival in the domain of religion of ideas attaching to the matriarchal system.' Cf. also below.
110 Evans (1901b: 94–6; 1902: 74). For changing interpretations regarding the supposedly female figures in this fresco, see also Chapter 1, page 6, with note 25.
111 Here it will suffice to remember that the National Union of Women's Suffrage Societies was founded in 1897 and was followed by the Women's Social and Political Union in 1903.
112 Taylor (1896). See also Hutton (1997). Indeed, *pace* Eller (2012), the notion of a Great Mother Goddess that could have dominated Minoan religion did not emerge suddenly in Evans's writings after he started digging at Knossos, and especially after 1903: see, e.g., Evans (1901b: 29), where he discusses Aegean seals showing a Goddess, which he considered to be a prototype of Rhea and Kybele; see also Evans (1901c: 185), where he points out the Anatolian similarities of clay and stone figurines found at Knossos and mentions the 'ultimate derivation, through intermediate types, from clay figures of a Babylonian Mother Goddess'. On Evans and his ideas about mother goddesses, see also Burns (2017).
113 Burkert (1985: 39).
114 Morris (2006). Other scholars, such as MacGillivray (2000: 193) and Gere (2009: 135), have suggested that Evans's belief in a Great Mother Goddess may have also been influenced by the loss of his mother at a tender age.
115 Cf. MacGillivray (2000: 180), citing Evans's notebooks and Harriet Boyd's report of her visit to Knossos, stating that Evans, in jest, had immediately named the now famous gypsum seat as the throne of Ariadne.
116 Evans (1901a: 122–4 and 131); cf. also Evans (1900: 42–3, n.1): 'The prominence of the female sex in the Mycenaean period – as illustrated by the cult-scenes on the signet-rings – might in itself favour the view that a queen had occupied the throne here ... But it must not be forgotten that the masks on the royal tombs of Mycenae were of the male sex. The leading part played by Goddesses and female votaries in the cult-scenes may have been due to the longer survival in the domain of religion of ideas attaching to the matriarchal system. This religious survival of matriarchy was, as is well known, a well-marked feature among the Phrygians at a much later period.' Note that here Evans is still using the label Mycenaean for the Cretan Bronze Age.
117 Evans (1903: 111).
118 Robinson (2002: 117 and n. 104).
119 On Harrison's visit to Knossos, see Robinson (2002: 136). Her membership of the managing committee of the British School at Athens is attested by the list of members published in the volumes of the journal *Annual of the British School at Athens*. Harrison was a member of the committee from the 1890s, while Evans joined in 1901; see also Momigliano (1999a: 28 and 77, n. 104). In 1922, when Harrison retired from Cambridge, Evans was signatory to a letter that raised £315 for her (Robinson 2002: 289).
120 See, e.g., Cerro (2017). An English edition of Sergi's 1895 *Origini e diffusione della stirpe mediterranea* appeared in 1901.
121 See, e.g., Poliakov (1974: esp. 267–8). The *Entente Cordial* rationalized colonial expansion above all, but also involved some protection against potential

German aggression and provided some balance to Germany's own diplomatic alliances.

122 Baikie (1910: 18).

123 Evans (1896).

124 Evans (1912).

125 Evans (1943: 365, citing a letter from Evans to Charles Bell of July 1912).

126 Evans (1912: 278). For Evans, the Aryan/Greeks were only latecomers to the Aegean, arriving there only around 1200 BC, i.e. towards the end of the Bronze Age.

127 MacGillivray (2000: 178–81, and relevant illustrations).

128 Evans (1901a: 124–5).

129 On Armenoid, Greek, and Mediterranean elements, see, e.g., Evans (1896; and 1921: 8); on 'negro' mercenaries, see Evans (1928: 755–7; and 1935: 887). Although some of Evans's views on this topic were clarified only in later writings published after the First World War, their origins go back to the 1890s (as his 1896 paper testifies).

130 Bandini (2003: 36–7).

131 See, e.g., discussion of anthropometric studies in Burrows (1907: 163–8).

132 Evans (1901b: 96).

133 Starr (1984). In this context, it is also worth mentioning that Willetts did present a pacifist view of Minoan Crete in his own works, and he did so in conscious opposition to what he considered to be 'Evans's ideas about kingship and aggressive Minoan imperialism' (Willetts 1977: 11). See also discussion of Hawkes and Willetts in Chapter 5.

134 Alexiou (1979: 41, n.1) cites in particular 'pacifist' works by Hutchinson, Spyridon Marinatos, Meyer, Higgins, and Branigan.

135 Castleden (1990: 168 and 171).

136 MacGillivray (2000: 195). The pacifist accusation is somewhat undermined by the fact that, a few lines earlier, MacGillivray had cited a passage from Evans extolling the powerful Minoan navy.

137 Gere (2009: 12 and esp. 14): '[W]hen he first went to the island of Crete, he explored a network of fortifications in the eastern part of the island and reveled in a description of a warlike society constantly feuding with itself. But his horror at the aftermath of the ignominious war that won Crete her independence caused Evans to turn his back on this evidence for Minoan belligerence and to reconstruct their world as a pacifist paradise.' Apart from the evidence discussed below, one may also wonder why the Cretan insurrection could have turned Evans into a pacifist, unlike his previous Balkan experiences: the latter were equally horrifying, but did not prevent him from finding military installations in his 1890s travels on Crete.

138 Evans used the phrase *Pax Minoica* in the third volume of his *Palace of Minos* (Evans 1930: 6). In an earlier publication, he compared his Golden Age of Crete to the *Pax Romana* (Evans 1928: 569–71). The phrase *Pax Minoica* is also used explicitly in a famous article by Spyridon Marinatos (1939: 427), and by many other scholars subsequently (e.g. Chryssoulaki 1999: 76).

139 Although Evans's views on the Minoan *thalassocracy* and especially the *Pax Minoica* are most eloquently expressed in his *Palace of Minos*, which was published after the First World War, they can be found *in nuce* in his earlier publications and in early drafts of the *Palace of Minos*, when it was still titled *The Nine Minoan Periods* and was mostly completed by the spring of 1914: see Momigliano (1999b).

140 See, for example, Evans (1901b: 44, and 1903: 59, with mentions of Minoan warrior divinities); see also Evans (1901b: 11, 43, 63, 75, 93, 95–6, especially on enslaved

barbarians). A simple word search of Evans's annual reports in the *Annual of the British School at Athens* (1900–5) reveals that discussions of battles, warlike scenes, weapons, and such themes appear frequently, whereas the terms peaceful and pacifism never do. The term 'peace' in fact appears only twice (Evans 1900: 6, and 1902: 22) and in conjunction with war (i.e. in Evans's description of war and peace scenes in the Miniature Frescoes and Town Mosaic fragments, which he compared to the Homeric description of the shield of Achilles). One may also note that in the index of *Palace of Minos* the terms 'peace' and '*Pax Minoica*' are not even listed, unlike the word 'Warriors', which has many entries.

141 See, e.g., Evans (1901a): 'Here, in his royal city of Knossos, ruled Minos, or whatever historic personage is covered by that name, and founded the first sea empire in Greece, extending his dominion far and wide over the Aegean isles and coasts.'

142 Seeley ([1883] 1971: 16): 'We seem, as it were, to have conquered and peopled half the world in a fit of absence of mind.'

143 On 'defensive imperialism' discourses current at the time, see, e.g., Adler (2008).

144 On Minoan empire as burdensome, see, e.g., Evans (1921: 2).

145 Evans (1921: 22–3). See also Evans (1928: 168–9, especially on Minoan conquest of a large part of the Greek mainland 'due to the commercial necessity of controlling' trade routes, especially to obtain silver, tin, amber, and other goods). See also Evans (1928: 371) on the 'process of overseas conquest which led to the wholesale colonization of Mainland Greece by men of Minoan stock'.

146 Cf. Herodotus, 1.171 and 3.122; Thucydides 1.4.

147 For the conquest of Cyprus, see, e.g., Evans (1921:15); for Libya, see, e.g., Evans (1928: 755–7, and 1935: 887).

148 Evans (1928: 571 and 626–7).

149 Evans (1912: 278, and 1928: 345–6 and 627).

150 For example, MacGillivray (2000: 195) blames Evans for creating the myth of his peaceful Minoans as early as 1901, while discussing this very passage in which, in fact, Evans extolls the effectiveness of the Minoan navy.

151 Evans (1901a: 122).

152 Evans (1921: 1–2).

153 Evans (1928: 569–71).

154 Evans (1930: 6).

155 See, e.g., Mosso (1907: 166–8), Hawes and Hawes (1909: 87, and index, sub voce 'Warrior or Harvester vase'), Baikie (1910: 124). The interpretation of the vase as representation of a 'military parade' is still reported in Harrel-Courtès (1967: 54).

156 See, e.g., Baikie (1910: 112).

157 Mosso (1907). On Mosso, see La Rosa (2001) and La Rosa and Militello (2006). Another popular volume extolling Minoan militarism is Baikie (1910: 169 and passim). Baikie (1910: 224–6) stressed that the Minoans were not as warlike as the Assyrians, and pointed out the absence of truculent themes in their art, but also noted that their military force was thoroughly organized: the 'genius' of the Minoans was allegedly more commercial than military – just like the British – but not necessarily peaceful. One can find an even less pacifist view of the Minoans in Hall's *Aegean Archaeology*, since the author suggests that the Bronze Age fortifications found on mainland Greece were actually built by Cretan colonists in the Middle Minoan period, because they were 'compelled to build a strong burgh ... to defy not the native enemy alone, but Time itself' (Hall 1915: 130).

158 See, e.g., Mosso (1907), esp. his chapter III, section III.

159 Mosso (1907: 137). Baikie (1910: 119), instead of socialist revolutions, refers to civil wars between Knossos and Phaistos.

160 Hawes and Hawes (1909: 36), who, nevertheless, suggest that Knossos may have been attacked and burned by the rival ruler of Phaistos at the close of the Middle Minoan II period (1909: 67).

161 Hawes and Hawes (1909: 147): 'it further appears that the increasing wealth of the Achaeo-Pelasgian lords attracted Minoan artists and artisans to the chief pre-Hellenic centres on the mainland – a peaceful invasion'. Hawes and Hawes (1909: 93) also remarked on the lack of walls around Gournia, and interpreted this as showing peacefulness: 'One sees no circuit walls, no "castle standing amid the huts of dependants," but an open unwalled settlement, evidently at peace with its neighbours.'

162 Hawes and Hawes (1909: 142–3).

163 Hawes and Hawes (1909: passim and esp. 59, 105).

164 Hawes et al. (1908). In these chapters she often uses the phrase 'I believe', clearly indicating that she is expressing her own views.

165 Allsebrook (1992), Fotou and Brown (2004).

166 For example, the popular volume *The Bull of Minos* by Leonard Cottrell warmly recommends *Crete: The Forerunner of Greece* (Cottrell 1955: 137). Recent reprints of this book have appeared by Nabu Press (19 October 2013) and CreateSpace Independent Publishing Platform (9 April 2014).

167 Also interesting in the dissemination of knowledge about Minoan Crete is the role of cruises to Crete, which started from the early 1900s – a theme that, however, I cannot examine in detail in the present work. We know, for example, that the renowned Baedeker's guide to Greece had nothing on Crete in its 1888 edition, whereas the 1904 edition included fifteen pages devoted to the island, and especially its Minoan discoveries: see Farnoux (1993: 103). We also know that the Hellenic Travellers' Club and other companies organized cruises that sometimes included Knossos in the 1900s and 1910s: see, e.g., Lunn (1925: 245–52). Duncan Mackenzie, when appointed first curator at Knossos in the late 1920s, was given an allowance of £30 to entertain visitors to the site: see Momigliano (1999a: 134).

168 Starr (1984: 9).

169 See, e.g., Papadopoulos (2005); cf. also Whitley (2006).

170 Reinach worked at the Musée des Antiquités nationales in Saint-Germain-en-Laye from 1887, and became its director in 1902; Pottier was a member of the département des antiquités orientales et de la céramique antique du musée du Louvre from 1884. He initiated the project *Corpus Vasorum Antiquorum*, which now documents ancient ceramics, especially Greek, in twenty-seven countries: http://www.cvaonline.org/cva/default.htm.

171 Anatole France was a frequent contributor to *La Revue de l'Art ancien et modern*. Flaubert first published *Madame Bovary* in *La Revue de Paris*.

172 Bradfer-Burdet (2005). See also Sherratt (2009), who comments that press exposure given to Knossos before the end of 1900, especially in British newspapers, made Evans something of a national celebrity. Reinach's brother, Adolphe, also wrote articles about Minoan as well as modern Crete: see Reinach (1919).

173 Pottier (1902a): 'Plus moderne encore et plus imprévue est la représentation de la femme. On en jugera par le spécimen que nous reproduisons ici. Quel poète ou quel artiste à l'imagination vagabonde eût osé s'imaginer sous cet aspect les femmes crétoises dans le palais de Minos? Qu'eût dit Racine, qu'eût dit Euripide lui-même, si on lui avait présenté sous ces traits l'imagine authentique d'une parente de Phèdre?

Comme toujours la réalité dépasse et déconcerte ce qui l'invention poétique a crée.
Cette chevelure ébouriffée, cette mèche provocante en « accroche-cœur » sur le front,
cet œil énorme et cette bouche sensuelle, qui sur l'original est tachée d'un violent ton
rouge, cette tunique a raies bleues, rouges et noires, cet flot de rubans rejeté dans le
dos à la mode des « suivez-moi, jeune homme », ce mélange d'archaïsme naïf et de
modernisme pimente, cette pochade qu'un pinceau a tracée sur un mur de Cnossos il
y a plus de 3.000 ans, pour nous donner la sensation d'un Daumier ou d'un Degas,
cette Pasiphaé qui ressemble à une habituée de bars parisiens, tout contribue ici à
nous surprendre, et pour tout dire, il y a dans la découverte de cet art inouï quelque
chose qui nous ahurit et nous scandalise.' See also Pottier (1902b).

174 Reinach (1904: 30ff.). The chapter is titled 'Quatrième leçon: art égéen, minoen et
mycénien'. For English translation, see Reinach (1907: 30–6).

175 Reinach (1907: 30–6). Regarding the 'decadence' of Mycenaean art, see also, e.g., Hall
(1915: 108). Despite the valiant efforts of the 'Viennese School' of Alois Riegl and
Franz Wickhoff of the late nineteenth–early twentieth century (Bianchi Bandinelli
1976: 110–15), the application of the biological notion of 'decadence' in art history
(and other fields) persisted for a considerable time.

176 Reinach (1907: 30–6).

177 Besides the publications briefly discussed in the main text, one should mention
Diedrich Fimmen's rigorous but ponderous *Zeit und Dauer der kretisch-mykenischen
Kultur* (1909), which did not have a single illustration except for a chronological
table, and Angelo Mosso's *Le Origini della Civiltà Mediterranea* (1910), which, like his
earlier *Escursioni nel Mediterraneo*, was immediately translated into English. For
publications in Greek, see Xanthoudides (1904 and 1909); see also the three volumes
of illustrations (fifty plates each) published by Maraghiannis between 1907 and 1915,
with introductions by Pernier, Karo, and Seager. For Polish publications, see Serrano
and Bzinkowski (2012). For Swedish coverage, see, e.g., Montelius (1905). One should
also mention the influential volumes of the series *Histoire de l'art dans l'antiquité:
Egypte, Assyrie, Perse, Asie Mineure, Grèce, Étrurie, Rome*, published by Hachette in
Paris between 1882 and 1914, of which the sixth volume (*La Grèce primitive, l'art
mycénien*, published by Perrot and Chipiez in 1894) was also translated into English
in 1894 as *Art in Primitive Greece* (London: Chapman and Hall). This volume
contained illustrations of material culture that, by the early 1900s, was recognized as
Minoan in origin.

178 Michaelis (1905 and 1908). Despite its title, this work covered a period considerably
longer than a century, since it also discusses antiquities in medieval Rome and
collections made in the sixteenth, seventeenth, and eighteenth centuries, and its
chronological table starts in 1790 and ends with the first decade of the twentieth
century.

179 Dussaud's (1910) and Burrows's (1907) volumes are referred to by Evans as 'luminous
surveys' in the 1914 proofs of the preface to his 'Nine Minoan Periods', the work that
eventually metamorphosed into the multi-volume *Palace of Minos* (Momigliano
1999b).

180 See Florensky (2002: 139–73).

181 Baikie's *The Sea Kings of Crete* went though at least four editions between 1910 and
1926.

182 For Atlantis and the fall of Crete, see the anonymous article 'The Lost Continent'
in *The Times* of 19 February 1909 (later attributed to T. K. Frost). See also Frost
(1913).

183 See Harrison (1903: 460, 482–3, 498–9, 566–8 and passim); see also Harrison (1912: x–xv, 159–211).

184 Murray (1907: 9 and 29).

185 Murray (1907: 29).

186 Myres (1911: 166).

187 See Díaz-Andreu (2008 and 2012). I am extremely grateful to Prof. Margarita Díaz-Andreu for information and discussion on this topic.

188 Mélida (1905), Bosch Gimpera (1912a and 1912b).

189 Bosch Gimpera (1980: 60, 64, and 214). He also recalls meeting Evans at a conference, and again in Oxford, when he delivered the 61st Rhind Lectures on Iberian art in 1936.

190 Baikie (1910: viii).

191 On Minoan priest-kings and princes, see, e.g., Hawes and Hawes (1909: passim). On Achaean Zeus replacing the Mother Goddess, see Hawes and Hawes (1909: 113). On the higher status of women before the arrival of the Achaean, see also Myres (1911: 210).

192 See Evans (1906).

193 Hawes and Hawes (1909: 65).

194 A third example is Burrows (1907: 135 and 163), who suggested that Crete was 'as much part of the East in the Minoan age as Constantinople is to-day', because the notion of 'Classical Greece as the bulwark of the West against the East' represented a very short chapter in Greece's ancient history, given that before Marathon, and after Alexander, Greece was not Western, and 'the Roman–Greek Empire was a good half Oriental'; and also that 'Minoan civilisation as a whole was, we saw, a native growth, rooted in the soil, and Oriental in the sense that Crete itself was an integral part of the East'.

195 Dussaud (1910) shows an interesting use of the term 'proto-history' instead of pre-history, which could underline the relative advancement and sophistication of Minoan Crete, but could also exemplify the growing use of words other than pre-history for romantic, nationalistic reasons, i.e. to suggest more continuity with historical people and nations: see Sherratt (1989: 171).

196 Hall (1913: ix).

197 See, e.g., Baikie (1910, 231) who wonders 'How much the Greek of the Classic period imbibed of the spirit of this gifted and artistic race [the Minoans]', and suggests that the Minoan love of beauty was inherited by their less artistic, but more masculine, northern conquerors, since it was this combination of love of beauty and virility that made the 'historic Greek the most brilliant type of humanity that the world has ever seen'. Cf. also Hawes and Hawes (1909: 150): 'In classical Greece we see the results of the mingling of two unusually gifted races – one autochthonous, the other immigrant – the former contributing the tradition and technical skill of a highly advanced native civilization, especially rich in art; the latter its heritage of Aryan institution, power of co-ordination, and an all-conquering language.' Similar ideas can be found in Myres (1911: 216): 'The Greeks of history are now revealed as the product of intense fusion.'

198 Farnoux (1996: 120–2).

199 For comparisons with Renaissance artists, see, e.g., Baikie (1910: 123, comparing Minoan work to that of Benvenuto Cellini). For comparison with William Morris, see Evans (1903: 5, suggesting that lilies in Minoan frescoes recall, but are even better than, Morris's wallpaper designs). Flinders Petrie in a letter of 1890 compared some

Minoan pottery with 'the savage neatness of Polynesian ornaments': see Fitton (1995: 114) and see Blakolmer (2006: 232), with further references. For comparisons to Japanese artists, see, e.g., Hawes and Hawes (1909: 81 and 121) and especially Myres (1911: 180–1): '[I]t is here that man first achieved an artistic style which was naturalist and idealist in one; acutely observant of the form and habit of living things, sensitive to the qualities and potentialities of raw materials, wonderfully skilled in the art of the potter, painter, gem-engraver, and goldsmith; and above all able to draw inspiration from other styles and methods, without losing the sureness of its own touch, or the power to impress its strong character on its works of art. There are moments when we might be in Japan instead of Crete.' For other comparisons made between Minoan and Japanese art, see also Farnoux (1996: 118) and Caloi (2017).

200 Dussaud (1910: 4–5): 'Cette découverte fit d'autant plus sensation qu'elle semblait avoir choisi son heure, celle où l'éducation du gout permettait de sentir le charme intime d'une technique moins sévère que celle des purs classiques.'

201 Ford ([1915] 1990: 43).

202 For more detailed discussion of Aegean allusions in Proust, including the passages discussed here, see Basch (2016); see also Momigliano (2018 and 2019, where, inadvertently, Basch's article is not mentioned).

203 See also Blakolmer (2017).

204 Bakst and Johnson (1990). The article was originally published in the Russian magazine *Apollon* (vol. 3, 1909, 46–61). Bakst also published a French version of his article ('Les forms nouvelles du classicisme dans l'art', in *La Grand Revue*, 1910), as reported by Pruzhan (1987: 241).

205 Bakst and Johnson (1990: 180).

206 Sideris (1976: 181 and 144, fig. 9) illustrates a photograph of the set of this drama, showing the entrance of a semi-imaginary Aegean Bronze Age palace: a portico provided with tapering columns, and stone friezes decorated with spirals and rosettes. These are largely modelled on well-known finds from Mycenae, especially from the illustrations of Perrot and Chipiez (1894) of the so-called Tomb of Atreus and the palace at Mycenae. Evans's excavations of 1900, however, had illustrated how many Mycenaean architectural elements were ultimately derived from Minoan Crete (cf., e.g., Evans 1900b, fig. 3), hence Sideris's 'Minoan' labelling.

207 A recent example of this use of Minoan sets, props, and costumes is the 2011 performance of Mozart's *Idomeneo* by Opera San Jose and the 2018 BBC/Netflix series *Troy: Fall of a City* (cf. Chapter 7).

208 On Bahaettin, see Ak (2004), Cadogan (2004: 538–40, figs. 49.2 and 49.3), Sarri (2007), Varouhakis (2015).

209 See Ak (2004: 56–65), Cadogan (2004: 538–40, figs. 49.2 and 49.3). The photos and sketch (now in the Vikelaia Library in Heraklion) show a two-storeyed building, with Minoan columns adorning a veranda and a balcony. As Cadogan has remarked, Bagge's sketch shows a frieze with running spirals, but in the building appearing in the photos the spirals were replaced by roundels, in a manner more closely reminiscent of the Knossian Town Mosaic house models.

210 Kazantzakis (1956: 354).

211 On the Minoan gold ring, see Dimopoulou and Rethemiotakis (2004), with earlier bibliography.

212 See, e.g. Varouhakis (2015: passim, esp. fig. 31, 104–15, and Appendix C).

213 See also Momigliano (2002).

214 Cf. Hamilakis (2006), especially his discussion of the 'ambivalent incorporation' of Crete into Greek national discourses. Cf. also Herzfeld (1991).

215 Caloi (2011: 84, and 2017: 73).

216 Translation by Scott Moncrieff, available at http://gutenberg.net.au/plusfifty-n-z. html#proust. French text: 'À la façon des décors de Sert, de Bakst et de Benois, qui, à ce moment, évoquaient dans les ballets russes les époques d'art les plus aimées – à l'aide d'œuvres d'art imprégnées de leur esprit et pourtant originales – ces robes de Fortuny, fidèlement antiques mais puissamment originales, faisaient apparaître comme un décor, avec une plus grande force d'évocation même qu'un décor, puisque le décor restait à imaginer, la Venise tout encombrée d'Orient où elles auraient été portées, dont elles étaient, mieux qu'une relique dans la châsse de Saint-Marc évocatrice du soleil et des turbans environnants, la couleur fragmentée, mystérieuse et complémentaire.' (Text available at http://www.gutenberg.org/files/60720/60720-h/60720-h.htm.)

217 De Osma (1980), Caloi (2011 and 2017).

218 Fortuny mentioned Angelo Mosso's Cretan publications as providing an incentive to his work (e.g. Mosso 1907 and 1910), even if these were published after he had already produced his 'Knossos scarves', and even if Fortuny drew inspiration from earlier publications by Evans and other scholars: see Caloi (2011: 83–99, and 2017: 71), hence the suggestions I make as to how he may have been introduced to Minoan Crete.

219 On Isadora Duncan and her visit to Knossos, see Momigliano (1999a: 68–9, and 2013, with further references). Gere (2009: 94) reports 1910 as the date of her visit to Knossos, but she does not provide evidence and references for this. A 1903 date could be equally if not more likely, since she was living in Greece at that time.

220 Caloi (2011: 43–7).

221 On Kupka and Aegean art, see brief discussion in Momigliano (forthcoming), with further references.

222 'Les costumes sont ceux-là même qu'on portait à Mycènes au XIIIe siècle et l'Acropole a été reconstruite d'après Schliemann, Dörpfeld et d'autres . . .'; letter from Kupka to Machar of 2 October 1906, cited in Sotheby's catalogue: http://www.sothebys.com/en/auctions/ecatalogue/2009/books-and-manuscripts-pf9005/lot.63.html.

223 For images of Kupka's watercolours, see http://www.sothebys.com/en/auctions/ecatalogue/2012/european-paintings/lot.16.html and http://book-graphics.blogspot.com/2013/08/les-erinnyes-illustrator-frantisek-kupka.html.

224 For more detailed discussion of Bakst and Minoan Crete, see Momigliano (2013 and especially 2017a).

225 Other Minoan ballets and dances are Ted Shawn's 1919 *Gnossienne* (cf. Chapter 4); John Taras's *Minotaur* (1947), with Minoan costumes by Joan Junyer (cf. Chapter 4); and Paul Taylor's *Images* (1977), with costumes by Gene Moore (cf. Chapter 6).

226 See Nijinsky (1937: 151): 'Leon Bakst did not understand what I wanted.' See also Spencer (2009: 72) citing Romola Nijinsky (1933): '"My idea of Greece is utterly different from Bakst's", she quotes him saying, adding that he actually disliked the artist's scenery. Mrs Nijinsky continues, "Duncan like Fokine understood Greece as the gracious billowy curves of the Parthenon friezes. Nijinsky with his Faune took an entirely different view. It is the severity of Attic carving, the simplicity and faith of the pre-Phidias sculptors against the charm and elegance of Praxiteles".' Although Romola Nijinsky attributes these ideas to her husband, they also appear in Bakst's 1909 artistic manifesto, cited above.

227 As cited in Spencer (2009: 86; cf. also Spencer 1973: 144).

228 On *La Furie*, see Humbert-Mougin (2006) and Boucher (2014a). On Jules Bois's occultism and feminism, see also Churton (2016) and Gazdar (2016).

229 Humbert-Mougin (2006: 210).

230 Boucher (2014a).

231 Chaineux even gave a lecture at the l'Académie des Inscriptions et Belles-Lettres on the dress of the 'Pelasgians, Aegeans, and Achaeans': see Chaineux (1908). The sets were reused a year later for a new production of Leconte de Lisle's *Erynnies*: see Humbert-Mougin (2006: 210, n.15).

232 See in particular the following comment by Doumic (1909): 'Donc les décors et les costumes sont du temps ; mais les âmes, les idées, les sentimens, les actes n'en sont pas. Ce seraient plutôt des âmes de maintenant, des idées d'aujourd'hui ou même d'après-demain. Le second caractère de la tragédie "vivante," suivant la formule de M. Jules Bois, consisterait, essentiellement à prêter une mentalité du XXe siècle après Jésus-Christ à des personnages du XXe siècle avant notre ère.' See also other reviews cited in Humbert-Mougin (2006) and Boucher (2014a).

233 Butler (1939), Goldhill (2002: 155, fig. 16).

234 Goldhill (2002: 108–77). Gere (2006b: 127–8).

235 Cf. Goldhill (2002: 135–6, fig. 15).

236 Goldhill (2002: 139).

237 See Styan (1982: 80); cf. also Goldhill (2002: 172–4).

238 Fischer-Lichte (2014: 133, n. 5). Cf. Goldhill (2002: 172–3, n. 188), Styan (1982: 84–5).

239 Styan (1982: 84–5).

240 Votive robe: see Evans (1903: 82, fig. 58); bridge spouted jar: see Evans (1903: 120, fig. 75). For Bakst's use of the same Minoan jar, see Momigliano (2017a: fig. 5.11A and B).

241 Pound (1914).

Chapter 4

1 Cf. Virgil, *Aeneid* 3, 104–5: 'Creta Iovis magni medio iacet insula ponto,/ mons Idaeus ubi et gentis cunabula nostrae' (in the middle of the sea lies Crete, the island of great Zeus, where is mount Ida and the cradle of our race).

2 Worth (1924: 81).

3 Koliopoulos and Veremis (2009: 68–88), Clogg (1986: 101–32).

4 Carabott (2006), Kostopoulou (2012).

5 Matton (1957: 201), Llewellyn Smith (1965: 100).

6 Momigliano (1999a: 132–3).

7 EAM: Εθνικό Απελευθερωτικό Μέτωπο, *Ethnikó Apeleftherotikó Métopo* (National Liberation Front); ELAS: Ελληνικός Λαϊκός Απελευθερωτικός Στρατός, *Ellinikós Laïkós Apeleftherotikós Stratós* (Greek National Liberation Army); EDES: Ελληνικός Δημοκρατικός Εθνικός Στρατός, *Ellinikós Dimokratikós Ethnikós Stratós* (National Democratic Greek Army).

8 EOK: Εθνική Οργάνωση Κρήτης or National Organization of Crete; see O'Ballance (1966: 60 and 91), Beevor (2005: 270), Janes (2013).

9 For a brief overview of excavations at Knossos, cf. Chapter 3. For reconstructions at Knossos, see Picard (1932), Kienzle (1998), Blakolmer (2017), all with further references; see also various responses discussed below. For Evans's use of the term 'reconstitution', see Evans (1927).

10 See, e.g., the work conducted by American archaeologist Carl Blegen at various mainland sites in Greece and Troy: McDonald (1967: 197–243), Fitton (1995: 155–65).

11 For German archaeological explorations on Crete during the Second World War, see, most recently, Flouda (2017), with further bibliography.

12 Pendlebury (1939).

13 Marinatos (1939 and 1971), Marinatos (2015: 146). On Frost's earlier connection between Plato's Atlantis and Minoan Crete, see Chapter 3; on Marinatos's excavations on Thera, see Chapter 5.

14 For accounts of archaeological discoveries in the Near East, see, e.g. Demargne (1938), Brion ([1937] 1948), Moorey (1991); for Greece, see Fitton (1995: 150–70), Karo (1959).

15 For the view that Mycenaean civilization was not a Minoan offshoot, but the result of the amalgamation of a strong Helladic/Mycenaean tradition and a veneer of Cretan traits, see, e.g., Wace and Blegen (1918), Karo (1959). For Pendlebury's views, see below.

16 This led to considerable academic dispute between Evans and Wace, which, nonetheless, did not impinge on their friendship: see Fitton (1995: 154–5), Momigliano (1999a: 129–31).

17 Blegen (1921: 125–6), Haley and Blegen (1928), Glotz (1923), and see also below. For suggestions of an even earlier date, cf. Hall (1928: 247, with notes 2 and 3). Hall (1928: 247–54), however, held the view of a racial-cultural (and non-Aryan) identity for the Minoans and Mycenaeans, while suggesting, at the same time, that Achaean/Aryan elements (though not yet speaking Greek) may have been part of the population conquered by the Minoans on mainland Greece. For Hall, Greek-speaking populations may have lived in northern Greece, but a substantial Aryan invasion into southern Greece, or Wiros' invasion, as he calls it (1928: 287–91), did not occur before the thirteenth century BC.

18 Besides the impact of Evans's views, the notion that the Mycenaeans were Achaean Greeks received less and less support, especially thanks to Ridgway's 1901 *Early Age of Greece*. See also Burns (1930: esp. 38–9).

19 Hrozný (1917).

20 Haley and Blegen (1928: esp. 150–4).

21 Cf. also Fitton (1995: 171).

22 Whitehead (1929: 24–44).

23 Momigliano (1999b). Glotz (1923 and 1925) still cites 'The Nine Minoan Periods, London, 1914' in his bibliography.

24 The French archaeologist Charles Picard described it as a 'Trésor' of pre-Hellenic Crete (1936: 194 and 211), and Evans himself, in the preface of the fourth volume, called his work an 'Encyclopaedia of Minoan cultural features, of its Art, and of its Religion' (1935: vii).

25 See Lapatin (2002: 153–75), Burns (2017: 160–1 and fig. 8.1).

26 On priest-kings, cf. Evans (1921: 1–2 and passim). On Minoan women, see esp. Evans (1930: 58–9, 227); on partial and regulated segregation of the two sexes, see also Evans (1930: 296, 349–50).

27 Note that despite the war, in 1916 Karo had made available to Evans the proofs of an article he had written on the Shaft Graves: see Momigliano (1999b: 496 and n. 9).

28 On the term 'Mycenaean', see Evans (1921: 1, 24, and 1935: 283, 294); on the move of the Minoan seat of government to Mycenae, see Evans (1921: 27, and 1935: 945).

29 On the end of Bronze Age, and arrivals of the Achaeans and Dorians, see, e.g., Evans (1921: 9–13, 28); on Evans's experience of a violent earthquake on Crete and earthquakes as agents of cultural-political change, see Evans (1928: 316–25).

30 See, e.g., Evans (1921: 25–8).

31 Evans's anti-Hellenic and anti-Aryan stance finds further illustration in the fact that the index of *Palace of Minos* lists no reference to Aryans or Indo-Europeans, even if there are some references to Hittite civilization.

32 On Evans's anti-Classicism, especially anti-Hellenism, see also Momigliano (2006). I should like to stress, however, that other important factors explain Evans's preference for Rome as a model for the Minoan empire: Evans lived in the British age of empire as encapsulated in Disraeli's Royal Titles Act of 1876, which made Queen Victoria 'Regina et Imperatrix', and many late nineteenth- and early twentieth-century British historians (pro or anti-empire) were much attracted to imperial Rome as a source of inspiration for historical comparison, if not necessarily as an example to imitate; see, e.g., Betts (1971). In addition, in the last quarter of the nineteenth century, Oxford had become an important centre for the study of Roman history, largely through the efforts of one of Evans's Oxford colleagues, Francis Haverfield, who had written eloquently about the civilizing role of Rome (e.g. Haverfield 1912). Finally, Evans himself always had a keen interest in Roman history: see, e.g., Joan Evans's (1964: 97) reminiscences of her half-brother's discussions 'of the minor Roman Emperors as if they had been personal friends'. On Athenian rhetoric of Ionian descent and the Delian League, see, e.g., Mac Sweeney (2013).

33 Blegen (1921: 125–6). For Hawes's pacifist views, cf. Chapter 3.

34 See, e.g., Fitton (1995: 155–65), McDonald (1967: 197–8).

35 Blegen (1941: 7–11); cf. McDonald (1967: 239–40).

36 Blegen (1958: 62). For Blegen's Hellenism and views on the 'Greek spirit', see also Lalaki (2012).

37 Fimmen (1909).

38 Fimmen (1921: 38) briefly discusses the 'Achaean' Catalogue of Ships in the *Iliad*, but in an uncommitted manner regarding its relationship to Bronze Age ethnic groups, remarking that the overlap between Mycenaean sites and those mentioned in the poem does not imply that that the *Iliad* is a record for the Mycenaean period, since many sites continued to be occupied in the Iron Age.

39 Bossert (1921, 1923, 1937a, 1937b). Bossert's main claim to fame, however, rests on his work in Anatolia, especially his 1940s excavation of the Hittite citadel of Karatepe in the Taurus Mountains, which yielded an important bilingual inscription in Phoenician and Hieroglyphic Luwian: see, e.g., Bossert and Alkım (1947).

40 The first, second, and third editions have, respectively, 272, 352, and 572 plates of illustrations. On fakes such as the 'Boston Goddess', see Lapatin (2002 and 2006).

41 For even more flamboyant illustrations about Minoan Crete by Krischen, see Krischen and Tischer (1921).

42 Bossert (1921: foreword).

43 Bossert (1921: 6).

44 Bossert (1921: 12–15).

45 Bossert (1921: 12–15); cf. Evans (1928: 279): 'A religion, indeed, so pervasive and that looked beyond the grave almost inevitably entailed a certain moral code. The weighing of the soul in its butterfly form, of which we have evidence, itself points to a standard that had, surely, its ethical side. It is at any rate a significant circumstance that, from the beginning to the end of Minoan Art, among all its manifold relics, – from its earliest to

its latest phase, – not one single example has been brought to light of any subject of an indecorous nature – a striking contrast, indeed, to the artistic records of Classical times. The *postscenia vitae* were at any rate sedulously concealed.'

46 Bossert (1921: 9): 'Der Charakter der kretisch-mykenischen Kunst kann wohl als uneuropäisch bezeichnet werden, wenn wir lediglich die Herkunft des Stiles ins Auge fassen. Sehen wir jedoch vorwärts statt rückwärts, so müssen wir zu- gestehen, daß das, was uns verwandt anmutete, eben jenes alte Erbgut sein muß, das diese vorindoeuropäischen Völker ihren Nachfolgern auf den Weg mitgaben. Ein Erbe, das treu bewahrt, sich bis in unsere Tage hinein auswirkt.' The idea that the history of Europe owes much to the East and to non-Indo-European people is also expressed, for example, in the preface of the first volume of the *Cambridge Ancient History*: 'The *Cambridge Ancient History* is designed as the first part of a continuous history of European people . . . The history of Europe begins outside Europe. Its civilization is so deeply indebted to the older civilizations of Egypt and south-western Asia that for the study of its growth the early history of these lands is more important than the barbarous life which Celts, Germans, and others lived within the limits of Europe' (Bury et al. (1923: v)). Note that the third edition of Bossert's work, besides omitting the introductory section and suspected forgeries, presents a more complex chronological table (1937b: 10–11), in which the Greek invasion of mainland Greece is marked at *c.* 2000 BC, and their invasion of Crete, the Cyclades, Cyprus, Sporades, and Rhodes at *c.* 1375 BC; this, in turn, is followed by the Dorian invasion in *c.* 1200–1100.

47 Bossert (1921: 18–19). On German expressionism, see, e.g., Elger (2018), with further references.

48 Bossert (1921: 17).

49 The English translation (Glotz, 1925a) was also reprinted in 2003 by publisher Kegan Paul. According to the World Catalogue, 140 editions were published between 1923 and 2013, in four languages, and are held by 1,719 WorldCat member libraries worldwide (http://www.worldcat.org/identities/lccn-n50-030595/). Glotz's ideas on the Aegean Bronze Age also found a wide audience through some of his later works on ancient Greek history, such as Glotz (1925b, see especially Chapters 2 and 3, on 'pre-Hellenic Crete' and 'The great Migrations: Achaeans and Dorians'). The 1923 volume had originally been assigned to Adolphe Reinach (nephew of Salomon and Theodore), who had died in the First World War, and was subsequently offered to Glotz.

50 Glotz (1923: 271, and 1925a: 234): with the French phrase 'fétiche bissexuel' Glotz was translating Evans's idea that the double-axe may have been a symbol of a divine male and female pair.

51 Glotz (1925a: 21–2) rejected the term 'Minoan' as used by Evans because it suggested a unity in the Aegean that did not really exist until after the fall of 'Minos'. Moreover, he considered the term 'Minoan' for the whole of the Bronze Age as misleading, because the Minoan 'dynasty' was, in any case, a relatively recent political system. Glotz even proposed a different periodization for Bronze Age Crete, which was based on an earlier work by the ethnologist Louis Franchet: 1) Neolithic and Chalcolithic phase (equivalent to Evans's EMI-III); 2) First Bronze Age (EM III-MM IA); 3) First Palace period, starting in *c.* 2000 BC (MM IB-MM IIIA); 4) Second palace period (MM IIIB-LMII, ending *c.* 1400 BC); and 5) Mycenaean Age (LM III), a system that clearly anticipates the Prepalatial, Protopalatial, and Neopalatial periodization suggested by Nikolaos Platon and subsequently refined by other scholars as Neolithic, Prepalatial,

Protopalatial, Neopalatial, Final palatial, and Postpalatial: see Momigliano (2007: 8), with further references. In effect, however, Glotz makes extensive use of Evans's Minoan system for chronological purposes, and even of the term Minoan to describe occasionally the culture of Bronze Age Crete.

52 Beckman et al. (2011).

53 Glotz (1925a: 48).

54 Glotz (1925a: 45).

55 Glotz (1925a: 55).

56 Glotz (1925a: 45).

57 Glotz (1925a: 44–6).

58 On Minoan–Mycenaean relations, see esp. Glotz (1925a: 45–6); on the subordinate position of women in Mycenaean society, see Glotz (1925a: 145). Wace's chapter for the *Cambridge Ancient History* series summed up the different views held at the time regarding Minoan–Mycenaean relations in the Late Minoan/Late Helladic period: 'The difference between these two views may be summed up in the question, "Was the dynasty which now arose at Mycenae Helladic or Minoan?"' His own answer was that Cretan domination was similar to that 'in which the Franks held the Morea after the Fourth Crusade, or the Dukes of Normandy England': see Wace (1923: 608–9). Wace, on the whole, gives Minoan Crete most of the glory, but also mentions that the Helladic people were 'vigorous' and that Mycenae eventually 'would eclipse the power and riches of Cnossos' (1923: 614–15).

59 Glotz (1925a: 52).

60 Glotz (1925a: 309).

61 The great Swedish historian of religions, Martin P. Nilsson, is another important scholar of this period who accepted the arrival of warlike Indo-Europeans in Greece around 2000 BC and the relative independence of Mycenaean Greece from Crete, although he believed that the Mycenaeans adopted much of Minoan religion. Nilsson too tried to elucidate the cultural differences between non-Aryan Minoans and Aryan Mycenaeans: see Nilsson (1927, especially introductory section on migrations, and 1933). Nilsson also rejected Evans's Minoan monotheism, preferring, instead, a polytheistic view of all Aegean prehistoric religions. Other rejections of Minoan domination and *thalassocracy* over mainland Greece appear in important specialist syntheses, such Arne Furumark's volume on Mycenaean pottery (1941) and Helen Kantor's (1947) on contacts between the Aegean and the Near East.

62 Pendlebury (1939: 226, 271, and 286). The view that mainland Greece was conquered by Crete was held by others, such as Hall (1928: 154), who believed that Knossos was overthrown by its former colonies and did not have a particularly peaceful view of the Minoan *thalassocracy* either: 'The L.M. II period ended with the catastrophic destruction of Knossos by a foreign enemy. Possibly her thalassocracy was no more popular than that of the Athenians was to be, a thousand years later': see Hall (1928: 198).

63 Pendlebury (1939: passim and esp. 237 and 289).

64 Regarding the physical differences between Minoans and Mycenaeans, see, e.g., Burns (1930: 33), who describes the Mediterranean race as 'slender, active type, black-haired, dark-eyed, artistic, not very war-like, of less stature and less heavily boned than either the rugged Alpine or the tall blonde Nordic types of central and northern Europe'.

65 For Etruscan and Japanese comparisons, see, e.g., above discussion of Bossert and Glotz; for comparison to children, see, e.g., Pendlebury (1939: 275), who defines

Minoan art as a 'curious mixture . . . of religious formalism and a real *joie de vivre* of a somewhat heartless and childlike nature'; for similar comparisons made in the period before the First World War, see Chapter 3. For the interwar period, also interesting is Snijder's *Kretische Kunst* (1936), which interpreted Minoan art as eidetic, and stressed the differences between Minoan and Mycenaean artistic as well as architectonic principles. In addition to the aforementioned works, George Glasgow's booklet *The Minoans* (1923), Charbonneaux's *L'art égéen* (1929), and P. Waltz's *Le monde égéen avant les Grecs* (1934) also continued to praise Minoan originality and beauty, while stressing the divergence between southern Minoans (Mediterranean) and northern Mycenaeans/Aryans, especially in terms of belligerence.

66 Pendlebury (1933: 27).

67 On the emergence of an interest in universal history after the First World War, see, e.g., Ziolkoswki (2008: 18–19); for discussions on the concept of decadence, see the issue dedicated to this topic in the journal *New Literary History* (vol. 34, no. 4, Autumn 2004), titled 'Forms and/of decadence'.

68 Wells ([1895] 2017: 77 and 40).

69 Wells ([1898] 2017: 185) and cf. Wells ([1895] 2017: 40–2).

70 Wells (1920: 214–15).

71 The first volume of *Der Untergang des Abendlandes* (1918) had the subtitle *Umrisse einer Morphologie der Weltgeschichte*, and the second (1922) *Welthistorische Perspektiven*.

72 On Spengler, see, e.g., Conte (1997); on his influence, especially on modern British literature, see Shaffer (1993: 121–42); on Spengler and the Aegean Bronze Age, see Sherratt (2006: 120–2), Gere (2009: 147–9).

73 Spengler (1928: 87–9).

74 On Kossinna and the culture-history turn in archaeology, see Trigger (1989: 163–6); on Childe and Minoan Crete, see Sherratt (2006).

75 Childe (1915); documents relating to Childe's 1915 travels in Greece, including a brief report, are kept in the archives of the British School at Athens.

76 Green (1981:18).

77 On Indo-Europeans in Greece and their characteristic features, see Childe (1926: esp. 56, 59, 60, and 81); on Minyan martial prowess, see also Childe (1925: 74).

78 Childe (1926: 57, 58, and 60).

79 Childe (1926: 57).

80 Childe (1925: 29); see also Sherratt (2006).

81 Childe (1926: 209). Cf. also Childe (1930), where he reiterates the essentially Mediterranean, almost Oriental character of the Aegean Bronze Age, and its later transformation into the very different and more distinctly European Hellenism in which Western civilization is so largely rooted.

82 Sherratt (2006: 113). Cf. also Renfrew (1987: 4).

83 On Childe's pacifism, see, e.g., Green (1981: 22–9).

84 See Waddell (1929: passim, and especially 295 and 498). For Kossinna's Aryanization of the Minoans, see Childe (1926: 169–70), where he refers to the German scholar's treatment of this subject in the 'unfinished monograph entitled *Die Indogermanen* in 1921'. Another book that seeks the origin of Aryan culture on Crete is Lidio Cipriani's *Creta e l'Origine Mediterranea della Civiltà*, published soon after the Italian occupation of Crete in the Second World War (1943), as discussed by La Rosa and Militello (2006). For the rise of Aryanism in the interwar period, see, e.g., Poliakov (1974), Mallory (1989: 266–72). For more racist views related to the Mediterranean/Oriental

Minoans vs. the superior Indo-European race, see also Schachermeyr (1939). An interesting article by the French excavator of Malia, Pierre Demargne (1938), provided a brief history of changing 'oriental' and 'western' views about Aegean art, re-evaluated the connections between Crete and the Near East (especially Syria and Anatolia), and critiqued the 'northern mirage' (a phrase alluding to a well-known 1903 article by Salomon Reinach, on the 'oriental mirage'), namely the exaggeration of Nordic elements in Mycenaean material culture, especially by German scholars: see esp. Demargne (1938: 39).

85 In the context of the Orientalization of Crete, besides the texts by Spengler and Childe discussed above, one could also mention Demargne (1938), where the French scholar argues for close links between Crete and the Near East, especially Asia Minor, and the popularizing work by Brion ([1937] 1948), which implicitly Orientalizes Minoan Crete by including it in a book on the resurrection of dead cities in Mesopotamia, Asia Minor, Syria, Palestine, Cyprus, and Egypt. On Brion see also below.

86 Boucher (2017).

87 For Minoan exhibitions, see Galanakis (2015); for cruises, see Basch and Farnoux (2006), Boucher (2017).

88 For example, the ninth issue of *Cahiers d'art* for 1926 included an article on 'Le counterpoint chez Debussy', which was juxtaposed with two Minoan images, i.e. the famous bull-leaping fresco and the throne room at Knossos; the second issue of 1927 had an article on 'Cnossos, figurines de faience', and the third issue an article by the museologist, musicologist, and ethnographer Georges-Henri Rivière ('Un sondage dans l'art égéen'), which showed pictures of various Minoan artefacts, including the chryselephantine statuette of the Boston snake goddess, and asked the readers' opinion about its genuineness. Issues published in the 1930s included articles by Spyridon Marinatos on the origin and development of Minoan art: see also Rentzou (2011), Stavroulaki (2016).

89 There are no *Minotaure* issues that include actual photographs and/or articles on Minoan subjects, but there is one article on the Archaic Greek temple of Artemis on Corfu in the very first issue, side-by-side works by Picasso, and another one on ancient Boeotian figurines by Jacques Prevert (next to works by Salvador Dali) (*Minotaure* 10 (15 December 1936)). The magazine contains plenty of bull and Minotaur images, but with no clear connection with Minoan iconography and material culture.

90 References to Ovid are linked to Skira's edition of his *Metamorphoses*, with illustrations by Picasso (1931). In connection with Picasso's alleged Cretomania, see also Momigliano (forthcoming, contra Gere (2009: 151–3)). Although Picasso never visited Crete (communication by Claude Picasso at the meeting organized by Branding Heritage, 'Contemporary Minoans', held at the Museum of London on 5 November 2019), he must have been aware of Minoan material culture, if only because of his close acquaintance with Zervos (on his friendship with Zervos, see, e.g. Penrose (1958: 259)). For Picasso's motifs, other sources seem more plausible than Minoan Crete. For example, Penrose (1958: 349) mentions a seventeenth-century book on Tauromachia by Jose Delgado (Pepe Ilo). I also remain unconvinced that Picasso's ceramic plate with octopus decoration (Cadogan 2004: 543) shows Minoan influence, since there are also plenty of octopus representation in Roman mosaics, including Romano-Spanish mosaics, which could have influenced the artist. The impression that Minoan Crete is not a particular source of inspiration is reinforced by the recent exhibition in Athens, titled 'Picasso and Antiquity. Line and Clay', which was part of a series of exhibitions on 'Divine Dialogues': see Stampolidis and Berggruen (2019). In

this exhibition, some Minoan and other ancient artefacts are juxtaposed to Picasso's works, but, as the curators admit, this is because of some generic formal similarities, not because the Spanish artist knew, and was inspired by, them: see Stampolidis and Berggruen (2019: 53). Indeed, some of the Minoan artefacts used in the exhibition were discovered after Picasso had produced his works. An example is a ceramic anthropomorphic vessel created by Picasso in 1951, which is compared to one discovered at Myrtos Pyrgos, a site excavated by Peter Warren in the late 1960s (Stampolidis and Berggruen (2019: 35, figs. 10 and 11)); another example is Picasso's 1956 ceramic plate with dancers, which is compared to a clay model from the tomb at Kamilari, which was excavated by Doro Levi in 1959 (Stampolidis and Berggruen (2019: 2012–13)).

91 I discuss various new literary genres mentioned at the beginning of this section in the following pages, except for detective stories and fantasy fiction. The only examples known to me which date from the period examined in this chapter are *Murder Gone Minoan* and *The Reign of Wizardry*. The former, by the American author Clyde B. Clason, was first published in 1939 (Clason [1939] 2003) and revolves around the disappearance of a valuable chryselephantine figurine of the Minoan snake goddess, held by an American private collector in his mansion-cum-museum on an island off the coast of California, which is being decorated with Minoan-style frescoes by an impoverished artist. As Ken Lapatin (2006) has shown, one of the merits of this detective story is that it illustrates how an actual forgery, the so-called Boston Goddess, has helped to shape modern perceptions of the Minoans. But I should like to add that *Murder Gone Minoan* is intriguing also for the way in which it curiously anticipates aspects of the much later Villa-Museum built by the American millionaire J. P. Getty in Malibu, even if this is based on the Villa of the Papyri in Herculaneum instead of Minoan Crete. *The Reign of Wizardry* by Jack Williamson was written in 1939 and first published in 1940 (see Williamson ([1940] 1981)). It offers a new version of the myth of Theseus and Ariadne, with a magical twist. Theseus is not an Athenian prince, but a mere Greek pirate who, with the help of Ariadne, brings to an end the evil, oppressive, despotic regime of King Minos, a king-god and warlock, whose great power is based on wizardry. References to Minoan material culture, however, are sparse in this work: just enough to give some local colour.

92 Merezhkovsky ([1925] 1926, 1927, and [1930] 1933); see also Momigliano (2017a).

93 Bedford (1975: 147), Pachmuss (1990: 87).

94 For a more detailed summary of this novel, see Momigliano (2017a).

95 The idea of the Minoans as ancestral to Christianity can also be found in H. A. L. Fisher's review of A. J. Toynbee's *A Study of History*, where survivals of Minoan religion are seen in Greek mysteries, and these, in turn, are seen as leading to Christianity: see Sherratt (2006: 118–19). Another combination of Minoan elements and Christianity can be seen in Giorgio Wenter Marini's 1925 lithograph for a monument dedicated to Federico Halbherr (who died in 1930), which reflects a homage to Halbherr's deep religiosity and achievements in Minoan archaeology: see La Rosa and Militello (2006: fig. 15.5).

96 Merezhkovsky ([1925] 1926: 40); cf. Groenewegen-Frankfort (1951: 216) and Chapter 5.

97 Merezhkovsky ([1925] 1926: 45).

98 Merezhkovsky ([1925] 1926: 62).

99 Merezhkovsky ([1925] 1926: 58 and 60).

100 Haggard also published a book, *Little Plays From the Greek Myths* (1929), with notes for children on how to act the plays.

101 Some information on Cheney is provided by his great-grandson, who states that he was a reporter during the First World War: see https://www.amazon.co.uk/Son-Minos-Novel-David-Cheney/dp/1417916737.

102 Cheney (1930: vii).

103 Their travels involve encounters with Phoenicians, Ligurians, Etruscans, Pile-Dwellers, Veneti, Hittites, and Trojans as well as flying with a primitive balloon provided with wings made of wax for steering.

104 Cheney (1930: 149). Cf. Cheney (1930: 186): 'no woman should ever be Minos'.

105 Cheney (1930: 238).

106 Cheney (1930: 6 and 210).

107 Cheney (1930: 25).

108 See, e.g., Cheney (1930: 9 and 90).

109 Cheney (1930: 36): 'new life will burn in the cold veins of Minoa'.

110 See http://www.lib.usm.edu/legacy/degrum/public_html/html/research/findaids/berry.htm.

111 Such as Hall (1901 and 1915), Glotz (1923), Burns (1930), and articles in the *Encyclopaedia Britannica*: see Berry (1933: 149).

112 I have not been able to carry out a systematic study of Minoan illustrations for children books, especially those focusing on Greek mythology, but I have examined over a dozen illustrated editions of one the most famous in the English language: Charles Kingsley's *The Heroes, or Greek Fairy Tales for my Children* (first published in 1855). Of the illustrated editions that were issued between 1900 and 1970 it seems that only one, published in1964, with an afterword by Mary Renault and illustrations by Federico Castellon, shows Minoan architecture and artefacts: cf. also Chapter 5.

113 Berry (1933: 51–2).

114 Berry (1933: 39).

115 Gudmundsson (1940: 408).

116 *The Egyptian* (1954), directed by Michael Curtis (see also Chapter 5).

117 The novel has been praised and studied among Egyptologists, with seminars organized on the occasion of the 100th anniversary of Waltari's birth in 2008: see, e.g., http://www.finland.gr/public/default.aspx?contentid=142603&contentlan=2&culture=en-US and http://www.finemb.org.uk/Public/default.aspx?contentid=141670&nodeid=35864&culture=en-GB. The alleged attention to detail and historical accuracy for things Egyptian does not fully apply to Minoan Crete, although it is clear that the author is familiar with some archaeological literature, including connections made between Crete and Plato's Atlantis. Waltari makes use of familiar Minoan images such as bare-breasted ladies and bull-leaping activities, intermingled with elements derived from Greek mythology, and the author's own creativity, especially to underline the overall picture of marvel. For example, Waltari (1949: 197) provides the Minoans not only with flushing toilets, but also with hot and cold water from silver pipes!

118 Waltari (1949: 196–7).

119 Waltari (1949: 215).

120 Waltari (1949: 198).

121 Waltari (1949: 220–1). This also illustrates how the identification of Minoan Crete with Atlantis was becoming more common (cf. Chapter 3).

122 Beaton (2006: 184).

123 Kazantzakis (1958: VI.352 and cf. VI.319).

124 Beaton (2006: 184, and 2008: 12).

125 See Kazantzakis (1969 and 1988) and discussion in Beaton (2008). The Minoan Mother Goddess makes a brief but beneficial appearance, as a kind of precursor of the Virgin Mary, in Kazantzakis's most famous work, *Zorba the Greek* (first published in 1946), when the narrator pays visits to a small Minoan settlement, which appears to be based on the site of Gournia, and to a nearby nunnery, which has an icon of the Virgin Mary that performs miracles.

126 Beaton (2006: 186, and 2008: 12).

127 Kazantzakis and Bien (2012: 569–70, letter to Emile Hermozious, 23 May 1943), see also Beaton (2008: 5–6, citing a 1943 article by Kazantzakis in *Nea Estia*, which discusses the same idea).

128 Gide's interest in the myth of this Attic hero is clearly attested in the 1930s (and may be traced back to at least 1911), and much of the novel was written in the early 1940s, while Gide was based in North Africa: see Pollard (1970); see also Ziolkowski (2008: 91–3).

129 Pollard (1970).

130 Gide (1949). Regarding Massimo Campigli, La Rosa and Militello (2006: figs. 15.3–15.4) suggested some possible connections between Minoan Crete and two of his works, *Donne alla toeletta* (1941) and *Profilo con cappello* (1944), as possibly indicated by the flounced skirts and profiles of his female figures. Similar flounced skirts, however, appear in many other earlier and later paintings by Campigli, such as *Le due amiche* (1937), *Le due sorelle* (1940), *Scuola di danza* (1941), *Gioco del Diablo* (1954), and *Carnevale* (1958). In other words, it seems that flounced skirts are too common in Campigli's *oeuvre* to be the result of concrete engagement with Minoan archaeology, unlike the illustrations for Gide (1949), which show more concrete points of contacts with Minoan iconography – from bare breasts to feathered crowns. As La Rosa and Militello (2006: 249) rightly observe, in the works of some Italian artists it is often too difficult, if not impossible, to disentangle the potential Minoan allusions from citations of generic archaic Mediterranean traits, which could be Minoan but also Etruscan, archaic Greek, Egyptian or even African. It is well known that Campigli, like D. H. Lawrence, was much taken by the Etruscans: a visit in 1927 or 1928 to the Museo di Villa Giulia and an encounter with Etruscan material culture acted as a catalyst in the transformation of his own art: cf. http://campigli.org/c3/artista_biografia.php, see also http://campigli.org/c3/scrupoli/Weiss2.pdf; see also Calandra (2017). It is likely that Campigli, unlike Gide, would not have seen in the Cretan artistic language some kind of decadence, but, like D. H. Lawrence (cf. below), would have perceived some kind of affinity between Etruscans and Minoans, some primordial, Mediterranean, and primitive essence.

131 Gide (1949: 23 and 31).

132 Gide (1949: 71).

133 Gide (1949: 50). For later views of the Minoans and their drug use, cf., e.g., Chapter 5 (esp. discussion of Jacquetta Hawkes).

134 Gide (1949: 65).

135 Gide (1949: 66) and cf. encounter in Kazantzakis's *Kouros*, discussed above.

136 For a useful list of French travellers in Greece in the period 1900–68, see Lebel (1969).

137 Boucher (2017: 125) reports that, on its route from Marseilles to China, the ocean liner *Aramis* called at Port Said and Djibouti (via the Suez Canal), Colombo, Penang,

Singapore, Saigon, and Hong Kong, but not in Crete. It is, nevertheless, interesting that this Neo-Minoan liner was chosen for a route to the Far East, perhaps illustrating a perception of Minoan Crete as suitably exotic and Oriental.

138 Waugh ([1930] 1985: 112).

139 Waugh ([1930] 1985: 112).

140 See discussion in Blakolmer (2006 and 2017), with further bibliography.

141 Waugh ([1930] 1985: 112–13).

142 De Lacretelle (1931: 153–92, and esp. 175–92).

143 Cf. De Lacretelle (1931: 181).

144 Mauclair (1934: 232–5). His reactions to Phaistos, Hagia Triada, and Malia are more positive, because he feels that they show no attempt to resuscitate what is dead.

145 Mauclair (1934: 245–50).

146 Mauclair (1934: 199 and 251).

147 Praz's account of his Greek journey first appeared in instalments in the newspaper *l'Ambrosiano* (April–June 1931), and was subsequently reprinted in his *Viaggio in Grecia* (1943), *Viaggi in Occidente* (1955), and *Il Mondo che ho visto* (1982): see Gabrieli and Gabrieli (1997).

148 Praz (1955: 26): 'un ritmo diverso'.

149 Praz (1955: 28): '... che dire di questa casetta che non evoca immagine più poetica di quella delle ritirate di certe stazioni nostrane?'

150 Praz (1955: 41): 'Il tempio perfetto, il metro del mondo'.

151 Hood (1995).

152 Hood (1995: 176).

153 Hood (1995: 177).

154 Brion ([1937] 1948: 286).

155 Brion ([1937] 1948: 289).

156 Humbert-Mougin (2006: 211). The essay is reprinted in Caillois's *Le Mythe et l'homme* (1938): cf. Caillois ([1938] 1972).

157 Caillois ([1938] 1972: 142).

158 Replicas of the 'snake goddesses' and other finds from the Temple Repositories were made by the Danish artist Halvor Bagge, who worked for Evans at Knossos in the mid-1900s (cf. Chapter 3). These were soon put on display in the Ashmolean, as shown by a photo of the Aegean collections as arranged in the 1910s: see Galanakis (2013: 22, fig. 18, on the left, and 50–1, figs. 73–6). I suggest that a replica in the Ashmolean inspired the poem because Huxley does not seem to have visited Crete (especially before 1917), whereas he is likely to have visited the museum while a student at Balliol.

159 Huxley (1917: 3). The poem is also available online at http://www.online-literature. com/aldous_huxley/4191/.

160 The poem dates to *c.* 1947: see Day-Lewis (1992: 374), MacDonagh and Lennox Robinsons (1958: 276), Stanford (2007). I suggest that visits to the Ashmolean may have been the source of inspiration for his poem too, since I have been unable to find any evidence that Day-Lewis visited Crete.

161 Lawrence (1932a); see also Cadogan (2004) and Roessel (2006). The poem is also available online at https://www.odyssey.pm/?page_id=1443.

162 Cadogan (2004, with further references).

163 Lawrence (1932b). In his volume on the Etruscans, Lawrence mused on Etruscan–Minoan affinities: for example, in his discussion of Tarquinia, Lawrence wonders whether the Etruscans were originally 'Lydians or Hittites with hair curled in a roll

behind, or men from Mycenae or Crete', and remarks that the Tomb of the Bulls 'suggests the old East: Cyprus, or the Hittites, or the culture of Minos of Crete': see Lawrence (1932b: 37, 107); see also text available online at http://gutenberg.net.au/ebooks09/0900381h.html.

164 One may also detect some sense of hope in a poem about Minoan Crete by Osip Mandelstam dated to 21 March 1937 (part of the third of his *Voronezh Notebooks*). At that time, about one year before his death in a concentration camp, the acclaimed Russian poet was in exile in Voronezh, having been arrested in 1934 for writing a poem that criticized Stalin. Yet he could find some solace and inspiration even in distant Minoan Crete, which he described as a blue and joyful island, famous for its potters, where well before Odysseus people sung: 'Give me back what is mine, Crete, / blue, soaring island, give me back my work, / and fill the fired vessel / from the breasts of the flowing goddess': see Mandelstam, McKane, and McKane (1996: 89). On Mandelstam and this poem, see also Hingley (1982: 216). Many other translations are available in print and online: see, e.g., Mandelstam and France (2014: 72), and https://issuu.com/uglyducklingpresse/docs/mandelstam and https://www.poetryintranslation.com/PITBR/Russian/MoreMandelstam.php.

165 See Chapter 3 and see also, e.g., above discussion of Bossert's work.

166 Cecchi (1936: 11). His Greek journey started with a brief stop in Corfu. Cecchi's Cretan sojourn included visits to Candia/Heraklion, Knossos, Phaistos, Hagia Triada, and Gortyn.

167 Cecchi (1936: 23–4).

168 Cecchi (1936: 18–22); see also the perceptive comments by La Rosa and Militello (2006).

169 Checchi (1936: 20–1, esp. the description of the new elements being like a cage for the old, and the 'Tabelloni in cemento armato, da fabbrica di prodotti chimici, accanto a purissimi alabastri dove la luce dei secoli dorme in una lattiscenza d'opale ...').

170 See Cecchi (1936: 22–4), who seems to echo here Evans's reference to Athenian chauvinism transforming Knossos into an ogre's den: see Evans (1921: 1).

171 Cecchi (1936: 24–5): 'la donna che ... attraverso l'amore avvia alla conoscenza ... irraggiungibile, e così presente ... ho perduto il mio appuntamento con te di tremila e cinquecento primavere.'

172 Checchi (1936: 17, 68, and 107–8, i.e. the section titled 'Dove riappare Arianna', where he adds further reflections on Minoan–Mycenaean art).

173 See esp. Checchi (1936: 69): 'capolavoro di prepotenza, d'individuale violenza'.

174 For pacifism, see Gere (2009: 153); for libidinal Minoans, see Roessel (2006: 198). For earlier impressions of Minoan and Mycenaean Greece, see also Miller's *First Impressions of Greece* (1973), which, albeit published later than *The Colossus of Maroussi*, was completed in November 1939. Hilda Doolittle (H.D.) is another author who alludes to Minoan Crete as a pacifist utopia in the interwar period: see Gere (2009: 177–94).

175 Roessel (2006: 200).

176 Roessel (2006: 199).

177 Keeley (1999: 5). In 1947, Durrell published *Cefalù*, a psychological novel set in Crete (later republished as *The Dark Labyrinth*), which involved a fictional Minoan site thought to be the real Minoan labyrinth. But in *Cefalù* the engagement with Minoan material culture and ideas about the Minoans is quite limited. Nevertheless, Evans's discoveries partly spurred Durrell's imagination, as did his visit to Crete during the

Second World War, before escaping to Egypt (for escape to Egypt, see Keeley (1999: 167–8)), and the novel contains clear allusions to Evans, with some interesting reflections about archaeology and psychoanalysis, authenticity and forgeries, and the blurring between reality and fiction. I also wonder whether the fact that one of the characters, the archaeologist Sir Juan Axelos, pretends that his finds are fakes could be an ironic allusion to Evans's reconstructions at Knossos, which create an impression of fakery among visitors: see, e.g., Bacchelli's description of Knossos as a fake antique (Chapter 5) and Hitchcock and Koudounaris (2002: 55), who call Knossos a 'shrine of the Fake'.

178 For another positive response to Evans's reconstructions, see the recollection of British artist John Craxton (cited in Cadogan (2004)), who first visited Crete in 1947 and lived on the island for a period (cf. also Chapter 6).

179 Miller (1941: 121–2).

180 Miller ([1939] 1973: 24).

181 Miller (1941: 150) and cf. Miller ([1939] 1973: 23): 'It is the softest spot of earth I know of. It is feminine through and through. I feel certain the site was chosen by the dynastic queen of Minos. It is the female line of the great dynasty which has given to the landscape its character, its charm, its subtlety – and its inexhaustible variety.'

182 Miller (1941: 85). Durrell (1969: 274) later used similar words to describe Mycenae: '[E]ach site in Greece has its singular emanation: Mycenae, for example, is ominous and grim – like the castle where Macbeth is laid. It is a place of tragedy, and blood. One does not get it from its history and myths – they merely confirm one's sensation of physical unease. Watch the people walking around the site. They are afraid that the slightest slip and they may fall into a hole in the ground, and break a leg. It is a place of rich transgressions, tears, and insanity.'

183 Miller (1941: 86). A jolly, happy-go-lucky impression of the Minoans also appears in Osbert Lancaster's *Classical Landscape with Figures* (1947: 205): 'a race of happy little extraverts [sic] unshadowed by the inhibiting preoccupations with the future life which so troubled the contemporary Egyptians and were quite unconcerned with the intellectual problems which engaged the fascinated attention of the classical Greeks'.

184 *Seven Days in New Crete* was published in the US as *Watch the North Wind Rise*. On Graves's *The White Goddess*, see also Firla and Lindop (2003), with further bibliography; on Graves and myth-making, see Zajko (2015); on Graves and matriarchy, see Ihm (2015).

185 Graves (1948: 10).

186 Cf. Chapter 3, p. 60 and Chapter 4, pp. 105, 113, 114.

187 All this is redolent of Frazer's *The Golden Bough* and Jane Harrison's *Prolegomena* and *Themis*, which were among the sources that Graves had used in *The White Goddess* (together with Glotz, Evans, and others).

188 Cf. Graves (1949: 268–9).

189 O'Prey (1984: 57–9, citing Grave's letter to James Reeves of 13 May 1949, discussing the progress of his '7 Days in New Crete'. In the same letter Graves also refers to a future collaboration on a ballet with Joan Junyer ('I'm also working on a mythical ballet with Joän Junyer by correspondence: he wants to do the *décor*'), who had already produced a mythical Minoan ballet in 1947 (cf. below).

190 Seymour (2003: 93–4); see also Evans (1943: 375).

191 Nigel Worth is the nom de plume of Royal Navy officer and author Noel Wright (1890–1975), who reached flag rank in the navy during the Second World War and

also wrote *The Wise Man of Welby* (1924), as well as works of non-fiction, mostly about naval matters, under his own name; see http://www.sf-encyclopedia.com/entry/worth_nigel.

192 Sidney Keyes's play *Minos of Crete*, written probably in the summer of 1940 and published posthumously in 1948, is another work that combines Minoan Crete and eroticism. In this play, however, actual elements of Minoan material culture are almost non-existent. Michael Meyer, the editor, reports that it was written while Keyes was still at school in Tonbridge before going up to Oxford, and that he had been reading Racine's *Phèdre* for the Higher Certificate, and James Baikie's *Sea Kings of Crete* – Keys's explanatory note to the play reports 'For a picturesque account of Minos legends, see Baikie's *Sea Kings of Crete* (also for photographs of Minos' throne and other antiquities).' Apart from this note, however, there is little or no evidence that Keyes engaged with Minoan finds and used them as an inspiration for his play; on the contrary, whenever he mentions the throne of Minos, for example, he describe it as being high up and reached by several steps – which is not what one finds at Knossos. In his explanatory note, Keyes also describes Minos as a 'modern character', the play as a 'psychological study of perversion and obsession', and his desire to create a play 'largely in erotic terms'. The eroticism seems, however, more inspired by ancient Greek texts and Racine than Minoan finds.

193 Worth (1924: 284).

194 Variation no. 26 is titled 'Die Schlangengöttin und ihr Feind', and is available at https://itunes.apple.com/us/album/wingate-symphony-no-2-kleet%C3%BCden-variationen-f%C3%BCr-orchester/356113128.

195 For the Linear A sign, see, e.g., Evans (1909: 273–93) and Mellink (1964). For a brief discussion of this work by Klee, now in a private collection, see also Momigliano (forthcoming), with further references; see also https://www.bildindex.de/document/obj00077308 and http://paulklee.fr/html/1940d.html#1940_317.

196 Frey (1997: 254): the two stops on Crete taking place on 23 December 1928 and 11 January 1929; cf. also Wada (1980: 65, 71).

197 Cited in Grohmann 1957, 381).

198 Paul Klee Foundation (1998–2004: vol. 9, no. 9313). The painting is now in the Berggruen Museum in Berlin (part of the Berlin Staatlichen Museen). Images can be seen at: https://www.artfritz.ch/MUSE/klee/index.html and https://paulklee.fr/html/1940c.html.

199 On Klee's use of chessboard patterns, see Klee and Artemis Group (1989: 54). One may wonder whether some other works produced by Klee more or less at the same time as *Stadtbild Knossos* (his opus no 9313) might contain references to his difficult sea journey of 1928 and other memory of things Cretan, such as his no. 9311 ('In trouble due to water'), no. 9312 ('In trouble due to aridity'), no. 9314 ('Museum industry'), no. 9315 ('Palaces'), and no 9316 ('navigare necesse'): see Paul Klee Foundation (1998–2004, vol. 9).

200 Morris (2017), with further references.

201 On this ballet and Junyer, see the special issue of *Dance Index* 6, no. 7 (1947), edited by Joan Junyer, available online at: https://archive.org/details/danceindexunse_27; see also https://www.nycballet.com/ballets/m/the-minotaur.aspx., and Ziolkowski (2008: 113 –14), who seems, however, unaware of Junyer's contribution and Minoan-styled costumes. I should like to thank Lynn Garafola for bringing this ballet to my attention. Another 1947 ballet that could, potentially, have some Minoan connection is Martha Graham's *Errand into the Maze*, based on a poem by Ben Belitt, with music

by Gian Carlo Menotti and stage design by Isamu Noguchi: Bannerman (2010), with further bibliography. Although Graham, a student of Ruth St Denis and Ted Shawn, must have been aware of Shawn's *Gnossienne* and Minoan Crete in general, as far as I can see this work shows no clear inspiration from the material culture of Bronze Age Crete.

202 *Dance Index* 6 (1947): 164.

203 For the 1923 production of *Phèdre*, see Chapter 3 and Momigliano (2017a); for Sköld's 1934 'Minoan style' *Medea*, see Hilleström (1956: 24) and http://www.apgrd. ox.ac.uk/productions/production/7821; for the 1942 production of Racine's *Phèdre*, see Humbert-Mougin (2006).

204 See further discussion in Chapter 5 (Robert Wise's *Helen of* Troy) and Chapter 7 (Wolfang Petersen's *Troy*).

205 Christian C. Schnell, 'The career of an archaeological object in the movies. The "Throne of Minos" as requisite and icon in *Helena* (1924) and *La Guerra di Troia* (1961)', paper presented at the conference 'Replica knowledge: histories, processes and identities', 2–4 February 2017, Berlin (Humboldt University); see also Winkler (2007a: 204) and https://www.edition-filmmuseum.com/product_info.php/language/ en/info/p163_Helena--Der-Untergang-Trojas.html.

206 I should like to thank my colleague Pantelis Michelakis, who first brought this image to my attention. On this film, see also Winkler (2007a: 205); see also http://www. fulltv.tv/movies/the-private-life-of-helen-of-troy.html, and https://www.pinterest. co.uk/pin/299207968970495367/.

207 Markatou (2008: 309–13).

208 See http://www.lykeionellinidon.gr/index_en.html; see also Psarra and Fournakari (2006).

209 Fournaraki (2011: 71), Florou (2016).

210 Markatou (2008: 309–13 and fig. 3).

211 Markatou (2008: 309–13).

212 On Kalliroi Parren, see Psarra and Fournakari (2006); on Anna Apostolaki, see Florou (2016).

213 On the 1930 Flag Ceremony, see Markatou (2008: 311–13). For later examples of Minoan elements in national pageantry, see Simandiraki (2005, on the opening ceremony of the 2004 Olympic Games in Athens); see also Solomon (2006: 167 and fig. 10.4, discussing a Minoan Ritual enacted by the Lyceum of Greek Women in 1995 in Heraklion). For exclusion of certain periods of Greek history from official narratives, parades, and pageants, such as the opening ceremony of the 2004 Olympics, see also Chapter 7.

214 Yalouri (2001: 39–40).

215 Hamilakis (2007: 179 and 185). See also http://metaxas-project.com/doube-axe-labrys-pelekys-metaxas-zeus-eon/. The Metaxas regime's choice of the *labrys* as one of its symbols may have been prompted more by its later association with the thunder-god Zeus than Minoan Crete. It may also be connected with Italian fascism, since one of its main emblems was the axe (and sometimes a double-axe) with the 'fasces' of Roman and Etruscan inspiration, such as the famous double-axe and fasces of the Etruscan 'Tomba del Littore' in the necropolis of Vetulonia. Nevertheless, many people would have perceived the *labrys* as a link to the Minoan world.

216 On the Heroon in Heraklion, see Cadogan (2004), Markatou (2008: 316–17), Philippides and Sgouros (2017).

217 Alušík (2004); for the 'Bull Staircase', see also Blakolmer (2006: 224–5, fig. 14.4).

218 Blakolmer (2017: fig. 3.3), Boucher (2014b: 174, cat. 313). See also another example in the Metropolitan Museum in New York: http://www.metmuseum.org/art/collection/search/500026.

219 Wängberg-Eriksson (1996), Long (2002: 212–13 and colour plate 16).

220 By coincidence, in 1920, only a few years before discovering this fresco, Evans had travelled to Stockholm to receive the Great Gold Medal of the Swedish Society of Anthropology and Geography: Evans (1943: 373).

221 Lancaster (1947: 70–1).

222 Philippides and Sgouros (2017: 30–1, 34).

223 Mitsotaki (1999: 22–3, 33, 40–3, 45). Greensted (2010: 138–40); Giorgos Kaloutsis (Florentini Kaloutsi's son), pers. comm. (email correspondence of 20 June 2019).

224 Giorgos Kaloutsis (pers. comm.: email correspondence of 20 June 2019).

225 Mitsotaki (1999: 21 and 42).

226 Mitsotaki (1999: 43–4).

227 Leontis (2018). Eva-Palmer Sikelianos also used Minoan and Mycenaean motifs in her textiles: see, e.g., Leontis (2018: fig. 10.1). On the friendship between Kaloutsi, Angelos Sikelianos, and his wife Eva Palmer Sikelianos, see Mitsotaki (2017). I am grateful to Artemis Leontis for providing this reference.

228 Hobsbawm (1994): his 'age of extremes', the title of the whole volume, covers the period from *c.* 1914 to 1991, and his 'age of catastrophes', the title of part I, covers the period from *c.* 1914 to 1945.

229 See, e.g., Potolsky (2004: v and x), Oram (2006), with further references.

230 See also Momigliano (2017b).

Chapter 5

1 See, e.g., Beevor (2005: 334–6, 341), Janes (2013: 197–205).

2 Hopkins (1977: 235) mentions that the initially slow growth of tourism after the Second World War gained pace under the dictatorship; Herzfeld (1991: 41) also refers to the 'heavy-handed promotion of large-scale tourism', especially in the 1960s.

3 Cf. also Chapter 2 and below.

4 Cottrell (1955: 218).

5 Ventris and Chadwick (1956: 13) and Chadwick (1967: 1). The dedication of *Documents in Mycenaean Greek* to Schliemann as the 'Father of Mycenaean Archaeology' also includes a passage from the latter's autobiography related to his aptitude for learning languages, and his particular fascination with Greek.

6 See, e.g., Ventris and Chadwick (1956: 10) and McDonald (1967: 313).

7 The story of Ventris's decipherment has been recounted many times, starting with John Chadwick's classic *The Decipherment of Linear B* (1st ed. 1958, 2nd ed. 1967); see also, e.g., Fitton (1995: 171–8) and Robinson (2002).

8 Hood (1967: 126) suggests that the notion that the decipherment 'came as a shock' is myth; instead, it 'came as welcome confirmation of what were already well-entrenched views'. See also McDonald (1967: 311–13).

9 See, e.g., Lorimer (1950: 125).

10 Wace (1956: xxvii and xxxi). Cf. also Wace's introduction to Cottrell (1955), and Fitton's (1995: 202) comments on classicists who do not show adequate appreciation of the importance of Bronze Age Greece.

11 For Luwian and Linear A, see, e.g., Palmer (1958 and 1961), Huxley (1961). For an attempt to link Linear A with Greek, see Nagy (1963). On the 'Orientalization' of the Minoans after the decipherment, see also Nixon (1995: 11–13).

12 For example, regarding the Minoan legacy to Mycenaean Greece (and via Mycenaean Greece to Western civilization), Graham (1962: 16) mentions various aspects of material culture (from architecture to the art of writing) and repeats Evans's idea that Minoan poetry may have influenced the Homeric epics (cf. Chapter 3).

13 Myres (1930: 538); cf. Renfrew (1987:6) and also his Runciman Lecture (4 February 2016, King's College London): 'Who were the Greeks? New insights from linguistics and genetics'.

14 Chamoux (1963: 16).

15 Deshayes (1969: 381, 441 and passim). Faure (1973: 368) similarly suggests that Minoan Crete is 'la première civilisation vraiment humaine de la Méditerranée'.

16 Deshayes (1969: 380–1). For de Lacretelle, cf. Chapter 4.

17 Vermeule (1964: ix).

18 Vermeule (1964: ix).

19 Bury et al. (1923: v). Faure (1973: 360–1) suggested that it is meaningless to talk of Minoan Crete as a 'European culture', since the notion did not really exist in the second millennium BC, and prefers to characterize Minoan culture as the first example of classicism that Europe has known.

20 See Matz (1973a and 1973b) and cf. also Matz (1962c). For traits such as passivity and dynamism being associated with East and West, see, e.g., Hobson (2004: 8, with further references). A more Oriental impression of Minoan Crete is also visible in Demargne (1964), whereas Faure (1973: 364) associates dynamism with the Minoans and contrasts it with the stagnation ('immobilisme') of the Orient.

21 Starr (1961: 37–8).

22 Starr (1961: 49).

23 Starr (1961: 55–7). See also Demargne (1964: 268) who suggested that the Greek Dark Age provided a significant hiatus between Mycenaean and Greek art, and the latter's true emergence occurred when it broke free from its most primitive aspects. Christian Zervos and his monumental and lavishly illustrated publications on the arts of Greece represent another interesting and comparable example that makes Minoan Crete, if not Oriental, at least a case *sui generis*, and regards Mycenaean Greece as not entirely 'Hellenic': see Zervos (1934, 1956, 1957, 1962, and 1967). In 1934, before the decipherment of Linear B, Zervos produced a book on the arts *in* Greece from prehistoric times to the eighteenth century AD, which included illustrations of the Neolithic, Cycladic, Minoan, Mycenaean, Geometric, Archaic, Classical (up to the fourth century AD), Byzantine, and post-Byzantine (illustrations are up to seventeenth century AD included) periods, but bypassed the Hellenistic, Roman, Frankish, Arab, and Ottoman periods. In 1956 and 1957 he produced two lavish volumes on Cycladic Art and on Neolithic-Minoan Crete. The latter includes illustrations of Linear B tablets but a highly sceptical view of Ventris's decipherment. No subsequent volume was devoted to Mycenaean Greece, but in 1962 Zervos published a book titled *The Birth of Civilisation in Greece* (my emphasis). The preface mentions that the purpose of the book is to trace the 'origines de la civilisation grecque', and 'civilisation' is equated with the Neolithic. Indeed the focus of this volume was the Neolithic of Thessaly and Macedonia, but also included many illustrations of Neolithic objects from Jericho, Iranian and Iraqi Kurdistan, and Cyprus. Finally, in 1969, just before his death in the following year, Zervos published a book on *Hellenic*

Civilisation, which started with the eleventh century BC. In other words, the Bronze Age Mycenaeans were not Greek enough, while the destruction of their palaces and the Dorian invasion provided the watershed leading to the emergence of the Greek *poleis*.

24 See, e.g., Hood (1961), Boardman (1962), and especially Palmer and Boardman (1963). A concise summary of the state of play in the mid-1960s can be found in Vermeule (1964: 136–9) and Harrell-Courtès (1967: 179–85). Cf. also Chapter 4 (discussion of Blegen's 1958 essay, which called for a re-examination of the stratigraphy and context of the Knossos tablets).

25 See, e.g., Driessen (1990 and 1997, with further bibliography).

26 Bennet (2000), Driessen (2008), Palaima (2010).

27 See Ventris and Chadwick (1956: 127 and 303–12). For more detailed discussion of textual evidence in the Linear B tablets concerning the polytheistic vs. monotheistic or dualistic nature of Minoan Religion, see Gulizio and Nakassis (2014).

28 See, e.g., James (1959: 128–60, Chapter V, on Crete and Greece).

29 Guthrie (1959: 39).

30 See, e.g., Marinatos and Hirmer (1960: 36).

31 Marinatos and Hirmer (1960: 36).

32 Goodison and Morris (1998a: 8, citing works by Peter Ucko and Andrew Fleming in particular).

33 Goodison and Morris (1998a: 8).

34 See, e.g., Marinatos (2010).

35 See list of excavations compiled by N. Karadimas and N. Momigliano available at https://bristol.academia.edu/NicolettaMomigliano (uploaded June 2019).

36 On Minoan villas, see Hägg (1997).

37 On Doro Levi's work, see Carinci (2007).

38 See Hood (1962), Hood and Cadogan (2011).

39 For an overview of John Evans's work, see Renfrew (2015, with further references); for Neolithic Knossos in particular, see Isaakidou and Tomkins (2008), with further bibliography.

40 Popham (1973), Popham et al. (1984).

41 Sackett and Popham (1970), with earlier references. For more recent explorations at Palaikastro, see MacGillivray and Sackett (2010), Bennet (2016: 11–12).

42 The structures at Chania/Kydonia at first were not initially recognized as part of a palace because the archival materials were discovered in later years: see Hallager (1974), with further bibliography. For Kato Zakros, see Platon (1971).

43 Warren (1972).

44 See, e.g., McDonald (1967: 330–3) and Fitton (1995: 182), with further bibliography.

45 Renault (1969: 82–3).

46 McDonald (1967: 333, referring to the work by physical anthropologist L. Angel).

47 See, e.g., Starr (1955), who argued that the Minoan *thalassocracy* was largely an Athenian invention to provide an antecedent to the Delian League (see also reply by Buck, 1962); Faure (1973: 260); cf. also Niemeier (2009) for an overview of historiography on the Minoan *thalassocracy*.

48 Cf. Chapter 4. Marinatos did not link the Minoan eruption of Santorini with Plato's myth of Atlantis explicitly in his seminal 1939 article in *Antiquity*, but he did so in print and in lectures by the 1950s: see Marinatos (1971).

49 The year 2017 marked the 50th anniversary of more or less continuous excavations at Akrotiri. For a popular account of this work up to 1979, see Doumas

(1983, with selected bibliography). See also, more recently, Doumas and Doumas (2016).

50 See Manning (2014: 15–17), with relevant bibliography and also Chapter 6. Note, however, that the authoritative third edition of the *Cambridge Ancient History*, published in 1973, still reports that the eruption of the volcano started in Late Minoan IA late, but the final cataclysm occurred in Late Minoan IB (see Matz (1973b: 558 and chronological tables at 822–3), and despite the fact that even Marinatos was beginning to recognize that the Theran eruption could not be responsible for all the devastation on Crete: see Marinatos and Hirmer (1960: 22–4).

51 For a recent overview, see Driessen (2019), with further bibliography.

52 See, e.g., Warren (2012), Adams (2017: 4–8).

53 See, e.g., the popular volume by Luce (1969, with several reprints) and Marinatos (1971).

54 Vidal-Naquet and Lloyd (1992: 323).

55 Boucher and Krapf (2014: 198, catalogue nos. 320–1).

56 On peaceful Minoans, their trading *entrepôts*, and the idea that Evans's *thalassocracy* is exaggerated, see, e.g., Furumark (1950), also quoted below; Hutchinson (1962: 98–9), Matz (1962a: 154; 1962c: passim; 1973a and 1973b: passim), Hawkes (1968: 65), Deshayes (1969: 90).

57 For an overview of the debate, see Broodbank (2004: 54–8) and Niemeier (2009).

58 On the New Archaeology, see Trigger (1989: 289–328).

59 Furumark (1950: 252–3).

60 Furumark (1950: 271): 'When seen under a wider historical aspect, the outstanding fact of Aegean history during the period c. 1550–1400 B.C. is the meeting between the highly differentiated Mediterranean culture of LM I–II Crete and the essentially European Middle Helladic civilization of the Greek Mainland . . . The whole Mycenaean cultural development means an "Auseinandersetzung" between Helladic and Minoan, resulting finally in the victory of the former element. After all, the insular civilization of Crete was only a picturesque episode, and its lasting contribution to European history is that it wakened Greece from its prehistoric slumber and brought it into contact with the civilizations of the Ancient East.' Besides this quotation, the Hellenism of Furumark is evident also in the following statement: 'Still, the reconstruction of the earliest Greek history remains one of the most important tasks of modern historical science. In my opinion it is even the principal *raison d'être* of Aegean archaeology' (Furumark (1950: 183)).

61 Groegenwegen-Frankfort (1951). The title *Arrest and Movement* comes from a line in T.S. Eliot's *Four Quartets* ('Burnt Norton'):

At the still point of the turning world. Neither flesh nor fleshless;
Neither from nor towards; at the still point, there the dance is,
But neither arrest nor movement. And do not call it fixity,
Where past and future are gathered. Neither movement from nor towards,
Neither ascent nor decline. Except for the point, the still point,
There would be no dance, and there is only the dance.

62 Groegenwegen-Frankfort (1951: 188).

63 Groegenwegen-Frankfort (1951: 216).

64 Gere (2009: 212–13).

65 Kerenyi (1976) and Hawkes (1968). See also Hawkes's later book, *Quest of Love* (1980), which is a curious 'autobiography' in which a woman retells, in a series of chapters,

moments in the lives she has led in previous incarnations, progressing from a nameless woman in earliest prehistory to her present self, and including a chapter on her incarnation as Ianissa, a Minoan woman

66 On Minoan pacifism, see, e.g., Cottrell (1955: 150): '[The Minoans] seemed quite uninterested in recording triumphs, battles, treaties and conquests, as had the Egyptians and the blood-lusting Assyrians. Instead they painted delightful scenes from nature, flowers and birds and trees, processions of noble youths like the cup-bearer and the even lovelier fresco of the Priest-King discovered near the south entrance, scenes of public ceremony, sport or ritual at which the Court ladies prinked and chattered ...'; see also Alsop ([1962] 1965: 235, referring to 'unwarlike Minoans'). For more examples of pacifist Minoans, see also Matz (1962a, 1962b, 1973a, and 1973b), Hutchinson (1962: 21, 91ff.), and Graham (1962: 13, 19–21), who comments on the idea that the peaceful character of Minoan Crete appears so strange, when compared to other ancient cultures, that it has 'encouraged the charge that the Minoans were decadent and enervated. Alas for more such "decadence"!' and that the Minoans were an 'odd medley of primitive and sophisticated elements ... a brilliant, gifted people', but 'were not a soft, lazy people, however much they may contrast with the vigorous and bellicose Mycenaean Greeks'; see also Schachermeyer (1964: 126–34, i.e. Chapters 14 and 15 on '"Mutterrechtliche" Züge in der minoischen Kultur' and 'Der minoische Friede'). Alexiou (1964: 34, and 1969: 29–30) points out that already in the Protopalatial period 'Peace and prosperity, the so-called Pax Minoica, reigned in Crete' and that the Old Palaces were destroyed by earthquakes, not human agency. See also Platon (1966: 50–1, 147–8, 161, 256–60). According to Higgins (1967: 18), 'The peaceful character of this civilization is noticeable even before the Palace period. It was to remain a Cretan peculiarity and contributed to no small extent to the rapid development of her culture'. Von Matt et al. (1968: 9–10) report that 'At the end of the pre-Palace period, around 2000 BC, peace and prosperity reigned on the island ... The Cretan were a happy, lively people ... Peace reigned on the island with the famous Pax Minoica'. Cf. also von Matt (1967a: 9–10, and 1967b: 9–10); Faure (1973: 318–21, 331–6), Willetts (1962: 9, 24, 29; 1969: 138–9; 1977: 48, 57, 64, 112, 128–9).

67 See, e.g., Schachermeyer (1964: 126–34).

68 Helen Brock (pers. comm). Ronald Willetts was also close to and influenced by the Marxist classicist George Thomson: see, e.g., obituary of Willetts in the *Independent*: https://www.independent.co.uk/arts-entertainment/obituaries-professor-ronald-willetts-1078631.html; see also Foxhall (2013: 8–10).

69 Willetts (1977: 112). See also Willetts (1962: 21): 'the collective customs of the clan tenaciously survived in Crete'; and Willetts (1977: 63) on 'tenacious collective traditions'. A strong sense of community, egalitarianism, and pacifism can also be detected in Branigan's volume on Prepalatial Crete, where the author suggests that slavery was not in the 'spirit' of the Minoans (Branigan 1970: 121).

70 Willetts (1977: 63).

71 Willets (1962: 25).

72 Willetts (1962: 32–7); see also Willetts (1977: 111–12), suggesting that Evans's ideas about kingship and 'aggressive Minoan imperialism' were derived from the fact that he excavated first the Late Bronze Age strata of Minoan Knossos, which reflect these socio-economic and political changes and a more militaristic culture.

73 The possibility of Minoan Crete being a matriarchy or a matrilineal society (though not necessarily so closely linked to pacifism) is also found in numerous other works of

this period, such as Platon (1966: 32 and 171), Harrel-Courtès (1967: 162), Branigan (1970: 124–5), and Hood (1971: 117–18).

74 Hawkes (1968: 18). On the idea of Classical Greece rising from the union of two gifted races, cf. Chapter 3.

75 Hawkes (1968: 149–56). The idea that the occupant of the 'throne' was female, probably a high priestess enacting epiphany, partly originates from a seminal paper by Helga Reusch (1958). See also Helen Waterhouse's 1974 paper 'Priest Kings?', published posthumously by Goodison and Hughes-Brock (2002).

76 See, e.g., Hutchinson (1962: 257–8), Matz (1973b: 572–3).

77 Graham (1962: 21).

78 On rejection of Linear B, see, e.g., Hood (1967: 9–10, and 1971: 8 and 113–15). On internecine wars on Crete and Minoan warfare, see, e.g., Hood (1967: 80, and 1971: 51 and 118–22). On Minoan colonialism, see Hood (1967: 74): 'In that imperialistic age it is difficult to believe that the kings of Crete did not attempt to expand their dominions like the contemporary Pharaohs of Egypt, whether by extorting tribute or even by planting colonies.' See also Hood (1967: 111–12, and 1971: 52–6).

79 On Hood's scepticism about women's freedom on Crete, but their importance in religion and possibility of matrilineality, see Hood (1971: 117–18).

80 Renfrew (1972), reprinted in 2011, with a foreword by John Cherry (2011) as well as new preface and introduction by Renfrew.

81 Cherry (2004: 1). See also Cherry (2011).

82 Renfrew (1972: xxv).

83 Renfrew (1972: 1–8).

84 Renfrew (1972: 3).

85 Renfrew (1972: 258 and 394).

86 Renfrew (1972: 325).

87 Renfrew (1972: 502).

88 Renfrew (1972: 433).

89 Clarke (1972).

90 Letter to the Editor of *Antiquity*, reported in the Editorial for *Antiquity* 47, no. 186 (June 1973); also reprinted in Daniel (1992: 80).

91 See, for example, the definition of 'reciprocity' as 'movements between correlative points of symmetrical grouping' (Renfrew (1972: 297)).

92 Cowper Powys ([1954] 2008: 217).

93 On the Minoan religious revolution, see Cowper Powys ([1954] 2008: 217). As to references to Minoan material culture in Cowper Powys's *Atlantis*, they do exist, but are rare. A mention of pillars that 'might have been found in the crypt of some sea-king's palace beneath the floor of the ocean' may or may not be an allusion to a typical element of Minoan architecture (Cowper Powys ([1954] 2008: 24)). A More likely reference to Minoan material culture is the mention of 'hieroglyphs' that are neither Achaean nor Hellenic (Cowper Powys ([1954] 2008: 168)), which could allude to the fact that Linear B had been deciphered, whereas Linear A, Cretan Hieroglyphic, and the Phaistos disk had not. There is also a remark on 'parchment rolls, either inscribed by the careful fingers and the exquisitely prepared pigments of ancient Sumeria or by the less careful and much more daring imagination of the artists of Crete' (Cowper Powys ([1954] 2008: 238)). But even his descriptions of submerged Atlantis (e.g. Cowper Powys ([1954] 2008: 208, 336, 421, 427–8) have nothing particularly Minoan in them (i.e. the appearance of Atlantis is more classicizing).

94 Cowper Powys (1947: 83). See also Myles (1973: 69).

95   For date in which the story is set, see Farrer ([1954] 2004: 26).
96   Farrer ([1954] 2004: 41). I have not been able to ascertain whether a restaurant
     named after King Minos did exist in the London Soho district in the 1950s, but at
     least two restaurants called The Minotaur opened in the British capital: one was
     active in the 1960s, and was frequented by Michael Ayrton, his wife, and
     stepdaughter: see Ayrton (1970: 5–8); the other opened in 2011 at the Old Vic
     tunnels: see http://www.steeletheshow.com/london-the-minotaur-1/ and
     https://www.telegraph.co.uk/travel/destinations/europe/uk/london/london-in-your-
     lunch-break/8821816/London-in-your-lunch-break-The-Minotaur-at-the-Old-Vic-
     Tunnels.html.
97   Farrer ([1954] 2004: 14). Since by 1953 'Mycenaean' Linear B had been deciphered,
     the phrase 'The many inscriptions written in letters no one could yet interpret' could
     be understood to be referring to 'Minoan' Linear A, Cretan Hieroglyphic, and the
     Phaistos disk or as indicating the novelty of the decipherment of Linear B, and the
     fact that a few scholars had not accepted its decipherment.
98   See, for example, Farrer ([1954] 2004: 101), where seal-stones are described as
     'very beautiful, and quite unlike anything else in ancient and modern art', and
     Farrer ([1954] 2004: 108), where a Marine Style vase is described in the following
     way: 'The design was beautiful – a kind of underwater garden of seaweed and
     sea-anemones and octopuses, so free and fluid that they seemed to wave as you
     looked at them . . .'. On an annual human sacrifice, cf. also Farrer ([1954] 2004:
     61and 101).
99   Farrer ([1954] 2004: 32).
100 Farrer ([1954] 2004: 27). The notion that Homeric Scheria could be identified with
     Corfu and represented some vague memory of Minoan Crete was quite common at
     that time: see, e.g., Shewan (1919). Sir Alban also appears to be partly inspired by Sir
     Mortimer Wheeler, who often appeared in the popular television quiz show *Animal,
     Vegetable, Mineral?* that ran from 1952 to 1959, since he is provided with attributes
     that closely recall this British archaeologist, such as his 'leonine head and impressive
     utterance' and the fact the he brought archaeology 'to the common man . . . not
     disdaining to enlist the aid of film, radio, and television': see Farrer ([1954] 2004: 8).
101 For Evans's acceptance and use of fakes, see, e.g., Karo (1959: 110–14), Lapatin (2002),
     Marinatos (2015: 74–105). Farrer's negative view of archaeologists and their use of
     fakes probably also derives from fact that in 1953 the famous Piltdown man was
     exposed as a hoax (see *Time Magazine*, 30 November 1953).
102 Dick (1972: 51).
103 Renault (1969: 81–2). The passage in *The Last of the Wine* which was the most likely
     starting-point for *The King Must Die*, is: 'There is a labyrinth in the heart of every
     man, and to each comes the time when he must reach its centre, and meet the
     Minotaur' (Renault (1956: 206)).
104 Renault (1969: 82–3).
105 Renault (1969: 83).
106 Sweetman (1993: 167–70), Zilboorg (2001: 151).
107 Sweetman (1993: 27–8, 36).
108 For Renault's use of the term Minyans for the pre-Hellenic inhabitants of Greece and
     the Cyclades, see, e.g., Renault (1958: 68–9, 342, 345). See also Renault (1962: 271):
     '[T]wo forms of divine kingship co-existed in Mycenaean Greece. The Pelasgian, or
     Shore Folk, and the Minoans worshipped the Earth Mother, whose king consort was
     an inferior, expendable figure, sacrificed after each cycle of the crops so that his youth

and potency could be forever renewed. Though in Crete a Greek conquest had brought hereditary kingship, parts of the old cult remained. Ariadne was its high Priestess by right of birth.'

109 See previous note and Renault (1958: 274), where Ariadne tells Theseus, 'But that is … only a mainland custom. Here in Crete no king has been sacrificed for two hundred years. We hang our dolls on the trees instead, and the Mother has not been angry.'

110 See Sweetman (1993: 177–8), Zilboorg (2001: 155–6).

111 See, e.g., Renault (1958: 57–8, 172).

112 Renault (1958: 190, 210, and 249).

113 Renault (1958: 208–9).

114 Renault (1958: 254–5). The Minoans' decline is also shown by other features, such as Renault's suggestion that trained slaves are used in the bull-leaping ceremonies, but in earlier times it was the noblest and bravest Cretans who performed in them (Renault (1958: 190)), an idea already used by others (e.g. Berry in *The Winged Girl of Knossos*: see Chapter 4).

115 Renault (1962: 36). See also Renault (1958: 342–60, esp. 355).

116 Renault (1958: 360).

117 Renault (1958: 256).

118 Renault (1964: 44).

119 Diodorus Siculus, 4.62. Apollodorus, Bibliotheca (Epitome, 1.18 and 5.22).

120 See Renault (1958: 342–4): while escaping from Crete, Theseus and his companions see that not only had Crete been struck by a violent earthquake, but also a tsunami, which has caused havoc at the port of Amnisos; moreover, while sailing towards Naxos they see a great column of smoke rising from Kalliste (Thera), they get covered in ash, and on getting closer to Kalliste they see that half of the island has disappeared.

121 See, e.g., Renault (1958: 249) and cf. Renault (1962: 33), where the fall of Crete is partly explained through maltreatment of serfs and slaves: 'Men are dangerous when they have nothing to lose.' Also note that in Renault's novels there is no slaying of a half-bull half-human Minotaur. Instead, Theseus kills King Minos (who asks to be killed) and his stepson (and self-anointed successor) Asterion, using a sacred double-axe.

122 Renault (1962: 193).

123 Sweetman (1993: 206).

124 Elisabeth Ayrton read English, Archaeology, and Anthropology at Newnham; see Hopkins (2011).

125 Ayrton (1963: 19, 21, 94–7, 188).

126 See, e.g., Ayrton (1963: 20, 93, 97–8). Arkas seems to share the love for the animal and natural world of his Minoan ancestors: he regards his female donkey, called Pasiphae, as beautiful as 'an ancient fresco, or a relief which might have graced the Palace of Knossos' (Ayrton, 1963: 10).

127 See, e.g., Ayrton (1963: 114, 190).

128 Ayrton (1963: 21). Minoan artefacts and the art of digging fascinate Arkas: although he is conducting an illegal excavation, he is torn by moral dilemmas, does not wish the site to be desecrated and information lost through carelessness, and at some point even contemplates contacting the Greek authorities; see Ayrton (1963: 24, 48, 114, and 187).

129 Ayrton (1963: 13).

130 Ayrton (1963: 145, 150–2).
131 Ayrton (1963: 190).
132 Ayrton (1963: 196).
133 On the Boston Goddess, cf. Chapter 4, page 93 with note 25.
134 Nyenhuis (2003: catalogue nos. 42, 18, and 192 – the latter, *Minoan Landscape II*, is also titled *Corn Rhyton*; see also catalogue nos. 144–7, 149, 183, 240, 278).
135 Nyenhuis (2003: catalogue nos. 312 and 316). The Minoan palette may also have influenced the use of deep blue colours in the former and warm earth colours in the latter.
136 Nyenhuis (2003: catalogue no.704).
137 Ayrton (1977).
138 The literary interest and inspiration is also evident from other writings, such as Ayrton (1962 and 1971). On the Athenian origins of Daedalus as a possible fifth-century Athenian invention, see Chapter 2; cf. also Berry's take on Daedalus as a dynastic term (like Minos) in *The Winged Girl of Knossos* (cf. Chapter 4).
139 Ayrton ([1967] 2015: 32): 'Everything points to victory for the sky-gods . . . the Cretan mother is dying.'
140 For the maze as the life of the artist/craftsman, see Ayrton ([1967] 2015: 319).
141 See, e.g., Ayrton ([1967] 2015: 23–4, 56, 74–5, 82, 92–4, 181, 202), referring to Minoan gold cups, flounced skirts, loin clothes, double-axes, frescoes, light-wells, horns of consecrations, and even to the reverence gesture of fist to forehead found on Minoan figurines. Ayrton, however, also takes some liberties: for example, one of the Knossian frescoes is described as a boar's hunt (something that is not found at Knossos, but on mainland Greece) and is located in a courtyard (Ayrton ([1967] 2015: 82)), something that, again, is not a Minoan custom; see also the idea that bronze tripods and cauldrons were given to Minos as tribute (Ayrton ([1967] 2015: 241)), which is anachronistic in a Bronze Age context, but suitable for the Early Iron Age. The novel also contains references to common ideas about Minoan sea power (Ayrton ([1967] 2015: 54, 66)); pacifism, i.e. the idea that the Minoans are more interested in commerce than war: see, e.g., Ayrton ([1967] 2015: 68–9, 76, 90, 126, 285); and the important status of women in Minoan society (Ayrton ([1967] 2015: 30, 66, 72).
142 Ayrton ([1967] 2015: 25).
143 Ayrton ([1967] 2015: 26).
144 Ayrton ([1967] 2015: 77).
145 Ayrton ([1967] 2015: 77).
146 Ayrton ([1967] 2015: 77).
147 Ayrton ([1967] 2015: 77–8). Cf. also Ayrton ([1967] 2015: 32, 75, and 82, for more evidence of Minoan decadence: '[G]o to Crete and learn from them. They have much to teach a boy of your talents and their time is clearly short. The Cretan mother is dying and the future is here. When I have taken Athens from Aegeus we will make it more golden and more splendid than Knossos. We shall exalt Demeter and her daughter there as equal as Athena, and Apollo and Poseidon, and both sexes will be served'; 'Crete is losing her vitality and her arts show it'; 'We are dying here in Crete.'
148 For allusion to writing in the Aegean Bronze Age and the decipherment of Linear B, see Ayrton ([1967] 2015: 30 and 70), referring to Greek as coming into general use on Crete as a second language and writing on both clay tablets and papyri.
149 Ayrton ([1967] 2015: 200).

150 Ayrton ([1967] 2015: 87).

151 Ayrton ([1967] 2015: 88).

152 Swann (1966: 82).

153 Swann (1966: 35).

154 Swann (1966: 6).

155 For bull-leaping, cf. below. For drugs and dancing, see, e.g., Swann (1966: 60): 'We linked hands and she led me through stately, meandering steps like those of the young virgins when they dance beside the River Kairatos, though the music seemed more appropriate to the opium-drugged priestesses of the Great Mother, when they yield themselves to ecstasy ...'

156 Swann (1966: 142).

157 Swann ([1971] 1975: 77 and 105).

158 Swann ([1971] 1975: 138).

159 Swann ([1971] 1975: 76).

160 Swann ([1971] 1975: 81).

161 Swann ([1971] 1975: 140–5).

162 Swann ([1971] 1975: 24). Cf. Kazantzakis (1973: 149–50): 'The Cretan bullfights were not like the barbarous ones in Spain ... Here the bullfight was a bloodless game. Man and bull played together.'

163 Swann ([1971] 1975: 139).

164 Swann (1966: 40, and 1977: 192).

165 Swann (1966: 116).

166 Swann (1977: 77).

167 Swann (1977: 97).

168 Swann (1977: 111).

169 Swann (1977: 150).

170 Swann (1977: 143).

171 Anderson (1977: 70–1) refers directly to Renault's novels.

172 Anderson (1971: 60).

173 Anderson (1971: 99).

174 Anderson (1971: 101–2).

175 Anderson (1971: 98 and 101–2).

176 Anderson (1971: 79).

177 Anderson (1971: 178).

178 Anderson (1971: 179).

179 Anderson (1971: 181).

180 Anderson (1971: 181 and 183).

181 Another reimagining of the myth of Theseus, Ariadne, and the Minotaur is *The Bull Leapers* (1970) by James Watson, an author who was a lifelong socialist and active member of Amnesty International, mostly famous for his books for young adults (see obituary in https://www.theguardian.com/books/2015/may/11/james-watson). The novel offers plenty of references to Minoan material culture that provide some local colour and some intriguing variations on the famous legend, such as the friendship between Theseus and another bull-leaper, the black Egyptian slave Piros, who shares the adventures and glory of the Athenian hero. Also, the wily Pasiphae becomes ruler for a period of eight years. If Watson's Pasiphae can be read as an incarnation of the alleged Minoan matriarchy, this is not cast in a good light, and *The Bull Leapers* does not offer any glimpses of redemption for the Minoan Mother Goddess, nor of her exacting some kind of revenge. 'On Polish 'Cretomania' in the Cold War see Ulanowska (2019).

182 Both poems are published in Quasimodo (1958); see also Quasimodo (1983). The English translation of 'Minotauro a Cnosso' is from La Rosa and Militello (2006: 247). See also https://www.nobelprize.org/prizes/literature/1959/quasimodo/biographical/.

183 See Lee (1968:19–20 and 24).

184 Brandi (2006: 44). Brandi (2006) is the 3rd edition of Brandi (1954). On Brandi's journey to Crete, see also La Rosa and Militello (2006: 249).

185 Brandi (2006: 27–8).

186 Brandi (2006: 30–3, 42–3).

187 Brandi (2006: 95–8). Brandi's views of Minoan Crete did not mellow with time: in two articles on Santorini and Atlantis, originally published in the newspaper *Corriere della Sera* in 1975, he wrote very appreciatively on the Akrotiri frescoes, which he found much superior to those of Knossos, and described the Minoan naturalism illustrated by pottery decorated with octopi as being almost repugnant: see Brandi (2006: 177–91).

188 Bacchelli (1965: 32–8, section on 'Micene fascinosa'); see also Bacchelli (1965: 191–2), on his second visit in 1962, with interesting meditations on the site as a skeleton.

189 Bacchelli (1965: 179–92, esp. 184–8, section on 'Creta la misteriosa', 208–19, sections on 'Uve e favole' and 'Creta la favolosa'). The negative impressions obtained after his actual visit to the island can be compared to the earlier enthusiastic clichés about the joie de vivre, naturalism, sensuality, vitality, love of colour and movement, etc. that Bacchelli used in his discussion of Cretan–Mycenaean art during his visit to Mycenae of 1958: see Bacchelli (1965: 34).

190 See, e.g., Evans (1912), Glotz (1925: 388).

191 Heidegger (1989 and 2005).

192 Heidegger (2005: 19).

193 Heidegger (2005: 22).

194 Heidegger (2005: 23).

195 Heidegger (2005: 24). For Spengler and de Lacretelle, cf. Chapter 4.

196 Heidegger (2005: 24)

197 Heidegger (2005: 30ff.).

198 De Richaud (1953: 367).

199 De Richaud (1953: 368): 'Si, comme le dit un philosophe chinois, "la tranquillité dans le désordre et le signe de la perfection", le Palais de Minos vous donnera une imagine parfaite de la perfection.'

200 De Richaud (1953: 370).

201 For dates of his journeys to Crete, see Lacarrière (1975: 119 and 149).

202 Lacarrière (1975: 120).

203 Lacarrière (1975: 122).

204 Lacarrière (1975: 178–9).

205 Lacarrière (1975: 122 and 179–82).

206 Lacarrière (1975: 121 and 137).

207 Lacarrière (1975: 124). For Miller's feminine perception of Phaistos, see Chapter 4.

208 Durrell (1969: 274): '[E]ach site in Greece has its singular emanation: Mycenae, for example, is ominous and grim – like the castle where Macbeth is laid. It is a place of tragedy, and blood. One doesn't get this from its history and myths – they merely confirm one's sensation of physical unease. Watch the people walking around the site. They are afraid that the slightest slip and they may fall into a hole in the ground, and break a leg. It is a place of rich transgressions, tears, and insanity.' For Miller's views of Mycenae, cf. Chapter 4.

209 For destruction of Minoan Crete, see Durrell ([1978] 2002: 106 and 117); for his lukewarm appreciation of Minoan art, see, e.g., Durrell ([1978] 2002: 93), describing the snake goddess as 'charming and pleasant as a piece of folklore but not really impressive as sculpture'; here he also suggests that the Ballets Russes influenced Minoan art as visible in the extensive restorations, a remark that reminds one of those made by Waugh, who saw, instead, the influence of *Vogue* (cf. Chapter 4). For Durrell's more appreciative views before the Second World War and before he visited Crete, see Chapter 4 (especially epigraph).

210 Durrell ([1978] 2002: 65): 'In these quiet precincts, which in fact may be simply administrative buildings, but which exhale the kind of equanimity and poise of an architecture at once beautifully proportioned and not too sweet, one feels the presence of a race that took life gaily and thoughtfully'; cf. also Durrell ([1978] 2002: 75): '... these faraway Minoan people, who sometimes make one think of China and sometimes of Polynesia. Bright, fresh and pristine are the little faces from the frescoes ... Candour and a smiling self-possession seem to be the characteristics of these people, but of course they guard their secrets very well.'

211 Durrell ([1978] 2002: 74).

212 Keeley (1961: 88). See also Roessel (2006: 203). In the context of libidinal Minoans, I should also like to mention the long poem *Encounter in Crete* (1971) by Hugo Manning, a Jewish-British journalist and poet who could list among his friends many important literary figures, such as Henry Miller, Lawrence Durrell, John Cowper Powys, and Jorge Luis Borges among many others; see http://norman.hrc.utexas.edu/fasearch/findingAid.cfm?eadid=00275. *Encounter in Crete* is inspired above all by the myth of Pasiphae and the bull, but there are a few nods to Minoan material culture, such as references to the Mother Goddess as a 'serpent-wreathed Lady', bull-games, double-axes, frescoes, Minoan plumbing, bare breasts, etc.: see, e.g., Manning (1971: 18–19, 21, 24, 34).

213 Keeley (1961: 87).

214 Keeley (1961: 88).

215 Keeley (1961: 88).

216 Keeley (1961: 88–9).

217 Keeley (1961: 91).

218 Keeley (1961: 91).

219 Kazantzakis (1973: 141–54, esp. 148–52).

220 Kazantzakis (1973: 149).

221 Kazantzakis (1973: 149).

222 Kazantzakis (1973: 151). Note, however, that there are no representations of snake goddesses in Minoan frescoes, and that the 'blue boys' had long been identified as monkeys by the time Kazantzakis was writing this passage.

223 Kazantzakis (1973: 151).

224 Beaton (2008: 22–3).

225 Beaton (2008: 22–3). Cf. also Beaton (2006: 187): 'the Minoans have become *Greek*'.

226 Hamilakis (2006: 156–60, esp. 158).

227 On Hellenizing the Minoans and Minoanizing the Greeks, see also Momigliano (2017b: 7).

228 Beaton (2006: 184); cf. also Beaton (2008: 22–3).

229 Cf. Chapter 4. With regard to the chronological setting, as far as I have been able to ascertain, most novels that are set at the time of the Greek–Mycenaean takeover of

Crete (often presenting the myth of Theseus and the Minotaur as symbolic of it) and were published in the periods examined in this and previous chapters, almost inevitably present a decadent view of the Minoans, ready to be defeated. Even Haggard's 1929 novel, *The Double Axe*, merely present the Dorian period as something even worse than the obnoxious regime of the last Minoans. One exception is Poul Anderson's novel *The Dancer from Atlantis* (cf. above).

230 The works by Elytis and Diktaios discussed below are examined by Beaton (2006), who also discusses the incorporation of the Minoans into Yannis Ritzos's poem *Romiosini*, through a brief allusion to Minoan frescoes.

231 Elytis (1980: 9, 10).

232 Beaton (2006: 188); see also Elytis (1980: 9–10).

233 Beaton (2006: 188); see also Elytis et al. (1997: 177).

234 Elytis (1980: 74); see also Beaton (2006: 188).

235 Diktaios (1974: 57–8 and 301–4). See also Beaton (2006).

236 Beaton (2006: 189).

237 Diktaios (1974: 324–6).

238 See Bosanquet (1909) and Murray (1909).

239 Beaton (2006: 189).

240 Diktaios (1974: 325).

241 In contrast to Diktaios's subtle reflections is the work of the anthropologist Aris Poulianos, who, in the 1970s, concluded that the Minoans spoke Greek on the basis of dubious physiognomic and craniometric studies: see Hamilakis (2006: 150).

242 Michalaros (1958). On Michalaros, see Karanikas (1983: 65–89). See also http://snaccooperative.org/ark:/99166/w61k0mh5.

243 See, e.g., Michalaros (1958: 19, 25, 29).

244 Michalaros (1958: 153).

245 Cadogan (2004: 537–8); see also note 246 below.

246 Vasso Fotou (pers. comm. in email of 4 September 2017), who has made enquiries in Ierapetra, has confirmed that the Dimarchio was built around 1967–8, and it seems likely that the Neo-Minoan airport terminal mentioned by Cadogan (cf. note 245 above) post-dates the Greek Civil War. Krapf (2019) illustrates other examples of vernacular and public buildings in Neo-Minoan style, both on Crete and beyond. These, however, mostly date to periods later than that discussed in this chapter, with a few exceptions, such as a private house in the Vyronas district in Athens – Krapf (2019: pl. CXXXIIb) – which could date between the 1950s and 1970s (T. Krapf, pers. comm. in email of 27 April 2019).

247 See Birkstead (2004: 55–6 and fig. 3.4).

248 Preziosi (2017); see also Birkstead (2004: 57). Birkstead (2004, esp. Chapters 2 and 3) also sees Minoan influences in the building created by Josep Lluís Sert for the Maeght foundation, but the alleged Minoan inspiration of some elements appears to me too generic and contrived.

249 See La Rosa and Militello (2006: 251–2, figs. 15.5 and 15.6), De Pirro (2012: 27, 32 and 52; 2013: esp. fig. 22). Other works by Novelli also contain references to the Phaistos disk: see De Pirro (2012: passim; 2013: 135).

250 Jean Arp's *Knossos* (1956) can be viewed at https://www.wikiart.org/en/jean-arp/abstract-composition-knossos.

251 Cocteau's image can also be viewed, for example at https://www.art-days.com/oeuvre/lithographie-gravure/lithographie-originale-taureaux-v-par-jean-cocteau/.

252 From the essay 'On a trip to Greece'; see Cocteau (1988: 229).

253 From the essay 'On Relative Freedoms'; see Cocteau (1988: 113).

254 Cocteau (1988: 113). In addition to the artists mentioned above, one may also note in passing the British artist Patrick J. Caulfield (1936–2005), who visited Crete in the early1960s and collected postcards of Minoan frescoes: he appreciated their 'simplicity and directness' as well their 'amusing and quite strong imagery': see https://www.tate.org.uk/context-comment/articles/fun-exotic-and-very-modern. A few art critics have detected some Minoan influence in his early work, but if so, this is at a very general and abstract level, in terms of bold colours and simplicity of line, rather than actual content and particular engagement with Minoan material culture.

255 Murnaghan and Roberts (2018: esp. Chapter 2, 'Classics in their own right').

256 Kingsley (1964), Renault (1964).

257 Solomon (2001) notes the following films, which I list here in chronological order: 1) Cecil B. DeMille's *Samson and Delilah* (1949), showing the Temple of Dagon decorated with Sumerian and Minoan motifs (the latter based on the idea that the Philistines originated from Crete: see Chapter 2); 2) *Queen of Sheba* (1953); 3) *The Egyptian* (1954); 4) *Ulysses* (1954 or 1955); 5) Robert Wise's *Helen of Troy* (1956); 6) *The Minotaur, The Wild Beast of Crete*, a.k.a. *Theseus against the Minotaur* (1960); 7) *Saffo, Venere di Lesbo*, a.k.a. *The Warrior Empress* (1960); 8) *The Trojan Horse* (1962); 9) *My Son, the Hero*, a.k.a. *Sons of Titans* and *Arrivano i Titani*. Nisbet (2006: 24) notes the use of a snake goddess statuette (and even plaster lions based on Mycenae's Lion Gate) in the 1961 film *The Colossus of Rhodes* directed by Sergio Leone. In addition, Minoan and other Aegean Bronze Age elements also appear in the 1975 film *The Man Who Would be King*, directed by John Houston and starring Sean Connery and Michael Caine: see Boucher and Krapf (2014: 196–7, fig. 197).

258 For the Hollywood film, see Solomon (2001: 246, fig. 159, showing a Minoan fresco in the background); see also http://www.tcm.com/mediaroom/video/1110263/ Egyptian-The-Original-Trailer.html and http://www.afi.com/members/catalog/ DetailView.aspx?s=&Movie=51196.

259 Winkler (2015a: 19). On this film, see also Nisbet (2006: 31–6), Winkler (2007a: 206).

260 The idea that the fall of Knossos prefigured the fall of Troy had already been used in other genres, e.g. in Guðmundsson's *Gyðjan og uxinn: skáldsaga* (The Goddess and the Bull: a novel, 1937), translated into English as *Winged Citadel* (cf. Chapter 4): see, e.g., Gudmunsson (1940: 399), where the Achaeans launch 1,000 ships against Knossos – which is an allusion to both Homer's *Iliad* (book 2) and the famous phrase 'Was this the face that launch'd a thousand ships, / And burnt the topless towers of Ilium' in Christopher Marlowe's *Doctor Faustus* (1604, Act V, Scene I).

261 https://www.imdb.com/title/tt0049301/quotes/qt3288703.

262 Wise produced a number of films that could be considered as feminist, or at least very sympathetic to female characters, e.g. *Mademoiselle Fifi* (1944) and *I Want to Live* (1958). The anti-war message may not be entirely explicit in *Helen of Troy*, which was produced only two years after the US became involved in the Vietnam War, but is crystal clear in *The Sand Pebbles* (1966).

263 On Minoans in science fiction, see Bourke (2014).

264 For the use of Minoan and Theran motifs in *Doctor Who* episodes in the 1960s and 1970s, see Boyes (2017) (consulted in October 2018); see also Bourke (2014).

265 This is now available at http://www.teche.rai.it/1953/10/notturno-a-cnosso/ and http://www.teche.rai.it/programmi/notturno-a-cnosso/.

266 Jacobs (1957); also cited in Farnoux (1993: 118–19), which provides an illustration showing the Knossian throne and Minoan columns.
267 See the website of the Virtual Museum Vallée (VmV) of Val D'Aosta, and its branch the Museo della Mucca (MuMu): http://www.vmv.it/.

Chapter 6

1 See, e.g., Koliopoulos and Veremis (2009: 159–60).
2 See, e.g., discussion of the Circular of the Minister of Culture and Science, 488/21-07-1982 in Galatsiatou (2003). See also Pantos (2013: esp. 94, n. 4); see also http://www.tap.gr/tapadb/files/nomothesia/nomoi/n.3028_2002.pdf: article 36.2, p. 3017, i.e. Νόμος 3028/2002 (Law 3028/2002), which introduced a maximum of three collaborations/*synergasies* for non-Greeks.
3 The clashes between Greek and foreign archaeologists are partly the result of the crypto- or quasi-colonial position of modern Greece since the nineteenth century and the appropriation of ancient Greece by Western Hellenism: cf., e.g., the discussion of the clash between Xanthoudidis and Halbherr over the excavation of the Kalyvia cemetery in Chapter 3.
4 Hamilakis and Yalouri (1996: 125–6), Hamilakis (2006).
5 On Crete and PASOK, see Featherstone and Katsoudas (1985: 33–4); on political influences on the Heraklion 1979 demonstrations, including resistance to US military presence on Crete, see Hamilakis and Yalouri (1996: 126–7).
6 http://www.aegeanprehistory.net/.
7 See list of excavations compiled by N. Karadimas and N. Momigliano available at https://bristol.academia.edu/NicolettaMomigliano and at https://www.researchgate.net/publication/333918486_Minoan_excavations_Crete_1900-2000_v_19_June_2019.
8 For the term 'New Wave', see Cherry (1994).
9 Gkiasta (2008: with further references, esp. fig. 4.1.5); see also the earlier overview in Driessen (2001).
10 See, e.g., Driessen (2001: 64).
11 For the Minoan Roads project, see Chryssoulaki (1999); see also http://www.hydriaproject.info/en/cases/crete/zakros/minoan_roads.html. For the Minoan Roads project and demystification of Minoan pacifism, see also Gere (2009: 16 and 225).
12 Waterhouse (1986: 99), Coldstream and Catling (1996).
13 For Palaikastro (start of new excavations in 1986), see MacGillivray and Sackett (1992 and 2010, with further references). For Kommos (start of excavations in 1976), see Shaw and Shaw (1995 and 2010, with further references). For Hagia Triada (start of new excavations in 1977), see La Rosa (2010 and 2014, with further references).
14 Karetsou (1981).
15 Sakellarakis (1988).
16 Lebessi (1992).
17 Sakellarakis (1996).
18 Nerokourou: Chryssoulaki (1997, with further bibliography); for Zominthos, see Papadopoulos and Sakellarakis (2013, with further bibliography).
19 Driessen (2002: vii).

20 Driessen et al. (2002b: ix), referring in particular to the state of knowledge reflected in Hägg and Marinatos (1987).

21 Halstead (1981: 201).

22 Driessen et al. (2002b: vii, ix–x).

23 See Manning (2014: 7–45 and appendix, with further bibliography).

24 See Driessen (2019).

25 Avaris: Bietak (2000, 2013) and Bietak et al. (2007); Tel Kabri: Niemeier and Niemeier (2000); Miletus: Niemeier and Niemeier (1999), all with further references.

26 Bietak et al. (2007: 145–50).

27 See, e.g., Cline (1998).

28 GORILA: Godart and Olivier (1976–85); CHIC: Olivier and Godart (1996).

29 Renfrew (1987).

30 Renfrew (1998). On the non-Indo-European origins of the words *wanax* and *basileus*, see also Palaima (1995).

31 On the Versailles effect in the Aegean Bronze Age, see Wiener (1984 and 2016).

32 For Anemospilia, see Sakellarakis and Sapouna-Sakellaraki (1981), Sakellarakis and Sakellarakis (1997: 268–311); see also https://www.nytimes.com/1984/08/19/magazine/the-secrets-of-crete.html. For Knossos, see Warren (1981a and 1981b), Wall et al. (1986), Whitehouse (1986: 97–8).

33 For instance, Anemospilia provided the first example of a tripartite shrine and possibly of a cult statue (a xoanon with clay feet), while Knossos offered a remarkable ritual assemblage dating to Late Minoan IB – a phase not very well represented within the palace.

34 Sakellarakis and Sapouna-Sakellaraki (1981).

35 See Branigan (1982) and Angeliki Rovatsou's 2017 interview with Sapouna-Sakellaraki, https://www.archaeology.wiki/blog/2017/07/19/meticulous-research-with-a-discerning-eye/. On reactions to the discoveries at Anemospilia and Knossos, see also Castleden (1990: 169–74), Mastrorakis and van Effenterre (1991: 75–6).

36 Cf. note above.

37 Platon (1981b: 173): 'La substitution au sacrifice humain d'un autre type d'offrandes, quoiqu'il ait été impose par des principes magique très anciens, est un autre exemple de supériorité morale' ('Though imposed by very ancient magic principles, the substitution of another type of offering for human sacrifice is another example of [Minoan] moral superiority').

38 Treuil et al. (1989: 315).

39 In addition to the works discussed in this section, readers may find it useful to consult Fitton (2002) and Hamilakis (2002): the former, aimed at the general public, gives a good idea of the general trends and consensus regarding the Minoans reached in the previous decade; the latter, aimed at specialists, offers a similar but more critical overview and presents a kind of manifesto for new approaches in the twenty-first century (see especially Hamilakis's introduction).

40 See, e.g., Warren (1989: 39–41). As the text and even the pagination of the main chapters remained the same in Warren (1975) and Warren (1989), in the following notes I shall simply refer to the second edition.

41 Warren (1989: 46).

42 Warren (1989: 41). Cf. also Warren (1989: 42), where the Minoans are described as brilliant craftsmen, with remarkable skills in naturalistic representation. Furthermore, Warren uses fairly antiquated craniological evidence from a couple of cemeteries to

suggest that, despite some variations, the Minoans represent a relatively homogenous group: Warren (1989: 75).

43 Warren (1989: 104); on peaceful evolution, disturbed only by natural causes, such as earthquakes, see also Warren (1989: 75). The popularizing 1975 volume *Lost World of the Aegean*, part of Time Life Books series 'The Emergence of Men', attributes the peacefulness of the Minoans, at least among themselves, to their dominance of the sea, the prominence of Knossos, a powerful religious network, and a homogenous population 'with a far better chance of living in peace with itself than the rest of the world's mixed- up, ethnically jangled, eternally moving, squabbling and rebellious peoples': Edey (1975: 66 and cf. also 59–60).

44 Warren (1989: 99 and 100).

45 Warren (1989: 75 and 100).

46 Warren (1989: 101). For a critique of this checklist approach, see Broodbank (2004: 56–7).

47 Warren (1989: 97).

48 Warren (1985: 94).

49 On the lack of 'individualism', see Warren (1989: 97), and on the main Minoan legacies, see Warren (1989: 136).

50 Platon (1981a: 11–12).

51 Platon (1981a: 255): 'caractère dynamique des nouveaux éléments raciaux'.

52 Cf. Platon (1981a: 256): 'aussi sa qualification de civilisation peut-elle être considérée comme heureuse'; on the egalitarian and peaceful character, see, e.g., Platon (1981a: 162–71, 285, 295) and Platon (1981b: 80–1). On Platon's egalitarian views of the Minoans also in popularizing works, see Hamilakis (2006: 150, n. 4). On the peaceful Minoan *thalassocracy*, see Platon (1981b: 179–81, esp. 180), where he suggests that ancient Greek sources, such as Thucydides and Diodorus, give a peaceful impression of the Minoan sea empire; see also Platon (1981b: 197 and 260), where he discusses the non-aggressive infiltration of the Minoans, thanks to the superiority of their culture, and the peaceful coexistence of Minoan and indigenous elements in the Aegean islands, at least in the initial phases.

53 See Platon (1981a: 162–8, 283–5), where he also refers to emergence of the Knossian kingdom as 'primus inter pares'; see also Platon (1981b: 80–1) on racial elements, the importance of religion, and the role of women in Minoan society.

54 On Minoan religion, see Platon (1981a and 1981b: passim) and especially Platon (1981b: 119–22).

55 For comparison between Minoan palaces and Tibetan temples, see Platon (1981a: 346).

56 See Platon (1981a and 1981b: passim, esp. 1981a: 286).

57 See, e.g., Platon (1981b: 13–22). A picture of theocratic kingship, peaceful colonial expansion in the Aegean, relative egalitarianism, love of nature, etc. also appears in the chapter on Neolithic and Minoan Crete written by Efi and Yiannis Sakellarakis for the two-volume work on the history of the island published by the Association of Municipalities & Communities in Crete: Sakellarakis and Sakellarakis (1987).

58 Treuil et al. (1989: 214 on 'primitive democracy', and 315 on Neopalatial intensification of 'royal power' and ritual).

59 Treuil et al. (1989: 231).

60 Treuil et al. (1989: 306–8).

61 Treuil et al. (1989: 318–23).

62 Watrous (1995: 411–12).

63 Dickinson (1994: 88): 'The effort expended on measuring skulls in an attempt to distinguish human types and trace migrations seems to have been entirely wasted . . .'; cf. also Dickinson (1994: 207).

64 Dickinson (1994: 266).

65 On human sacrifice and cannibalism, see Dickinson (1994: 266); on the development of weapons and its connection with the emergence of palatial society, see Dickinson (1992: 201) and cf. the views already expressed by Renfrew (1972: 325) on the development of metallurgy, especially on Crete, as being linked to military requirements; on Cretan internal conflicts and the presence of fortifications, see Dickinson (1994: 301 and 303).

66 Dickinson (1994: 302). For important debates and different opinions about Minoan and Mycenaean elites, see papers in Rehak (1995).

67 On the Mother Goddess and Minoan priestesses, see Dickinson (1994: 257–9 and 265).

68 Cadogan (1976: 9 and 54–5).

69 Gimbutas (1974 and 1982); Gimbutas and Dexter (1999).

70 See, e.g., Gimbutas (1974: 236–8; 1982: 236–8) and Gimbutas and Dexter (1999: 149–55).

71 Castleden (1990: 159 and 177).

72 Castleden (1990: 124 and passim for polytheism; 159 for 'euphoria minoica').

73 Castleden (1990: 177).

74 Castleden (1996: xiv).

75 Castleden (1990: passim, especially 1–8, 34–5 on Mycenaean takeover; 124 on Mother Goddess; 162–8, 175 on matrilineality).

76 Castleden (1990: 178).

77 Castleden (1990: 140); for Merezhkovsky's Minoan eunuchs cf. Chapter 4.

78 Castleden (1990: 175–7).

79 Quotations from Castleden (1990: 4 and 17). On the importance of women in Minoan society, see Castleden (1990: passim, and esp. 13, 28–9, 32).

80 For the ceremonial role of the *wanax*, who was 'living in the shadow of a Labyrinth run by powerful priestesses as an earthly parallel to the Minoan myth of a relatively insignificant male god, Velchanos, who was subordinate to a more powerful goddess', see Castleden (1990: 28–9); for the importance of priestesses and power-sharing with the lawagetas, see Castleden (1990: 175–6).

81 On rejection of Mycenaean takeover of Crete, see Castleden (1990: 34–5).

82 Wunderlich (1974), originally published in German under the title *Der Stier Europa trug: Kretas Geheimnis und das Erwachen des Abendlandes* (1972).

83 Evasdaughter (1996: 1).

84 Evasdaughter (1996: 53).

85 Evasdaughter (1996: 165).

86 Evasdaughter (1996: 2 and 171–6). Interestingly, the Mycenaeans at first appear in a good light and as 'Goddess-loving', since they had been deeply influenced the Minoans: see Evasdaughter (1996:174–6, 181). But, in the end, they succumb to their increasing aggressiveness: Evasdaughter (1996: 172). The Dorians are the final straw: Evasdaughter (1996: 178, 181).

87 In this period, in addition to the works discussed below, four 'Minoan' poems appeared in Lorand Gaspar's *Egée suivi de Judée* (1980), dedicated to Giorgos Seferis and the fishermen of Patmos, in the section 'Fouilles' (Excavations). The poems have titles that

refer to the Evans–Mackenzie periodization of Minoan Crete: Néolithique II, Minoen Ancien, Minoen Moyen III, and Minoen Récent I (Aiguières d'Hagia Triada). Unlike many authors and poets discussed in this section, the award-winning Hungarian-born French poet, physician, writer, photographer, and translator does not appear to explore the darker side of the Minoans, but his poems convey the sense mystery and magic incantation of Minoan Crete as well as Gaspar's sensuous, physical response to the joy, colour, and movement of Minoan objects and iconography, as shown, for example, in these verses from his 'Minoen Moyen III' (Gaspar 1980: 23): 'Hommes glabres aux longs cheveux, / ceints de pagnes, huilés de combats, / l'arc tendu à l'extrême du mouvement, / moissonneurs et porteurs d'offrandes – / ruissellement de haches et de bijoux – / dames bleues et hommes aux longs cheveux/ qu'avez-vous vu de si incompréhensible? / qu'était cette clameur sur vous seuils? / an – 1570' ('Beardless men with long hair, / girdled with loincloths, oiled from the fights, / the bow stretched to the extreme of movement, / reapers and bearers of offerings – / dripping with axes and jewels – / blue ladies and men with long hair / what did you see so incomprehensible? / what was this clamor on your thresholds? / year – 1570').

In the mid-1980s, the famous Argentinian writer Jorge Luis Borges visited Knossos, on the occasion of receiving an honorary degree from the University of Crete in Rethymnon: see Sifakis et al. (1985); see also https://www.cretalive.gr/ opinions/o-mporches-kai-to-allo-panepisthmio-krhths. A picture of Borges in the Grand Staircase at Knossos accompanies his brief composition 'El Laberinto': Borges and Kodama (1986: 58). One finds, however, little evidence of his engagement with the material culture of Minoan Crete in this or other writings, with the possible exception of a reference to the 'temple of the Axes' in his 'La casa de Asterión', first published in *Los Anales de Buenos Aires* in May 1947 (reprinted in Borges 2000: 170–2), which shows at least his knowledge of Evans's interpretation of the word 'labyrinth' as meaning the 'House of the Double Axe' (cf. Chapter 3).

88 The novel was partly inspired by the discovery of the famous Cape Gelidonya shipwreck in 1954, subsequently excavated by George Bass and his team in the 1960s. See Michaels ([1975] 1989: 56).

89 Michaels ([1975] 1989: 56 and 192).

90 Michaels ([1975] 1989: 30–2).

91 Michaels ([1975] 1989: 35). Her reaction to Evans's reconstructions are described as follows:'Most archaeological sites are pretty boring, just low foundation walls, drab brown brick and gray stone . . . although purists criticize his restorations . . . the result is so handsome you can't condemn him . . . they give some idea of how gay and bright the place looked like in its heyday': Michaels ([1975] 1989: 33).

92 Michaels ([1975] 1989: 173).

93 Michaels ([1975] 1989: 174–5).

94 Michaels ([1975] 1989: 76).

95 Michaels ([1975] 1989: 174–5).

96 Michaels ([1975] 1989: 125). Incidentally, some of the pottery found by Ariadne is a strange mixture of Kamares and Late Minoan IB – (Michaels ([1975] 1989: 128, 140, 153) – which would link more closely the fall of Knossos with the eruption of Thera.

97 Caldecott (2007: 202, 204, 217).

98 Caldecott (2007: 65). On the spirit healer (from Bristol), see Caldecott (2007: 44 and 77).

99 Caldecott (2007: 65–6).

100 Besides numerous references to bull-leaping interspersed in the novel, allusions to Minoan material culture include, for example, descriptions of frescoes: see Caldecott (1979: passim, especially interesting is the reference to the female character Ierii as a fresco painter (1979: 6)); see also references to seal-stones worn on wrists (1979: 35); the Malia gold wasp pendant (1979: 75); the 'snake goddesses' and their staring glance, which is explained as resulting from the use of hallucinatory drugs in rituals (1979: 100); and the Phaistos disk (1979: 156).

101 The only exceptions are some explicit references to labyrinths as mazes (but not as the House of the Axe) and an implicit reference to the Minotaur myth, which can be elicited from a scene describing the encounter between the Queen of Ma-ii and a bull, in which 'she and the bull were staring at each other, each half animal, half human': Caldecott (1979: 109).

102 Caldecott (1979: 86; see also 13–15, 17, 22, and 135: 'The Bull and the Lily must be at peace – they are the two sides of One Reality – to worship the one without the other is to create imbalance . . .').

103 Caldecott (1979: 8): 'It was only at funerals that acrobats could show their skills and dance with the beast to show man's defiance of death, his desire for new life'; see also Caldecott (1979: 15 and 107), where Caldecott explains that, if the bull-leaper is killed, there is no chance of reincarnation/rebirth for the deceased.

104 Caldecott (1979: 78). Quilla had already appeared as a bull-leaper from Crete in Caldecott's earlier work, *The Tall Stones*: see Caldecott (2007: 33).

105 Caldecott (1979: 165).

106 Caldecott (1979: 178).

107 Burns (2017); Aburrow (2018: 258–9).

108 http://www.minoan-brotherhood.org/.

109 http://www.minoan-brotherhood.org/.

110 For the Neo-Pagan Greek group Labrys, see http://www.labrys.gr/en/index.html. For Perry's Modern Minoan Paganism, see https://www.facebook.com/groups/1502335483312496/; see also http://www.lauraperryauthor.com and pers. comm. (email of 20 February 2018); see also Chapter 7.

111 https://news.artnet.com/exhibitions/the-brooklyn-museum-judy-chicago-dinner-party-1131506 (7 November 2017).

112 Most of the authors discussed in this section on 'feminist novels and other works' (e.g. Lawton, Christ, Brindel, Dintino, and Hand) explicitly acknowledge the influence of Gimbutas; see also https://feminismandreligion.com/2017/10/23/the-impact-of-marija-gimbutas-on-my-life-and-work-by-carol-p-christ/. Lawton describes Minoan Crete as 'the last and longest ever bastion of truly civilised living', where women had 'leading positions' in society and lived a 'life without fear or oppression' (1977: 19), and she marshals Minoan archaeology, anthropology, biology, psychology, and Marxism to suggest that society would be better off not only if it were liberated from patriarchy, but also monogamy. Chicago's *The Dinner Party* celebrates mythical and historical women in Western civilization and includes the Minoan 'snake goddess' among the diners; moreover, in the 'Heritage Panels', Chicago explicitly refers to the patriarchal takeover in the section next to the image of the snake-brandishing Knossian figurine: see https://www.brooklynmuseum.org/eascfa/dinner_party/place_settings/snake_goddess and https://www.brooklynmuseum.org/eascfa/dinner_party/heritage_panels/panel. See also http://www.judychicago.com/gallery/the-dinner-party/dp-artwork/ (all consulted at the suggestion of Christine Morris). Eisler's influential volume presents a multi-disciplinary discussion of the

evolution from peaceful to violent societies from prehistory to the present, in which Minoan Crete features as an example of her 'gylany', a type of society in which gender relations are not hierarchical, but understood in terms of partnership: Eisler (1987: 105). Marilyn Coffey's poems offer alternative, feminist retellings of well-known Greek myths pertaining to Crete, from Europa and the Bull to Theseus and the Minotaur. Although her engagement with the material culture of Minoan Crete is minimal, the subtitle of her volume tell us that she imagines that her verses are fragments dug up at Knossos, and in the poem 'The Goddess, of herself' she explains that her premise is that 'Once upon a time, the entire Aegean Sea, including the island of Crete, was governed by the Great Goddess . . . around whom serpents twine': Coffey ([1991] 2014: 4). Christ's autobiographical volume describes the path that led her to organize many pilgrimages to Crete since the 1980s. These are still going strong today, and the participants are promised that 'You will learn about a Society of Peace where [a] Goddess was revered as the Source of Life, women were honored, people lived in harmony with nature, and there was no war. You will celebrate the grace and joy of life in sacred places and find the wellsprings of your own creativity and power.' See https://www.goddessariadne.org/.

113   In Brindel's *Ariadne* (1980) and *Phaedra* (1985), Theseus orders the killing of as many priestesses as possible and even commits matricide and double filicide: he kills not only his son Hyppolitus, because of the latter's devotion to a Goddess cult and abhorrence of violence, but also a daughter he fathered with Phaedra. Riebe's *Palast der blauen Delphine* (1994) is set in Crete *c.* 1500 BC and is another retelling of the myth of Ariadne, Theseus, and the Minotaur as symbolic of the struggle between matriarchy and patriarchy. The main character is Asterios – the son of Queen Pasiphae and a bull-leaper – who becomes the first male priest of the Great Mother, represents both a male and female part in his priestly role, and has visions of an impending natural disaster. Sreevivasan's *The Moon Over Crete* is a novel written for children aged eight–twelve, which tells the adventures of an eleven-year-old American girl, Lily, who travels back to Minoan Knossos with the help of Mrs Zinn, her music teacher. On Crete, she experiences for the first time in her life what it is like to live in an egalitarian society, where women held equal or even higher status than men. During her Knossian sojourn, Lily dreams of the future eruption of Thera and Mycenaean takeover, and although she would like to stay in Crete forever, the Queen of Knossos persuades her that she can be more useful back in her country, where she can draw inspiration from her Cretan experience and the Goddess to 'help men and women to work together again': Sreenivasan (1994: 117). Dintino's *Ode to Minoa* (1999), which is provided with the sequel *Stories They Told Me* (Dintino 2003), tells the story of Aureillia, a young Cretan girl who becomes a Snake Priestess, and can predict the future through visions induced by snakebites. These prophetic visions include the demise of the happy Cretan egalitarian society (in which men and women enjoy complete equality and a satisfactory sex-life), the emergence of a male-dominated world after the Mycenaean takeover of Crete (post-Theran eruption), and much later episodes of female oppression, such as the burning of witches and the introduction of female genital circumcision. Yet, the Minoan past (with a touch of New Age) offers a glimmer of hope for the future: through meditation and a close connection with nature, Aurellia and other women can find new powers and meaning in their life. There are also some notable Cretomanic novels by male authors (or co-authored by male authors), which show feminist touches in

their portrayal of Minoan Crete, such as Richard Purtill's 'Kaphtu' trilogy (1979, 1980, 1983); Les Cole's *The Sea Kings: The Prophecy* (1996); John Dempsey's *Ariadne's Brother: A Novel on the Fall of Crete* (1996); Philippe Bonifay's graphic novel *Messara* (1994–6), with illustrations by Jacques Terpant; Heidi Neale and Nick Manolukas's *The Coming of the New Millennium* (1998) (*non vidi*, but cited in Roessel 2006). Other relevant works by women authors include Suzanne Frank's *Shadows on the Aegean* (1998) (a mixture of Minoan archaeology and Plato) and Doris Orgel's *Ariadne, Awake!* (1994) (*non vidi*).

114 Hand ([1999] 2001: 107). Besides examples of the Minoans' sexual versatility and prowess discussed in previous chapters, in works of the last quarter of the twentieth century these features are also highlighted, for example in Dempsey's *Ariadne's Brother* and Les Cole's *The Sea Kings: The Prophecy*. In the former, the reader gets the impression that one of the best things about the Minoans is their attitude to sex, which they consider to be a religious experience, especially when both partners feel the presence of the divinity through orgasm – Minoan men do not stop sexual intercourse after ejaculation, and always wish to provide their female partners with a good climax: see, e.g., Dempsey (1996: 127 and 303). Cole's *The Sea Kings* is a kind of *Bildungsroman* about Tanuati of Amnisos, and has at least the merit of having a more original chronological setting than most novels about Minoan Crete, since it covers the period 1734–1729 BC, instead of revolving around the Theran eruption and fall of Knossos; see also Coles (1996: 384). The work reminds one of Waltari's *Sinuhe the Egyptian*, because it is a romp through various adventures, including many sexual ones, experienced by the protagonist during his travels in various Mediterranean regions, from Crete to the Levantine coast, Babylon, Egypt, Libya, mainland Greece, and the Cycladic islands. Cole describes the Minoans as a people mostly interested in sea commerce, the pleasures of the flesh, and the arts, who treat women as equals, not as objects; see, e.g., Cole (1996: 55 and 275). Although they are not as warlike as the Mycenaeans, Cole describes the Minoans as prepared to fight: they train for war to defend their commercial interests: Cole (1996: 67); and are prepared to die in battle to defend the Cretan ideal: 'free seas, free trade, Peace forever' – Cole (1996: 366).

115 Hand ([1999] 2001: 376).

116 See, e.g., Wolf (1984), i.e. *Cassandra: A Novel and Four Essays*. The original German title of the essay section, *Voraussetzungen einer Erzählung: Kassandra*, could also be translated as 'preconditions of a narrative'. The Minoans also make cameo appearances in Wolf's later book, *Medea: Stimmen* (1996), published in English as *Medea: A Modern Retelling* (1998). For example, one of the characters in this later novel is a Cretan woman called Arethusa, who had migrated to Corinth, together with a former bull-leaper, after Crete was struck by earthquakes and tsunamis caused by the Theran eruption: Wolf (1998: 117–18, 131). Arethusa is a 'gem cutter', whose 'head had the same profile as the jewels that she cut out of their stone', and 'wore a dress that emphasized her narrow waistline and left much of her breasts bare': Wolf (1998: 117).

117 Another example of the Minoanization of the Trojans in novels published in the last quarter of the twentieth century is *Daughter of Troy* (1998) by Sarah B. Franklin (pen name of D. J. Duncan), where one finds references to older matriarchal/matrilineal societies, and where many elements of material culture (such as ceremonial female dress, frescoes, an alabaster throne) are derived not only from Mycenaean Greece but also from Minoan Crete and Theran frescoes.

118 See Wolf (1984: 13), where Cassandra says, 'War gives people their shape. I do not
     want to remember them that way, as they were made and shattered by war ... [Priam]
     was the husband of the ideal queen; that gave him special privileges. I can still see
     him: night after night he used to go in to my often-pregnant mother, who sat in her
     megaron, in her wooden armchair, which closely resembled a throne ... I, Father's
     favorite and interested in politics like none of my numerous siblings, was allowed to
     sit with them and listen to what they were saying'; see also Wolf (1984:102–3, 108,
     and 126), discussing how the Trojans are becoming like Greeks because of war and
     the Greek's poor treatment of women.

119 Wolf (1984: 49). In addition, and although this is not an exclusively Minoan feature,
     the Trojans have scribes who use clay tablets for palace accounts, which are baked in
     the flames of Troy: see Wolf (1984: 32, 36, and esp. 78, where Cassandra remarks that
     'The scribes' tablets, baked in the flames of Troy, transmit the palace accounts, the
     records of grain, urns, weapons, prisoners. There are no signs of pain, happiness, love.
     That seems to be extreme misfortune').

120 Wolf (1984: 273 and 287).

121 Visit to Crete: see Wolf (1984: 182–205); visit to Argos and Mycenae, see Wolf (1984:
     214–19). Wolf did not visit Troy (as this would have required another visa from
     Turkey).

122 Wolf (1984: 193).

123 Wolf (1984: 193 and 197).

124 Wolf (1984: 195).

125 Wolf (1984: 194).

126 Wolf (1984: 197).

127 Wolf (1984: 203).

128 Wolf (1984: 205).

129 Wolf (1984: 197).

130 On Knossian cannibalism and Archanes-Anemospilia human sacrifice, described as
     the 'corpse in the cellar', see Wolf (1984: 199). On the debate about the Minoan
     palaces as kingly residences and/or ceremonial centres, see Wolf (1984: 195–6); on
     her disbelief regarding the alleged *Pax Minoica* and Minoan egalitarianism, see Wolf
     (1984: 200). Wolf also questions the idea that the lack of fortification can be
     interpreted as indicating that the Minoans 'were a peace-loving people' (1984: 202).

131 Wolf (1984: 200). See also Wolf (1984: 201): '... we stroll through the ruins of Knossos
     and Phaestos ... seeing what we *want* to see'.

132 On her acceptance of the idea of female divinity, see Wolf (1984: 200). She cites as her
     sources Engels, Bachofen, Robert Graves, and the Marxist classicist George Thomson
     (see also Chapter 5, discussion of Willetts), but must have been aware of Gimbutas if
     only through discussions with her acquaintances. See also Wolf (1984: 194–5, 238,
     242–3), where she repeats the idea that in remote antiquity the chief deity was female,
     an earth goddess, and refers to early matriarchal societies

133 Wolf (1984: 195).

134 Wolf (1984: 224). Cf. also Wolf's admission (1984: 212) that her 'grip on the distant,
     the primordial past is, I am aware, likewise a remedy against this indissoluble sadness.
     By now it has almost become a grip on the future again, the flight backwards takes
     the form of a flight forward.' The sadness she refers to is the disappointment created
     by the outcome of the Greek Civil War, communism, Stalinism, etc. The idea of a
     consciously (or unconsciously) idealized past as models also appears in her later
     novel, *Medea: A Modern Retelling*, where Medea tells of the Colchian legends 'where

just Queens and Kings ruled, where the people lived in harmony with one another, and where property was so evenly distributed that no one envied anyone else ... this ideal was so tangible to us Colchians that we measured our life by it': see Wolf (1998: 73).

135 Wolf (1984: 199).

136 Wolf (1984: 183).

137 Wolf (1984: 192). She even mentions a suggestion that Priam resembled a Minoan sovereign more than an Achaean one: Wolf (1984: 205).

138 Wolf (1984: 202).

139 Wolf (1984: 231).

140 On Wolf's musings on the close chronology of the fall of Knossos and Troy, see also, e.g., Wolf (1984: 183, 233, and esp. 247: 'Cassandra lived between two disasters: the volcanic eruption of Thera/Santorin circa 1500 BC and the invasion of the Dorians ... circa 1200 BC. In the interval, perhaps in the middle of the thirteenth century BC came her personal disaster: the fall of Troy'). On Minoan bards, see Wolf (1984: 233): 'Highly skilled bards schooled by Minoan culture and living in Ionia took up the themes of the Achaeans, which had been handed down in individual songs.'

141 Brindel, for example, explicitly refers to the notion that male bards do not tell stories of rape but sing about heroes, and also tell lies – see Brindel (1980: 240): '... our story, like all others, is being told by liars. This is why I must write this for you. So that you will know what really happened. So that you will listen for Her [the Goddess's] voice.' Cf. also Brindel (1985: 88, 104, 223).

142 See, e.g., Hand's own preface and 'commentary' to her novel, which list as facts many debatable points (beside the matriarchy/patriarchy issue), such as the absence of warfare, violence, and slavery ([1999] 2001: i–v and 376–80).

143 In addition to the works by DeLillo, Jones, Porter, Beaton, and Padel discussed in this section, and in connection with the themes of memory and the exploration of the self, I should like to thank the late John Stallworthy for bringing to my attention his poem 'The thread' (Stallworthy (1998: 235–6)), first published in the *Poetry Nation Review* for March–April 1995, https://www.pnreview.co.uk/cgi-bin/scribe?item_id=1940, where one finds the following verses on Knossos: 'It was all coming back. Perhaps not all, / but rooms behind closed doors came back to me, / a corridor, curtains, a gallery, / and the staircase down to the hall- / the hall now filled with píthoi wall to wall, / those man-sized storage jars you see / in the palace of Knossos. Should / I go on? The thread did. Seeing it run / ahead of me, over the flagstones, / under the bolted door, suddenly I could / hear what the swarm was saying, understood / what had been done to me, what I had done.'

144 DeLillo (1982: 84).

145 DeLillo (1982: 85).

146 DeLillo (1982: 85).

147 DeLillo (1982: 116).

148 DeLillo (1982: 133). On the growing appreciation of objects, their agency, materiality, entanglements with humans, etc. (the 'material turn' and 'material-culture turn'), see, e.g., Latour (2005), Miller (2005), Ingold (2007), Bennett and Joyce (2010), Hicks (2010); Hodder (2012). On the 'sensory turn', see, e.g., Howes (2006, 2013, 2018) and, in a Minoan context, Hamilakis (2013).

149 DeLillo and his wife lived in Greece during the late 1970s–early 1980s, and the story was inspired by the earthquakes they experienced there (pers. comm., letter of 11 March 2015).

150 By the time this story was written, current views on the male gender of bull-leapers in Minoan iconography had not yet reached the wider public. On recent interpretations of the Toreador fresco as representing only male figures, see Chapter 1, n. 25.

151 DeLillo ([1988] 2011: 66–7).

152 In a personal communication, DeLillo commented further on Kyle's feelings of 'strangeness and distance . . . nothing but indelible mystery' for the object (letter of 11 March 2015).

153 DeLillo (pers. comm.: letter of 11 March 2015).

154 On the idea of the modern Minoan replica as a 'relic', see transcript of 'Don DeLillo in conversation with Jonathan Franzen' (broadcast on 24 October 2012), available at https://www.nypl.org/audiovideo/angel-esmeralda-don-delillo-conversation-jonathan-franzen.

155 DeLillo ([1988] 2011: 72).

156 Crawford (1983: 47). Indeed, Jones openly acknowledges the influence of papers such as those published by Bintliff (1984) and Crawford (1983), among others.

157 Jones (1991: 27 and 70, describing Charles's struggle with his project of 'The Golden Age', which falls apart; 120–1, describing how, instead of teaching about Minoan Crete, he takes a critical approach to historiography, structuralism, and the deconstruction of Evans's romantic image).

158 Jones (1991: 9).

159 Jones (1991: 10).

160 Jones (1991: 13).

161 Jones (1991: 55).

162 Jones (1991: 32).

163 Jones (1991: 54–5).

164 Jones (1991: 62).

165 Jones (1991: 62).

166 Jones (1991: 58).

167 Porter (1996: ix). The book is divided into six sections: 'Crete'; 'This Weird Solidarity'; 'Missolonghi'; 'Bone-burning Tunes'; 'Cigarettes'; and 'Summer 92'. The first contains the forty-one poems inspired by the island and provides the title for the whole collection. The connections with Crete in the other sections are difficult to detect, except for the second one: 'This Weird Solidarity' presents poems on Osip Mandelstam, Anna Akhmatova, and Marina Tsvetayeva, and Porter used some verses from a poem on Minoan Crete by Mandelstam (cf. Chapter 4, n. 164) as the epigraph for the Cretan section in her 1996 volume (Porter (1996: 1)). On Porter and her Minoan poems, see also Morris (2020).

168 Cf. Porter (1996: 11, 'Gorgeous Breasts', and 26, 'Bull-leaping').

169 Porter (1996: 28).

170 Porter (1996: 6).

171 McCredden (2014: 273).

172 Porter (1996: 25).

173 Porter (1996: 21, 'Exuberance with bloody hands').

174 Porter (1996: 41, 'The laws of volcanoes', and 44, 'The Power and the Glory').

175 Porter (1996: 48, 'The beautiful friend', and 37, 'Blue Monkey flying through an orchard').

176 Porter (1996: 23, 'Atlantis', where Lithuanian pogroms are mentioned in the epigraph); for comparison with Nazis, see Porter (1996: 43, 'Triumph of the Will').

177 Beaton (1995: 130–2).

178 Beaton (1995: 303). Cf. also Beaton (1995: 169, for palaces as residences of peaceful priest kings; 170–1, for palaces as residence of exploitative decadent rulers; 235, for strange ceremonies involving the mixing of 'prodigious quantities of wine and blood').

179 Beaton (1995: 264).

180 Beaton (1995: 260). Cf. the volume's epigraph, taken from Thomas Mann's *The Magic Mountain*, which alludes to the idea that behinds civilization there is also a blood sacrifice.

181 Beaton (1995: 44).

182 Freud (1953–74, vol. 2: 139), also cited in Gere (2002), where one can find a more detailed discussion of Freud's use of archaeological metaphors.

183 https://www.ruthpadel.com/about/greece-and-crete/. Padel was also the first woman elected Oxford's Professor of Poetry, but resigned less than a fortnight after the vote, following allegations of her involvement in a smear campaign against her main rival, Derek Walcott: see, e.g., https://www.theguardian.com/books/2009/may/25/ruth-padel-resigns-oxford-poetry-professor.

184 Padel (1990: 53).

185 Padel (1990: 62–3).

186 Padel (1990: 78).

187 Padel (1990: 12).

188 Padel (1990: 64–5).

189 https://www.ruthpadel.com/article/summer-snow/.

190 Batsaki (2013: 225); on Galanaki's postmodern stance, see also Katsan (2013: 130–55), Beaton (2017).

191 *The Century of Labyrinths* tells the semi-fictional story of two families: that of Minos Kalokerinos and Christos Papaoulakis, the schoolteacher who helped the former on his excavations at Knossos. The century of the title starts in 1878, with Kalokairinos's dig (cf. Chapter 3), and ends in 1978, with the visit to the sanctuary at Kato Symi Viannou by a descendent of Papaoulakis and his niece, who is an archaeologist called Ariadne. 'Growing up next door to Knossos and "The other Ariadne"' is a brief autobiographical piece that portrays Knossos as both a *milieu* and *lieu de mémoire* (Momigliano (2019: 632)), and provides a retelling of the myth of Theseus, the Minotaur, and Ariadne, from Ariadne's perspective. For Minoan elements in Galanaki's work, see Beaton (2006 and 2017), Kopaka (2017).

192 Galanaki (1996: 15).

193 Beaton (2017: 175). Beaton (2006: 190) has also highlighted the playful modernist stance of another Cretan author, Dimitris Kalokyris, in his book *Lexilogio*, where he asks the Phaistos 'hard disk' to be re-examined as a 'database': Kalokyris (1997: 169). As Beaton (2006: 190) has remarked, 'No less postmodern than the deliberate flippancy of this remark is its implicit nod towards popular culture and contemporary technology: already, during the 1990s, the same image had been adopted as its logo by the Crete-based IT company Forthnet.'

194 Beaton (2006: 194).

195 http://www.eikastikon.gr/zografiki/panagiotakis_cv.html. Dozens of Panagiotakis's paintings can be seen on his Facebook page, https://www.facebook.com/roussetos.panagiotakis; he has also illustrated the 2014 novel for children *Travels in Time: Minoan Crete* by Mary Black (pen name of Maria Mavrogiannaki). Two of his illustrations also appear on the dust jacket of Hamilakis and Momigliano (2006).

196 On Panagiotakis's use of Minoan elements since the mid-1950s, see pers. comm. (Facebook/Messenger, 15 December 2018).

197 Panagiotakis (pers. comm).

198 In the context of Cretan–Hellenic identities, one should also mention the establishment of the maritime transportation company Minoan Lines, founded in 1972, which uses as its logo the Knossian Prince of Lilies; the first ferry, appropriately named *Minos*, was deployed on the Heraklion–Piraeus route in the summer of 1971, and the first international line (between Greece and Italy) started in 1981; some of the ferries deployed in the 1980s and 1990s are also named after mythological characters, such as Ariadne, Phaedra, Ikarus, Pasiphae, and Daedalus: see https://www.minoan.gr/en/page/4510/history. As expressions of more specific Cretan identity in the period examined in this Chapter, one may include, for example, the painting by A. Markakis, *Representation of the Minoan Villa of Hagia Triada 3667 years ago* and Neo-Minoan architecture, such as the private houses decorated with Minoan columns, horns of consecrations, and double-axes in the village of Petrokephali (Messara) and Heraklion: see Hamilakis (2006: 154, figs. 9.5–9.6), Solomon (2006: 169, fig 10.6).

199 Craxton settled in Chania in the 1960s, but left Greece during the dictatorship, returning only in 1977: see http://www.fitzmuseum.cam.ac.uk/gallery/craxton/; see also Chapter 4, n. 178.

200 Opus no. 65: see Kane (1996) and also http://ptamd.org/artists-dances/taylor-repertoire-alphabetically/ and https://www.nytimes.com/2016/03/19/arts/dance/review-a-program-of-premieres-by-paul-taylors-american-modern-dance.html.

201 Boucher and Krapf (2014: 196–9).

202 La Rosa and Militello (2006: 251) give a 2002 date for this, but other sources suggest it was first published in 1988: see https://inducks.org/s.php?c=I%20TL%201720-A; https://comicvine.gamespot.com/topolino-1720-topolino-e-il-disco-di-festos/4000-184785/ and http://disney.fumetto-online.it/index.php?txtdis=scala%20guido&collana=classici%20walt%20disney%202serie&langCode=fr&COLLANA=TOPOMISTERY&vall=1.

203 Uderzo (1996). See also https://www.asterix.com/ and Boucher and Krapf (2014: 195, fig. 56).

204 Minoan elements also appear in the award-winning graphic novel series *Age of Bronze* by Eric Shanower, which started in 1998. In these works one can see, for example, that Helen's physiognomy is partly based on an Archaic Greek statue (the so-called Peplos Kore), while her dress is inspired by that worn by female figures in Mycenaean frescoes, which in turn derived from earlier Minoan prototypes: http://age-of-bronze.com/. On Shanower's use of the peplos kore, see also Momigliano (2013: 44 and n. 34). Note that since 2018, all the *Age of Bronze* volumes have been reissued in full colour.

205 Laura and Lo Duca (1989) (*non vidi*), but see https://en.todocoleccion.net/comics-cupula/el-toro-blanco-laura-lo-duca~x113567747; https://www.tebeosfera.com/publicaciones/toro_blanco_el_1989_la_cupula.html; and https://losmejorescomics.com/el-toro-blanco/.

206 See asterias.gr and https://asterias.gr/work/coca-cola-seasonal-lebs-greece/.

207 Morris (2020).

208 https://stargate.fandom.com/wiki/The_Broca_Divide. In the *SG-1* series (season 1), there are also references to Linear A in the 'Brief Candle' episode: see https://www.gateworld.net/sg1/s1/brief-candle/transcript/; see also Bourke (2014).

Chapter 7

1   Hawkes (1967: 174). Cf. de Maistre (1853: 264, letter of 27 August 1811): 'Toute nation a le gouvernement qu'elle mérite.'

2   One exception discussed in this volume is Cheney's *Son of Minos* (cf. Chapter 4).

3   On the persistence of the idea of female bull-leapers, see, e.g., information provided by the popular National Geographic: https://www.nationalgeographic.org/media/bull-leaping/. Even explanatory materials available in museums are silent on the issue: see, e.g., https://www.penn.museum/sites/expedition/bulls-and-bull-leaping-in-the-minoan-world/. For the idea that bull-leapers in the Toreador fresco are all male, see Chapter 1, with n. 25.

4   On terms such as post-postmodern, post-humanist, and meta-humanist, see Ferrando (2013).

5   For the pageant at the opening ceremony of the 2004 Athens Olympics, and performances of Minoan-inspired dances and Minoan culinary events, see below.

6   Cf. note 18 below.

7   For example, the work *Pulsar*, by the Armenian artist Albert Vardanyan: see Momigliano (2017b: fig. I.2).

8   Such as *A Restoration* (2016), by the acclaimed artist Elisabeth Price, which was on show at the Ashmolean Museum: https://www.ashmolean.org/event/elizabeth-price-restoration.

9   Such as the spring–summer 2017 collection by Mary Katranzou: see https://www.marykatrantzou.com/collections/spring-summer-2017/; on Katrantzou's collection, see also Morris (2020). For other fashion and jewellery, see also below, discussion of 'Contemporary Minoans'.

10 See, e.g., 'The role of women in the art of ancient Greece': https://www.rwaag.org/, and especially the page on dress: http://www.rwaag.org/skirt; see also the comments on 'Ancient Minoan Culture Illustrated with Barbies' at http://www.weirduniverse.net/blog/comments/ancient_minoan_culture_illustrated_with_barbies/.

11 Calcutt (2000a).

12 Books: see, e.g., Manfredi and Manfredi (2014); play scripts: see, e.g., Calcutt (2000b and 2002).

13 For example, Pierret and Denoël (2005).

14 Such as the group Modern Minoan Paganism founded by Laura Perry in 2014 (cf. Chapter 6 and below).

15 Such as Wolfang Petersen's film *Troy* (2004) and the BBC/Netflix series *Troy: Fall of a City* (2018): https://www.bbc.co.uk/programmes/b09szdtr. The latter, in particular, used Minoan columns, frescoes, and objects very liberally throughout its episodes, and once again associates Minoans and Trojans. For Minoan elements in Petersen's film, see Winkler (2007a: 206; 2007b: plates 12–14; 2015b: 19), Cavallini (2015: 68 and 73), Petersen (2015: 29).

16 Some incomplete lists of novels related to Minoan Crete available on the Internet show dozens of books published after 1999: see, e.g., https://www.goodreads.com/list/show/93110.Crete_Minoans_Fiction and https://en.wikipedia.org/wiki/Fiction_set_in_ancient_Greece. See also the list posted by Laura Perry on the Ariadne's Tribe Facebook Group: https://www.facebook.com/notes/ariadnes-tribe-modern-minoan-paganism/minoan-themed-historical-fiction-and-related-works/1680461362166573/. Bourke (2014) discusses Laura Reeve's 'Major Ariadne Kedros' science-fiction novels, where the Minoans appear as an alien race. The aforementioned lists tend to be biased

in favour of books in English (or in English translation). A few examples of books in other languages (published after 1999) include Ivano Mingotti's *Minoica* (2016); Sabine Wassermann's *Die Stiertänzerin: Historischer Roman* (2018); and Jacque Lafarge's *Le testament d'Issasara: Une épopée au temps des Minoens* (2018). Some allusions to Minoan material culture also appear in Victor Pelevin's intriguing retelling of the myth of the Minotaur in his *The Helmet of Horrors* (2006), originally written in Russian, which portrays the labyrinth as an Internet chat-room.

17 Other examples of twenty-first-century novels that show little, if any, influence of Greek mythology include Jay Starre's erotic novel *Lusty Adventures of the Prince of Knossos* (2009) (*non vidi*); Alison Fell's *The Element -inth in Greek* (2012), which focuses on the relatively neglected figure of Alice Kober, who contributed to the decipherment of Linear B; Gavin Scott's trilogy *Age of Treachery* (2016), *Age of Olympus* (2017), and *Age of Exodus* (2018), which is inspired by the history of Minoan archaeological research and features a fictional Oxford don, Duncan Forrester, who gets tantalizingly close, but never quite manages to decipher an important Minoan inscription; and the 'Gods and Warriors' quintet of children's novels by Michelle Paver (2012–16).

18 See the Minoan Amusement Park at the Out of the Blue Capsis Elite Resort in Aghia Pelagia, built in 2010 (Marianthi Panteri, pers. comm., email of 18 April 2019), where children can play the 'Archaeologist Game' in a labyrinth full of Minoan features, and the winner reaches Ariadne's clew, while the loser falls into the Minotaur's trap: see https://capsis.com/en/children-activities.html. See also the Labyrinth Park, a family entertainment destination that was designed by Adrian Fisher and built by the Giakoumakis firm, located near Hersonnisos on the road to Lasithi, and opened to the public in 2013 (pers. comm. from info@labyrinthpark.gr, email of 17 April 2019). In this amusement park, Minoan elements are mixed indiscriminately with later Greek myths, including the Trojan War: children and adults can venture into the labyrinth, escape from Atlantis, and play with a laser maze inside a huge Trojan Horse; see http://www.labyrinthpark.gr/en/home. For other examples of Minoan elements in other theme park attractions, see Carlà-Uhink and Freitag (2018).

19 Williamson (2018: 7, 'Swimming with the Bull', and 14–15, 'The Minotaur Speaks'). For many other contemporary modern poems inspired by Minoan Crete, see, e.g., the poetry website and community Poetry Soup at https://www.poetrysoup.com/poems/minoan.

20 Images of this opera are available at http://www.shomler.com/osj/idomeneo/ and http://news.harker.org/opera-san-jose-opens-harker-concert-series-season-on-a-spectacular-note/.

21 Samuel (2008: 215). See also Samuel's essay 'The Music of the Minotaur', in the programme of *The Minotaur* available at the performance, and http://www.boosey.com/cr/news/Birtwistle-interview-explores-new-opera-The-Minotaur/11545&LangID=1.

22 Harsent (2008: 49–53).

23 Birtwistle, pers. comm. (interview of 23 November 2015). In addition to the snake priestess, several references to Minoan Crete appear in the programme of *The Minotaur* available at the performance, namely in the essays 'Around the Minotaur' by Ruth Padel and 'Of Bulls and Minotaurs' by John Lord, which are accompanied by illustrations of famous Knossian artefacts such as the Charging Bull and Toreador frescoes, the 'snake votary', and the Bull's head rhyton in steatite from the Little Palace, together with relevant images of works by Antonio Canova, Nicholas Poussin, Peter

Paul Rubens, and Michael Ayrton. Padel's essay is also available at https://www.ruthpadel.com/article/around-the-minotaur/.

24 See Mulvey (1989). Berger (1972) still provides useful insights on ways of looking at females in art.

25 Many versions of the Athens Olympics opening ceremony are available on YouTube. For a commentary on the Minoan themes, see Simandiraki (2005).

26 Morris (2009: 243).

27 Momigliano (2017b: 6).

28 On the 'Contemporary Minoans' exhibition and conference, see, e.g., http://www.brandingheritage.org/images/events/BH_Contemporary_Minoans_Crete_2018.pdf; http://www.brandingheritage.org/el/news-el/250-minoikos-politismos-apotelesmata-draseon-kriti-maios-2018; and http://www.bbc.com/culture/event/20180501-contemporary-minoans. Brands represented in the exhibition included Sophia Kokosalaki, Mary Katrantzou, Ancient Greek Sandals, Spyridon Tsagarakis, Zeus+Dione, Polina Sapouna-Ellis, Croquis by Qupa, Faye Chatzi, Philomela, Klotho, Xenia Nefelly, Vlachou-Marmarometry, Voula Karampatzaki, Anna Kitsou Ceramic Jewellery, and Anaktae.

29 Presentations by archaeologists, politicians, and artists who took part in the 'Contemporary Minoans' events are available at https://www.youtube.com/playlist?list=PLWZEON72L_1Qj_IgqNd90TkcNrkMZfZ15.

30 Tracks of Giant Squid's *Minoan* album are available at https://giantsquid.bandcamp.com/album/minoans; for the lyrics, see http://www.darklyrics.com/lyrics/giantsquid/minoans.html.

31 Interview with Gregory, 21 October 2010, in the journal *Burning Ambulance* available at https://burningambulance.com/2014/10/21/premiere-giant-squid/; cf. also Gregory (pers. comm., email of 7 December 2015).

32 Interview with Gregory, 21 October 2010 (see n. 31, above).

33 Not all is doom and gloom in Giant Squid's *Minoan* album, since it includes a cheeky take on Sir Arthur Evans and his reconstructions, as illustrated in the song named after this British archaeologist, where he appears as a driven, determined, rich man, who is prepared to 'buy the whole bloody island' to fulfil his dreams, finds the ruins 'too old', and so 'will make some new ones' (https://giantsquid.bandcamp.com/track/sir-arthur-evans).

34 Perry (2013 and 2016). See also the Facebook group, https://www.facebook.com/groups/1502335483312496/.

35 https://www.minoantastes.com/. Morrison is an archaeologist who has written her doctoral dissertation on Minoan cooking vessels, has a considerable fieldwork experience on Crete, and is also a potter.

36 See https://www.minoantheater.gr/about-us/ and https://greece.greekreporter.com/2019/07/17/cretes-minoan-theater-a-reinvestment-in-excellence-and-spirit/.

37 See https://www.minoantheater.gr/about-us/. Minoan Theater also offers another example of the interweaving of Minoan material culture and Greek mythology, because one of its dances refers to the myth of Theseus and Ariadne.

38 See https://www.minoantheater.gr/about-us/.

39 On the restorations of the Temple Repositories snake goddess figurines, see also Bonney (2011).

40 Sweetman (1993: 303).

41 Pers. comm.

Bibliography

Abadía, O. M. (2009), 'The History of Archaeology as Seen Through the Externalism-Internalism Debate: Historical Development and Current Challenges', *Bulletin of the History of Archaeology* 19, no. 2: 13–26.

Aburrow, Y. (2018), *The Night Journey: Witchcraft as Transformation*, Morrisville, NC: Lulu Press.

Ackroyd, P. (2006), *The Fall of Troy*, London: Chatto and Windus.

Adams, E. (2017), *Cultural Identity in Minoan Crete: Social Dynamics in the Neopalatial Period*, Cambridge: Cambridge University Press.

Adler, Eric (2008), 'Late Victorian and Edwardian Views of Rome and the Nature of "Defensive Imperialism"', in *International Journal of the Classical Tradition*, Vol. 15, no. 2, 187–216.

Ak, S. A. (2004), *Fotoğraf ve Karpostallarıyla. Girit'ten Istanbul'a Bahaettin Rahmi Bediz. Beyaz atlı fotoğrafçı 1875-1951*, Istanbul: Iletişim yayınları.

Alberti, B. (2002), 'Gender and the Figurative Art of Late Bronze Age Knossos', in Y. Hamilakis (ed.), *Labyrinth Revisited: Rethinking 'Minoan' Archaeology*, 98–117, Oxford: Oxbow Books.

Alcock, S. E. (2002), 'Cretan inventions', in S. E. Alcock (ed.), *Archaeologies of the Greek Past: Landscape, Monuments, and Memories*, 99–131, Cambridge: Cambridge University Press.

Alcock, S. E. and J. F. Cherry (2006), '"No Greater Marvel": a Bronze Age Classic at Orchomenos', in J. I. Porter (ed.), *Classical Pasts: The Classical Traditions of Greece and Rome*, 69–87, Princeton, NJ: Princeton University Press.

Alexandri, A. (2009), 'Envisioning Gender in Aegean Prehistory', in K. Kopaka (ed.), *Fylo: Engendering Prehistoric 'Stratigraphies' in the Aegean and the Mediterranean. Proceedings of an International Conference, University of Crete, Rethymno 2-5 June 2005*, 19–24, Liège and Austin: Université de Liège Histoire de l'art et archéologie de la Grèce antique and University of Texas at Austin Program in Aegean Scripts and Prehistory.

Alexiou, S. (1964), *Μινωικός πολιτισμός*, Heraklion: Spyros Alexiou Sons.

Alexiou, S. (1969), *Minoan Civilization*, Heraklion: Spyros Alexiou Sons.

Alexiou, S. (1979), 'Τείχη και Ακροπόλεις στη Μινωική Κρήτη (Ο μύθος της μινωικής ειρήνης)', *Κρητλογία* 8: 41–56.

Allsebrook, M. ([1992] 2002), *Born to Rebel: The Life of Harriet Boyd Hawes*, Oxford: Oxbow Books.

Alsop, J. ([1962] 1965), *From the Silent Earth*, London: Secker and Warburg.

Alušík, T. (2004), 'Minoan–Mycenaean Elements in the Work of Josip Plečnik at the Prague Castle', *Studia Hercynia* 8: 59–66.

Anderson, P. (1971), *The Dancer From Atlantis*, New York: Doubleday.

Anonymous (1932), 'Minoan Culture', *Man* 32 (September): 213–14.

Antoninus (1992), *The Metamorphoses of Antoninus Liberalis*, trans F. Celoria, London: Routledge.

Armstrong, R. (2006), *Cretan Women: Pasiphae, Ariadne, and Phaedra in Latin Poetry*, Oxford: Oxford University Press.

Aslan, C. C. and C. B. Rose (2013), 'City and Citadel at Troy from the Late Bronze Age through the Roman Period', in S. Redford and N. Ergin (eds.), *Cities and Citadels in Turkey: From the Iron Age to the Seljuks*, 7–38, Leuven: Peeters.

Ayrton, E. (1963), *The Cretan*, London: Hodder and Stoughton.

Ayrton, M. (1962), *The Testament of Daedalus*, London: Methuen.

Ayrton, M. (1970), *The Minotaur*, London: Genevieve Restaurants.

Ayrton, M. (1971), 'The Making of a Maze', in M. Ayrton, *The Rudiments of Paradise: Various Essays on Various Arts*, 293–305, London: Secker and Warburg.

Ayrton, M. (1977), *The Graphics of Michael Ayrton*, Somerset, UK: Bruton Press.

Ayrton, M. ([1967] 2015), *The Maze Maker*, Chicago: University of Chicago Press.

Bacchelli, R. (1965), *Viaggi all'Estero e Vagabondaggi di Fantasia*, Milan: Mondadori.

Bachofen, J. J. (1861), *Das Mutterrecht*, Stuttgart: Verlag Von Krais and Hoffmann.

Baikie, J. (1910), *The Sea Kings of Crete*, London: A. and C. Black.

Baird, S. W. (2007), *The Minoan Psychopath*, Osprey, FL: Sheppard Baird Publishing.

Bakst, L. and R. Johnson (1990), 'Bakst on Classicism: "The Paths of Classicism in Art"', *Dance Chronicle* 13, no. 2: 170–92.

Bammer, A. (1990), 'Wien und Kreta: Jugendstil und minoische Kunst', *Jahreshefte des Österreichischen Archäologischen Instituts in Wien* 60: 129–51.

Bandinelli, R. B. (1976), *Introduzione All'archeologia Classica Come Storia Dell'arte Anctica*, Rome and Bari: Laterza.

Bandini, G. (2003), *Lettere dall'Egeo. Archeologhe italiane tra 1900 e 1950*, Firenze: Giunti.

Bannerman, H. (2010), 'Ancient Myths and Modern Moves: The Greek-inspired Dance Theatre of Martha Graham', in F. Macintosh (ed.), *The Ancient Dancer in the Modern World: Responses to Greek and Roman Dance*, 255–76, Oxford: Oxford University Press.

Barber, R. (2008), 'Giorgio De Chirico and Greek Prehistory', in C. Gallou, M. Georgiadis, and G. M. Muskett (eds.), *Dioskouroi Studies Presented to W.G. Cavanagh and C.B. Mee on the Anniversary of their 30-year Joint Contribution to Aegean Archaeology*, 137–43, BAR International Series S1889, Oxford: Archaeopress.

Barrett, W. S. (ed.) (1964), *Euripides: Hippolytos*, Oxford: Clarendon Press.

Barthélemy, J. J. (1788), *Voyage du jeune Anacharsis en Grèce*, Paris: Par.

Basch, S. (2016), 'Proust à Cnossos ou le cosmopolitisme archéologique. Échos de la Grèce archaïque et reflets de la crétomanie Art nouveau dans "À la recherche du temps perdu"', in A. Compagnon and N. Mauriac Dyer (eds.), *Du côté de chez Swann ou le cosmopolitisme d'un roman français*, 103–30, Paris: Honoré Champion.

Basch, S. and A. Farnoux (eds.) (2006), *Le Voyage en Grèce 1934–1939. Du périodique de tourisme à la revue artistique. Actes du colloque international organisé à l'École française d'Athènes et à la Fondation Vassilis et Eliza Goulandris à Andros (23–26 Septembre 2004)*, Athens: École française d'Athènes.

Basedow, M. (2007), 'Troy without Homer: The Bronze Age–Iron Age Transition in the Troad', in S. P. Morris and R. Laffineur (eds.), *Epos: Reconsidering Greek Epic and Aegean Bronze Age Archaeology. Proceedings of the 11th International Aegean Conference / 11e Rencontre égéenne internationale, Los Angeles, UCLA – The J. Paul Getty Villa, 20–23 April 2006*, 49–58, Liège and Austin: Université de Liège Histoire de l'art et archéologie de la Grèce antique and University of Texas at Austin Program in Aegean Scripts and Prehistory.

Batsaki, Y. (2013), 'In "Third Space" Between Crete and Egypt in Rhea Galanaki's *The Life of Ismail Ferik Pasha*', in B. Sahar, Y. Batsaki, and D. Angelov (eds.), *Imperial Geographies in Byzantine and Ottoman Space*, 225–43, Hellenic Studies Series 56, Washington, DC: Center for Hellenic Studies.

Bietak, M., N. Marinatos, and C. Palivou (2007), *Taureador Scenes in Tell el-Dab'a (Avaris) and Knossos*, Vienna: Verlag der Österreichischen Akademie der Wissenschaften.

Beaton, R. (1995), *Ariadne's Children*, London: Weidenfeld and Nicolson.

Beaton, R. (2006), 'Minoans in Modern Greek literature', in Y. Hamilakis and N. Momigliano (eds.), *Archaeology and European Modernity: Producing and Consuming the 'Minoans'*, 183–95, Padova: Bottega d'Erasmo (Ausilio).

Beaton, R. (2008), 'Kazantzakis the Cretan: Versions of the Minoan Past from the Author of *Zorba the Greek*', *Kampos: Cambridge Studies in Modern Greek* 16: 1–23.

Beaton, R. (2009), 'Epilogue', in M. Llewellyn-Smith, P. M. Kitromilides, and E. Calligas (eds.), *Scholars, Travels, Archives: Greek History and Culture through the British School at Athens: Proceedings of a Conference Held at the National Hellenic Research Foundation, Athens, 6–7 October 2006*, 217–21, London: British School at Athens.

Beaton, R. (2017), 'Minoans and the Postmodern Critique of National History: Two Novels by Rhea Galanaki', in N. Momigliano and A. Farnoux (eds.), *Cretomania: Modern Desires for the Minoan Past*, 173–9, London and New York: Routledge.

Beckman, G. M., T. R. Bryce, and E. H. Cline (eds.) (2011), *The Ahhiyawa Texts*. Atlanta, GA: Society of Biblical Literature.

Bedford, C. H. (1975), *The Seeker: D.S. Merezhkovskiy*, Laurence: University of Kansas Press.

Beekes, R. (2010), *Etymological Dictionary of Greek*, Boston and Leiden: Brill.

Beevor, A. (2005), *Crete: The Battle and Resistance*, London: Murray.

Bennet, J. (1997), 'Homer and the Bronze Age: Framing the question', in I. Morris and B. Powell (eds.), *A New Companion to Homer*, 511–33, Leiden: Brill.

Bennet, J. (2000), 'Linear B and Linear A', in D. Huxley (ed.), *Cretan Quests: British Explorers, Excavators and Historians*, 129–37, London: British School at Athens.

Bennet, J. (2016), 'The Work of the British School at Athens 2015–2016', *Archaeological Reports* 62: 7–22.

Bennett, T. and P. Joyce (eds.) (2010), *Material Powers: Cultural Studies, History and the Material Turn*, London: Routledge.

Berger, J. (1972), *Ways of Seeing*, London: Penguin.

Berlin, I. (1953), *The Hedgehog and the Fox: An Essay on Tolstoy's View of History*, London: Weidenfeld and Nicolson.

Bernal, M. (1987), *Black Athena*, New Brunswick, NJ: Rutgers University Press.

Berry, E. (1933), *The Winged Girl of Knossos*, New York and London: D. Appelton.

Beschi, L. (1984), 'La Cultura Antiquaria Italiana a Crete: Premesse di un Impegno Scientifico', in Scuola Archeologica Italiana di Atene, *Creta Antica: Cento Anni di Archeologia Italiana*, 19–25, Rome: De Luca.

Betts, R. F. (1971), 'The Allusions to Rome in British Imperialist Thought of the Late Nineteenth and Early Twentieth Century', *Victorian Studies* 15, no. 2: 149–59.

Biesantz, H. (1964), 'Die kretisch-mykenische Kunst', in H. Biedermann, H. Biesantz, and J. Wiesner (eds.), *Das Europäische Megalithikum*, 369–90, Ullstein Kunstgeschichte 4, Frankfurt and Berlin: Ullstein.

Bietak, M. (2000), 'Rich beyond the Dreams of Avaris: Tell el-Dab'a and the Aegean world – A Guide for the Perplexed. A response to Eric H. Cline', *Annual of the British School at Athens* 95: 185–205.

Bietak, M. (2013), 'The Impact of Minoan Art on Egypt and the Levant: A Glimpse of Palatial Art from the Naval Base of Peru-nefer at Avaris', in J. Aruz, S. Graff, and

Y. Rakic (eds.), *Cultures in Contact: From Mesopotamia to the Mediterranean in the Second Millennium B.C.*, 188–99, New York and New Haven, CT: Metropolitan Museum of Art and Yale University Press.

Bietak, M., N. Marinatos, and C. Palivou (2007), *Taureador Scenes in Tell el-Dab'a (Avaris) and Knossos*, Österreichische Akademie der Wissenschaften Denkschriften der Gesamtakademie 43, Untersuchungen der Zweigstelle Kairo des Österreichischen Archäologischen Institutes 27, Vienna: Verlag der Österreichischen Akademie der Wissenschaften.

Bintliff, J. (1984), 'Structuralism and Myth in Minoan Studies', *Antiquity* 58, no. 222: 33–8.

Birksted, J. (2004), *Modernism and the Mediterranean: The Maeght Foundation*, Aldershot: Ashgate.

Black, M. (2014), *Travels in Time: Minoan Crete*, Astoria, NY: Seaburn Books.

Blakolmer, F. (2006), 'The Arts of Bronze Age Crete and the European Modern Style: Reflecting and Shaping Different Identities', in Y. Hamilakis and N. Momigliano (eds.), *Archaeology and European Modernity: Producing and Consuming the 'Minoans'*, 219–40, Padova: Bottega d'Erasmo (Ausilio).

Blakolmer, F. (2010), 'Images and Perceptions of the Lion Gate Relief at Mycenae During the 19th century', in F. Buscemi (ed.), *Cogitata Tradere Posteris. Figurazione dell'architettura antica nell'Ottocento*, 49–66, Rome: Bonanno.

Blakolmer, F. (2017), 'The Artistic Reception of Minoan Crete in the Period of Art Déco: The Reconstruction of the Palace at Knossos … and Why Arthur Evans was Right', in N. Momigliano and A. Farnoux (eds.), *Cretomania: Modern Desires for theMinoan Past*, 39–69, London and New York: Routledge.

Blegen, C. W. (1921), *Korakou: A Prehistoric Settlement near Corinth*, Boston and New York: American School of Classical Studies at Athens.

Blegen, C. W. (1941), 'Preclassical Greece', in *University of Pennsylvania Bicentennial Conference, Studies in the Arts and Architecture*, 1–14, Philadelphia: University of Pennsylvania Press.

Blegen, C. W. (1958), 'A Chronological Problem', in E. Grumach (ed.), *Minoica. Festschrift zum 80. Geburtstag von Johannes Sundwall. Deutsche Akademie der Wissenschaften zu Berlin. Schriften der Sektion für Altertumswissenschaften, 12*, 61–6, Berlin: Akademie Verlag.

Bloedow, E. F. (1999), 'Heinrich Schliemann and Relative Chronology: The Earliest Phases', *L'antiquité Classique* 68, no. 1: 315–25.

Blouet, A., A. Ravoisié, A. Poirot, F. Trézel, and F. Gournay (1831–8), *Expédition scientifique de Morée, ordonnée par le gouvernement français. Architecture, sculptures, inscriptions et vues du Péloponèse, des Cyclades et de l'Attique, mesurées, dessinées, recueillies et publiées*, Paris: Firmin Didot.

Boardman, J. (1962), 'The Knossos Tablets: Again', *Antiquity* 36, no. 141: 49–51.

Boardman, J. (2002), *The Archaeology of Nostalgia: How the Greeks Re-created their Mythical Past*, London: Thames and Hudson.

Bonifay, P. (1994–6), *Messara*, Paris: Dargaud.

Bonney, E. M. (2011), 'Disarming the Snake Goddess: A Reconsideration of the Faience Figurines from the Temple Repositories at Knossos', *Journal of Mediterranean Archaeology* 24, no. 2: 171–90.

Borges, J. L. (2000), *Labyrinths*, London: Penguin.

Borges, J. L. and M. Kodama (1986), *Atlas*, Barcelona: Edhasa.

Borgna, E., I. Caloi, F. M. Carinci, and R. Laffineur (eds.) (2019), *MNHMH / MNEME: Past and Memory in the Aegean Bronze Age, Proceedings of the 17th International*

Aegean Conference, University of Udine, Department of Humanities and Cultural Heritage, Ca' Foscari University of Venice, Department of Humanities, 17–21 April 2018, Leuven and Liège: Peeters.

Bosanquet, R. C. (1902), 'Excavations at Palaikastro', *Annual of the British School at Athens* 8: 286–316.

Bosanquet, R. C. (1909), 'The Palaikastro Hymn of the Kouretes', *Annual of the British School at Athens* 15: 339–56.

Bosch-Gimpera, P. (1912a), *La civilització crètica-micènica*, Estudis de prehistoria grega [(I)], Estudis Universitaris Catalans 6, 181–98, 272–81.

Bosch-Gimpera, P. (1912b), *La civilització crètico-micènica*, Estudis de prehistoria grega [(II)], Estudis Universitaris Catalans 7, 9–35.

Bosch-Gimpera, P. (1980), *Memòries*, Barcelona: Edicions 62.

Bossert, H. T. (1921), *Alt Kreta: Kunst und Kunstgewerbe im Ägäischen Kulturkreise*, Berlin: Ernst Wasmuth.

Bossert, H. T. (1923), *Altkreta: Kunst und Handwerk in Griechenland, Kreta und auf den Kykladen während der Bronzezeit*, Berlin: Ernst Wasmuth.

Bossert, H. T. (1937a), *Altkreta: Kunst und Handwerk in Griechenland, Kreta und auf den Kykladen während der Bronzezeit*, Berlin: Ernst Wasmuth.

Bossert, H. T. (1937b), *The Art of Ancient Crete from the Earliest Times to the Iron Age*, London: Zwemmer.

Bossert, H.T. and U. B. Alkım (1947), *Karatepe: Kadirli ve dolayları; ikinci ön-raport*, İstanbul: Pulhan Basımevi.

Boucher, A. (2014a), '*La Furie* de Jules Bois, une pièce préhistorique habillée rue de la Paix', in A. Boucher (ed.), *La Grèce des origins: entre rêve et archéologie*, 162–3, Paris: Réunion des Musées Nationaux – Grand Palais.

Boucher, A. (2017), 'The Ocean-liner *Aramis*: A Voyage to the Land of Minos and Art Deco', in N. Momigliano and A. Farnoux (eds.), *Cretomania: Modern Desires for theMinoan Past*, 124–56, London and New York: Routledge.

Boucher, A. (ed.) (2014b), *La Grèce des origins: entre rêve et archéologie*, Paris: Réunion des Musées Nationaux – Grand Palais.

Boucher, A. and T. Krapf (2014), 'Des jeux Olympiques aux Mangas Japonais: l'Art Egéenne est Partout', in A. Boucher (ed.), *La Grèce des origins: entre rêve et archéologie*, 195–9, Paris: Réunion des Musées Nationaux – Grand Palais.

Bourke, E. (2014), 2014. 'The Image of the Minoan in Science Fiction', *Foundation: The International Review of Science Fiction* 43, no. 118: 9–18.

Boyes, P. (2017), 'A Visual Guide to the Aegean Bronze Age in Doctor Who', https://ancworlds.wordpress.com/2017/09/25/a-visual-guide-to-the-aegean-bronze-age-in-doctor-who/.

Brandi, C. (1954), *Viaggio nella Grecia Antica*, Florence: Vallecchi.

Brandi, C. (2006), *Viaggio nella Grecia Antica*, 3rd edition, preface E. Siciliano, Rome: Editori Riuniti.

Branigan, K. (1970), *The Foundations of Palatial Crete: A Survey of Crete in the Early Bronze Age*, London: Routledge and Kegan Paul.

Branigan, K. (1982), 'The Unacceptable Face of Minoan Crete?', *Nature* 299, no. 5880 (September): 201–2.

Branigan, K. (1992), 'The Early Keep Knossos: A Reappraisal', *Annual of the British School at Athens* 87: 153–63.

Brindel, J. R. (1980), *Ariadne*, New York: St Martin's Press.

Brindel, J. R. (1985), *Phaedra*, New York: St Martin's Press.

Brion, M. ([1937] 1948), *La Résurrection des Villes Mortes: Mésopotamie, Syrie, Palsetine, Égypte, Perse, Hittites, Crète, Chypre*, Paris: Payot.

Broodbank, C. (2004), 'Minoanisation', *Proceedings of the Cambridge Philological Society* 50: 46–91.

Brown, A. (1986), 'I propose to begin at Gnossos', *Annual of the British School at Athens* 81: 37–44.

Brown, A. (1993), *Before Knossos . . . Arthur Evans's Travel in the Balkans and Crete*, Oxford: Ashmolean Museum.

Brown, A. and K. Bennett (2001), *Arthur Evans's Travels in Crete 1894–1899*, BAR International Series 1000, Oxford: Archeopress.

Bryce, T. (2006), *The Trojans and their Neighbours*, London and New York: Routledge

Buck, R. J. (1962), 'The Minoan Thalassocracy Re-examined', *Historia: Zeitschrift für Alte Geschichte* 11: 129–37.

Burkert, W. (1985), *Greek Religion*, Oxford: Blackwells.

Burns, A. R. (1930), *Minoans, Philistines, and Greeks B.C. 1400–900*, London and New York: Kegan Paul and Trench Treubner, A. Knopf.

Burns, B. E. (2010), *Mycenaean Greece, Mycenaean Commerce, and the Formation of Identity*, Cambridge: Cambridge University Press.

Burns, B. E. (2017), 'Cretomania and Neo-paganism: The Great Mother Goddess and Gay Male Identity in the Minoan Brotherhood', in N. Momigliano and A. Farnoux (eds.), *Cretomania: Modern Desires for the Minoan Past*, 157–70, London and New York: Routledge.

Burrow, J. W. (1982), 'Editor's Introduction', in J. W. Burrow (ed.), Charles Darwin, *The Origin of Species*, 1–49, Harmondsworth: Penguin.

Burrows, R. W. (1907), *The Discoveries in Crete and Their Bearing on the History of Ancient Civilisation*, London: Murray.

Bury, J. B. (1913), *A History of Greece to the Death of Alexander the Great*, 2nd edition, London: MacMillan.

Bury, J. B., S. A. Cook, and F. E. Adcock (1923), *The Cambridge Ancient History*, vol. 1: *Egypt and Babylonia to 1580 B.C.*, Cambridge: Cambridge University Press.

Butler, E. (1935), *The Tyranny of Greece Over Germany: A Study of the Influence Exercised by Greek Art and Poetry over the Great German Writers of the Eighteenth, Nineteenth and Twentieth Centuries*, Cambridge: Cambirdge Univerity Press.

Butler, E. (1939), 'Hofmannsthal's Elektra: a Graeco-Freudian Myth', *Journal of the Warburg Institute* 2: 164–75.

Cadogan, G. (1976), *Palaces of Minoan Crete*, London: Barrie and Jenkins.

Cadogan, G. (2004), '"The Minoan distance": The impact of Knossos upon the twentieth century', in G. Cadogan, E. Hatzaki, and A. Vasilakis (eds.), *Knossos: Palace, City, State. Proceedings of the Conference in Herakleion organised by the British School at Athens and the 23rd Ephoreia of Prehistoric and Classical Antiquities of Herakleion, in November 2000, for the Centenary of Sir Arthur Evans's Excavations at Knossos*, 537–45, London: British School at Athens.

Cadogan, G., E. Hatzaki, and A. Vasilakis (eds.) (2004), *Knossos: Palace, City, State. Proceedings of the Conference in Herakleion organised by the British School at Athens and the 23rd Ephoreia of Prehistoric and Classical Antiquities of Herakleion, in November 2000, for the Centenary of Sir Arthur Evans's Excavations at Knossos*, British School at Athens Studies 18, London: British School at Athens.

Caillois, R. ([1938] 1972), *Le Mythe et L'homme*, Paris: Gallimard.

Calandra, E. (2017), 'Massimo Campigli e la folgorazione per l'arte etrusca', *Annali della Fondazione per il Museo 'C. Faina'* 24 : 371–384 (special volume dedicated to the Atti del XXIV Convegno Internazionale di Studi sulla Storia e l'Archeologia dell'Etruria on the topic of *Gli etruschi nella cultura e nell'immaginario del mondo modern*, edited by G. M. Della Fina).

Calcutt, D. (2000a), *The Bull Beneath the Earth* (play first broadcast on 1 March 2000 on BBC Radio 4), https://archive.org/details/ THEBULLBENEATHTHEEARTH.

Calcutt, D. (2000b), *The Labyrinth: The Dramatized Story of Theseus and the Minotaur*, Oxford: Oxford University Press.

Calcutt, D. (2002), *Daedalus and Icarus*, Oxford: Oxford University Press.

Caldecott, M. (1979), *The Lily and the Bull*, London: Rex Collings.

Caldecott, M. (2007), *Multi-Dimensional Life*, n.p.p.: Mushroom eBooks, https://www.mushroom-ebooks.com/index.html.

Calder, W. M. (1999), 'Behind the Mask of Agamemnon', *Archaeology* 52, no. 4, https://archive.archaeology.org/9907/etc/calder.html.

Caloi, I. (2011), *Modernità Minoica. L'arte Egea e l'Art Nouveau: il Caso di Mariano Fortuny y Madrazo*, Periploi 4, Florence: Florence University Press.

Caloi, I. (2017), 'The Minoan Woman as the Oriental Woman: Mariano Fortuny's Knossos Scarves and Ruth St. Denis', in N. Momigliano and A. Farnoux (eds.), *Cretomania: Modern Desires for theMinoan Past*, 71–83, London and New York: Routledge.

Cameron, P. (2003), *Crete*, Blue Guides, London: A and C Black Publishers.

Carabott, P. (2006), 'A Country in a "State of Destitution" Labouring Under an "Unfortunate Regime": Crete at the Turn of the 20th Century (1898–1906)', in Y. Hamilakis and N. Momigliano (eds.), *Archaeology and European Modernity: Producing and Consuming the 'Minoans'*, 39–55, Padova: Bottega d'Erasmo (Ausilio).

Carinci, F. M. (2007), 'Doro Levi and Minoan Archaeology (1950–1980): History of a Heresy without Stakes', *Creta Antica* 8: 401–17.

Carlà-Uhink, F. and F. Freitag (2018), '(Not So) Dangerous Journeys: The Ancient Mediterranean and Ancient Mythological Sea Travelers in European Theme Park Attractions', in H. Kopp and C. Wendt (eds.), *Thalassokratographie: Rezeption und Transformation antiker Seeherrschaft*, 283–300, Berlin and Boston: De Gruyter.

Castleden, R. (1989), *The Knossos Labyrinth: A New View of the 'Palace of Minos' at Knossos*, London: Routledge.

Castleden, R. (1990), *Minoans: Life in Bronze Age Crete*, London: Routledge.

Castleden, R. (1996), 'Foreword', in S. Evasdaughter, *Crete Reclaimed: A Feminist Exploration of Bronze Age Crete*, xiv–xvi, Loughborough, UK: Heart of Albion Press.

Cavallini, E. (2015), 'In the Footsteps of Homeric Narrative: Anachronisms and Other Supposed Mistakes in *Troy*', in M. M. Winkler, *Return To Troy: New Essays on the Hollywood Epic*, 65–85, Leiden: Brill.

Cecchi, E. (1936), *Et in Arcadia Ego*, Milan: Hoepli.

Ceram, C. W. (1999), *Gods, Graves, and Scholars: The History of Archaeology*, London: Folio Society.

Cerro, G. (2017), 'Giuseppe Sergi: The portrait of a positivist scientist', *Journal of Anthropological Sciences* 95: 109–36.

Chadwick, J. (1967), *The Decipherment of Linear B*, 2nd revised edition, Cambridge: Cambridge University Press.

Chaineux, D. (1908), 'Le costume des habitants primitifs de la Grèce (Pélasges, Égéens, Achéens)', *Comptes rendus des séances de l'Académie des Inscriptions et Belles-Lettres*

52ᵉ année, no. 5 : 316, at https://www.persee.fr/issue/crai_0065-0536_1908_num_ 52_5.

Chamoux, F. (1963), *La Civilisation Grecque, à L'époque Archaïque et Classique*, Paris: Arthaud.

Charbonneaux, J. (1929), *L'Art égéen*, Paris and Brussels: Van Oest.

Chatzidakis, J. (1931), Ιστορία του Κρητικού Μουσείου και των αρχαιολογικών ερευνών εν Κρήτη, Athens: Athens Archaeological Society.

Chaudhuri, N. C. (1974), *Scholar Extraordinary: The Life of Professor the Rt. Hon. Friedrich Max Müller*, Londra: Chatto and Windus.

Cherry, J. F. (1994), 'Regional survey in the Aegean: The "New Wave" (and after)', in P. N. Kardulias (ed.), *Beyond the Site: Regional Studies in the Aegean Area*, 91–112, Lanham, MD: University Press of America.

Cherry, J. F. (2004), 'Chapter 14 Revisited: Sites, Settlements and Population in the Prehistoric Aegean since *The Emergence of Civilisation*', in J. C. Barret and O. Halstead (eds.), *The Emergence of Civilisation Revisited*, 1–20, Oxford: Oxbow Books.

Cherry, J. F. (2011), 'Foreword', in C. Renfrew, *The Emergence of Civilisation: The Cyclades and the Aegean in the Third Millennium BC*, xxi–xxvi, Oxford and Oakville, CT: Oxbow Books, David Brown Book Co.

Childe, V. G. (1915), 'On the Date and Origin of Minyan Ware', *Journal of Hellenic Studies* 35: 196–207.

Childe, V. G. (1916), 'The Influence of Indo-Europeans in Prehistoric Greece', B.Litt. dissertation, University of Oxford.

Childe, V. G. (1925), *The Dawn of European Civilization*, London: Kegan Paul.

Childe, V. G. (1926), *The Aryans*, London: Kegan Paul.

Childe, V. G. (1930), 'Review of J.L. Myres, *Who were the Greeks?*', *Nature* 126: 340–1.

Choiseul-Gouffier, M. (1782), *Voyage Pittoresque De La Grèce*, Paris: n.p.

Christ, P. C. (1995), *Odyssey With the Goddess: A Spiritual Quest in Crete*, New York: Continuum.

Chryssoulaki, S. (1997), 'Nerokourou Building I and Its Place in Neopalatial Crete', in R. Hägg (ed.), *The Function of the 'Minoan Villa': Proceedings of the Eighth International Symposium at the Swedish Institute at Athens, 6–8 June 1992*, 27–32, Stockholm: Paul Åströms.

Chryssoulaki, S. (1999), 'Minoan Roads and Guard Houses – War Regained', in R. Laffineur (ed.), *POLEMOS: Le contexte guerrier en Égée á l'âge du Bronze. Actes de la 7e Rencontre égéenne internationale Université de Liège, 14–17 avril 1998. Aegaeum: Annales d'archéologie égéenne de l'Université de Liège et UT-PASP 19*, 75–85, Liège: Histoire de l'art et archéologie de la Grèce antique; Austin, TX: Program in Aegean Scripts and Prehistory.

Churton, T. (2016), *Occult Paris: The Lost Magic of the Belle Époque*, Rochester, VT: Inner Traditions, Bear & Co.

Cipriani, L. (1943), *Creta e l'Origine Mediterranea Della Civiltà*, Florence: Marzocco.

Clarke, D. (1973), 'Archaeology: The Loss of Innocence', in *Antiquity* 47, no. 185: 6–18.

Clason, C. B. ([1939] 2003), *Murder Gone Minoan*, Lyons, CO: Rue Morgue Press.

Cline, E. H. (1991), 'Hittite Objects in the Bronze Age Aegean', *Anatolian Studies* 41: 133–43.

Cline, E. H. (1994), *Sailing the Wine-Dark Sea: International Trade and the Late Bronze Age Aegean*, BAR International Series S591, Oxford: Tempus Reparatum.

Cline, E. H. (1998), 'Rich beyond the dreams of Avaris: Tell el-Dab'a and the Aegean world – a Guide for the Perplexed', *Annual of the British School at Athens* 93: 199–219.

Cline, E. H. (1999), 'The Nature of the Economic Relations of Crete with Egypt and the Near East during the Late Bronze Age', in A. Chaniotis (ed.), *From Minoan Farmers to Roman Traders: Sidelights on the Economy of Ancient Crete*, 115–44, Stuttgart: Franz Steiner Verlag.

Cline, E. H. (2014), *1177 BC: The Year Civilization Collapsed*, Princeton, NJ: Princeton University Press.

Cline, E. H., A. Yasur-Landau, and N. Goshen (2011), 'New Fragments of Aegean-Style Painted Plaster from Tel Kabri, Israel', *American Journal of Archaeology* 115, no. 2: 245–61.

Cocteau, J. (1953), *Journal d'un inconnu*, Paris: Grasset.

Cocteau, J. (1988), *The Diary of an Unknown*, trans. J. Browner, New York: Paragon House.

Coffey, M. ([1991] 2014), *A Cretan Cycle: Fragments Unearthed from Knossos*, Santa Barbara, CA: Bandanna Books, https://www.academia.edu/8314240/ A_Cretan_ Cycle_Fragments_Unearthed_at_Knossos.

Coldstream, J. N. (1988), 'Some Minoan Reflexions in Cretan Geometric Art', in J. H. Betts, J. T. Hooker, and J. R. Green (eds.), *Studies in Honour of T.B.L. Webster*, vol. 2, 23–32, Bristol: Bristol Classical Press.

Coldstream, J. N. (1991), 'Knossos: An Urban Nucleus in the Dark Age?', in D. Musti, A. Sacconi, L. Rocchetti, M. Rocchi, E. Scafa, L. Sportiello, and M. E. Giannotta (eds.), *La Transizione dal Miceneo all'Alto Arcaismo, Dal Palazzo alla città*, 287–99, Rome: Consiglio Nazionale delle Ricerche.

Coldstream, J. N. (1998), 'Minos Redivivus: Some Nostalgic Knossians of the Ninth Century BC (A Summary)', in W. G. Cavanagh and M. Curtis (eds.) with J. N. Coldstream and A. W. Johnston (co-eds.), *Post-Minoan Crete, Proceedings of the First Colloquium on Post-Minoan Crete held by the British School at Athens and the Institute of Archaeology, University College London, 10–11 November 1995*, 58–61, London: British School at Athens.

Coldstream, J. N. (2000), 'Evans's Greek Finds: The Early Greek Town of Knossos, and its Encroachment on the Borders of the Minoan Palace', *Annual of the British School at Athens* 95: 259–99.

Coldstream, J. N. and H. W. Catling (1996), *Knossos North Cemetery: Early Greek Tombs*, London: British School at Athens.

Coldstream, J. N. and G. L. Huxley (1972), *Kythera: Excavations and Studies Conducted by the University of Pennsylvania Museum and the British School at Athens*. London: Faber & Faber.

Cole, L. (1996), *The Sea Kings: The Prophecy*, Ventura, CA: House of Adda Press.

Conte, D. (1997), *Introduzione a Spengler*, Rome and Bari: Laterza.

Cossu, U. (1989), *Le Ninfe*, Rome: Editrice Comic Arts.

Cottrell, L. (1955), *The Bull of Minos*, 2nd revised edition, London: Pan Books.

Crawford, O. G. S. (1957), *The Eye Goddess*, London: Phoenix House.

Crawford, S. (1983), 'Re-evaluating Material Culture: Crawling Towards a Reconstruction of Minoan Society', in O. Krzyszkowska and L. Nixon (eds.), *Minoan Society: Proceedings of the Cambridge Colloquium, 1981*, 47–53, Bristol: Bristol Classical Press.

Culler, J. (2013), 'Lévi-Strauss: Good to Think With', *Yale French Studies* 123: 6–13.

Curtius, L. (1913), *Die Antike Kunst*, vol. 2: *Der klassische Stil*, Berlin: Akademische Verlagsgesellschaft Athenaion.

D'Agata, A. L. (1994), 'Sigmund Freud and Aegean Archaeology, Mycenaean and Cypriote Material from his Collection of Antiquities', *Studi Micenei ed Egeo-Anatolici* 34: 7–41.

D'Agata, A. L. (2010), 'The Many Lives of a Ruin: History and Metahistory of the Palace of Minos at Knossos', in O. Krzyszkowska (ed.), *Cretan Offerings: Studies in Honour of Peter Warren*, 57–69, British School at Athens Studies 18, London: British School at Athens.

Damiani-Indelicato, S. (1988), 'Were Cretan Girls Playing at Bull-Leaping?', *Cretan Studies* 1: 39–47.

Daniel, G. (1992), *Writing for Antiquity: An Anthology of Editorials from Antiquity*, London: Thames and Hudson.

Darling, J. K. (2004), *Architecture in Greece*, Westport, CT: Greenwood Press.

Davies, N. (1996), *Europe: A History*, Oxford: Oxford University Press.

Day-Lewis, C. (1992), *The Complete Poems of C. Day-Lewis*, Stanford, CA: Stanford University Press.

De Lacretelle, J. (1931), *Le Demi-dieu ou le Voyage de Grèce*, Paris: Grasset.

DeLillo, D. (1982), *The Names*, New York: Alfred A. Knopf.

DeLillo, D. ([1988] 2011), 'The Ivory Acrobat', in Don DeLillo, *The Angel Esmeralda: Nine Stories*, 55–72, London: Picador (originally published in *Granta* 12 (Autumn 1988), https://granta.com/the-ivory-acrobat/).

De Maistre, J. (1853), *Lettres et opuscules inédits du comte Joseph de Maistre, Tome 1 / précédés d'une notice biographique pars son fils le comte Rodolphe de Maistre*, Paris: Varon, https://gallica.bnf.fr/ark:/12148/bpt6k246120/f3.item.

Demargne, P. (1938), 'Crète–Égypte–Asie: Perspectives d'hier et d'aujourd'hui', *Annales de l'Ecole des Hautes Etudes de Gand* 2: 31–66.

Demargne, P. (1964), *Aegean Art: The Origins of Greek Art*, London: Thames and Hudson.

Dempsey, J. (1996), *Ariadne's Brother: A Novel on the Fall of Bronze Age Crete*, Athens: Kalendis and Co.

De Osma, G. (1980), *Mariano Fortuny: His Life and Work*, London: Aurum Press.

De Pirro, A. (2012), '"Le regole del gioco permettono infinite partite". Giochi linguistici, magie verbali e lingue inventate nelle opere su carta di Gastone Novelli. Studio delle fonti e del contest', doctoral dissertation, University of La Sapienza, Rome.

De Pirro, A. (2013), '*Il Vocabolario* di Gastone Novelli. Una nuova lettura', *Storia Dell'Arte* 135, new series 35 : 124–47.

De Renzi, S. (1845), *Storia della Medicina Italiana vol. II*, Napoli: Filiatre-Sebezio, https://archive.org/stream/StoriaDellaMedicinaInItalia2/storia-medicina-ita-2#page/n0/mode/2up.

De Richaud, A. (1953), 'Créte', in D. Ogrizek (ed.), *La Gréce*, 361–82, Paris: Odé.

Deshayes, J. (1969), *Les Civilisations de L'Orient Ancien*, Paris: Arthaud.

Detorakis, T. (1990), *Ιστορία της Κρήτης*, Heraklion: Typokretas G. Kazanakēs (trans. J. C. Davis as *History of Crete*, 1994).

Díaz-Andreu, M. (2008), 'Revisiting the "Invisible College": José Ramón Mélida in Early 20th Century Spain', in N. Schlanger and J. Nordbladh (eds.), *Histories of Archaeology: Archives, Ancestors, Practices*, 121–9, Oxford: Berghahn Books.

Díaz-Andreu, M. (2012), *Archaeological Encounters: Building Networks of Spanish and British Archaeologists in the 20th Century*, Newcastle: Cambridge Scholars.

Dick, B. F. (1972), *The Hellenism of Mary Renault*, Carbondale: Southern Illinois University Press.

Dickinson, O. T. P. K. (1994), *The Aegean Bronze Age*, Cambridge: Cambridge University Press.

Dickinson, O. T. P. K. (2009), 'Ahhiyawan Questions', *Δῶρον: τιμητικός τομός για τον καθηγητή Σπύρο Ιακωβίδη*, ed. Δανιηλίδου, Δέσποινα Σειρά Μονογραφιών 6, 275–84, Athens: Ακαδημία Αθηνών, Κέντρον Ερεύνης της Αρχαιότητος.

Dickinson, O. T. P. K. (2012), 'Schliemann's contribution to Greek Bronze Age Archaeology: Was He Really the "Father of Mycenaean Archaeology"?', in G. S. Korres, N. Karadimas, and G. Flouda (eds.), *Archaeology and Heinrich Schliemann a Century After his Death. Assessments and Prospects: Myth – History – Science*, 391–400, Athens: Giorgios Styl. Korres.

Diktaios, A. (1974), *Τα Ποιήματα (1934–1965)*, Athens: Dodone.

Dimopoulou, N. and G. Rethemiotakis (2004), *The Ring of Minos and Gold Minoan Rings: The Epiphany Cycle*, Athens: Ministry of Culture Archaeological Receipts Fund.

Dintino, T. C. (1999), *Ode to Minoa: A Novel*, Pittsburgh: Sterling House.

Dintino, T. C. (2003), *Stories They Told Me*, Bloomington, IN: iUniverse.com (2nd edition, 2014, Wise Strega Books).

Di Vita, A. (2000), 'F. Halbherr e l'archeologia italiana a cavallo fra il XIX e XX secolo', *Creta Antica* 1: 113–28.

Doumas, C. (1983), *Thera: Pompeii of the Ancient Aegean: Excavations at Akrotiri, 1967–79*, London: Thames and Hudson.

Doumas, C. and A. Doumas (2016), *Prehistoric Thera*, Athens: John S. Latsis Public Benefit Foundation.

Doumic, R. (2009), 'Revue Dramatique – 14 Mars 1909', *Revue des Deux Mondes* 50 (1909): 444–55, https://fr.wikisource.org/wiki/Revue.dramatique_-_14_mars_1909.

Driessen, J. (1990), *An Early Destruction in the Mycenaean Palace at Knossos: A New Interpretation of the Excavation Field-notes of the South-east Area of the West Wing*, Acta Archaeologica Lovaniensia, Monographiae 2, Leuven: Katholieke Universiteit Leuven.

Driessen, J. (1997), 'Le Palais de Cnossos au MR II–III: Combien de Destructions?', in J. Driessen and A. Farnoux (eds.), *La Crète Mycénienne: Actes de la Table Ronde Internationale Organisée par l'École Française d'Athènes (26–28 Mars 1991)*, BCH Supplément 30, 113–34, Athens: École française d'Athènes; Paris: De Boccard Édition-Diffusion.

Driessen, J. (2001), 'History and Hierarchy: Preliminary Observations on the Settlement Pattern in Minoan Crete', in K. Branigan (ed.), *Urbanism in the Aegean Bronze Age*, 51–71, London and New York: Sheffield Academic Press.

Driessen, J. (2002), 'Foreword', in J. Driessen, I. Schoep, and R. Laffineur (eds.), *Monuments of Minos: Rethinking the Minoan Palaces; Proceedings of the International Workshop 'Crete of the hundred palaces?' held at the Universite Catholique de Louvain, Louvain-la-Neuve, 14–15 December 2001*, vii, Aegeum 23, Liège: Université de Liège.

Driessen, J. (2008), 'Chronology of the Linear B Texts', in Y. Duhoux and A. M. Davies (eds.), *A Companion to Linear B: Mycenaean Greek Texts and their World*, vol. 1, 69–79, Bibliothèque des cahiers de l'Institut de Linguistique de Louvain 120, Leuven: Peeters.

Driessen, J. (2019), 'The Santorini Eruption: An Archaeological Investigation of its Distal Impacts on Minoan Crete', *Quaternary International* 499: 195–204.

Driessen, J., I. Schoep, and R. Laffineur (eds.) (2002a), *Monuments of Minos: Rethinking the Minoan Palaces; Proceedings of the International Workshop 'Crete of the hundred palaces?' held at the Universite Catholique de Louvain, Louvain-la-Neuve, 14–15 December 2001*, Aegaeum 23, Liège: Université de Liège.

Driessen, J., I. Schoep and R. Laffineur (2002b), 'Introduction', in J. Driessen, I. Schoep, and R. Laffineur (eds.), *Monuments of Minos: Rethinking the Minoan Palaces; Proceedings of the International Workshop 'Crete of the hundred palaces?' held at the Universite Catholique de Louvain, Louvain-la-Neuve, 14–15 December 2001*, ix–x, Liège: Université de Liège.

Duhoux, Y. (1982), *L'Étéocrétois: Les Textes – la Langue*, Amsterdam: J.C Gieben.

Durrell, L. (1947), *Cefalù*, London: PL Editions Poetry.

Durrell, L. (1958), *The Dark Labyrinth: A Novel*, London: Harborough Publishing.

Durrell, L. (1969), *Spirit of Place: Letters and Essays on Travel*, ed. A. Thomas, London: Faber & Faber.

Durrell, L. ([1978] 2002), *The Greek Islands*, London: Faber & Faber.

Dussaud, R. (1910), *Les Civilisations Préhelléniques dans le Bassin de la Mer Egée: Études the Protohistoire Orientale*, Paris: Paul Geuthner.

Dyson, S. L. (1998), *Ancient Marbles to American Shores: Classical Archaeology in the United States*, Philadelphia: University of Pennsylvania Press.

Dyson, S. L. (2014), *The Last Amateur: The Life of William J. Stillman*, Albany, NY: SUNY Press.

Edey, M. A. (1975), *Lost World of the Aegean*, New York: Time Life Books.

Eisler, R. T. (1987), *The Chalice and The Blade: Our History, Our Future*, San Francisco: HarperCollins.

Elger, D. (2018), *Expressionism: A Revolution in German Art*, trans. H. Beyer, Cologne: Taschen.

Eller, C. (2012), 'Two Knights and a Goddess: Sir Arthur Evans, Sir James George Frazer, and the Invention of Minoan Religion', *Journal of Mediterranean Archaeology* 25, no. 1: 75–98.

Elytis, O. (1980), *To Axion Esti*, trans. and annotated E. Keeley and G. Savidis, London: Anvil Press.

Elytis, O., J. Carson, and N. Sarris (1997), *The Collected Poems of Odysseus Elytis*, Baltimore, MD, and London: Johns Hopkins University Press.

Engels F. (1884), *Origin of the Family, Private Property and the State*, Hottingen and Zürich: Verlag der Schweizerischen Volksbuchhandlung.

Evans, A. J. (1883), 'Review of Schliemann's *Troja*', *Academy* 24: 437–9.

Evans, A. J. (1894), 'Primitive Pictographs and prae-Phoenician Script from Crete and the Peloponnese', *Journal of Hellenic Studies* 14: 270–372.

Evans, A. J. (1895), *Cretan Pictographs and Prae-Phoenician Script, with an Account of a Sepulchral Deposit at Hagios Onuphrios near Phaestos in its Relations to Primitive Cretan and Aegean Culture*, London: Quaritch.

Evans, A. J. (1896), '"The Eastern Question" in Anthropology', in *Report of theSixty-Sixth Meeting of the British Association for the Advancement of Science, Held at Liverpool in September 1896*, 906–922, https://archive.org/stream/reportofbritisha 96brit/ reportofbritisha96brit_djvu.txt and https://www.biodiversitylibrary.org / bibliography/2276#/summary.

Evans, A. J. (1900), 'Knossos: Summary report of the excavations in 1900', *Annual of the British School at Athens* 6: 3–70.

Evans, A. J. (1901a), 'The Palace of Minos', *Monthly Review*, March 1901: 115–32.

Evans, A. J. (1901b), 'The palace of Knossos: Provisional report of the excavations for the year 1901', *Annual of the British School at Athens* 7: 1–120.

Evans, A. J. (1901c), 'The Neolithic settlement at Knossos and its Place in the History of Early Aegean Culture', *Man* 1: 184–6.

Evans, A. J. (1902), 'The palace of Knossos: Provisional report of the excavations for the year 1902', *Annual of the British School at Athens* 8: 1–129.

Evans, A. J. (1903), 'The palace of Knossos: Provisional Report for the year 1903', *Annual of the British School at Athens* 9: 1–153.

Evans, A. J. (1904), 'The palace of Knossos', *Annual of the British School at Athens* 10: 1–62.

Evans, A. J. (1905), 'The palace of Knossos and its dependencies', *Annual of the British School at Athens* 11: 1–26.

Evans, A. J. (1906), *Essai de classification des époques de la civilisation minoenne*, London: Quaritch.

Evans, A. J. (1909), *Scripta Minoa: The Written Documents of Minoan Crete, with Special Reference to the Archives of Knossos*, Oxford: Clarendon Press.

Evans, A. J. (1921), *The Palace of Minos: A Comparative Account of the Successive Stages of the Early Cretan Civilization as Illustrated by the Discoveries at Knossos*, vol. 1, London: Macmillan.

Evans, A. J. (1927), 'Work of Reconstitution in the Palace of Knossos', *Antiquaries Journal* 7, no. 3: 258–67.

Evans, A. J. (1928), *The Palace of Minos: A Comparative Account of the Successive Stages of the Early Cretan Civilization as Illustrated by the Discoveries at Knossos*, vol. 2, London: Macmillan.

Evans, A. J. (1930), *The Palace of Minos: A Comparative Account of the Successive Stages of the Early Cretan Civilization as Illustrated by the Discoveries at Knossos*, vol. 3, London: Macmillan.

Evans, A. J. (1935), *The Palace of Minos: A Comparative Account of the Successive Stages of the Early Cretan Civilization as Illustrated by the Discoveries at Knossos*, vol. 4, London: Macmillan.

Evans, J. (1943), *Time and Chance: The Story of Arthur Evans and his Forebears*, London: Longmans, Green and Co.

Evans, J. (1964), *Prelude and Fugue: An Autobiography*, London: Museum Press.

Evasdaughter, S. (1996), *Crete Reclaimed: A Feminist Exploration of Bronze Age Crete*, Loughborough: Heart of Albion Press.

Evely, D., H. Hughes-Brock, and N. Momigliano (eds.) (1994), *Knossos: A Labyrinth of History: Papers Presented in Honour of Sinclair Hood*, Oxford: British School at Athens and Oxbow Books.

Farnoux, A. (1993), *Cnossos: L'archéologie d'un Rêve*, Paris: Gallimard (trans. D. Baker as *Knossos: Unearthing a Legend*, London: Thames and Hudson, 1996).

Farnoux, A. (1996), 'Art Minoenne et Art Nouveau', in P. Hoffmann and P. L. Rinui (eds.), *Antiquités Imaginaries: La Référence Antique dans L'art Moderne, de la Renaissance à Nos Jours. Actes de la Table Ronde du 29 avril 1994*, 109–26, Paris: École Normale Supérieure.

Farrer, K. ([1954] 2004), *The Cretan Counterfeit*, Boulder, CO: Rue Morgue Press.

Faure, P. (1973), *La vie Quotidienne en Crète au Temps de Minos (1500 avant Jésus-Christ)*, Paris: Hachette.

Fawkes, A. G. (2001), *Cartoons of Cyprus*, Nicosia: Moufflon Press.

Featherstone, K. and D. K. Katsoudas (1985), 'Change and Continuity in Greek Voting Behaviour', *European Journal of Political Research* 13: 27–40.

Fell, A. (2012), *The Element -inth in Greek*, Dingwall, Ross-shire: Sandstone Press.

Ferrando, F. (2013), 'Posthumanism, Transhumanism, Antihumanism, Metahumanism, and New Materialisms: Differences and Relations', *Existenz* 8, no. 2: 26–32.

Fimmen, D. (1909), *Zeit und Dauer der kretisch-mykenischen Kultur*, Leipzig and Berlin: B. G. Teubner.

Fimmen, D. (1921), *Die Kretisch-mykenische Kultur*, Leipzig: Teubner.

Finley, M. I. (1954), *The World of Odysseus*, New York: Viking Press.

Finley, M. I. (1968), *Aspects of Antiquity*, London: Chatto and Windus.

Firla, I. and G. Lindop (eds.) (2003), *Graves and the Goddess: Essays on Robert Graves's The White Goddess*, Selinsgrove, PA, and London: Susquehanna University Press, Associated University Press.

Fischer-Lichte, E. (2014), *Dionysus Resurrected: Performances of Euripides' The Bacchae in a Globalizing World*, Chichester: Blackwell.

Fitton, J. L. (1995), *The Discovery of the Greek Bronze Age*, London: British Museum.

Fitton, J. L. (2002), *Minoans*, London: British Museum.

Florensky, P. (2002), *Beyond Vision: Essays on the Perception of Art*, ed. N. Misler, trans. W. Salmond, London: Reaktion.

Florou, V. (2016), 'Anna Apostolaki: A Forgotten Pioneer of Women's Emancipation in Greece', *Archivist's Notebook*, 1 January 2016, https://nataliavogeikoff.com /2016/01/01/anna-apostolaki-a-forgotten-pioneer-of-womens-emancipation-in-greece/.

Flouda, G. (2017), 'Archaeology in the War Zone: August Schörgendorfer and the *Kunstschutz* on Crete during World War II', *Annual of the British School at Athens* 112: 341–77.

Ford, F. M. ([1915] 1990), *The Good Soldier: A Tale of Passion*, ed. T. C. Moser, Oxford: Oxford University Press.

Forsdyke, E. J. (1925), *Catalogue of the Greek and Etruscan Vases in the British Museum*, vol. 1, part 1: *Prehistoric and Aegean Pottery*, London: British Museum and Quaritch.

Fotiadis, M. (2016), 'Aegean Prehistory without Schliemann', *Hesperia* 85, no. 1: 91–119.

Fotou, V. and A. Brown (2004), 'Harriet Boyd Hawes (1871–1945)', in G. M. Cohen and M. S. Joukowsky (eds.), *Breaking Ground: Pioneering Women Archaeologists*, 198–273, Ann Arbor: University of Michigan Press.

Foucault, M. (1984), 'Des Espace Autres', *Architecture, Mouvement, Continuité* 5 : 46–49; English translation: https://foucault.info/documents/heterotopia/foucault.hetero Topia.en/.

Fournaraki, E. (2011), 'Bodies that Differ: Mid- and Upper-class Women and the Quest for "Greekness" in Female Bodily Culture (1896–1940)', in E. Fournaraki and Z. Papakostantinou (eds.), *Sport, Bodily Culture and Classical Antiquity in Modern Greece*, 49–85, London: Routledge.

Fournaraki, E. and Z. Papakostantinou (eds.) (2011), *Sport, Bodily Culture and Classical Antiquity in Modern Greece*, London: Routledge.

Foxhall, L. (2013), *Studying Gender in Classical Antiquity*, Cambridge: Cambridge University Press.

Frank, S. (1998), *Shadows on the Aegean*, New York: Warner Books.

Franklin, S. B. (1998), *Daughter of Troy*, New York: Harper Torch.

Frazer, R. M. (ed) (1966), *The Trojan War: The Chronicles of Dictys of Crete and Dares the Phrygian*, trans. with Introduction and Notes R. M. Frazer, Bloomington and London: Indiana University Press.

Freud, S. (1916), *Wit and Its Relation to the Unconscious*, trans. A.A. Brill, New York: Moffat, Yard and Co., www.bartleby.com/279/.

Freud, S. (1953–74), *The Standard Edition of the Complete Psychological Works of Sigmund Freud*, trans. J. Strachey, London: Hogarth Press.

Frey, S. (1997), 'Dokumentation über Paul Klees Reisen ans Mittelmeer', in U. Gerlach-Laxner and E. Schwinzer (eds.), *Paul Klee: Reisen in den Süden: Reisefieber Praecisiert*, 242–64, Ostfildern-Ruit: G. Hatje.

Frost, K. (1913), 'The Critias and Minoan Crete', *Journal of Hellenic Studies* 33: 189–206.

Furumark, A. (1941), *The Mycenaean Pottery: Analysis and Classification*, Stockholm: Kungl, Vitterhets.

Furumark, A. (1950), 'The Settlement at Ialysos and Aegean History c. 1550–1400 B.C.', *Opuscula Archaeologica* 6: 150–271.

Gabrieli, V. and M. Gabrieli (1997), *Bibliografia Degli Scritti di Mario Praz*, 2nd revised edition, Rome: Edizioni di Storia e Letteratura.

Galanaki, R. (1989), *Ο βίος του Ισμαήλ Φερίκ Πασά*, Athens: Agra.

Galanaki, R. (1996), *The Life of Ismail Ferik Pasha*, trans. K. Cicellis, London: Peter Owen.

Galanaki, R. (2002), *Ο αιώνας των λαβυρίνθων*, Athens: Kastaniotis.

Galanaki, R. (2017), 'Growing up Next Door to Knossos and "The Other Ariadne"', in N. Momigliano and A. Farnoux (eds.), *Cretomania: Modern Desires for the Minoan Past*, 189–94, London and New York: Routledge.

Galanakis, Y. (2015), 'Exhibiting the Minoan Past: From Oxford to Knossos', in S. Cappel, U. Günkel-Maschek, and D. Panagiotopoulos (eds.), *Minoan Archaeology: Perspectives for the 21st Century*, 17–34, Louvain: Presses Universitaires de Louvain.

Galanakis, Y. (ed.) (2013), *The Aegean World: A Guide to the Cycladic, Minoan and Mycenaean Antiquities in the Ashmolean Museum*, Oxford: Ashmolean Museum.

Galanakis, Y., E. Tsitsa, and U. Günkel-Maschek (2017), 'The Power of Images: Re-Examining the Wall Paintings from the Throne Room at Knossos', *Annual of the British School at Athens* 112: 47–98.

Galatsiatou, P. (2005), 'Ξένες Αρχαιολογικές Σχολές στην Ελλάδα. Το νομικό και θεσμικό πλαίσιο', MA dissertation, Πάντειο Πανεπιστήμιο – Τμήμα Επικοινωνίας, Μέσων και Πολιτισμού – Μεταπτυχιακό πρόγραμμα πολιτιστικής διαχείρισης, https://www.academia.edu/31960977/ΞΕΝΕΣ_ΑΡΧΑΙΟΛΟΓΙΚΕΣ_ΣΧΟΛΕΣ_ΣΤΗΝ_ΕΛΛΑΔΑ_Μεταπτυχιακή_εργασία.

Gallavotti, C. (1957), 'Labyrinthos', *Parola del Passato* 12: 161–76.

Ganz, T. (1993), *Early Greek Myth: A Guide to Literary and Artistic Sources*, Baltimore, MD, and London: Johns Hopkins University Press.

Gaspar, L. (1980), *Égée: Suivi de Judée*, Paris: Gallimard.

Gazdar, K. (2016), *Feminism's Founding Fathers: The Men Who Fought for Women's Rights*, Alresford, UK: John Hunt Publishing.

Georgakopoulos, K. (2009), 'The Aegean and Anatolia in the late Bronze Age: Interconnections, Intermediaries and Interpretations', PhD dissertation, University of Liverpool.

Georgakopoulos, K. (2012a), 'Minoan–Anatolian relations and the Ahhiyawa Question: A Re-assessment of the Evidence', *Talanta* 44: 137–56.

Georgakopoulos, K. (2012b), 'A Note on a Hittite Bull-Leaping Scene and its Minoan Perspectives', in N. C. Stampolidis, A. Kanta, and A. Giannikouri (eds.), *Athanasia: The Earthly, the Celestial and the Underworld in the Mediterranean from the Late Bronze and the Early Iron Age. International Archaeological Conference, Rhodes, 28–31 May, 2009*, 111–114, Aegean Library 3041, Heraklion: University of Crete.

Gere, C. (2002), 'Inscribing Nature: Archaeological Metaphors and the Formation of New Sciences', *Public Archaeology* 2: 195–208.

Gere, C. (2006a), 'Cretan Psychoanalysis and Freudian Archaeology: H.D.'s Minoan Analyis with Freud in 1933', in Y. Hamilakis and N. Momigliano (eds.), *Archaeology and European Modernity: Producing and Consuming the 'Minoans'*, 211–18, Padova: Bottega d'Erasmo (Ausilio).

Gere, C. (2006b), *The Tomb of Agamemnon: Mycenae and the Search for a Hero*, London: Profile Books.

Gere, C. (2009), *Knossos and the Prophets of Modernism*, Chicago: University of Chicago Press.

Gerhard, E. (1849), *Über das Metroon zu Athen und über die Göttermutter der griechischen Mythologie*, Berlin: Gedruckt in der Druckerei der Königlichen Akademie der Wissenschaften.

German, S. C. (2000), 'The Human Form in the Late Bronze Age Aegean', in A. E. Rautman (ed.), *Reading the Body: Representations and Remains in the Archaeological Record*, 95–110, Philidelphia: University of Pennsylvania Press.

Gesell, G. C. (2004), 'History of American Excavations on Crete', in L. P. Day, M. S. Mook, and J. D. Muhly (eds.), *Crete Bryond the Palaces: Proceedings of the Crete 2000 Conference*, 1–18, Philadeplphia: Instap Academic Press.

Gibson, A. G. G. (ed.) (2015), *Robert Graves and the Classical Tradition*, Oxford: Oxford University Press.

Gide, A. (1946), *Thésée*, Paris: Gallimard.

Gide, A. (1949), *Theseus*, trans. J. Russell, lithographs M. Campigli, London and Verona: New Directions and Officina Bodoni.

Gimbutas, M. (1974), *The Gods and Goddesses of Old Europe, 7000 to 3500 BC: Myths, Legends and Cult Images*, London: Thames and Hudson.

Gimbutas, M. (1982), *The Goddesses and Gods of Old Europe, 6500–3500 BC: Myths and Cult Images*, London: Thames and Hudson.

Gimbutas, M. and M. R. Dexter (1999), *The Living Goddesses*, Berkeley and London: University of California Press.

Gkiasta, M. (2008), *The Historiography of Landscape Research on Crete*, Leiden: Leiden University Press.

Glasgow, G. (1923), *The Minoans*, London: Jonathan Cape.

Glotz, G. (1923), *La Civilisation Égéenne*, Paris: Renaissance du livre.

Glotz, G. (1925a), *The Aegean Civilization*, London and New York: Kegan Paul and Knopf.

Glotz, G. (1925b), *Histoire Grecque: Des Origines aux Guerres Médiques*, Paris: Presse Universitaires de France.

Godart, L. and J. P. Olivier (1976–85), *Recueil des Inscriptions en Linéaire A*, vols. 1–5, Paris: Dépositaire, P. Geuthner.

Goldhill, S. (2002), *Who Needs Greek? Contests in the Cultural History of Hellenism*, Cambridge: Cambridge University Press.

Goodison, L. and H. Hughes-Brock (2002), 'Helen Waterhouse and her "Priest-Kings?"', *Cretan Studies* 7: 89–96.

Goodison, L. and C. Morris (1998a), 'Introduction: Exploring Female Divinity; From Modern Myths to Ancient Evidence', in L. Goodison and C. Morris (eds.), *Ancient Goddesses: The Myths and the Evidence*, 6–21, London: British Museum Press.

Goodison, L. and C. Morris (eds.) (1998b), *Ancient Goddesses: The Myths and the Evidence*, London: British Museum Press.

Gorogianni, E., P. Pavúk, and L. Girella (eds.) (2016), *Beyond Thalassocracies: Understanding Processes of Minoanisation and Mycenaeanisation in the Aegean*, Oxford: Oxbow Books.

Grafton, A. (1981), 'Prolegomena to Friedrich August Wolf', *Journal of the Warburg and Courtauld Institutes* 44: 101–29.

Graham, J. W. (1962), *The Palaces of Crete*, Princeton, NJ: Princeton University Press.

Graves, R. (1948), *The White Goddess: A Historical Grammar of Poetic Myth*, London: Faber & Faber.

Graves, R. (1949), *Seven Days in New Crete*, London: Cassel and Co.

Graves, R. (1955), *The Greek Myths*, Harmondsworth: Penguin Books.

Green, S. (1981), *Prehistorian: A Biography of V. Gordon Childe*, Bradford-on-Avon: Moonraker.

Greensted, M. (2010), *The Arts and Crafts Movement: Exchanges between Greece and Britain (1876–1930)*, M.Phil thesis, University of Birmingham, http://etheses.bham. ac.uk/1110/.

Gregory, M. E. (2008), *Evolutionism in Eighteenth-century French Thought*, New York: Peter Lang.

Groenewegen-Frankfort, H. A. (1951), *Arrest and Movement: An Essay on Space and Time in the Representational Art of the Ancient Near East*, London: Faber & Faber.

Grohmann, W. (1957), *Paul Klee*, 2nd edition, London: Humphries.

Grote, G. (1846), *History of Greece*, vol. 1, London: Murray.

Guðmundsson, K. (1937), *Gyðjan og uxinn: skáldsaga*, Reykjavík: Ólafur Erlingsson.

Gudmundsson, K. (1940), *Winged Citadel*, trans. B. Mussey, New York: Henry Holt and Co.

Gulizio, J. and D. Nakassis (2014), 'The Minoan Goddess(es): Textual Evidence for Minoan Religion', in D. Nakassis, J. Gulizio, and S. A. James (eds.), *KE-RA-ME-JA: Studies Presented to Cynthia W. Shelmerdine*, 115–28, Prehistory Monographs 46, Philadelphia: INSTAP Academic Press.

Guthrie, W. K. C. (1959), 'Early Greek Religion in the Light of the Decipherment of Linear B', *Bulletin of the Institute of Classical Studies* 6: 35–46.

Hägg, R. (ed.) (1997), *The Function of the 'Minoan Villa': Proceedings of the Eighth International Symposium at the Swedish Institute at Athens, 6–8 June 1992*, Stockholm: Paul Åströms.

Hägg, R. and N. Marinatos (eds.) (1987), *The Function of the Minoan Palaces: Proceedings of the Fourth International Symposium at the Swedish Institute in Athens, 10–16 June, 1984*, Stockholm: Svenska institutet i Athen.

Hales, S. and J. Paul (2011), 'Introduction: Ruins and Reconstructions', in S. Hales and J. Paul (eds.), *Pompeii in the Public Imagination from its Rediscovery to Today*, 1–14, Oxford: Oxford University Press.

Haley, J. B. and C. Blegen (1928), 'The Coming of the Greeks', *American Journal of Archaeology* 32: 141–54.

Hall, H. R. (1901), *The Oldest Civilization of Greece*, London and Philadelhia: Nutt and Lippincott.

Hall, H. R. (1913), *The Ancient History of the Near East*, London: Methuen.

Hall, H. R. (1915), *Aegean Archaeology: An Introduction to the Archaeology of Prehistoric Greece*, London: P.L. Warner.

Hall, H. R. (1928), *The Civilization of Greece in the Bronze Age (the Rhind Lectures 1923)*, London: Methuen.

Hallager, E. (1974), 'Linear A and Linear B Inscriptions from the Excavations at Kastelli, Khania 1964–1972', *Opuscula Atheniensia* 11: 53–86.

Halstead, P. (1981), 'From Determinism to Uncertainty: Social Storage and the Rise of the Minoan Palace', in A. Sheridan and G. Bailey (eds.), *Economic Archaeology: Toward an Integration of Ecological and Social Approaches*, 187–213, Oxford: British Archaeological Reports.

Halstead, P. (1988), 'On Redistribution and the Origin of Minoan–Mycenaean Palatial Economies', in E. B. French and K. A. Wardle (eds.), *Problems in Greek Prehistory: Papers Presented at the Centenary Conference of the British School of Archaeology at Athens, Manchester, April 1986*, 519–30, Bristol: Bristol Classical Press.

Hamilakis, Y. (2006), 'The Colonial, the National, and the Local: Legacies of the "Minoan" Past', in Y. Hamilakis and N. Momigliano (eds.), *Archaeology and European Modernity: Producing and Consuming the 'Minoans'*, 145–62, Padova: Bottega d'Erasmo (Ausilio).

Hamilakis, Y. (2007), *The Nation and its Ruins: Antiquity, Archaeology, and National Imagination in Greece*, Oxford: Oxford University Press.

Hamilakis, Y. (2013), *Archaeology and the Senses: Human Experience, Memory, and Affect*, New York: Cambridge University Press.

Hamilakis, Y. (ed.) (2002), *Labyrinth Revisited: Rethinking 'Minoan' Archaeology*, Oxford: Oxbow Books.

Hamilakis, Y. and N. Momigliano (eds.) (2006), *Archaeology and European Modernity: Producing and Consuming the 'Minoans'*, Padova: Bottega d'Erasmo (Ausilio) (special volume of *Creta Antica*, no. 7).

Hamilakis, Y. and E. Yalouri (1996), 'Antiquities as Symbolic Capital in Modern Greek Society', *Antiquity* 70: 117–29.

Hand, J. ([1999] 2001), *Voice of the Goddess*, Cardiff, CA: Pacific Rim Press.

Harloe, K. C. and N. Momigliano (2018), 'Introduction. Hellenomania: Ancient and Modern Obsessions with the Greek Past', in K. Harloe, N. Momigliano, and A. Farnoux (eds.), *Hellenomania*, Oxford and New York: Routledge.

Harrel-Courtès, H. (1967), *Les Fils De Minos*, Paris: Plon.

Harrison, J. E. (1903), *Prolegomena to the Study of Greek Religion*, Cambridge: Cambridge University Press.

Harrison, J., G. Murray, and F. Cornford (1912), *Themis: A Study of the Social Origins of Greek Religion*, Cambridge: Cambridge University Press.

Harsent, D. (2008), *The Minotaur: An Opera*, London: Boosey and Hawkes.

Haverfield, F. (1912), *The Romanisation of Roman Britain*, 2nd edition, Oxford: Clarendon Press.

Hawes, C. H. and H. B. Hawes (1909), *Crete the Forerunner of Greece*, London and New York: Harper and Brothers.

Hawes, H. B., B. E. Williams, R. B. Seager, and E. H. Hall (1908), *Gournia, Vasiliki and other Prehistoric Sites on the Isthmus of Hierapetra, Crete; Excavations of the Wells–Houston–Cramp Expeditions, 1901, 1903, 1904*, Philadelphia: American Exploration Society.

Hawkes, J. (1967), 'God in the Machine', *Antiquity* 41: 174–80.

Hawkes, J. (1968), *Dawn of the Gods*, London: Chatto and Windus.

Hawkes, J. (1980), *Quest of Love*, London: Chatto and Windus.

Heidegger, M. (1989), *Aufenthalte*, Frankfurt am Main: Klostermann.

Heidegger, M. (2005), *Sojourns: The Journey to Greece*, trans. J. P. Manoussakis, New York: State University of New York Press.

Herzfeld, M. (1991), *A Place in History: Social and Monumental Time in a Cretan Town*, Princeton, NJ: Princeton University Press.

Herzfeld, M. (2002), 'The Absence Presence: Discourses of Crypto-colonialism', *South Atlantic Quarterly* 101, no. 4: 899–926.

Hicks, D. (2010), 'The Material-cultural Turn: Event and Effect', in D. Hicks and M. C. Beaudry (eds.), *The Oxford Handbook of Material Culture Studies*, 25–98, Oxford: Oxford University Press.

Higgins, R. A. (1967), *Minoan and Mycenaean Art*, London: Thames and Hudson.

Hilleström, G. (1956), 'Sverige (Sweden)', in R. Hainaux (ed.), with foreword by J. Cocteau and preface by K. Rae, *Stage Design Throughout the World Since 1935*, 24–5, London: George G. Harrap and Co.

Hingley, R. (1982), *Nightingale Fever: Russian Poets in Revolution*, London: Weidenfeld and Nicolson.

Hitchcock, L. A. (2000), 'Engendering Ambiguity in Minoan Crete: It's a Drag to be a King', in M. Donald and L. Hurcombe (eds.), *Representations of Gender from Prehistory to the Present*, 69–86, London: Palgrave Macmillan.

Hitchcock, L. A. and P. Koudounaris (2002), 'Virtual discourse: Arthur Evans and the reconstruction of the Minoan palace at Knosso', in Y. Hamilakis (ed.), *Labyrinth Revisited: Rethinking 'Minoan' Archaeology*, 40–58, Oxford: Oxbow books.

Hobsbawm, E. (1994), *The Age of Extremes: The Short Twentieth Century, 1914–1991*, London: Michael Joseph.

Hobson, J. M. (2004), *The Eastern Origins of Western Civilization*, Cambridge and New York: Cambridge University Press.

Hodder, I. (2012), *Entangled: An Archaeology of the Relationships between Humans and Things*, Malden, MA, and Oxford: Wiley-Blackwell.

Hoeck, K. (1823–9), *Kreta. Ein versuch zur Aufhellung der Mythologie und Geschichte der Religion und Verfassung dieser Insel, von den ältesten Zeiten bis auf die Römer-Herrschaft*, 3 vols., Göttingen: Rosenbuch.

Hogarth, D. G. (1903), 'The Cretan Exhibition', *Cornhill Magazine* 81, New Series (March 1903): 319–32.

Hogarth, D. G. (1908), 'Aegean Religion', in J. Hastings (ed.), *Encyclopaedia of Religion and Ethics*, vol. 1, 141–8, New York: Charles Scribner's Sons.

Hogarth, D. G. and R. C. Bosanquet (1899), 'Archaeology in Greece, 1898–9', *Journal of Hellenic Studies* 19: 319–29.

Holland, R. and D. Makrides (2006), *The British and the Hellenes: Struggles for Mastery in the Eastern Mediterranean 1850–1960*, Oxford: Oxford University Press.

Hood, S. (1961), 'The Date of the Linear B Tablets from Knossos', *Antiquity* 35, no. 137: 4–7.

Hood, S. (1962), 'Stratigraphic Excavations at Knossos, 1957–61', in *Πεπραγμένα του Α' Διεθνούς Κρητολογικού Συνεδρίου (Ηράκλειο 23–26 Σεπτεμβρίου 1961)*, in *Κρητικά Χρονικά*, vols. 15–16: 92–8.

Hood, S. (1967), *Home of the Heroes: The Aegean before the Greeks*, London: Thames and Hudson.

Hood, S. (1971), *The Minoans: Crete in the Bronze Age*, London: Thames and Hudson.

Hood, S. (1987), 'An Early British Interest in Knossos', *Annual of British School at Athens* 82: 85–94.

Hood, S. (1995), 'Collingwood on the Minoan civilization of Crete', *Collingwood Studies II*: 175–9.

Hood, S. (2020), *The Masons' Marks of Minoan Knossos*, ed. L. Bendall, London: British School at Athens.

Hood, S. and G. Cadogan (2011), *Knossos Excavations, 1957–1961: Early Minoan*, London: British School at Athens.

Hood, S. and D. Smyth (1981), *Archaeological Survey of the Knossos Area*, London: British School at Athens.

Hood, S. and W. Taylor (1981), *The Bronze Age Palace At Knossos: Plan and Sections*, London: British School at Athens.

Hopkins, J. (2011), 'Ayrton [née Walshe/Balchin], Elisabeth Evelyn', *Oxford Dictionary of National Biography*, https://doi.org/10.1093/ ref:odnb/49561.

Howes, D. (2006), *Empire of the Senses: The Sensual Culture Reader*, Oxford: Berg.

Howes, D. (2013), *The Expanding Field of Sensory Studies*, https://www.sensorystudies.org/ sensorial-investigations/the-expanding-field-of-sensory-studies/.

Howes, D. (2018), *Senses and Sensation: Critical and Primary Sources*, London: Bloomsbury.

Hrozný, B. (1917), *Die Sprache der Hethiter: ihr Bau und ihre Zugehörigkeit zum indogermanischen Sprachstamm*, Leipzig: Hinrichs.

Huby, P. (2000), *Pasiphae*, Stockport: Dewi Lewis.

Humbert, J. (1994), 'Egyptomania: A Current Concept from the Renaissance to Postmodernism', in J. Humbert, M. Pantazzi, and C. Ziegler (eds.), *Egyptomania: Egypt in Western Art 1730–1930*, 21–6, Ottawa: National Gallery of Canada.

Humbert-Mougin, S. (2006), 'La "crétomanie" dans les arts de la scène en France au temps de la revue *Le Voyage en Grèce*', in S. Basch and A. Farnoux (eds.), *Le Voyage en Grèce 1934-1939. Du périodique de tourisme à la revue artistique*, 205–18, Athens: École française d'Athènes.

Hurwit, J. M. (1999), *The Athenian Acropolis: History, Mythology and Archaeology from the Neolithic Era to the Present*, Cambridge: Cambridge University Press.

Hutchinson, R. W. (1962), *Prehistoric Crete*, Harmondsworth, Middlesex: Penguin.

Hutton, R. (1997), 'The Neolithic Great Goddess: A Study in Modern Tradition', *Antiquity* 71: 91–9.

Huxley, A. (1917), *Jonah*, Oxford: Holywell Press.

Huxley, G. (1961), *Crete and the Luwians*, Oxford: Vincent-Baxter Press.

Huxley, G. (1968), *Minoans in Greek Sources: A Lecture*, Belfast: Queen's University of Belfast.

Huxley, G. (1994), 'On Knossos and her Neighbours (7th century to mid-4th century B.C.)', in D. Evely, H. Hughes-Brock, and N. Momigliano (eds.), *Knossos: A Labyrinth of History. Papers Presented in Honour of Sinclair Hood*, 123–33, Oxford: British School at Athens and Oxbow Books.

Ihm, S. (2015), 'Robert Graves's *The Greek Myths* and Matriarchy', in A. G. G. Gibson (ed.), *Robert Graves and the Classical Tradition*, 165–80, Oxford: Oxford University Press.

Ingold, T. (2007), 'Materials against Materiality', *Archaeological Dialogues* 14, no. 1: 1–16.

Isaakidou, V. and P. Tomkins (2008), *Escaping the Labyrinth: The Cretan Neolithic in Context*, Oxford: Oxbow Books.

Jacobs, E. P. (1957), *L'Enigme de l'Atlantide*, Brussels: Éditions du Lombard.

James, E. O. (1959), *The Cult of the Mother-goddess: An Archaeological and Documentary Study*, London: Thames and Hudson.

Janes, C. (2013), *The Eagles of Crete: An Untold Story of Civil War*, Scotts Valley, CA: CreateSpace Independent Publishing Platform.

Jauss, H. (1982), *Toward an Aesthetic of Reception*, trans. B. Timothy, Minneapolis: University of Minnesota Press.

Jenkyns, R. (1980), *The Victorian and Ancient Greece*, Cambridge, MA: Harvard University Press.

Jones, R. (1991), *Prince of the Lilies*, Fitzroy, Victoria, Australia: McPhee Gribble.

Jusdanis, G. (2004), 'Farewell to the Classical: Excavations in Modernism', *Modernism/ Modernity* 11, no. 1: 37–53.

Kane, A. (1996), 'A Catalogue of Works Choreographed by Paul Taylor', *Dance Research: The Journal of the Society for Dance Research* 14, no. 2: 7–75.

Kantor, H. J. (1947), *The Aegean and the Orient in the Second Millennium B.C.*, Bloomington, IN: Principia.

Karadimas, N. (2009), 'Prolegomena to Aegean Archaeology: From the Renaissance Until 1875', PhD dissertation, University of Bristol.

Karadimas, N. (2015), 'The Unknown Past of Minoan Archaeology: From the Renaissance Until the Arrival of Sir Arthur Evans in Crete', in S. Cappel, U. Günkel-Maschek, and

D. Panagiotopoulos (eds.), *Minoan Archaeology: Perspectives for the 21st Century*, 3–15, Louvain-la-Neuve: Presses Universitaires de Louvain Series.

Karadimas, N. and N. Momigliano (2004), 'On the term "Minoan" before Sir Arthur Evans's Work in Crete (1894)', *Studi Micenei ed Egeo Anatolici* 46: 243–58.

Karanikas, A. (1983), 'Greek-American Literature', in R. J. Di Pietro (ed.), *Ethnic Perspectives in American Literature: Selected Essays on the European Contribution: A Source Book*, 65–89, New York: Modern Language Association of America.

Kardamitzi-Adami, M. (2009), *Ανάκτορα στην Ελλάδα*, Athens: Melissa.

Karetsou, A. (1981), 'The Peak Sanctuary of Mt. Juktas', in R. Hägg and N. Marinatos (eds.), *Sanctuaries and Cults in the Aegean Bronze Age. Proceedings of the First International Symposium at the Swedish Institute in Athens, 12–13 May 1980*, 137–53, Stockholm: Svenska Institutet i Athen.

Karo, G. (1959), *Greifen am Thron: Erinnerungen an Knossos*, Baden-Baden: B.Grimm.

Katsan, G. (2013), *History and National Ideology in Greek Postmodernist Fiction*, Madison, NJ: Farleigh Dickinson University Press.

Kazantzakis, N. (1952), *Zorba the Greek*, trans. C. Wildman, London: J. Lehmann.

Kazantzakis, N. (1956), *Freedom or Death*, trans. J. Griffin, preface A. Doolaard, New York: Simon and Schuster.

Kazantzakis, N. (1958), *The Odyssey: A Modern Sequel*, trans. F. Kimon, London: Secker and Warburg.

Kazantzakis, N. (1969), *Three Plays: Christopher Columbus, Melissa, Kouros*, trans. A. Giannakas-Dallas, New York: Simon and Schuster.

Kazantzakis, N. (1973), *Report to Greco*, trans. P. Bien, London: Faber & Faber.

Kazantzakis, N. (1988), *At The Palace of Knossos*, trans. T. Vasils, London: Peter Owen.

Kazantzakis, N. and P. Bien (2012), *The Selected Letters of Nikos Kazantzakis*, Princeton, NJ: Princeton University Press.

Keeley, E. (1961), *The Gold-Hatted Lover*, London: Faber & Faber.

Keeley, E. (1999), *Inventing Paradise: The Greek Journey 1937–1947*, Evanston, IL: Northwestern University Press.

Kerenyi, K. (1976), *Dionysos: Archetypal Image of Indestructible Life*, trans. R. Manheim, London: Routledge and Kegan Paul.

Keyes, S. (1948), *Minos of Crete: Plays and Stories*, ed. M. Meyer, London: Routledge.

Kienzle, P. (1998), 'Conservation and Reconstruction at the Palace of Minos at Knossos', PhD dissertation, University of York, http://etheses.whiterose.ac.uk/9787/.

Kingsley, C. (1856), *The Heroes, or Greek Fairy Tales for My Children*, Cambridge: Macmillan.

Kingsley, C. (1964), *Theseus: A Greek Legend Retold by Charles Kingsley with an Afterword by Mary Renault, Illustrated by Federico Castellon*, New York and London: Macmillan.

Klee, P. (1920), *Schöpferische Konfession*, Berlin: E. Reiss, https://upload.wikimedia.org/wikipedia/commons/1/1c/Schoepferische_Konfession_-_Paul_Klee.pdf.

Klee, P. and Artemis Group (1989), *Paul Klee 1879–1940*, London: Artemis Fine Arts.

Klee, P. and H. Read (1948), *Paul Klee on Modern Art*, London: Faber & Faber.

Koliopoulos, J. S. and T. M. Veremis (2009), *Modern Greece: A History Since 1821*, A New History of Modern Europe, Chichester: Wiley-Blackwell.

Kopaka, K. (1989–90), 'Μίνωος Καλοκαιρινού, Ανασκαφές στην Κνωσό', *Παλίμψηστον* 9, no. 10: 5–69.

Kopaka, K. (2004), 'Η Κνωσός πριν τον Καλοκαιρινό. Μια λησμονημένη μητρόπολη των πηγών', in G. Cadogan, E. Hatzaki, and A. Vasilakis (eds.), *Knossos: Palace, City, State. Proceedings of the Conference in Herakleion organised by the British School at Athens*

and the 23rd Ephoreia of Prehistoric and Classical Antiquities of Herakleion, in
   November 2000, for the Centenary of Sir Arthur Evans's Excavations at Knossos,
   497–512, London: British School at Athens.
Kopaka, K. (2015), 'Minos Kalokairinos and his Early Excavation at Knossos: An Overview,
   a Portrait and a Return to the Kephala Pithoi', in C. F. Macdonald, E. Hatzaki, and
   S. Andreou (eds.), *The Great Islands: Studies of Crete and Cyprus presented to Gerald
   Cadogan*, 143–61, Athens: Kapon.
Kopaka, K. (2017), 'Rhea Galanaki's *The Century of the Labyrinths*: A Dialogue between
   Literature and Archaeology That Starts with Minos Kalokairinos', in N. Momigliano
   and A. Farnoux (eds.), *Cretomania: Modern Desires for the Minoan Past*, 180–8, London
   and New York: Routledge.
Kopytoff, I. (1988), 'The Cultural Biography of Things: Commoditization as Process', in
   A. Appadurai (ed.), *The Social Life of Things: Commodities in Cultural Perspective*,
   64–91, Cambridge: Cambridge University Press.
Kostopoulou, E. (2012), 'The Art of being Replaced: The Last of the Cretan Muslims
   between the Empire and the Nation State', in J. S. Nielsen (ed.), *Religion, Ethnicity and
   Contested Nationhood in the Former Ottoman Space*, 129–46, Leiden: Brill.
Kouremenos, A. (2016), 'The Double Axe (λάβρυς) in Roman Crete and Beyond: The
   Iconography of a Multi-faceted Symbol', in J. E. Francis and A. Kouremenos (eds.),
   Roman Crete: New Perspectives, 43–57, Oxford: Oxbow Books.
Krapf, T. (2019), 'Searching for Neo-Minoan Architecture', in E. Borgna, I. Caloi, F. M. Carinci,
   and R. Laffineur (eds.), *MNHMH / MNEME: Past and Memory in the Aegean Bronze Age,
   Proceedings of the 17th International Aegean Conference, University of Udine, Department of
   Humanities and Cultural Heritage, Ca' Foscari University of Venice, Department of
   Humanities, 17–21 April 2018*, 709–12, Aegaeum 43, Leuven and Liège: Peeters.
Kriga, D. (2011), 'Οι μινωικές δεξαμενές καθαρμών και τα ιουδαϊκά mikweh. Ίδια
   αρχιτεκτονική μορφή – διαφορετικές λειτουργίες', in *Πεπραγμένα του Ι' Διεθνούς
   Κρητολογικού Συνεδρίου (Χανιά 1–8 Οκτωβρίου 2006)*, vol. A3, 797–817, Chania:
   Φιλολογικός Σύλλογος 'Χρυσόστομος'.
Krischen, F. and G. Tischer (1921), *Ein Festtag am Hofe des Minos / 50 Steinzeichnungen
   von Fritz Krischen*, Berlin: Schoetz and Parrhysius.
Krzyszkowska, O. (2000), 'The Eye of the Beholder: Some Nineteenth Century Views of
   Aegean Glyptic', in W. Müller (ed.), *Minoisch-mykenische Glyptik: Stil, Ikonographie,
   Funktion. V. Internationales Siegel-Symposium Marburg, 23–25 September 1999*, 149–63,
   Berlin: Gebr. Mann.
Krzyszkowska, O. (2005), *Aegean Seals: An Introduction*, London: Institute of Classical
   Studies.
Krzyszkowska, O. and L. Nixon (1983), *Minoan Society: Proceedings of the Cambridge
   Colloquium, 1981*, Bristol: Bristol Classical Press.
Lacarrière, J. (1975), *L'été Grec: Une Grèce Quotidienne de 4000 Ans*, Paris: Plon.
Lafarge, J. (2014), *Le Testament d'Issasara: Une Épopée au Temps des Minoens*, Paris:
   Books on Demand.
Lagrange, M. J. (1908), *La Crète Ancienne*, Paris: Librairie Victor Lecoffre.
Lalaki, D. (2012), 'On the Social Construction of Hellenism: Cold War Narratives of
   Modernity, Development and Democracy for Greece', *Journal of Historical Sociology* 25:
   552–77.
Lambropoulos, V. (2010), 'Unbuilding the Acropolis in Greek Literature', in S. Stephens and
   P. Vasunia (eds.), *Classics and National Culture*, 182–98, Oxford: Oxford University
   Press.

Lamprey, L. (1928), *Children of Ancient Greece*, London: Harrap.

Lancaster, O. (1947), *Classical Landscape with Figures*, London: Murray.

Lapatin, K. (2002), *Mysteries of the Snake Goddess: Art, Desire, and the Forging of History*, Boston and New York: Houghton Mifflin.

Lapatin, K. (2006), 'Forging the Minoan Past', in Y. Hamilakis and N. Momigliano (eds), *Archaeology and European Modernity: Producing and Consuming the 'Minoans'*, 89–105, Padova: Bottega d'Erasmo (Ausilio).

La Rosa, V. (1984), 'Gli Scavi e le Ricerche di età Minoica', Scuola Archeologica Italiana di Atene, *Creta Antica: Cento Anni di Archeologia Italiana*, 35–42, Rome: De Luca.

La Rosa, V. (2000), 'Ti Abbraccio Fraternamente: Lettere di J. Chatzidakes a F. Halbherr', *Atti dell'Accademia Roveretana degli Agiati* 7, no. 10: 7–112.

La Rosa, V. (2001), 'Lo Scavo di Festòs Nella Letteratura Archeologica Italiana', in *I Cento Anni Dello Scavo di Festòs (Roma, 13–14 dicembre 2000)*, 25–49, Rome: Accademia Nazionale Dei Lincei.

La Rosa, V. (2010), 'Ayia Triada', in E. H. Cline (ed.), *Oxford Handbook of the Bronze Age Aegean (ca. 3000–1000 BC)*, 495–508, Oxford: Oxford University Press.

La Rosa, V. (2014), 'La Conclusione dei Lavori ad Haghia Triada: Le Campagne 2010–2012', *Creta Antica* 15: 129–241.

La Rosa, V. and P. Militello (2006), 'Minoan Crete in 20th-century Italian Culture', in Y. Hamilakis and N. Momigliano (eds.), *Archaeology and European Modernity: Producing and Consuming the 'Minoans'*, 241–58, Padova: Bottega d'Erasmo (Ausilio).

Latour, B. (2005), *Reassembling the Social: An Introduction to Actor-Network Theory*, Oxford: Oxford University Press.

Lawrence, D. H. (1932), *Last Poems*, Florence: G. Orioli.

Lawrence, D. H. (1932b), *Etruscan Places*, http://gutenberg.net.au/ebooks09/0900381h.html.

Lawton, E. (1977), *The Inevitability of Matriarchy*, London: Community Press.

Lebel, M. (1969), *Le Voyage de Grèce: Bibliographie de Voyageurs Français en Grèce au XXe Siècle (1900–1968)*, Sherbrooke, Canada: Editions Pauline.

Lebessi, A. (1992), 'Syme', in J. Myers, E. E. Myers, and G. Cadogan (eds.), *The Aerial Atlas of Ancient Crete*, 268–71, Berkeley: University of California Press.

Leconte de Lisle, C. M. R and F. Kupka (1908), *Les Erinnyes: Tragédie Antique*, Paris: Romagnol.

Lee, L. (1968), *The Cretan Flute and Other Poems*, Dublin: Dolmen Press.

Leontis, A. (1995), *Topographies of Hellenism: Mapping the Homeland*, Ithaca, NY, and London: Cornell University Press.

Leontis, A. (2018), 'Fashioning a Modern Self in Greek Dress: The Case of Eva Palmer Sikelianos', in K. Harloe, N. Momigliano, and A. Farnoux (eds.), *Hellenomania*, 212–32, Abingdon, UK, and New York: Routledge.

Lévi-Strauss, C. (1963), *Totemism*, trans. R. Needham, Boston: Beacon Press.

Llewellyn Smith, M. (1965), *The Great Island: A Study of Crete*, London: Longmans.

Long, C. (2002), *Josef Frank: Life and Work*, Chicago and London: University of Chicago Press.

Lorimer, H. L. (1950), *Homer and the Monuments*, London: Macmillan.

Lubbock, J. (1865), *Pre-Historic Times, As Illustrated by Ancient Remains, and the Manners and Customs of Modern Savages*, London: Williams and Norgate.

Luce, J. V. (1969), *The End of Atlantis: New Light on an Old Legend*, Norwich: Thames and Hudson.

Lunn, H. S. (ed.) (1925), *Aegean Civilizations: Lectures by Dr Caton; L.R. Furneaux; The late Rev. J. Gow, D.D.; The Venerable S.R. James, Archdeacon of Dudley; W. Allan Jamieson,*

M.D.; Walter Leaf, Litt.D.; The late Professor Sanday and Others, London: Epworth Press.

Macaulay, R. (1953), *Pleasure of Ruins*, London: Weidenfeld and Nicolson.

MacDonagh, D. and E. S. Lennox Robinson (1958), *The Oxford Book of Irish Verse, XVIIth–XXth century*, Oxford: Oxford University Press.

MacGillivray, J. A. (2000), *Minotaur: Sir Arthur Evans and the Archaeology of the Minoan Myth*, London: Jonathan Cape.

MacGillivray, J. A. (2009), 'Thera, Hatshepsut, and the Keftiu: Crisis and Response', in D. A. Warburton (ed.), *Time's Up! Dating the Minoan Eruption of Santorini*, 154–70, Athens and Aarhus: Danish Institute at Athens, Aarhus University Press.

MacGillivray, J. A. and L. H. Sackett (1992), 'Palaikastro', in J. Myers, E. E. Myers, and G. Cadogan (eds.), *The Aerial Atlas of Ancient Crete*, 222–31, Berkeley: University of California Press.

MacGillivray, J.A. and L.H. Sackett (2010), 'Palaikastro', in E.H. Cline (ed.) *The Oxford Handbook of the Bronze Age Aegean (ca. 3000–1000 BC)*, Oxford: Oxford University Press, 571–581.

MacGregor, A. (ed.) (2008), *Sir John Evans, 1823–1908: Antiquity, Commerce and the Natural Science in the Age of Darwin*, Oxford: Ashmolean Museum.

Mac Sweeney, N. (2013), 'Being Ionian: The Ionian League, Ionian Migrations and Smyrna', in N. Mac Sweeney (ed.), *Foundation Myths and Politics in Ancient Ionia*, 157–97, Cambridge: Cambridge University Press.

Magnan, J.-M. (1965), *Taureaux*, Paris: Michèle Trinckvel.

Mallory, J. P. (1989), *In Search of the Indo-Europeans: Language, Archaeology and Myth*, London: Thames and Hudson.

Mandelstam, O. (2014), *Poems of Osip Mandelstam*, trans. P. France, New York: New Directions Books.

Mandelstam, O., R. McKane, and E. McKane (1996), *The Voronezh Notebooks: Osip Mandelstam, Poems 1935–1937*, Newcastle-upon-Tyne: Bloodaxe Books.

Manfredi, V. M and D. Manfredi (2014), *Odisseo. Le imprese straordinarie del re di Itaca*, Milan: Mondadori.

Manning, H. (1971), *Encounter in Crete*, London: Enitharmon Press.

Manning, S. W. (2014), *A Test of Time and a Test of Time Revisited: The Volcano of Thera and the Chronology and History of the Aegean and East Mediterranean in the Mid-second Millennium BC*, 2nd edition, Oxford: Oxbow Books.

Maraghiannis, G. and G. Karo (1911), *Antiquités Crétoises: Deuxième Série*, Candia: Maraghiannis.

Maraghiannis, G., L. Pernier, and G. Karo (1907), *Antiquités Crétoises: Première Série*, Vienna: Angerer.

Maraghiannis, G. and R. B. Seager (1915), *Antiquités Crétoises: Troisième Série*, Candia: Maraghiannis.

Marchand, S. L. (1996), *Down from Olympus: Archaeology and Philhellenims in Germany, 1750–1970*, Princeton, NJ: Princeton University Press.

Marinatos, N. (1989), 'The Bull as an Adversary: Some Observations on Bull-hunting and Bull- leaping', *Ariadne* 5: 23–32.

Marinatos, N. (1994), 'The "Export" Significance of Minoan Bull-hunting and Bull-leaping Scenes', *Ägypten und Levante* 4: 89–93.

Marinatos, N. (2010), *Minoan Kingship and the Solar Goddess: A Near Eastern Koine*, Urbana and Chicago: University of Illinois Press.

Marinatos, N. (2015), *Sir Arthur Evans and Minoan Crete: Creating the Vision of Knossos*, London: I.B. Tauris.

Marinatos, S. (1939), 'The Volcanic Destruction of Minoan Crete', *Antiquity* 13, no. 52: 425–39.

Marinatos, S. (1971), *Some Words about the Legend of Atlantis*, 2nd edition, Athens: General Direction of Antiquity.

Marinatos, S. and M. Hirmer (1960), *Crete and Mycenae*, trans. J. Boardman, London: Thames and Hudson.

Markatou, D. F. (2008), 'Archaeology and Greekness on the Centenary Celebrations of the Greek State', in D. Damaskos and D. Plantzos (eds.), *A Singular Antiquity: Archaeology and Hellenic Identity in Twentieth-century Greece*, 309–20, Athens: Benaki Museum.

Martindale, C. (1993), *Redeeming the Text: Latin Poetry and the Hermeneutics of Reception*, Cambridge: Cambridge University Press.

Mastorakis, M. and M. van Effenterre (1991), *Les Minoens: L'âge d'or de la Crète*, Paris: Armand Colin.

Matt, L. von, S. Alexiou, N. Platon, and H. Guanella (1967a), *Das antike Kreta*, Zürich: NZN-Buchverlag.

Matt, L. von, S. Alexiou, N. Platon, and H. Guanella (1967b), *La Crète Antique*, Paris: Hachette.

Matt, L. von, S. Alexiou, N. Platon, and H. Guanella (1968), *Ancient Crete*, London: Thames and Hudson.

Matton, R. (1957), *La Crète au Cours des Siècles*, Athens: Institut Français D'Athènes.

Matz, F. (1962a), *Crete and Early Greece: The Prelude to Greek Art*, London: Methuen.

Matz, F. (1962b), *Kreta und frühes Griechenland: Prolegomena zur griechischen Kunstgeschichte*, Baden-Baden: Holle.

Matz, F. (1962c), *Minoan Civilization: Maturity and Zenith*, Cambridge Ancient History Revised Edition of Volumes I & II, Cambridge: Cambridge University Press.

Matz, F. (1973a), 'The Maturity of Minoan Civilization', in E. I. S. Edwards, C. J. Gadd, N. Hammond, and E. Sollberger (eds.), *The Cambridge Ancient History*, vol. 2, part 1: *History of the Middle East and Aegean Region c. 1800–1380 B.C.*, 141–64, Cambridge: Cambridge University Press.

Matz, F. (1973b), 'The Zenith of Minoan Civilization', in E. I. S. Edwards, C. J. Gadd, N. Hammond, and E. Sollberger (eds.), *The Cambridge Ancient History*, vol. 2, part 1: *History of the Middle East and Aegean Region c. 1800–1380 B.C.*, 557–81, Cambridge: Cambridge University Press.

Mauclair, C. (1934), *Le Pur Visage de la Grèce*, Paris: Grasset.

McCredden, L. (2014), 'Crete: Dorothy Porter, Exuberance, and the Limits of Art', *Journal of Australian Studies* 38, no. 3: 271–80.

McDonald, W. A. (1967), *Progress into the Past: The Rediscovery of Mycenaean Civilisation*, Bloomingtom: Indiana University Press.

McDonald, W. A. and C. G. Thomas (1990), *Progress into the Past: The Rediscovery of Mycenaean Civilisation*, 2nd edition, Bloomingtom: Indiana University Press.

McEnroe, J. C. (1995), 'Arthur Evans and Edwardian Archaeology', *Classical Bulletin* 7: 3–18.

McEnroe, J. C. (2010), *Architecture of Minoan Crete: Constructing Identity in the Aegean Bronze Age*, Austin: University of Texas Press.

McGowan, E. (2011), *Ambiguity and Minoan Neopalatial Seal Imagery*, Uppsala: Åström Förlag.

Mélida, J. R. (1905), 'Nota Sobre la Arquitectura Miceniana en Iberia: La Acrópolis de Tarragona', *Revista de Arquitectura y Construcción* 6–10: 38–47.

Mellink, M. J. (1964), 'Lycian Wooden Huts and Sign 24 on the Phaistos Disk', *Kadmos* 3: 1–7.

Merezhkovsky, D. ([1925] 1926), *The Birth of the Gods: Tutankhamon in Crete*, trans. N. A. Duddington, London: Dent and Sons.

Merezhkovsky, D. (1927), *Akhnaton: King of Egypt*, trans. N. A. Duddington, London and Toronto: Dent and Sons.

Merezhkovsky, D. ([1930] 1933), *The Secret of the West: Atlantis-Europe*, trans. J. Cournos, London: Jonathan Cape.

Michaelis, A. (1905), *Die Archäologischen Entdeckungen des Neunzehnten Jahrhunderts*, Leipzig: Seeman.

Michaelis, A. (1908), *A Century of Archaeological Discoveries*, London: Murray.

Michaels, B. (1975), *The Sea King's Daughter*, New York: Dodd, Mead and Co.

Michaels, B. ([1975] 1989), *The Sea King's Daughter*, New York: Berkley Books.

Michalaros, D. (1958), *The Minoan*, Chicago: Athene Editions.

Milchhöfer, A. (1883), *Die Anfänge der Kunst in Griechenland*, Leipzig: F.A. Brockhaus.

Miller, D. (ed.) (2005), *Materiality (Politics, History, and Culture)*, Durham, NC, and London: Duke University Press.

Miller, H. (1941), *The Colossus of Maroussi*, New York: New Directions.

Miller, H. (1973), *First Impressions of Greece*, Santa Barbara, CA: Capra Press.

Mingotti, I. (2016), *Minoica*, Piazza Armerina: Nulla Die.

Mitchison, N. (1931), *Boys and Girls and Gods*, London: Watts and Co.

Mitsotaki, Z. (1999), *Florentini Kaloutsi and the Art of Crete from the Minoan Period to the Present*, Athens: Benaki Museum.

Mitsotaki, Z. (2017), 'Φλωρεντίνη Καλούτση ... Εργάζεται απείρως θετικώτερα υπέρ της ελευθερίας της Ελληνίδος γυναικός, από κάθε κοινωνιολογούσαν φεμινίστριαν', http://iscreta.gr/2017/03/φλωρεντίνη-καλούτση-εργάζεται-απε/.

Momigliano, A. (1966), *Studies In Historiography*, London: Weidenfeld and Nicholson.

Momigliano, N. (1996), 'Evans, Mackenzie, and the History of the Palace at Knossos', *Journal of Hellenic Studies* 116: 166–9.

Momigliano, N. (1999a), *Duncan Mackenzie: A Cautious Canny Highlander and the Palace of Minos at Knossos*, BICS Supplement 72, London: University of London, Institute of Classical Studies.

Momigliano, N. (1999b), 'A Note on A.J. Evans's *The Palace of Minos: A Comparative Account of the Successive Stages of the Early Cretan Civilization as Illustrated by the Discoveries at Knossos*', in P. B. Betancourt, V. Karageorghis, and R. Laffineur (eds.), *Meletemata: Studies in Aegean Archaeology presented to Malcolm H. Wiener as he enters his 65th year*, 493–501, Liège and Austin: Université de Liège, Histoire de l'art et archéologie de la Grèce antique; University of Texas at Austin: Programs in Aegean Scripts and Prehistory.

Momigliano, N. (2000a), 'Crete', in G. Speake (ed.), *Encyclopedia of Greece and the Hellenic Tradition*, 414–17, London and Chicago: Fitzroy Dearborn Publishers.

Momigliano, N. (2000b), 'The Old Palace Period', in D. Huxley (ed.), *Cretan Quests: British Explorers, Excavators and Historians*, 100–12, London: British School at Athens.

Momigliano, N. (2002), 'Federico Halbherr and Arthur Evans: an Archaeological Correspondence (1894–1917)', *Studi Micenei ed Egeo-Anatolici* 44: 263–318.

Momigliano, N. (2006), 'Sir Arthur Evans, Greek Myths, and the Minoans', in P. Darcque, M. Fotiadis, and O. Polychronopoulou (eds.), *Mythos: La Préhistoire Égéenne du XIXe au XXIe Siècle après J.-C. Table Ronde International, Athènes, 21–23 Novembre 2002,* 73–80, Bulletin de Correspondence Hellénique, Supplement 46, Paris: Ecole Française.

Momigliano, N. (2010), 'Review of T. Ziolkowski *Minos and the Moderns* (Oxford, 2008)', *International Journal of the Classical Tradition* 17, no. 2: 310–14.

Momigliano, N. (2013), 'Modern Dance and the Seduction of Minoan Crete', in M. G. Morcillo and S. Knippschild (eds.), *Imagines II. Seduction and Power: Antiquity in the Visual and Performing Arts*, 35–55, London: Bloomsbury.

Momigliano, N. (2017a), 'From Russia with Love: Minoan Crete and the Russian Silver Age', in N. Momigliano and A. Farnoux (eds.), *Cretomania: Modern Desires for the Minoan Past*, 84–110, London and New York: Routledge.

Momigliano, N. (2017b), 'Introduction', in N. Momigliano and A. Farnoux (eds.), *Cretomania: Modern Desires for the Minoan Past*, 1–16, London and New York: Routledge.

Momigliano, N. (2018), 'Minoici a Parigi: memoria e archeologia minoico-micenea nelle pagine di *À la recherche du temps perdu* di Marcel Proust', in G. Baldacci and I. Caloi (eds.), *Rhadamanthys: Studi di archeologia minoica in onore di Filippo Carinci per il suo 70° compleanno/Studies in Minoan archaeology in honour of Filippo Carinci on the occasion of his 70th birthday*, 293–8, Oxford: BAR Publishing.

Momigliano, N. (2019), 'Memory and Modern Receptions of the Aegean Bronze Age', in E. Borgna, I. Caloi, F. M. Carinci, and R. Laffineur (eds.), *MNHMH / MNEME, Past and Memory in the Aegean Bronze Age: Proceedings of the 17th International Aegean Conference, University of Udine, Department of Humanities and Cultural Heritage, Ca' Foscari University of Venice, Department of Humanities, 17–21 April 2018*, 629–38, Leuven: Peeters.

Momigliano, N. (forthcoming), 'Aegeomania', in L. A. Hitchcock (ed.), *A Companion to Aegean Art and Architecture*, Blackwell Companions to the Ancient World.

Momigliano, N. and A. Farnoux (eds.) (2017), *Cretomania: Modern Desires for the Minoan Past*, London and New York: Routledge.

Montelius, O. (1905), *Konung Minos' Palats: Arthur Evans' Upptäckter vid Knossos på Kreta*, Stockholm: Wahlström and Widstrand, http://dbooks.bodleian.ox.ac.uk/books/PDFs/302404500.pdf.

Moore, D. (2013), *Dawn of Discovery: The Early British Travellers to Crete*, Cambridge: Cambridge Scholars Publishing.

Moorey, P. R. S. (1991), *A Century of Biblical Archaeology*, Cambridge: Lutterworth Press.

Morand, P. ([1960–1] 2011), 'La Crète: L'île où le soleil se lève Asie, se couche Europe', in P. Morand, *Bains de Soleil*, 110–29, Paris: Nicholas Chauduh.

Morgan, L. H. (1877), *Ancient Society*, Chicago: C.H. Kerr.

Morris, C. (2007), 'An Ardent Lover of Cretan Freedom: J. D. Bourchier, 1850–1920', in J. V. Luce, C. Morris, and C. Souyoudzoglou-Haywood (eds.), *The Lure of Greece: Irish Involvement in Greek Culture, Literature, History and Politics*, 111–22, Dublin: Hinds.

Morris, C. (2009), 'The Iconography of the Bared Breast in Aegean Bronze Age Art', in K. Kopaka (ed.), *Fylo: Engendering Prehistoric 'Stratigraphies' in the Aegean and the Mediterranean. Proceedngs of an International Conference, University of Crete, Rethymno 2–5 June 2005*, 243–9, Liège and Austin: Université de Liège and University of Texas Press.

Morris, C. (2017), 'Lord of the Dance: Ted Shawn's Gnossienne and its Minoan Context', in N. Momigliano and A. Farnoux (eds.), *Cretomania: Modern Desires for the Minoan Past*, 111–23, London and New York: Routledge.

Morris, C. (2020), 'The Usable Past: Minoans Reimagined, in B. Davis and R. Laffineur (eds.), *ΝΕΩΤΕΡΟΣ. Studies in Bronze Age Aegean Art and Archaeology in*

Honor of Professor John G. Younger on the Occasion of His Retirement, 629–38, Leuven and Liège: Peeters.

Morris, I. (1994), 'Archaeologies of Greece', in I. Morris (ed.), *Classical Greece: Ancient History and Modern Archaeologies*, 8–47, Cambridge: Cambridge University Press.

Morris, S. P. (1992), *Daidalos and the Origins of Greek Art*, Princeton, NJ: Princeton University Press.

Mosso, A. (1907), *Escursioni nel Mediterraneo e gli scavi di Creta*, Milan: Treves (trans. as *Palaces of Crete and their Builders*, London: Unwin).

Mosso, A. (1910), *Le Origini della Civiltà Mediterranea*, Milan: Treves (trans. as *The Dawn of Mediterranean Civilization*, London: Unwin).

Müller, K. O. (1824), *Geschichten hellenischen Stämme und Städte: die Dorier*, Breslau: Max and Komp.

Müller, K. O. (1825), *Prolegomena zu Einer Wissenschaftlichen Mythologie*, Göttingen: Vendenhoeck and Ruprecht.

Müller, K. O. (1830), *Handbuch der Archäologie der Kunst*, Breslau: Max.

Müller, K. O. (1832–5), *Denkmäler der alten Kunst*, 5 vols., Göttingen: Dietrich.

Mulvey, L. (1989), *Visual and Other Pleasures*, London: Palgrave Macmillan.

Murnaghan, S. (2007), 'Review of C. Martindale and R.F. Thomas (eds.) 2006, *Classics and the Uses of Reception* (Oxford: Blackwell)', *Bryn Mawr Classical Review*, http://bmcr. brynmawr.edu/2007/2007-07-19.html.

Murnaghan, S. and D. H. Roberts (2018), *Childhood and the Classics: Britain and America, 1850–1965*, Oxford: Oxford University Press.

Murray, G. (1907), *The Rise of the Greek Epic*, Oxford: Clarendon Press.

Murray, G. (1909), 'The Hymn of the Kouretes', *Annual of the British School at Athens* 15: 357–65.

Myles, G. F. (1973), 'The Interaction between Landscape and Myth in the Novels of John Cowper Powys', PhD dissertation, University of British Columbia, https://open.library. ubc.ca/cIRcle/collections/ubctheses.

Myres, J. L. (1901), 'Abstract of the Report of the Committee of the British Association on Explorations in Crete', *Man* 1, no. 1: 4–7.

Myres, J. L. (1911), *The Dawn of History*, New York and London: Holt and Co. and Williams and Norgate.

Myres, J. L. (1930), *Who Were the Greeks?*, Berkeley: University of California Press.

Myres, J. L. (1933), 'The Cretan Labyrinth: A Retrospect of Aegean Research. The Huxley Memorial Lecture for 1933', *Journal of the Royal Anthropological Institute* 63: 269–312.

Nagy, G. (1963), 'Greek-like Elements in Linear A', *Greek, Roman, and Byzantine Studies* 4, no. 4: 181–211.

Neale, H. and N. Manolukas (1998), *The Coming of the New Millennium*, Berkeley, CA: Labrys.

Nencioni, G. (1967), 'Agnizioni di lettura', *Strumenti Critici* 2: 191–8.

Neumann, E. (1955), *The Great Mother: An Analysis of the Archetype*, London: Routledge and Kegan Paul.

Niemeier, B. and W. D. Neimeier (1999), 'The Minoans of Miletus', in P. B. Betancourt, V. Karageorghis, and R. Laffineur (eds.), *Meletemata: Studies in Aegean Archaeology presented to Malcolm H. Wiener as he enters his 65th year, Vol. II*, 543–54, Liège and Austin: Université de Liège, Histoire de l'art et archéologie de la Grèce antique; University of Texas at Austin: Programs in Aegean Scripts and Prehistory.

Niemeier, B. and W. D. Niemeier (2000), 'Aegean Frescoes in Syria–Palestine: Alalakh and Tel Kabri', in S. Sherratt (ed.), *The Wall Paintings of Thera: Proceedings of the First*

International Symposium, Petros M. Nomikos Conference Centre, Thera, Hellas, August 30–September 4, 1997, 763–802, Athens: Thera Foundation.

Niemeier, W. D. (2009), '"Minoanisation" Versus "Minoan Thalassocrassy" – An Introduction', in C. F. Macdonald, E. Hallager, and W. D. Niemeier (eds.), *The Minoans in the Central, Eastern and Northern Aegean – New Evidence: Acts of a Minoan Seminar 22–23 January 2005 in collaboration with the Danish Institute at Athens and the German Archaeological Institute at Athens*, 11–29, Athens: Danish Institute at Athens.

Niemeier, W. D. and B. Niemeier (1998), 'Minoan Frescoes in the Eastern Mediterranean', in E. H. Cline and D. Harris-Cline (eds.), *The Aegean and the Orient in the Second Millennium*, 69–97, Liège and Austin: Université de Liège and University of Texas Press.

Nijinsky, R. (1933), *Nijinsky*, London: V. Gollancz.

Nijinsky, V. (1937), *The Diary of Vaslav Nijinsky*, ed. R. Nijinsky, London: Gollancz.

Nilsson, M. P. (1927), *The Minoan–Mycenaean Religion and Its Survival in Greek Religion*, Lund: C.W.K. Gleerup.

Nilsson, M. P. (1933), *Homer and Mycenae*, London: Methuen.

Nisbet, G. (2006), *Ancient Greece in Film and Popular Culture*, Bristol: Bristol Phoenix.

Nixon, L. (1995), 'Gender Bias in Archaeology', in L. Archer, S. Fischler, and M. Wyke (eds.), *Women in Ancient Societies: 'An Illusion of the Night'*, 1–23, Basingstoke: Macmillan.

Nora, P. (1989), 'Between Memory and History: *Les Lieux de Mémoire*', *Representations* 26: 7–24.

Nora, P. (1996), 'General Introduction: Between Memory and History', in P. Nora, *The Realms of Memory: Rethinking the French Past*, trans. A. Goldhammer, New York: Columbia University Press.

Nyenhuis, J. E. (2003), *Myth and the Creative Process: Michael Ayrton and the Myth of Daedalus, the Maze Maker*, Detroit: Wayne State University Press.

O'Ballance, E. (1966), *The Greek Civil War 1944–1949*, London: Faber & Faber.

Obsomer, C. (2003), 'Hérodote II 148 à L'origine du Mot Labyrinthos? La Minotauromachie Revisitée', *Cretan Studies* 9: 105–86.

Olivier, J.-P. and L. Godart (1996), *Corpus Hieroglyphicarum Inscriptionum Cretae*, Paris: De Boccard.

Olivier, L. (2011), *The Dark Abyss of Time: Archaeology and Memory*, trans. A. Greenspan, Lanham, MD, New York, Toronto, and Plymouth: Altamira Press.

O'Prey, P. (1984), *Between Moon and Moon: Selected Letters of Robert Graves 1946–1972*, London: Hutchinson.

Oram, A. (2006), '"A Sudden Orgy of Decadence": Writing about Sex between Women in the Interwar Popular Press', in L. Doan and J. Garrity (eds.), *Sapphic Modernities*, New York: Palgrave Macmillan.

Orgel, D. (1994), *Ariadne, Awake!*, with illustrations by B. Moser, New York: Viking Juvenile Press.

Pachmuss, T. (1990), *D.S. Merezhkovsky in Exile: The Master of the Genre of Biographie Romancée*, New York: Peter Lang.

Padel, R. (1990), *Summer Snow*, London: Hutchinson.

Palaima, T. G. (1995), 'The Nature of the Mycenaean Wanax: Non-Indo-European Origins and Priestly Functions', in P. Rehak (ed.), *The Role of the Ruler in the Prehistoric Aegean. Proceedings of a Panel Discussion presented at the Annual Meeting of the Archaeological Institute of America, New Orleans, Louisiana, 28 December 1992*, 119–42, Liège and Austin: Université de Liège, Histoire de l'art et archéologie de la Grèce antique and Program in Aegean Scripts and Prehistory, University of Texas at Austin.

Palaima, T. G. (2010), 'Linear B', in E. H. Cline (ed.), *Oxford Handbook of the Bronze Age Aegean (ca. 3000–1000 BC)*, 356–72, Oxford: Oxford University Press.

Palmer, L. R. (1958), 'Luvian and Linear A', *Transactions of the Philological Society* 57: 75–100.

Palmer, L. R. (1961), *Mycenaeans and Minoans: Aegean Prehistory in the Light of the Linear B Tablets*, London: Faber & Faber.

Palmer, L. R and J. Boardman (1963), *On the Knossos Tablets. (The find-places of the Knossos tablets. By L. R. P. The date of the Knossos tablets. By J. B.)*, Oxford: Clarendon Press.

Panagiotaki, M. (2004), 'Knossos and Evans: Buying Kephala', in G. Cadogan, E. Hatzaki, and A. Vasilakis (eds.), *Knossos: Palace, City, State. Proceedings of the Conference in Herakleion organised by the British School at Athens and the 23rd Ephoreia of Prehistoric and Classical Antiquities of Herakleion, in November 2000, for the Centenary of Sir Arthur Evans's Excavations at Knossos*, 513–30, London: British School at Athens.

Panagiotopoulos, D. (2001), 'Keftiu in Context: Theban Tomb-paintings as a Historical Source', *Oxford Journal of Archaeology* 20: 263–83.

Pantos, A. P. (2013), 'Το θεσμικο πλάισιο των άνάσκάφων στην ελλάδά άπο τον 20o στον 21o άιωνά', https://anaskamma.files.wordpress.com/2013/06/06_pantos.pdf.

Papadopoulos, C. and Y. Sakellarakis (2013), 'Virtual Windows to the Past: Reconstructing the "Ceramics Workshop" at Zominthos, Crete', in F. Contreras, M. Farjas, and F. J. Melero, (eds.) *Fusion of Cultures. Proceedings of the 38th Annual Conference on Computer Applications and Quantitative Methods in Archaeology, Granada, Spain, April 2010*, 47–54, Oxford: Archaeopress.

Papadopoulos, J. K. (2005), 'Inventing the Minoans: Archaeology, Modernity and the Quest for European Identity', *Journal of Mediterranean Studies* 18: 87–149.

Pashley, R. (1837), *Travels in Crete*, Cambridge and London: Pitt Press, J. Murray.

Paton, S. (1994), 'Roman Knossos and the Colonia Julia Nobilis Cnossus', in D. Evely, H. Hughes-Brock, and N. Momigliano (eds.), *Knossos: A Labyrinth of History. Papers Presented in Honour of Sinclair Hood*, 141–53, Oxford: British School at Athens and Oxbow Books.

Paton, S. (2000), 'Hellenistic and Roman Crete', in D. Huxley (ed.), *Cretan Quests: British Explorers, Excavators and Historians*, 174–81, London: British School at Athens.

Paul Klee Foundation (1998–2004), *Paul Klee: Catalogue Raisonné*, ed. Paul Klee Foundation (Museum of Fine Arts, Berne), London: Thames and Hudson.

Paver, M. (2012), *Gods and Warriors: The Outsiders*, London: Puffin.

Paver, M. (2013), *Gods and Warriors: The Burning Shadow*, London: Puffin.

Paver, M. (2014), *Gods and Warriors: The Eye of the Falcon*, London: Puffin.

Paver, M. (2015), *Gods and Warriors: The Crocodile Tomb*, London: Puffin.

Paver, M. (2016), *Gods and Warriors: Warrior Bronze*, London: Puffin.

Pelevin, V. (2006), *The Helmet of Horrors: The Myth of Theseus and the Minotaur*, trans. A. Bromfield, Edinburgh: Canongate.

Pendlebury, J. D. S. (1933), *A Handbook to the Palace of Minos at Knossos: With Its Dependencies*, London: Macmillan.

Pendlebury, J. D. S. (1939), *The Archaeology of Crete: An Introduction*, London: Methuen.

Penrose, R. (1958), *Picasso: His Life and Work*, London: Gollancz.

Perrot, G. and C. Chipiez (1894), *Histoire de l'Art dans l'Antiquité: Tome VI, La Grèce Primitive, l'Art Mycénien*, Paris: Hachette.

Perry, L. (2013), *Ariadne's Thread: Awakening the Wonders of the Ancient Minoans in Our Modern Lives*, Winchester and Washington, DC: Moon Books.

Perry, L. (2016), *Labrys and Horns: An Introduction to Modern Minoan Paganism*, n.p.p.: Potnia Press.

Peters, J. P. (1901), 'Notes on Recent Theories of the Origin of the Alphabet', *Journal of the American Oriental Society* 22: 177–98.

Petersen, D. (2015), 'Live from *Troy*: Embedded in the Trojan War', in M. M. Winkler (ed.), *Return To Troy: New Essays on the Hollywood Epic*, 27–47, Leiden: Brill.

Philippides, D. and O. Sgouros (2017), 'Identity and Freedom: Some Observations on Minoan and Contemporary Greek Architecture', in N. Momigliano and A. Farnoux (eds.), *Cretomania: Modern Desires for the Minoan Past*, 25–38, London and New York: Routledge.

Picard, C. (1932), 'Au Pays du Griffon: Cnossos Ressuscitée', *La revue de l'Art* 41: 3–18.

Picard, C. (1936), 'La Crète au Déclin de la Civilisation "Minoenne"' (Review of Evans, A. *Palace of Minos*, vol. 4), *Journal des Savants* 5: 193–213.

Pierret, M. and J. Denoël (2005), *Les Déesses: T.1 La Grande Île*, Grenoble: Glenat.

Platon, N. (1966), *Crete*, Geneva: Nagel; Cleveland and New York: World Publishing Co.

Platon, N. (1971), *Zakros: The Discovery of a Lost Palace of Ancient Crete*, New York: Scribner.

Platon, N. (1981a), *La Civilisation Egéenne: Du Néolithique au Bronze Récent*, Paris: Albin Michel.

Platon, N. (1981b), *La Civilisation Egéenne: Le Bronze Récent et la Civilisation Mycénienne*, Paris: Albin Michel.

Poliakov, L. (1974), *The Aryan Myth: A History of Racist and Nationalist Ideas in Europe*, trans. E. Howard, London: Chatto and Heinemann for Sussex University Press.

Pollard, P. (1970), 'The sources of Andre Gide's "Thésée"', *Modern Language Review* 65, no. 2: 290–7.

Popham, M. R. (1973), 'The Unexplored Mansion at Knossos: A Preliminary Report on the Excavations from 1967 to 1972. Part I: The Minoan Building and its Occupation', *Archaeological Reports* 19: 50–61.

Popham, M. R. (1978), 'Notes from Knossos, Part II', *Annual of the British School at Athens* 73: 179–87.

Popham, M. R., J. Betts, M. Cameron, H. Catling, D. Evely, R. Higgins, and D. Smyth (1984), *The Minoan Unexplored Mansion At Knossos*, London: British School at Athens.

Porter, D. (1996), *Crete*, Melbourne: Hyland House.

Porter, J. I. (2004), 'Homer: The History of an Idea', in R. Fowler (ed.), *The Cambridge Companion to Homer*, 324–43, Cambridge: Cambridge University Press.

Porter, J. I. (2005), 'What Is "Classical" about Classical Antiquity? Eight Propositions', *Arion: A Journal of Humanities and the Classics* 13, no. 1: 27–62.

Porter, J. I. (2006), 'What is "Classical" about Classical Antiquity', in J. I. Porter (ed.), *Classical Pasts: The Classical Traditions of Greece and Rome*, 1–65, Princeton, NJ: Princeton University Press.

Potolski, M. (2004), 'Introduction', *New Literary History* 35, no. 4: v–xi.

Pottier, E. (1902a), 'Une excursion a Cnossos dans l'ile de Créte', *La Revue de l'Art Ancien et Modern* 12: 81–94 and 161–72.

Pottier, E. (1902b), 'Le Palais de Roi Minos', *La Revue de Paris* 15: 169–99 and 827–50.

Powys, J. C. (1947), *Obstinate Cymric: Essays 1935–47*, Carmarthen, Wales: Druid Press.

Powys, J. C. ([1954] 2008), *Atlantis*, London: Faber & Faber.

Praz, M. (1955), *Viaggi in occidente*, Florence: Sansoni.

Prent, M. (2003), 'Glories of the Past in the Past: Ritual Activity at Palatial Ruins in Early Iron Age Crete', in R. M. Van Dyke and S. E. Alcock (eds.), *Archaeologies of Memory*, 81–103, Malden, MA, and Oxford: Blackwell.

Preziosi (2017), 'Orthochronicity and its (Dis)contents: Cretomania and Frank Lloyd Wright', in N. Momigliano and A. Farnoux (eds.), *Cretomania: Modern Desires for the Minoan Past*, 17–24, London and New York: Routledge.

Proust, M. (1913–27), *À la Recherche du Temps Perdu*, Paris: Gallimard.

Pruzhan, I. (1987), *Léon Bakst: Sets and Costume Designs, Book Illustrations, Paintings and Graphic Works*, London: Viking.

Psarra, A. and E. Fournaraki (2006), 'Parren, Callirhoe (born Siganou) (1859–1940)', in F. de Haan, K. Daskalova, and A. Loutfi (eds.), *Biographical Dictionary of Women's Movements and Feminisms in Central, Eastern, and South Eastern Europe: 19th and 20th Centuries*, 402–7, Budapest: Central European University Press.

Purtill, R. (1979), *The Golden Gryphon Feather*, New York: DAW Books.

Purtill, R. (1980), *The Stolen Goddess*, New York: DAW Books.

Purtill, R. (1983), *The Mirror of Helen*, New York: DAW Books.

Quasimodo, S. (1958), *La Terra Impareggiabile*, Milan: Mondadori.

Quasimodo, S. (1983), *Complete Poems*, trans. J. Bevan, London: Anvil Press Poetry.

Rehak, P. (ed.) (1995), *The Role of the Ruler in the Prehistoric Aegean*, Liège: Université de Liège.

Reinach, S. (1893), 'Le Mirage Oriental', *L'Anthropologie* 4: 539–78 and 699–732.

Reinach, S. (1904), *Apollo: Histoire Générale des Arts Plastiques Professée en 1902–1903 à l'École du Louvre*, Paris: Hachette.

Reinach, S. (1907), *Apollo: An Illustrated Manual of the History of Art throughout the Ages*, New York: Scribner.

Reinach, S. (1919), 'Bibliographie d'Adolphe Reinach', *Revue Archéologique* 9, 5th series: 193–7.

Renan, E. (1899), *Prière sur l'Acropole*, Paris: E. Pelletan.

Renault, M. (1956), *The Last of the Wine*, London: Longman, Green and Co.

Renault, M. (1958), *The King Must Die*, London: Longman, Green and Co.

Renault, M. (1962), *The Bull from the Sea*, London: Longman, Green and Co.

Renault, M. (1964), 'How Much is True?', in C. Kingsley, *Theseus: A Greek Legend Retold by Charles Kingsley with an Afterword by Mary Renault, Illustrated by Federico Castellon*, 42–5, New York and London: Macmillan.

Renault, M. (1969), 'Notes on the King Must Die', in T. McCormack (ed.), *Afterwords: Novelists on their Novels*, 81–7, New York, Evanston, IL, and London: Harper and Row.

Renfrew, C. (1972), *The Emergence of Civilisation: The Cyclades and the Aegean in the Third Millennium B.C.*, London: Methuen and Co.

Renfrew, C. (1987), *Archaeology and Language: The Puzzle of Indo-European Origins*, London: Jonathan Cape.

Renfrew, C. (1998), 'Word of Minos: The Minoan Contribution to Mycenaean Greek and the Linguistic Geography of the Bronze Age Aegean', *Cambridge Archaeological Journal* 8, no. 2: 239–64.

Renfrew, C. (2015), 'John Davies Evans, 1925–2011', *Biographical Memoirs of Fellows of the British Academy* 14: 141–63.

Rentzou, E. (2011), 'The Minotaur's Revolution: On Animals and Politics', *L'Esprit Créateur* 51, no. 4: 58–72.

Reusch, H. (1958), 'Zum Wandschmuck des Thronsaales in Knossos', in E. Grumach (ed.), *Minoica: Festschrift zum 80. Geburtstag von Johannes Sundwall*, 334–56, Berlin: Akademie-Verlag.

Ricoeur, P. ([1984]1990), *Time and Narrative*, vol. 1, Chicago: University of Chicago Press.

Ridgway, W. (1901), *The Early Age of Greece*, vol. 1, Cambridge: Cambridge University Press.

Riebe, B. (1994), *Palast der Blauen Delphine*, Munich and Zürich: Piper.

Rizzo, M. (1984), 'Le Prime Esplorazioni', Scuola Archaeologica Italiana di Atene, *Creta Antica: Cento Anni di Archeologia Italiana*, 53–68, Rome: De Luca.

Robinson, A. (2002), *The Life and Work of Jane Ellen Harrison*, Oxford: Oxford University Press.

Robinson, W. A. (2002), *The Man Who Deciphered Linear B: The Story of Michael Ventris*, London: Thames and Hudson.

Roessel, D. (2006), 'Happy Little Extroverts and Bloodthirsty Tyrants: Minoans and Mycenaeans in Literature in English after Evans and Schliemann', in Y. Hamilakis and N. Momigliano (eds.), *Archaeology and European Modernity: Producing and Consuming the 'Minoans'*, 197–208, Padova: Bottega d'Erasmo (Ausilio).

Romeo, I. (2010), 'Europa's Sons', in T. Whitmarsh (ed.), *Local Knowledge and Microidentities in the Imperial Greek World*, 69–85, Cambridge: Cambridge University Press.

Rouse, W. H. D. (1901), 'The Double Axe and the Labyrinth', *Journal of Hellenic Studies* 21: 268–74.

Runnels, C. (2007), *The Archaeology of Heinrich Schliemann: An Annotated Bibliographic Handlist*, 2nd edition, Boston: Archaeological Institute of America.

Ruse, M. (1979), *The Darwinian Revolution: Science Red in Tooth and Claw*, Chicago: University of Chicago Press.

Sackett, L. H. and M. Popham (1970), 'Excavations at Palaikastro VII', *Annual of the British School at Athens* 65: 203–42.

Sakellarakis, E. and Y. Sakellarakis, (1987), 'Νεολιθική και Μινωική Κρήτη', in N. Panagiotakis (ed.), *Κρήτη:ιστορία και πολιτισμός*, vol. 1, 1–130, Crete: Syndesmos Topikon Enoseon Dimon and Koinotiton Kretes.

Sakellarakis G. and E. Sakellarakis (1997), *Archanes: Minoan Crete in a New Light*, Athens: Ammos.

Sakellarakis, I. and E. Sapouna-Sakellaraki (1981), 'Drama of Death in a Minoan Temple', *National Geographic* 159, no. 2: 204–23.

Sakellarakis, J. A. (1988), 'The Idaean Cave: Minoan and Greek Worship', *Kernos* 1: 207–14.

Sakellarakis, Y. (1996), 'Minoan Religious Influence in the Aegean: The Case of Kythera', *Annual of the British School at Athens* 91: 81–99.

Samuel, R. (2008), 'Birtwistle's *The Minotaur*: The Opera and a Diary of its First Production', *Cambridge Opera Journal* 20, no. 2: 215–36.

Sarri, M. (2007), 'The Turkish-Cretan who Captured History', *ΣΤΙΓΜΕΣ Κρητικό περιοδικό* 84, http://stigmes.gr/br/brpages/articles/behaedin.htm.

Schachermeyr, F. (1939), *Zur Rasse und Kultur im minoische Kreta*, Heidelberg: Winter.

Schachermeyr, F. (1964), *Die minoische Kultur des alten Kreta*, Stuttgart: W. Kohlhammer.

Schachermeyr, F. ([1964] 1979), *Die minoische Kultur des alten Kreta*, Stuttgart: W. Kohlhammer.

Schacter, D. L. (2001), *The Seven Sins of Memory: How the Mind Forgets and Remembers*, Boston and New York: Houghton Mifflin.

Schacter, D. L., J. Y. Chiao, and J. P. Mitchell (2003), 'The Seven Sins of Memory: Implications for the Self', *Annals of the New York Academy of Sciences* 1001: 226–39.

Schliemann, H. (1875), *Troy and Its Remains*, London: John Murray.

Schoep, I. (2010), 'The Minoan "Palace-Temple" Reconsidered: A Critical Assessment of the Spatial Concentration of Political, Religious and Economic Power in Bronze Age Crete', *Journal of Mediterranean Archaeology* 23, no. 2: 219–43.

Scott, G. (2016), *The Age of Treachery*, London: Titan Books.

Scott, G. (2017), *The Age of Olympus*, London: Titan Books.

Scott, G. (2018), *The Age of Exodus*, London: Titan Books.

Scuola Archeologica Italiana di Atene (1984), *Creta Antica: Cento Anni di Archeologia Italiana*, Rome: De Luca.

Seeley, J. R. ([1883] 1971), *The Expansion of England*, Chicago: University of Chicago Press.

Seltman, C. T. (1935), 'Review of *Palace of Minos*, vol. 4', *Nature* 136, no. 3432 (10 August): 202–3.

Sergi, G. (1895), *Origine e diffusione della stirpe mediterranea: induzioni antropologiche*, Rome: Società Editrice Dante Alighieri.

Sergi, G. (1901), *The Mediterranean Race: A Study of the Origin of the European People*, London: Walter Scott.

Serrano, M. and M. Bzinkowski (2012), 'Marcin Czermiński and his Eyewitness Account of the Minoan Excavations in Crete at the Beginning of the 20th Century', *Studies in Ancient Art and Civilization* 16: 249–67.

Seymour, M. (2003), *Robert Graves: Life on the Edge*, London: Scribner.

Shaffer, B. W. (1993), *The Blinding Torch: Modern British Fiction and the Discourse of Civilization*, Amherst: University of Massachusetts Press.

Shapland, A. (2013), 'Jumping to Conclusions? Bull-leaping in Minoan Crete', *Society and Animals* 21: 194–207.

Shaw, J. W. and M. C. Shaw (2010), 'Kommos', in E. H. Cline (ed.), *The Oxford Handbook of the Bronze Age Aegean (ca. 3000–1000 BC)*, 543–55, Oxford: Oxford University Press.

Shaw, J. W. and M. C. Shaw (eds.) (1995), *Kommos 1: An Excavation on the South Coast of Crete. The Kommos Region and Houses of the Minoan Town. Part I: The Kommos Region, Ecology, and Minoan Industries*, Princeton, NJ: Princeton University Press.

Shaw, M. (2004), 'The "Priest-King" Fresco from Knossos: Man, Woman, Priest, King, or Someone Else?', in A. Chapin (ed.), *ΧΑΡΙΣ: Essays in Honor of Sara A. Immerwahr*, 65–84, Hesperia Supplement 33, Princeton, NJ: American School of Classical Studies at Athens.

Sherratt, A. (1989), 'V. Gordon Childe: Archaeology and Intellectual History', *Past and Present* 125: 151–85.

Sherratt, A. (2006), 'Crete, Greece and the Orient in the Thought of Gordon Childe (with an Appendix on Toynbee and Spengler: the afterlife of the Minoans in European Intellectual History)', in Y. Hamilakis and N. Momigliano (eds.), *Archaeology and European Modernity: Producing and Consuming the 'Minoans'*, 107–26, Padova: Bottega d'Erasmo (Ausilio).

Sherratt, S. E. (1996), 'With Us but Not of Us: The Role of Crete in Homeric Epic', in D. Evely, I. S. Lemos, and S. Sherratt (eds.), *Minotaur and Centaur: Studies in the Archaeology of Crete and Euboea Presented to Mervyn Popham*, 87–99, Oxford: Tempus Reparatum.

Sherratt, S. E. (2009), 'Representations of Knossos and Minoan Crete in the British, American and Continental Press, 1900–c.1930', *Creta Antica* 10: 619–49.

Shewan, A. (1919), 'The Scheria of the Odyssey', *Classical Quarterly* 13, no. 1: 4–11.

Sideris, G. (1976), *Το Αρχαίο Θέατρο στη Νέα Ελληνική Σκηνή 1817–1932*, Athens: Ikaros.

Sifakis, G. M., N. Vagenas, and J. L. Borges (1985), *Ο Μπόρχες στην Κρήτη. Η Τελετή Αναγόρευσης του Χόρχε Λουίς Μπόρχες σε Επίτιμο Διδάκτορα της Φιλοσοφικής Σχολής του Πανεπιστημίου Κρήτης*, Athens: Stigmi.

Simandiraki, A. (2005), 'Minoan archaeology in the Athens 2004 Olympic Games', *European Journal of Archaeology* 8, no. 2: 157–81.

Snijder, G. A. S. (1936), *Kretische Kunst: Versuch Einer Deutung*, Berlin: Gebr. Mann.

Snodgrass, A. (1983), 'Archaeology', in M. Crawford (ed.), *Sources for Ancient History*, 137–84, Cambridge: Cambridge University Press.

Solomon, E. (2006), 'Knossos: Social Uses of a Monumental Landscape', in Y. Hamilakis and N. Momigliano (eds.), *Archaeology and European Modernity: Producing and Consuming the 'Minoans'*, 163–82, Padova: Bottega d'Erasmo (Ausilio).

Solomon, J. (2001), *The Ancient World in the Cinema*, New Haven, CT, and London: Yale University Press.

Spencer, C. (1973), *Leon Bakst*, London: Academy Editions.

Spencer, C. (2009), *Bakst in Greece*, Athens: Gema.

Spengler, O. (1918), *Der Untergang des Abendlandes: Umrisse Einer Morphologie der Weltgeschichte*, Vienna and Leipzig: Braumüller.

Spengler, O. (1922), *Der Untergang des Abendlandes: Welthistorische Perspektiven*, Vienna: Braumüller.

Spengler, O. (1928), *The Decline of the West*, vol. 2: *Perspectives of World-history*, trans. C. F. Atkinson, New York: Knopf.

Spratt, T. A. B. (1865), *Travels and Researches in Crete*, London: J. van Voorst.

Spratt, T. A. B. (1879), 'Paper on Certain Archaic Gems Procured in Crete and the Aegean Islands', *Proceedings of the Society of Antiquaries*: 118–23.

Sreenivasan, J. (1994), *The Moon Over Crete*, Duluth, MN: Holy Cow.

Stallworthy, J. (1998), *Rounding the Horn: Collected Poems*, Manchester: Carcanet.

Stampolidis, N. C. and O. Berggruen (eds.) (2019). *Picasso and Antiquity. Line and Clay*, Athens: Museum of Cycladic Art.

Stampolidis, N. C. and A. Kotsonas (2006), 'Phoenicians in Crete', in S. Deger-Jalkotzy and I. S. Lemos (eds.), *Ancient Greece: From the Mycenaean Palaces to the Age of Homer*, 337–60, Edinburgh: Edinburgh University Press.

Stanford, P. (2007), *C. Day-Lewis: A Life*, London: Continuum.

Starr, C. G. (1955), 'The Myth of the Minoan Thalassocracy', *Historia: Zeitschrift für Alte Geschicthe* 3: 282–91.

Starr, C. G. (1961), *The Origins of Greek Civilization 1100–650 B.C.*, New York: Alfred A. Knopf.

Starr, C. G. (1984), 'Minoan Flower Lovers', in R. Hägg and N. Marinatos (eds.), *The Minoan Thalassocracy: Myth and Reality. Proceedings of the Third International Symposium at the Swedish Institute in Athens, 31 May–5 June, 1982*, 9–12, Gothenburg: Paul Åströms Förlag.

Starre, J. (2009), *Lusty Adventures of the Prince of Knossos*, Herndon, VA: STARbooks.

Stavroulaki, E. (2016), 'L'image de la Grèce dans la revue *Cahiers d'Art* (1926–1960)', *La Revue des Revues* 55, no. 1: 66–81.

Stone, J. R. (2002), *The Essential Max Müller: On Language, Mythology, and Religion*, Londra: Palgrave Macmillan.

Stoneman, R. (2010), *Land of Lost Gods: The Search for Classical Greece*, 2nd revised edition, London: I.B. Tauris.

Stuart, J. and N. Revett (1762–1816), *The Antiquities of Athens: Measured and Delineated*, 4 vols., London: J. Haberkorn.

Stuart, J., N. Revett, W. Newton, W. Reveley, J. Woods, C. R. Cockerell, W. Kinnard, T. L. Donaldson, W. Jenkins, and W. Railton (1825), *The Antiquities of Athens: Measured and Delineated*, London: Priestly and Weale.

Styan, J. L. (1982), *Max Reinhardt*, Cambridge: Cambridge University Press.

Swann, T. Burnett (1966), *Day of the Minotaur*, New York: Ace Books.

Swann, T. Burnett (1971), *The Forest Forever*, New York: Ace Books.

Swann, T. Burnett ([1971] 1975), *The Forest Forever*, St Albans: Mayflower Books.

Swann, T. Burnett (1977), *Cry Silver Bells*, New York: Daw Books.

Sweetman, D. (1993), *Mary Renault: A Biography*, London: Chatto and Windus.

Tittel, K. (1903), 'Der Palast Zu Knossos', *Neue Jahrbücher für Das Klassische Altertum Geschichte und Deutsche Literatur und für Padagogik* 11: 385–409.

Traill, D. A. (1995), *Schliemann of Troy: Treasure and Deceit*, New York: St. Martin's Press.

Traill, D. A. (2014), 'Heinrich Schliemann, 1822–90, and Sophia Schliemann, 1852–1932: Searching for Homer's World', in B. Fagan (ed.), *The Great Archaeologists*, 2–77, London: Thames and Hudson.

Treuil, R., P. Darcque, J. Poursat, and G. Touchais (1989), *Les Civilisations Egéennes du Néolithique et de l'Âge du Bronze*, Paris: Presses Universitaires de France.

Trigger, B. G. (1989), *A History of Archaeological Thought*, Cambridge: Cambridge University Press.

Tsigakou, F. M. (1981), *The Rediscovery of Greece: Travellers and Painters of the Romantic Era*, London: Thames and Hudson.

Tylor, E. B. (1896), 'The Matriarchal Family System', *The Nineteenth Century* 40: 81–96.

Tzachili, I. (2005), 'Excavations on Thera and Therasia in the 19th Century: A Chronicle', *Journal of Mediterranean Archaeology* 18, no. 2: 231–57.

Uderzo, A. (1996), *La Galère d'Obélix*, Paris: Albert René.

Ulanowska, A. (2019), review of Nicoletta Momigliano and Alexandre Farnoux (eds), *Cretomana: Modern Desires for the Minoan Past*, in Aegeus Reviews (https://www.aegeussociety.org/en/review_category/aegean-book-reviews/)

Unsworth, B. (2004), *Crete*, Washington, DC: National Geographic.

Unwin, N. C. (2017), *Caria and Crete in Antiquity: Cultural Interactions between Anatolia and the Aegean*, Cambridge: Cambridge University Press.

Vaio, J. (1990), 'Gladstone and the Early Reception of Schliemann in England', in W. M. Calder III and J. Cobet (eds.), *Heinrich Schliemann Nach Hundert Jahren*, 415–30, Frankfurt: V. Klostermann.

Van de Mieroop, M. (2016), *A History of the Ancient Near East ca. 3000–323 BC*, 3rd edition, Chichester: Wiley Blackwell.

Van den Bosch, L. (2002), *Friedrich Max Müller: A Life Devoted to Humanities*, Leiden: Brill.

Vandersleyen, C. (2003), 'Keftiu: A Cautionary Note', *Oxford Journal of Archaeology* 22: 209–12.

Van Steen, G. (2011), 'Rallying the Nation: Sport and Spectacle Serving the Greek Dictatorships', in E. Fournaraki and Z. Papakostantinou (eds.), *Sport, Bodily Culture and Classical Antiquity in Modern Greece*, 117–50, London: Routledge.

Varouhakis, V. (2015), 'L'archéologie enragée: Archaeology and National Identity under the Cretan State (1898–1913)', PhD. dissertation, University of Southampton.

Ventris, M. and J. Chadwick (1956), *Documents in Mycenaean Greek: three hundred selected tablets from Knossos, Pylos and Mycenae*, Cambridge: University Press.

Vercoutter, J. (1956), *L'Egypte et le Monde Égéen Préhellénique: Étude Critique des Sources Égyptiennes (du Début de la XVIIIe à la Fin de la XIXe Dynastie)*, Cairo: l'Institut Français d'Archéologie Orientale.

Vermeule, E. T. (1964), *Greece in the Bronze Age*, Chicago and London: University of Chicago Press.

Vermeule, E. T. (1975), *The Art of the Shaft Graves of Mycenae, Lectures in Memory of Louise Taft Semple, Delivered April 30 and May 1, 1973, the University of Cincinnati*, Norman: University of Oklahoma Press.

Vernetti, Laura Pérez and J.-M. Lo Duca (1989), *El Toro Blanco*, Barcelona: La Cupula.

Vidal-Naquet, P. and J. Lloyd (1992), 'Atlantis and the Nations', *Critical Inquiry* 18, no. 2: 300–26.

Voutsaki, S. (2002), 'The "Greekness" of Greek Prehistory: An Investigation of the Debate 1876–1900', *Pharos* 10: 105–22.

Voutsaki, S. (2003), 'Archaeology and the Construction of the Past in Nineteenth Century Greece', in H. Hokwerda (ed.), *Constructions of Greek Past: Identity and Historical Consciousness from Antiquity to the Present*, Groeningen: Brill, 231–55.

Wace, A. J. B. (1923), 'Early Aegean Civilization', in J. B. Bury, S. A. Cook, and F. E. Adcock (eds.), *The Cambridge Ancient History*, vol. 1: *Egypt and Babylonia to 1580 B.C.*, 589–615, Cambridge: Cambridge University Press.

Wace, A. J. B. (1956), 'Foreword', in M. Ventris and J. Chadwick, *Documents in Mycenaean Greek: three hundred selected tablets from Knossos, Pylos and Mycenae*, xvii–xxx, Cambridge: University Press.

Wace, A. J. B. and C. W. Blegen (1918), 'The Pre-Mycenaean Pottery of the Mainland', *Annual of the British School at Athens* 22: 175–89.

Wada, S. (1980), *Paul Klee and his Travels*, Tokyo: Nantenshi Gallery

Waddell, L. A. (1929), *The Makers of Civilization in Race and History: Showing the Rise of the Aryans or Sumerians, their Origination and Propagation of Civilization, their Extension of it to Egypt and Crete, Personalities and Achievements of their Kings, Historical Originals of Mythic Gods and Heroes with Dates from Rise of Civilization about 3380 B.C. Reconstructed from Babylonian, Egyptian, Hittite, Indian and Gothic Sources*, London: Luzac and Co.

Walde, C. (2005), 'Labyrinth', in *Brill's New Pauly: Encyclopaedia of the Ancient World*, 139–41, Leiden and Boston: Brill.

Wall, S., J. Musgrave, and P. Warren (1986), 'Human Bones from a Late Minoan IB House at Knossos', *Annual of the British School at Athens* 81: 333–88.

Waltari, M. (1945), *Sinuhe Egyptiläinen Viisitoista Kirjaa Lääkäri Sinuhen Elämästä n. 1390–1335 e. Kr*, Helsinki: Porvoo.

Waltari, M. (1949), *Sinuhe the Egyptian: A Novel*, trans. N. Watford, London: Putnam.

Waltz, P. (1934), *Le monde Égéen avant les Grecs*, Paris: A. Colin.

Wängberg-Eriksson, K. (1996), 'Anakreon (Catalogue Entries Nos. 77–78)', in N. Striztel-Levine (ed.), *Josef Frank, Architect and Designer: An Alternative Vision of the Modern Home*, 228–9, New Haven, CT: Yale University Press.

Warren, P. M. (1972), *Myrtos: An Early Bronze Age Settlement in Crete*, London: British School at Athens.

Warren, P. M. (1975), *The Aegean Civilizations*, Oxford: Elsevier-Phaidon.

Warren, P. M. (1981), 'A. Knossos: Stratigraphical Museum Excavations, 1978–1980. Part I', *Archaeological Reports* 27: 73–92.

Warren, P. M. (1981b), 'Minoan Crete and Ecstatic Religion: Preliminary Observations on the 1979 Excavations at Knossos and Postscript on the 1980 Excavations at Knossos', in R. Hägg and N. Marinatos (eds.), *Sanctuaries and Cults in the Aegean Bronze Age: Proceedings of the First International Symposium at the Swedish Institute in Athens, 12–13 May 1980*, 155–66, Stockholm: Svenska Institutet i Athen.

Warren, P. M. (1985), 'Minoan Palaces', *Scientific American* 253: 94–103.

Warren, P. M. (1989) *The Aegean Civilizations: From Ancient Crete to Mycenae*, Oxford: Phaidon.

Warren, P. M. (2000), 'Early Travellers from Britain and Ireland', in D. Huxley (ed.), *Cretan Quests: British Explorers, Excavators and Historians*, 1–8, London: British School at Athens.

Warren, P. M. (2012), 'The Apogee of Minoan Civilization: The Final Neopalatial Period', in
    H. Mantzourani and P. Betancourt (eds.), *Philistor: Studies in Honor of Costis Davaras*,
    255–72, Philadelphia: INSTAP Academic Press.

Wassermann, S. (2018), *Die Stiertänzerin: Historischer Roman*, Hamburg: Edel Germany
    GmbH.

Waterhouse, H. (1986), *The British School at Athens: The First Hundred Years*, London:
    British School at Athens and Thames and Hudson.

Watrous, V. (1995), 'Review of *The Aegean Bronze Age* by Oliver Dickinson', *American
    Anthropologist* 97, no. 2, new series: 411–12.

Watson, J. (1970), *The Bull Leapers*, London: Gollancz.

Waugh. E. ([1930] 1985), *Labels: A Mediterranean Journal*, London: Penguin.

Wells, H. G. (1920), *The Outline of History, Being a Plain History of Life and Mankind*, New
    York: Macmillan Co., http://www.gutenberg.org/files/45368/45368-h/45368-h.htm.

Wells, H. G. (1922), *The Secret Places of the Hearth*, London: Cassell.

Wells, H. G. ([1895] 2017), *The Time Machine*, London: Gollancz.

Wells, H. G. ([1898] 2017) *The War of the Worlds*, London: Gollancz.

West, M. L. (1997), *The East Face of Helicon: West Asiatic Elements in Greek Poetry and
    Myth*, Oxford: Clarendon Press.

West, M. L. (2007), *Indo-European Poetry and Myth*, Oxford: Oxford University Press.

Whitehead, A. N. (1929), *The Aims of Education and Other Essays*, London: Williams and
    Northgate.

Whitley, J. (2006), 'The Minoans: A Welsh Invention?', in Y. Hamilakis and N. Momigliano
    (eds.), *Archaeology and European Modernity: Producing and Consuming the 'Minoans'*,
    55–67, Padova: Bottega d'Erasmo (Ausilio).

Wiener, M. H. (1984), 'Crete and the Cyclades in LM I: The Tale of the Conical Cups', in
    R. Hägg and N. Marinatos (eds.), *The Minoan Thalassocracy: Myth and Reality.
    Proceedings of the Third International Symposium at the Swedish Institute in Athens,
    31 May–5 June, 1982*, 17–26, Gothenburg: Paul Åströms Förlag.

Wiener, M. H. (2016), 'Beyond the Versailles Effect: Mycenaean Greece and Minoan
    Crete', in J. Driessen (ed.), *RA-PI-NE-U: Studies on the Mycenaean World Offered to
    Robert Laffineur for His 70th Birthday*, 365–78, Leuven: Presses Universitaires de
    Louvain.

Wilde, O. ([1891] 1913), *Intentions*, London: Methuen.

Willetts, R. (1962), *Cretan Cults and Festivals*, London: Routledge and Kegan Paul.

Willetts, R. (1969), *Everyday Life in Ancient Crete*, London and New York: Batsford,
    Putnam.

Willetts, R. (1977), *The Civilization of Ancient Crete*, London: Batsford.

Williamson, C. (2018), *Visiting the Minotaur*, Bridgend: Seren.

Williamson, J. ([1940] 1981), *The Reign of Wizardry*, London: Sphere Books.

Winkler, M. M. (2007a), 'The Trojan War on the Screen: An Annotated Filmography', in
    M. M. Winkler (ed.), *Troy: From Homer's Iliad to Hollywood Epic*, 201–15, Malden, MA:
    Blackwells.

Winkler, M. M. (2015a), 'Wolfang Petersen on Homer and *Troy*', in M. M. Winkler (ed.),
    Return To Troy: New Essays on the Hollywood Epic, 16–26, Leiden: Brill.

Winkler, M. M. (ed.) (2007b), *Troy: From Homer's Iliad to Hollywood Epic*, Malden, MA:
    Blackwells.

Winkler, M. M. (ed.) (2015b), *Return To Troy: New Essays on the Hollywood Epic*, Leiden:
    Brill.

Wolf, C. (1983), *Kassandra*, Darmstadt and Neuwied: Hermann Luchterhand.

Wolf, C. (1984), *Cassandra: A Novel and Four Essays*, trans. J. van Heurck, New York: Farrar, Straus and Giroux.

Wolf, C. (1996), *Medea: Stimmen*, Munich: Luchterhand.

Wolf, C. (1998), *Medea: A Modern Retelling*, trans. J. Cullen, intro. M. Atwood, London: Virago.

Worth, N. (1924), *The Arms of Phaedra: A Tale of Wonder and Adventure*, London: Mills and Boon.

Wunderlich, H. G. (1974), *The Secret of Crete*, trans. R. Winston, New York: Macmillan.

Xanthoudides, S. (1904), *Ο Κρητικός πολιτισμός: ήτοι τα εξαγόμενα των εν Κρήτη ανασκαφών*, Athens: Sakellariou.

Xanthoudides, S. (1909), *Επίτομος ιστορία της Κρήτης: από των αρχαιοτάτων χρόνων μέχρι των καθ' ημάς*, Athens: Ελληνική Εκδοτική Εταιρεία.

Yalouri, E. (2001), *The Acropolis: Global Fame, Local Claim*, Oxford and New York: Berg.

Zajko, V. (2015), 'Scholarly Mythopoiesis: Robert Graves's *The Greek Myths*', in A. G. G. Gibson (ed.), *Robert Graves and the Classical Tradition*, 181–200, Oxford: Oxford University Press.

Zervos, C. (1934), *L'art en Grèce des temps préhistoriques au début du XVIIIe siècle*, Paris: Cahiers d'Art

Zervos, C. (1956), *L'art de la Crète néolithique et minoenne*, Paris: Cahiers d'art.

Zervos, C. (1957), *L'art des Cyclades du début à la fin de l'Âge du Bronze, 2500–1100 avant notre ère*, Paris: Cahiers d'Art.

Zervos, C. (1962), *Naissance de la civilisation en Grèce*, Paris: Cahiers d'art.

Zervos, C. (1969), *La Civilisation Hellénique*, Paris: Cahiers d'art.

Zilboorg, C. (2001), *The Mask of Mary Renault: A Literary Biography*, Columbia and London: University of Missouri Press.

Ziolkowski, T. (2008), *Minos and the Moderns: Cretan Myth in Twentieth-Century Literature and Art*, Oxford: Oxford University Press.

Index

Abu-Hafs-Umar 30
A Century of Archaeological Discoveries
    (Michaelis) 71
*A Cretan Cycle: Fragments Unearthed from
    Knossos* (Coffey) 206
Aegan Civilizations, The (Warren) 196–7
Aegean Bronze Age
    artefacts in other regions 32
    and Crete *see* Bronze Age Crete
    and the European Classical Tradition 41
    excavations of sites 38, 91–2, 139,
        144–8, 190–5
    marginal position of 11–12, 21,
        245n.38
    and Mariano Fortuny y Madrazo 77
    and Mary Renault 157, 240
    new language of Cretan ruling elite 22
    organization of palaces 231
    a period of artistic decadence 98
    storytelling and poetry in 27
    as a succession of *thalassocracies* 148
    three hegemonies of 97
    un-Hellenic character of 72, 140
Aegean Bronze Age, The (Dickinson) 198–9
Aegisthus 27
Aerope 27
Aeschylus 207
Agamemnon 27, 38, 42–5, 171
Agamemnon (Aeschylus) 207
Age of Bronze (Shanower) 303n204
Aghia Irini on Kea 146
Ahhiyawa 20
Ain Shems 51
Akhmatova, Anna 301n.167
Akhnaton: King of Egypt (Merezhkovsky)
        104–5
Akkadian Empire 20
Akrotiri on Thera (Santorini) 3, 146–8,
        192
Á la recherche du temps perdu (Proust) 74,
        77, 261n.216

Albania 89
Alcestis (Nea Skini) 76–7, 260n.206
Alcock, S. E. 28–9, 248n.51
Alexiou, Stylianos 65
Alfred, Prince 43, 251n.33
À l'ombre des jeunes filles en fleurs (Proust)
        74–5
Altertumswissenschaft (Wolf) 34
Alt Kreta (Bossert) 94–5
amusement parks 234, 305n.18
Ancient Crete (Willetts) 150
Ancient Greek Sandals (company) 237
Ancient History of the Near East (Hall)
        73
ancient responses to Minoan Crete
    from Arab to Ottoman 30–6
    Hellenistic and Roman Minoans 28–30
    Minoan interaction with major
        civilizations 18–21
    Minoans under Near Eastern eyes'
        18–21
    Minoans under Greek eyes 21–8
Ancient Society (Morgan) 60
Anderson, Poul 162, 164–5, 185
Anemospilia 194–5, 202, 209 (*see also*
        Archanes-Anemospilia)
Angioletti, Giovanni Battista 183
Annual of the British School at Athens
        (Evans) 93
Antigone (Sophocles) 154
*Antiquities of Athens Measured and
        Delineated, The* (Stuart/Revett) 34
Apesokari, Messara 90
Aphrodite 61, 182, 191
Apollodorus 25
Apostolaki, Anna 129
Aptera 33, 248n.68
Aramis (ocean liner) 103, 114
Archaeology of Crete (Pendlebury) 98
'Archaeology: the loss of innocence'
        (Clarke) 153

Archanes-Anemospilia 3, 15, 188, 193–5, 211, 224, 292n.33 (*see also* Anemospilia)
Argolid 98
Ariadne 10, 26, 61, 114, 121, 126, 154, 165, 247n.34, 286n.181
Ariadne (Brindel) 206–7
Ariadne's Children (Beaton) 194, 215–16
Ariadne, wife of Dionysus (Panagiotakis) 219
Arkadi monastery 30–1
Arms of Phaedra: A Tale of Wonder and Adventure (Worth) 124
Arp, Jean (Hans) 179
Arrest and Movement (Groenewegen-Frankfort) 105, 149, 280n.61
Art Nouveau 6, 38, 114
Aryanism 15, 62, 230–1
Aryans, The (Childe) 102–3
Ashmolean museum 119, 157
Assyria 37, 68, 71, 174
Asterios (Cretan prince) 25
Athenian Panathenaic Stadium 129
Athens Archaeological Society 144
Athens Olympics (2004) 236
Atlantis 10, 38, 71, 185
Atlantis (Panagiotakis) 234
Atlantis (Cowper Powys) 154–5
At the Palace of Knossos (Kazantzakis) 111–12
Atreus 27, 228
Avaris, Egypt 192–3
Axis powers 90
Ayios Giorgos, Kythera 191
Ayrton, Elisabeth 159, 284nn.126, 128, 285n.147
Ayrton, Michael 159–60

Bacchelli, Riccardo 168–70, 185, 287n.189
Bachofen, J. J. 60
Bagge, Halvor 76, 260n.209, 272n.158
Bahaettin Rahmi Bediz 76
Baikie, James 71–2, 195
Bakst, Léon 74–6, 78–1, 85–6, 126, 221, 229
Balkan Wars (1912–13) 88–9
Ballets Russes 2, 80, 126, 288n.209
Ballets Russes de Monte Carlo 126
Baritakis, Ali 89

Barrault, Jean-Louis 126
Barthélemy, Jean-Jacques 34
Barye, Antoine-Louis 115
basileus 193
Bastaki, Anna 239
Battle of Crete (1941) 89
Beaton, Roderick 111, 174–7, 194, 215–16, 218, 302n.193
Beethoven Frieze (Klimt) 13
Beginning of Art in Greece, The (Milchhöfer) 44
Behaeddin, Rhamizade *see* Bahaettin
Belle Époque 3, 5, 14, 69–83, 85, 88, 103, 118, 124, 181
Berlin, Isaiah 45
Berry, Erick 107
Bietak, Manfred 192
Billy Sunday (Jones) 213
Birth of the Gods, The (Merezhkovsky) 104–6, 111, 200
Birtwistle, Sir Harrison 5, 235–6, 305–6n.23
Blake and Mortimer (Jacobs) 183
Blegen, Carl 22, 91–2, 94, 140, 148, 181, 263n.17
Bloch, Raymond 141
'blond beast' (Nietzsche) 40–1
Blouet, Guillaume-Abel 34
Borges, Luis 295n.87
Bosanquet, R. C. 50, 54
Bosch-Gimpera, Pere (Pedro) 72
Bosnian War (1992) 215
Bossert, Helmut Theodor 94–7, 264–5nn.39,45–6
'Boston Goddess' 93, 95, 157, 160, 265n.40, 268n.88, 269n.91
Bourdelle, Antoine 115
Bovril billboards 116
Bowra, Maurice 119
Boyd, Harriett 51, 54 *see also* Hawes
Boys and Girls and Gods (Mitchison) 107
Brandi, Cesare 168, 287n.187
Braniga, Keith 194
Brindel, June Rachuy 206–7, 210, 300n.141
Brion, Marcel 118, 135–6
British School at Athens 50
Bryher (A.W. Ellerman) 1
Buczynski, Edmund ('Eddie') 205

Bull from The Sea, The (Renault) 143, 154, 157, 159, 170
bull-leaping
  captive youths trained in 9, 24
  and Coca-Cola 222
  a 'cruel sport' 64
  emblematic in Minoan iconography 20–1
  the famous 'Toreador fresco' 59
  no female participants 6, 233, 244n.25
  and the Olympic Games 237
Bull of Minos, The (Cottrell) 150
Bull Staircase, Prague Castle 132
Burgon, Thomas 32, 248n.65
Burkert, Walter 60
Bury, J. B. 97
Butler, Eliza Marian 34
Byzantine Empire 29–30, 38, 41

Cadogan, Gerald 178–9, 199
Cahiers d'Art (magazine) 103
Caillois, Roger 118
Caldecott, Moyra 204–5
Caloi, Ilaria 78
Cambridge Ancient History (series) 97, 142, 278n.19
Cambridge Ritualists 61, 71
Campigli, Massimo 113
cannibalism 15, 22, 123, 190–6, 202, 209, 231
Carter, Elliot 126
Cassandra 11, 182, 208–10
Cassandra: A Novel and Four Essays (Wolf) 15
Castellon, Federico 180
Castleden, Rodney 65, 200–1
Catteau, Charles 132
Caulfield, Patrick J. 180, 290n.254
Caylus, Comte de 32
Cecchi, Emilio 121
Cefalù *see Dark Labyrinth, The* (Durrell)
Century of Labyrinths, The (Galanaki) 43, 217, 250–1n.29, 302n.191
Chacot, Jean-Martin 60, 83
Chadwick, John 3, 141, 143
Chagall, Marc 6
Chalice and The Blade: Our History, Our Future (Eisler) 206

Chamber of Commerce Work and Industry, Ljubljana 132
Chamoux, François 141
Chania palace 50, 145, 279n.42
Charioteer, The (Renault) 157
Charmed lives in Greece: Ghika, Craxton, Leigh Fermor (British Museum) 221
Chatzidakis, Iosif 44, 76, 90, 251n.36
Chatzi, Faye 237
Cheney, David 106
Cherry, John 152–3
CHIC (Corpus Hieroglyphicarum Inscriptionum Cretae) 193
Chicago, Judy 206
child burials 24
Childe, Vere Gordon
  and Colin Renfrew 154
  first visit to Crete 90
  and Germanic tradition of culture-historical archaeology 101–2
  and language of ruling classes on Crete 140
  Marxist archaeologist 150–1
  publications 14, 102–3
  and racial stereotyping 103, 267n.81
Children of Ancient Greece (Lamprey) 107
Chloé (fashion house) 221
choros (dancing floor) of Ariadne 57
Christakis, Kostis 237
Christ, Carol P. 188, 206
Christian Cretans 76
Christianity 105, 143
Clarke, David 153
Clepsydra (Athens Olympics) 237
Cline, Eric 20
Clytemnestra (Collier) 83, 85
Coca-Cola bottle 222, 233
Cocteau, Jean 179–80
Coffey, Marilyn 206
Coldstream, Nicolas 23–4
Cold War 90, 138, 148–50, 178, 188, 230
'Collection Les Grandes Civilisations' 141
Collier, John 83
Collingwood, R. G. 114, 116, 118
Colonia Iulia Nobilis Cnossus 29
Colossus of Maroussi, The (Miller) 121, 171
'Coming to Mycenae' (Lee) 166–8
Comparetti, Domenico 48
Constantine of Greece, King 43, 89

Constantine II, King 139
'Contemporary Minoans' (exhibition) 237
Cordo, Simone di 31
Cornhill Magazine 56
Cossu, Ugolino 222
Cowper Powys, John 154–6, 282n.93
Crawford, O. G. S. 143
Craxton, John 221, 274n.178
Cretan Counterfeit, The (Farrer) 155–6
Cretan Cults and Festivals (Willetts) 150
Cretan Exploration Fund 50
Cretan Hegemonies
    first (c. 2000–1750 bc) 97
    second (c. 1700–1400bc) 97
    third Mycenaean Hegemony
        (c. 1400–1200 bc) 97
Cretan Hieroglyphic 22
Cretan leap 129
Cretan Pictographic 12, 52
Cretan, The (Ayrton) 159
Crete (Porter) 15, 214–15, 301n.167
Crete Reclaimed (Evasdaughter) 200–2
Crete: The Forerunner of Greece (Hawes/
    Hawes) 68, 73
Cretomania
    after the Belle Époque 124
    amidst world and civil Wars 103–16,
        118–26, 129, 132, 134
    ancient 191
    in the Cold War 154–83
    influence of novels 142
    and *La Furie* (Bois) 60
    in the late Belle Époque 9, 14, 38–9,
        74–83, 85, 88, 181
    and Minoan femininity 126
    in the new millennium 240
    and Paul Morand 2–3, 77, 88, 229,
        243n.6,
    in Poland 286n.181
    in a postmodern world 202–24
    resurgence of in 21st century 233
Cry Silver Bells (Swann) 162, 164
Cult of The Mother-Goddess, The (James)
    143
Cup Bearer fresco 63
Curtis, Michael 180
Curtius, Ernst 41
Cyclades 32, 95, 146, 152, 157, 2010,
    265n.46, 278 n.23, 283n.108,

298n.114 *see also* Aghia Irini,
    Akrotiri, Santorini, Thera
Cyclopaean masonry 33

Daedalus 10, 26, 35, 161
Damvergis, Ioannis 129
Dancer from Atlantis, The (Anderson) 162,
    164–5
Dancing Lady fresco 57
D'Annunzio, Gabriele 115–16
Dark Labyrinth, The (Durrell) 173–4n.117
Darwin, Charles 33–4, 45
Das Mutterrecht (Bachofen) 60
Daughter of Troy (Franklin) 207, 298n.117
Dawkins, R. M. 76
Dawn of European Civilization, The
    (Childe) 14, 102
Dawn of the Gods (Hawkes) 151
Dawn of History, The (Myres) 72
Day-Lewis, Cecil 119–20, 272n.160
Day of the Minotaur (Swann) 162–3
Debussy, Claude 81
Decipherment of Linear B (Chadwick) 153
Decline of the West, The (Spengler) 100–1,
    135
De Lacretelle, J. 115–16, 141, 168, 170
Delian League 94
DeLillo, Don 6, 15, 188, 210–13, 300n.149
De Richaud, André 170
De Sanctis, Emilia 64
De Sanctis, Gaetano 49, 64
Deshayes, J. 141, 174
'Desperately foreign' (Finley) 12, 245n.40
Diaghilev, Sergei 2, 128, 155
Dickinson, John 45
Dickinson, Oliver 198–9, 240
Dictys of Crete 29
Die Dorier (Müller) 35
Die Kretisch-mykenische Kultur (Fimmen)
    94–5
Die minoische Kultur des alten Kreta
    (Schachermeyer) 151
Diktaios, Aris 176–7
Dimarchio (City Hall) 179, 289n.246
Dinner Party, The (Chicago) 206
Diodorus Siculus 29
*Dionysos: Archetypal Image of
    Indestructible Life* (Kerenyi) 150
Dionysus 26, 72, 219

Doctor Who (tv programme) 182–3
Documents in Mycenaean Greek (Ventris and Chadwick) 139, 143
Doolittle, Hilda *see* H.D.
Dorian invasion 35–6, 97, 106
Dörpfeld, Wilhelm 42, 50, 181
Double Axe: A Romance of Ancient Crete (Haggard) 106
Doumas, Christos 146
Durrell, Lawrence 121, 171, 273–4n.177, 287nn.208–10
Dürrenmatt, Friedrich 235
Dussaud, René 71, 73–4, 259–60nn.195, 199
Dyplous Pelekys (atelier of F. Kaloutsi) 132, 134

EAM/ELAS 90, 138
Early Iron Age 8, 23–5, 27, 49, 72, 202, 228
    Minoans under Near Eastern eyes 18–21
Eastern Question 56
EDES 90
Egée suivi de Judée (Gaspar) 202, 294–5n.87
Egypt
    Aegean Bronze Age finds in 41
    hieroglyphics in 47
    and Keftiu 176
    and Minoan Crete 18, 21, 102, 116
    Minoan interaction with 18
    periodization of Old, Middle, and New Kingdom 54
    and the Ptolemaic dynasty 28
    relationship with other Oriental civilizations 67, 72–3
    texts of 19
Egyptian, The (film) 180, 270n.116
Eisler, Riane 206
Elektra (Reinhardt/von Hofmannsthal) 78, 83
Elektra (Strauss) 83
Elgin Marbles 73, 189
El Greco *see* Theotokopoulos, Domenikos
Elisabeth II, Austro-Hungarian Empress 42
el-Khandak 30
Ellerman, Annie Winifred *see* Bryher

El Toro Blanco (Laura Perez-Vernetti and J.M. Lo Duca) 222
Elytis, Odysseus 175–6
Emergence of Civilisation, The (Renfrew) 145, 152–3
Encounter in Crete (Manning) 288n.212
Engels, F. 60
Entente Cordial (1904) 62
EOK 90
Ericson, Estrid 132
Erinnyes (de Lisle) 79
Erotokritos (Kornaros) 30
Errand into the Maze (Graham) 275n.201
Et in Arcadia Ego (Cecchi) 121
Eteocretans 35, 49, 51
Etruscan Places (Lawrence) 121
Etruscans 96, 99, 121, 122, 270n.103, 271n.130.
Etruscan tombs 54
euphoria minoica 200
Euripides 27, 76, 126
Europa 25, 219
Europa and the Bull 25
European Renaissance 10
European Union 189, 197
Evans, Joan 45–7, 92, 157
Evans, John 145
Evans, Margaret 46
Evans, Sir Arthur
    and Ali Baritakis 89
    anti-Aryan stance 62–3
    choice of the label 'Minoan' 36
    early stages of research 33
    and Émile Gilliéron 12
    epoch-making excavations of 2–3, 17, 246n.2
    ethnic affinities between Minoans and Etruscans 121
    and glory of Tiryns and Mycenae 22
    and Glotz 97–8
    grandiose imperialist vision of 15
    and Greece 24, 152, 175
    and Heinrich Schliemann 48
    and Homer 27
    and human sacrifice 195
    idea of Minoan palaces as palace-temples 192
    and Kalokairinos's Mycenaean building find 44

and Knossos excavations 2–3, 5, 6, 31,
  61–2, 83, 90, 105, 183, 229
and Knossos tablets 30, 95, 139, 143
Minoan analogy with Rome 99
and Minoan military action 21
and Minoan monotheism 60,
  254n.114–16
and Minoan music and poetry 169
and the Minoans 65–70, 74, 209,
  255nn.138–41,145,167
multi-ethnic view of the Minoan
  world 64
and the name Minos 59
pan-Minoan model of 88, 91–4, 148,
  264n.32
prestige and dominance in the field of
  Aegean studies 135
and Priest-Kings 113, 196, 224
purchase of one quarter of the Kephala
  44–5
and reconstruction of the 'Prince of
  Lilies' 176
rediscovery of Minoan Crete 54, 56–7,
  59, 253n.89
road to Knossos 45–9, 251nn.49–
  50,52,54
and Robert Graves 123–4
and the snake votary 240
and supreme female divinity 60, 72, 93
and *The Palace of Minos* 92–3, 97, 230
tripartite chronological scheme of 73
view of Minoans 14, 65–9
Evans, Sir John 45, 47, 252n.70
Evasdaughter, Susan 200–2, 294n.86
Everyday Life in Ancient Crete (Willetts)
  150
Expédition scientifique de Morée 34
Eye Goddess, The (Crawford) 143

Fabricius, Ernst 48
Fallmerayer, Jakob Philipp 38
Farnoux, Alexandre 12
Farrer, Austin 155
Farrer, Katharine 155, 283nn.96–100
feminism 60, 96, 124–6, 188, 202, 206, 210,
  230–3
Fimmen, Diedrich 94–5, 97, 264n.38
Finley, Moses 142
First Cemetery, Athens 42

First World War 3, 14, 31, 51–2, 71–2,
  89–90, 92–6, 215
Fitton, Lesley 2–3
Flag Ceremony in Athens 129, 276n.213
Flaubert, Gustave 69
Florensky, Pavel 71
Ford, Ford Madox 74–5
Forest Forever, The (Swann) 162
Fortuny y Madrazo, Mariano 77–8, 86,
  221, 261n.218
Fotiadis, Mihalis 33–4
Foucalt, Michel 4, 15, 228
4th of August Regime 89
France, Anatole 69
François Vase 27
Frank, Josef 132
Frazer, James 60
Freedom and Death (Kazantzakis) 31,
  76
Freeman, Edward Augustus 46
Freeman, Margaret 47
French School in Athens 44
Freud, Sigmund 1–2, 16, 60, 83, 124, 216
Frickenhaus, August 72
From the Silent Earth (Alsop) 150
Frost, T. K. 147
Fukishimi Daiichi nuclear disaster 238
Furumark, Arne 149, 185, 280n.60

Gabinetto Segreto (Secret Cabinet) 6
Galanaki, Rhea 15, 43, 217–18
Garden of Eden 123–4, 135
Gaspar, Lorand 294–5n.87
Geometric domed lids 24, 246n.21
George, Prince of Greece 50
Gere, Cathy 2, 40, 65, 255n.137
Gerhard, E. 60
Germany 41, 50, 89–90, 96
Giant Squid (rock band) 5, 238
Gide, André 97, 106, 111–14, 119, 126, 161,
  271nn.128, 130
Gilliéron, Émile 12
Gimbutas, Marija 144, 195, 199–201, 206,
  296–7n.112
GIS (Geographical Information System)
  190
Gladstone, William 42, 54
Glotz, Gustave 97–8, 169, 197, 230,
  265nn.49–51, 266n.58

Gnossienne (Shawn) 126, 221
Goddess Movement 188, 195
Goddess pilgrimage tours 206
Gold-Hatted Lover, The (Keeley) 171–3
Goncourt, Edmond de 115
Good Soldier, The (Ford) 74
GORILA (Godart, Olivier Recueil des
Inscriptions en Lineaire A) 193
Goscinny, René 221
Graeco-Turkish War 68
Graham, Martha 275n.201
Graves, Robert 97, 123, 126, 153, 155, 157,
195, 274n.189
*Great Mother, The: An Analysis of the
Archetype* (Neumann) 143
Great Mother, The (Panagiotakis) 219–20
Great Powers Club 21
Greece
ancient narratives inspired by Minoan
ruins 228
archaeological history 189, 291n.3
and the Bronze Age 48, 62–3, 91–2, 96,
139
and Bronze Age Crete 96, 140–1, 185
Civil War 88, 90, 129
conquest by Rome 29, 98
constitution of ancient 41
continuity between Bronze and Iron
Ages 142–3, 278–9n.23
and dictatorship in 138–9
differences between mainland and
Crete 95
discovery of Mycenae 56
and the Early Iron Age 8, 72, 197
fall of the Junta to the new millennium
188–90
golden Classical age of 40
government's gift of Knossian throne
replica 43
historical and literary tradition of 175
Homeric 38, 40
independence of (1832) 30
and Indo-European people from the
Caspian region 97
institutional and economic problems
of 89
male-dominated pantheon of religion
59, 254n.109
Minoan conquest of 102

and Minoan Crete 116, 140
Minoan Crete antithesis of 118
Minoan elements attested on 91
and Minoan hegemony 93
Minoans under Greek eyes 21–8
and the monarchy 90, 138
nebulous heroic past of 34
otherness of 118
and Persia 73
powerful myths of 11–12
relationship of literature to
postcolonialism/postmodernism 217
the soul of 174–5
and the surrounding world 9–10,
245n.30
troops to Asia Minor 89
unification with Crete (1913) 50, 64,
88, 89
the unsurpassed pinnacle of
civilization 74, 259n.197
and *Volkgeist* 94
and War of Independence 38
Greece in the Bronze Age (Vermeule) 141
Greek Archaeological Service 144
Greek Islands, The (Durrell) 171
Greek Myths (Graves) 153, 157
Gregory, Aaron John 238
Griffin fresco 183
Groenewegen-Frankfort, Henriette 105,
149–50, 174
Grote, George 36, 41
'Growing up next door to
Knossos'(Galanaki) 217
Guðmundsson, Kristmann 110
Gullberg, Hjalmar 126
Guthrie, W. K. C. 143
Guys, Constantin 118

Haggard, Audrey 106
Hagia Triada 24, 28, 83, 115, 129, 183, 191,
214
Hagios Onuphrios 48
Halbherr, Federico 17, 44, 47–8, 50–1, 54,
62
Hall, H. R. 40, 59, 73, 253n.105
Halstead, P. 192
Handbuch and Denkmäler (Müller) 35
Hand, Judith 207
Harrison, Jane 60–1, 71–2, 195

Harsent, David 235
Harvester Vase (Hagia Triada) 67
Hassoulier, Bernard 48
Hattusili I 20
Hawes, Charles Henry 68
Hawes, Harriet Boyd 68, 96, 98, 148,
    257n.161
Hawkes, Jacquetta 65, 150, 200, 228,
    280–1n.65
Hazzidakis *see* Chatzidakis
H.D. 1–2, 243n.3
Heidegger, Martin 169–70
Helena (Noa) 129
Hélène de Sparte (Verhaeren/Bakst) 80,
    85
Helen of Troy (film) 180, 182
Hellenomania 34
Heraklion Museum 114–16, 121, 209
Herder, Johann Gottfried 100, 101
Herodotus 8–9, 27, 175
Heroes, or Greek Fairy Tales for My
    Children (Kingsley) 180
Heroic Age of Excavation 2–3
Heroon (Kyriakos) 129
'Heterotopia of Hellenism' (Leontis) 34
heterotopia 4, 15, 228
Hippolyta 157
Hippolytus (Euripides) 26–7
historical novels 104, 269n.91, 270n.112
History of Greece (Grote) 36
Hittites
    and the Ahhijawa texts 97
    and Hrozný's decipherment 91
    Minoan–Anatolian relations 20–1
    rule of much of Asia Minor 91–2
Hobsbawm, Eric 134–5, 230
Hodder, Ian 195
Hoeck, Karl 35–6, 40, 54, 228
Hofmannsthal, Hugo von 78, 83
Hogarth, D. G. 50–1, 54, 56–7, 59, 145
Home of the Heroes (Hood) 151–2
Homer 8, 27, 35–6, 42, 140–1, 181, 183
Hood, Sinclair 116, 140, 145, 151–2
House of the Double Axe *see* labyrinth
House of the Frescoes, Knossos 132,
    277n.220
Hrozný, Bedrich 91
Huby, Peter 233–4
Hugo, Jean 126

human sacrifice 15, 24, 190–6, 202, 209,
    224, 231, 246–7n.25
Hüseyindede Tepe vase 20
Huxley, Aldous 119–20
Huxley, George 193

Idaean cave 29, 31, 44, 191
Idomeneo (Mozart) 235
Idomeneus 27
Iliad 27
Iliou Melathron (Schliemann) 41–2
Images (Taylor) 221
Imperial Museum, Constantinople 44
Inevitability of Matriarchy, The (Lawton) 4,
    206
INSTAP (Institute for Aegean Prehistory)
    189–90
International Court of Justice 43
Isles in the Middle of the Great Green 19–20
Isopata Ring 200
Italian Archaeological Mission 50, 90
Italy 50, 89
'Ivory Acrobat, The' (DeLillo) 6, 210

Jacobs, Edgar P. 183
James, E.O. 143
'Jeux d'ombre sur l'Hellade' (Caillois) 118
Jolas, Betsy 250n.11
Jones, Rod 213
Joubin, Andre 44
Journal d'un inconnu (Cocteau) 180
Jules Bois, Henry Antoine 60, 82–3, 229
Julia Paradise (Jones) 213
Jung, Carl 200
Junyer, Joan 126, 274n.189

Kalokairinos, Minos 11, 17, 31, 42–4, 47,
    49, 52, 235
Kalokyris, Dimitris 302n.193
Kaloutsi, Florentini 132, 221, 237
Kalyvia affair 50
Kamares cave 49, 76, 252n.69
Kamilari Minoan tomb 28
Kaphtor/Caphtor 20
Karadimas, N. 33
Karahöyük 20
Karamanlis, Konstantinos 188–9
Karo, Georg 91, 95
Kassandra (Wolf) 207–10

Kato Symi Viannou 191
Kato Zakros palace 138–9, 145
Kazantzakis, Nikos 30–1, 76, 111–12,
    118–19, 173–5, 195, 271n.125,
    288n.222
Keeley, Edmund 171, 287n.212
Keftiu 19–21
'Keftiu' (Diktaios) 176
Keftiu people 63
Kemal, General Mustafa (Ataturk) 89
Kephala tou Tselevi (Knossos) 43, 51
Kerenyi, Károly 150
Keyes, Sidney 275n.192
King Must Die, The (Renault) 6, 143, 154,
    157, 159, 170
Kingsley, Charles 180
Klee, Paul 6, 13, 124–5, 275n.199
Klimt, Gustav 12–13
Knossian Theatral Area 61
Knossos (1956) (Arp) 179
Knossos
    Antiquity to Mid-19th Century
        22–33
    Cold War and 1960s 139, 143–5, 149,
        151, 158–87
    heroic age of excavations 2, 49–54,
        56–7, 61, 63–6
    as heterotopia and *lieu de mémoire* 4
    late Belle Époque 69–70, 72, 74–8, 80,
        83, 85
    Mid-19th Century to First World War
        41, 43–8
    Minoan cultural legacies 188–229, 234,
        240
    palace 4, 243–4n.13
    and the World Wars 89–90, 92, 95–9,
        104–12, 115–16, 119–25, 135
Knossos Labyrinth, The (Castleden) 200
'Knossos' (Lee) 166–8
Knossos and the Prophets of Modernism
    (Gere) 65
Knossos scarves 77
Kokalos, king 26
Kokosalaki, Sophia 237–8
Kommos 24, 191
Korakou (Blegen) 94
Korda, Alexander 129
Kornaros, Vincenzo 30
Kossinna, Gustaf 103

Kouros (Kazantzakis) 111–12
Kreta (Hoeck) 35
Krischen, Fritz 95
Kritiki Politeia (1898–1913) 31, 89–90, 229
Kronos 25
KULP (Knossos Urban Landscape
    Project) 227
Kupka, František 79, 82, 86
Kyriakos, Dimitrios 129
Kythera 21, 192

Labels: A Mediterranean Journal (Waugh)
    114
Labrys 205
Labrys (Ayrton) 161
labyrinth
    of Gide 114
    as Internet chat-room 305n.16
    and King Minos 25, 29, 72
    and the Minotaur 62, 88
    real Cretan 57
    true location of 44
Lacarrière, Jacques 170–1, 185
La Chronique des arts et de la curiosité
    69
La civilisation égéenne (Glotz) 97, 194,
    197–8, 230
La Créte ancienne (Lagrange) 71
La Furie (Jules Bois) 60, 82–3
La Galère d'Obélix (comic) 221–2
Lagerfeld, Karl 147, 221
Lagrange, Marie Joseph 71
Lamprey, Louise 107
Lancaster, Osbert 132
L'Après-midi d'un Faune (Ballets Russes)
    80, 221
La résurrection des villes mortes (Brion)
    118
La Revue de l'Art ancient et moderne 70
La Revue de Paris 69–70
larnakes (clay coffins) 24
Last of the Wine, The (Renault) 157
Late Geometric period 25
Lathbury, Maria Millington 45
Lawrence, D. H. 120–1, 125, 272–3n.163
Lawton, Elizabeth 16, 206
Le Corbusier 179
Le Côté de Guermantes (Proust) 75
L'écuyère (Chagall) 6

Le demi-dieu ou le Voyage de Grèce (De Lacretelle) 115
Lee, Lawrence 166–8
Leighton, Frederic 250n.24
'Le mirage oriental' (Reinach) 48
L'Enigme de l'Atlantide (comic) 183
Le Ninfe (Cossu) 222
Lenin, Vladimir 112
Leontis, Artemis 34
Le Petit Temps 69
Le pur visage de la Grèce (Mauclair) 115
Les civilisations préhelléniques dans le bassin de la mer égée (Dussaud) 71, 73
L'été grec (Lacarrière) 170
Levi, Doro 144–5
Lewis, C. S. 155
Library/Bibliotheca, The (Apollodorus) 25–7
Liebig Extract of Meat Company 116, 183
Life of Ismail Ferik Pasha. Spina nel Cuore, The (Galanaki) 217–18
Lily and the Bull, The (Caldecott) 202, 204–5, 207, 296nn.100–1
Lindsay, Norman 124
Linear A
    and Antonino Nacci 179
    discovery of tablets 193
    and the Luwian language 140
    not deciphered 12, 21–2
    one of three main scripts 52
Linear B
    decipherment of 3, 12, 15, 92, 137–43, 152, 154, 173, 175–9, 183, 230
    evidence for writing in the Aegean 52
    and Linear A 21
    and Mary Renault 146
    and tablets from Knossos 19, 22, 27, 95, 192, 201
Lion Gate, Mycenae 35, 42, 168, 250n.24
Lisle, Leconte de 79
Lloyd George, David 89
Lo Duca, J.M. 222
Lorrain, Jean 116
Louis XIV, King 75
Lubbock, Sir John 33
Lucius Septimius 29
Luwian, Anatolian 193
Lyceum of Greek Women 129

Lycian wooden hut 125
Lyell, Charles 34

Macaulay, Rose 11, 83
MacGillivray, Sandy 65, 255n.136
Mackenzie, Duncan 45, 51–2, 63, 78
Macmillan, George 50
Madonna (singer) 195
Magnan, Jean-Marie 179
Makarios III, Archbishop 139
Malia 33, 90, 116, 144, 160, 191, 192, 204, 219 268n.64, 272n.144, 296n.100
Mallarmé, Stéphane 81
Manchester Guardian 46–7
Mandelstam, Osip 273n.164, 301n.167
Manning, Hugo 288n.212
Marchand, Suzanne 40
Mari, city of 20
Marian Age 60
Mariani, Lucio 49
Marinatos, Spyridon 3, 90–1, 129, 144, 146, 185, 192
Markatou, Dora 129
Marshall Plan 138
Martini, Christina 237
Massine, Léonide 126
'Material Girl' (Madonna) 195
Matsch, Franz von 42
Matz, Friedrich 142
Maucaulay, Rose 74
Mauclair, Camille 115–16, 168
Maze Maker, The (Ayrton) 160–1, 285nn.141, 148
Medea (Euripides) 126
Medea (Wolf) 298n.116
Medicine (Klimt) 12–13
Megali Idea (Great Idea) 89
Mehmet IV, Sultan 30
Mélida, José Ramón 72
Mellink, Machteld J. 141
Merezhkovsky, Dmitry 104–6, 111, 118–19, 135, 150, 195, 200
Mertz, Barbara Louise *see* Michaels, Barbara
Mesopotamian/Ugaritic texts 20
Metamorphoses (Ovid) 12
Metaxas, General Ioannis 89
Metaxas regime 129, 276n.215
'Micene' (Quasimodo) 165–6

Michaelis, Adolf 54, 56, 71, 258n.178
Michaels, Barbara 202–3, 295nn.88, 91, 96
Michalaros, Demetrios 177–8
'Middle of the World, The' (Lawrence) 120
Milchhöfer, Arthur 44, 54, 228
Miletus, Turkey 25–6, 192–3
Miller, Henry 121–2, 135, 171, 185, 274n.181–3
mini-palaces 191
Minoan ashlar walls 24
Minoan Brotherhood 5, 205, 239
'Minoan Experiences' 239
'Minoan Flower Lovers' (Starr) 65, 69
Minoan (Giant Squid) 238, 306n.33
Minoanization 21–2
Minoan landscape (Ayrton) 160
Minoan pacifism 65–8, 150, 281n.66
'Minoan Porcelain' (Huxley) 119
Minoan Psychopath, The (Sheppard Baird) 234
Minoan Roads project 191
Minoans: Crete in the Bronze Age (Hood) 151–2
Minoans (Giant Squid) 5
Minoan Sisterhood 5, 205, 239
Minoans: Life in Bronze Age Crete (Castleden) 200
Minoan Tastes (Morrison) 239
Minoan Theater (Bastaki) 239
Minoan, The (Michalaros) 177–8
Minos, King
    and Arthur Evans 59, 180
    claim to his stepfather's kingdom 26–7
    famous Greek stories of 10, 23
    and his wife Pasiphae 75
    island of 42
    labyrinth of 4, 25, 29, 72
    and Platonic dialogue 228
    site of palace 42–5
    throne of 114–15, 183, 235
    unsavoury 106
Minotaur (Birtwistle) 5, 235
Minotaur as calf (Ayrton) 161
Minotaure (magazine) 103–4, 268n.88–9
Minotaur HMS 43
'Minotauro a Cnosso' (Quasimodo) 165–6
Minotaur (Panagiotakis) 234

Minotaur, the
    an instrument of Minos's revenge 26
    and Bacchelli 169
    in ballet form 126
    and his labyrinth 10–12, 62, 88
    images in Greek art 27
    legend of 194
    in Minoan art 10–11, 22
    and Theseus 25, 57, 59, 114, 180, 235, 288–9n.229
Minotaur, The (ballet) 126, 275–6n.201
Minotaur, The (Birtwistle) 235
Minotaur, The (Junyer) 126
Minotaurus: Eine Ballade (Dürrenmatt) 235
Mitchison, Naomi 107
Modern Minoan Paganism (Perry) 5, 205, 239
Monastiraki site 90
Monthly Review (magazine) 56
Moore, Gene 221
Morand, Paul 2–3, 77, 229
Morgan, L. H. 60
Morris, Christine 60, 126, 222
Morrison, Jerolyn 239
Morris, Sarah 24
Mosso, Angelo 68, 82, 256n.157
Mount Juktas 29, 191
Müller, Karl Otfried 35–6, 41, 54, 228
Murray, Gilbert 71–2, 83, 140, 157
Muslims 89
Mycenaeanization 22
Mylonas, George 146
Myres, J. N. L. 153–4
Myres, John L. 44, 72, 79, 97, 140–1
Myrtos (Fournou Koryfi) 145

Nacci, Antonino 179
Names, The (DeLillo) 15, 210–13
Napoleonic Wars 34
Naquet, Vidal 147
National Liberation Front (*see* EAM/ ELAS)
Nea Demokratia (New Democracy) 188–9
Nea Skini 76, 77
neoliberalism 231
Neolithic period 193, 199
Neopalatial motifs 24

Neptos company 104
Nero, Emperor 30
Neumann, E. 143
New Age spiritualism 205
New Archaeology 148, 154, 190, 195–6
Newbery Honor award 107
Newton, Charles T. 44
New Wave surveys 190, 224
Night Labrys (Ayrton) 160–1
Nijinsky, R. 261n.226
Nijinsky, V. 221, 261n.226
Nilsson, Martin P. 98, 266n.61
Noa, Manfred 129
Notturno a Cnosso (radio documentary) 183
Novelli, Gastone 179

octopus vases 132
    Catteau 132
    Geometric 24
    Minoan 283n.98
    Picasso 268n.90
Ode to Minoa (Dintino) 237
Odyssey: A Modern Sequel, The (Kazantzakis) 111–12
Odyssey with the Goddess (Christ) 206
Odyssey, The (Homer) 32, 111
Oedipus Rex (Reinhardt) 83
Olympic Games (Athens 2004) 5
'On the date and origin of Minyan Ware' (Childe) 102
On the Origin of Species (Darwin) 33
Orestes 27
Origin of the Family, Private Property and the State (Engels) 60
Origins of Greek Civilization 1100–650 B.C. (Starr) 142
'other Ariadne, The' (Galanaki) 217
Ottoman Empire 17, 30, 42–3, 76, 89, 229
Outline of History (Wells) 99–100
Ovid 12, 27, 104, 268n.90

Pact of Chalepa (1878) 42–3
Padel, Ruth 216–17
Palace of Knossos 56
Palace of Minos 3, 17, 74–5
Palace of Minos, The (Evans) 14, 65–6, 88, 92–4, 97, 104, 135, 230, 263n.24
Palaces of Minoan Crete (Cadogan) 199

Palaikastro 33, 50, 145, 191
Palestine Exploration Fund 51
Palmer, Leonard 193
Palmer-Sikelianos, Eva 134
Panagiotakis, Roussetos 188, 218–20, 234
Pan-Hellenic Games 129
Papadimitriou, Yannis 146
Papandreou, Andreas 189
Papaoulakis, Christos 43
Paquin, Jeanne 81
Paris 69–71, 182
Parren, Kalliroi 129
Pasch van Krienen, Count 32
Pashley, Robert 33, 35–6, 50–1
Pasiphae (Huby) 233–4
PASOK 189
Pater, Walter 74
'Paths of Classicism in Art, The' (Bakst) 75
Pax Minoica 65–6, 94, 135, 196–7, 209
Peatfield, Alan 217
Pendlebury, John 90, 98–9, 266n.62
Perez-Vernetti, Laura 222
Perry, Laura 205, 239
Persian Wars 182
Petrie, Flinders 41–2
Phaedra 26, 114
Phaedra (Brindel) 206–7
Phaistos 17, 20, 24, 51, 122, 144, 209
Phaistos disk 12–13, 52, 125, 176, 179
'Phaistos Disk' (song) 238
Phèdre (Racine) 112, 126
Phèdre (Rubinstein) 81, 126
Phelps, Fanny (Frances) 45
Phidias 75
Picasso, Claude 268n.90
Picasso, Pablo 12, 103, 245n.42, 268n. 89, 268–9 n. 90
Plato 10, 28, 38, 71, 147, 185
Platon, Nikolaos 145, 194, 197–9, 292n.137, 293nn.52–7
Plečnik, Jože 132
Pliny 29
Point of Departure (Ayrton) 161
Polygnotus 73
polytheism 196
polythira 54
Pompeii 5–6, 54, 73
Popham, Mervyn 145

Porter, Dorothy 15, 214–15
Poseidon 26
positivist fallacy (Snodgrass) 31–2
postmodernism 195, 231, 233–41
Postprocessual Archaeology 195
Pottier, Edmond 69–71, 103, 257–8n.173
Pound, Ezra 1, 86
Praxiteles 75
Praz, Mario 116, 168, 183
Prent, Mieke 23–4
Preziosi, Donald 179
Priam, King 38, 42
Prière sur l'Acropole (Renan) 40
Priest-King 123, 199
Prince of Lilies 175–6, 179, 199, 217, 240
Prince of the Lilies (Jones) 213–14
Princes de Nacre et de Caresse (Lorrain)
    116
Private Life of Helen of Troy, The (Korda)
    129
Prolegomena (Müller) 35
Prolegomena to the Study of Greek Religion
    (Harrison) 61, 71, 195
Proto-Indo-European 34
Proust, Marcel 74–5, 77–8
Psychro 17, 28, 49, 51, 54, 218, 235
Pyrgos Minoan Villa 28

Quasimodo, Salvatore 15, 165–6, 168,
    185
Quest of Love (Hawkes) 280–1n.65
Quintus Caecilius Metellus 'Creticus' 29

Rahmizade Behaeddin *see* Bahaettin
    Rahmi Bediz
Ramesses VI 19
Rascoe, Burton 106
Reinach, Salomon 48, 69–71, 103
Reinhardt, Max 78, 83
Renan, Ernest 40
Renault, Mary
    and cannibalism 195
    and Greek mythological narratives 158,
        225, 232
    and hybrid Greek-Minoan dynasty 6
    and Linear B 143, 146
    and Minoan arts and crafts 158
    and the Minoan Mother Goddess 154,
        157

novels an insight into Greek past 240
    royal sacrifice 157
    and *The King Must Die* 170
    and Theseus and the Minotaur 164,
        180, 185, 284nn.120–1
Renfrew, Colin 141, 145, 152–4, 193
Report to Greco (Kazantzakis) 112, 173–5
republic of St Titus (1363) 30
Revett, Nicolas 34
Rhea (goddess) 25, 59
Rise of the Greek Epic (Murray) 71–2
Rodenwaldt, Gerhard 91
Roman erotica 6
Rome
    comparison with Minoans 99
    engagements with Minoan remains
        29–30
    most visible remains at Knossos 33
    and the *Pax Romana* 66
    remains at sto Katsouni near
        Makryteichos 44
Rubinstein, Ida 81, 126
ruin cults 24, 246n.23
Russia 50

sack of Constantinople (1204) 30
Sackett, Hugh 145
Sakellarakis, Efi 3, 193, 194
Sakellarakis, Yannis 3, 144, 193, 194
Sandwith, Thomas B. 44
Santorini volcano 10, 21, 91, 146, 171, 192,
        196, 280n.50 *see also* Thera
Savignoni, Luigi 49
Schliemann, Heinrich
    and Bronze Age Greece 62, 91
    excavations at Mycenae 11, 33, 83, 86,
        228–9
    excavations at Troy 3, 181
    Hellenization/Europeanization of the
        Aegean Bronze 59
    'hero for the age of Wagner and
        Nietzsche' 45
    'Heroic' period of excavations on Crete
        37–8, 40–2, 40n.11
    and the Homeric Achaeans 73
    and Kalokairinos's Mycenaean building
        find 44
    Opera and novels on his life and work
        40, 250n.11

plan to dig at Knossos 44
reliance on ancient Greek mythological narratives 57
a romantic, revolutionary Hellenist 36
and shaft graves 146, 168
and Sir Arthur Evans 48
stimulus provided by his discoveries 47
Scully, Vincent 179
Sea Kings of Crete, The (Baikie) 71
Sea King's Daughter, The (Michaels) 202–4, 295n.88
Second Athenian League 147
Second International 68
Second World War 90, 138, 231
Secret of Crete, The (Wunderlich) 201–2
Secret of the West: Atlantis–Europe, The (Merezhkovsky) 105
Sergi, Giuseppe 62–3, 197
Sesostris I 19
Seven Days in New Crete (Graves) 123
Shaft Graves, Mycenae 42, 91, 138–9, 146, 168
Shawn, Ted 126, 221
Sheppard Baird, W. 234
Sherratt, S. E. 102
Sikelianos, Eva Palmer 237
Sinuhe the Egyptian (Waltari) 110–11, 180, 270n.117
Sköld, Otte 126
Smith, William Robertson 60
snake goddesses 13, 116, 119–20, 125, 129, 162, 179, 235–6, 272n.158
Snake Goddess and her Foe, The (Klee) 13, 124–5
Snijder, G.A.S. 233, 267n.65
Snodgrass, Anthony 31–2
Society for the Promotion of Hellenic Studies 63
solar myths 62
Solomon, J. 180, 290n.257
Son of Minos (Cheney) 106
Soviet Union 188
Spanish–American War 68
Spartali, Marie 44
Spengler, Oswald 100–2, 112–13, 116, 134–5, 170
Spirit of Place (Durrell) 171
Spratt, Thomas 33–6, 50–1, 248–9n.72

Stallworthy, John 300n.143
Stargate (film series) 224
Starr, Chester 65, 69, 142, 255n.133
'Statuette-Late Minoan' (Day-Lewis) 119–20
Stillman, William James 17, 44
Stone Age
  Neolithic 33
  Palaeolithic 33
Stories They Told Me (Dintino) 237
'Stratification of Aegean Culture, The' (Florensky) 71
Strauss, Richard 83
Stuart, James 34
Sublime Porte 30
Summer Snow (Padel) 216–17
Swann, Thomas Burnett 162
Symphony no. 2: Kleetüden; Variationen Für Orchester Nach Paul Klee (Wingate) 125

Taramelli, Antonio 49
Taras, John 126
TARDIS 183
Taureaux (Magnan) 179
Tavola degli ornamenti (Novelli) 179
Taylor, Paul 221
Telemachus 32
Tel Kabri, Israel 192–3
Tell el-Dab'a *see* Avaris, Egypt
temple-palaces 4, 202, 243
Terror Antiquus (Bakst) 80
thalassocracy
  and Aegean Bronze Age 148
  as an Athenian invention 279n.47
  establishment of 22
  fall of 164
  Greek sources on 146
  and John Pendlebury 98
  Mycenaean–Greek rebellion against 135
  and the Neopalatial period 196
  seen as a peaceful enterprise 197
  and Sir Arthur Evans 65–6, 93–4
Theban tombs 19
'The Ivory Acrobat' (DeLillo) 15
Theochari, Alexandra 237
Theophaneia (Panagiotakis) 219–20
Theotokopoulos, Domenikos 30
Thera 38, 192 *see also* Santorini

Thésée (Gide) 106–7, 111–12, 126, 161
'The settlement at Ialysos and Aegean
        history c. 1550–1400 B.C.'
        (Furumark) 149
Theseus
        and Ariadne 114, 154, 165, 286n.181
        Athenian hero 28, 157, 185
        in ballet form 126
        connection with Crete 26
        and Hippolyta 157
        Ionian Attica, the home of 25
        and the Minotaur 25, 57, 59, 114, 180,
            235, 288–9n.229
tholos tombs 32, 40
Thomsen, Christian Jürgensen 33
Three-Age system 33
Throne Room (Panagiotakis) 221, 303n.198
Thucydides 8–9, 27
Thutmose III, pharaoh 192, 198
Thyestes 27
Tiberius 29
Tibetan Lamas 197
Tilley, Christopher 195
*Time and Chance: The Story of Arthur
        Evans and his Forebears* (Evans)
        45–4
Time Machine, The (Wells) 99, 123
Tiryns 24, 33, 40, 42, 56
To Axion Esti (Elytis) 175–6
tomb of Zeus 33
Topography of Power (research group) 191
Topolino e il Disco di Festòs (comic) 221
Toreador Fresco, Knossos 5–6, 59–60, 209,
        244n.25
Travels in Crete (Pashley) 33
Travels and Researches in Crete (Spratt) 33
Treaty of London (1913) 89
Treuil, R. P. 198
Triumph of Achilles, The (Matsch)
Trojan War 9, 22, 25, 27, 29, 35, 36, 42, 76,
        106, 136, 154, 158, 182, 305n18
Troja (Schliemann) 47
Troy
        association with Greek myths 51
        belonged to the Mycenaean culture 210
        excavations at 38
        fate of 182, 290n.260
        portrayal in film 180
        swastikas of 42

Truman Doctrine 138
Tsipopoulou, Metaxia 237
Tsirkas, Stratis 177
Tsountas, Christos 42, 73, 91, 229
Tsvetayeva, Marina 301n.167
Turkey 20, 64, 89, 139
Twain, Mark 40
Tylor, E. B. 60, 254n.112
Tyranny of Greece over Germany, The
        (Butler) 34

Uderzo, Albert 221
United Kingdom 90
United States 90
Unsworth, Barry 240
Upbringing of Zeus, The (Panagiotakis) 219

Van Effenterre, Henri 198
Venizelos, Eleftherios 89, 129
Venn-Thomas, Edward 123
Ventris, Michael 3, 11–12, 92, 139, 141,
        143
Verhaeren, Emil 80
Vermeule, Emily 141, 240–1
Versailles 56
Viaggio nella Grecia Antica (Brandi) 168
Victoria, Queen 61
Vietnam War 138, 150, 188
View of Knossos (Klee) 125
Villa Ariadne 51
Visiting the Minotaur (Williamson) 234
Voice of the Goddess (Hand) 207
Voronezh Notebooks (Mandelstam)
        273n.164
Voskos (Craxton) 221
*Voyage du jeune Anacharsis en Grèce dans
        le milieu du IVe siècle* (Barthélemy)
        34
Voyage pittoresque de la Grèce (Choiseul-
        Gouffier) 34

Wace, Alan 22, 91, 97, 140, 148
Waddell, L. A. 103, 267–8n.84
Waltari, Mika 110–11
wanax 193, 201, 294n.80
Warren, Peter 3, 145, 194, 196–8,
        292–3n.42–3
Warrior Vase *see* Harvester Vase (Hagia
        Triada)

Wartburg 56
War of the Worlds, The (Wells) 99
Watteau, Jean-Antoine 118
Waugh, Evelyn 114, 122
Wellcome, Henry 51–2
Wells, H. G. 99–100, 102, 108, 122–3
Wenter Marini, Giorgio 269n.95
*White Goddess: A Historical Grammar of
    Poetic Myth* (Graves) 123
Whitehead, A. N. 145, 148
Wiener, Malcolm H. 189–90
Wilde, Oscar 235
Willetts, R. F. 65, 150, 255n.133, 281n.72
Williamson, Claire 234
Winckelmann, Johann Joachim 34, 62, 73,
    83, 86, 170
*Wine-press of Vathypetro and Throne
    Room, The* (Panagiotakis) 219
Wingate, Jason Wright 125
Winged Citadel (Guðmundsson) 110
Winged Girl of Knossos, The (Berry) 107–8,
    110
Wise, Robert 180–2, 290n.262

Wolf, Christa 15, 188, 207–10,
    298–300nn.116, 118–19, 132, 134,
    140
Wolf, Friedrich Augustus 34–5
World of Odysseus, The (Finley) 142
Worth, Nigel 124
Wotan 200
Wright, Frank Lloyd 179
Wunderkammer (cabinets of curiosities) 32
Wunderlich, H. G. 201–2

Xanthoudidis, Stephanos 50, 90

Zavoli, Sergio 183
Zervos, Christian 103, 268n.90, 278–9n.23
Zeus 25, 29
Zeus Cretagenos 29
Zeus and Europa (Panagiotakis) 218–19
Ziller, Ernst 41
Zimri-Lim, King 20
Ziolkowski, T. 12, 27
Zominthos 191
Zoumboulides, Nikolaos 132